This Happy Land

JUDAIC STUDIES SERIES

Leon J. Weinberger, General Editor

This Happy Land

THE JEWS OF COLONIAL AND ANTEBELLUM CHARLESTON

JAMES WILLIAM HAGY

The University of Alabama Press
Tuscaloosa & London

Manufactured in the United States of America
designed by zig zeigler

∞

The paper on which this book is printed meets the minimum requirements of American National Standard for Information Science-Permanence of Paper for Printed Library Materials, ANSI Z39.48-1984

0-8173-1288-9 (pbk: alk. paper)

Library of Congress Cataloging-in-Publication Data

Hagy, James William.
This happy land : the Jews of colonial and antebellum Charleston / James W. Hagy
p. cm. — (Judaic studies series)
Includes bibliographical references and index.
ISBN 0–8173–0576–9
1. Jews—South Carolina—Charleston—History. 2. Reform Judaism—South Carolina—Charleston—History. 3. Charleston (S.C.)—History—Colonial period. ca. 1600–1775.
4. Charleston (S.C.)—History—1775–1865.
5. Charleston (S.C.)—Ethnic relations. I.Title.
II. Series: Judaic studies series (unnumbered)
F279.C4H34 1992
975.7'915—dc20 92-12171
CIP

British Library Cataloguing-in-Publication Data available

Contents

List of Illustrations and Tables

ILLUSTRATIONS

TABLES

Introduction

The view that many people have of Jews and Jewish life in America derives largely from the great waves of immigrants who arrived in the United States from the middle of the nineteenth century onward. But Jews have resided in this country almost from the beginning, and the early communities were decidedly different from those such as New York's Lower East Side. No place illustrates this more than Charleston, South Carolina. Jews had arrived and had begun to take their place in that city by the 1690s. For a generation after the American Revolution, more Jews resided in Charleston than in any other city in North America. There they gained full economic and political rights much earlier than elsewhere in the western world. They held public office and voted. They attended medical schools and entered the arts and professions. They participated in intellectual affairs in the community. They adopted the way of life of other white southerners. Some grew rich and powerful. All deeply appreciated the economic, social, and political opportunities offered to them. Again and again, they referred to their home as "the Happy Land"; it was their New Jerusalem, New Palestine—the Promised Land. By freely mingling with their neighbors and absorbing the rationalistic ideas of freedom of conscience and equality of the Enlightenment, the Jeffersonian concepts of adapting to time and place, the southern views on slavery, and Charlestonian practices of good living, they lived contented lives. All this affected their religious outlook. They played a leading role in transforming American Judaism by creating the Reformed Society of Israelites in 1824 and making Beth Elohim a Reform synagogue by 1836. In the process, as one observer noted, they had become "Americans to the core." Even more, they were Charlestonians. Because of the size of the community and the religious innovations developed by them, they helped shape the experience of all Jews in America.

Two books on the Jews of Charleston have previously appeared. The first was by Barnett Elzas, *The Jews of South Carolina from the Earliest Times to the Present Day* (1905). In the years that have passed since the publication of the volume, many new sources have become available. The second book was written by Charles Reznikoff and Uriah Z. Engelman. Entitled *The Jews of Charleston: A History of an American Jewish Community*, it was published in 1950. Reznikoff and Engelman rewrote the findings of Elzas but did very little new research on the colonial and antebellum periods. Neither book deals with many aspects of daily life.

I began this study out of curiosity as to why Reform Judaism in America should originate in Charleston, a city more often known for its conservatism and its aristocratic values. I found I could not understand the movement without looking at the people involved. Thus, this became a full study of Judaism and Jewish life in Charleston before the Civil War.

Since few personal accounts were written by the Jews of Charleston, their history had to be traced largely through public and synagogue records. Fortunately, the South Carolina Archives has preserved vast quantities of documents dealing with the Jews of the state.

The narrative herein is heavily noted; however, because of the large number of people involved, references had to be eliminated in places. For example, a sentence or list referring to dozens of people would require pages of notes. The appendix eliminates the need for such dense citation. There, one can find basic biographical information on all named individuals and the sources from which this has been drawn. To reduce the length of documentation in the appendix, I have used the abbreviations listed below. Those with asterisks are used in the text, the footnotes, and the table notes as well.

AF = Henry Aaron Alexander, *Notes on the Alexander Family of South Carolina and Georgia and Connections*. Atlanta, 1954. AF21 refers to page 21 of this work.

AJA = *American Jewish Archives*, a periodical.

BS-BI = *Brith Shalom Beth Israel: 130th Anniversary, 30th Anniversary Merger, January 13, 1985, 20th Teveth, 5745*. Charleston, 1985

C = Federal Census. Thus, 1830C is the 1830 census.

CB = Cash Book of Beth Elohim, followed by year.

*CO = Colonial Office, Public Records Office, London.

Courier = *The Courier*, a Charleston newspaper.

D = Charleston city directory. Thus, D1794 is the directory of 1794. See the City Directories section of the Bibliography for a complete listing.

DR = Death records of Charleston.

E = Barnett A. Elzas, *The Jews of South Carolina*. Philadelphia, 1905.

EBS = Barnett A. Elzas, *The Jewish Cemeteries of Congregation Berith Shalome at Charleston, S.C.* Charleston, 1910.

EC = Barnett A. Elzas, *Old Jewish Cemeteries of Charleston, S.C.* Charleston, 1903. EC23 refers to page 23 of this work.

EG = Barnett A. Elzas, *The Jewish Cemeteries at Georgetown, S.C.* Charleston, 1910.

EJCC = Barnett A. Elzas, *Jewish Cemeteries at Columbia, S.C.* Charleston, 1910.

EJCO = Barnett A. Elzas, *The Jewish Cemeteries of Orangeburg, S.C.* Charleston, 1910.

EL = Barnett A. Elzas, *Leaves from My Historical Scrapbook*. Charleston, 1907.

EM = Barnett A. Elzas, *Jewish Marriage Notices from the Newspaper Press of Charleston, S.C. (1775–1906)*. New York, 1917.

ENJC = Barnett A. Elzas, *New Jewish Cemeteries of K. K. Beth Elohim at Charleston, S.C.* Charleston, 1910.

EP = Barnett A. Elzas, "Death, Funeral and Obituary Notices in the Newspapers of Charleston, S.C." Manuscript in New York Historical Society; copy in American Jewish Archives, Cincinnati, Ohio.

FSSC = Agnes Leland Baldwin, *First Settlers of South Carolina, 1670–1700*. Easley, S.C., 1985.

"House Journal, 1783–1784" = "House Journal" in *Journals of the Privy Council, 1783–1789,* ed. Adele Stanton Edwards. Columbia, S.C., 1971.

JF = Jacobi Genealogy by Svend Jacobi, American Jewish Archives.

*JR = Judgement Roll, Court of Common Pleas, South Carolina Archives. JR, 1707, 43a would cite Judgement Roll, 1707, item 43a. Judgement Rolls from 1703 to 1790 are from the South Carolina Court of Common Pleas. From 1791 to 1839 they are from the Charleston District, Court of Common Pleas.

LF = Genealogical Records of the Descendants of David Lopez and Priscilla Moses, American Jewish Archives.

MF = Harold Moïse, *The Moïse Family of South Carolina*. Columbia, S.C., 1961.

Min. = Minute Book of Beth Elohim.

MJSC = Harold Moïse, *The Jewish Cemetery at Sumter, S.C.: A Transcription of the Names and Dates on the Tombstones, 1874–1912*. Sumter, S.C., 1942.

Mort. = Mortgage Books in S.C. Archives.

*MR = Miscellaneous Records in the State Archives. MR2V.248 would cite vol. 2V, p. 248.

*MS = Marriage Settlements, South Carolina Archives. MS13.148 would cite vol. 13, p. 148.

OJCS = B. H. Levy, *Savannah's Old Jewish Community Cemeteries*. Macon, Ga., 1983.

*PRO = Public Records Office, London.

RB = Joseph R. Rosenbloom, *A Biographical Dictionary of Early American Jews: Colonial Times through 1800*. Lexington: University of Kentucky, 1960. I cite this only when he has information that differs from my data.

*RMC = Register Mesne Conveyance Office, Charleston County.

Rogers = George C. Rogers, Jr., *The History of Georgetown, South Carolina.* Columbia, S.C., 1970.

SCA = Records in S.C. Archives. SCA-1709–44 means that there are records on this person for these dates. These records may be located by the indexes of the Miscellaneous Records or the Combined Index.

SCHM = *South Carolina Historical Magazine*. SCHM8.18 would cite vol. 8, p. 18.

SCM = Brent H. Holcomb, *South Carolina Marriages, 1688–1799.* Baltimore, Md.,1983.

SFF = Malcolm Stern, *The First Jewish Families of America: 600 Genealogies.* Cincinnati, Ohio, 1979.

SP = *Southern Patriot*, a Charleston newspaper.

*T = Thomas J. Tobias, *The Hebrew Orphan Society of Charleston, S.C., Founded 1801: An Historical Sketch.* Charleston, 1957.

TBS = Thomas J. Tobias, *The Hebrew Benevolent Society of Charleston, S.C., Founded 1784, The Oldest Jewish Charitable Society in the United States.* Charleston, 1965.

*W = Charleston County Will Book. Those used were the typed copies found in the Register Mesne Conveyance Office, Charleston County, and the Charleston County Library. W45.234 would cite Will Book vol. 45, p. 234.

*WIM = Wills, Inventories, and Miscellaneous Records, South Carolina Archives. WIM (1716–21), 35, would cite the bound volume covering the years 1716–21, p. 35.

Wolf = Lucien Wolf, *The History and Genealogy of the Jewish Families of Yates and Samuel of Liverpool.* London, 1901.

Yates, Samuel and Lazarus = Yates, Samuel and Lazarus Family Manuscript, American Jewish Archives.

Other abbreviations for seldom-used sources give enough information that the sources can be found in the bibliography.

Chapter 1

Origins

"Under the present state of emigration from all countries of Europe, many of our people, driven from their native land by various circumstances, seek refuge in this our free and happy country."

—Samuel Valentine, 1848.[1]

". . . there are in these happy United States, not more than *six thousand* [Jews]. . . . in South Carolina, about one thousand two hundred."

—Isaac Harby, 1826.[2]

The Jews who lived in Charleston before the Civil War came from many places. Whatever their origins, their long history weighed heavily on them. The sufferings of their ancestors had served as constant reminders of the need to be wary of their neighbors. In coming to the New World, they sought a homeland where they could live in peace and security. Initially, most of them were Sephardic Jews whose homeland had once been Spain and Portugal but who had since moved on to places such as the Netherlands and England. As time passed more and more were Ashkenazic Jews, those who had lived in Central Europe. Eventually the latter greatly outnumbered the Sephardic element. For a time Charleston had more Jews than any other city in North America. In this chapter I attempt to determine the countries from which Jews came to settle in Charleston and how many resided in the town.

Just when the first Jew lived in Carolina cannot be determined. A curious and extremely difficult to read letter in the Shaftesbury Papers, written when Charles Town was still at its original site at Albemarle Point in 1671, states something to the effect: "I Pray God send more thankfull spirits & grate-

1. Quoted in "Fifty-Sixth Anniversary of the Hebrew Benevolent Society of Charleston, S.C.," 49.

2. From a memorandum prepared by Harby for Samuel Gilman in Gilman, "Harby's Discourse on the Jewish Synagogue."

full harts . . . than those stubborn, hard harted, stiff-necked, and rebellious Jews."[3] Obviously the unknown writer did not find Jews to be subservient, but it is not clear if he is referring to Jews in Charleston or is reacting to some previous experience. Jews from Barbados could have been among the earliest settlers. That island had begun to experience economic troubles and over-population, and as a result a considerable number of people left for the mainland colonies. Many of the first non-Jewish residents of Charleston came from there. A study of the 1679–80 census in Barbados revealed that of 404 households in Bridgetown, 54 were Jewish.[4] Some of these Jews possibly made their way to Carolina.

The first mention of a Jew living in Charleston occurs in 1695. Governor John Archdale relates that soon after he took office, a group of Yamasee Indians, who then lived in Georgia and in the lower part of Carolina, captured four Spanish-speaking Indians, three men and one woman, near St. Augustine. When the captives were brought to Charleston, Archdale questioned them by using a "Jew for an Interpreter," and this otherwise unknown man discovered that the Indians were Roman Catholics. Therefore, instead of selling the captives into slavery, which was the normal practice, Archdale had them returned to the Spanish governor at St. Augustine.[5] The Jewish interpreter had apparently been in the colony for some time and most likely was a Marrano, a term used for Jews in Spain, since he knew the Spanish language.

In 1697 four Jews appended their signatures to a petition by the Huguenots requesting full citizenship. For the first time in records of early Charles Town, names of individual Jews appear. Three were Simon Valentine, Jacob Mendis, and Abraham Avila. The fourth name cannot be deciphered. Valentine was a merchant and later an owner of a farm. As "an alien of the Jewish nation" he was naturalized on May 26, 1697. He has been identified with Simon Valentyn van der Wilden or Simon Valentine of New York, a nephew and heir of Asser Levy. The latter was a Jew who arrived in New Amsterdam from Brazil in 1654 and was the only Jew remaining there when the English took it in 1664. Rabbi Malcolm Stern, the preeminent Jewish genealogist in America, has argued that Van der Wilden means "from Wilna" in seventeenth-century Dutch, and Leo Hershkowitz recently discovered a letter in Amsterdam signed by Asser Levy of Vilna. This would mean that Valentine's family originally came from Lithuania—thus, Ashkenazic Jews. Valentine resided in Jamaica for some

3. Shaftesbury Papers, section IX, bundle 48, no. 85, PRO. Printed in W. Noel, ed., *Calendar of State Papers, Colonial Series, 1669–1774*, 27 vols. (London, 1860–1926), 186–87. The printed version differs somewhat from my reading. The document is extremely difficult to decipher.

4. In Barbados the English residents "disliked and distrusted the Jews, although all agreed that they were less pestilential than the troublesome Quakers." Samuel, "A Review of the Jewish Colonists in Barbados," 8–9. For close connections between the islands and Carolina see Dunn, "The English Sugar Islands and the Founding of South Carolina."

5. Archdale, *A New Description of That Fertile And Pleasant Province of Carolina*, 22.

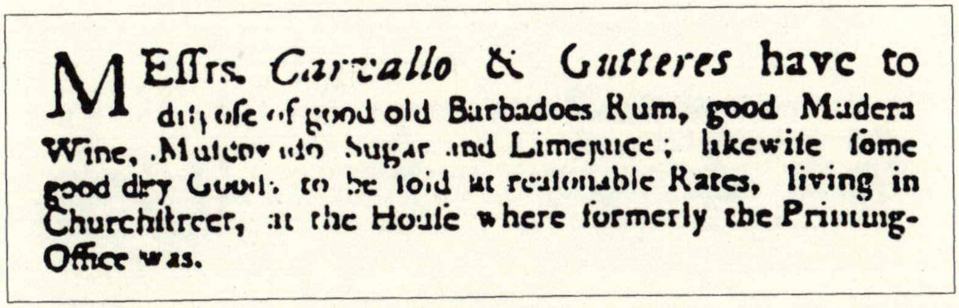

MEſſrs. *Carvallo* & *Gutteres* have to diſpoſe of good old Barbadoes Rum, good Madera Wine, Muſcovado Sugar and Limejuice; likewiſe ſome good dry Goods to be ſold at reaſonable Rates, living in Churchſtreet, at the Houſe where formerly the Printing-Office was.

1. First known Jewish advertisement in Charleston by Carvallo and Gutteres. (*South-Carolina Gazette,* August 17, 1734.)

time, but South Carolina records indicate that he spent about fifteen years in the colony.[6] Jacob Mendis and Abraham Avila had Spanish surnames, and there is little reason to doubt their background. They probably came to Charles Town from New York or the Caribbean. Avila and Valentine had some association because Avila granted power of attorney to Valentine in 1698.[7] Besides Samuel Mincks, they were the only Jews known to be in Charleston in the seventeenth century.[8]

Before 1750, the number of Jews in Charleston remained small. Jacob Marcus has stated that the Jews seem to have left Charleston after 1715 and the community died out; however, this does not seem to be the case.[9] Moses Modina appeared in the records in 1703,[10] David Riz between 1705 and 1707,[11] David Valentine between 1711 and 1712,[12] Aron Cohen in 1712,[13] Nathan Mordecai in 1715,[14] Isaac Emanuel in 1722,[15] Jacob Dias Carvallo and Aaron DeMuttos Gutteres in 1734,[16] Joseph Tobias in 1737,[17] Samuel Levy, Moses Solomon,[18] Isaac DePass in 1738,[19]

6. Friedman, "Jacob Mears and Simon Valentine of Charleston"; Stern, "Charleston's First Jews"; Rosendale, "An Early Ownership of Real Estate"; WIM (1694–1704), 362, 428; WIM (1714–1717), 196–98. Jacob Mears of Jamaica charged that Valentine, who had lived in Jamaica, had left the island to return to Charleston but had failed to pay money due him. The suit was filed in 1701.

7. WIM (1694–1704), 129.

8. Elzas believed that "Mincks" might be a misspelling of "Mendes," especially since Mincks was often associated with Simon Valentine. See Elzas, "The First Jew in South Carolina," *News and Courier*, Mar. 3, 1907, reprinted in *Leaves from My Historical Scrapbook*. Elzas believed that all the early Jews were Sephardic.

9. Marcus, *Colonial American Jew*, 1: 345.

10. Elzas, "First Jew in South Carolina," in *Leaves from My Historical Scrapbook.* I have been unable to locate the document referred to by Elzas.

11. Bullock v. Riz, South Carolina Court of Common Pleas, JR, 1705–07, 681.

12. Symond Valentine v. David Valentine, JR, 1711–12, 61a. Rosenbloom, *Biographical Dictionary*, 171, indicates that David Valentine was in New York by 1695.

13. WIM (1716–21), 35.

14. WIM (1714–17), 196–98.

15. Simpson v. Emanuels, JR, 1722, 87a.

16. *South-Carolina Gazette*, Aug. 17, 1734; JR, 1737, 52a; Jacob Dias Carvallo and Aaron DeMuttos Gutteres v. David Alexander, JR, 1737, 52a.

17. Joseph Tobias v. Thomas Beasley, JR, 1738–39, 25a.

18. MR2F.300.

19. *South-Carolina Gazette*, Mar. 30, 1738. He was naturalized in 1744. MR2F.112.

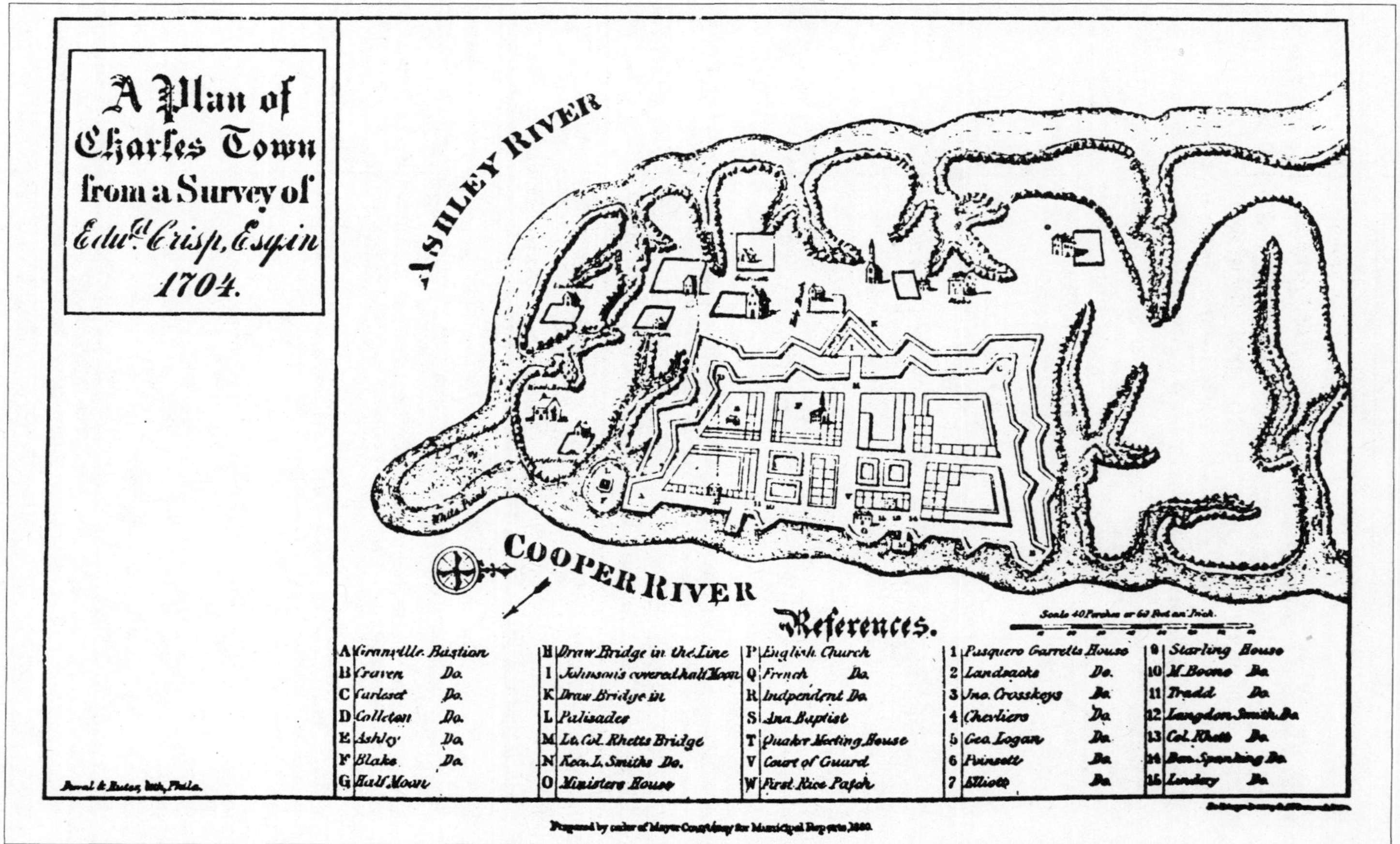

2. The walled city of Charleston, 1704. (From Thomas Petigru Lesesne, *History of Charleston County* [Charleston, 1901].)

Moses DeMattos in 1739,[20] and Joseph Frank in 1743.[21] Some of these people apparently lived in the town for several years before appearing in records. Many of the early Jews seem to have been of Sephardic stock. The D'Oliveira, Tobias, and DaCosta families came from London. No doubt, most of the others came from that city as well. At the same time, Ashkenazic Jews probably were always present.

Each person identified probably had a household of additional people. A good example of a person with several relatives in his home was Jacob D'Oliveira, who died in Charleston in 1751. In his will he repeats the Sh'ma, the Jewish equivalent of a statement of faith (Hear O Israel: The Lord our God, the Lord is One), and asked to be buried according to Jewish rites. He left bequests to the Portuguese Synagogue in London and £10 for each male Jew who washed and anointed his body. Three of the witnesses to his will were Jewish: David Lopez D'Oliveira, Isaac DaCosta, and Solomon Isaacs, all of whom here appear in records for the first time. In addition, Jacob D'Oliveira mentions his daughter Leah, who married Joseph Tobias. They had four children, Joseph, Jacob, Reinah, and Judith.[22] The D'Oliveira household therefore appears to have contained eight people, the two D'Oliveiras and six members of the Tobias family. Other Jewish households probably came close to that number.

20. *South-Carolina Gazette*, Aug. 25, 1739. He was naturalized in 1741. MR2E.lll, 2F.112.

21. MR2F.3.

22. W6.635.

In London the Spanish and Portuguese Jews generally prospered, and some accumulated great wealth. Many ran small shops, and yet many others had little or no means of livelihood. The poorest usually belonged to the Ashkenazic group. Members of the Sephardic community, including Moses DaCosta and Francis Salvador, raised funds to send poor Jews, both Spanish-Portuguese and Germans, to Georgia. Initially they had hoped to establish an entirely Jewish settlement but eventually decided to send them to Oglethorpe's new settlement in Savannah. They hired a ship, the *William and Sarah*, which arrived in Savannah on July 11, 1733, with forty-two Jews aboard. The trustees of Georgia did not want them, but their charter excluded only slaves and Catholics. Almost immediately the Jews founded Mikve Israel, the third synagogue in America, the first two being in New York and Newport. In 1740 James Oglethorpe invaded Spanish territory and attacked St. Augustine. When he failed to conquer it, most of the Sephardic Jews, remembering the terrible persecutions in Spain and fearing the Spanish might take Savannah, left the city. Some of them went to Charleston. By 1741 only one family remained in Savannah.[23]

A scheme similar to that for Georgia

23. Rubin, *Third to None*, 2–17; Sheftall, "The Sheftalls of Savannah," 65–78; Stern, "New Light on the Jewish Settlement of Savannah"; Morgan, "Judaism in Eighteenth-Century Georgia"; Elzas, *Jews of South Carolina*(1905), 30; Jones, "The Settlement of the Jews in Georgia."

was drawn up in 1737 to establish a Jewish community in Carolina. The leaders of the Spanish-Portuguese effort in London were Solomon DaCosta, Francis Salvador, and Benjamin Mendes DaCosta. As early as October 1747 James Peyne, a London merchant, petitioned the Commissioners for Trade and Plantations to grant him land in South Carolina.[24] Within a few months in a new petition he stated that he planned to settle "Foreign Protestants and others as will shew themselves attached to Your Majesty's Person and Government."[25] By December 1747 a Mr. Hamilton had become associated with him in the project. At the time Peyne reportedly was in Languedoc obtaining persons for the settlement.[26] On December 22, 1747, Hamilton attended the meeting of the commissioners accompanied by Solomon DaCosta. DaCosta reported that he had agreed with Hamilton "for the settlement of several of their poor in South Carolina" and subscribed a sum of money for that purpose. By this time the promoters of the scheme were requesting 200,000 acres of land.[27] Peyne and Hamilton sought to justify their request by pointing out that the area could produce tar and other naval goods and that they had settlers ready. Besides the Jews, they claimed that a Dr. Hempe was ready to provide as many German Protestants as needed. Various meetings were held and petitions received from Hamilton in the first half of 1748. The board became suspicious of Hamilton, and in July it decided to consult with Solomon DaCosta to see if the proposals of Hamilton still had the support of the Jewish merchants. DaCosta did not respond until September, stating that he, Francis Salvador, and Benjamin Mendes DaCosta spent the summer months in the country and came to London only once or twice a week to take care of affairs. Then the Jewish merchants reaffirmed their support of Hamilton. But on December 8, 1748, the board again wrote DaCosta seeking assurance of his continued support. On the twelfth he replied that his group had been interested in only 200,000 acres, not three times that amount, and that Hamilton "should not have scrupled to increase it." Apparently, Hamilton had asked for much more. DaCosta's letter was read to the board on December 13, and the group immediately denied the petition of Hamilton for the grant since he failed to "induce them to think that he can carry his Proposals into Effect."[28] Obviously, Peyne, who disappeared early in these events, and Hamilton were manipulators who were interested only in their profits. They misled the Jewish promoters.

Because the scheme failed, Barnett Elzas, the author of *The Jews of South*

24. Petition of Peyne, Oct. 26, 1747, CO 5/371, PRO; *Acts of Privy Council of England, Colonial Series*, 4: 60–61.

25. Petition of Peyne, received Dec. 1747, CO 5/371, PRO.

26. *Journal of the Commissioners for Trade and Plantations from January 1711/12 to December 1749*, 264.

27. Ibid., 265, Dec. 22, 1747.

28. Elzas, *Documents Relative to a Proposed Settlement*, 14.

Carolina, concluded that "the Jews who came here from London, came not as a colony, but as individuals and that those who came did not belong to the pauper class." But a tradition among the Jews of Charleston related that they had come as a group under the leadership of Moses Cohen in the 1730s.[29] Though the DaCosta-Salvador attempt to found a colony in Carolina came to little, a group may have come out under the leadership of Moses Cohen because the number of Jews in the town reached a point that a congregation could be established in 1749, only shortly after the demise of the attempt to establish a colony in South Carolina. Those who formed the congregation came from London, were mostly Spanish-Portuguese Jews, and followed the ritual as observed at Bevis Marks synagogue in London.[30] Also lending credence to the idea of a group's coming from London was the fact that soon after this the Salvador and DaCosta families bought a great deal of land in the Ninety-Six District of South Carolina that became known as the Jews' Lands.[31]

Although the Jews in Charleston in the early years largely came from Sephardic stock, a few were Ashkenazic in origin. Some Ashkenazim, however, had apparently moved to areas where the Sephardim dominated and seem to have assimilated into that group. Also, they possibly intermarried with the Spanish-Portuguese. Individuals and families are therefore very difficult to classify. Furthermore, many family names can be either Sephardic or Ashkenazic, especially those such as Levy and Cohen. In the narrative and the tables that follow an attempt has been made to identify the origins of the Jews in Charleston and the changing nature of the immigration into the city. Unfortunately, the sources are so numerous that they cannot be listed. The most important are Stern's *First Jewish Families of America*, the death records of Charleston, Elzas's *Jews of South Carolina*, the cash books and minute books of Synagogue Beth Elohim, wills, city directories, and documents in the South Carolina Archives.

Some idea of the origins of the Jews in Charleston can be deduced from those for whom a place of birth is indicated. Of 3,083 Jews believed to have lived in Charleston before the Civil War, the place of birth for 1,517 has been recorded. The greatest number was born in South Carolina (869 people). For some, the place of birth is simply listed as South Carolina (321). This designation could mean Charleston as well as the rest of the state, especially for those who appear in the federal censuses of 1850 and 1860. Although a person may have lived in Charleston and had been born there, the records might simply give the birthplace as South Carolina. Another 548 were listed as having been born in Charleston. Thus, at least 57 percent of the people for whom a birthplace is listed were born in the state. In addition, many of those for whom no

29. Ibid., 1.

30. Levin, "The Jewish Congregation of Charleston," 337

31. Elzas, "The Jews' Lands in Abbeville," *News and Courier*, April 7, 1907, reprinted in *Leaves from My Historical Scrapbook*.

place of birth is listed were very likely natives of South Carolina. For the 321 born in South Carolina outside of Charleston, the only places of birth that are given are Ashepoo (2 people), Beaufort (3), Black Mingo (1), Branchville (1), Camden (5), Columbia (7), Edgefield (1), Georgetown (12), Jacksonboro (1), Mt. Pleasant (1), Oakland (1), Pendleton (1), Sullivan's Island (1), and Sumter (6). This pattern may well reflect the distribution of Jews throughout the state.

Jews who crossed the Atlantic and who settled in Charleston at some time came from at least twenty-three places, including one who was born at sea. The greatest number came from Germany (27 percent), England (24 percent), Poland (17 percent), Prussia (12 percent), and the Netherlands (6 percent). Smaller numbers came from places as diverse as Denmark and Italy. Oftentimes, these people lived in the city for a while and then moved elsewhere. Tables 1–3 below are for all men, women, and children who are believed to have lived in Charleston by 1861 but were born outside South Carolina. In some cases very little other information is known about them. If no definite date can be assigned to them, they have not been included in the list at the end of the chapter. (See Table 1.)

Table 1

Old-World Birthplaces of 478 Jewish Men, Women, and Children Resident in Early Charleston

Germany	131
England	114
Poland	83
Prussia	57
Netherlands	28
France	18
Russia	14
Denmark	7
Bohemia	6
Portugal	4
Ireland	2
Gibraltar	2
Europe	2
Wales	1
Sweden	1
Scotland	1
Madeira	1
Italy	1
Galacia	1
Barbary States	1
Austria	1
At Sea	1
Algiers	1

Note: The borders of central and eastern Europe changed many times. The places of birth as given in the records have been accepted as given.

Jews from the New World can be divided into two major groups, those born in the West Indies and those born in North America. At least seven West Indian islands supplied residents for Charleston. Jews had long lived there and had an especially strong presence in Jamaica, where they still figure prominently. Members of the Moïse family fled the island of Haiti, as did many other Europeans when the slaves rose up in rebellion in the 1790s. This experience, no doubt, affected their attitudes thereafter. More people, however, came from St. Croix, Jamaica, and Curaçao. (See Table 2.)

People from a number of other colonies or states came to reside in Charleston as well. Most were born in states

Table 2
Caribbean Birthplaces of 40 Jewish Men, Women, and Children Resident in Early Charleston

St. Croix	9
Jamaica	9
Curaçao	8
Haiti	6
St. Thomas	4
St. Eustatius	2
West Indies	1
Guadeloupe	1

Table 3
Birthplaces, Excluding South Carolina, of 130 Native-Born Jewish Men, Women, and Children Resident in Early Charleston

New York	40
Georgia	33
Pennsylvania	19
Virginia	13
Rhode Island	9
North Carolina	3
New Jersey	2
Louisiana	2
Connecticut	2
Ohio	1
Mississippi	1
Massachusetts	1
Maryland	1
Maine	1
Florida	1
California	1

with considerable Jewish communities such as New York (31 percent), Georgia (25 percent), and Pennsylvania (15 percent), and Rhode Island (7 percent). Usually they came from the cities of New York, Savannah, and Newport. (See Table 3.)

Although no particular pattern can be seen for Jews coming into Charleston from other colonies, with the exception from Georgia during the Revolution, the nature of the immigration by foreign-born Jews changed over the years: The Ashkenazic element gradually surpassed the Sephardim. Conditions in both the United States and Europe affected the flow of people into the community. Since men are more likely than women to appear in records soon after their arrival, only they have been used to see how the nature of immigration altered. Furthermore, only men to whom a fixed date can be assigned are included in Tables 4–7. All these individuals may be found in the list at the end of the chapter. The date in South Carolina was compared with the place of birth. The first men for whom information exists were in the city at the time the synagogue was organized in 1749. From 1749 through 1775, and thus to the beginning of the American Revolution, records can be located for 21 men: 10 came from England, 8 from Germany, 2 from the Netherlands, and 1 from St. Eustatius. These numbers are small, but they seem to give a fair idea of the origins of the Jews in the city, although more possibly were present from the West Indies than the records indicate.

Beginning with the Revolution, more national, state, and local records are available giving names of people in the city. Of special importance is the federal census of 1790. In addition, cash books survive from Beth Elohim beginning in 1800. All contributors to the synagogue are listed there, and this provides a roll of most of the Jewish men in the city. Information on 77 men from seventeen places has been found for the years 1776–1800. As before, the English continued to dominate, although the West Indies almost matched them. The percentage of immigrant Jews who were English coming into the city did decline, no doubt as a result of the Revolution and the ill-will that continued afterward. he last quarter of the eighteenth century was the greatest period for the West Indian Jews to migrate to the city. They came from St. Croix (4), Haiti (4), St. Thomas (2), Jamaica (3), Curaçao (2), Guadeloupe (1), and West Indies (1). Also during this time, central and eastern European Jews began to come to the city: 6 from Poland, 1 from Bohemia, and 1 from Prussia. Some of these came to the area with the troops. (See Table 4.)

Table 4
The Origins of 77 Jewish Men of Record in Charleston, 1776–1800

Place	*Percentage*	*Number*
England	29	22
West Indies	22	17
Germany	16	12
Netherlands	14	11
Poland	8	6
France	5	4
Bohemia	1	1
Prussia	1	1
Portugal	1	1
Ireland	1	1
Denmark	1	1

Ira Rosenwaike used the first federal census, which was taken in 1790, to estimate the Jewish population of Charleston and other cities. He reckoned the population to be 200; however, he missed at least five households, and the census counters apparently failed to find all the residents in the city. Also, all the federal censuses have names of people who are likely to be Jewish but for which there is no proof. Therefore, the number should be somewhat larger —perhaps 225–250. The population of Charleston at the time was 16,359, of which 8,089 were whites. The Jews thus constituted about 3 percent of the white population. In 1787, 7 of the 275 voters (2.54 percent) in municipal elections for intendent and wardens in the city were Jews.[32] In the Charleston directory for 1790, they made up about 5 percent of the entries; however, poor people often did not appear in the directories. Rosenwaike calculated that at the time only about 1,500 Jews lived in the entire country, whose population was 3,929,000—slightly more than the population of South Carolina in the 1990 census. Thus, the Jews in Charleston made up a considerable proportion of the Jewish population of the United States. New York in 1790, according to Rosenwaike, had the largest number of

32. The voters were Alexander Alexander, Jacob Cohen, Gershon Cohen, Isaac DaCosta, Philip Hart, Jacob Jacobs, and Marks Lazarus. "Poll Lists, Charleston Municipal Elections, 1787."

Jews, with about 242 people. Charleston was second and Philadelphia third. Charleston may have had as many Jews as New York because of the influx of people during and after the Revolution who do not appear in the census. Rosenwaike also estimated that by 1800 the Jewish population of Charleston, about 400 people, had surpassed that of other cities in America.[33] This number is low. The cash book for 1800 for Beth Elohim shows at least 142 contributors and perhaps 148 to the synagogue (six names cannot be read, which could be duplicates). If each of these represents the head of a household, which usually averaged five or six people, the number would be substantially higher than Rosenwaike estimated. Elzas figured the total to be about 500.[34] However, 600 might be more accurate.[35]

During the first quarter of the nineteenth century there were at least 63 foreign-born Jewish men who appeared for the first time in the records. The British contingent increased once again to more than half, while the number from the islands declined with one each from Curaçao, St. Croix, and St. Eustatius. (See Table 5.)

Table 5
The Origins of 63 Jewish Male Newcomers of Record in Charleston, 1801–1825

Place	*Percentage*	*Number*
England	51	32
Germany	21	13
Netherlands	13	8
West Indies	5	3
Prussia	3	2
Poland	3	2
France	3	2
Wales	2	1

By 1820 Charleston ranked above New York and Philadelphia for the number of Jewish residents in the city. According to Rosenwaike, Charleston had 674 Jews, 96 households south of Boundary (Calhoun) Street and 13 in the Neck area, north of that street. He, however, missed 19 households representing 120 people.[36] In 1811 Philip Cohen informed Hannah Adams that about 700 Jews lived in Charleston,[37] and in 1826 Isaac Harby calculated the number in the congregation of Beth Elohim to be about 600.[38] Therefore, the number in Charleston must have

33. Rosenwaike, "Estimate and Analysis," 23–60; U.S., Census Department, *Heads of Families at the First Census*. Rosenwaike omits Joshua Canter, Joseph Emanuel, Abraham Lyon, Joseph Myers, and Eleazer Phillips. He includes Hymon Hart; however, I cannot find him in the records.

34. Elzas, *Jews of South Carolina*, 132.

35. For various estimates, see Marcus, *To Count a People*, 204–6.

36. They are Isaac Barrett, John Cantor, Joseph Cardoza, Samuel Cohen, Isaac DaVega, Zachariah Florance, Philip Frideburg, Jacob Harris, Simon Moses Hart, H. M. Hertz, Celia Jacobs, Abraham Jones, Elias Jones, Moses Josephs, Henry Lazarus, Henry Morris, Mrs. E. Moses, Simon Moses, Solomon Solomons.

37. Adams, *History of the Jews*, 2, 217.

38. Gilman, "Harby's Discourse on the Jewish Synagogue."

been close to 800 in 1820.[39] New York had the second highest number (about 550), while Philadelphia was third (about 450). Charleston, including the Neck, had a total population of 37,471, of which only 14,958 were whites.[40] Black slaves and free persons of color constituted 60 percent of the residents. The Jews made up about 5 percent of the white population in Charleston. Nationwide, they constituted approximately 0.03 percent.[41]

From 1826 through 1850 the immigrants to Charleston changed considerably from those who had previously arrived in the city. The period saw dramatic developments in both Europe and America. The United States headed toward the Civil War. In Europe liberal or nationalistic revolutions occurred in 1830 and again in 1848, but eventually the conservative elements regained power. Then Bismarck began to unify Germany, and borders began to change. Also, technological innovation made it possible for steamships to ply the Atlantic, thus greatly shortening the trip from Europe to America. Whereas earlier sailing ships had navigated southward with the winds and then proceeded into southern ports such as Charleston, they now took a northerly route and landed in New York. In addition, ship travel became cheaper, and people of little means could make the journey to the New World. The number of Jewish immigrants into Charleston increased, but older Jewish residents were moving away. By 1850 the U.S. census began to list persons by name and give their place of birth. As a result, more information is available on residents of Charleston. In this period few arrived from England whereas Germany, Poland, Prussia, and Russia accounted for about 71 percent of the newcomers. Heretofore the majority of the immigrant Jewish population appears to have had English as its first language. That now changed and would continue to change in the following decade. About 80 percent would have spoken another tongue. This factor, no doubt, made the Jewish residents of the city appear far more foreign than they had before. (See Table 6.)

Since most Jewish immigrants settled in the northern states by this time, New York with about 1,150 Jews and possibly Philadelphia with approximately 750 surpassed Charleston's Jewish population by 1830. By using the census of that year, Rosenwaike figured the number of Jews in Charleston to have declined to 650.[42] Again, he failed to find a few people in the census returns.[43]

39. This figure is higher than other estimates. See Marcus, *To Count a People*, 204. Isaac Harby believed that about 1,200 Jews lived in South Carolina; however, he seems to have been far off the mark. Only a few families lived in places such as Georgetown, Sumter, and Columbia, and isolated families operated country stores at other places. Only Charleston had a synagogue.

40. Rosenwaike, "Jewish Population of 1820."

41. Rosenwaike, *On the Edge of Greatness*, 17.

42. Ibid., 30, 113–15. The figures on p. 115 have been scrambled and cannot be interpreted.

43. Moses M. Cohen, Abraham Jones, Elias Jones, Samuel B. Jones, William Lambert,

Table 6
The Origins of 88 Jewish Male Newcomers of Record in Charleston, 1826–1850

Place	*Percentage*	*Number*
Germany	33	29
Poland	23	20
England	18	16
Prussia	9	8
Russia	6	5
Netherlands	2	2
France	2	2
Denmark	2	2
West Indies (Curaçao)	1	1
Sweden	1	1
Madeira	1	1
Europe	1	1

Thus, the total may have been closer to 700.

Though the number of Jewish residents in the city decreased, some sources would lead one to think otherwise. For example, the Charleston directory for 1822 has 108 entries for Jews, but the one for 1831 has 118. In the Charleston directory of 1835 there are 131 listings; in 1841, 94; in 1852, 115; and in 1859, 122. One problem, however, is that neither city directories nor censuses are ever complete. Most authorities assume that the federal census takers missed about 10 percent of the population. The city directories were issued by private individuals wishing to make a profit by selling the guide. Some tried to collect the names of all residents, but most did not succeed. The directories served principally as business guides and to a lesser extent as a social register. Slaves never appeared in them and the poorest whites only occasionally; the free persons of color began to appear in the 1830s. The latter, however, either had a separate listing at the back or were noted by some designation such as "fpc."

The 1850 federal census contained about 500 names of Jews living in the city. In 1861 Charleston held its own census because the city claimed that the federal 1860 census had missed a large number of people. The enumerators located every house and business in the city and listed the owners and heads of the households. If a house had several occupants, for example, two businesses on the ground floor and a residence or boarding house on the upper floor, each was assigned a number. As a result, 143 Jewish households or businesses, excluding duplications, were found. Unfortunately, the 1861 census takers listed only the head of the household and not the other occupants.[44]

Even though the 1851–61 period is shorter than earlier segments of time examined, it does reveal a continuing change in the nature of the Jewish immigrants. Only 6 or 7 percent of the newcomers spoke English as their native language. (See Table 7.)

Clearly, the Jewish population of Charleston constantly changed. Not only did the total number decline but

Joseph Marks, Rachel Myers, Alexander Solomons, and Solomon Solomons.

44. Ford, *Census of Charleston.*

Table 7
The Origins of 83 Jewish Male Newcomers of Record in Charleston, 1851–1861

Place	*Percentage*	*Number*
Poland	35	29
Prussia	29	24
Germany	20	17
England	5	4
Russia	2	2
France	2	2
Bohemia	2	2
West Indies (Jamaica)	1	1
Scotland	1	1
Europe	1	1

many of the Sephardic Jews moved away or disappeared while the Ashkenazic element grew larger and changed. Over time, more and more Jews came from Eastern Europe. A group that had once been largely English-speaking immigrants became German or Yiddish speaking, especially after 1840. The Jews of the city, therefore, were never a monolithic group; they probably had as many languages among themselves as the general population had. They also followed various religious traditions and customs. Though most would adapt to southern mores, tensions existed within the community. Very likely, as well, the latecomers found it more difficult than their predecessors to blend into the general white population. Nevertheless, the varied backgrounds of the group produced a colorful history.

COLONIAL AND ANTEBELLUM JEWS OF CHARLESTON, LISTED BY PLACE OF BIRTH (EXCLUDING SOUTH CAROLINA) AND DATE OF FIRST RECORD IN SOUTH CAROLINA

Only persons to whom a fixed date can be assigned are included in this list.

Algiers
  David, Leonie, 1858
At sea
  Moses, Rebecca (Phillips), 1807
Barbary States
  Barrett, Starr, 1788
Bohemia
  DeLieben, Israel, 1790
  Lewith, Henry, 1859
  Lewith, Magdalena, 1852
  Weiskopf, Leopold, 1851
  Weiskopf, Rose, 1860
Bohemia, Polnau
  Pool, Isaac, 1800
California
  Hart, Daniel, 1860
Connecticut, Norwalk
  Isaacks, Sampson Mears, 1804
Connecticut, Wilton
  Moses, Esther (Isaacks), 1800
Curaçao
  Hertz, Esther (Peixotto), 1839
  Motta, Jacob Ares, 1801
  Myers, Rachel (Peixotto), 1839
  Peixotto, Joshua, 1829
  Peixotto, Rachael de David de Isaac (Suares), 1826
  Suares, David, 1799;
  Suares, Jacob, 1799
Denmark
  Canter, Jacob, 1785

Jacobs, Jacob Simon, 1840
Jacobs, Mathilda, 1860
Denmark, Copenhagen
Jacobi, Moritz [Morris], 1850
England
Abrahams, Elias, 1813
Alexander, Moses, 1800
Alexander, Rachel (Anderson), 1767
Barnett, Woolf, 1840
Carvalho, Sarah Nunes (D'Azevedo), 1814
Cohen, Moses, 1749
Cohen, Moses, 1796
Cohen, Nathan A., 1827
Dyer, Francis Polock (Ellis) (Abrahams), 1821
Emanuel, N., 1849
Goldsmith, Henry, 1821
Goldsmith, Morris, 1803
Harris, Hyam [Henry], 1800
Hart, Godfrey, 1850
Hyams, Daniel, 1818
Hyams, Hannah, 1807
Israel, Naphtali H., 1838
Jacobi, Nathaniel, 1850
Jacobs, M., 1859
Jacobs, Moses, 1823
Jacobs, Myer, 1811
Levy, Levine L., 1838
Levy, Polly, 1850
Levy, R., 1804
Levy, Sarah (Sally) C., 1813
Lipman, Abraham, 1809
Loryea, Abraham, 1850
Lyon, Judith (Cohen), 1790
Marks, Sarah (Harris), 1808
Mordecai, Goodman, 1808
Moses, Myer [Meyer], 1767
Myers, Michael, 1800
Nathan, Abraham, 1785
Nathan, Rachel, 1850
Nathans, Nathan, 1801
Phillips, Jacob, 1780
Sampson, Elias, 1805
Sampson, Jane, 1829
Sampson, Sampson, 1841
Samuels, Elizabeth, 1850
Samuels, Moses [also Samuel], 1859
Simpson, Jacob, 1821
Simpson, Rebecca, 1824
Solomons, Hyam, 1782
Wineberg, Janetta (Nachman), 1844
Wineman, Philip, 1851
Wolfe, Benjamin, 1827
Woolf, Sarah (Moses), 1829
Zachariah, Amelia, 1850
England, Bristol
Cohen, Barnet A., 1800
England, Canterbury
Simons, Sampson, 1780
England, Hull
Jacobs, David, 1850
England, Liverpool
Chapman, Edwin, 1860
Lazarus, Phoebe (Yates), 1834
Levy, Fanny (Yates), 1837
Sampson, Joseph, 1834
England, London
Abrahams, Rebecca DeLyon, 1785
Alexander, Abraham, 1767
Alexander, Abraham, Jr., 1800
Alexander, Judah, 1790
Barnard, Alexander, 1805
Benjamin, Rebecca (DeMendes), 1820
Benjamin, Solomon A., 1831
Cardoza, Abraham Nunez, 1750
Carvalho, David Nunes, 1809
Carvalho, Emanuel Nunes, 1807
Carvalho, Sarah (Moreira), 1811
Cohen, Aaron Nathan, 1838
Cohen, Abraham, 1750
Cohen, Clara (Harris), 1797
Cohen, Jonas, 1818

DaCosta, Isaac, 1749
DaCosta, Isaac, 1769
D'Azevedo, Benjamin, 1805
D'Azevedo, Isaac Cohen, 1794
Emanuel, Joseph [Joel], 1790
Harby, Solomon, 1781
Hart, Bella (Levy), 1788
Hyams, Henry, 1809
Hyams, Miriam (Levy), 1806
Hyams, Mordecai, 1812
Hyams, Samuel, 1800
Jacobs, Israel, 1775
Joseph, Daniel M., 1818
Levin, Jacob, 1822
Levin, Lewis, 1807
Levy, Hannah (Abrahams) (Levy), 1796
Lipman, Ralph, 1820
Marks, Humphrey [Mordecai], 1788
Marks, Mark, 1804
Morris, Ainsley, 1812
Moses, Cecilia, 1812
Moses, Hannah (Lazarus), 1802
Moses, Reuben, 1818
Moses, Sally, 1809
Moses, Solomon, 1808
Nathan, Solomon, 1799
Nathans, Nathan, 1805
Polock, Elias C., 1835
Salvador, Francis, 1773
Salvador, Joseph, 1784
Simons, Montague, 1780
Simons, Moses, 1782
Simons, Samuel, 1772
Simons, Saul, 1780
Solomon, Phineas, 1841
Solomons, Mark, 1805
Woolf, Isaac, 1806

England, St. Edmunds
Sampson, Joseph, 1817
Sampson, Samuel, 1823

England, Woolwich
Levy, Lyon, 1785

Europe
Triest, Maier, 1850

Europe, Pousseau
Housseau, Simond, 1852

France
Cohen, Manuel, 1845
Haas, Adolph Godchaux, 1858
Haas, E., 1857
Labatt, David, 1796

France, Bayonne
Torres, Sarah (D'Aquilar), 1800

France, Bordeaux
DePass, Jacob Samuel, 1820
Esdra, Joseph Eugene, 1835
Esdra, Pauline, 1841
Henry, Esther Lucile (Esdra), 1836
Huchet, Elonide (Esdra), 1839
Mannahan, Esther Desirée (DePass) (Heydenfeldt), 1815
Rodrigues, Esther, 1798
Rodrigues, Moïse [Moses], 1806
Sasportas, Abraham, 1778
Torres, Abraham, 1799

France, Mezieres
Mantoue, Benjamin, 1855

France, Strasbourg, Alsace
Moïse, Abraham, 1791

Georgia
Cohen, Rebecca (Sarzedas), 1761
Levy, Nathaniel, 1860

Georgia, Augusta
Canter, Judith, 1828
Moïse, Benjamin Franklin, 1852
Moïse, Thomas Jefferson, 1849
Ottolengui, Rosalie Cecile (Moïse), 1854

Georgia, Savannah
Abrahams, Rachel, 1814
Cardozo, Jacob Nunes, 1794
Cohen, Bella, 1785
DeLaMotta, Emanuel, 1830

DeLaMotta, Jacob Canter, 1807
DeLyon, Isaac, 1762
DeLyon, Levi Sheftall, 1819
DePass, Joseph, 1808
Levy, Sarah (Cardozo), 1780
Minis, Abigail, 1781
Minis, Philip, 1780
Mordecai, Samuel, 1779
Moses, Esther (DeLyon), 1783
Myers, Frances (Minis), 1794
Myers, Levy Julian, 1849
Sarzedas, Moses, 1790
Sheftall, Benjamin, 1780
Tobias, Virginius Jenkins, 1827

Georgia, Spirit Creek
Lopez, John Hinton, 1833

Germany
Abrahams, ———, 1857
Alexander, S., 1850
Baruc, Bernard S., 1855
Belitizer, Caroline, 1850
Belitizer, Isaac, 1850
Belitizer, Jacob, 1850
Belitizer, Theodore, 1850
Bernstein, ——— F. [Burnstine], 1858
Bernstein, H., 1860
Bernstein, Nathan, 1855
Boas, B., 1860
Cohen, ———, 1858
Cohen, Cecilie (Bentschner), 1845
Cohen, Elijah, 1850
Cohen, Hannah, 1850
Cohen, Leopold, 1849
Cohen, Moses, 1772
Cohen, Philip Jacob, 1772
Cohen, Samuel J., 1804
Dittenhoefer, Isaac, 1836
Elias, Levy, 1858
Friedlander, M. J., 1838
Goldberg, Jacob, 1850
Goldberg, Miriam, 1850
Goldberg, Moses, 1850
Goldstein, Abraham, 1855
Goldstein, David, 1860
Goldstein, Fanny, 1860
Goldstein, Harriett, 1854
Goldstein, Henrietta, 1860
Gouthalk, Isaac, 1859
Harris, ———, 1860
Hart, Alexander Moses, 1797
Hyneman, L., 1839
Jacob, Sarah, 1860
Jacobs, Jacob, 1763
Jacobs, S. L., 1860
Jacobs, Sarah, 1850
Jacobson, J. J., 1850
Kleber, ———, 1849
Labatt, Catherine, 1816
Lazarus, Frances, 1822
Lehman, Hannah, 1850
Leman, ———, 1849
Levy, Cossman, 1838
Levy, Samuel, 1782
Loeb, Daniel, 1851
Meyer, Jacob, 1840
Moses, Abraham, 1800
Moses, Levy, 1793
Myers, M., 1849
Pearlstein, Mary, 1851
Petska, Barnet, 1850
Petska, Eleanor, 1850
Petska, Rosa Gesler, 1850
Sampson, Sarah, 1818
Schlichter, ———, 1839
Seaman, Lenard, 1859
Seckendorf, G., 1850
Seckendorf, Hannah, 1850
Seckendorf, Isaac (1), 1850
Seckendorf, Isaac (2), 1850
Solomons, Cecilia (Cohen), 1785
Solomons, Hart, 1799
Solomons, Levy [also Levi], 1783
Solomons, Mark, 1806

Sommers, Edward, 1840
Stern, Miriam (Lehman), 1857
Triest, Caroline, 1856
Vanderveri, Rebecca, 1825
Weinberg, Fanny, 1843
Wetherhahn, L., 1850
Wetherhahn, Sipporah, 1855
Germany, Altona
Somers, Anton, 1851
Germany, Anspach
Phillips, Aaron, 1807
Germany, Bavaria
Cohn, Sophia M., 1855
Drey, Nathan, 1848
Jacobs, Rebecca, 1860
Pinkussohn, Elizabeth, 1860
Rice, Hannah, 1850
Triest, Joseph, 1855
Germany, Berlin
Jacoby, Seigismond A., 1860
Germany, Bremen
Abrahams, Alexander Hezekiel, 1821
Abrams, Abram, 1852
Goldstein, Charlotte, 1860
Germany, Budingen
Mairs, Levy, 1821
Mairs, Simon, 1803
Germany, Buseck
Phillips, Jonas, 1756
Germany, Coblentz
Davis, Moses, 1809
Germany, Dedesdorf
Elias, Levy, 1830
Germany, Frankfurt
Harris, Hannah (Leman), 1851
Germany, Hamburg
Abrahams, Catherine Cohen, 1815
Cohen, Eleanor S., 1849
Furst, Daniel H., 1840
Hart, Moses, 1780
Hart, Philip, 1749
Germany, Hannover
Bernstein, H., 1838
Moses, Isaiah, 1800
Oppenheim, Hertz Wolff, 1821
Germany, Hessen, Budingen
Mairs, Seligman, 1850
Germany, Hildesheim
Hertz, Alexander, 1804
Hertz, Handel Moses, 1802
Germany, Holtzheim
Wetherhahn, Marcus, 1838
Germany, Koenigsburg
David, Joseph, 1763
Germany, Mannheim
Davis, Hannah (Levy) (Hart) (DeLieben), 1809
Hart, Daniel, 1792
Hart, Hymon N., 1791
Hart, Nathan, 1802
Hart, Samuel, 1767
Joseph, Israel, 1764
Noah, Manuel, 1793
Germany, Neustadt
Zacharias, Selig, 1861
Germany, Oberdorff
Cohen, Jacob I., 1776
Germany, Oberelsbach
Lyons, Isaac, 1805
Germany, Obrigheim
Emanuel, Henrietta, 1852
Germany, Prussia
Levin, Hannah, 1856
Germany, Schwersenz
Baum, Elkan, 1855
Germany, Wurtenburg
Goldstein, Hannah, 1860
Germany, Wurzburg
Lewis, David, 1804
Gibraltar
DaVega, Sarah [Sol], 1758

Guadeloupe
  Aarons, Jacob, 1785
Haiti, Port-au-Prince
  Moïse, Aaron, 1791
  Moïse, Benjamin, 1791
  Moïse, Cherie, 1791
  Moïse, Hyam, 1791
  Moïse, Sarah, 1791
  Tobias, Rachel (Aarons), 1785
Ireland
  Lazarus, ———, 1857
Ireland, Dublin
  Hyams, Solomon M., Sr., 1790
Jamaica
  DeLeon, Jacob, 1796
  DePass, Ralph, 1785
  Jacobs, Abigail, 1860
  Jacobs, Julia Matilda (Lyon), 1860
  Schwerin, Caroline (Suares), 1841
Jamaica, Kingston
  Jacobs, Henry Samuel, 1859
  Milhado, Benjamin, 1796
  Milhado, Hannah DePass, 1796
Madeira
  Ricardo, Joseph, 1849
Maine
  Levy, Jane, 1860
Maryland
  Hart, Gerstine, 1860
Maryland, Baltimore
  Lazarus, Esther (Lyons), 1808
Massachusetts, Boston
  Woolf, Rachel (Andrews) (Moses), 1790
Mississippi, Woodwille
  Moïse, Theodora Sydney (Moïse), 1850
Netherlands
  Aarons, Levi, 1786
  Abrams, Eliza, 1824
  Cantor, Jacob, 1784
  DeYoung, Moses, 1819
  Harris, Clara, 1822
  Harris, Jacob, 1797
  Jacobs, Barnard [Barnett], 1800
  Levy, Nathan, 1805
Netherlands, Amsterdam
  Azuby, Abraham, 1784
  Azuby, Esther, 1784
  Benedix, Isaac, 1787
  Cohen, Jacob A., 1796
  DeLange, Lucas, 1829
  D'Oliveira, Jacob Lopez, 1751
  Joseph, Moses, 1818
  Moses, Lyon, 1781
  Moses, Solomon, 1794
  Nathan, Henry, 1809
  Rothchild, M. C., 1841
  Solomons, Israel, 1800
  Solomons, Joseph, 1780
  Solomons, Sampson, 1819
  Spitz, I. A., 1818
Netherlands, Gronigen
  Lazarus, Jacob, 1805
Netherlands, The Hague
  Hart, Moses, 1761
Netherlands, Rotterdam
  Goldsmith, Isaac Moses, 1803
New Jersey
  Levy, Catherine (Bowers), 1850
  Nathan, Frank, 1850
New York
  Abrahams, Hyam, 1794
  Andrews, Zalegman, 1844
  Cardozo, David Nunez, 1775
  Cohen, Philip Melvin, 1829
  DeLeon, Hannah (Hendricks), 1839
  Ellis, Myer J., 1818
  Emanuel, Charlotta, 1850
  Emanuel, Rosetta, 1850
  Emanuel, Sarah, 1850
  Gollinger, Augusta, 1860

Gollinger, Hannah, 1860
Gollinger, Simon, 1860
Isaacks, Judith Rachel (Mears), 1806
Isaacks, Moses, 1800
Isaacs, Jacob, 1830
Jacobs, Samuel, 1794
Lazarus, Gershon Clarendon, 1837
Lazarus, Hetty Maria (Gomez) (Hart), 1850
Lazarus, Rachel DeTorres (Benjamin), 1772
Levy, Eliza, 1850
Levy, Joseph, 1757
Marks, Samuel Mandel, 1800
Massias, Abraham A., 1804
Moses, Rebecca (Jackson), 1860
Phillips, Abraham, 1809
Pinkussohn, Abram, 1860
Seixas, Abraham, 1825
Seixas, Abraham Mendes, 1777
Whippey, Catherine Francis, 1858
Whippey, Cornelius Frances, 1858
Williams, Rebecca, 1820

North Carolina
Prince, Mary Ann (Cortissoz), 1850

North Carolina, Beaufort
Henry, Esther, 1823

Pennsylvania
Dessau, Rebecca, 1850
Goldberg, Rachel, 1850
Goldberg, Rebecca, 1850

Pennsylvania, Philadelphia
Carvalho, David Nunes, 1852
Cohen, Rebecca (Phillips), 1836
DeLeon, Abraham, 1809
DeLeon, Isabella (Bilha) (Moïse), 1860
Hannay, Hannah, 1821
Levy, Almeria (DeLeon), 1819
Mordecai, Isabel Rebecca (Lyons), 1850
Mordecai, Joseph [Joseph D.?], 1808
Moses, Esther Mendez (Phillips), 1845
Moses, Franklin J., 1825
Noah, Mordecai Manuel, 1807
Phillips, Jonas Altamont, 1837
Phillips, Naphtali, 1807

Poland
Beretz, Solomon, 1850
Broadman, J., 1841
David, Berrin, 1860
David, Jacob, 1860
David, Joseph, 1860
David, Mary Ann, 1860
David, Matilda, 1860
David, Woolf, 1860
Davis, Benjamin, 1837
Davis, Mordecai, 1850
Epstein, N., 1860
Epstein, Phillip, 1858
Goldstein, Jacob, 1855
Hart, Susan, 1860
Hyams, Jacob, 1825
Isear, J. A., 1857
Jacubowsky, Simon David, 1860
Lazarus, Abraham, 1860
Lazarus, Lena, 1860
Lazarus, Rose, 1857
Levin, ———, 1855
Levin, Esther, 1860
Levin, Harris A., 1860
Levin, Harris D., 1861
Levin, Matilda, 1860
Levin, Woolf, 1860
Levy, Marcus, 1839
Levy, Marks, 1850
Livingstain, Abraham, 1840
Loewenburg, Joseph, 1860
Loewenburg, Rachel, 1860
Lyon, Mordecai, 1782
Lyons, ———, 1861
Lyons, Joseph, 1860
Moses, Rachel, 1850

Nathan, Myer, 1841
Pollock, Solomon, 1781
Poznanski, Gustavus, 1836
Poznanski, Hyam, 1839
Rosenband, Nathan I., 1855
Samuel, ——— Mrs., 1859
Samuel, M., 1850
Samuel, S., 1850
Solomons, Alexander, 1798
Weinglass, Lewis, 1850
Winstock, M., 1850
Zachariah, Jonathan, 1850
Poland, Goslin, Posen
Phillips, Casper, 1850
Poland, Neustadt, Posen
Bentschner, Esther (Falk), 1857
Bentschner, Isaac, 1854
Bentschner, Jacob, 1854
Bentschner, Wolff, 1858
Cohen, Grune (Jacobi), 1851
Poland, Plock
Petska, David, 1849
Poland, Posen
Holz, Minna, 1857
Zacharias, Ephraim P., 1855
Zacharias, Isidore, 1849
Zacharias, Jane, 1860
Zacharias, Mina, 1860
Zacharias, Robert, 1860
Zacharias, Simon, 1860
Poland, Posen, Krotoszyn
Zacharias, Rosalia, 1860
Poland, Posen, Lissa
Isear, Anna (Mintz), 1857
Poland, Posna
Cohen, Abraham, 1800
Poland, Russian
Isear, Abraham, 1861
Livingston, Hannah, 1830
Mintz, Etel, 1861
Mintz, Joseph, 1851
Pearlstein, J., 1856
Poland, Warsaw
Ehrlich, Morris, 1851
Hart, Sarah, 1845
Jones, Israel, 1850
Prince, Sarah B., 1861
Poland, Wartha
Cohen, Hartwig, 1815
Poland, Zamosc
Cohen, Mordecai, 1788
Poland, Zobnau
Levy, Moses Clava, 1783
Portugal
Marks, Joseph, 1790
Prussia
Breslau, Moses, 1840
Breslau, Myers, 1824
Bush, Jacob, 1854
Cohen, Hannah, 1860
David, R. L., 1861
Dessauer, M. H., 1858
Goldstein, Aaron, 1854
Goldstein, David, 1860
Gollinger, ———, 1860
Gollinger, Herman, 1860
Hart, Caspar, 1859
Hart, Pauline, 1860
Hyman, Amelia, 1860
Hyman, Charles, 1860
Jacoby, Bertha, 1860
Jacoby, Hannah, 1860
Jacoby, Isadore, 1860
Jacoby, Rudolph Robinson, 1860
Manassen, Amelia, 1850
Morris, Elias, 1852
Moses, Henry, 1782
Phillips, Isidore, 1850
Rich, Arnethena, 1860
Rich, Hannah, 1860
Rich, Phillip, 1860
Rosenfeld, Jacob, 1844
Solomons, Bennett, 1860
Valentine, Samuel, 1818

Weinberg, B. A., 1848
Wolfe, Simon, 1860
Zacharias, Yetta, 1860
Prussia, Bielefeld
Meyer, Emil Joseph, 1857
Prussia, Bornbaum
Borck, Roschen, 1858
Prussia, Breslau
Hoffman, Henrietta, 1860
Prussia, Fraustadt
Berge, Mortiz, 1838
Hoffman, Rudolph, 1852
Pecare, Rosel, 1833
Prussia, Kreyankeh
Pinkussohn, Pinkus, 1859
Prussia, Kurnick
Schwerin, Julius, 1841
Prussia, Lessau
Dublin, Henry, 1855
Prussia, Neustadt
Benjamin, David, 1855
Bentschner, Hester, 1856
Bentschner, Isidor Wolff, 1852
Falk, Abraham, 1852
Jacobi, Wolf Jacob, 1849
Rich, Eva, 1860
Wolfe, Esther, 1860
Zacharias, Moses L., 1860
Prussia, Posen
Bush, Minna, 1857
Prussia, Posen, Neustadt
Rich, Lippmann, 1860
Prussia, Rogarsen
Prince, George, 1839
Prussia, Schwersenz
Baum, Jacob, 1854
Rhode Island, Newport
Elizer, Eleazer, 1791
Elizer, Hannah, 1822
Elizer, Priscilla, 1796
Lopez, David, 1793
Mordecai, Esther (Marache), 1803
Rhode Island, Swansea
Isaacks, Abraham Mears, 1800
Russia
Fabian, Henrietta H., 1841
Goldman, L. Jacob, 1861
Hyman, Moses, 1851
Livingston, Lewis S., 1850
Loryea, Aaron, 1850
Loryea, Esther, 1845
Schur, Barnet, 1850
Schur, Bella, 1850
Schur, David, 1847
Schur, Henrietta, 1850
Russia, Courland
Loryea, Isaac, 1849
Russia, St. Petersburg
Housseau, Dorthea (Abramowitch), 1852
St. Croix
Benjamin, Judah Philip, 1820
Canter, Isaac, 1800
Canter, John, 1800
Canter, Joshua, 1790
DeLaMotta, Emanuel, 1800
DeLaMotta, Sarah (Canter), 1796
DePass, Rachel (DeLaMotta), 1784
Levy, Rebecca (Benjamin), 1823
St. Eustatius
Benjamin, Philip, 1820
Moses, Philip, 1774
St. Thomas
Abendanone, Grace, 1807
Abendanone, Hyam, 1800
Abendanone, Joseph, 1785
Peixotto, Grace, 1850
Scotland, Glasgow
Loewenstein, Abraham Levin, 1854
Sweden, Stockholm
Hirsch, John M., 1841
Virginia
Epstein, Isabella, 1860
Jacobs, Rebecca, 1858

Mordecai, Harriet, 1823
Mordecai, Judith, 1820
Trager, Eva (Jacobs), 1860
Virginia, Petersburg
Moïse, Esther (Lyon), 1854
Samuel, Samuel, 1850
Virginia, Richmond
Emanuel, Nathan, 1851
Seixas, David Cardozo, 1848
Wales, Swansea
Cohen, Esdaile P., 1818
West Indies
Vierga, Joseph, 1780

❖

CHAPTER 2

Acceptance

"Here, on these shores of liberty, thy suffering people have found an asylum and a refuge; here they can serve Thee, without fear, in a manner most pleasing to Thee. O Lord, may thy watchful eye rest graciously on this beloved country."

—Jacob Rosenfeld, 1847[1]

Jews have always been noted as a distinct people. Flavius Josephus, the Roman-Jewish historian of the first century, remarked, "Since . . . we have had a peculiar way of living of our own, there was no occasion offered us in ancient ages of intermixing."[2] Charlestonians have also commented about this. For example, J. L. E. W. Shecut in 1819 stated: "There can be no argument that goes more fully to illustrate the correct principles of our government, than that of a reference to the Jews who have settled among us. All other classes of citizens, however their peculiar tenets might have differed . . . were as one family. . . . The Jews were the only settlers . . . whose religious principles differed."[3] Jacob Barrett Cohen in 1884 stated, "The Jews occupy a peculiar place in history."[4] Finally, an American Jewish historian, Abraham J. Peck, remarked in 1987 that Judaism in the South was that "other peculiar institution."[5] The purpose of this chapter is to investigate how well these "peculiar" people fit into the society of Charleston.

Viewing Jews as separate and treating them differently, especially in a negative way, has become known as anti-Semitism. David A. Gerber has defined this as: (1) believing that Jews are different and alien in faith, physiognomy, and psychology; (2) seeing Jews as power-hungry, materialistic, aggressive, dis-

1. "Discourse by Rosenfeld," 327.

2. *Against Apion*, I, 12.

3. Shecut, *Medical and Philosophical Essays*, 30.

4. Cohen, *Judaism and the Typical Jew*, 9.

5. Peck, "That Other Peculiar Institution." The first peculiar institution was slavery.

honest, or clannish; (3) feeling that the above negative qualities result from a manifestation of ill-will toward others; (4) making Jews the object of social discrimination or denying them social and legal rights based on the perception that they are different, alien, and malevolent.[6]

In colonial and antebellum Charleston, Jews received better treatment than in most places in the world. There, for the first time in modern western history, they achieved citizenship, won the right to vote, and held public office. Yet, even there, economic and political progress took time. The accomplishments of Charleston's Jews are a matter of public record. Personal feelings, on the other hand, are more difficult to document.

When in Europe, many Jews suffered persecution, pogroms, disabilities, restrictions, confinement to ghettoes, special taxes, registration, rejection, and expulsion. In England, the Netherlands, and a few other scattered places, however, the treatment, at least in the seventeenth and eighteenth centuries, was notably better. The English granted freedom of worship to Jews in 1674 and reaffirmed this freedom in 1685. Not until 1753, though, could they become citizens, and even then they could not vote.[7] The situation was much the same in the Netherlands. Neither the Dutch nor the English ever created ghettoes. Yet, in both places Jews lived apart from the rest of the population and were thought of as aliens.

In much of the New World the Jews faced similar problems. The Portuguese drove them from Brazil, and the Spanish and French banned them from their colonies, although they were usually ignored if they happened to "slip in." The English found it expedient to be tolerant abroad because they wished to populate their colonies, especially with those who could produce wealth for the mother country. Therefore, they allowed dissenters (non-Anglican Protestants), who also suffered disabilities in England, and others to settle in the New World—except for Roman Catholics, whom they feared for both political and religious reasons. Since Jews arrived in very small numbers, they did not threaten British political authorities. Furthermore, many of them possessed considerable wealth and often had international trade connections. In sum, they could prove useful. At the same time, Jews sought greater economic opportunities. Thus, they began to arrive in South Carolina in the seventeenth century and have continued to come since.

Religious Toleration in Early Carolina

The colony openly received religious dissenters. The charter granted to the proprietors in 1663 called for the establishment of the Church of England, although indulgences could be granted to those people who did not conform to the Anglican church.[8] The second charter, put forth in 1665, again promised toler-

6. Gerber, "Anti-Semitism," 3.
7. Morris, "Civil Liberties," 27.
8. Parker, *North Carolina Charters*, 76–89.

ance for people of different beliefs or practices.[9] After Anthony Ashley Cooper, later Lord Shaftesbury, took over direction of the enterprise in 1669,[10] more liberal promises were made. John Locke, the close friend, physician, and confidant of Cooper, is generally credited with having drawn up the *Fundamental Constitutions*, the proposed framework of government for the colony. Though the social and political systems of Carolina were not very enlightened, the ideas of religious freedom found in the *Fundamental Constitutions* were quite liberal, if not revolutionary for the time. The charter, however, did have some conservative religious elements. For example, it called for the establishment of the Church of England,[11] required all residents to acknowledge that a God existed and was to be publicly worshiped,[12] and compelled everyone seventeen or older to be a member of a religion or profession. Yet, freedom of religion was guaranteed to "Jews, Heathens, and other Dissenters from the purity of the Christian Religion" in the belief that if they were exposed to the "truth," they would be won over. Therefore, seven or more persons agreeing on their religious principles could constitute a church or profession. Furthermore, no one could "use any reproachful, reviling or abusive Language against the Religion of any Church or Profession."[13] Although the provincial parliament never officially accepted the *Fundamental Constitutions*, these regulations were the basic laws for the colony for the first thirteen years of its existence, and many were later incorporated into statutes.[14] The *Fundamental Constitutions* set the tone for religious interactions in Carolina. Only Rhode Island, chartered in 1644, offered such freedom for the Jews, and that colony later rescinded it.

The promise of religious freedom in the *Fundamental Constitutions* attracted many non-Anglicans to the colony. According to one source, two-thirds of the people in Carolina could be classified as dissenters.[15] The Huguenots of France were the most notable group of Protestants. They began to arrive in 1680, and many more followed, especially after 1685 when Louis XIV of France revoked the Edict of Nantes and took away their religious freedom. Although aliens were allowed to settle in Carolina, the *Fundamental Constitutions* did not address economic rights. The ability to own shops, engage in trade, work as craftsmen, in other words make a living, was a privilege and not a right for aliens, much as it is in the United States today. The Jews and Huguenots excelled as shopkeepers and traders, especially in international commerce. The possible loss of their livelihood greatly concerned them. As early as 1692, the English in the colony questioned the right of

9. Ibid., 91–104.

10. For Shaftesbury, see Haley, *The First Earl of Shaftesbury*.

11. Article 96 of second version issued on Mar. 1, 1670. Parker, *North Carolina Charters*, 132–64.

12. Article 95.

13. The second version of *The Fundamental Constitutions* is used here. Parker, *North Carolina Charters*, 132–64.

14. Salley, "The Fundamental Constitutions."

15. Rivers, *Sketch of History*, 217.

the French to perform marriages, to bear legitimate offspring, and to inherit property. The British Navigation Act of 1660 already threatened aliens. This law required that all goods imported or exported from English colonies be carried in English ships that Englishmen had built and that Englishmen owned. Also, the captains and at least three-fourths of the crews of ships had to be English. These laws seem to have been largely ignored, but in 1665 the English accused Jews of monopolizing the trade of Barbados and dealing principally with "their tribe in Holland."[16] Because of concern for their economic rights in Carolina, the Huguenots in 1693 petitioned the proprietors, who responded that the group enjoyed the same privileges as the English.[17]

Another more serious threat appeared in 1696 when the English parliament debated making comprehensive changes in the navigation laws. The proposed act would have excluded any person who was not a native-born British subject from conducting trade in any of the colonies. A group of Huguenots and Jews in London intervened on behalf of their coreligionists in Carolina. The Jewish leaders stated that Jews had traded in the colonies without difficulty for more than forty years and should be permitted to continue. The two groups succeeded. Parliament continued to allow their people to trade in the colonies.[18]

Citizenship

The Huguenots and Jews realized that new threats could develop in the future but that if they could obtain citizenship in Carolina, they would have economic rights. Thus, in 1697 Simon Valentine, Abraham Avila, and Jacob Mendis and another man joined with sixty Huguenots in signing a petition to Governor John Blake requesting citizenship. The governor supported them and so notified the legislature in his address to that body. In response, the assembly, noting that several inhabitants of the colony had transported themselves to the province in the hope of enjoying religious liberty, passed a law that granted citizenship to all aliens, their wives, and children, whatever their nation of origin. At the same time, the legislature ruled that full freedom of conscience and worship would be granted to all Christians, excepting Roman Catholics.[19]

Apparently, this ruling would exclude the Jews, but the authorities seemingly grouped them with the Protestants. At least they were not papists! The Charleston Jews were pragmatic and apparently worried little about how they gained citizenship, because at least two of them did so. Simon Valentine took out his citizenship papers first on May 26, 1697.[20] Abraham Avila followed suit on August 3, 1698.[21] The documents refer

16. Morris, "Civil Liberties," 29.

17. *Journals of Assembly for 1693*, ed. Salley, 31.

18. Morris, "Civil Liberties," 30.

19. *Statutes*, 2: 131–33; Wallace, *History of South Carolina*, 1: 417; *Journals of Assembly for 1697*, ed. Salley, 27.

20. Elzas, *Record of the First Naturalization*.

21. Elzas, "First Jew in South Carolina," in *Leaves from My Historical Scrapbook*.

to these men as aliens of the "Jewish Nation" who had been born outside the realm of the crown of England. Their papers also stated that naturalization granted them the rights and privileges given to "all Protestants."

After they won citizenship, the Huguenots and Jews joined with the Anglicans against the dissenters in the political battles in the province. The struggle centered on control of the assembly. In 1701 the dissenters lost in elections for the parliament. They then claimed that the Anglicans had allowed strangers, indentured servants, paupers, free Negroes, and unqualified aliens to vote. During the next elections, in the fall of 1703, considerable violence and alleged illegal voting occurred. By this time the Huguenots had begun to intermarry with the Anglicans and join in business matters with them. The Anglican party put a Frenchman on the ballot in order to show its acceptance of them. The result was that the Anglicans won a majority of the seats. This time dissenters in Colleton County charged that "Jews, Strangers, Sailors, Servants, Negroes, & almost every *French* Man" in Craven and Berkeley counties had been allowed to vote.[22]

This is the first reported instance of Jews' voting in South Carolina and perhaps in America; however, considering the nature of voting requirements in South Carolina, Jews possibly had been casting ballots for some time. The proprietors had based the right to vote on a property qualification only. Virtually anyone could vote who owned fifty acres of land. This law limited the suffrage for shopkeepers in Charleston but favored the nascent aristocracy.

Obviously, servants, aliens, and men from ships could not have met the voting requirements. Simon Valentine very likely could, as he was a citizen and at some point acquired a 350-acre plantation; so also could Mordecai Nathan, who was joint owner of that estate and owned another by himself.[23] Possibly, the two men purchased the land in order to have full political rights, as both were merchants. Other Jews likely did not own property and could not legally vote, regardless of citizenship. Apparently, though, the election laws were largely ignored, at least by the dominant party. The dissenters' complaint quoted above does illustrate that enough Jews lived in Charleston to be of concern to any who opposed them.

Religious Restrictions

Meanwhile, the Church of England party found strong support in Governor Nathaniel Johnson (1703–9). In May 1704 he hastily summoned the legislature to an early session and quickly pushed through a religious bill. Introduced on May 4, the bill received its second and third readings on May 5, and the governor and council ratified it on May 6. The bill passed the House by a vote of 12 to 11, with 7 members being absent.[24] This measure required members of the House to take communion

22. Rivers, *Sketch of History*, 459.

23. WIM (1714–17), 196–98.

24. Rivers, *Sketch of History*, 217–19.

according to the rites of the Anglican church, as was the case in England, and to take an oath to that effect. Having very strong beliefs about the nature of the communion, many dissenters could not do this in good conscience.[25]

The dissenters, incensed with the alleged voting irregularities in 1703, had already dispatched John Ash to London to set forth their complaints. Although he died before completing his work, Ash managed to accuse "Simon Valentine, the Jew" of taking part in a questionable deal with the governor, a charge that he admitted he could not prove.[26] John Boone replaced Ash as the spokesman for the dissenters in London. By that time the Exclusion bill keeping dissenters from the assembly had passed. Boone employed Daniel Defoe, who wrote a pamphlet entitled *Party-Tyranny* that pressed the charges of the dissenters and exclaimed, "Blush, Gentlemen-Proprietors, and be asham'd for your Petty Sub-Tyrants."[27] When the proprietors showed little interest in the complaints, the House of Lords asked the queen to veto the act, which required the taking of the sacraments according to the rites of the Anglican church. The monarch referred the matter to the Board of Trade, which ruled in 1706 that the act was null and void.[28]

Meanwhile at the November 1704 meeting, the South Carolina assembly made the Church of England the established church.[29] At the same time, it eliminated any religious qualification for voting, allowed voters to take an oath "according to his forme of profession," and denied the vote or the right to sit in the assembly to aliens. The assembly did give resident aliens the right to acquire land and carry on all business affairs.[30] By these laws Jews could vote only if they were British subjects and owned property. Alien Jews had the right to claim land and make valid bargains and sales. When they had to take oaths, they swore allegiance to Queen Anne on the New Testament or according to their profession.

The election law remained on the books until 1716, when the assembly required voters to be professing Christians.[31] In 1717, 1721, and 1745 the assembly restated these provisions and in 1721 took away the ability to swear oaths according to one's profession.[32]

Then, in 1759, the lawmakers required voters and officeholders to be Protestants.[33] This law remained in force until the Revolution. Considering the laxity of enforcement of previous laws on these matters, we may reasonably assume that some Jews may have continued to vote as they had through much of the colonial period.

25. *Statutes*, 2: 232–35.

26. Ash, *Present State of Affairs*, in Salley, *Narratives*, 265–76.

27. Defoe, *Party-Tyranny*, in Salley, *Narratives*, 257.

28. Rivers, *Sketch of History*, 221–25; Wallace, *History of South Carolina*, 1: 68–107.

29. *Statutes*, 2: 236–46.

30. Ibid., 249–51.

31. Ibid., 688.

32. Ibid., 3: 2–3, 136–37, 656–57.

33. Ibid., 4: 98–101.

Naturalization

Meanwhile, in 1740 the British parliament passed an act that naturalized foreign Protestants, Jews, and Quakers (but not Roman Catholics) who had lived in the colonies for seven years and who took an oath or made an affirmation of loyalty to the crown. Jews could omit the words "upon the true Faith of a Christian" from their oath.[34] A number of Jews in Charleston took the opportunity to acquire citizenship. Among these were Joseph Tobias and Moses DeMattos in 1741,[35] Mordecai Myers in 1771,[36] and Isaac DePass in 1774.[37]

Effects of the American Revolution

During the American Revolution a number of South Carolina Jews served in civil and military positions. Whether or not they took their oaths on the "holy evangelists" or even took oaths is unknown. In revolutionary America such legal niceties could easily be forgotten.

One Jew, Francis Salvador, served in the revolutionary legislature and as an officer in the military but died in battle, the first Jew to fall in the American Revolution.[38] Salvador's family, like many Sephardic Jews, had moved from Portugal to Amsterdam, and from Amsterdam to London. The family acquired wealth and a coat of arms in 1745, the grant for which can be found in a damaged condition in the museum of Beth Elohim Synagogue in Charleston. Francis Salvador's father died when Francis was about two years of age. His mother obtained a good education for him and his brother, Moses. His inheritance, which was substantial, allowed him to live well in France and England with his wife and cousin Sarah, a daughter of Joseph Salvador; the latter had purchased 100,000 acres of land in upstate South Carolina in the Ninety-Six District as early as 1755.[39] Joseph Salvador sold some of these lands to Francis Salvador, who soon arrived in Charleston.[40] The person who had arranged the transfer of land from Joseph Salvador to Francis was Richard Andrews Rapley, an earlier émigré from London.[41] After reaching Charleston, Salvador traveled to his lands, which he called Coronaca, also referred to as Cornacre, where Rapley already lived. He then advertised for an overseer with knowledge of indigo, and he purchased slaves.[42]

At the time Salvador came to America, relations between Britain and America were rapidly coming to a climax. The South Carolinians held elections on December 19, 1774, in the Ninety-Six District for representatives to the first and second sessions of the First Provincial Congress in Charleston. Salvador and Rapley were chosen as two of the ten

34. Rosendale, "An Act Allowing Naturalization"; Schappes, *Documentary History*, 26–30.

35. MR2E.110, 111.

36. MR2P.77.

37. MR2F.112.

38. Elzas, *Jews of South Carolina*, 68–77.

39. RMC Book F3, 333.

40. *South-Carolina Gazette*, Dec. 6, 1773.

41. MR4M.286.

42. *South-Carolina and American General Gazette*, Sept. 9, 1774.

3. Salvador Memorial, City Hall Park. (Photograph by Michael Whittemore.)

deputies for the district. At the congress, which met first on January 11, 1775, Salvador served on a number of committees, including one "to draw up a declaration of the motives upon which the proceedings of the present Congress are grounded"; another "to enquire into the conduct of John Dunn, Esq.," who was reprimanded for his failure to remain neutral in the events transpiring between Great Britain and America; one to look into the supplies of ammunition; and one to look into the "state of the interior parts of the country." He was subsequently returned to the Second Provincial Congress on November 1, 1775, and he served in both sessions. At that time he carried out a number of tasks, including investigating the proper salaries for officials, and served along with Charles Coatesworth Pinckney to "examine and compare" the engrossed copy of the 1776 constitution of South Carolina with the "rough draught thereof."[43]

The congress deemed itself the General Assembly of South Carolina upon the adoption of the constitution, and Salvador thus sat in that body until it adjourned on April 11, 1776. By July of that year the frontier area in which Salvador lived began having serious troubles with Indians and "white Scopholites." In letters dated July 18 and July 19, 1776, Salvador reported on events. The militia forces had increased to 600 men, and Salvador carefully advised W. H. Drayton of the problems being encountered.[44] On July 31, 1776, Indians attacked the militia; Salvador fell in battle, and an Indian took his scalp. He died within three-quarters of an hour at the age of twenty-nine.[45] "The whole army regretted his loss, as he was universally loved and esteemed by them."[46] Salvador found acceptance among his rural compatriots. More surprising, Salvador almost immediately joined with the rebels upon his arrival despite the fact that most of his family lived in London and could possibly have been harmed by his actions.

At first, the Revolution changed little for the Jews. The South Carolina Constitution of 1776, which Salvador had examined along with Pinckney, provided that the qualifications for voting should be the same as those required by law, which meant the election law of 1759.[47]

The next constitution, which the legislature passed in 1778, however, gave the vote to free white men who believed in a God and a future state of reward and punishments, were at least twenty-one years of age, had been a resident for a year, and owned fifty acres of land or a town lot. Upon demand of election officials, voters had to take an oath that they met these qualifications. To sit in either the House or Senate one had to be a Protestant.[48] The Jews could vote but not hold office. Furthermore, Protestantism became the established religion,

43. *Extracts from the Journals*, 6, 24, 49, 88, 100, 101, 177, 241, 254.

44. Gibbes, *Documentary History*, 24–26.

45. Drayton, *Memoirs*, 2: 339–50.

46. London *Rembrancer* for 1776, part 2, p. 320.

47. *Constitution, 1776*, art. XI.

48. *Constitution, 1778*, arts. XII and XIII.

although any religious group that acknowledged one god and a future state of rewards and punishments would be tolerated, and individuals could take oaths according to their beliefs. Article XXXIII allowed for the incorporation of churches.

The Supreme Court of South Carolina ruled shortly after the promulgation of the 1778 constitution that both it and the constitution of 1776 were invalid because they had been only legislative acts and could be changed at any time by the assembly. Therefore, a constitutional convention met in Columbia in 1790 and wrote a third constitution. This document eliminated religious qualification for voting or holding office. Furthermore, it provided for "the free exercise and enjoyment of religious profession and worship, without discrimination or preference." The Constitution of 1790 also allowed for the incorporation of religious bodies.[49] Shortly afterward the leaders of the Kahal Kadosh Beth Elohim synagogue petitioned for incorporation. When this petition was approved by the state, they built a meeting house on Hasell Street, which they dedicated in 1794. The basic laws of the state remained in effect until the Reconstruction period.

When the American colonies broke away from England, they issued the Declaration of Independence, which promised equality to all men. After the failure of the Confederation, the Constitution of 1787 and the amendments that became law in 1791 eliminated all religious tests for office, established equality for white men, and established religious freedom. These, however, were federal laws and did not necessarily affect state elections.

The Sunday Laws

Though Jews could fully participate in business and elections, and could stand for office in South Carolina, they still faced a problem with the Sunday laws. One of the basic requirements of Judaism was the commandment to "Remember the Sabbath and to keep it Holy." The Sabbath or seventh day was a day of worship and rest. Furthermore, rule 25 of the Constitution of 1820 of Beth Elohim stated, "Any person or persons publicly violating the Sabbath, or other sacred days, shall be deprived of every privilege of the Synagogue and the services of its officers." Violators could be readmitted only upon payments of fines and penalties as the officers might see fit. The 1836 constitution, however, said nothing about this matter.

The Christians had moved the day of worship from the seventh day to the first, and they sought to enforce worship and rest on Sunday. In 1682 the South Carolina legislature passed Act Number One, which required the observance of Sunday as the Lord's Day.[50] This act was reaffirmed in 1685 and 1712. According to the 1712 law, which is the first to have survived, no one was allowed to work, travel, participate in sports or

49. *Constitution, 1790*, arts. I, VIII.

50. Passed 1682. Reference to it can be found on p. v of *Statutes*, vol. 2, and in Act 28, passed in 1685. The first twenty-two acts have not survived.

pastimes, or cause servants to work on Sunday. According to the act, "the holy keeping of the Lord's Day is a principle part of the true service of God."[51]

In October 1776 a grand jury in Charleston recommended "that Jews and others may be restrained from allowing their negroes to sell goods in shops, as such a practice may induce other negroes to steal and barter with them." The jurors considered this to be a "profanation of the Lord's Day."[52] Whether or not anything came of this recommendation is unknown; however, the city council of Charleston in 1801 passed an ordinance that made it a crime for a person "to exercise any worldly labor, business or work of their ordinary callings, on the Lord's Day," "to sale, or sell in any shop, warehouse, or otherwise any goods, wares of merchandize whatsoever," or to participate in any sports, pastimes, public exercises, or exhibitions or games. Furthermore, no one could disturb church services or employ any slave, with the exception of "necessary occasions for the family."[53] For observant Jews this ordinance caused a serious financial hardship. Charleston businesses stayed open six days a week. If Jews observed their Sabbath as well, they had to close two days of the week, including the busiest day—Saturday. Columbia had a similar law, and in 1833 city officials prosecuted a Jew in that city for operating a store on Sunday. The man contended that the law was unconstitutional because it established a religion. The court ruled against him, stating that the ordinance served the good of society and of law and order.[54]

On a Sunday in July 1840 a black man went to the back door of a store kept by Jacob Meyer, a German-born Jew on upper King Street outside the city limits in the Charleston Neck area. The man purchased a pair of suspenders. When he came out of the building, he was arrested. The state then tried Meyer for violating an 1837 law that made it illegal for shopkeepers in the Charleston Neck area to trade with slaves or persons of color on Sunday or after 9:00 P.M. in the winter or 10:00 P.M. in the summer. The jury found Meyer guilty, and the Court of Appeals refused to order a new trial.[55]

Although Meyer did not question the right of the state to require him to close on Sundays, Solomon A. Benjamin did. On Sunday, December 21, 1845, Benjamin, an Orthodox Jew born in London who operated a clothing shop at 48 East Bay Street, sold a pair of gloves to W. C. Gatewood, a black man. According to the charges, Benjamin then exposed additional goods such as coats, pantaloons, gloves, and other articles of clothing for sale. The defendant, through his counsel, admitted selling the gloves to Gatewood but claimed not to have displayed other goods. The court found him guilty and fined him $40. Benjamin appealed his conviction on the grounds he was a

51. *Statutes*, 2: 13, 396–97.

52. Reznikoff and Engelman, *Jews of Charleston*, 288.

53. *Digest of Ordinances* (1844), 272–73.

54. Friedenberg, "Jews and Sunday Laws," 102.

55. State v. Meyer, *South Carolina Law Reports, November 1842 to May 1843*, 285–89.

Jew and the law could not compel him to observe the Christian Sabbath. He cited the eighth article of the 1790 constitution, which guaranteed the "free exercise and enjoyment of religious profession and worship, without discrimination or preference . . . forever" and maintained that the law interfered with and violated the free exercise and enjoyment of his religion and discriminated against him. He could not be forced to observe and keep the Christian Sunday in addition to his own Sabbath. The city's attorney contended that the law was a police regulation and not a religious one. At the same time he claimed that "Christianity is a part of the common law of the land, with liberty of conscience to all." Furthermore, according to the judge, the constitution of 1790 did not abolish the Christian religion. "It only grants toleration to all religions, the Christian Religion still being the law of the land." In rendering his decision, the judge stated that he admired "the remnant of Israel, scattered among us, and all the other civilized nations of the earth." He then referred to Exodus 31:16, which reads, "The Israelite people shall keep the sabbath, observing the sabbath through the ages as a covenant for all time." He also quoted *Jerusalem,* in which the German Jewish philosopher Moses Mendelssohn (1729–86) argued, "As long as the Almighty does not make known to us changes of the law in accordance with time, place and circumstance, our subtle reasoning cannot release us from the rigid obedience which we owe the law." The judge thus emphasized that Benjamin had the duty to observe his Sabbath. But he stated that there was "no violation of the Hebrew's religion, in requiring him to cease from labor on another day than his Sabbath, *if he is left free to observe the latter according to his religion.*" He then ruled that the observance as required by law was a police matter, not a religious one, and did not cause the man to desecrate his own Sabbath. Benjamin remained guilty.[56] Only in 1983 did the General Assembly make a general relaxation of the Sunday laws, 323 years after the legislature passed Law Number One.

56. Not all Jews agreed on the question of the "Blue Laws." An editorial entitled "Sunday Laws" in *Sunday Times and Noah's Weekly Messenger*, Feb. 13, 1848, refers to this case. The editorial was probably written by M. M. Noah, who had lived in Charleston and who later tried to create a Jewish colony in America. "A very interesting case, involving the constitutionality of Sunday Laws was argued before the Court of Errors in Charleston, South Carolina, on an appeal from the decision of the recorder of the city, who decided that it was not unlawful for an Israelite to vend goods on the first day of the week called the Lords day, and that the ordinance against it was in violation of the constitution of the United States and that of the state. The judge concurred and reversed the decision of the court below, sustaining the Sunday laws. Freedom of religion means a mere abolition of all religious disabilities. You are free to worship God in any manner you please; and this liberty of conscience cannot be violated. . . . If the Israelites possessed a government of their own, they would assuredly prohibit labor on the Sabbath day. It would be their duty to do so, enjoined by their own law. Why prohibit the Christian from enforcing the same regulations? The question ought not to have been raised. Respect to the laws of the land we live in, is the first duty of good citizens of all denominations."

Sensitivity toward Jews

The state courts in Charleston seem to have been sympathetic to the Jews when it came to the composition of juries. Although the records of the Charleston District, Court of General Sessions, are not very complete and often give little information, they show, if the list of jurors is given, that normally when a case involved a Jew, one or more others could be found on the jury. Jury duty for Jews did occasionally pose a problem. An example of the dilemma posed can be found in a letter from Abraham Ottolengui to a judge in 1829. He had been called to serve on a jury on a Saturday. He wrote the judge stating that such an action would violate the Sabbath, "a thing I have never done in all my life." Moreover, the case might "last until Monday a holy day among our nation & they being at present without a regular minister, that duty is performed by me."[57] Whether or not the judge accepted his plea is not known. Someone did see reason to preserve the request.

Problems of Exclusion

Some state governors also presented problems for the community. Two instances made deep impressions on the Jews, who worked as a group to try to change the attitudes of the governors. In the first example, in March 1812, Governor Henry Middleton called for a day of thanksgiving. He asked "all Christian denominations to have services in their respective churches." Middleton did not mention the Jews. The members of Beth Elohim viewed this with considerable displeasure. They wrote the governor protesting their exclusion, pointing out that they constituted "no unimportant portion of the community." The governor quickly replied in a letter to the congregation that the failure to include the Jews had been an oversight and was unintentional. Furthermore, he hoped they would join with other religious societies in the state "in a devotional action that would assuredly be most acceptable to the Almighty." Governor Middleton could be excused in overlooking Beth Elohim; it was the only synagogue in the state. Having made their point, the members of the congregation held a religious assembly on the date set aside for thanksgiving, at which time Myer Moses, who was noted for his speeches, delivered an "excellent discourse."[58]

A similar incident occurred after September 9, 1844, when Governor James H. Hammond of South Carolina issued a proclamation stating that "it becomes all Christian nations to acknowledge at stated periods, their dependence on Almighty God." Therefore, he called on "citizens of all denomination to assemble at their respective places of worship, to offer up their devotions to God their creator, and his Son Jesus Christ, the Redeemer of the World." At the time there were two Jewish congregations in Charleston, and members of

57. A. Ottolengui to Judge Bay, Oct. 9, 1829, South Caroliniana Library, Columbia, S.C.

58. Levin, "The Jewish Congregation of Charleston," 435–37.

both sought to have the Jews included. They approached the governor unofficially without success. Hammond ignored the entreaties. Therefore, about one hundred Jews met and drew up a protest to the governor. They explained that not only had they been excluded, but they found his proclamation offensive in that it referred to the nation as a Christian one and recognized Jesus as the Messiah. They pointed out that the South Carolina constitution had established religious freedom without discrimination or preference. This time the governor responded. He stated that "it did not occur to me, that there might be Israelites, Deists, Atheists, or any other class of persons in the State who denied the divinity of Jesus Christ." Even so, he did not think that he would have changed the language of his proclamation as he "lived in a Christian land" and was the "chief magistrate of a Christian People." Furthermore, he stated that he had addressed his proclamation to the Christian community, and others could ignore it if they wished. He went on to say that the Jews had inherited "the same scorn for Jesus Christ which instigated their ancestors to crucify him." Hammond therefore would not amend his actions and treated the Jews with disdain—if not contempt. As a result the Jews held another public meeting at the Masonic Hall, where Michael Lazarus and Samuel Valentine spoke against the proclamation and the reply of the governor. They appointed a committee to deliberate on the matter. The committee duly gave its report and published its proceedings in newspapers in Charleston and Columbia. However, they experienced no success in dealing with Hammond.[59]

Observations by Visitors

Contempt for the Jews can also be found in observations made by a writer who visited Charleston in 1852. J. Benwell, an Englishman, said that the Jews were numerous and influential in the city and monopolized many of the corporate honors. According to him, avarice was their besetting sin. He claimed that they worked their slaves beyond endurance and forced many of them to labor on Saturday nights in order to bring in more money. If the slaves did not earn enough, they received cruel punishments. A critic of Benwell, however, says that the Englishman had no love for Jews and therefore willingly repeated any hearsay about them.[60] Nonetheless, someone in the city must have told him what he wanted to hear.

Other writers reported a different situation. Hannah Adams in *A History of Jews* reported that the Carolinians were open and hospitable and that some individual Jews held municipal offices and one was a state representative. Furthermore, according to her informant (Jacob Cohen), visitors from every denomination often crowded the seats in the synagogue.[61] Also, when Isaac M. Wise came to Charleston in 1850, he spoke at Beth

59. The proclamation, the letters, and the proceedings can be found in "The Israelites of South Carolina." See also Kohler, "Phases in the History of Religious Liberty."

60. Benwell, *An Englishman's Travels*, 205–6; Steen, "Charleston in the 1850's."

61. Adams, *History of the Jews*, 2: 217.

Elohim. He stated, "The magnificent temple was filled Saturday morning with the fine gentlemen and ladies, Jews and Christians, the sons and daughters of the first families; even a colonel and his granddaughters sang in the choir."[62] I. J. Benjamin, a German Jew who visited America between 1859 and 1862, stated, "the southern states . . . outdid, in many respects, the northern states in hospitality. The white inhabitants felt themselves united with, and closer to, other whites—as opposed to the Negroes." He also pointed out that only the southern states had sent Jewish men such as Judah Benjamin and David Yulee to the U. S. Senate and had elected Henry Hyams as lieutenant governor of Louisiana. "In Charleston," he wrote, "Israelites occupy the most distinguished places."[63]

Participation in Civic Events

The Jews of Charleston also participated in great events. When Lafayette visited Charleston on his grand tour of America, one of those accompanying him was A. Levasseur. He stated that when Lafayette met with dignitaries in Charleston, "we saw all the members of the clergy arrive, assembled under the direction of the Rev. Dr. Farnham, whom they had chosen for their orator. Among them were seen Episcopalians, Presbyterians, Jews, Roman Catholics, and German and French Protestants. To witness their touching union, and the testimonies of their reciprocal liberality, one might have thought that they all belonged to the same communion."[64]

In 1791 the Jews also played a role when the city authorities decided to build an orphan house. All the religious organizations in the city were called upon for assistance. Beth Elohim enthusiastically invited city authorities, the commissioners of the orphan house, and the citizenship at large to attend services in the synagogue on August 21, 1791. The *hazan* Abraham Azuby led a religious service in which the Hebrew and Spanish had been translated into English. After that, Joseph Myers spoke to the gathering of dignitaries. The commissioners of the orphan house responded immediately and reported a "handsome collection" amounting to £48 and 5 shillings.[65] A week later Gershon Cohen wrote Mordecai Sheftall of Savannah about the event. He sent a copy of the prayers used and the speech of Myers. Cohen claimed that he "never saw more decorum & Decent Behaviour in a Place of Worship" in his life. He especially praised the *hazan* and four men and four boys who performed the services. They had practiced for a week, and the tunes were "Delightfully Pretty." Cohen also wrote a Jew in New York City describing the events. In his letter he defended the fact that the services were held on a Sunday. The Jews had not imitated the Christians, he claimed, but chosen a day on which both

62. Wise, *Reminiscences*, 144.

63. Benjamin, *Three Years in America*, 2: 76.

64. Levassuer, *Lafayette in America*, 2: 47–48.

65. Levin, "The Jewish Congregation of Charleston," 385–86.

Christians and Jews could gather. Furthermore, he felt that the event would help to secure stronger links between the two groups.[66]

Another instance when the Jews took part in a community event was in 1813. Mrs. S. M. Drayton on behalf of The Ladies' Benevolent Society of the city contacted the officers of Beth Elohim pointing out that the organization had, from its inception, asked a church each year to hold services at which an address would be given and a collection taken for the benefit of the poor. The ladies had selected Beth Elohim for that year. Nathan Hart, the president of the congregation, responded that they would happily participate, but they did not have a regular minister at the time and no English speech could thus be given. Furthermore, a collection could not be made on the Sabbath because handling money on that day was forbidden by the faith. However, free-will offerings would be made on another day and the proceeds given to the society. Later Mr. Hart turned over $250 for charity.[67]

The Jews also participated in the most elaborate funeral ever held in Charleston, that of John C. Calhoun in 1850. The committee of citizens to make arrangements for the event included M. C. Mordecai and David Lopez. Also, the Hebrew Orphan Society and the Hebrew Benevolent Society were given positions in the parade as it proceeded from Citadel Square, down Boundary Street, turned left on King Street, and left again on Hasell past the synagogue, to Meeting, down Meeting to South Bay. From there, the procession marched along the Battery to East Bay and then up East Bay to Broad Street to the City Hall.[68]

Gentile Support

From time to time Charlestonians supported the Jewish community. For example, when the synagogue was consecrated in 1794, a "numerous concourse of ladies and gentlemen" of the city attended. Furthermore, one of the newspapers remarked:

> We can perceive those little prejudices and weaknesses that have for years disgraced the human character to be wearing off, and safely pronounce, that injured people, in the blessed climate of America, to have realized their promised land. The shackles of religious distinctions are now no more; the oppressive and cramping capitation tax, that has for ages scattered them upon the face of the earth, is here unknown; they are here admitted to the full privileges of citizenship, and bid fair to flourish and be happy.[69]

Another instance was on August 28, 1840, when citizens met in Charleston as a result of the Damascus case, an incident in which Roman Catholics and Muslims accused Jews in Syria of killing

66. Marcus, *American Jewry*, 182–83.

67. Levin, "The Jewish Congregation of Charleston," 435–36.

68. Thomas, *The Carolina Tribute*, 71, 79, 80.

69. *South-Carolina State Gazette & Timothy & Mason's Daily Advertiser*, Sept. 20, 1794.

a monk in order to obtain his blood for use in the baking of the Passover bread.[70] Certainly, this meeting showed community support and acceptance of the Jews —and also demonstrated the anti-Catholic sentiment of the country at the time. Another occasion came in 1847. The Hebrew Benevolent Society, for the first time calling on the entire city for help, held a benefit ball for the purpose of raising funds. The Saint Andrew's Society donated its hall for use, which meant that the function had to be held strictly according to "temperance principles." Men and women from all denominations attended. Since tickets cost $5 per person and the receipts amounted to $1,250, as many as 250 people may have attended. Obviously, the event succeeded for charity and for the Jewish community.[71]

Jews in Public Office

Charlestonians also chose Jews for public office, something noted by travelers to the city. Election to office and appointments to local boards or positions in public service apparently came about in most cases because of the qualifications of the individuals involved. At other times Charlestonians appear to have been sensitive to the group and placed representatives from the Jewish population on commissions and boards. Some served more than others and apparently were appointed for their potential contributions or status.

70. *Proceedings of a Public Meeting on the 28th August, 1840.*

71."Benevolent Society," 310.

As early as 1757 and again in 1760, Joseph Levy received appointments from the governor as a lieutenant in the provincial forces.[72] Not long afterward Moses Lindo became the inspector of indigo and later the appraiser of all dyes and drugs produced in North America.[73] Other early appointments included Joseph Tobias as "a Linguister or Interpreter for the Spanish Language,"[74] Isaac DaCosta as interpreter of Spanish and Portuguese, Abraham Alexander as a clerk in the Treasury Office, and Abraham M. Seixas as warden of the workhouse.[75] When running for office in the 1790s, Seixas composed a doggerel that read:

> The man I love, who will avow
> He is my friend or foe;
> But he who come with double face,
> I do despise as being base.

He lost the election.[76]

From 1800 to the Civil War, Jews held numerous federal, state, and city appointive jobs. Indeed, the names provided here are incomplete, as lists of board members and such can be found only occasionally. Appointive jobs included: assessor (2 Jews); master of the workhouse; clerk of the court; clerk, gauger, measurer, and inspector at the customs house (11); justice of the peace (8); constable, deputy sheriff, jailer, city

72. MR2K.506; 2L.306.

73. MR2M.170; 2P.256.

74. *Journals of the Commons House, 1745–1746*, 50–51; Tobias, "Joseph Tobias."

75. MR2S.331; 2U.29; Charleston directory, 1794; Reznikoff, *Jews of Charleston*, 103–4, 185–86.

76. Marcus, *United States Jewry*, 86.

FIRE DEPARTMENT.

GEORGE A. BOWMAN, Chief.

ASSISTANTS.

1st. S. G. Courtenay, 2d. M. H. Nathan, 3d. C. Wienges.

4. M. H. Nathan's service in the Fire Department as noted in the city directory. (Gazlay, *The Charleston City and General Business Directory for 1855.*)

guard, police warden, and deputy U.S. marshal in the field of law enforcement (21); magistrate (2); paymaster for U.S. Army; positions in the post office (2); register in equity; and positions in the city and state treasury offices (3). By and large, law enforcement attracted Jews who chose not to go into business. Jews also served on many commissions and boards in the city. These include: Free Schools (1), Health (9), Marine Hospital (2), Markets (2), Orphan House (1), Pilotage (2), Poor House (3), Public Schools (1), Roads (1), Shirras Dispensary (1), and Streets and Lamps (1). In addition, Levi Myers served as apothecary general to the militia of the state.

Charlestonians and South Carolinians also elected Jews to public office. Philip Phillips represented the city in the lower house of the state assembly in 1834–35, Myer M. Cohen in 1835–36, and Mordecai C. Cohen in 1845–46. Mordecai C. Cohen also served in the state senate from 1855 to 1858. Lyon Levy, who had long service in the state treasury office, was elected as the state treasurer in 1817, a position he occupied until 1822. Of those with appointive and elective positions, Mordecai C. Cohen held the greatest number. In addition to being a state representative and senator, he served on at least five commissions in the city. A man of great wealth, he assumed his position in the community and received duties and honors in return.[77] On a whole, most people in Charleston seem to have been very receptive to the Jews as a separate group.

Housing Patterns

Because Charlestonians did not restrict housing, Jews dwelled where they wished.[78] The 1790 directory lists 56 places of business or residences of Jews in the city, about 5 percent of the en-

77. Charleston directory, 1790, 1794, 1800, 1801, 1802, 1803, 1806, 1807, 1809, 1813, 1816, 1819, 1822, 1829, 1831, 1835–36, 1837–38; 1840–41, 1849, 1852, 1855, 1859; Reznikoff, *Jews of Charleston*, 103–4, 204–5.

78. In order to find where the Jews lived and worked, I examined the directories for the years 1790, 1809, 1831, and 1852. These cover approximately twenty-year intervals. Directories did not appear every year, and some possibly are missing. The first directory for Charleston that attempted to list all businesses, if not residents, was issued in 1790. The one published in 1809 was the first to give addresses for people in the Charleston Neck area, then the district above Boundary (Calhoun) Street. The other two were chosen because they came about two decades apart.

tries. Although the directory obviously omits blacks and poor people, it probably does include a considerable proportion of the Jews because most of them engaged in some sort of business and would have wanted to be listed.[79] Although the Jews scattered throughout the city, many clustered on King Street, already in the eighteenth century the most important street for businesses. There, 46 percent of them located their businesses, homes, or both.[80]

In later years this same pattern holds true. In 1809 the Jews continued to live almost anywhere in the city, with the highest number concentrated on King Street (55 percent). For the 110 entries in the directory of that year, the Jews lived in 25 locations.[81] In 1831 Jews can be found in 31 locations. The highest concentrations were on King Street, with 26 percent, and East Bay Street, with 15 percent. Another 6 percent lived in the market area. Otherwise, members of the group tended to be widely scattered, living and working in many different locations.[82] In 1852 the Jews were located in 52 areas in Charleston, with the greatest concentrations being in the commercial regions of King Street, with 19 percent, and East Bay Street, with 12 percent. The next highest concentration can be found on Meeting Street, with 9 percent.[83] Over the

79. The streets where they lived were Beresford's Alley (2), Champney's Row (1), Church Street (2), Clifford Street (2), East Bay Street (6), The Exchange (3), King Street (26), Lynch's Lane (1), Meeting Street (2), Moore Street (1), Motte's Wharf (1), Pinckney Street (1), Queen Street (2), Short (1), Tradd (2), Union Street Continued (2).

80. In 1790 very few Jews, as well as other residents of the city, had both a business and home address. Indications are that most people had businesses with homes above them.

81. The places were Beaufain (1), Bedon's Alley (1), Beresford's Alley (1), Broad Street (1), Champney's Row (4), Church Street (4), Church Street Continued (1), Cock Lane (1), East Bay Street (4), The Exchange (2), Guignard Street (1), King Street (61), King Street Road (1), Legare Street (1), Liberty Street (1), Meeting Street (3), Meeting Street Road (1), Orange Street (3), Queen Street (1), Savage Street (1), St. Philip's Street (2), Swinton's Lane (2), Tradd Street (7), Trott Street (2), Wentworth Street (3).

82. They are Archdale Street (1), Beaufain Street (4), Boundary Street (1), Broad Street (4), Champney's Street (2), Church Street (1), Clifford Street (3), Coming Street (1), Cordes Wharf (1), East Bay Street (18), Elliott Street (1), George Street (2), Guignard Street (2), Hasell Street (5), King Street (31), Kunhardt's Wharf (1), Magazine Street (2), Market Street (7), Meeting Street (3), Montague Street (1), New Street (1), Orange Street (1), Queen Street (2), Savage Street (1), South Bay Street (2), St. Philip's Street (3), State Street (3), Stoll's Alley (2), Tradd Street (4), Vendue Range (3), Wentworth Street (5).

83. The locations are Adger's Wharf (2), Aiken Row (1), American Hotel, (1), Amherst Street (1), Anson Street (1), Archdale Street (1), Atlantic Wharf (3), Bank of South Carolina (2), Bedon's Alley (1), Beaufain Street (6), Broad Street (5), Brown's Wharf (1), Burns Lane (1), Calhoun Street (3), Chalmer's Street (1), Chapel Street (4), Charleston Hotel (1), Church Street (6), College Street (2), Coming Street (2), Court House Square (2), Custom House (2), Dewee's Wharf (1), East Bay Street (25), Friend Street (1), Gillon Street (1), Green Street (2), Hayne Street (5), Horlbeck Alley (2), King Street (39), Laurens Street (1), Lightwood's Alley (3), Market Street (5), Meeting Street (18), Minority Street (1),

years with the opening of new areas of the city, the Jews dispersed ever more widely. By 1852 a number of people had separate residences from their places of business, the most popular streets for homes being King, Wentworth, Meeting, Beaufain, and St. Philip's.

With the exception of the tendency to concentrate along the business streets, no distinct geographical pattern can be seen for the Jewish residents of Charleston. On some streets, such as King and East Bay, they formed a considerable element, but other businessmen and women always outnumbered them. They seem to have lived on virtually every street in the city at some time. Absolutely no discriminatory pattern can be seen in the location of homes and businesses.[84]

The Jews of Charleston could also purchase property anywhere they wished. From the beginning they owned country estates and houses in the city. Fortunately, the city of Charleston took a census of every building in the city in 1861 and listed the owners and occupants. As a result, the extent of property holding at one time can be examined. The census shows that Jews owned 396 houses and businesses in the city. These represented 143 separate owners, occupants, or establishments. Some people owned a considerable amount of property. For example, the estate of Isaac Barrett had 29 buildings scattered throughout the city but mostly on King and Meeting streets. In addition, Moses D. Hyams owned 23 buildings, Joshua Lazarus 20, the estate of Nathan Nathans 18, and Benjamin A. Rodrigues 11. Forty-two owners occupied buildings they owned. The rest were occupied by other whites (165), by Jews (35) who in some cases were relatives, free persons of color (19), or slaves (17). The owners of buildings not owned by the Jews who were using them were other whites (49), Jews (35), and free people of color (2).[85]

Business Relations

Obviously, in conducting their businesses, Jews had to deal largely with non-Jews. The ordinary buying and selling of goods seem to have been no problem; however, when it came to close business relationships, Jews and other whites remained somewhat distant. Yet a number of business partnerships between Jews and others were formed from time to time. Nevertheless, the partnerships that survived over a period of several years, judging from their listings in city directories, tended to be within Jewish families. (See Table 8.)

Nassau Street (2), New Street (1), Pinckney Street (1), Pitt Street (1), Queen Street (4), Rutledge Street (1), Short Street (1), Smith Street (3), Society Street (2), Southern Wharf (1), St. Philip's Street (7), State Street (2), Tradd Street (5), Vendue Range (4), Wall Street (1), Warren Street (1), Wentworth Street (11).

84. Examinations of other city directories reveal that this pattern holds up and many other streets are represented. Addresses for people at the time of their deaths, though limited in number, substantiate the information in the directories, with the exception that a few more seem to have lived on Coming Street.

85. Ford, *Census of Charleston*.

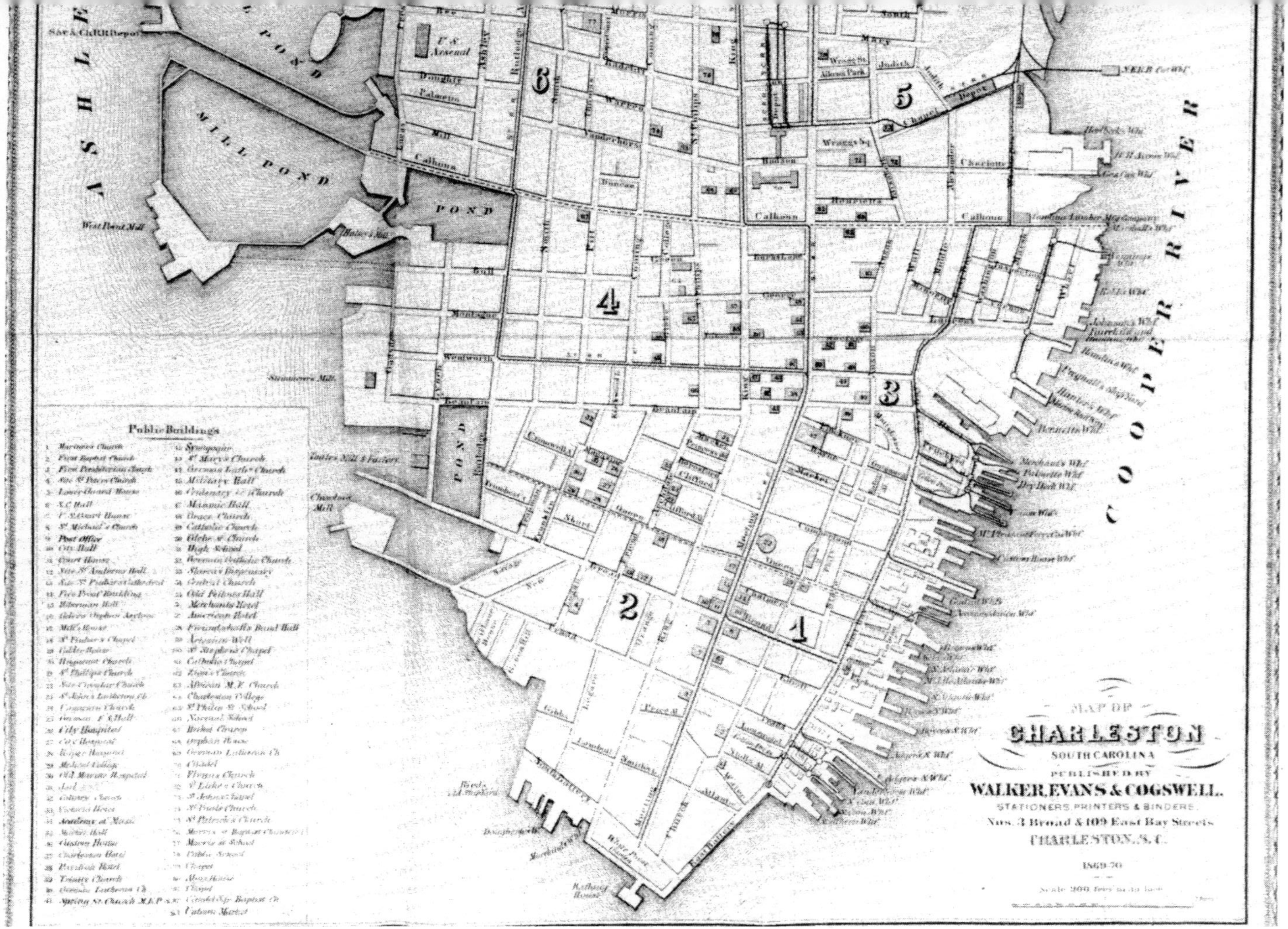
ASHLEY
MILL POND
POND
POND
Public Buildings
COOPER RIVER
MAP OF
CHARLESTON
SOUTH CAROLINA
PUBLISHED BY
WALKER, EVANS & COGSWELL.
STATIONERS, PRINTERS & BINDERS.
Nos. 3 Broad & 109 East Bay Streets
CHARLESTON, S.C.
1869-70

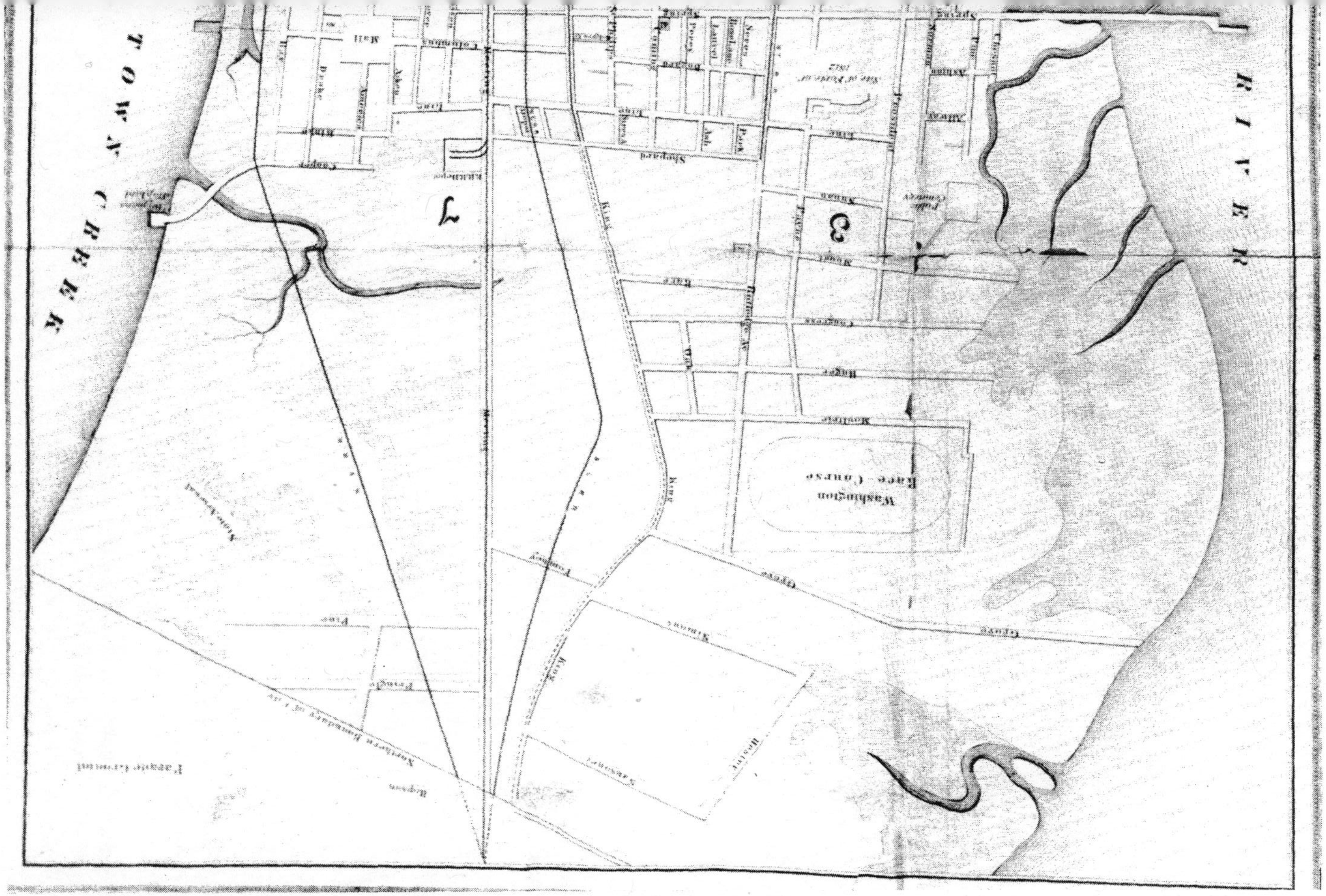

5. Map of Charleston, 1869. (Courtesy of Special Collections, College of Charleston Library.)

Table 8
Examples of Partnerships in Charleston between Jews and Others

Year Formed	*Name of Firm*	*Partners*
1758	DaCosta & Farr	Thomas Farr, Jr., and Isaac DaCosta
1779	Stevens, Henry & Co	Abraham DaCosta, Jervis H. Stevens, Joseph Johnson, and David Menzes
1792	DaCosta, Worthington & Kirby	Abraham DaCosta, Joseph Worthington, and Nicholas Kirby
1798	Moses, Isaac & Co.	Isaac Moses and John Stewart
1809	Mordecai & DeBow	
1820	Brown & Moses	Joshua Brown and Myer Moses
1820	Staley & Moses	Christian Staley and Isaac C. Moses
1821	Ballund & Sarzedas	Alexander Ballund and David Sarzedas, Jr.
1831	F. A. Colburn & Co.	Frederick A. Colburn and Isaac Mordecai
1834	B. P. Colburn & Co.	Benjamin P. Colburn and Isaac Mordecai
1837	J. Cohen Jr. & Co.	Jacob Cohen, Jr., and R. A. Long.
1838	Kinloch & Mordecai	George Kinloch and Thomas Mordecai
1840	Flex & Levy	Michael Flex and Marks Levy
1859	Brown & Hyams	George W. Brown and Mordecai Hyams
1859	Cohen, Willis & Co.	A. N. Cohen, Jr., B. G. Willis, and Israel Ottolengui
1859	Hyams, Mordecai, Brown & Hyams	
1859	Mordecai & Co.	M. C. Mordecai, I. E. Hertz, J. A. Enslow, J. R. Mordecai

Sources: Records in South Carolina Archives, 1758–1859.

From time to time legal agreements were made. Records in the state archives show that 9 of these were between Jews,[86] and 5 were between Jews and others.[87] When it came to giving power of attorney to someone, Jews gave this authority to other Jews 36 times[88] and to non-Jews 17 times.[89] Non-Jews gave it to Jews only 9 times.[90] These records tend to indicate that the non-Jews were hesitant about dealing with the Jews and that the Jews preferred to keep matters among themselves.

Some idea of business relationships

86. MR3M.133; 3S.175; 5C.225; 5D.19; 5M.226; 5X.517; 5Y.302; 5X.244.

87. MR2U.202, 369; 5H.332; 5M.3; 5P.55.

88. MR2P.257; 2T.359, 361; 2U.249, 554; 3B.392; 3E.406; 3F.140, 248; 3H.99, 30, 196; 3U.99, 248; 3V.117, 160, 533; 3Z.337; 4C.14; 4E.470; 5L.314, 424; 40.67; 4Q.246, 423, 495; 4T.301, 496; 4W.111, 126, 358, 388, 394; 4Z.38.

89. WIM (1722–1726), 1726; MR2X.571; 30.81; 3Q.89, 324, 325, 553; 3R.259; 3U.221; 3V.431; 3W.203; 3Y.201; 4E.194; 4F.243; 4G.412; 4Q.528; 4S.221.

90. MR3C.166; 3E.19, 484; 3K.34; 3Q.606, 3V.315; 3W.162; 3Z.154; 4C.363.

Table 9
Patterns of Jewish and Gentile Relationships in 200 Civil Cases in Charleston, 1705–1824

Jews v. Gentiles	46.0%
Gentiles v. Jews	40.0%
Jews v. Jews	10.0%
Jews and Gentiles v. Gentiles	2.0%
Gentiles v. Jews and Gentiles	1.5%
Jews and Gentiles v. Jews	0.5%

Note: Sample was randomly selected from 2,000 cases of record. The Plaintiff is named first. *Sources:* Records of Court of Common Pleas, South Carolina Archives.

can be obtained from civil cases. Approximately two thousand records can be found between 1705 and 1824 in which Jews were involved. These cases typically deal with the nonpayment of debts or the settlement of estates. All residents seem to have used the courts as a debt- collection service; the number of cases is enormous. A random sample of 200 of these shows that the Jews of the city had active commercial relationships with non-Jews but rarely joined with Gentiles in cases. (See Table 9.)

Personal Relationships

Relationships on a more personal level also show that Christians had their differences with Jews. An example is correspondence received by Isaac DaCosta from John Joachim in 1770. Much of the letter deals with a discussion the two men had in Charleston regarding a passage in Isaiah 7:14 regarding a virgin, which had been translated by some to mean Mary, mother of Jesus. The conclusion of the letter states, "we are persuaded, and thousands among us earnestly pray for it, that the Vail of Moses may be taken away from the face of our elder Brethren the Jews, that there may be one Shepherd and one Sheepfold, that the Heathen may trust in his Name and all Israel be saved!"[91] Though the exchange between the two may have been courteous, it also reveals that the author viewed Jews as heathens because they had not accepted Jesus as the Messiah.

In the December 1, 1778, edition of the Charleston *Gazette* a letter to the editor signed by "An American" said that he had witnessed several carriages and loaded horses come into Charleston from Georgia. "Upon inspection of their faces and enquiry, I found them to be of the Tribe of Israel, who after taking every advantage in trade the times admitted fled here for asylum with their ill got wealth turning their backs on their country." In reply to this attack, an unknown writer to the *South-Carolina and American General Gazette* stated that the people in the caravan were women and children and that at the time there was not a single Georgia Israelite in Charleston. The writer went on to say that the Jews were as staunch as other citizens of Carolina in support of the Revolution, and "I hope their further conduct will be such as will invalidate the malicious and designing fallacy of the author of the piece alluded to."[92] The letter in the *Gazette* reflects many of the contemporary negative feelings toward Jews. The

91. John Joachin Zubly to Isaac DaCosta, [1770 ?], American Jewish Archives.

92. Response was in *South-Carolina and American General Gazette*, Dec. 3, 1778.

writer saw them as aliens whose physiognomies set them apart. And worst of all, perhaps, they were viewed as materialistic. Their flight from Savannah only proved to him their inferiority.

In 1800 someone using the initials A. B. wrote to the Charleston *Times* claiming that "a federal or state officer affected to join in worship with the Jews" and afterward distributed election tickets. A few days later another person using the initials C. D. wrote on the subject. Then a Jew identifying himself or herself as E. F. responded. The Jewish writer claimed that the article by A. B. was altogether void of truth and candor and that it "most wantonly asperses the Hebrew nation." According to this person, no state officer was in the synagogue enclosure after the service was finished; consequently, no tickets could have been distributed by him, as alleged, for electioneering purposes. The writer felt that the charges were intended as a slur upon the congregation. He stated that the votes of the Jews were not for sale, and they had not "prostituted the temple of the Most High, for electioneering purposes."[93] Obviously, a state official had attended worship at the synagogue in hopes of getting votes.

Sometimes personal differences resulted in violence. In 1818 Nancy McDowall of Charleston claimed that Rebecca Solomons, her husband Aaron, and her son Shane Audler had attacked her. She deposed that Mr. and Mrs. Solomons threw brickbats at her in her own yard, cutting her head and severely wounding her. Also, Shane threatened to come in her house and beat her. Moreover, she claimed that he threw a dead fowl at her. McDowall claimed that she believed her life was in danger and wanted a peace bond. Rebecca Solomons, however, swore that McDowall threw a dead fowl over the fence and hit her in the face. Mrs. Solomons tossed it back, only to have Mrs. McDowall pitch it at her again in the evening. McDowall, she claimed, then grossly insulted and abused her "and called her a damned Jew bitch." The court, either believing the Solomons or confused by all the claims about fowls, refused to return an indictment.[94] Obviously, some Jews did not get along with their neighbors.[95]

Some Jews felt slighted and left out, although they would have had difficulty proving that they were unacceptable to their peers. Joseph Lyons, the son of Isaac Lyons and Rachel Cohen Lyons, attended South Carolina College (now University), where he graduated in 1822. Although he went on to receive his medical degree from the University of Pennsylvania, he wrote: "I have passed through without being distinguished with even the paltry honor of an appointment on the Exhibition, which was a piece of injustice, which would not have annoyed me but from the evidence

93. Charleston *Times*, Oct. 16, 1800.

94. State v. Rebecca Solomon, Aaron Solomon, Shane Audler, May Session, 1818, Bills of Indictment, Court of General Sessions.

95. Aaron Solomons may not have been the best of neighbors. In 1811 he was pardoned for an assault. MR4C.557.

6. Fanny Yates of Liverpool, later the wife of Jacob C. Levy of Charleston. (Portrait by Thomas Sully. Courtesy of the Corcoran Gallery.)

of prejudice which it indicated against me."[96]

Wealth and culture did not change the fact that some Jews felt uneasy in social situations. Jacob C. Levy and Joshua Lazarus, both from well-to-do Charleston Jewish families, received good educations. Their families sent them to Europe to further their training. The two visited Liverpool, where

96. Reznikoff, *Jews of Charleston*, 109–10. The experiences of Ludwig Lewisohn, the author and critic, were much like those of Joseph Lyons. He attended the College of Charleston at the turn of the twentieth century. His classmates did not invite him to their parties, which they openly discussed before him despite the fact that at the time he attended the Methodist Church and even taught Sunday School there. He also failed to gain admission to a fraternity. Upon graduation, according to his semi-autobiographical *Up Stream*, he obtained a teaching position at what is now Porter-Gaud School. But a local clergyman denounced him in a letter to the Charleston *Courier*, and he lost the job. Although all his statements cannot be verified, they show the lack of acceptance of Jews. Ludwig Lewisohn, *Up Stream* (New York, 1926), chapter IV, pp. 89–119.

Jacob Levy met and fell in love with Fanny Yates, whom he married. Afterward, he returned with her to Charleston. According to a family history, the "foreign bride was the admiration of the whole city. It is said that at her first appearance in the dress circle of the old Charleston Theatre in Broad St., the whole house rose in tribute to her matchless beauty." The Levys lived on East Bay near the homes of the Heywards, the Laurens, and other important Charleston families. Mrs. Levy was the leader of the "best Jewish society." Her husband enjoyed books and had an impressive library in the home. When his business interests took a turn for the worse, he devoted his time to the Charleston Library Society, "then the resort of the 'illumaniti' of Charleston." The children of the couple, all girls, were sought for marriage by the "most polished & wealthy young Israelites" as intermarriages between Jews and Christians were then unusual. The glowing family history then suddenly shifts moods. The author states:

> About forty years ago, Mr. Levy removed with his family to Savannah, Georgia, where they at once took social rank with the best people in that eminently refined society—a marked contrast, in its liberal tone, to the narrow-minded bigotry of Charleston people. In Charleston, the higher circles were closed to Jews.

The author goes on to relate, however, that the "broadened social circle had its dangers" because the female members of the Levy family in Savannah married Christians, and Judaism lost them.[97]

Most Jews seem to have been free to make choices in virtually all personal matters. For example, they obtained medical care from the physician of their choice. The death records of Charleston show that the Jews who died in the city between 1821 and 1861 were attended by 41 different physicians; only two doctors in this list, Columbus DaVega and Jacob DeLaMotta, were Jewish. Neither Jewish physician had large numbers of Jewish patients. DeLaMotta, who received his degree in 1810, served in the War of 1812 and practiced medicine in Charleston, New York, and Savannah. His main concern, in Charleston, was his pharmacy, which he operated in Charleston from 1825 until his death in 1845.[98] DaVega obtained his medical degree in 1852. Following that, he served in the Crimean War (1853–56) before setting up practice in Charleston. In other words, he did not reside very long in the city during the period between 1821 and 1860. The physicians with the most Jewish patients were Eli Geddings, Edward North, and Henry R. Frost, then recognized among the best in the city.[99]

Frequently, relations between Jews and Christians seemed warm. An ex-

97. Yates, Samuel and Lazarus Families, American Jewish Archives.

98. Waring, *History of Medicine in South Carolina, 1670–1825*, 209–10; Tobias, "Many-Sided Dr. De La Motta."

99. Waring, *History of Medicine in South Carolina, 1825–1900*.

ample occurred in 1802 when General Christopher Gadsden gave the congregation three volumes of the Mishnah and two of the works of Moses Maimonides. Gadsden stated in the letter accompanying them that he had "long had a particular regard" for the congregation. His gift especially pleased the elders of the congregation, and they thanked him warmly for the "ancient and valuable" works.[100] Another example occurred in 1858 when a severe yellow fever epidemic ravaged Charleston. Mrs. Elizabeth Bonnell and her father John Drummond took care of the sick and dying members of a Jewish family who came down with the fever. The Hebrew Orphan Society passed resolutions thanking them for their assistance and presented Mrs. Bonnell with a copy of a Bible and a letter of thanks to her father.[101]

Perhaps the best example of Jewish participation in life in Charleston is provided by the Masons. The first known Jewish member of a Charleston masonic lodge was Isaac DaCosta in 1753. He and others actively took part in and served as officers of a number of organizations: King Solomons Lodge Number 1, La Candeur Lodge Number 12, La Reunion Francaise Number 45, Orange Lodge Number 14, and Friendship Lodge Number 9. Also, four of the nine founders of the Supreme Council of Scottish Rite Masonry were Jewish: Emanuel DeLaMotta, Abraham Alexander, Israel DeLieben, and Moses C. Levy. Such activity, however, was not unique for Charleston. Quite early, Jews participated in masonry in America. The Masons believed in toleration and equality, and they practiced what they professed—at least for the white male members of human society. The Masons also used the Hebrew system of dating and believed in universalism. Thus, Jews did not have to overcome any religious problems when they took part. In return, the Masons often helped to dedicate synagogues, including Beth Elohim.[102]

All in all, most Charlestonians saw a need to include Jews in many events. When it came to business associations, the relationships between Jews and others were somewhat less close. And social events seem to have been more segregated. At the same time, many Jews, perhaps, did not want to participate fully in the often vacuous social gatherings. Despite some standoffishness on both sides, the Jews of Charleston fared much better than in most places in the world. With few exceptions, they felt so much at home that Myer Moses could proclaim in 1806, "the Almighty gave to the Jews what had long been promised them, namely a second Jerusalem! . . . . I am so proud of being a sojourner in this promised land."[103] Isaac Harby,

100. Levin, "The Jewish Congregation of Charleston," 388–89.

101. Tobias, *Hebrew Orphan Society*, 16.

102. Oppenheim, "Jews and Masonry"; Harris, *Eleven Gentlemen of Charleston*, 571–73.

103. Moses, *An Oration*, 6, 18, 19.

two decades later, expressed largely the same sentiment, stating, "America truly is the land of promise spoken of in our ancient Scriptures; that this is the region to which the children of Israel, if they are wise, will hasten to come."[104]

The Jews often found it easy to mix with other Charlestonians because so many of them came from London. Some obviously were well educated and urbane. Furthermore, they did not dress in an unusual manner. Even though the Jews did some things differently from the rest of the population, they found Charlestonians to be more tolerant of unconventional citizens than were people in most European and American cities. Also, Judaism emphasizes the enjoyment of life, an attitude widely shared among the sociable Charlestonians. In addition, not only did the Jews assume their duties in government and charity, but Jewish shopkeepers and merchants were needed for the economic development of Charleston. Finally, they were not viewed as a racial threat, as were the African Americans, or as a religious menace, as were the Catholics.

104. Harby, *Discourse*.

Chapter 3

Sense of Community

"Its object is to aid the poor and needy stranger, who may be compelled to seek an asylum in this free and happy country."

—Isaac Leeser in 1848[1]

Jacob R. Marcus, the noted historian of American Jews, stated, "For Christians, it is Christ who is all important; for Jews, it is Jews who are all important." The concern for other Jews is paramount. Despite their diversity, they feel a kinship because "Jews did not join the group, they were born into it."[2] As a group, the Jews of Charleston sought to preserve their religious heritage, look after common interests, and take their place in the city. Nevertheless, they had their differences with their neighbors and within their group.

The first Jews known by name appear together in the same record when Simon Valentine sold a slave to Samuel Mincks.[3] The next document having to do with Jews shows Abraham Avila giving power of attorney to Valentine.[4] These men certainly felt some sort of kinship—being Jewish, no doubt, counted more than language or national background. By the middle of the eighteenth century, enough Jews had reached the city that they could express their sense of community by founding institutions such as synagogues, cemeteries, social service institutions, and schools, and by taking joint actions from time to time.

Sources

Unfortunately, the early history of the community is difficult to trace because most of the records before 1838 have disappeared. These could have been lost or destroyed during the Civil War, although some may yet come to light. Nathaniel Levin had access to them in

1. "Benevolent Society," 310.
2. Marcus, *United States Jewry*, 310.
3. WIM (1694–1704), 362.
4. Ibid.

the 1840s because he quotes directly from them, and the disputants in a religious conflict that went to the courts in that same decade had at least the minute book for 1784. The records may have been taken by the orthodox members who formed Synagogue Shearith Israel; its records have disappeared. Because they saw themselves as carrying forth the traditional faith, they could have felt the records belonged to them. Most of the history of the first ninety years of the congregation must be recreated from the writings of Levin and a much shorter account found in J. L. E. W. Shecut, *Medical and Philosophical Essays*, written in 1819. Levin's history, entitled "The Jewish Congregation of Charleston," appeared in the first volume of the orthodox Jewish magazine *The Occident* in 1843–44. He mentions the records several times. He seems to have carefully gone through them extracting the most important events, and, on occasion, he quotes documents in their entirety.

The Synagogue

In America, Jewish community life has centered on the synagogue. In ancient Israel the temple in Jerusalem occupied the foremost place in religious life, but after the destruction of Jerusalem by the Romans, the temple no longer existed. Thereafter the synagogue became the chief Jewish institution. The word, which is Greek in origin, means "assembly." In Yiddish *shul* or "school" was synonymous with synagogue, while the Hebrew *bet ha-knesset* means "meeting house." Worship in the synagogue is a group activity, and Jewish practice requires a *minyan*, or ten males over the age of thirteen, for services to take place. Just when a *minyan* could be formed in Charleston is unknown. Shecut says, "As soon as ten men could assemble (and which the Hebrew law requires, for public worship) they provided themselves with a place, as suitable as their slender means could command." Shecut continues, "A vestry was afterwards organized, and a minister called from England, to exercise the sacred functions of his office."

Both Shecut and Levin are vague about the first meetings. Levin states that enough Jews had gathered in the city by 1750 and then relates that the records of the first meeting come from the second day of the Jewish year 5510, which corresponds to September 14, 1749 (old style), or September 3, 1749 (new style). He names the following people as being present in the city at the time: Moses Cohen, Isaac DaCosta, Joseph Tobias, Meshod Tobias, Moses Pimienta, David D'Oliveira, Abraham DaCosta, Mordecai Sheftall, Levi Sheftall, Michael Lazarus, and Abraham Nunez Cardoza. Levin does not say that this information comes from the minutes; he does point out that descendants of many of these individuals still lived in the city. He probably obtained this from some of them, because it is unlikely that Meshod Tobias and Levi Sheftall helped to constitute a *minyan*—both were only nine years of age at the time.[5] Without these two, the group would have been short of a *minyan;* however, a number of

5. Stern, *First Jewish Families of America*, 267, 298.

7. The founding of Beth Elohim. Mural by William Halsey. (Photograph courtesy of Beth Elohim Synagogue.)

other Jews appear to have resided in the city at the time, a possibility that Levin does not exclude. Others then living in Charleston, if not before, were Abraham Cohen, Philip Hart, and Jacob Lopez D'Oliveira.

"At the first meeting of which any record exists," on the evening of the second day of Rosh ha-Shanah, thus technically the third day of the year as the Jewish day begins at sunset, the organizers elected Moses Cohen, the person most responsible for forming the group, as the *haham* (chief rabbi) and head of the *beth din* (religious court), Isaac DaCosta as *hazan* (reader), Joseph Tobias as *parnass* (president of the congregation), and Philip Hart as *mohel* (the person who performs circumcisions).[6]

6. Levin, "The Jewish Congregation of Charleston," 337.

They also adopted the name of Kahal Kadosh Beth Elohim, or Holy Congregation of the House of God. The organizers were Sephardic Jews with the exception of Philip Hart and the Sheftalls.

Levin points out, "In this year [1749] they associated themselves as a religious society,"[7] a fact confirmed by a document surviving from 1775.[8] They established as their form of worship the Minhag Sephardim of the Spanish-Portuguese Jews, "as observed by the congregations of London and Amsterdam."[9] Levin points out that the first congrega-

7. Ibid.

8. Minutes of a meeting of Isaac DaCosta, Abraham DaCosta, Isaac DaCosta, Jr., Isaac DeLeon, and Jacob Tobias, Jan. 25, 1775, American Jewish Historical Society.

9. Levin, "The Jewish Congregation of Charleston," 338.

tion was strictly orthodox in its obedience of the written and oral laws, and anyone who violated the Sabbath or religious holidays could expect heavy penalties and loss of membership in the synagogue. As in London, the organizers established the *adjunta* as the ruling body. This consisted of eighteen men whom the congregation elected each year. In turn, the *adjunta* chose a *parnass* and other officers. The officers could make rules and regulations "for the peace, harmony, and good government of the people."[10]

The society used a small wooden house on Union Street (now State) near Queen as its first place of worship until 1757, when it moved to 318 King Street, near Hasell. The new meeting house had much more room than the earlier one and stood some distance off the street. In 1764 the congregation moved again, this time to a building on Beresford Street (now Fulton), near King.[11] A visitor to the city in 1765 mentions a meeting house of the Jews,[12] an indication that the building was substantial enough to be noted.

Internal Divisions

The first indications of division in the community appeared early. Moses Cohen, who Shecut indicates was brought over from London, had been recognized as the first rabbi of the congregation, although no proof exists that he was ordained. "Rabbi" probably meant that he was knowledgeable about Jewish law. As he did not receive a salary from the synagogue, he earned his living as a shopkeeper. Apparently things went well under his leadership. When he died in 1762 he was fifty-three years of age and seems to have served as rabbi until that time. Abraham DaCosta apparently succeeded him. DaCosta had studied in London under the chief rabbi of the Portuguese Jews, Isaac Nieto. For a living he engaged in trade and shipping. A misunderstanding developed between DaCosta and some of the congregation, and "the reverend gentleman resigned his office."[13] Levin, in his account of the early history of the congregation, seems to indicate that this happened in 1764.

The *Gazette* of August 18, 1766, notes the arrival of the Reverend Mr. Alexander on the ship *Queen Charlotte* from London. Abraham Alexander, who was born in London, the son of Rabbi Joseph Raphael, apparently had been sent out by Bevis Marks congregation. He made his living as a scrivener (a person who wrote letters and other documents for people), an operator of a dry goods store, and as a clerk and auditor in the customs house. He served in the Revolution and lived out his life in Charleston, where he died in 1816.[14]

Apparently problems continued after the resignation of DaCosta, for on January 25, 1775, five men met to air their

10. Ibid.
11. Ibid.
12. Hewatt, *Historical Account*, 2: 290.
13. Ibid.
14. Elzas, *Old Jewish Cemeteries*, 40; Charleston Directory, 1790, 1794, 1803, 1806, 1807, 1809, 1813, 1816; Stern, *First Jewish Families of America*, 8.

grievances.[15] They were Abraham DaCosta; Isaac DaCosta, brother of Abraham; Isaac DaCosta, Jr., the son of Abraham; Jacob Tobias, who married Rachel DaCosta on May 20 that year; and Isaac DeLeon, who had married Rinah Tobias. They claimed that Emanuel Abrahams and Myer Moses had "on severall instances acted directly contrary to the original institution & rules entered into for the regulation" of the congregation. In order to maintain peace, to avoid confusion and discord, they had "tamely submitted" for a long time "in hopes that cool reasons & deliberation (after they had their vanity satisfied by some time ruling their own way) would at last have made them sensible of their improper behaviour & put things upon a just & equitable footing, according to the original institution." But this strategy had not worked; the two had continued to act in the same way and to "arrogate to themselves rights of their own creation of an arbitrary nature." Furthermore, they had altered rules, laws, and other matters as well as added new ones without the "proper sanction of the number of persons, agreeable to the original Laws of the first institution of the Congregation of Beth Elohim in its originall rules." Unfortunately, the men do not indicate the exact nature of their complaints except to state that in 1771 Abrahams had "taken it upon himself" along "with the consent of some others equally illegally admitted with himself into the Junta, to expell an Old Adjunto, who was one of the first establishers [apparently Abraham DaCosta] from serving in his turn as parnass," despite the fact that the man had paid his "arrears," or annual dues, some months before. Abrahams had been told at the time that he had acted illegally. Despite this, "he & the rest persevered in the matter." Therefore, the individuals at the meeting decided that Isaac DaCosta and Isaac DaCosta, Jr., should send a letter to Emanuel Abrahams, Myer Moses, and Israel Joseph telling them of their grievances and asking them to meet with them and to examine the laws of the congregation "provided they come with cool Tempers."

Isaac DaCosta then told the group that Jacob Tobias had "generously granted a seven Years lease of his two rooms, over the westernmost part of his new house in Hasell Street for the use of a Synagogue *pro tempore*." The group agreed that Tobias should have a prayer in his honor in the synagogue the following morning and also on the night of every Yom Kippur thereafter during his life. Thus it seems that the group had already decided to meet separately, if it had not already done so.

Next, Isaac DaCosta announced that he had purchased with the consent of those present part of a lot belonging to Patrick Hinds on King Street "for the purpose of building a Synagogue thereon." Each of the men present had given bonds for building, for a total of £416 and 10 shillings. DaCosta contributed the largest amount, £180. He also wrote the congregation of Shearith Israel of

15. The minutes of their meeting have been classified as a "Fragment of Congregational Minutes"; however, it was a meeting of individuals who discussed writing to congregational officers.

New York in an attempt to raise money for building a synagogue, but that congregation begged off.[16]

The minutes of the meetings indicate that friction had grown within the congregation to such an extent that the dissidents had decided to form their own synagogue. Tobias provided his house on a temporary basis for "a synagogue" and DaCosta purchased another lot for the permanent use of "a synagogue." They were not talking about *the* synagogue then in existence. Obviously, the movement had been under way for some time, and they seem to have anticipated the outcome of the meeting with Abrahams.

By the time the split in the congregation was developing, a number of changes had occurred among the members of Beth Elohim. Some of the founders had died: Abraham Nunez Cardoza in 1762, Joseph Tobias in 1761, Moses Pimienta in 1765, and Moses Cohen in 1762. Meanwhile, a number of immigrants had arrived in Charleston. Among these were Samuel Hart, of Mannheim, Germany, who had arrived by 1767; Philip Jacob Cohen, of Germany, who arrived by 1772; and Moses Cohen, also from Mannheim, who was in the city by 1772. Furthermore, Israel Joseph, who was one of the people to be written to by the dissenters in 1775, came from Germany in 1764. Not all new arrivals were German, for Myer Moses and Emanuel Abrahams, with whom the dissidents differed so strongly, came from London. Abrahams was in Charleston by 1761, and Moses by 1767. These men were all Ashkenazic.

Differences between the new members and the old apparently resulted in two congregations, the new members being predominantly a German congregation but retaining control of Kahal Kadosh Beth Elohim and the older Sephardic group forming a new Spanish-Portuguese group. Clearly, the DaCosta and related families had become displeased with events in Charleston.

The rival groups possibly functioned through the early parts of the American Revolution. Jacob Tobias, however, died on November 11, 1775, less than six months after his marriage. Further changes occurred when the British occupied Charleston in 1780. A number of Jews fled, including Isaac DaCosta. The British seized his property, and when he refused to take a loyalty oath, they banished him.[17] By December 13, 1781, he arrived in Philadelphia, where he took a leading role in founding the Spanish-Portuguese synagogue, Mikveh Israel, in that city. The organizational meeting for Mikveh Israel took place on May 17, 1782. DaCosta served as the temporary chairman but was not selected to be a member of the *adjunta*.[18]

16. "Also a letter from Mr. Isaac Decasta of Charleston requesting Assistance toward building a synigog. Which letter being red, Resolved that it is not in the power of the congregation at Present to Give any Moneys toward any of these uses" in "From the 2nd Volume of Minutes Books," 139.

17. *The Royal Gazette*, Mar. 14, 1781, supplement.

18. Morais, "Mickve Israel Congregation," 13–15.

The Old Synagogue

During the British occupation of Charleston from 1780 to 1782, the Spanish-Portuguese meetings very likely collapsed as members dispersed. As for Beth Elohim, Shecut says, "In 1780 they assembled in Hasell street, at the old Synagogue, lately occupied by Mr. Little, as a cotton gin manufactory." Levin relates that "Jacob Tobias purchased a lot and brick building in Hasell Street for 310 guineas, which was then occupied by a Mr. Little, as a cotton-gin manufactory." Levin appears to have taken much of his information from Shecut; however, as noted above, Tobias had died by this time and Robert Little, a carpenter and later lumber merchant, is never listed at that address. Very likely the property came from Joseph Tobias, who was guardian for his children, who were in line to acquire the property of Jacob after his mother died.[19] Levin, furthermore, states that the congregation had a surplus of funds and purchased the building from Tobias in 1781 for the same amount that he had paid. They "arranged it in a suitable manner for their worship, and it was ever afterwards termed the 'Old Synagogue'."[20] The Tobias family, however, did not sell the land to the congregation until December 10, 1794.[21] By this time a new synagogue had been built.

The information is very confusing, but it would seem that the Tobias property probably lay to the back of the King Street tenement of Jacob Tobias and could be reached from Hasell Street. It could have been used as a meeting house when the dissidents broke away but later passed to the control of Beth Elohim. The marriage settlement between Abraham DeLyon, son of Isaac DeLyon and Sarah Sheftall, in 1785 tends to confirm this interpretation. DeLyon agreed to provide $^1/_6$ of a dwelling in Charleston on King Street where Jacob Tobias lived and $^1/_6$ of a lot on which the synagogue in Charleston was then located.[22]

Cemeteries

Meanwhile, a cemetery had been established. In 1754 Isaac DaCosta purchased a plot of land on Coming Street to be used for his family for burial purposes. In 1764, possibly the year when he had a falling out with some of the congregation and resigned as *hazan*, DaCosta transferred this property to Beth Elohim. In the deed he stated that "it would be a convenient place for the Burial Ground of the Jews' Congregation in general." He conveyed the property in return for £70 with the stipulation that the cemetery be used for those "who do and shall conform to the Jewish rites and ceremonies in general" and who observed the regulations of Beth Elohim.[23] This burial ground is known as the Coming Street Cemetery, the oldest Jewish cemetery still existing in the South.[24]

19. W18.1.

20. Levin, "The Jewish Congregation of Charleston," 338–39.

21. RMC Book M6, 45, 48.

22. MS1.224.

23. RMC Book C3, 108.

24. Tobias, "Tombstones That Tell a Story."

Everyone had to be buried in the congregational cemetery except "certain family places of interment already established, namely, that of the *Tobias* family."[25] By the 1830s the Coming Street Cemetery had been divided into *carreras*, or family plots. These were reserved to the parents, their children, and other people for whom they were legally responsible. Should a family fail to keep up its contributions for two years, it would lose claim to the *carrera* except in cases where the family members had moved out of the state. Families then would be allowed a grace period of three years.[26]

After the British evacuated Charleston in 1782, most of the Jews who had departed for Philadelphia and elsewhere returned. Among these was Isaac DaCosta; however, he died on November 23, 1783, as a result of having gotten a splinter in his hand.[27] His family did not bury him in the Coming Street Cemetery, but in what became known as the DaCosta Cemetery, which was located between Hanover and Amherst streets in the suburb of Hampstead. Since DaCosta had been responsible for the establishment of the Coming Street Cemetery, it would seem that problems continued to disturb the congregation. The 1836 constitution of the congregation considered the cemetery to be the property of the Isaac DaCosta family. His near relatives could be buried there, but "no other person; not even such persons as have relations already deposited there."[28] The DaCosta Cemetery became property of Beth Elohim in 1847.[29]

25. *New Constitution of Beth Elohim* (1837), 11.

26. Ibid., 11–12.

27. *The Gazette of the State of South-Carolina*, Nov. 27, 1783.

Beth Elohim Unveh Shallom

Elzas, in his research, found evidence of a second congregation but rejected the idea as being "exceedingly improbable."[30] However, Solomon Breibart has concluded that it was very probable two synagogues had existed.[31] Indeed, there is ample evidence for this. The first indication is the burial of Isaac DaCosta outside the Coming Street Cemetery. Also, Moses Molina, who died in late 1785, left a bequest to the Portuguese Jewish Congregation of Beth Elohim Unveh Shalom, not Kahal Kadosh Beth Elohim.[32] On February 3, 1786, the Charleston *Evening Gazette* reported that "YESTERDAY the Portuguese Jewish Congregation of this City, called '*Beth Elohim Unve Shallom*' or the House of the Lord and Mansion of Peace, Proceeded to their burying ground in Hampstead [DaCosta Cemetery], in order to lay the Foundation Stones of the Wall." Isaac DaCosta, Samuel DaCosta, Joseph DePalacios, Joseph Benzakin, and Joseph Abendanone, all Sephardic Jews, laid the stones.[33] Later in that year (No-

28. *New Constitution of Beth Elohim*, 11.

29. Minute Book of Beth Elohim, Oct. 3, 1847.

30. Elzas, *Old Jewish Cemeteries*, 104.

31. Breibart, "The Synagogues"; idem, "Two Jewish Congregations."

32. W21.774.

33. The newspaper Breibart quotes has not survived. However, a researcher found a clip-

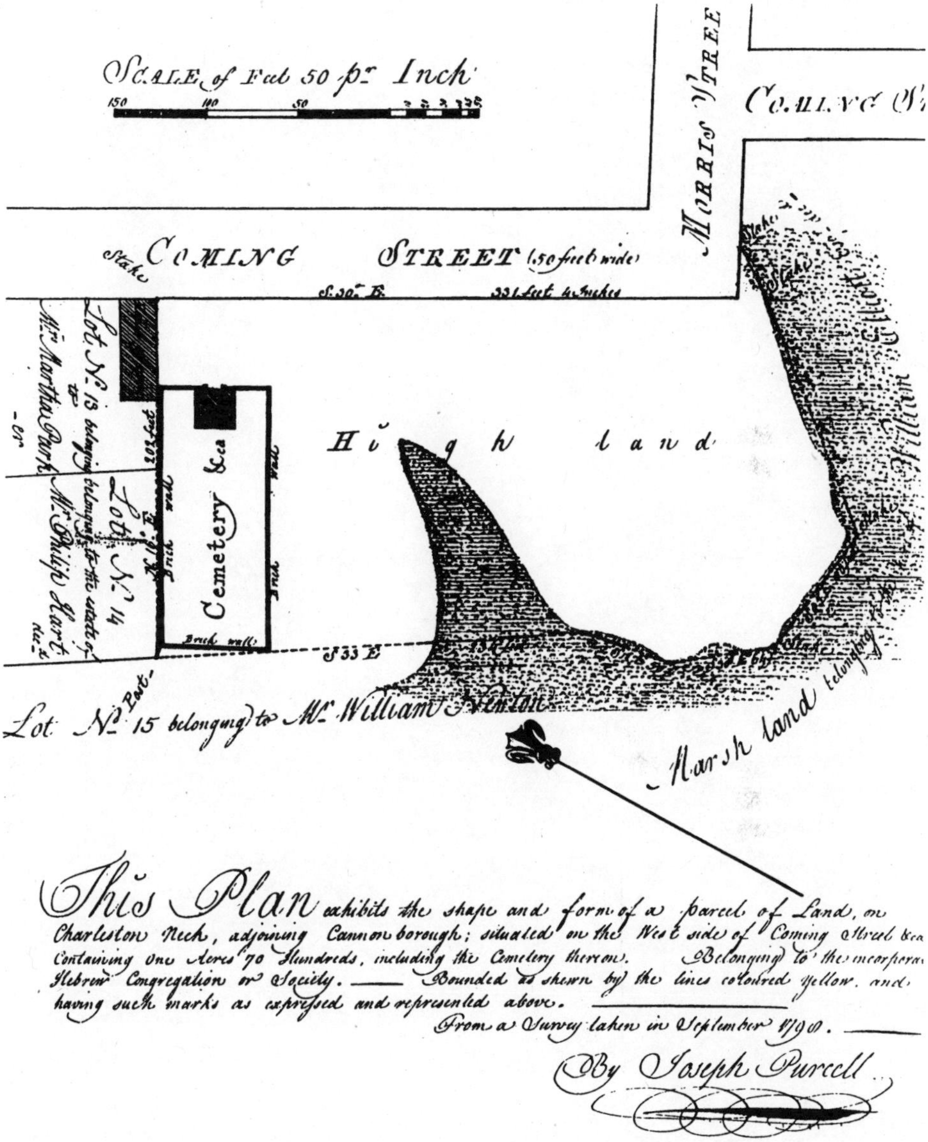

8. 1790 map showing location of Coming Street Cemetery. (Courtesy of Beth Elohim Synagogue.)

9. Coming Street Cemetery. (Photograph courtesy of Beth Elohim Synagogue.)

vember 11, 1786) Joseph Salvador, in a codicil to his will, provided a bequest to Joseph DaCosta for "the Portuguese Jews Congregation in Charleston known as Beth Elohim Unveh Shallom, or the House of the Lord and the Mansion of Peace." At the same time he left a legacy to Gershon Cohen for "the German Jewish Congregation in the city of Charleston, known by the Name of Beth Elohim, or the House of God."[34] Two days after Salvador drew up this codi-

ping somewhere in the files of the Charleston Library Society. Solomon Breibart has a handwritten copy of the advertisement, but no one knows where the clipping was found.

34. W22.94.

10. Tomb of Catherine Lopez. (Photograph courtesy of Beth Elohim Synagogue.)

cil, an advertisement appeared in the Charleston *Post and Advertiser* offering for sale tenements at 21–22 Beresford Street with a "brick building, the upper part of which is the SYNAGOGUE for the PORTUGUESE JEWISH CONGREGATION." Finally, Solomon Breibart discovered a document dated 1794 that indicated that Emanuel DeLaMotta had been penalized by the *adjunta* of Beth Elohim for having buried his father in the Portuguese Cemetery because they feared that this "would tend to cause a Scism in the congregation and revive the distinction of *portuguese* & Todeska [German]."[35] One may conclude that a Portuguese synagogue was located on Beresford Street where Beth Elohim had been, and that Beth Elohim, now dominated by Germans, was on Hasell Street in back of the Tobias property, where the Portuguese Jews had worshiped.

The notion that the Germans had control of K.K. Beth Elohim helps explain an important statement in a civil suit in

35. Breibart, "Two Jewish Congregations," 362. The advertisement was found in the papers of the Charleston Library Society.

the 1840s. The court ruled that "the Congregation had existed prior to 1784, as an incorporated society, called the 'Kaal Kadosh Beth Elohim.' Some of the old books are lost, but one, yet in the possession of the congregation, shews that on the 15th August, 1784, the congregation adopted the 'Minhog Sephardim' (viz: the Portuguese Ritual), as practiced in London and Amsterdam."[36] The same information is found in an unofficial version of the trial.[37] Both sources on the trial earlier indicated that the Spanish-Portuguese rituals as practiced in Amsterdam and London had been initiated when the congregation began. A plausible explanation for establishing them in 1784 would be that they had been abandoned earlier by Beth Elohim.

Azuby

Other important changes occurred in 1784. According to Levin, Abraham Alexander resigned that year as *hazan*. The congregation lacked religious leadership for some time until they hired Rev. Abraham Azuby, "a man well versed in our laws, who afforded much satisfaction and pleasure to his flock."[38] Azuby, of Spanish-Portuguese stock, came from Amsterdam. The 1790 city directory lists him as a rabbi, and the 1796 edition gives his profession as "High Priest of the Jewish Synagogue" at 207 King Street. He served until 1805. The congregation thought very highly of him, and his term of office was one of the most dynamic of the Charleston Jewish community.

The Benevolent Society

The Hebrew Benevolent Society was also founded in 1784. Although the synagogue handled many works of charity, members of the community decided to form an additional agency for this purpose. As Thomas J. Tobias pointed out in a history of the organization, the founders were probably influenced by the fact that several such charitable societies for various ethnic groups already existed in the city.[39] Moreover, *hevrot* (sing. *hevra*), or "pious associations" such as these were common and go far back into Jewish history.[40] For example, the Jews of Columbia, South Carolina, founded their Hebrew Benevolent Society long before establishing their synagogue.[41] The existence of such a society told the community at large that the Jews intended to take care of their own people. Furthermore, separate funds could be created, which would not necessarily take support away from the synagogue, and men who were not officers of the synagogue, nor even members, could fulfill their duties to perform good works. The other organizations in the city included the Saint George Society for the English, the Saint Andrew's Society for the Scots, the Huguenot Society

36. "The State v. Ancker," in *Reports of Cases*, 2: 247.

37. *State ex rel. A. Ottolengui*, 10.

38. Levin, "The Jewish Congregation of Charleston," 339.

39. Tobias, *Hebrew Benevolent Society*, 2.

40. Marcus, *United States Jewry*, 320–21.

41. Elzas, *Jews of South Carolina*, 246–47.

for the French Protestants, the German Friendly Society, and later the Hiberian Society for the Irish. Over time, they developed into social organizations more than charitable ones, and the Jews, no doubt, found themselves attracted by such fraternal institutions. The official Hebrew name of the society was Hebra Gemilut Hasadim, or Society for Deeds of Loving Kindness. The seal of the organization gave the date of the founding, the angel of death, and the biblical quotation "Charity Delivers from Death" (Proverbs 10:2).[42] The belief is that philanthropy saves the giver rather than the receiver from death, the concept of charity being one of the most profound of Jewish ideas. Despite the existence of the Benevolent Society, the 1836 constitution of Beth Elohim provided that the trustees could grant any sum they wished up to $25 for an individual and $50 for a family,[43] and cash books indicate that the poor received aid from time to time.

At first the organization probably took care of burying the dead, as is shown by the case of *The State v. Solomon Moses*. In 1801 a group of men from the Benevolent Society were preparing the body of a deceased member of the congregation at the home of Abraham Torres when Solomon Moses entered the place and demanded to take part. Simon M. Hart told him that he needed the permission of the society to do so. Moses then struck Hart in the face with his fist. Hart took the case to the courts, which fined Moses only $1 in view of the fact that the Hebrew congregation had required him to make amends. An excerpt of the minutes of the *adjunta* shows that it fined him £3 and required to him to read a confession in the synagogue. Had he not done this, he would have lost all rights and privileges in the synagogue, which was tantamount to excommunication. On November 2, 1801, Moses paid the fine imposed by the court, and on May 12, 1802 he made a statement that he had complied with the demands of the *adjunta*.[44] On June 9, 1802, the governor pardoned him of "so much of a sentence for an assault as relates to imprisonment."[45] Whether this is a separate case or not is unclear.

Although Tobias says that the organization is the oldest of its type in the United States, it seems to have disappeared from time to time. The Benevolent Society received bequests from congregational members from 1787 to 1811, which indicates it operated for those years.[46] It ceased to operate at some time, for it was revived and reorganized on October 20, 1824. On December 18, 1830, the legislature incorporated it.[47] When reconstituted in 1824, it appears to have taken on a larger scope of activities than before, and after its incorporation it no longer came under control of Beth Elohim.

The organization played a significant

42. Tobias, *Hebrew Benevolent Society*, 4. Although the seal gives the founding date as 1774, the society in the 1840s believed that it had been founded in 1791.

43. *New Constitution of Beth Elohim*, 21.

44. Elzas, *Jews of South Carolina*, 154–55.

45. MR3Q.591.

46. Tobias, *Hebrew Benevolent Society*, 5–7.

47. Ibid., 7–8.

role in disasters, especially outbreaks of yellow fever in the years 1838, 1854, and 1858, when the organization cared for many in the city. During the yellow fever epidemic in 1838 the Benevolent Society advertised in the Charleston *Courier*: "Sick persons requiring aid from this society, can have it to the utmost extent of its funds" by calling representatives of the society.[48] No restrictions as to the origins or beliefs of persons were mentioned, illustrating the Jewish practice of taking care of their own people first but then helping others.

In 1848 the president of the organization, Samuel Valentine, gave a report of the year's events. He told of the large number of poor and sick who had been helped with food, clothing, and care. The needs for assistance came mostly from the newly arrived immigrants, who tended to be poor, without friends or relatives, and unable to speak English. The society had never refused aid when asked, he said, despite the fact that some people were later found to be undeserving and impostors. The organization had taken the position that it was better to give aid to five people who did not deserve it than to deny one who did.[49] In 1855 the society considered going even further with its benevolence by establishing a Jewish hospital in Charleston as a "proper asylum" for "the sick and needy Israelite at all times, but more particularly during the prevalence of the epidemics of our inhospitable climate."[50] Such an institution, however, never came into being. In 1858, in response to a raging epidemic, the Benevolent Society supplied aid to thirty-eight adults and eight children. Of these people, thirty died. It also assisted seven strangers to leave the city at the time of the outbreak of disease.[51] The society thus provided help to a limited number of persons on a regular basis and performed extraordinary service when crises hit the community. Moreover, members used the association as a social organization where they could hear speeches, make innumerable toasts, eat good food, and otherwise enjoy themselves.[52]

Other Cemeteries

Although many of the Jews of the city seem to have cooperated in providing relief for their friends and neighbors, they did not always want to be buried together. In 1793 Rebecca Mendes DaCosta, the widow of Moses Mendes DaCosta, who had probably come to America with Joseph Salvador, added a codicil to her will in which she left money to the Portuguese Jewish synagogue and instructed her executor to purchase a lot in Hampstead to be used "for the sole purpose of being a burial ground for my family and the Portuguese Jews."[53] Her wishes, as far as is known, were ignored. Then in 1798 Henry Moses, Solomon Moses, Meyer Derkheim, Samuel Hyams, Benjamin

48. Ibid., 8, 14.

49. "Fifty-Sixth Anniversary of the Hebrew Benevolent Society of Charleston, S.C."

50. Leeser, "Testimonial of Members."

51. "Hebrew Benevolent Society of Charleston, South Carolina."

52. Tobias, *Hebrew Benevolent Society*, 7–17.

53. W29.666.

Tores, and Solomon Harby decided to establish a new cemetery in Hampstead. Although they stated that the cemetery could be used for anyone professing Judaism, they divided all the plots among themselves. In meetings, of which they kept minutes, they approved the purchase of the land and arranged for the laying out of the plots. At their last recorded gathering, in September 1799, they accepted the resignation of Solomon Moses, because he was a "very poor man," and returned his funds to him.[54] The burial ground became the Hanover Street Cemetery. The founders came from both Ashkenazic and Sephardic backgrounds, and its creation apparently did not represent a schism in the community, although it is unclear why these individuals thought they needed another cemetery. One of the original trustees, Henry Moses, was interred there. So were several members of the Harby family and the wife of Samuel Hyams.[55]

The Orphan Society

The Jewish community next established the Hebrew Orphan Society. Jewish children could be placed in the city orphanage; nevertheless, a group of Jews met on July 15, 1801, to found the Hebrew Orphan Society. Apparently seeing the role of the Charleston Orphan House as too narrow and possibly afraid of Christian training of the youth, the founders of the Hebrew Orphan Society planned to relieve widows, and to educate, clothe, and maintain orphans and children of indigent parents. The organizers hoped to inculcate piety, morality, and industry in the orphans, and to seek out children with exceptional talents for special training. The individuals could then "freely assume an equal station in this favored land with the cheering conviction that their virtues and acquirements may lead them in every honor and advantage their fellow citizens can attain." Actually, the community had few Jewish orphans, but occasionally widows and children of poor parents needed help. In 1802 the legislature incorporated the society as Abi Yetomin Ubne Ebyonim, or Society for the Relief of Orphans and Children of Indigent Parents. After the reconstitution of the Benevolent Society in 1824, the two organizations overlapped in their responsibilities. Nevertheless, the Orphan Society acquired a stately building, the former Bank of the United States, at the corner of Broad and State streets. The building was large enough that it could be used as the place of worship when the synagogue burned in 1838. In the early days of the organization no children are known to have been housed there. Instead, the society assigned the few orphans in the city to families who received financial assistance to care for them.[56] Children of poor families also obtained aid, one of those possibly being Judah Benjamin,

54. Minutes of the Trustees of the New Burial Ground, Oct. 14; Nov. 18, 1798; Sept. 23, 1799, American Jewish Archives; RMC Book W6, 397; Elzas, *Old Jewish Cemeteries*, 109.

55. Elzas, *Old Jewish Cemeteries*, 110–11.

56. Tobias, *Hebrew Orphan Society*, 10, 13, 14, 17.

11. Hebrew Orphan Society Building. Now occupied by offices. (Photograph by Michael Whittemore.)

later the secretary of state for the Confederacy, although this has never been proved.[57] Isaac Harby was "at one time, the teacher of the children on its bounty."[58] For a while before the Civil War some children stayed in the house, although no records of them can be found.[59] All in all, the organization seems to have done quite a bit of good for poor children and widows; however,

57. Evans, *Judah P. Benjamin*, 13.

58. Moïse, "Memoir," in Moïse and Pinckney, *A Selection from the Miscellaneous Writings*, 26.

59. In 1857 Maurice Mayer, the *hazan*, wrote a letter to the trustees about the Hebrew children in the Orphan House. Minute Book of Beth Elohim, Nov. 1, 1857.

abject poverty among the Jews of the city seems to have been unusual.

Political Action

In addition to founding institutions, the Jews of Charleston actively worked together in 1790 when the constitutional convention met in South Carolina. In this instance, the Jews thought of themselves as a community. Levin states that "as none of our brethren were delegated to that convention, they determined to support such persons as were of known sterling integrity, and liberal sentiments."[60] They gave their "undivided support" to a group of candidates. Christopher Knight, one of the winners, felt himself "greatly obliged to the assistance I received . . . at the late election" and sent a donation of 50 guineas to the congregation for the use of the poor or "any such matter" as the vestry should think appropriate. Jacob Cohen, president of the congregation, reported the donation to the board, but they returned the money so that it could not be "suggested at some future period that the members of our community were to be bought."[61]

Incorporation

The vigorous activities of the Jewish community paid off, because the 1790 constitution of South Carolina allowed for religious freedom and the incorporation of organizations such as synagogues. Therefore, the congregation acted to become a legal entity. The petition, dated January 7, 1791, stated that incorporation would "be conducive to the decent and regular exercise of their religion, and public worship of the great Jehovah and Almighty ruler of the Universe." Philip Hart and Isaac DaCosta signed the petition as "wardens" (apparently, the two presidents) and Moses C. Levy as treasurer. J. I. Cohen, Dores Benjamin, Israel Joseph, and Gershon Cohen also signed the document.[62] The group was equally divided between Sephardic and Ashkenazic Jews, and all had apparently been born outside the United States. Obviously, the congregation had reconciled its differences and carefully balanced the two groups. On February 19, 1791, the legislature passed a bill for the incorporation of "the Jewish Congregation at Charleston, called Beth Elohim or House of God."[63]

A New Synagogue

The board also decided in September 1791 to buy a lot on Hasell Street adjacent to the "Old Synagogue" as a place to construct a new meeting house.[64]

60. Levin, "The Jewish Congregation of Charleston," 339.

61. Ibid., 339–40.

62. General Assembly Papers, Petitions, 1791, No. 14, South Carolina Archives.

63. *Journal of the House of Representatives, 1791*, 16, 40, 48, 107, 108–9, 128, 150, 253, 300; *Statutes*, 1: 162–63.

64. RMC Book H6, 10.

They selected five trustees. Of these Abraham Cohen came from London; Jacob Jacobs, whose family origins are unknown, married the widow of Abraham Sarzedas, who came from Santo Domingo; Gershon Cohen, who probably came from London, married a member of the Sarzedas family; and Israel Joseph and Philip Hart came from Germany. This board thus seems to have consisted of three Sephardic and two Ashkenazic members. The members of the building committee then raised funds for construction, frequently advancing their own money when needed. In addition to seeking contributions from local sources, they called on other congregations for support. Shearith Israel of New York, Bevis Marks in London, and a congregation on Barbados sent aid. The cornerstones were laid on September 14, 1792. For the ceremonies the congregation first gathered in the old synagogue for prayers, then marched in procession to the new site. Those who had given most laid the eight stones, four for the building and four for the porch. Each stone bore the name of the person who laid it, the date of the event, as well as inscriptions in Hebrew and English. The congregation followed Masonic tradition in doing this.[65] When the builders completed the structure, consecration services took place on Friday, September 19, 1794. The congregation invited the civil, military, religious, and political figures of the city and state, as well as the general public. One of the local newspapers reported the events the following day.[66]

In addition to building the new synagogue, the congregation added to its holdings, purchasing the Tobias property and another parcel of land.[67] By 1809 the congregation completed the construction of a *mikva*, a ritual bath, and soon afterward an oven for baking *matzah*, or Passover bread.[68] By 1810 the communal facilities reached their height. The Jews of Charleston at the time appear to have been diligent in their faith—the presence of a *mikva* often indicates that. Some evidence of the level of religious observance comes from Rebecca Samuel, who commented on the subject in two letters that she wrote her parents in Hamburg, Germany. One is dated January 12, 1791, and she apparently wrote the other later. At the time she lived in Petersburg, Virginia, which she disliked because, as she claimed, the Jews were poor. She asserted they had been beggars in Germany before coming to America with German troops. She reported in her second letter that she and her family planned to move to Charleston after Passover. In Petersburg there was a lack of "*Yehudishkeit*" or Jewishness, but in Charleston "there is a blessed community of three hundred Jews."[69] The Samuels indeed made the move at some point, because in 1806 Hyman Samuel,

65. Levin, "The Jewish Congregation of Charleston," 386.

66. *South-Carolina State Gazette & Timothy & Mason's Daily Advertiser*, Sept. 20, 1794.

67. Breibart, "The Synagogues," 221.

68. Levin, "The Jewish Congregation of Charleston," 387–88.

69. Marcus, *American Jewry*, 51–54.

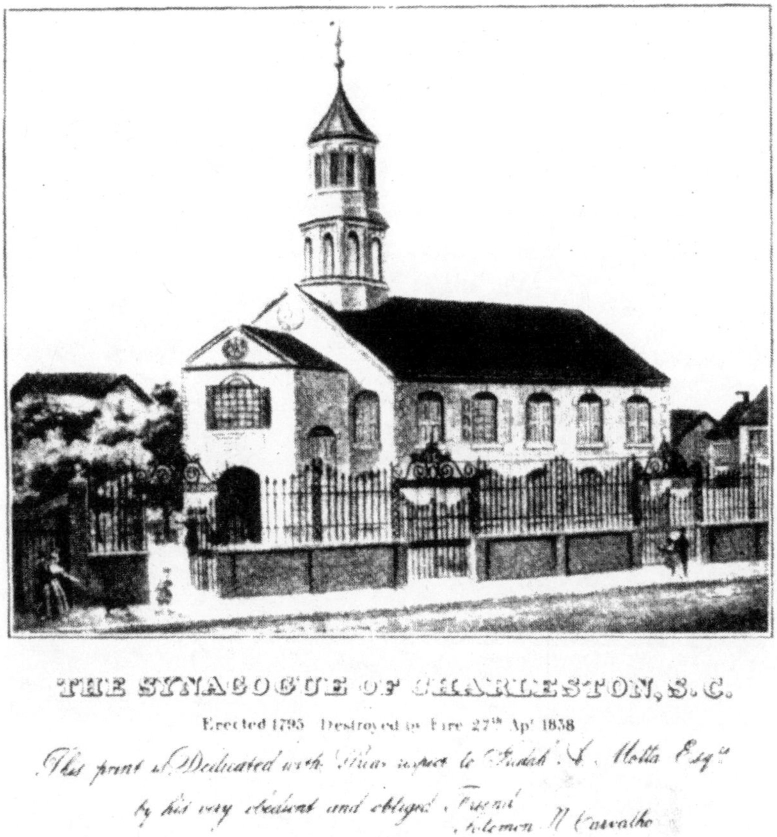

12. Exterior of Beth Elohim. Destroyed by fire in 1838. (By Solomon N. Carvalho. Photograph courtesy of Beth Elohim Synagogue.)

her husband, appears in the city directory as a watchmaker, the profession he had followed in Petersburg. Another report came from about 1810 when Jacob Cohen reported to Hannah Adams that the Jews of the city "strictly observed" the religious rites, customs, and holidays, though they were "ameliorated with the social liberality, which pervades the minds and manners of the inhabitants of civilized countries."[70] A third report comes from Sally Lopez, who lived until 1902 to the age of ninety-six. She reported to Barnett Elzas when he was doing his research on the community that Rebecca Benjamin, the mother of Judah Benjamin, kept her shop open on the Sabbath, something

70. Adams, *History of the Jews*, 2: 217.

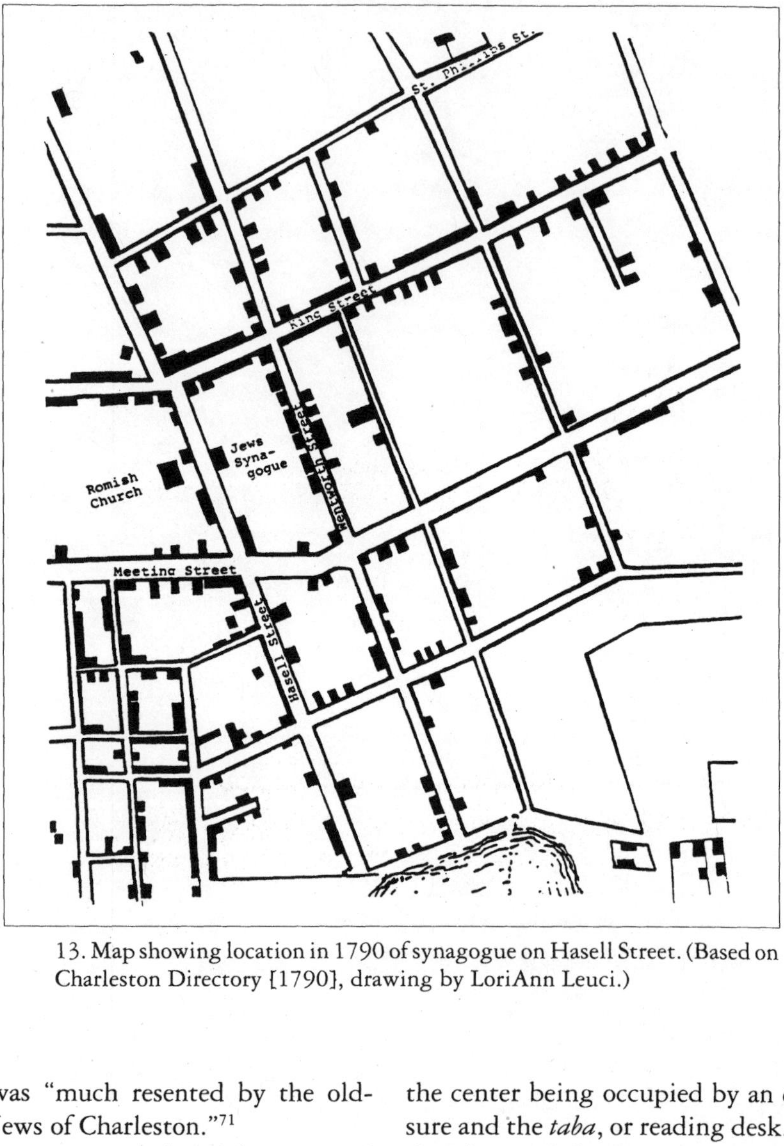

13. Map showing location in 1790 of synagogue on Hasell Street. (Based on Charleston Directory [1790], drawing by LoriAnn Leuci.)

that was "much resented by the old-time Jews of Charleston."[71]

The synagogue of 1794 impressed those who saw it. Built in the Georgian style, it blended well with its surroundings. The interior conformed to the requirements of Sephardic worship, with the center being occupied by an enclosure and the *taba*, or reading desk. Here the *hazan* led the congregation in prayers. The women sat in galleries separately from the men. Fortunately, Solomon N. Carvalho painted the synagogue before it burned. In September 1838 he offered the congregation the painting for such compensation as the board might find proper. They gave him

71. Elzas, *Leaves from My Historical Scrapbook*.

14. Interior of Beth Elohim. (By Solomon N. Carvalho. Photograph courtesy of Beth Elohim Synagogue.)

$50.[72] Carvalho then had lithographs made of the interior and exterior. The synagogue looked very much like those in London and Amsterdam.

The Jews of Charleston not only cooperated with one another but with their coreligionists in Philadelphia, New York, and Richmond in 1790 to congratulate George Washington on his election as president. Various groups throughout the country had been doing this, and the Jews wanted to take their place with them. Members of Beth Elohim, led by Jacob Cohen, first drafted a letter. Over several months, the other congregations joined with them, and a letter went out on Decem-

72. Minute Book of Beth Elohim, Sept. 20, Oct. 21, 1838.

ber 13, 1790. Shortly after that, Washington replied.[73] Their cooperative gesture represented a rare instance of the joining together of Jews from different cities. The cooperation had not come easily. A number of Jewish institutions did not work with the rest, and Washington got three separate letters from Jewish groups. Strongly believing that each group should run its own affairs, the Jews resisted any movement toward centralized control.

Hazanim

Most of the accomplishments in establishing institutions came when Azuby served as the *hazan*. The breach within the community had been repaired, the Benevolent Society created, the Hebrew Orphan Society established, and the new synagogue constructed. Beth Elohim enjoyed its happiest, most unified, and most prosperous time. When Azuby died in February 1805 after nearly twenty years of service, "the congregation sustained a severe loss."[74] In order to show its appreciation, the congregation paid his wife, Esther Azuby, his salary until a new *hazan* was hired and provided her with a rent-free house. Even after they had settled on a new reader, they continued to supply her with an annual stipend and a house.[75] When she died, she left a bequest to the synagogue.[76]

Since no one in the community had the training to serve as *hazan*, the congregational leaders wrote Bevis Marks in London asking for a new religious leader. Most of their letter deals with their "happy situation which makes us feel that we are men." They pointed out that America offered civil and religious liberty and that no distinctions existed between the clergy of differing denominations. They were "freely tolerated" and "participated in all the rights and blessings of this happy country." The only thing they needed was a *hazan* "of merit and classical education" who would bring honor on himself and the community.[77] They gave the leaders at Bevis Marks authority to choose a new *hazan* for them, who announced the vacancy in the synagogue and placed a notice on a board in the yard of the religious center. Bevis Marks did point out to Beth Elohim that *hazanim* frequently proved difficult to find because young men who began religious studies often turned to commerce and trade to make their living. Two men applied to Bevis Marks for the position, Benjamin Cohen D'Azevedo and Abraham Ottolengui. D'Azevedo was the son of the chief Spanish-Portuguese rabbi in London; Ottolengui had been born in Charleston and was in London studying at the time, but was only sixteen years of age. The authorities at Bevis Marks deemed him too young to be selected for such a post or, for that matter, to even read prayers in the synagogue.

73. Schappes, *Documentary History*, 82–84; Marcus, *American Jewry*, 167.

74. Levin, "The Jewish Congregation of Charleston," 389.

75. Ibid.

76. W30.855.

77. Levin, "The Jewish Congregation of Charleston," 390, provides the text of the entire letter.

D'Azevedo led the services in Bevis Marks for a week to the general satisfaction of the congregation, and they chose him to be the *hazan* for Beth Elohim. He, his wife, and four children set out for Charleston on the *Wanderer*. D'Azevedo brought with him a letter of introduction from London.[78] Shortly after the new *hazan* arrived in Charleston, the congregation found him unacceptable. Not only was he sickly but, in their opinion, he did not meet the "necessary qualification." They paid him for his troubles and sent him back to England.[79]

London having failed them, the congregation then turned to its own members for leadership. Among those serving were Emanuel DeLaMotta, Ralph Amesquita, Moses C. Levy, and Jacob Suares. By 1806 Suares had been chosen as the permanent *hazan*. He then served until 1811, when Emanuel Nunes Carvalho replaced him.[80]

Born in London and the son of an artisan, Carvalho studied Hebrew and other eastern as well as modern languages. He left London in 1799 to serve Nidhe Israel Congregation in Barbados, but he proved not to be very suitable and departed for New York, where he arrived in 1806. There he taught Hebrew and other languages privately and for the Polonies Talmud Torah School of Shearith Israel. Citing the great expense of living in New York, he asked the vestry of Shearith Israel in 1809 to increase his pay from $800 to $1,300 per year. Beth Elohim, he reported, had "once again" offered him the position of *hazan*, and he would accept if not given the raise, especially in view of the fact that his health was not good and the warm climate would better suit him. The leaders made arrangements with him to stay,[81] but in 1811 he accepted the position of *hazan* at Beth Elohim, "then the best post on the continent."[82] In Charleston he not only served as the reader but established a school where he taught Spanish and Hebrew.[83] According to Mordecai Manuel Noah, who lived in the city, Carvalho got into trouble with the *adjunta*. He taught the children to sing the concluding psalm in the morning service "in a very handsome manner which in a measure did away with the discordance which attends every Synagogue." Then "for a whim or caper" he forbade the children to sing the psalm any longer. The *adjunta* tried to prevail on him to reinstate it. When he refused, they suspended him for five days. Carvalho then "collected a rabble composed of all the vagrant Jews & had a petition signed by them to give him redress." He gave this to the *parnass*, who could not act on his own authority. A riot resulted in the synagogue and "in a short time the whole meeting parnass & all were bat-

78. Letters from Bevis Marks to the Parnassim of Beth Elohim, March 19, May 8, July 3, July 25, 1806, American Jewish Archives.

79. Levin, "The Jewish Congregation of Charleston," 390.

80. Ibid.

81. DeSola Pool, *An Old Faith in the New World*, 217–18.

82. Marcus, *United States Jewry*, 276.

83. Adams, *History of the Jews*, 2: 219.

tling with clubs & bruising boxing, etc during which his reverence & brother & friend Lipman came off with a few thumps." As a consequence he lost "the small remnant of respectability & character" he had.[84]

The troubles that began in the synagogue did not stay there, as members hurled charges against one another in the courts. Jacob David claimed that Abraham Goldsmith, the clerk of the synagogue, "violently and grossly assaulted him" when he struck him in the face without provocation,[85] while Abraham Goldsmith declared that Jacob David had struck him.[86] Furthermore, Simon N. Hart accused Israel Davis of assault,[87] and Israel Davis swore that Simon N. Hart and Mary Hart violently assaulted him.[88] The court refused to indict any of them. The incident obviously occurred shortly after Carvalho arrived in Charleston, as the court cases are dated 1811 and Noah's letter 1812. Apparently, Carvalho did not completely lose his creditability as Noah indicates, because he stayed in the city until 1814. Such incidents did occur elsewhere. Jacob Marcus has remarked, "Squabbles in God's house were almost as traditional as the liturgy itself; one sometimes suspects that these quarrels testified to a rugged spiritual health."[89] This statement certainly fits the situation at Charleston. Men and women fought over the changes that Emanuel Carvalho had introduced and then withdrawn, and the "handsome manner" of singing, without doubt, made an impression on boys who sang in the choir. A few years later the young men of the congregation sought to bring about dramatic changes in the liturgy. Many were probably the same individuals who sang in the choir. Furthermore, this incident showed that the congregation was willing to make minor innovations in its liturgy.

Two later cases that grew out of a dispute in the synagogue may have been related. They involved Nathan Hart and David N. Carvalho. Carvalho claimed that on November 21, 1818, he was "assaulted, insulted and abused by Nathan Hart in the Hebrew synagogue."[90] The court refused to indict Hart, but Hart succeeded in bringing charges against Carvalho. Carvalho appealed, but the higher court ruled that disturbing a congregation was an indictable offense at common law even if the defendant was a member. Although this dispute could have involved any number of differences, it may be related to the later reform movement: David N. Carvalho became a member of the Reformed Society of Israelites in the 1820s, and Nathan Hart led the opposition to reforms in the late 1830s.

In 1818 Hartwig Cohen became the

84. Noah to Naphtali Phillips, May 10, 1812, in Goldberg, *Major Noah,* 51–52.

85. State v. Goldsmith, 1811, Court of General Sessions.

86. State v. Jacob David, 1811, Court of General Sessions.

87. State v. Israel Davis, 1811, Court of General Sessions.

88. State v. S. M. Hart, 1811, Court of General Sessions.

89. Marcus, *United States Jewry*, 265.

90. State v. Nathan Hart, 1819, Court of General Sessions.

hazan and led the services for a number of years. Eventually, Solomon Cohen Peixotto, also a resident of the city, replaced him and served until his death in 1835.[91]

Religious Education

Keeping the faith alive in Charleston required training for young Jews. Nathaniel Levin made this clear in a speech he delivered in 1842. He stated, "it becomes our duty to . . . teach them to cling to *that* which we can prove to have been *before all human charters*, the '*first born*' of the rights of man, the indefeasible inheritance of every genuine worshipper of the God of Abraham, of Isaac and of Jacob."[92] Knowledge of Hebrew and Spanish posed a particular problem because the Sephardic services called for almost exclusive use of these languages. Some Sephardic congregations used Portuguese and Spanish for prayers, while others used Ladino, which is a Spanish dialect that includes many Hebrew words. With one exception, the references at Beth Elohim are to Spanish; however, Isaac Harby in 1825 spoke of "bad Spanish and Portuguese."[93] From the earliest times men in the community taught Jewish subjects and languages. J. Barrett Cohen in 1884 said that Moses Cohen, the "rabbi" in 1749, was the first teacher of Jewish law in South Carolina and one of the first in America.[94] At the same time Moses Pimienta lived in Charleston. He was "learned in the laws, . . . taught the Jewish youth, and manifested an untiring zeal for the advance of the religion of our forefathers in this country."[95]

Another early teacher was "Rabbi Moses Eleizar" or Moses Elias, who apparently lived in the community in the second half of the eighteenth century. Both the 1820 and 1836 constitutions required that the second *escaba*, or prayer for the dead, be made for him "because he was a learned man in the laws of God, and until his death had taught the youth of this Congregation, and manifested unremitted zeal to promote religion in this country." The first prayer was for Moses Cohen. Another teacher, Raphael DaCosta Amesquita, judging by his epitaph, enjoyed a favorable reputation as an instructor. The inscription at his grave says he was "a truly honest and pious man, who devoted all his life to the instruction of youths in the Jewish religion."[96] He died in 1821. After being turned down for the position of *hazan*, Abraham Ottolengui returned to America, and the Charleston directory of 1807 indicates he was a teacher that year. He possibly taught Hebrew. When Gustavus Poznanski arrived in the city to serve as *hazan*, he privately taught Hebrew to boys.[97] Such haphazard pri-

91. Levin, "The Jewish Congregation of Charleston," 435.

92. Levin, "Address Delivered Before the Society for the Instruction of Jewish Youth," 165.

93. Harby, *Discourse*, 8.

94. Cohen, *Judaism and the Typical Jew.*

95. Levin, "The Jewish Congregation of Charleston," 29.

96. Elzas, *Old Jewish Cemeteries*, 71.

97. Minute Book of Beth Elohim, Nov. 26, 1838.

vate instruction for young Jews probably had been the practice during most of the early years in Charleston. Very likely the boys learned little more than how to pronounce the Hebrew used in services, because by the 1820s few knew the language, especially those born in the United States.

Two other promoters of the faith in Charleston, Isaac Pinto and Emanuel Nunes Carvalho, wrote some of the earliest Jewish books in America. Pinto, a merchant by profession, lived in the city a number of years. He has been credited with translating the first Jewish prayerbook into English in America, although this has never been proven.[98] Another author, Emanuel Nunez Carvalho, published the first Hebrew text by an American Jew after he returned to Philadelphia; apparently, he had used it while in Charleston. The book is divided into two parts, one containing lessons and the other grammar. The language lessons consist of lists of unrelated words and their translations. The vocabulary words have no relation to one another, and there is no text from which they are taken. The author may have had a purpose in choosing the words, but he never explains what it is. The second part of the book introduces the Hebrew alphabet, although students would have to know this to work in the first part of the book, and grammar. The grammar section could help one begin to understand the language. All in all, his methods of teaching must have left much to be desired.[99]

An important development came about in 1838. In that year Sally Lopez proposed to the leaders of the synagogue that she be authorized to establish, along with other female members of the community, The School of Israel to promote the knowledge of "our sacred Religion among the children of our congregation." Gustavus Poznanski, as *hazan*, promised his full support and recommended that the school be held on Sunday. He suggested the name Religious Exercise for Jewish Youths. The organization, however, became known as the Hebrew Society for the Instruction of Jewish Youth in Charleston. The trustees approved the expenditure of funds for the purchase of books and other materials, and the second Sunday school for Jewish boys—and girls—in America began operation.

The school met in the Tabernacle, a temporary structure erected after the synagogue had been destroyed by fire. Poznanski at first opposed using the building as it was a place of worship, but the trustees approved its use, provided a curtain separated the place of learning from the rest of the meeting place.[100] Sally Lopez in establishing this school followed the example of Rebecca Gratz of Philadelphia, who had begun a similar one shortly before. According to tra-

98. *Evening Service of Roshashanah and Kippur.*

99. Carvalho, *A Key to the Hebrew Tongue*; Chomsky, "Hebrew Grammar and Textbook Writing," 123, 128–30.

100. Minute Book of Beth Elohim, Nov. 11, 26, Dec. 29, 1838; Jan. 17, Mar. 11, 1839.

dition, Miss Gratz assisted in the creation of the school in Charleston by sending copies of her lessons to Sally Lopez. By 1845 a Miss Simpson ran the school, but Penina Moïse replaced her that year.[101]

When Julius Eckman became the *hazan* of Beth Elohim in 1850, he wrote the board of trustees, "I intend to open, with the beginning of next month, a Hebrew school, to which I will devote several evening hours weekly." The board approved his use of the Tabernacle for this purpose "so long as the scholars do no mischief to the premises."[102] Apparently, the unruly boys had little interest in the study of Hebrew.

Leadership

Although the *hazan* of the synagogue was the most visible representative of the community, he was only an employee of the congregation. Power lay in the hands of the corporate officials. The first surviving document giving a complete view of the administrative structure of Beth Elohim is the constitution of 1820.[103] The preamble states that this was a new constitution, which indicates that others had preceded it. Very likely, some restlessness in the congregation motivated its promulgation. The rules provided that a person had to attend services at the congregation for one year before he could apply to become a *yahid*, or full member. Only the *yahidim* could hold office. The government of the congregation consisted of a *general adjunta* of twenty-five members who served for three-year terms. They took over the administrative powers "formerly exercised by the people at large."[104] When elections were held, at least eighteen of the new *general adjunta* could already be serving in office while seven had to be elected from the *yahidim* at large. The *general adjunta* (essentially an electoral college) then chose the *private adjunta* (a board or vestry) of seven members. From among these, they annually chose a *parnass presidenta* (presiding president), a *parnass residenta* (president elect), and a *gabbay* (treasurer). The *parnass presidenta* served for the first six months, to be followed by the *parnass residenta*.

This oligarchical government left little power to the individual members. On the other hand, the *parnass presidenta* had considerable authority. He presided at services, over paid officers, and at public meetings. He could "call before the Private Adjunta any person or persons, who may misbehave either in Synagogue, its enclosures during divine service, or other legal occasions or meeting." He called regular meetings at the *private adjunta* at least once a month. The *general adjunta* along with the *parnassim* and the *private adjunta* chose the other officials necessary for operating the synagogue. These included the *hazan*, the *shamas* (sexton), the *shohet* (ritual butcher), the *shomar* (watchman),

101. "Hebrew Society for the Instruction of Jewish Youth"; Engelman, "Jewish Education in Charleston," 57.

102. Minute Book of Beth Elohim, June 29, 1850.

103. *Constitution of the Hebrew Congregation of Kaal Kadosh Beth-Elohim.*

104. Ibid., Rule 2.

and the *parnass* of the cemetery. By this time the congregation paid the officials.

The leaders of the synagogue sought to maintain tight control over the members living in the city. All had to pay annual dues and to purchase seats for their wives. Newly arrived individuals had to become members after a year if they wanted to be married, buried, or otherwise participate in community affairs. If they refused but later changed their minds, they had to pay their back dues as if they had been members. No one could erect a synagogue or hold service within five miles of Charleston or be buried in any but the congregational burial ground.[105] The leaders soon found that they could not prevent other services from being held, but the refusal to bury wayward Jews was a strong inducement for conformity. Additionally, no one could be accepted as a member who married contrary to Jewish law or who had renounced his faith. Anyone violating the Sabbath or other holy days would lose all privileges and would be subject to fines. Following traditional Jewish practice, the congregation neither encouraged nor interfered with making proselytes, but a convert would have to produce satisfactory credentials from a congregation that had a chief rabbi and a Hebrew consistory or *bet din*, "provided, he, she, or they, are not people of colour." Finally, none of these regulations could be easily changed. The Constitution of 1820 required two-thirds of the members, excluding the *private* and *general adjuntas*, to petition for amendments. These two bodies would then meet, twenty of whom would form a quorum, and if two-thirds of them agreed, they could institute amendments that "shall become binding and of full force in this Congregation."[106] All told, members found themselves under a very authoritative form of government.

This constitution remained in effect until 1825, when a new one was written.[107] The 1825 constitution has not been located; however, in light of the fact that it grew out of a serious division in the congregation, it probably was as strict if not stricter than the 1820 document.

In 1836 the congregation adopted a new constitution with thirty-four articles.[108] It came about after a general meeting on February 23, 1836, and went into effect on Rosh ha-Shanah that year.[109] Article 1 of that set of laws reaffirmed the Minhag Sephardim. The government of the congregation was vested in a board of trustees, no longer known as the *adjunta*, which consisted of five people. The first five board members—Moses C. Levy, Nathan Hart, Abraham Ottolengui, H. M. Hertz, and Isaiah Moses—held office for life. Upon their death or removal from the city,

105. An exception was made for the Tobias family, the near relatives of Isaac DaCosta, and Emanuel DeLaMotta, his wife, and his children.

106. *Constitution of the Hebrew Congregation of Kaal Kadosh Beth-Elohim*, Rule 14.

107. The preamble of the 1836 constitution stated that it was amending the "Constitution framed for its government in 1825."

108. *New Constitution of Beth Elohim*.

109. This information is found in the Preface, ibid.

they could be replaced by new members whose terms were limited to three years. The trustees chose the president, or *parnass president*, for the term of one year and a vice president, or *parnass segan*, who could replace the president in case of sickness, death, or temporary absence. The president controlled the religious services, the paid employees, and the decorum in the synagogue. Persons living in the city could become *yahidim*, or voting members, after two years' residence and application to the board. The *hazan* would be elected initially for a two-year trial period. If he passed that test, he received a lifetime appointment. The final article provided for various fines for transgressions such as failing to attend a general meeting of the congregation where a constitutional issue was to be decided.

The 1820 and 1836 constitutions give a good idea of the funding of the synagogue. Normal funds came from annual subscriptions and the leasing of seats. In 1820 the annual dues amounted to $11; in 1836 they had risen to $15 per year for members and $5 for widows. In 1820 the seats for women were auctioned off to the highest bidder; however, in 1836 seats, whether for men or women, cost $5 (first class), $4 (second class), and $2 (third class). The seats had the names of the occupants on the back, and no other person could occupy them without the permission of the proprietor. The president assigned separate seats for strangers and people who had not paid their dues. In addition to the normal funding, the synagogue had the *kaaren kayematt*, or permanent fund, which had been established in 1791. This endowment came from contributions, bequests, interest, and dividends. In 1820 it had a separate treasurer. In 1836 the congregation changed this office to a separate board, which then elected a treasurer from its own members. The income had to be invested in good bonds, which were secured by mortgages on real estate within the city or state or stock in banks located in the city. Members of the congregation could borrow from the permanent fund provided they gave the necessary security. When these funds accumulated interest of at least $1,000, money could be used to pay the *hazan* or other congregational expenses. Not many congregations had funds such as these. Indeed, the reasons given in the preface for the new constitution were the "advancement and prosperity of Kaal Kadosh Beth Elohim." A separate fund went toward the maintenance of the cemeteries.

The 1836 constitution retained the 1820 prohibitions against marriage outside the faith and restrictions about accepting converts, including people of color. It required three-quarters of the members to amend it. The congregational government was somewhat less oligarchical than that described in the earlier document.

Another change came with a new constitution in 1840. It contained only fifteen articles and increased the board to seven members, who were to be elected every three years. They had to live within one mile of the city. The trustees elected the president, vice president, and treasurer for one-year terms. The board, rather than the president, had control over all the civil and religious concerns of the congregation. Any resident of the city could become a *yahid*, or voting member, if he had attained the age of twenty-one, was under no religious disabilities, and had been approved by the board. Strangers had to pay dues for three years before becoming full members. Because a rival synagogue, Shearith Israel, had been established by that time, anyone who habitually attended services at any other place of worship in the city had to pay annual dues of $100, while those for a member in good standing was $15. Also, one-third of the *yahidim* could call for a constitutional meeting, at which time any changes had to be passed by two-thirds of those present. This constitution, accordingly, gave broader powers to the trustees and the full members. Although it did not exclude people who attended services at another synagogue, they had to pay dearly for the privilege should they want to have a voice in the affairs of Beth Elohim.[110]

Concern for Other Jews

One of the problems for the community was the itinerant Jews who appeared from time to time. Some had real needs and sought help where they could. They knew they would be likely to find assistance from other members of the faith. A few were no more than beggars. Occasionally, needy persons received only enough assistance to get to another city. An example occurred in 1815 when the congregational leaders sent a blind and penniless Mrs. Levy to Philadelphia for medical care with nothing more than a letter of introduction. On another occasion, two men "dressed in the Moorish habit" arrived in Charleston. When questioned by a law officer because they looked suspicious, they reacted strongly. According to the officer, the men became impertinent and vulgar. Soon a mob gathered. Eventually the authorities discovered that they were of the "Jewish nation" and took the two men to the home of a woman on East Bay Street who understood their language.[111]

The community also showed concern for other Jewish congregations in the United States and abroad. When Jewish communities needed help, they normally wrote other cities asking for aid. One example of Charleston's helping occurred in 1825 when an appeal came from a new congregation in Cincinnati. After the synagogue in Charleston burned in 1838, Cincinnati returned the favor.[112]

More distant incidents involving Jews also concerned the Jews of Charleston. The first of a number of very serious events in the nineteenth century took place when thirteen members of the Jewish community of Damascus were thrown in jail, tortured, and then executed on the charge that they had committed a ritual murder of a French priest

110. This constitution has not been located, but parts can be reconstructed from the case of State v. Ancker, which is discussed later.

111. Reznikoff, *Jews of Charleston*, 51–52. Apparently they came from North Africa.

112. Schappes, *Documentary History*, 177–79, 608.

in order to obtain blood to put in the Passover bread. One of the most heinous charges against Jews, the accusation had appeared repeatedly over the centuries despite the fact that the use of blood in the Passover bread would have been an utmost defilement. The Jewish communities in France and Britain sent representatives to protest this event to the ruler of Egypt, as he then controlled the area. President Martin Van Buren of the United States also sent a formal protest. Mayor Henry L. Pinckney and all religious leaders of Charleston organized a protest meeting on August 28, 1840. Pinckney spoke, as well as the Honorable Alfred Huger, Bishop John England, the Reverend Dr. Brantley, the Reverend Dr. Palmer, the Honorable James S. Rhett, and B. F. Pepoon. The attendance of Bishop England at the assembly is especially noteworthy, as French priests as well as Muslims had spread the story. The assembly passed resolutions condemning the actions, which they sent to Van Buren. The following day the Jews met at the Hebrew Orphan House, where J. C. Levy served as chair and spoke of a "smoking volcano, that might again rage with the fury of the Middle Ages." He stated that the atrocities "demand an expression of public opinion co-existensive with the length and breadth of this republican land." Levy also claimed that the meeting of the previous evening was an "unbought homage to truth and toleration, and to the integrity and purity of our ancient faith." Aaron Moïse, Sr., stated, "The people of Charleston had shown practically what they understood by equality of rights and true liberality." "They were now ready to raise their voices in behalf of wounded Israel." Moïse also said that "the citizens of his native city had been the first in the New World to stand forth in defence of principles so clearly cherished by freemen." This group also passed resolutions to be sent to the president of the United States demanding that some action be taken.[113] Such unity in Charleston was a rare occurrence.

In 1855 the Jews of Charleston and America again became concerned when the United States negotiated a secret treaty with Switzerland regarding trade. What troubled the Jews was that some of the cantons in Switzerland forbade their coreligionists to reside or trade there. The treaty between the United States and Switzerland recognized and accepted this, and the Swiss government rejected the application of an American to trade there because he was a Jew. A heated debate in the Charleston newspapers came about in 1857 when Maurice Mayer, the minister at Beth Elohim, wrote the *Daily Courier* pointing out that although the treaty "may well be worthy of Russian politics," it was "a disgrace to this republic." He called on the Jews of the city to forget their religious differences and to act together to have the treaty changed. He also appealed to the Christians for "assistance in this holy cause."[114] A few days later "A Jew" responded claiming that Mayer was "either ignorant of the subject, or had allowed a hasty and impetuous zeal,

113. *Proceedings of a Public Meeting on the 28th August, 1840.*

114. *Daily Courier*, Aug. 13, 1857.

to get the better of his reasoning powers." He claimed that the rights of American Jews were in no way molested. On the other hand, the cantons of Switzerland had the same relationship to their federal government as the states in the United States. The national government could not interfere in state or canton matters. The writer argued that a Swiss citizen who was a Negro or mulatto could be thrown in jail or forcibly kept on board ship if he entered the port of Charleston. "And it will not do to argue that the negro is of an inferior race, while the Jew is the equal of the Swiss in moral, mental and social qualities: this is no doubt true, but it is begging the question." Mayer responded to the attack on August 21, and "A Jew" attacked him again on August 25. Then on August 29, J. N. C. (Jacob Nunes Cardozo) joined in. The letters continued until September 17, with Cardozo demolishing the arguments of his opponent.[115] According to another source, the Jews of Charleston met and forwarded a memorial to the president of the United States demanding that the treaty be rescinded. Eventually this problem was resolved in Switzerland when the cantons did away with many of the laws forbidding Jews to trade there.[116]

As the difficulties with the Swiss treaty were being settled, another problem broke out. This involved Edgardo Mortara, the son of a Jewish family that lived in Bologna, then a part of the Papal States in Italy. A Christian family maid claimed that about a year after Edgardo's birth in 1851 when the child became sick, she secretly baptized him. She did not tell anyone about this until 1858, when she went to the offices of the Inquisition. The archbishop of Bologna then ordered that the child be seized from his family. Officials arrived late at night and took the boy away. This action immediately became a rallying point for the Jews of Europe and America. It also caused much anti-Catholic sentiment on both sides of the Atlantic. Penina Moïse of Charleston showed how she felt by one of her poems. The first stanza reads:

> I grieve for thee Mortara! a Hebrew sister grieves
> For that dread stroke, which more than death, thy home and heart bereaves,
> Oh! every chord of sympathy vibrated in my breast,
> When o'er the broad Atlantic came the news of that arrest:
> Which breaking through each ordinance of Heaven and of Earth,
> Has torn a helpless infant from the authors of its birth
> Consigning to a stranger's care, and to a bigot's creed
> A child of Abraham's covenant—one of his chosen seed.

After Sir Moses Montefiore of London called on the Jews of America to take action, meetings were held in many communities, including Charleston. The Jews of Charleston met in the Masonic hall, where Daniel Ottolengui

115. Ibid., Aug. 19, 24, 25, 31, Sept. 3, 4, 14, 17, 1857.

116. Strock, "Switzerland and the Jews," 7–52.

spoke. Again they made protests to the president of the United States. In this case the national government denounced the events but took no action. In the end nothing could be done, and the church raised Edgardo Mortara in its institutions, and he later became a priest. He died in Belgium a month before the Nazis took that country; had he lived, the Germans would have classified him as a Jew.[117]

The Jews of Charleston had a strong sense of community. They worked together to promote their faith and to care for their people. They also showed concern for their coreligionists in other parts of the world. Despite the fact that they had their differences, they could work together when they felt it necessary. And even when the synagogue split, the Hebrew Orphan Society and the Benevolent Society continued to unite the members of the faith. Fortunately, they lived in a land where they could form their own organizations and fight among themselves at the same time. Many Jews in other parts of the world lacked such luxuries.

117. Korn, *The American Reaction to the Mortara Case.*

CHAPTER 4

Living in Charleston

"Have you ever been on the Battery? 'Tis a beautiful promenade, with the sea washing its base, and on a moonlight night, . . . its surroundings are all provocatives of love."

—Raphael Jacob Moses, 1890s[1]

"The Inhabitants are wealthy,—Gay—& hospitable."

—George Washington, 1791[2]

Charleston offered much for the Jewish residents. Besides living how and where they pleased, they could take part in the activities of the city and could make a living in the profession they chose. If so inclined, they also could enjoy attending concerts, going to the theater, and engaging in intellectual pursuits. At the same time the city made demands on the residents. Its climate, diseases, wars, and racial tensions created problems for all who dwelled there. This chapter deals with the ways Jews adapted to the city and the ways they met their responsibilities as citizens.

In 1769 a Captain Martin composed a poem that captured some aspects of life in Charleston. He wrote:

Black and white all mix'd together,
Inconstant, strange, unhealthy
weather
Burning heat and chilling cold
Dangerous both to young and old
Boisterous winds and heavy rains
Fevers and rhumatic pains
Agues plenty without doubt
Sores, boils, the prickling heat and
gout
Musquitos on the skin make blotches
Centipedes and large cock-roaches
Frightful creatures in the waters
Porpoises, sharks and aligators
Houses built on barren land
No lamps or light, but streets of sand
Pleasant walks, if you can find 'em
Scandalous tongues, if any mind 'em
The markets dear and little money

1. Raphael Jacob Moses to his daughter Mrs. James Whyte in Marcus, *Memoirs of American Jews*, 1: 169.

2. Salley, *President Washington's Tour*. Washington's description dates from the time of his visit to Charleston.

Large potatoes, sweet as honey
Water bad, past all drinking
Men and women without thinking
Every thing at a high price
But rum, hominy and rice
Many a widow not unwilling
Many a beau not worth a shilling
Many a bargain, if you strike it,
This is Charles-town, how do you
like it?[3]

Blacks and Whites

Blacks and whites did intermingle in Charleston. The house of a rich plantation owner or merchant might sit beside one filled with slaves. Sometimes whites rented their houses from well-to-do free persons of color. The Jews of the city, being white skinned, joined with the dominant race. As a group, most of them quickly adopted the attitudes of the slaveholding society. Some had previously resided in slaveowning territories such as the West Indies and had become familiar with the practice, but many who came straight from Europe owned slaves. Indeed, a large percentage of the Jews of the city who could afford to own slaves did so. The first two people identified as Jews in South Carolina owned slaves; in fact, Simon Valentine sold one to Samuel Mincks in 1696.[4] Over the years other Charleston Jews readily adopted the practice.

When the United States took the first census in 1790, the enumerators listed 53 Jews as the heads of households in Charleston.[5] Of these 29, or 55 percent had slaves; however, other records show that at least 15 additional Jews listed in the 1790 census held slaves at some time, raising the percentage of those who owned slaves to no less than 83 percent. The Jewish families that owned slaves in 1790 held a total of 93 people, with Philip Hart having the greatest number—15. The average in a Jewish household appears to have been approximately three slaves. (See Table 10.)

Over time, urban slaveholding increased. In 1830, 87 percent of the white households in Charleston had slaves. For the Jews the percentage was 83 percent.[6] By the middle of the nineteenth century, the Jews who owned slaves held an average of approximately 5.5 slaves. Females constituted 57 percent of the slaves and males 43 percent. Some people owned several, such as Morris Goldsmith with 16, Hannah Myers with 15, and M. C. Mordecai with 14. Most slaveowners, however, had only 1 to 3, and many recent immigrants to the city had none.[7] No one seemed bothered by the practice. Even Samuel Maas, an immigrant from Germany who had been in the country but four weeks, could write his parents a letter in which he supported slavery. Maas stated that only the black Africans could tolerate the heat, humidity, and hard work encoun-

3. Merrens, *The Colonial South Carolina Scene*, 220–21.

4. WIM (1694–1704), 362.

5. This excludes three entries: two for firms, Cantor and Solomons plus Hart and DaCosta, and one for Moses Levy, who is listed twice.

6. Rosenwaike, *On the Edge of Greatness*, 68.

7. 1850 U.S. Census.

Table 10
Slaveowning Jews in Early Charleston

Names	*Number of Slaves*	*Names*	*Number of Slaves*
Abendanone, Joseph	4	Levy, Solomon	0*
Abrahams, Emanuel	4	Lopez, Aaron	2
Abrahams, Jacob	1	Lyon, Abraham	1
Abrahams, Judith	0*	Lyon, Mordica	1
Alexander, Abraham	0*	Moses, Abraham	0*
Barrett, Solomon	0*	Moses, Barnet	2
Canter, Joshua	0*	Moses, Henry	0*
Cantor, Jacob	1	Moses, Isaac	1
Cohen, Gershon	6	Moses, Lyon	4
Cohen, Jacob	0*	Moses, Philip	0*
Cohen, Moses	0*	Phillips, Benjamin	0*
DaCosta, Isaac	6	Phillips, Eleazer	2
DaCosta, Samuel	0*	Pollock, Solomon	4
DaCosta, Sarah	5	Sasportas, Abraham	4
DeLyon, Isaac	2	Seixas, Abraham	5
Emanuel, Joseph	0*	Simons, Sampson	2
Hart, Philip	15	Simons, Samuel	2
Hart, Simon	1	Solomons, Hyman	0*
Jacobs, Jacob	0*	Spitzer, Bernard	0*
Jones, Samuel	3	Tobias, Joseph	3
Joseph, Israel	1	Tongues, Mark	1
Lazarus, Marks	2	Woolf, Rachel	6
Levy, Moses	2		

*Owned slaves at times other than the 1790 census.

Sources: U.S. Census Department, *Heads of Families at the First Census of the United States in the Year 1790: South Carolina.* MR4G.208 (Judith Abrahams); MR4A.116, 3X.428, 3G.239, 4A.116 (Abraham Alexander); W45.741 (Solomon Barrett); MR3N.424, 4P.321, 3X.125, (Joshua Canter); MR4I.203 (Jacob Cohen); MR2Q.230, 4C.592, 2Q.184 (Moses Cohen); MR3D.109 (Samuel DaCosta); MR3C.1 (Joseph Emanuel); MR3I.132, 2T.480, 3A.105 (Jacob Jacobs); MR4A.324, 4X.229, 4A.426 (Solomon Levy); MR3E.363 (Abraham Moses); MR4Q.320 (Henry Moses); MR3T.7 (Philip Moses); MR4X.397 (Benjamin Phillips); MR3H.286, 2W.106 (Hyam Solomons); MR2S.500 (Bernard Moses *or* Moses Bernard *or* Barand Moses Spitzer). For several of the individuals who owned many slaves only a few records are listed. For a guide to the abbreviations for sources, see the list of abbreviations in the Introduction.

Table 11
Slaveowning Jews in Charleston, 1850

Names	*Number of Slaves* *Total*	*Male*	*Female*	*Names*	*Number of Slaves* *Total*	*Male*	*Female*
Abrahams, Alexander	2	1	1	Lazarus, Michael	6	3	3
Abrahams, Elias	1	0	1	Levy, Elias	10	6	4
Barrett, Jacob	9	6	3	Levy, L. L.	7	5	2
Benjamin, Philip	4	2	2	Levy, Moses	13	7	6
Cohen, Hartwig	3	2	1	Levy, Sarah	2	0	2
Cohen, J.	1	0	1	Lipman, Samuel	4	2	2
Cohen, Jacob	10	3	7	Lopez, David	14	6	8
Cohen, M.	3	1	2	Lopez, H. G.	10	3	7
Cohen, N. A.	3	1	2	Moïse, Abraham	2	1	1
Cohen, Nancy	4	3	1	Mordecai, ——	12	5	7
Cohen, Philip	4	1	3	Mordecai, M. C.	14	8	6
Cohen, R. M.	2	2	0	Mordecai, T. W.	2	1	1
Cohen, Selina	2	1	1	Moses, Gershon	1	0	1
DaVega, Grace	3	1	2	Moses, Levy	2	2	0
DeLaMotta, Emanuel	2	0	2	Moses, Levy, Sr.	11	3	8
DeLange, Martha	8	2	6	Moses, Lyon	1	1	0
DeLeon, Isabella	2	0	2	Moses, Reuben	2	2	0
Emanuel, N.	3	1	2	Moses, Solomon	11	5	6
Goldsmith, Morris	16	8	8	Motta, Sarah	6	0	6
Hertz, Isaac	2	1	1	Myers, Hannah	15	8	7
Hyams, M. D.	8	2	6	Oppenheim, H. W.	4	1	3
Jacobs, Myer	6	1	5	Ottolengui, Abraham	13	7	6
Josephs, C.	1	0	1	Rodrigues, B. A.	6	3	3
Lazarus, B. D.	8	4	4	Rodrigues, Benjamin	4	2	2
Lazarus, G.	3	1	2	Solomons, Ellen	4	1	3
				Sommers, E.	2	0	2

Note: Some persons owned slaves at two or more addresses.
Sources: U.S. Census, 1850.

tered in the Carolina Low Country.[8] Polish, German, English, and Sephardic Jews all purchased slaves. Slaveholding was the way of the South. (See Table 11.)

Although many Jews of Charleston owned slaves, they seem not to have held great numbers. Most Jews appeared only once or twice in the bills of sale of slaves in the South Carolina Archives. Only 18 people show up ten or more times either buying or selling slaves. The highest number purchased by a person was 29,

8. Marcus, *United States Jewry*, 588.

and the highest number sold was 31. Mostly the transactions were small and extended over a few years. The two people involved most in buying and selling slaves were Mordecai Cohen and Isaiah Moses, both of whom owned plantations. Four others were vendue masters (auctioneers) or commission merchants or both, and two earned their living as brokers. Very likely, they purchased slaves that people brought to them to sell, held them for a while, and then sold them at a profit. A number of bills of sale list names of slaves and show them being purchased and sold within a few months.[9] Although many bills of sale apparently were never recorded, those that survive should give an idea who dealt most in slaves. (See Table 12.)

Among Jews, as among other whites, the largest owners of slaves were plantation owners. However, even they did not hold great numbers. Entries in city directories and other sources show that several men considered themselves planters from time to time.[10] A book written in 1884 states that Jacob Ottolengui of Charleston owned a plantation near the Savannah River with a thousand slaves.[11] Bertram Korn in his *Jews and Negro Slavery in the Old South* repeated the story and refers to him as a speculator in slaves; however, evidence for this statement is lacking.[12]

Since slaves cost a good deal of money, people often fought court cases over them. In 1834 M. C. Mordecai acted as the agent for the brig *Encomium* and contracted with John Waddell to transport several slaves from Charleston to New Orleans. During the voyage the ship wrecked on one of the Bahama Islands despite the fact that the captain was on the deck, the weather was pleasant, and the stars were shining brightly. According to Mordecai, the captain bore the responsibility for the wreck and "did not care a *damn*" for the slaves. Authorities in the Bahamas took charge of the human cargo and liberated them, since slavery had been abolished in British territories. Seven of the slaves, however, came back to Charleston, where authorities returned them to Waddell at the cost of $200. Waddell then demanded that Mordecai repay his commission of $100 for arranging their shipment. Mordecai refused, so Waddell took him to the courts and, when he did not receive satisfaction, appealed the decision; however, the judges found Mordecai not to be liable.[13]

9. Some people did not make good purchases. Alexander Isaacs purchased a slave woman and her five children on Jan. 1, 1864, as the war was coming to an end.

10. The following men are listed as planters in city directories and other records: Jacob Barrett, Barnet A. Cohen, David Daniel Cohen, Mordecai Cohen, Solomon Cohen, Isaac DaCosta, Myer Jacobs, Edward Levy, Isaac Lyons, Samuel Mincks, Isaiah Moses, Josiah Moses, Nathan Nathans.

11. Scott, *Random Recollections*, 83.

12. Korn, *Jews and Slavery*, 107. There are only two transactions for slaves for him found in the South Carolina Archives; they show that he purchased nine slaves in 1845 and sold five in 1860. MR6A.360; 6E.229.

13. "John Waddell v. M.C. Mordecai," *Reports of Cases at Law*, ed. Hill, 2: 366–72. For the wreck of the *Encomium*, see the Charleston *Courier*, Feb. 20, 1834.

Table 12
Slave Purchases and Sales by Jewish Slaveowners with Ten or More Recorded Transactions

Name	*Directory Listings*	*Slaves* *Bought*	*Slaves* *Sold*	*Years*	*Number of Transactions*
Barrett, Isaac B.	Store, merchant, VM and CM, factor	16	18	1817–29	10
Cohen, Mordecai	Merchant, shop, planter	25	26	1795–1838	27
Davis, Hannah L. H. D.	Shop	17	12	1803–35	23
DeLeon, Mordecai H.	Physician, VM and CM	8	4	1813–20	11
Lazarus, Marks	Shop	17	17	1786–1834	11
Levy, Lyon	Clerk, State Treasurer's Office, shop, accountant	11	1	1792–1824	10
Levy, Solomon	Shop, merchant	21	9	1809–28	21
Mordecai, Benjamin	Broker	17	31	1847–60	29
Mordecai, Moses Cohen	Accountant, merchant, VM	13	6	1827–49	14
Moses, Esther D.		2	8	1795–1817	10
Moses, Isaac	Shop, auctioneer	14	7	1794–1820	13
Moses, Isaiah	Grocer, merchant and planter, shop	29	29	1809–45	14
Moses, Levy	Store	12	23	1803–37	12
Moses, Simon	Store, broker	16	21	1813–32	27
Nathan, Solomon	Shop	7	7	1799–1817	10
Sasportas, Abraham	Merchant	3	24	1779–1806	13
Tobias, Abraham	Merchant, auctioneer, accountant, VM	16	8	1816–37	16
Woolf, Rachel A. M.	Shop	15	9	1814–25	16

Note: VM = vendue merchant; CM = commission merchant.
Sources: These bills of sales for these transactions may be found in the Miscellaneous Records of the South Carolina Archives. Because 287 transactions are tabulated here, the individual records are not listed.

Two other cases involved the soundness of slaves. Benjamin A. Rodrigues sold a female slave named Hannah to R. W. Habersham of Georgia on December 23, 1840. T. M. Hume had served as the agent and sold the slave for $550 in cash. Rodrigues executed a bill of sale but refused to warrant the "soundness" of the slave because he had not obtained a warranty when he bought her. Rodrigues said he knew of no disease except that she had "slight rheumatism in her arm and shoulder." According to Rodrigues, Hannah was a good washer and ironer, and the only reason he sold her was that "he had too many in his yard, having bought a younger woman some time before." Habersham took Hannah back to Georgia with him. After Hannah complained of being sickly for several months, Habersham took her to two doctors, who found that "Hannah was seriously diseased in the ovaria and uterus, having *schirrous* tumors in these parts of the size of the double fists." They concluded that the growths were cancerous and incurable. Habersham then brought Hannah back to Charleston, where doctors Prioleau and Ogier examined her and stated she must have had the tumors for the past year. Rodrigues, who was a doctor by training and a dentist by practice, then had the slave examined by three other doctors—Geddings, Frost, and Elfe. They stated that they could not say how long the tumors had existed without pathological dissection. Dr. Frost testified that he had treated Hannah for diarrhea before she was sold, and he did not believe that she had the tumors at the time. The jury, however, decided that since the price was a good one for Hannah that there was an implied warranty of her soundness, and Rodrigues was liable. Rodrigues appealed the decision but failed to get a higher court to reverse the lower court's finding.[14]

A similar case involved Solomon Cohen, Jr. In 1837 he bought from Mrs. Harriett Pinckney Rutledge two slaves, Bella and her son James, in trust for Henrietta Y. Cohen. In 1838 Henry L. Pinckney, mayor of Charleston, committed Bella to the "maniac department" of the poor house because she was "dangerous to the neighborhood, by a habit she had of throwing pieces of fire about her room." The authorities at the poor house then demanded that Cohen pay fifty cents per day for her care. Cohen claimed that he had rescinded the sale because Bella had been warranted sound. A jury, however, ruled he could not rescind a sale and that he had to pay the $35.88 demanded by the poor house. Cohen also lost on appeal.[15]

A slave named Cain also caused problems for Joshua Canter. A court found the man guilty of burglary and larceny on November 6 and sentenced him to death by hanging on November 15, 1799. The court recompensed Canter at the rate of £70; however, the owner did not feel that this amount was sufficient as he had paid £76 for the slave. He appealed to the General Assembly, asking for the full value. Apparently, he did not succeed.[16]

Some Jewish people were actively involved in slave trading as vendue masters, commission merchants, or both. People went to them to buy or sell slaves. The auctioneers or merchants charged a fee for these services and did

14. "R.W. Habersham v. B. A. Rodrigues," *South Carolina Law Reports from November 1842 to* May *1843*, ed. Spears, 2: 294–99.

15. City Council v. Cohen, *South Carolina Law Reports, November, 1843 to May, 1844*, ed. Spears, 2: 342–50.

16. Joshua Canter, Petition to General Assembly, No. 1651, (1799).

Prime Field Negros and House Servants.

BY B. MORDECAI, 5 State-street.

At private sale—

TOM, 25 years of age, superior **coachman and house servant.**

JOHN, 21 years of age, superior **coachman and house servant.**

LILBURN; 24 years of age, superior **coachman and house servant**

ISAAC, 22 years of **age,** house **servant,**

DRUCILLA, 20, seamstress, **washer and ironer, and house servant.**

ELVY, 18, seamstress, washer and ironer, and house servant.

AMELIA, 22, seamstress, **tailoress, washer, and house servant.**

LYDIA, 40, cook, washer and ironer.

LOUISA, 40, cook, washer and ironer..

PATSY, 19, seamstress, **cook, washer and ironer, and child's nurse.**

CAROLINE, 17 **years old, prime field hand.**

LUCY, 19 years old, **prime field hand.**

BETSY, 17 years old, **prime field hand.**

MARGARET, 16 years old, **prime field hand.**

CATHERINE, 16 years old, **prime field hand.**

MILLY, 17 **years old, prime field hand.**

OCTAVIA, 16 years old, **prime field hand.**

SALINA, 16 years old, **prime field hand.**

MARY, 28 years old, **prime field hand.**

NANCY and 2 children, 20 years old, prime field hand.

SARAH and child, 30 years old, prime field hand.

SUSAN, 30 years old, prime field hand.

SARAH, 18 years old, prime field hand.

CAROLINE, 18 years old, prime field hand.

SAUNDERS, 22, field hand.

BENJAMIN, 25, **field hand.**

SAMPSON, 30, **field hand.**

SAM, 16, field hand and plough boy.

MOSES, 33, field hand and cooper.

LINDSAY, 27, **field hand.**

HENRY, 20, field hand.

ISAAC, 18, **field hand.**

LAWRENCE, 45, **field hand.**

BYRON, 22, field hand.

DAVE, 25 years of **age,** laborer.

NAT, 30 years of **age,** laborer **and sailor.**

HENRY, a superior coat, **pantaloon and vest maker, 22 years old.**

thimtuwthfin7 **January 1**

15. Advertisement of slaves by B. Mordecai. (*Daily Courier*, March 24, 1840.)

16. Advertisement of slaves by Jacob Ottolengui. (*Daily Courier*, January 3, 1857.)

not own the slaves any more than they owned the land, houses, furniture, or other goods they sold for a commission.

The way the system worked can be illustrated by a dispute between Benjamin Mordecai and Moritz J. Jacobi. In November or December 1858 Jacobi put three slaves (Horace, Matilda, and their son Horace) into the hands of Mordecai to be sold. Mordecai agreed to sell them for 2.5 percent commission. Jacobi boarded the slaves, but they visited the office of Mordecai almost every day for about three weeks. Meanwhile, Jacobi sold the slaves himself. Mordecai sued him, claiming that he should be paid the commission because the slaves were never withdrawn from him. A number of brokers testified that Mordecai had followed the usual practice in his handling of the slaves. The appeals court, however, ruled that Mordecai could not collect the commission, although he could possibly recover any expenses that he had incurred.[17]

For many of the vendue masters and brokers, selling slaves constituted a small part of their business. Nonetheless, Frederic Bancroft concluded that the terms of "broker" or "auctioneer" denoted slave traders. Those who shunned the slave trade, he says, advertised as cotton brokers, insurance brokers, or such.[18] The newspaper advertisements do not support his contention. Goods other than slaves made up the bulk of trade for most auctioneers.

In addition to purchase, slaves could be acquired as gifts, as bequests in wills, or when estates were settled. At least 58 slaves belonging to Jews changed

17. "B. Mordecai v. M.J. Jacobi," *Reports of Cases at Law*, ed. Richardson, 12: 547–49.

18. Bancroft, *Slave Trading in the Old South*, 173–76.

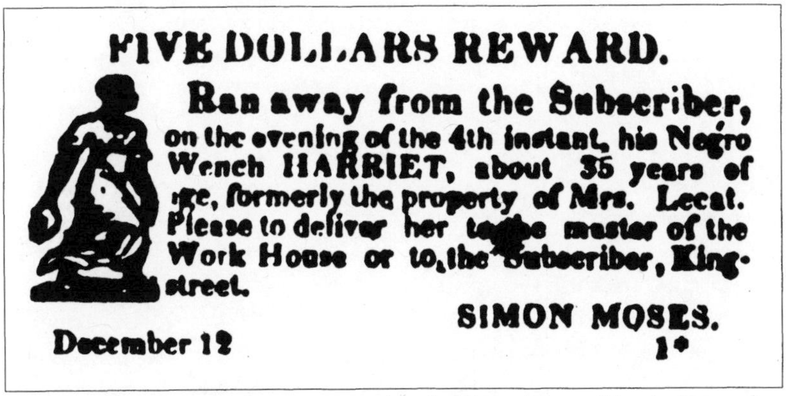

FIVE DOLLARS REWARD.

Ran away from the Subscriber, on the evening of the 4th instant, his Negro Wench HARRIET, about 35 years of age, formerly the property of Mrs. Lecat. Please to deliver her to the master of the Work House or to the Subscriber, King-street.

SIMON MOSES.

December 12 1*

17. Advertisement for a runaway slave by Simon Moses. (*Courier*, December 12, 1826.)

hands as gifts between 1761 and 1823. Mostly, people gave slaves to other members of their families for servants. They apparently had a fondness for both the slaves and their relatives. For example, Joseph Tobias gave Reinah Tobias DeLyon (his daughter) a slave in 1761,[19] and in 1818 Sarah Moïse gave two slaves to Cheri Moïse (her son) in trust for Penina Moïse (her daughter); however, Sarah Moïse reserved the use of the slaves during her lifetime.[20] Obviously, she wanted things settled before she died. Abraham Isaacs took a similar tack in 1823 when he presented two slaves to P. Cornell but kept the right to use them during his life.[21] He may have wanted to see that the slaves received good care after his death. A number of the people who wrote wills mentioned their slaves. Some provided for their disposition. For example, Israel Joseph left his slaves to Miriam Joseph, his wife.[22]

By working closely with their masters, some slaves earned the gratitude of their owners and, as a result, gained their freedom. For many years slave owners in South Carolina could dispose of their slaves as they wished; however, as disputes over slavery grew stronger and whites came to fear the blacks, who were in the majority, the state restricted the rights of the owners. A law in 1800 made the manumission of slaves difficult. An owner had to come before a justice and "five indifferent freeholders" and attest to the character and ability of the person to earn a living. Another law in 1820 forbade the freeing of slaves except by legislative act, and one in 1841 made it a crime to send slaves outside the state in order that they might obtain their freedom.[23]

Over the years at least ten Jews man-

19. MR2L.459.
20. MR4R.198.
21. MR4Z.240.
22. W29.673–78.
23. *Statutes*, 11: 168.

umitted eleven slaves altogether, beginning with Thomas Cohen in 1772 and ending with Samuel Hyams in 1811.[24] In addition, Judith Hyams cooperated with Ann Horry in removing three slaves from the state in 1831,[25] and Rachel D'Azevedo provided in her will that four slaves were to be protected by her daughter and that after that they were to be treated as if they were free.[26] Also, Solomon I. Barrett stated in his will that a slave by the name of Samuel should be freed. Unfortunately, he wrote his will in 1850,[27] when the slave could not legally be manumitted. The slave's only hope was to be treated as free by the family. Thus, Jacob DeLaMotta made his slaves free in practice if not in law. He provided in 1845 that his slaves Anna Maria Simmons and her son Augustus would belong to his sister Rachel. The slaves, however, were to be treated with leniency and to be allowed to earn their own wages. He instructed his sister not to sell them because they were family servants.[28] In a similar vein, David Pereyra Brandon recommended his faithful "servant and friend Juelitt or Julien," a free black, to relatives. They should give him some of Brandon's clothes and watch over him because he was the best friend Brandon ever had.[29]

Some men possibly cohabited with slaves or free blacks—"colored concubines were common among single men."[30] In fact, the legislature did not outlaw marriages between races until 1865. One possible example of a Jew's living with a slave could be Samuel B. Jones, who died in 1801. In his will he gave money to his slave Jenny, who was to be freed along with her son Emanuel if this had not been done during his lifetime. He also left goods and money to a mulatto, Nanny.[31] Jones mentioned no relatives in his will. Also, Benjamin Davids (d. 1831) left bequests to a free black by the name of Elsey for her faithful service. He also was single.[32] In addition, Samuel Simons, who died in 1824, left $1,400 and two slaves to his housekeeper Maria Chapman, a free person of color.[33] One man who may have been Jewish, Sherry Sasportas, recognized Catharine Maria Sasportas, a free mulatto woman, as his lawful wife and made her a sole trader in 1817 so that she might engage in business for herself.[34] And a relationship between a free woman of black and Indian blood and either Isaac N. Cardozo or Jacob N. Cardozo produced Francis Lewis Cardozo, one of the leading figures in South Carolina during the Reconstruction. Neither of the men married.[35]

24. MR2P.220, 227; 3H.286; 30.380, 670; 3Q.280; 4C.592.
25. MR5K.475.
26. W43.556–57.
27. W45.741–42.
28. W43.834–35.
29. W41.755–56.
30. Wallace, *South Carolina: A Short History*, 487.
31. W31.189.
32. W39.903.
33. W36.972–74.
34. MR40.165–66. See Chapter 8 for a discussion of what it meant for a woman to be a sole trader.
35. Korn, "Jews and Negro Slavery," 117–19.

A contemporary of the Cardozos in Charleston, Billy Simmons, was black, a slave, and a Jew. Information on him appeared in Jewish periodicals as early as 1856. Dr. Julius Eckman, who had been the *hazan* at Beth Elohim from 1850 to 1852 wrote an article in his newspaper, the *Weekly Gleaner* of San Francisco, on July 16, 1857. Eckman had encountered Old Uncle Billy Simmons in 1853 in the streets of Charleston. He reported that he saw Simmons attend synagogue on Yom Kippur "for some hours with an exemplary devotion." On another occasion during the heat of summer he observed Simmons walking in the streets without shoes. He offered to provide the slave with shoes and clothing, but Simmons refused, insisting that he would not accept charity while he could work. He did ask for some religious books so that he could learn more about his faith.

Simmons related that his father had told him that they were Rechabites, a tribe of Israelites, that existed in Africa.[36] According to Jeremiah 35, the Rechabites led ascetic lives and would not drink wine, build houses, sow fields, plant vineyards, or own things. An account by Maurice Mayer, the *hazan* from 1852 to 1859, in an article in *Allgemeine Zeitung des Judenthums* says that Simmons, who belonged to the congregation, claimed that he originally came from Madagascar by way of the Barbary States. He arrived with his Jewish master in the United States when he was very young. When Mayer knew him, Simmons was about seventy years of age. Mayer insisted that Simmons was "the most observant of those who go to the synagogue" and that he sat in the nave of the synagogue with his white coreligionists.[37] Another source states that in his later years he sometimes asserted that he had been born on the Waccamaw River in South Carolina. Yet he bore African markings, and most people believed he had come from that continent.[38]

Article 23 of the 1820 constitution and article 21 of the 1836 constitution of Beth Elohim excluded "people of color" from membership. The provisions of the 1840 constitution on this matter are unknown; however, Simmons apparently could not join the congregation. Indeed, since he was a slave, it would be unlikely that he could have afforded the fees. Although a B. M. Simmons became a member in 1839,[39] this apparently was not Billy Simmons.

Death worried Billy Simmons; he told Mayer the thing that concerned him most was his desire to be buried among other Jews. Mayer vowed that he would do everything in his power to see that this was done; however, by the time of Simmons's death, Mayer had left the city. No one knows where Simmons is buried.

While he lived, Simmons earned his

36. Reprinted in "Old Billy," 3–4; Melnick, "Billy Simmons," 3–8.

37. Vol. 21, p. 339. A translation can be found in Reznikoff, *Jews of Charleston*, 279.

38. Charleston *Daily Courier*, Dec. 12, 1859. If Simmons came from Africa, he possibly could have arrived with Moses DaVega, Sarah DaVega, and Starr Barrett.

39. Minute Book of Beth Elohim, July 24, 1839.

18. Billy Simmons. (*Centennial Edition of News and Courier*, 1903. Photograph courtesy of Special Collections, College of Charleston.)

keep delivering newspapers. A striking figure, he wore a high-crowned old hat on the job, but on weekends he wore a shining silk hat, a black suit, and a frilly white shirt.[40] An obituary that appeared on the front page of the *Daily Courier* described him as "unusually intelligent, shrewd, and quick at learning." Also: "Punctuality, promptness and fidelity at work were his invariable characteristics, and were exhibited to the last without claiming or accepting any of the privileges of age, and frequently without complaint under sufferings and attacks of asthma."[41] Eckman in the *Weekly Gleaner* stated that "he was universally respected by his co-religionists."[42] He was a remarkable man.

Although other Jews of Charleston accepted Billy Simmons, most whites viewed Africans with something akin to terror. Slaves constituted a majority of the population by the early eighteenth century. In 1739 a rebellion occurred on the Stono River when slaves armed themselves and killed twenty-one people. The governor suppressed the Stono Rebellion with great severity, and authorities increasingly feared their servants. On occasion, blacks who rose up were burned to death as punishment.[43] In Charleston the greatest problem occurred in 1822 when white residents of the city believed that Denmark Vesey, a free black, organized an uprising. Highly irregular and controversial trials found thirty-five blacks guilty and ordered them executed.[44] One of these, a man by the name of Mavidore, belonged to Mordecai Cohen. Mavidore was hanged on July 26.[45] The city also built The Citadel above Boundary Street to control the slaves.

On the whole, the Jews of Charleston supported the institution of slavery and the repressive measures that resulted. Isaac Harby and Jacob Cardozo owned and edited two of the local newspapers, the *Southern Patriot* and the *Evening News*, both of which favored slavery. In a series of editorials written in 1824 under the pseudonym of Junius, Harby attacked the abolitionists. He stated that South Carolina "can never consent to those newfangled doctrines, which, if carried to any extent might not only jeopardize the well-being of the Planting States, but . . . shake the 'married calm' of the whole Union."[46] A few days later he said that during the debate over the Missouri Compromise "our eyes opened to the character and sentiments of certain men" who had attempted to *"destroy the guarantee*, which secures the possession of slaves to their owners."[47] Jacob Cardozo believed that slavery had benefited both owners and slaves.[48] On the na-

40. "Uncle Billy: The First Carrier."

41. "Death of an Old Servant," Charleston *Daily Courier*, Dec. 12, 1859.

42. *Jewish Chronicle* [London], May 11, 1860, reprinting an article in *The Gleaner*.

43. Wallace, *South Carolina: A Short History*, 183–86.

44. Hamilton, *An Account of the Late Intended Insurrection*; Kennedy and Parker, *An Official Report of the Trials*.

45. Hamilton, *An Account of the Late Intended Insurrection*, 47.

46. Moïse and Pinckney, *A Selection from the Miscellaneous Writings*, 94–95.

47. Ibid., 134–35.

48. Cardozo, *Reminiscences*. Chap. 2 laments the destruction of the way of life of the Old South.

tional level, no major works by Jews on the subject appeared until 1861. At that time M. J. Raphall of New York wrote *Bible View of Slavery*, which generally supported the institution, and Moses Mielziner's dissertation at the University of Giessen, *Slavery amongst the Ancient Hebrews*, was translated from the German for the same reason.

Further evidence concerning the views among Charleston Jews about slavery can be found in the speech by Judah Barrett Cohen to the first anniversary meeting of the South Carolina Historical Society, in which he proclaimed that "the state of South Carolina is bound to reverence those men to whom she owes her position to the present day. She owes much to Sir John Yeamans, who first introduced slaves,—that incallucable benefit to our soil and necessity to our climate."[49] Also, Eleanor Cohen, daughter of Philip Melvin Cohen, fled with her family to Columbia during the Civil War. At the end of the conflict she wrote in her diary: "Slavery is done away with. . . . How it makes my southern blood boil to see them [Yanks] in the streets! . . . I, who believe in the institution of slavery, regret deeply its being abolished. I am accustomed to have them wait on me, and I dislike white servants very much."[50]

Differences between the North and South over slavery and other issues became pronounced in the 1820s, especially after the "Tariff of Abominations" passed in 1828. South Carolinians, led by John C. Calhoun, began to claim they had the right to nullify federal laws they believed to be unconstitutional. Charlestonians sharply differed on this issue, so much so that violence occurred on occasion. When Congress renewed the tariff in 1832, the Nullification Congress met in Charleston. The participants declared the tariffs of 1828 and 1832 null and void. The state legislature began to prepare for war, and Calhoun resigned as vice president of the United States. Congress reacted with the "Compromise Tariff," which offered relief, and in 1833 the nullification of the tariff was revoked.[51]

Four Jews from South Carolina attended the Nullification Convention. Two of them, Philip Phillips and Chapman Levy, were Unionists and opposed nullification, while Philip Cohen and Myer Jacobs favored it.[52] Only one of these, Philip Cohen, lived in Charleston at the time. Eventually the crisis passed and nullification died away. Then relations between the two sections of the country worsened again, and the cry for secession from the Union gained more and more favor in the city. By the time of the annual dinner of the Hebrew Orphan Society in 1858, the members omitted their usual toast to the president of the nation.[53] On the support of the southern causes, the Jews of Charles-

49. Cohen, "Oration Delivered on the First Anniversary of the South Carolina Historical Society," 104–17.

50. Marcus, *The American Jewish Woman*, 260–68.

51. Wallace, *South Carolina: A Short History*, 390–403.

52. Reznikoff, *Jews of Charleston*, 100–101.

53. Tobias, *Hebrew Orphan Society*, 16.

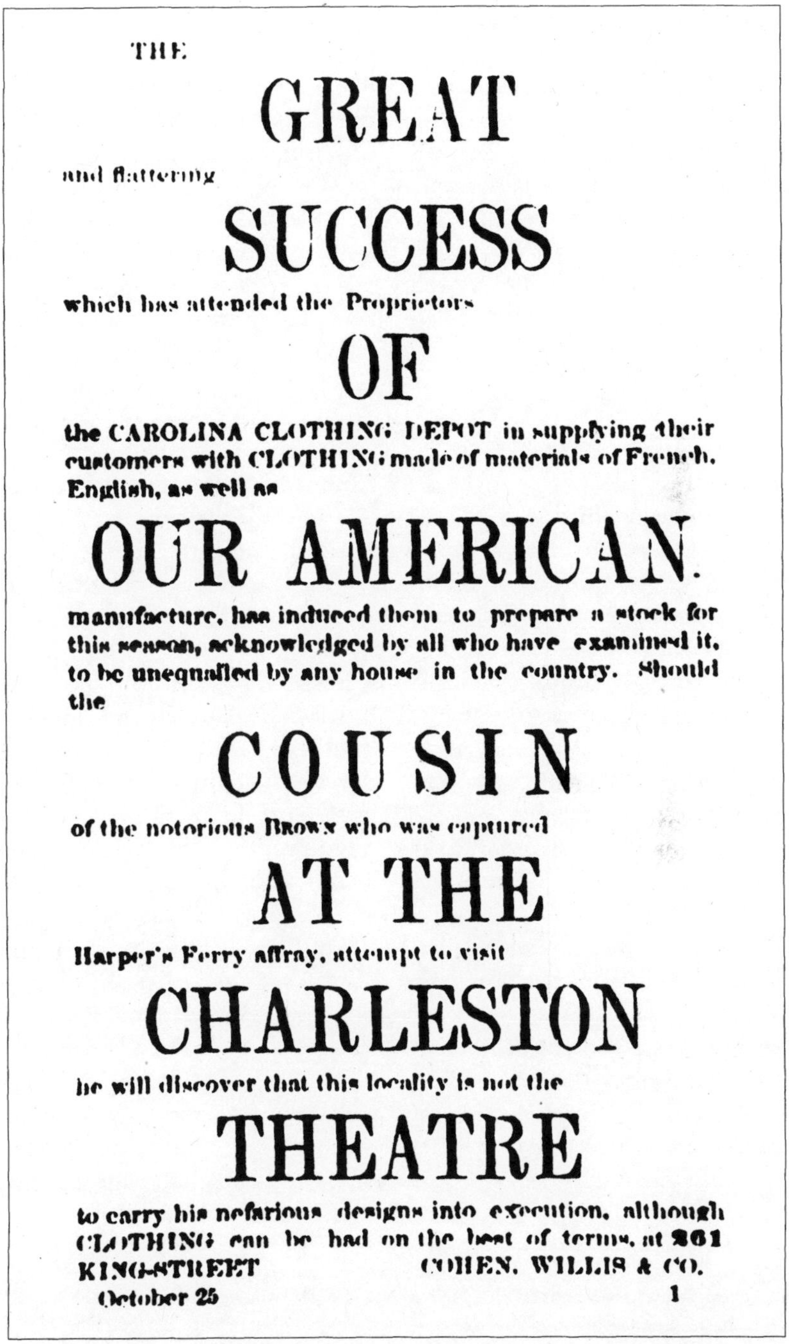
THE

GREAT

and flattering

SUCCESS

which has attended the Proprietors

OF

the CAROLINA CLOTHING DEPOT in supplying their customers with CLOTHING made of materials of French, English, as well as

OUR AMERICAN

manufacture, has induced them to prepare a stock for this season, acknowledged by all who have examined it, to be unequalled by any house in the country. Should the

COUSIN

of the notorious BROWN who was captured

AT THE

Harper's Ferry affray, attempt to visit

CHARLESTON

he will discover that this locality is not the

THEATRE

to carry his nefarious designs into execution, although CLOTHING can be had on the best of terms, at 261 KING-STREET COHEN, WILLIS & CO.

October 25 1

19. Advertisement by a Jewish firm with a political message. (*Daily Courier*, October 25, 1857.)

ton stood together with other whites, and when the conflict erupted into war, they fought and died along with other residents of the city. It was Philip Cohen's daughter Eleanor who detested seeing Yanks in the streets of Columbia at the end of the war. Despite this, she married a Yankee Jew, Benjamin B. Seixas, on August 2, 1865, and moved away to New York, where she died in 1874.[54]

Inconstant Weather

Wars only occasionally ravaged Carolina, but the climate constantly plagued the people. Winters could be mild and enjoyable, but sometimes they featured bone-chilling hard freezes as well. The heat and humidity of summer was constant and proved virtually unbearable. The immigrants from England, Holland, Germany, and Poland faced temperatures nearing 100 degrees Fahrenheit with high humidity. In order to try to escape the heat and the diseases associated with it, Charlestonians who could afford to do so left for summer resorts. Some went to slightly higher pine-covered ground inland such as Summerville, which gets its name from this custom. Others went to the surrounding islands, especially Sullivan's Island, for the ocean breezes. After the introduction of the railroad, a number of people made an annual migration to the mountains of North Carolina, especially to Flat Rock. Many Charlestonians still spend summers there. As early as 1765 Charlestonians also went farther north, particularly to Newport, Rhode Island. By the middle of the nineteenth century Saratoga Springs, New York, had become a favorite cool place for them to visit. The Jews of the city seem to have taken advantage of these opportunities as well. They had close commercial ties up and down the eastern seaboard, especially with Newport in the early days. Abraham Ottolengui had a house for sale on Sullivan's Island in 1857; Dr. Jacob DeLaMotta spent the summer taking the waters in Saratoga Springs, and Thomas J. Mordecai and his family spent the summer of 1858 there.[55]

Even worse than the heat were the hurricanes that blew in from the Caribbean with tremendous destructive force during the summer and autumn. In a few hours a hurricane could destroy more property than an invading army. These storms could not be predicted, and few preparations could be made for them. Periodically, they wrought havoc on the city and throughout the Carolina Low Country. One of the worst hit the coast in 1752. The September issue of *Universal Magazine* reported that year that Charleston had the greatest drought ever known, and the rice, indigo, and corn had suffered extremely. By the time the news of this hardship

54. Marcus, *United States Jewry*, 582, points out that, though evidence is slight, there appears to have been no hostility toward northern Jews by those Jews living in the Confederacy.

55. Brewster, *Summer Migrations and Resorts*, 3–102; Charleston *Daily Courier*, Aug. 19, 1858; Tobias, "The Many Sided Dr. De La Motta," 218.

reached London, a great hurricane struck on September 14 and 15. The force of the tidal surge, which rose ten feet above spring tides, and the winds drove vessels on shore from the harbor. The gale tore roofs off houses, and people reportedly stood up to their necks in water in their houses. The storm practically leveled the city. Then on September 30, another hurricane unleashed its fury on the city.[56]

Fevers and Pains

Greater suffering than that caused by violent weather came on a regular basis to Charleston in the form of contagious diseases. The hot, humid climate of Carolina made conditions ripe for epidemics, and the habits of residents of the city made matters worse. Animal and human filth filled the streets, and the city made only desultory attempts to clean up the waste. People used outdoor privies and drank water from nearby cisterns and wells. Rotting carcasses, standing water, and the lack of knowledge about transmission of diseases brought devastating results. Sickness and death occurred all too frequently.

Information on sickness and death comes from the death records of Charleston which began in 1821. Although these records are incomplete and sometimes inaccurate, they give a good idea of the difficulties of living in the city. Furthermore, two physicians from Charleston, John L. Dawson and H. W. DeSaussure, made a study of all deaths in the city from 1822 through 1848, which allows for comparison to be made between the Jews and the rest of the white population. The blacks of the city lived such different lives that their health status is not usually compared with that of the whites.[57]

From 1822 through 1848, the deaths of 138 Jews were recorded in the death records with the amount of information differing from one entry to another. Nevertheless, most entries are complete or nearly complete.

The number of deaths per year varied considerably. For example, in 1836 none was recorded but in 1827 there were thirteen and in 1841 there were fourteen. The number of Jewish deaths generally corresponds with the rise and fall in the number of deaths among the rest of the white population.

The hot months especially brought disease and death. This resulted from the fact that conditions were worst in the summer for the breeding of diseases or their carriers. The deaths of Jews steadily increased from March and reached their peak in July (18 percent), when they began to decline again. Jewish deaths peaked earlier during the "Sickly Season" than did deaths of other whites, possibly as a result of immigrants' not having developed immunity to local diseases.

56. *Universal Magazine* (London), Dec. 1752, 283–84, 580–82.

57. Dawson and DeSaussure, *Census of the City of Charleston*, 183–261. For information on the death records, see James W. Hagy, "The Death Records of Charleston," *South Carolina Historical Magazine* 91 (1990): 32–44.

Immigrant Jews especially feared yellow fever. Also known as strangers' fever, the disease rarely attacked the native-born population, with the exception of an occasional child, as they had developed an immunity. The fever baffled doctors for centuries. Not until the beginning of the the twentieth century did physicians learn that a mosquito transmitted the disease from one person to another. When the fever struck, many fled the city. Those who remained lived in terror of catching the disease.[58] Of the eleven Jews in Charleston who died from strangers' fever, ten were born in Europe. Both among the Jewish population and the general white population, males contracted yellow fever more frequently than females, possibly as a result of working outside and being exposed to the carriers to a greater extent.[59]

The leading causes of death as given in the death records indicate as much about the state of medicine of the time as about the nature of the diseases. The leading causes were: (1) old age, 16 percent; (2) yellow fever, 9 percent; (3) apoplexy, 6 percent; (4) consumption, 6 percent; (5) dropsy, 5 percent; (6) croup, 5 percent; (7) diarrhea, 4 percent; (8) debility, 4 percent; (9) bilious fever, 4 percent; and (10) malaria, 4 percent. The greatest differences between the Jews and the whole white population was that the Jews were less likely to have died of consumption and were more likely to have old age given as the cause of their deaths.

Other causes listed in the death records include such diverse factors as diabetes, drowning, fits, insanity, strangling, and sunstroke. Childbirth, although generally believed to have killed many women of the time, does not appear often as a cause of death among the Jews or the rest of the population. Only two Jewish women are reported to have died from this. On the other hand, four children died from "teething." Also, internal disorders, which would have been difficult to diagnose, do not appear often. The coroner held an inquest on the death of one Jewish male but could not determine the cause.

Of the persons whose cause of death is known, only one died of an accident and one committed suicide in jail. The last was twenty-six-year-old Israel Valentine, whose epitaph states that he was "A devoted son who in the prime of manhood offered up his life a voluntary sacrifice on the altar of parental affections, invoking as his last expression the forgiveness of his God." The death records give the cause of death while the notice in the newspaper only gave the parents' name and time of the funeral.[60]

At the time of death the average Jewish male was forty and the average female thirty-seven, with the oldest female dying at eighty-six and the oldest

58. Duffy, *Epidemics in Colonial America*, 138–61; Farley, "The Mighty Monarch of the South"; Waring, *History of Medicine in South Carolina, 1825–1900*, 30–36; Duffy, "Yellow Fever in Colonial Charleston"; Simons, *A Report on Strangers Fever.*

59. Simons, *A Report on Strangers Fever*, 14.

60. Elzas, *Old Jewish Cemeteries*, 87; *Southern Patriot*, July 12, 1850.

male at ninety-four.[61] The average age of Jews is very much affected by the high death rate among young children, with 21 percent dying before the age of three. Jewish infants were more likely to die at this age than other whites, but they were far more fortunate than blacks, 35 percent of whom died by the age of four.

One Jewish female, however, reportedly lived a very long life. This was Mrs. Starr Barrett, who died in Charleston on January 9, 1820, after a long and eventful life. Her family buried her in the Coming Street Cemetery, where her tombstone states that she was about one hundred years old. Other sources, however, state that she lived even longer. The Charleston Directory of 1819 listed her as a resident of Guignard Street and as aged 120 years, as did her death notice, which appeared on January 14, 1820, in the *Southern Patriot*, one of the Charleston newspapers.

Her obituary, which an admiring relative apparently composed, stated that she had been born in the year 1699 of the Christian Calendar and 1078 After the Hegira, the Muslim reckoning of time. The use of the Muslim calendar was appropriate (although 1078 A.H. does not correspond to 1699 A.D. but to 1667–1668) because Mrs. Barrett, according to the source, had been born in one of the Barbary States of North Africa, possibly under the control of the emperor of Morocco. Her family later moved to Spain. For a variety of reasons she became a great traveler, and she "visited, with no unobservant eye the four corners of the globe." Furthermore, she spoke with fluency English, Spanish, Italian, and French. In addition, she knew Morisco or Frank, the language used along the coast of north Africa, and Hebrew. She could speak, write, and translate Arabic. For many years her mind was keen; she could distinctly remember a battle that took place in Spain in 1707 and an attack by the Spanish on Gibraltar in 1727, at which time she was near the scene of action. She was supposed to have lived in London for thirty or forty years and to have come to the United States in 1780 at the age of eighty and to have lived in Charleston for forty years.[62] Whether Mrs. Barrett was 120 years old or not cannot be determined now, so long after her death, but even if she were only one hundred years of age, she still was the longest lived member of the Jewish community of Charleston so far discovered.

Although drowning was far down the list of causes of death, many people viewed it as a particularly horrible way of dying. Aside from being accidental,

61. Long-lived Jewish residents of Charleston of the early nineteenth century included Solomon Moses, who died in 1828 at the age of ninety-four; Sarah Woolf, in 1831 at ninety-three; Solomon Aarons, in 1821 at ninety; Bella Levy Hart, in 1851 at eighty-eight; Sarah Cohen Cardozo, in 1853 at eighty-seven; Clara Harris, in 1822 at eighty-six; Rachel D. B. Lazarus, in 1847 at eighty-five; Reuben Moses, in 1850 at eighty-five; Rose Levy, in 1812 at eighty-five; and Mordecai Cohen, in 1848 at eighty-five.

62. The only other Jews living on Guignard Street at the time were Sarah and Moses DaVega. Mrs. DaVega was born in Gibraltar and was therefore probably a relative of Starr Barrett.

drowning could involve a number of people at the same time. Such occurrences were especially sad when several members of a family went down with a boat at sea. On October 7, 1837, the steam packet *Home* departed from New York bound for Charleston. On board were several members of the Jewish community of Charleston. From early in the voyage the boat experienced difficulty. First, it grounded on a sandbar near Sandy Hook, New Jersey, and had to wait for the tide to float it off. When it neared Cape Hatteras, a strong storm struck and, according to one of the passengers on board, the captain "had to press the vessel by steam and canvass," which possibly resulted in a leak later. Soon water flooded the ladies' cabin and floated their trunks. The crew then mustered the passengers to bail. In addition to the other difficulties, according to the first mate, the captain was drunk. The bailing failed to save the ship, and soon the rising water had drowned the fire in the boilers. Early in the afternoon the women were provided with strips of blanket so they could be tied to parts of the boat should they sink. By eleven o'clock at night the water in the boat had almost submerged the deck. Many passengers loaded into two life boats, only to be swamped and drowned by the waves. Finally, the boat struck a sandbar, but waves crashed over the boat, sweeping passengers over the side to their deaths. The pounding sea smashed the boat apart destroying everything. Sixty-seven passengers including twenty from Charleston perished. Of these, four were Jews. They were Sarah C. Levy and her daughters, Olivia and Frances, and Philip S. Cohen. The city mourned its losses, and angry citizens called for an investigation. The mayor appointed a committee of twenty-one leading citizens, including Jacob N. Cardozo and Henry J. Harby, which conducted a series of hearings. After that, the city required safety inspections for steam ships.[63]

Fires

While people who went to sea risked being drowned, all feared being burned when at home. Charlestonians typically built wooden houses close together. Furthermore, when fires broke out, men could do little to stop them. The fear of fire pervaded the city, especially when everyone knew that discontented blacks might set fires to get revenge for their

63. "Narrative of the Loss of the Steam-Packet Home," appendix to Smyth, *Two Discourses on the Occasion of the Great Fire*; *Proceedings of the Citizens and City Council of Charleston, in Relation to the Destruction of the Steamboat Home*; Pinckney, *Report; Containing a Review of the Proceedings of the City Authorities.*

Records indicate that the following Charleston Jews died by drowning; Abram Cohen in 1833 at the age of seven; Philip S. Cohen in 1837 at twenty-seven; Priscilla Cohen in 1860 at forty-five; Rachel Lopez Cohen in 1833 at thirty-eight; David D'Oliviera in 1763; Nathan Drey in 1848 at twenty-seven; Eleazer Elizer in 1821; ——— Hart in 1744; ——— Levy in 1834 at twenty-five; Frances Levy in 1837 at twenty-four; Olivia Levy in 1837 at twenty-two; Samuel Levy in 1802; Sarah Cardozo Levy in 1837 at fifty-seven; Henry Lewis in 1850; Judith Polock Minis in 1819; Abraham Phillips in 1813.

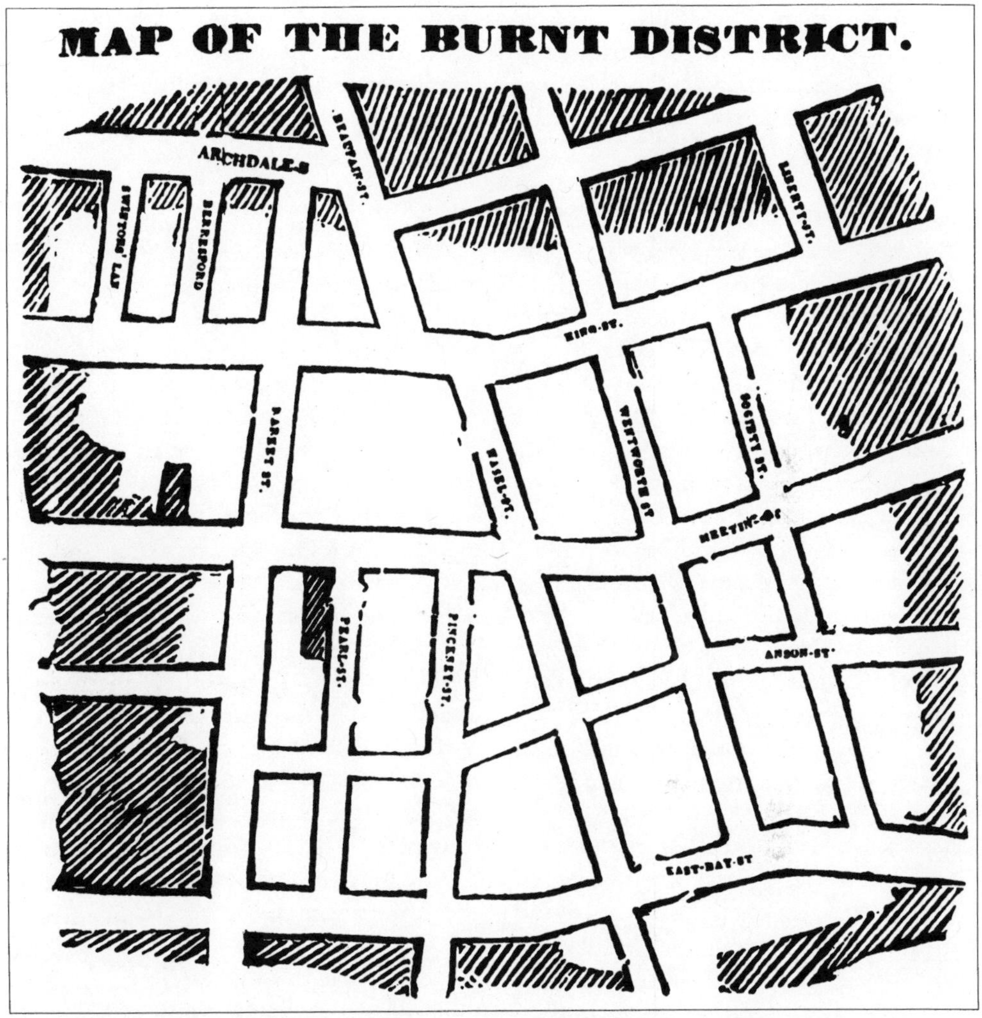

20. The path of destruction of the fire of 1838. (*Mercury*, May 1, 1838.)

treatment. Most of the great buildings of the city burned at some time, only to be replaced with new structures. Countless citizens suffered the loss of a home.[64]

The worst fire broke out about 9:00 P.M. on Friday evening April 27, 1838, in a fruit store near the corner of Beresford and King streets. The fire rapidly spread across the city, destroying about 560 houses and businesses as well as 598 subsidiary structures. Four white fire fighters and several blacks died in the

64. For the problems created by fires see Pease and Pease, "The Blood-Thirsty Tiger," 281–85.

inferno. Following the fire, disputes raged over the effectiveness of the mayor and the fire companies. Immediately after the fire the mayor called an emergency meeting of the city council, which ordered the commander of the militia to patrol the streets. On a motion of M. C. Mordecai, one of the members, the council appointed a Committee in Relation to the Late Fire. Mordecai served on that committee. The council also opened up the Citadel, the Orphan House, the Poor House, the Medical College, the Saint Andrew's Society building, the Hebrew Orphan House, and the German Friendly Society buildings for housing. A few days later after a mass meeting a Committee of Thirty began to take actions to get the city back on its feet, the feeling being that "the fate of Charleston for the next half century" was at stake.[65]

The fire of 1838 struck especially hard at the Jewish community. A good portion of the business district fell to the flames. Of the 560 dwellings and businesses destroyed, Jews owned or rented 69. Mordecai Cohen lost twelve and Moses C. Levy five. Several individuals owned at least four structures each that the fire devoured. In addition, the congregation owned two houses that fell.[66] Even worse, the "awful conflagration, which devastated our city, laid our beautiful place of worship in ruins." Moses C. Levy rushed to the synagogue to save the sacred scrolls.[67] The building, however, had to be replaced by a people who had suffered personal losses as well.

Wars

Living in Charleston also meant that residents had to be prepared to fight in military campaigns. In fact, virtually all adult males had to serve in the militia during the colonial period. The Militia Act of 1696 provided that the governor commanded the militia, with lieutenants, captains, or majors in charge of companies. The officers summoned the men between the ages of sixteen and sixty to drill at least every two months. Although the primary concern of the militia was to control the slaves, units could be called up for other emergencies. In the early years troubles flared with Indians and the Spanish from time to time. On occasion, the governors called on volunteers to serve outside the province.[68] The Jews of Charleston had to serve along with everyone else; in fact, the Jew used by Governor John Archdale in 1696 as an interpreter probably was on militia duty at the time.

The first Jew known to serve as an officer was Joseph Levy, the son of Moses Levy and Grace Mears Levy. In 1757 the governor appointed him as a "lieutenant of foot" in Captain Gaillard's Company of the South Carolina Regiment of Foot.[69] At the time their concern was the

65. Charleston *Mercury,* April 30–May 9, 1838; Smyth, *Two Discourses on the Occasion of the Great Fire*; "The Great Fire of April, 27th," in Pinckney, *Report; Containing a Review of the Proceedings of the City Authorities.*

66. The Charleston *Mercury,* April 30, 1838, listed the buildings destroyed.

67. Levin, "The Jewish Congregation of Charleston," 439.

68. Cole, "A Brief Outline of the South Carolina Colonial Militia."

69. MR2K.506.

Cherokees in the upper part of the state and North Carolina. Then in 1760 Levy received an appointment as a lieutenant in the Company of the Regiment of Buffs in the South Carolina Regiment.[70] The following year he recruited volunteers in North Carolina for Colonel Middleton's regiment.[71]

When the Revolution broke out, many of the Jews of Charleston participated. As one of the principal cities in North America, Charleston became an important objective for the British. Thus on June 28, 1776, Admiral Sir Peter Parker and General Sir Henry Clinton attacked Fort Sullivan (later Fort Moultrie) on Sullivan's Island. They failed to take the place. Militia forces from the city served there, among whom were Marks Lazarus[72] and Abraham Cohen. The latter, according to his widow, had to sleep in the open air and as a result acquired pleurisy.[73] Others possibly served on Sullivan's Island.

For the next two years the British concentrated on the north. Then in 1778 they returned to the South and captured Savannah. Militia forces from Charleston served at Beaufort in February 1779 and in an ill-fated attempt to retake Savannah in 1779. So many Jews of Charleston served in a company formed by Captain Richard Lushington that it has become known as the Jews' Company. According to a contemporary account, the company left Charleston on January 23, 1779, under the command of Lushington and proceeded to Port Royal. There they met with the enemy on a Wednesday and "Came off victorious Saturday." An unidentified member of the company, probably Jacob I. Cohen, wrote his will before going into battle.[74] This company also fought at Savannah. One of the men from the company, Ephraim Abrams, was wounded at Beaufort.[75] Although Lushington's company had a considerable number of Jews, they served in other militia units as well.[76]

In 1780 the British launched a new attack on Charleston. After occupying the surrounding sea islands, they marched across James Island and crossed the Ashley River to the north of Charleston. The British fleet then entered the harbor, meeting little resistance. After being besieged and bombarded for forty-two days, the American commander surrendered on May 12, 1780.

During the siege citizens in the town, hoping to prevent a slaughter, sent three

70. MR2L.306.

71. *South-Carolina Gazette*, April 11, 1761.

72. Revolutionary War Pension Application W21, 558, National Archives.

73. Revolutionary War Pension Claim R9931, National Archives.

74. Hühner, "Some Additional Notes." Elzas was scathing in his criticism of an earlier article by Hühner. He stated, "We have no record of Jacob I. Cohen as a member of Lushington's Company, and who Isaiah Isaacs is we cannot imagine." Hühner, in reply, published two certificates signed by Lushington for these two men. They lived in Richmond as well as Charleston. See Ezekiel and Lichtenstein, *History of the Jews of Richmond*, 13–20.

75. Elzas says that Joseph Solomon was killed.

76. Rezneck, *Unrecognized Patriots*, 47, says that the Jews of the city mobilized into one unit. This was not the case.

petitions to the American commander asking him to surrender. One from "diverse Inhabitants of Charlestown" contained 300 names, including 15 Jews (5 percent). A second from militiamen from outside Charleston had 111 signatures, none of which were those of Jews. A third of "divers Country Militia" contained 346 signatures, including those of 14 Jews (4 percent).[77] When the Americans capitulated, the continental troops marched out carrying unloaded rifles. The militia, being "too ragged to march," disarmed and returned to their homes. The British declared all of the citizens to be prisoners of war.[78]

Some idea of conditions in the city can be gained from letters written by Abigail Minis and Frances Sheftall during the siege and occupation. Along with most other Jews from Savannah, Abigail Minis fled rather than remain under British control. The royal governor in Charleston considered the Jews "to a man to have been violent rebels and persecutors of the King's loyal subjects."[79] To try to make ends meet, Mrs. Minis wrote one of the American generals in January 1780, seeking payment for provisions that the family had furnished for the American forces attacking Savannah.[80] As a native Charlestonian, Frances Sheftall fared somewhat better. She also came to Charleston after the fall of Savannah and the imprisonment of her husband, Mordecai Sheftall, and her son Sheftall Sheftall. She stayed with the Jacobs family and assured her husband that Mr. Jacobs had "been a father to your children." Her children attended school, and she used £2,000 from a Mr. Cape to do "a little business." On the other hand, she felt "very miserable" because her husband and son were in so much distress. She could not send them supplies because the British forces lay off the bar at Charleston at the time she wrote a letter. She did manage to send her husband some money by "a Jew gentleman . . . by the name of Mr. Levy."[81] Mrs. Sheftall pleaded with the British to release her husband, as "I have not it in my power to support him during his imprisonment."[82] In another letter, on August 20, 1780, she related the events of the siege, during which she "retreated into the Country" with her family along with "a great many of our people." According to her, "there was scarce a woman to be seen in the streets" during the cannonading. After the town surrendered, she returned to Charleston and rented a house on St. Michael's Alley "at the rate of 50 pounds sterling a year and where the money is to come from god only know for their is nothing but hard Money goes here and that I can assure you is hard enough to be got." She had begun to take in needlework to make a living. Her slaves all fell ill, and one of them, Little Billey, died of yellow fever. In addition, a smallpox epidemic had hit Charleston. The children all got

77. Elzas, *Jews of South Carolina*, 349.

78. Uhlendorf, *Seige of Charleston*, 349.

79. Rezneck, *Unrecognized Patriots*, 41.

80. Letter of Abigail Minis, Jan. 15, 1780, American Jewish Archives.

81. Frances Sheftall to Mordecai Sheftall, Mar. 3, 1780, American Jewish Archives.

82. Letter of Frances Sheftall, n.d., American Jewish Archives.

through that safely, but now she had to pay doctor's bills in addition to the rent. She related that her brother-in-law Levi had not returned, and Isaac, one of his children, had just been buried after being sick for three weeks. Furthermore, quite a number of other children had died, including the grandchildren of Isaac DeLyon, a child of Mrs. Mordecai, and Rachel Moses, daughter of Mrs. Myer Moses, who had the misfortune to be killed along with her nurse by a cannonball during the siege.[83] Rachel Moses may have been the only Jewish female to die as a result of military action in the Revolution.

During the occupation the British at first sought to convince the people that they were more interested in reconciliation than punishment. They issued a proclamation that offered pardons for "past treasonable offences," provided one pledged allegiance to Great Britain. On June 3, 1780, 110 of the "principal and most respectable inhabitants of Charleston" sent a memorial to Clinton offering him their "warmest Congratulations" and pledging their allegiance.[84] No Jewish names are on that list; however, another petition in August or September of 1780 contained 166 names, of which 7 were Jews.[85] The commandant of Charleston exiled residents who refused to pledge their allegiance or sent them off to disease-ridden prison ships in the harbor. One of those sent out to the ship *Torbay* to be punished was Jacob Cohen.[86] Benjamin Nones, Isaac DaCosta, Sr., his wife and two children, and Abraham Mendes Seixas had to leave the city. DaCosta and Seixas went to Philadelphia.[87]

Meanwhile, some of the prisoners taken at Savannah had been exchanged by the British, among them Mordecai Sheftall and Sheftall Sheftall. They also went to Philadelphia, where they sought permission to go to Charleston and Savannah under a flag of truce to bring money and food to the imprisoned American troops. Sheftall Sheftall unsuccessfully sought funds from the Georgia delegation to the Congress then meeting in Philadelphia but managed to get a flag and passports from Admiral Robert Digby. He arrived on the sloop *Carolina Packet* bringing food and money and managed to take out his family, that of Abraham Seixas, and a number of others, a total of about seventy people.[88]

When the tide of war began to turn for the Americans, Governor John Rutledge of South Carolina called a meeting of the legislature at Jacksonboro. The revolutionaries began to make plans to punish all those who had shown loyalty

83. Frances Sheftall to Mordecai Sheftall, Aug. 20, 1780, American Jewish Archives.

84. Hough, *Siege of Charleston*, 149–52; Barnwell, "Addressers of Clinton and Arbuthnot"; Stoesen, "The British Occupation of Charleston."

85. *Royal South-Carolina Gazette*, Sept. 21, 1780.

86. Webber, "Joseph Smith's Diary," 282.

87. Ibid., 81–83. The prayerbook of Seixas says that the British banished him. See: Reznikoff, *Jews of Charleston*, 50.

88. Mordecai Sheftall to President of Congress, Nov. 21, 1789, Sheftall Sheftall to Georgia Delegation, Dec. 22, 1780, Mordecai Sheftall to Congress, Apr. 24, 1781, in Marcus, *American Jewry*, 269–71; Webber, "Joseph Smith's Diary, " 208.

to the British. They decided to banish them under pain of death, confiscate their possessions, or to amerce (assess) their property.[89] The revolutionaries suspected anyone who remained in Charleston during the occupation. After the British withdrew in October 1782, loyalists could expect to be punished. (See Table 13.)

By and large the Jews of Charleston seem to have favored the rebel cause. The nine men who remained in the city and declared their loyalty to the crown had little choice if they wanted to make a living. Many important South Carolina officials before and after the Revolution did the same. Furthermore, the Jews did not fit the pattern for loyalists, who tended to be young men who held church or crown positions or practiced a profession.[90] The Jews who swore allegiance to the crown presumably did not suffer any consequences. On the other hand, Isaac DeLyon, a saddler by trade who came to Charleston from Savannah after its fall, had his property amerced at 12 percent of its value for his sympathies.[91] Two other men, Levi Sheftall and a member of the Abraham family, supplied information to the British commanders.[92]

Charleston's Jewish community received a number of newcomers during the Revolution. When the American authorities sought to root out the loyalists in 1783, they questioned the newly arrived Jews. Elzas discovered the minutes of testimony in the office of the South Carolina secretary of state. The documents have since been lost or destroyed; however, other records of these individuals have survived. The investigation showed that Samuel Levy and Levy Solomon had come in with Hessian troops but deserted them, that Montague Simons had arrived in America two years earlier in order to join three of his brothers in Charleston, and that Mordecai Lyon had arrived with a wife and child from Poland. Gershon Cohen and Jacob Jacobs attested to the honesty and good character of each of them. Jacob Jacobs, in fact, had known Levy Solomon since childhood, as they came from the same hometown. Another arrival, Moses Levy, said that he had been put on board a British ship of war at an early age. He, however, chose the American side and joined the crew of the ship *Dawes*, which departed from Jamaica for New York. The crew decided to put the ship into Wilmington, North Carolina, and join the American cause. Like the others, he petitioned to be made a citizen of South Carolina.[93] All remained in the city. (See Table 14.)

As a result of their participation in the Revolution, the Jews in the city reached

89. *Statutes*, 4: 516–20; Levett, "Loyalism in Charleston."

90. Andreano and Werner, "Charleston Loyalists," 164–68.

91. Webber, "Joseph Smith's Diary," 109. He petitioned the legislature stating that he was a good citizen but that in order to support his family he had been forced to take protection. "House Journal, 6 January 1783–17 March 1783," *Journals of the Privy Council, 1783–1789*, 54.

92. J. Wemyss to Cornwallis, July 25, 1780, Reese, *The Cornwallis Papers*, 364–65.

93. Elzas, *Jews of South Carolina*, 98–99; General Assembly Papers, Petitions, 1783, Nos. 27, 205; "House Journal, 6 January 1783–17 March 1783," in *Journals of the Privy Council, 1783–1789*, 12, 36, 37, 54, 84, 242, 253; Marcus, *American Jewry*, 236–37.

Table 13
Jewish Men in Charleston during the Revolution

Name	Activities
Aarons, Solomon	Lushington's co. Petition of inhabitants.
Abrahams, Emanuel	Unknown militia unit. Petition of militia. Advertised during occupation.
Abrahams, Joseph	Advertised during occupation.
Abrahams, Judah	Unknown militia unit. Petition of militia.
Abrams, Ephraim	Lushington's co.
Alexander, Abraham	Sumter's Brigade, lt.; Hill's regiment, lt. Loyalty oath in 1780.
Cardozo, David N.	Savannah Grenadiers. Peter Boquet's co., sgt major. Suffered wound in leg. Loyalty oath in 1780.
Cohen, Abraham	Unknown militia unit, pvt. Petition of militia. Advertised during occupation.
Cohen, Gershon	Petition of inhabitants. Advertised during occupation.
Cohen, Jacob	Prison ship *Torbay.* Later in Philadelphia.
Cohen, Moses	Lushington's co. Petition of militia.
Cohen, Philip Jacob	From Savannah. Banned by the British from there. Petition of militia. Loyalty oath in 1780.
DaCosta, Abraham	James Bentham's co., sgt. major. Advertised during occupation.
DaCosta, Isaac, Jr.	James Bentham's co., pvt. Petition of inhabitants.
DaCosta, Isaac, Sr.	Banished.
DaCosta, Joseph	James Bentham's co., pvt.
DaCosta, Samuel	Went to Philadelphia.
DePalacios, Joseph	Petition of inhabitants.
Eliazer, Moses	James Bentham's co., pvt. Loyalty oath in 1780.
Hart, Philip	Unknown militia unit. Petition of inhabitants.
Henry, Aaron	Lushington's co.
Jacobs, Frederick	Unknown militia unit.
Jacobs, Israel	Fled to Philadelphia.
Jacobs, Jacob	Petition of inhabitants. Advertised during occupation.
Jones, Samuel	Petition of militia.
Lazarus, Marks	Douill's co. Lushington's co., pvt., sgt. major. Petition of inhabitants. Loyalty oath in 1780.
Levy, Ezekiel	Lushington's co. Fled to Philadelphia
Marks, Samuel	George Turner's co.
Minis, Philip	Unknown militia unit. Fled Savannah. Petition of inhabitants.
Mordecai, Samuel	Petition of militia.[a]
Moses, ——	Lushington's co.

Table 13
(Continued)

Name	*Activities*
Moses, Abraham	Petition of inhabitants.
Moses, Attival	Lushington's co.
Moses, Barnard	Lushington's co. Petition of militia.
Moses, Jacob	Petition of militia.
Moses, Myer	James Bentham's co., pvt. Petition of inhabitants.
Moses, Philip	Petition of militia. Loyalty oath in 1789. Went to Philadelphia.
Myers, Joseph	Petition of inhabitants. Loyalty oath in 1780.
Nones, Benjamin	Served in Ga. under Gen. Pulaski. Banished. Militia.
Phillips, Nathan	Lushington's co.
Pollock, Cushman	From Savannah. Banned by the British from return.
Pollock, Samuel	James Bentham's co., pvt. Petition of militia.
Pollock, Solomon	Unknown militia unit. Express rider.
Sarzedas, David	Habersham's regiment of Georgia, lt. Petition of inhabitants.
Sasportas, Abraham	Fled to Philadelphia.
Seixas, Abraham M.	Lushington's co. Went to Philadelphia.
Sheftall, Levi	Fled from Savannah. Loyalist.
Sheftall, Mordecai	Deputy commissary general in Ga. Col. In Philadelphia.
Simons, Sampson	Unknown militia unit.
Simons, Samuel	Lushington's co.
Simons, Saul	Loyalty oath in 1780.
Solomon, Joseph	Unknown militia unit.
Solomon, Zadok	Lushington's co. Petition of inhabitants.
Solomons, Isaac	Lushington's co. Petition of inhabitants.
Solomons, Myer	Unknown militia unit. Petition of militia.
Viegra, Joseph	Loyalty oath in 1780.

[a]Mordecai was Isaac Harby's father-in-law. Harby stated that he "was a brave grenadier in the regular American army, and fought and bled for the liberty he lived to enjoy and to hand down to his children." *North American Review,* July 1826, p. 73.

Sources: Orderly Book in New York Public Library cited in Elzas, *Jews of South Carolina,* 91–92; Hühner, "Some Additional Notes"; Harris, *Eleven Gentlemen of Charleston,* 49; Revolutionary War Pension Claims W20830, R9931, S39061, W21558, National Archives; Robert Bentham Simons, "Regimental Book of Captain James Bentham, 1778–1780," 13–18; Payroll Records of Samuel Marks During His Service in the Revolutionary War, South Carolina, 1779–1780, American Jewish Archives; *Royal South-Carolina Gazette,* Sept. 21, 1780; Reznikoff and Engelman, *Jews of Charleston,* 47, 48, 50, 272; Marcus, *American Jewry,* 269–71; Rezneck, *Unrecognized Patriots,* 37, 41, 126; Schappes, *Documentary History,* 93–96. Marcus, *United States Jewry,* 54, estimates that no more than 100 males served in the armed forces during the revolution. If so, a substantial number of them served in South Carolina.

Table 14
Newly Arrived Jews in Charleston during the Revolution

Name	*From*	*In U.S*	*In Charleston*	*Occupation*
Harris, Henry				Tailor
Levy, Moses	Royal Navy			
Levy, Samuel	Germany		1780	Sutler with Hessians
Lyon, Mordecai	Poland		1780	Tailor
Moses, Henry	Prussia	1779	1780	
Simons, Montague	London	1789	1780	Clerk
Simons, Moses			1781	
Solomon, Levy	Germany	1780		Shopkeeper[a]
Solomons, Hyam	England		1781	
Woolf, Solomon				

[a]Had served a Hessian general but left him.
Sources: Elzas, *Jews of South Carolina,* 98, 99; General Assembly Papers, Petitions, 1783, Nos. 27, 205; "House Journal, 6 January 1783–17 March 1783," in *Journals of the Privy Council, 1783–1789,* 36, 37, 54, 84, 242, 253

new heights of acceptance—at least on the part of one person. A letter to a newspaper of the time states:

> He who hates another man for not being a christian, is himself not a christian.—Christianity breathes love, peace, and good-will to man. The Jews have had a considerable share in our late Revolution. They have behaved well throughout. Let our government invite the Jews to our State, and promise them a settlement in it. It will be a wise and politic stroke—and give a place of rest at last to the tribe of Israel.
> A WELLWISHER TO THE STATE.[94]

Conflict with the British did not end with the Revolution. The War of 1812 followed, but this clash did not dislocate life in Charleston as much as the Revolution. Those Jews known to have served in this conflict held higher positions than did those in the Revolution, and all were native born. Abraham Phillips volunteered on the day the war broke out. The navy assigned him to the U.S. frigate *Constellation*. Off Norfolk, a scouting cutter overturned, and he died at sea.[95] Levi Harby also volunteered for the navy only to be captured by the British, who imprisoned him for nearly two years. Eventually he escaped and received command of a ship. Afterward he continued to serve and rose to the rank of captain. When the Civil War came, he resigned his commission and served the Confederacy along the coast of Texas.[96]

94. *South-Carolina Gazette and General Advertiser*, Aug. 30, 1783.

95. Alexander, *Notes on the Alexander Family*, 62.

96. Elzas, *Jews of South Carolina*, 143–44; Hühner, "Jews in the War of 1812," 190–94; Rezneck, *Unrecognized Patriots*, 185–86; Heitman, *Historical Register*, 315, 365, 366, 696;

A number of Charlestonians fought in the Seminole Wars in Florida. One of them, Meyer M. Cohen, served as an officer and wrote an account of the expedition entitled *Notices of Florida and the Campaigns*. Among other things, he reported some of the humor that the troops devised in order to cope with the situation. One way was to put out a newspaper that included a "List of Deaths":

> Starved to death, 10; surfeit from too much food, 0; lock jaw from picking teeth with a bayonet, 5; drop-sy—down the well, 1; drowned by the sound of the drum, voices, 3; consumption—of beans, 5; died in the Greece-ian war of fat pork, 7; sick—of parade, 63; choked by coffee grounds, 8; total 105 being 39 more than ever were in garrison.

Joshua Peixotto fought in both the Seminole Wars and the Mexican War, and Jacob Valentine, the youngest member of the Palmetto Regiment in the latter war, was severely wounded at Churubusco.[97] The lists of those who served in these wars are probably incomplete. Nevertheless, they show that the Jews of Charleston fought in every major conflict that arose. Although all able-bodied men had to serve in the militia during the Revolution, this was not the case in the other wars. Not only did Jews volunteer to perform, they excelled at supplying troops and providing medical care.

Duels

The southern penchant for using violence to settle differences also expressed itself in private warfare or dueling. Jews fought in at least two duels in the city. One involved Mordecai Manuel Noah, whose father moved the family to Charleston when his offspring were young and then abandoned them. After that, the children lived in a number of places. Always involved in politics, Noah received an appointment from the president of the United States to be the American consul to Riga but rejected it,

Marcus, *United States Jewry*, 103. Other Jews from Charleston who served in the military during the War of 1812, along with the highest rank achieved and branch in which they served, were: Isaac Nunez Cardozo, Army; Hyam Cohen, 1st Lieutenant, Army; Philip Cohen, 1st Lieutenant, Army; Solomon Cohen, Midshipman, Navy; Jacob DeLaMotta, Surgeon, Army; Abraham DeLeon, Surgeon's Mate, Army; Abraham Massias, Major, Army; Myer Moses, Captain, Militia. (Abraham Massias was in and out of Charleston over the years.)

97. Jews from Charleston who served in the Seminole Wars were Hyam Cohen, Assistant Paymaster; Jacob Cohen, Washington Volunteers; Myer M. Cohen, Washington Volunteers; Philip Melvin Cohen, surgeon to troops in Charleston Harbor; Solomon Heydenfeldt; Columbus Moïse, Washington Volunteers; Thomas Whitlock Mordecai, 16th Regiment; Joshua Peixotto, 16th Regiment; and Gershon Poznanski, killed. Elzas, *Jews of South Carolina*, 206–7; Stern, *First Jewish Families of America*, 252.

Those who served in the Mexican War all served in the Palmetto Regiment: J. Frideberg, Orlando Levy, Isaac Lyons, Joshua Peixotto, and Jacob Valentine. Elzas, *Jews of South Carolina*, 207; "Fifty-Sixth Anniversary of the Hebrew Benevolent Society," 46.

as he wanted to go to the Barbary States. In 1812 just after he turned down the appointment to Riga, Noah returned to Charleston. An opponent of DeWitt Clinton and a War Hawk, he began to participate in politics and put his thoughts into writing. Using the name of Diodorus Sicilus, he published *A Letter Addressed to the Members of the Legislature of South Carolina Examining the Claims and Qualifications of Dewitt Clinton to the Presidency of the United States* (Charleston, 1812). He also began to write a series of articles entitled "Oriental Correspondence" for the *Times* of Charleston under the name of "Muly Malak." In an article in the April 15 issue he pretended to be a visitor writing back to the Middle East explaining the ways of life in Charleston. On June 2 he reported on a political gathering regarding the war fever then developing between the United States and Britain. In an article in the newspaper he attacked one of the opponents as being timid and believing that the United States should "purchase peace by submission." Two days later Joshua W. Toomer identified himself as the speaker and stated that he wanted to give a "fair and explicit explanation of some expressions used by me in the debate" which had been "so grossly misrepresented by a writer in your paper who bears the character, as well as the name of an unchristian Turk." A few days later Toomer demanded a duel; however, another man settled the dispute by convincing Toomer that the insult had not been personal. Noah "was entirely satisfied with the issue, having no desire to kill my opponent"; however, he then became involved in a dispute with William Crafts, who challenged Noah to a duel. Crafts fell ill, and that duel never came off. But then a Jew, John Cantor, challenged Noah over a "trifling" matter, and Noah would "neither accept explanation nor apology." A duel then took place before a large gathering at the Charleston Race Course. Noah injured "the puppy by the name of John Cantor" in the leg, thus finally ending the affair. Shortly after this Noah received his appointment to the Barbary States.[98]

According to a diary kept by a Charlestonian, another duel occurred between a Moïse and a Cohen at the race course on February 10, 1834. The account states that Cohen lost and died two days later of wounds. No further information on this duel has been found.[99] Despite the fact that the legislature outlawed duels in 1810,[100] the state did not prosecute the men involved. South Carolina "gentlemen" saw duels as acceptable behavior for settling personal affronts with people of equal rank. Usually they horsewhipped or caned social inferiors, or, as shown by a dispute between Dr. Edward Chisholm and Gershon P. Cohen, they refused to fight at all.[101]

98. Charleston *Times*, Apr. 15, June 2, 4, 1812; Sarna, *Jacksonian Jew*, 1–11; Goldberg, *Major Noah*, 53–67; Courtney, *Eulogy, Hon. William Crafts*.

99. Diary of Jacob F. Schirmer, Feb. 10, 1824, South Carolina Historical Society.

100. *Statutes*, 5: 671.

101. Williams, "The Code of Honor."

Crimes

Ordinary people did not challenge others to a duel; they often fought in the streets. Authorities could do little because modern law enforcement had not yet developed. The watch looked out for fires, major disturbances, and wayward blacks during the night, and constables, among many other duties, served as peace officers during the day.[102] Normally, people had to swear out warrants against one another or capture suspected criminals and take them off to the guard house. After swearing out a "peace surety," some people took no other action against persons with whom they had disputes. Others failed to press charges when the cases came up, and juries often refused to indict people.

Assault cases appear more often than others. In one case Rebecca M. Harris, Esther Harris, and Abraham Harris, for some unstated reason, threatened Elizabeth Denton on the streets. She went to the court to obtain a surety of peace against them.[103] In another, Susan Salts claimed that Elizabeth Hart struck her several blows and bit her hand.[104] Also, Marie Smith claimed that Benjamin Phillips assaulted her and knocked her down for no known reason while she stood in the door of her house.[105]

Other cases involved men such as Eleazer Phillips. Dan Joy claimed that Phillips stole a sheep belonging to him "and did also bake away the carcass and hide."[106] In addition, the court indicted Elias Solomons for running a disorderly house. The authorities claimed that he had harbored, entertained, and encouraged three slaves to gamble. Witnesses testified that he maintained "a certain common, ill-governed and disorderly house" where slaves came "together for the purpose of drinking, gaming, carousing and rioting" at "unlawful times and at night as in day."[107]

As well as being fined or imprisoned, people convicted of crimes could receive the sentence of being pilloried. This happened to "Jacob Ramos (a Jew)" for "receiving a Sum of Money . . . of which Mr. William Somerfall was some Time since robbed, by a Negro, who was convicted of & hanged for the Robbery." To his last breath, the slave claimed that Ramos had excited him to commit the robbery and had received the money. Upon conviction, Ramos had to stand in the pillory for an hour, pay a fine of £350, and receive 39 lashes. During the time he stood in the pillory "he was most severely & incessantly pelted by an enraged Populace; who nevertheless were so orderly, as not to use any other

102. Jordan, "Police Power and Public Safety."

103. State v. Rebecca Harris, Esther Harris and Abraham Harris, May 1818, Court of General Sessions.

104. State v. Elizabeth Hart, July 1813, Court of General Sessions, South Carolina Archives.

105. State v. Benjamin Phillips, Jan. 1821, Court of General Sessions, South Carolina Archives.

106. State v. Eleazer Phillips, Apr. 1819, Court of General Sessions, South Carolina Archives.

107. State v. Elias Solomons, Jan. 1802, Court of General Sessions, South Carolina Archives.

Materials than rotten eggs, Apples & Onions."[108]

Two Jewish men committed crimes for which they received the death penalty. The court sentenced both to hang. Levi Cohen was to hang on June 23, 1786; however, the governor remanded the sentence to thirty days.[109] Also, Abraham O. Valentine was sentenced to be hanged for stealing a slave in 1806. The governor also pardoned him.[110] Obviously, in both cases the governors considered the punishment far too great for the crimes. (See Table 15.)

Jews occasionally came to blows with one another, but these seem mostly to have resulted from disputes within the synagogue. From time to time other disputes arose. For example, Solomon J. Cohen charged that Alexander Marks "shamefully" said that Cohen "was a damd Rascal & thief" and "was undeserving of the appellation of an officer which hurted my feeling much so that I went over to ask why he so abused me. The moment I did so he in a great passion takes down a sword draws it over my head and swore if I spoke a word he would chop me to pieces."[111] In another case, Moses Rodrigues claimed that Philip Gomez struck him in the chest with an umbrella and called him a brigand and gave him much abuse.[112] In only one instance did a case go to a jury, which reached a guilty verdict. This case involved Isaac Marks who, according to Moses Hyams, came up behind Hyams in the public streets and assaulted him with a stick. The jury, although declaring Marks guilty, recommended the "utmost leniency." The records do not show what sentence followed.[113] In addition, Solomon Tobias pled guilty to charges of assaulting Simon Moses. On July 9, 1815, Moses took out a peace surety against Tobias, stating he feared personal violence. Then on January 9, 1816, according to Simon, Tobias grossly assaulted him by hitting him several times.[114] A more emotional case came up when Jacob Moses claimed that Moses DeYoung and Mrs. DeYoung assaulted and beat his three-year-old son. When Mr. Moses and his wife "went forward to rescue and protect their infant from the violence and cruelty," according to the testimony, DeYoung and his wife furiously beat the Moseses with a stick and an umbrella. The Moses family, however, did not pursue the charge.[115] (See Table 16.)

Because of the nature of the records, the number of attacks against Jews is harder to detect.[116] Solomon Moses was

108. *South-Carolina Gazette*, Nov. 1, 1773.

109. MR2V.218.

110. MR3W.699.

111. State v. Alexander Marks, 1810, Court of General Sessions, South Carolina Archives.

112. State v. Philip Gomez, 1806, Court of General Sessions, South Carolina Archives.

113. State v. Isaac Marks, 1834, Court of General Sessions, South Carolina Archives.

114. State v. Solomon Tobias, 1816, Court of General Sessions, South Carolina Archives.

115. State v. Moses DeYoung and Rachel DeYoung, 1823, Court of General Sessions, South Carolina Archives.

116. The manuscript records of the criminal court have not been indexed. Although one can determine the defendant of an action by the name of the case, one must read the entire record to find others involved.

Table 15

Charleston Jews Accused of Committing Crimes against non-Jews

Name	*Crime*	*Last Known Action of Court*	*Punishment*
Canter, Emanuel	Larceny	Not guilty	
Cohen, Levi	Burglary	Guilty	To be hanged; respited to 30 days.
Davis, Israel	Assault	No bill	
Frideburg, Philip	Theft	Quashed	
Gomez, Philip	Assault	Nolle prosequi	
Harris, Rebecca M., Esther, and Abraham	Assault	Indicted	
Harris, Solomon and Henry	Negro stealing	No bill	
Hart, Elizabeth	Assault	Unknown	
Jacobs, Samuel	Forgery	Guilty	Imprisoned, pilloried, pardoned
Levy, Joseph	Assault	Guilty	
Levy, Joseph L.	Stealing	True bill/Not guilty	
Mairs, Simon	Assault	No bill	
Marks, Alexander	Assault	Guilty	Imprisoned, fined, pardoned
Marks, Mark	Assault	Pled guilty	
Moses, Solomon	Assault	Guilty	Imprisoned, fined, pardoned
Moses, Solomon	Assault	Guilty	Imprisoned, fined, pardoned
Moses, Solomon	Assault	Guilty	Pardoned
Philips, Benjamin	Assault	Guilty	Fined
Phillips, Aaron	Trading with Negroes	Unknown	
Phillips, Aaron	Selling liquor w/o license	Indicted	
Phillips, Eleazer	Killed a sheep	Guilty	Fined
Phillips, Philip	Receiving stolen goods	True bill	
Pollock, Levy	Larceny	Guilty	Pardoned if left state
Pollock, Levy	Receiving stolen goods	Not Guilty	
Pollock, Levy	Receiving stolen goods	Not Guilty	
Ramos, Jacob	Robbery	Guilty	Pilloried, fined
Solomon, Aaron	Assault	Guilty	Pardoned
Solomon, Mark	Assault	Nolle prosequi	
Solomons, Rebecca Audler	Assault	Indicted	

Table 15
(Continued)

Name	*Crime*	*Last Known Action of Court*	*Punishment*
Solomons, Aaron	Assault	Guilty	
Solomons, Elias	Disorderly house	Indicted	
Solomons, Mark	Assault	No bill	
Solomons, Mark and Hetty	Assault	No bill	
Solomons, Moses	Assault	Indicted	
Solomons, Solomon	Assault	Guilty	Imprisoned, fined
Solomons, Solomon and Aaron	Assault	Nolle prosequi	
Tobias, Isaac	Assault	No bill	
Tobias, Solomon	Assault	Unknown	
Valentine, Abraham O.	Negro stealing	Guilty	Death, pardon

Sources: The records for Jews accused of committing crimes are found in the following: MR2V.218; 3B.103; 3G.379; 3Q.591; 3Q.594; 3V.142; 3W.699; 3V.5; 4B.284; 4C.557; State v. Aaron Phillips, 1819; State v. Aaron Solomons, 1810; State v. Benjamin Philips, 1821; State v. Charles Macklin and Joseph L. Levy, 1818; State v. Eleazer Phillips, 1819; State v. Elias Solomons, 1802; State v. Elizabeth Hart, 1813; State v. George Wood and Emanuel Canter, 1837; State v. Isaac Tobias, 1835; State v. Levy Pollock, 1814; State v. Levy Pollock, 1815; State v. Mark Marks, 1809; State v. Mark Solomons, 1806; State v. Mark Solomons, 1807; State v. Mark Solomons and Hetty Solomons, 1811; State v. Philip Frideburg, 1809; State v. Philip Phillips, 1818; State v. Rebecca Solomon, 1818; State v. Rebecca M. Harris, Esther Harris and Abraham Harris, 1818; State v. Simon Mairs, 1814; State v. Solomon Harris and Henry Harris, 1820; State v. Solomon Solomons, 1820; State v. Solomon Solomons and Aaron Solomons, 1809; State v. Solomon Tobias, 1816; *Gazette,* Nov. 1, 1773.

assaulted twice in his law enforcing role. Simon Moses charged others with assault on three occasions. One man, he claimed, beat him with his fists and kicked him in the groin at his house on King Street. Three witnesses supported his claim; however, Moses did not follow through on the case. Hayman Levy did pursue a case of theft. He stated that he was walking along Broad Street at 10:00 P.M. when a man stole two gold seals worth $21 which were attached to his watch. The watch ribbon broke and the man did not get it. The accused man was found guilty. In addition, David Hyams testified that a man broke the window glass of his house and struck his wife several blows. And Rachel Woolf stated that a man entered her shop and stole a coat. He fled running toward Black Birds Alley. Samuel Sampson pursued and caught him and recovered the coat as well. Sampson said, "I whipped him & sent him away from shop." The following day, Sampson's son saw the man passing back and forth in front of

Table 16
Legal Disputes between Jews in Antebellum Charleston

Case	*Accuser*	*Charge*	*Result*
State v. A. N. Nathans, 1806	Isaac M. Seixas	Assault	Nolle prosequi
State v. Mark Solomon, 1806	Isaac Emanuel	Assault	Nolle prosequi
State v. Philip Gomez, 1806	Moses Rodrigues	Assault	Nolle prosequi
State v. Abraham Goldsmith, 1810	Jacob David	Assault	Indicted
State v. Alexander Marks, 1810	Solomon I. Cohen	Assault	No bill
State v. Israel Davis, 1811	Simon N. Hart	Assault	No bill
State v. Jacob David, 1811	Abraham Goldsmith	Assault	No bill
State v. S. M. Hart, 1811	Israel Davis	Assault	No bill
State v. Solomon Tobias, 1816	Simon Moses	Assault	Pled guilty
State v. Nathan Hart, 1819	David N. Carvalho	Assault	No bill
State v. Abraham Ottolengui, 1821	Florance Levy	Assault	No bill
State v. Moses and Rachel DeYoung, 1823	Solomon Moses	Assault	Nolle prosequi
State v. Alice Solomons, 1825	Toy Audler	Assault	No bill
State v. Isaac D. Marks, 1834	Moses Hyams	Assault	Guilty

Table 17
Jews as Victims or Accusers in Court in Antebellum Charleston

Case	*Victim or Accuser*	*Charge*
State v. John Smith, 1810	J. C. Levy	Assault
State v. H. B. Toomer, 1816	Levy Pollock	Assault
State v. John Smith, 1816	Hayman Levy	Theft
State v. James Thompson, 1816	Solomon Moses	Assault
State v. John Smith, 1817	Solomon Moses	Assault
State v. Zachariah Wheeler, 1824	Simon Moses	Assault and battery
State v. William Martin, 1826	R. Woolf and S. Sampson	Larceny
State v. Charles Drayton, 1830	Myer Audler	Trading with slaves
State v. David Hines, 1831	Simon Moses	Assault
State v. James Allen, 1831	Simon Moses	Assault
State v. Charles Drayton, 1832	Isaac Emanuel	Assault
State v. George Markham, 1835	David and Elizabeth Hyams	Assault and battery

the shop. They chased him again, caught him, and took him to the guard house. The jury did not indict the man, apparently believing he had received enough punishment at the hands of Sampson. (See Table 17.)

Despite the problems of thieves, insurrections, wars, hurricanes, fires, and disease, Charleston flourished as one of the great cities of America until the 1820s. After that, economic decline set in and making a living became more difficult, but still for the Jews, the city provided a happy home.

"This is Charles-town,
how do you like it?"

Chapter 5

The Birth of Reform Judaism

> "In this happy land . . . equality of laws and freedom of conscience leave you a wide and cheerful field to act upon."
> —Isaac Harby, 1825[1]

On November 21, 1824, about a dozen men in Charleston gathered in what they called a Convention of Israelites.[2] Over the next month others joined with them. They began a movement to bring about changes in the worship services at Beth Elohim that soon developed into an attempt to alter drastically Judaism as they knew it. Obviously filled with enthusiasm, these young men assumed that their actions would bring an immediate response. They compared themselves to Martin Luther, who set off the Protestant Reformation when he nailed his Ninety-Five Theses to the cathedral door in Wittenberg, Germany, in 1517. The reformers in Charleston, however, did not meet with the reaction they anticipated. American Judaism did not suddenly transform. Nevertheless, their proposals ranked among the most radical within the Jewish faith during the first half of the nineteenth century.

The Petition

The group of men who wanted changes drew up a petition, written by Abraham Moïse, which they transmitted to the president of the congregation and the *adjunta* on December 23, 1824.[3]

1. Harby, *Discourse*, 1.

2. The Charleston directory for 1831 was prepared by Morris Goldsmith, the secretary of the Reformed Society. He gave the date of the founding as Jan. 16, 1825. The same date appears in the constitution of the organization. But the meetings had begun in November, and later this was accepted as the founding date. Harby to Jefferson, in Moïse and Pinckney, *A Selection from the Miscellaneous Writings*, 36.

3. Extract from the Minutes of Meeting of the Convention of Israelites, Held on the 16th January, 1825, in Elzas, *The Reformed Society*, 53. At the time H. M. Hertz served as the secretary of the *adjunta*. Elzas indicates that Israel Moses was the president. There may

The petitioners stated that they had "witnessed with deep regret, the apathy and neglect which have been manifested towards our holy religion. As inheritors of the *true faith*, and always proud to be considered by the world as a portion of 'God's chosen people,'" they were pained to see the decay of the system of worship that had long distinguished the Jews. They went on to say that they had "ingenuously investigated the reasons which may have led them from the Synagogue" and were of the opinion that defects in the mode of worship were the sole causes of problems. They stated they only wanted to secure the "future welfare and respectability of the nation." They could not "place before their children examples which are only calculated to darken the mind and withhold from the rising generation the more rational means of worshipping the true God."

Samuel Gilman (1791–1858), a minister in Charleston, described the services that the reformers wanted to change in an article in the *North American Review.*[4] Though he refers to services in synagogues, he probably had specific knowledge of those at Beth Elohim. Gilman stated that when one entered a synagogue, one noticed the assembly sitting or standing in an indifferent mood with their heads covered. The "Priest," surrounded by a few attendants, presided on a platform in the center of the building. Once, he reported, when the *hazan* conducted the prayers, a leading member of the congregation crossed the floor and discussed the Hebrew phrasing with another worshiper. The conversation, however, soon turned to other matters. The liturgy was almost entirely in Hebrew, although there were occasional prayers in Spanish, especially to announce the amount of money given to the synagogue by members. Almost no one understood the Spanish. The prayers consisted of readings and responses in a chant that rose and fell according to the passage. Because of the speed with which the prayers were read, the services concluded in about three hours. Had the prayers been read at a normal rate, the service would have taken five. As the exercise continued, people came and went and children played. No sermon could be heard, but on some occasions the reader instructed the congregation about correct procedures to be followed.

The petition contains the specific changes the group wished to see in the religious services in the synagogue. Above all, they sought to introduce English. The *hazan* should repeat parts, possibly all, of the Hebrew prayers in English because "not every one . . . has the means, and many have not the time, to acquire a knowledge of the Hebrew language" and English was "the language of the country." Furthermore, the reading of the *Parasa* (Torah) in Hebrew neither instructed nor entertained. But if the *hazan* "like all other ministers" would deliver a discourse based on a

---

have been two people by that name in Charleston at the time. One of them was born in 1787 in Charleston and died in 1849 in Florida. The name could have been mistaken for German-born Isaiah Moses, 1772–1857, who was a member of the *adjunta* in 1820 and bitterly opposed reform. He also served as a trustee of Shearith Israel synagogue in the 1840s.

4. Gilman, "Harby's Discourse on the Jewish Synagogue."

verse or chapter, the people, especially children, would become better acquainted with the teachings of Judaism. Every "reflecting and liberal mind" should see the advantages of these innovations. The changes, in turn, "would lead to more decency and decorum" in the synagogue and would elicit "regard from Jew and Gentile." They pointed out that the Roman Catholics, the German Lutherans, and the French Protestants all worshiped in this fashion. They emphasized that they did not intend to destroy their institutions "but to accommodate them to the progress of time, and change of situation and circumstances." The petitioners questioned if in the history of the civilized world there could be found a people "addressing the *Creator* in a language not understood *by that people*." The memorialists found it "indeed surprising, that heretofore no innovation has even been *attempted*," though the *adjunta* contained "many very enlightened and intelligent members."

Next they sought to shorten the service. The length caused those conducting the service to rush through many portions. Normally services began at 9:00 A.M. on the Sabbath and concluded at noon; however, if the prayers were read as they should be, worshipers could still be there until 2:00 P.M. Superfluous portions could be eliminated.

Then they requested "the favor of a patient hearing" on changes they wanted in the way offerings were made. They considered the method employed to be useless and improper. Offerings were given in Spanish, a "language of a people from whom we have suffered, and continue to suffer, so much persecution" and that few understood. Article 11 of the 1820 constitution provided that money offered at services could be deducted from the annual dues. Therefore, they saw the system of offerings as unnecessary and "an idle and absurd indulgence." Also, those who had fulfilled their dues felt induced to go out of the building to avoid having to contribute against their will. If people wanted to give more than their dues, another method should be worked out, and the time taken up by the offerings could be used for a discourse, especially one addressed to the young people. The whole system, the petitioners believed, set "an ill example to our children, and draws upon us the eyes of the strangers."

Finally, the reformers concerned themselves with bringing new members into the synagogue. Some individuals had wandered away from the faith. In them, the *adjunta* had "fair subjects for the holy work of reformation." Should the synagogue officials change the mode of worship to one that could be understood by these wanderers, they could be won back. In addition, in what might be a call for missionary work among non-Jews, the petitioners indicated that other religious groups zealously extended their means of worship to all quarters of the globe, and in the process made many inducements. But they "the mere remnant of a great nation" were "disregarding the fairest opportunities of increasing our own numbers, and at the same time neglecting the brightest prospects of enlarging our resources, and effectually perpetuating our national character."

In concluding their call for changes in the synagogue, the group stated that the petitioners did not wish to eliminate any ceremonies that distinguished them from gentiles. What they wanted was "to preserve and perpetuate the principles of Judaism in their utmost purity and vigour." These were all the alterations that the petitioners could "in reason and moderation require."

To bolster their demands, the petitioners then referred to "the reformation which has been recently adopted by our brethren in Holland, Germany, and Prussia" and gave an excerpt from the *Frankfurt Journal* telling of extensive changes made in the synagogues there. Various honors could no longer be auctioned, swaying during prayers was to end, reading prayers too loudly was to be stopped, profane songs were to be eliminated, striking Haman during Purim was strictly forbidden, children under the age of five were to be barred from attendance, the distribution of sweets to children on the eves of festivals was prohibited, and sermons were to be delivered in German.[5] The conclusion of the petition stated:

> Thus . . . it appears that no climes, not even tyranny itself, can forever fetter or control the human mind; and that even amidst the intolerance of Europe, our brethren have anticipated the free citizens of America in the glorious work of reformation; let us then hasten to the task with harmony and good fellowship. We wish not to *overthrow*, but to *rebuild*; we wish not to *destroy*, but to *reform* and *revise* the evils complained of; we wish not to *abandon* the institutions of Moses, but to *understand and observe them*; in fine, we wish to worship God, not as *slaves of bigotry and priestcraft*, but as the enlightened descendants of that chosen race, whose blessings have been scattered throughout the land of Abraham, Isaac and Jacob.

By reaffirming their Judaism, the group emphasized that they considered themselves reformers and not revolutionaries. Yet the document is highly inflammatory, and despite the call for "harmony and good fellowship," it attacked the form of worship as practiced by their fathers, brothers, cousins, and neighbors. Calling them slaves of bigotry and priestcraft was extremely unlikely to be met with sympathy.

When the petition came before the private *adjunta*, the secretary read the entreaty, at which point the *parnass* ruled that the mode of proposing changes was unconstitutional. Therefore, he would not allow any debate. He stated that the fourteenth rule of the constitution provided the appropriate method for proposing changes, and should that be complied with, the petition would be considered. H. M. Hertz, the secretary, returned the memorial to the group on January 10, 1825.[6] The president ruled correctly. Rule 1 of the

5. To the President and members of the Adjunta of Kaal Kadosh Beth Elohim of Charleston, South, Carolina, in Elzas, *The Reformed Society*, 44–53.

6. H. M. Hertz to Aaron Phillips, Jan. 10, 1825, in Elzas, *The Reformed Society*, 55.

1820 constitution provided that the congregation would follow the Minhag Sephardim. The petitioners wanted to modify that form of worship. Furthermore, rule 14 stated that changes to the constitution could be proposed by the *parnassim* and the *adjunta* or by a petition of two-thirds of the subscribing *yahidim*, excluding the members of the private and public *adjuntas*.

The forty-seven did not constitute two-thirds of the *yahidim*; indeed, a majority of them did not belong to the congregation. The cash book for 1823 of Beth Elohim, which ran from September of that year to September 1824, is the closest one available for these events. It lists 153 people who contributed to the synagogue. Although a few entries have two names, such as Michael and Benjamin Lazarus or Cherie and Aaron Moïse, most are for one person only. Twenty-four of the reformers, slightly more than half, are not listed in 1823, though seven of them had contributed in 1819, the previous year for which records have survived. None of the Harby family made contributions during 1815, 1819, or 1823. The last existing record showing they had paid their dues was in 1814, when Solomon and Isaac Harby purchased seats. Some of the reformers were still young in 1824 and apparently occupied seats leased by their fathers. Others may not have been in the city. Three had married outside the faith. These, Levy J. Abrahams, Theodore Sydney Moïse, and Isaac Tobias, would not have been eligible to have membership in the synagogue. They constituted part of those whom the petitioners pointed out might be won back. Those who married outside the faith had no choice but to leave the synagogue, and their children could never be admitted. Others may well have been excluded because of the restrictive nature of the constitution. Thus, this group appears to have been disenchanted with the services in the synagogue and its leaders for some time, apparently from the time of the adoption of the 1820 constitution.[7]

The reformers wanted to simplify and shorten their services to make them more comprehensible, edifying, and enjoyable. This, they believed, would bring back those people who had withdrawn from the synagogue and would prevent their children from leaving the faith in the future. The petitioners wanted to look good in the eyes of their Protestant neighbors. They also believed institutions should be accommodated to the time and place in which they existed, something that the 1820 constitution had recognized.[8] They sought a "more rational means of worshipping" which would "meet the views of the *liberal*." As "free citizens of America" they believed that they had the right to worship as they pleased.

7. Cash Books exist for 1814, 1815, 1819, and 1823. Isaac Harby had contributed in 1811 as well.

8. The Preface stated, "it becomes no less proper than necessary, that all human institutions, and legal provisions for the government of men, when united into societies, should receive, such additions, and undergo such alterations and improvements, as important changes and local circumstances may require."

Why in Charleston?

Because of the importance of the reform movement, a number of people have investigated the reformers' group and given a variety of interpretations. The chief of these are described and assessed below.

The Rising Middle Class

One author has maintained that "this impulse came from the needs of the rising Jewish middle class."[9] The best way to judge this conclusion is to look at the individuals involved and to compare the reformers with the *adjunta*.

The *adjunta* came to power with the congregational constitution of 1820. In that year the average age of the *adjunta* members was approximately fifty-six years, although the dates of birth of two are not known. By the end of 1824 three of them, Emanuel DeLaMotta, Lyon Moses, and Samuel Simons, had died. At least eighteen members (72 percent) were foreign born; only four are known to have been born in the United States, with three of these in Charleston. The largest number of foreign born (six) came from England, the second greatest (five) from Germany, with fewer (two) from the Netherlands. Other homelands were Haiti, Ireland, Poland, Jamaica, and St. Croix. Thus, this body was aging and largely European. Many of them would have had come from a very traditional Jewish world. (See Table 18.)

Most of the members of the *adjunta* were solid members of the middle class who stayed put. All of them can be found in the city directories over a number of years. Abraham Lipman has the least number of entries; he showed up in three directories over a period of six years. On the other hand, Marks Lazarus can be found in fourteen directories over a forty-five year period. The members held a variety of positions such as accountant, retail store operator, merchant, broker, and vendue master. Two of them, Isaiah Moses and Isaac Lyons, owned plantations at one time. All of them married except for Samuel Simons, and five of them married a second wife when the first one died. The city directory of 1822, which is the closest one available for the period, along with those from later dates, provides a means of comparing the members of the *adjunta* with the reformers. (See Table 19.)

Overall, these men had accomplished a great deal in life, enjoyed a high standard of living, and occupied positions of importance in their community. They would not favor disturbance of the status quo. Anyone who sought to bring about changes would have a difficult, if not impossible, time of it.

The petitioners in 1824 numbered forty-seven. No list of them is known to have survived; however, the Reformed Society of Israelites issued a constitution in 1825 that forty-three Jews in Charleston supported. Apparently, four had decided not to continue to demand reform or had left the community. This group differs remarkably from the *adjunta* of 1820; only one member can be found in both the *adjunta* and the Reformed Society—Jacob Lazarus. Fewer records exist for the people in this group. Their aver-

9. Schappes, *Documentary History*, 171.

Table 18
The *Adjunta* of 1820: Origins

Name	*Year Born*	*Place Born*
Alexander, Abraham, Jr.	1771	London, England
Cardozo, David Nunez	1753	New York
Cohen, Moses	1768	England
Cohen, Philip	1781	Charleston
DeLaMotta, Emanuel*	1760	St. Croix
DeLeon, Jacob	1764	Jamaica
Harris, Hyam (Henry)	1764	England
Hart, Nathan	1784	Mannheim, Germany
Hart, Simon Moses	1763	Germany?
Hertz, Handel Moses	1780	Hildesheim, Germany
Hyams, Solomon M., Sr.	1753	Dublin, Ireland
Joseph, Joseph J.		S.C.?
Lazarus, Jacob	1781	Gronigen, Netherlands
Lazarus, Marks	1757	Charleston
Levy, Lyon	1764	Woolwich, England
Levy, Moses Clava	1750	Zobnau, Poland
Levy, Simon L.		
Lipman, Abraham	1778	England
Lyons, Isaac	1774	Oberelsbach, Germany
Mairs, Simon	1765	Budingen, Germany
Moïse, Aaron	1783	Haiti (Santo Domingo)
Moses, Isaiah	1772	Hanover, Germany
Moses, Lyon*	1748	Amsterdam, Netherlands
Moses, Myer	1779	Charleston
Simons, Samuel*	1761	London, England

*Dead by 1825
Sources: See the appendix.

age age in 1825 was approximately thirty-three years, about two decades younger than the *adjunta*. The fathers of six of them served on the board: Isaac N. Cardozo was the son of David Nunez Cardozo; Henry Hyams was the son of Simon M. Hyams; Michael Lazarus was the son of Marks Lazarus; David Cardozo Levy and Lyon Levy were the sons of Lyon Levy; and Isaac Clifton Moses was the son of Myer Moses. Six of them were age twenty or below, and none was older than fifty-nine. The youngest was Joseph Goldsmith, who was only twelve or thirteen years of age. Equally striking is the fact that at least twenty-six of them (60 percent) were born in the United States, with nineteen of these in South

Table 19
The *Adjunta* of 1820: Occupations

Name	*Occupation in 1822*	*Years in Directories*
Alexander, Abraham, Jr.	Not listed	1801, 1802, 1803, 1806, 1813, 1831, 1835
Cardozo, David Nunez	Not listed	1796, 1801, 1802, 1803, 1806, 1807, 1809, 1813, 1816, 1819, 1829, 1831
Cohen, Moses	Merchant	1796, 1801, 1802, 1803, 1807, 1809, 1813, 1816, 1819, 1822
Cohen, Philip	None given	1801, 1802, 1807, 1809, 1813, 1819, 1822, 1831, 1849, 1855, 1859
DeLaMotta, Emanuel	Not listed	1801, 1802, 1803, 1806, 1807, 1809, 1813, 1819
DeLeon, Jacob	None given	1796, 1801, 1802, 1803, 1806, 1807, 1813, 1822
Harris, Hyam (Henry)	Merchant	1807, 1816, 1819, 1822
Hart, Nathan	Hardware merchant	1806, 1807, 1809, 1816, 1819, 1829, 1831, 1835, 1838, 1841
Hart, Simon Moses	Not listed	1790, 1801, 1803, 1807, 1809, 1813
Hertz, Handel Moses	Not listed	1813, 1816, 1831, 1835, 1838
Hyams, Solomon M., Sr.	Merchant	1790, 1794, 1801, 1802, 1803, 1816, 1819, 1822, 1831, 1835
Joseph, Joseph J.	Merchant	1801, 1802, 1806, 1809, 1816, 1822, 1835, 1838, 1841
Lazarus, Jacob	Merchant	1807, 1813, 1819, 1822
Lazarus, Marks	None given	1790, 1794, 1801, 1802, 1803, 1807, 1809, 1813, 1816, 1819, 1822, 1829, 1831, 1835
Levy, Lyon	None given	1794, 1796, 1801, 1803, 1806, 1807, 1809, 1813, 1819, 1822, 1831
Levy, Moses Clava	Merchant	1790, 1794, 1796, 1801, 1802, 1803, 1806, 1807, 1809, 1816, 1819, 1822, 1831, 1835, 1838
Levy, Simon L.	Merchant	1802, 1803, 1806, 1807, 1809, 1813, 1816, 1819, 1822
Lipman, Abraham	Not listed	1813, 1816, 1819
Lyons, Isaac	None given	1809, 1813, 1816, 1819
Mairs, Simon	Merchant	1809, 1816, 1819, 1822, 1829, 1831

Table 19
(Continued)

Name	*Occupation in 1822*	*Years in Directories*
Moïse, Aaron	Clerk	1807, 1809, 1813, 1816, 1819, 1822, 1829, 1831, 1835
Moses, Isaiah	Planter	1801, 1802, 1803, 1806, 1807, 1809, 1813, 1822, 1829, 1831, 1835
Moses, Lyon	Not listed	1790, 1794, 1796, 1801, 1802, 1803, 1806, 1807, 1809, 1813, 1816, 1819
Moses, Myer	Auctioneer	1806, 1807, 1809, 1813, 1816, 1819, 1822
Simons, Samuel	Merchant	1790, 1794, 1802, 1803, 1806, 1807, 1809

Sources: Charleston city directories for the years listed for each entry.

Carolina. Six came from England. Approximately 90 percent had English as their first language. Only four persons are known to have come from non-English countries, two from Germany and two from the Netherlands. (See Table 20.)

The occupations of the members of the Reformed Society differed dramatically from their elders. Twelve of them cannot be found in any directories, and only twenty can be found in directories for the 1820s. In general, they held jobs rather than ran their own businesses. Occupations include those of clerk, jailer, deputy marshal, printer, editor, blacksmith, author, teacher, and portrait painter. They were far less "middle class" than the *adjunta* and remained so throughout their lives. (See Table 21.) It would seem, then, that one cannot maintain that this reform impulse came from the rising middle class.

The Split in the Congregational Church

Lou H. Silberman claims that "what happened in Charleston was derivative and its proximate source is to be found within the context of Protestantism in Charleston in the years immediately preceding the founding of the Reformed Society."[10] Because Samuel Gilman wrote a review of Isaac Harby's anniversary speech to the Reformed Society of Israelites in 1826, Silberman sees a connection between developments in the Independent or Congregational church and the synagogue. In 1815 the church employed Anthony Forster on a temporary basis when one of its pastors became ill. Two years later the minister died, and a bitter dispute broke out about

10. Silberman, "American Impact," 94.

Table 20
The Members of the Reformed Society: Origins

Name	*Year Born*	*Place Born*
Abrahams, Levy J.[a]		U.S.
Benjamin, Philip	1780	St. Eustatius
Cardozo, Isaac N.	1793	Charleston
Carvalho, David Nunes	1784	London, England
Cohen, Esdaile P.[b]	1792	Swansea, Wales
Cohen, Jacob[b]	1796	Georgetown, S.C.
Goldsmith, Henry[a]		England
Goldsmith, Joseph H.[a]	1813	Charleston
Goldsmith, Morris	1778	England
Harby, Henry Jefferson[a]	1799	Charleston
Harby, Isaac[a]	1788	Charleston
Harby, Levi Myers[a]	1793	Georgetown, S.C.
Harris, Jacob[b]	1766	Netherlands
Hertz, Jacob E.	1776	Germany
Hyams, Henry[b]	1793	London, England
Hyams, Moses Kosciusko[a]	1798	S.C.
Hyams, Samuel	1766	London, England
Jacobs, Myer	1791	England
Labatt, Abraham Cohen	1802	Charleston
Lazarus, Jacob[b]	1781	Gronigen, Netherlands
Lazarus, Michael	1786	Charleston
Levy, Bernard[b]	1789	Charleston
Levy, David Cardozo[a]	1805	Charleston
Levy, Emanuel	1784	Charleston
Levy, Hayman	1795	New York
Levy, Lyon	1803	Charleston
Levy, Solomon[a]	1770	
Lyon, George[a]		
Moïse, Abraham	1799	Charleston
Moïse, Isaac	1800	Charleston
Moïse, Jacob	1798	Charleston
Moïse, Theodore Sydney[a]	1808	Charleston
Mordecai, Isaac D.	1805	U.S. (Charleston?)
Mordecai, Thomas Whitlock[a]	1806	U.S.
Moses, Isaac Clifton	1781	S.C.
Moses, Jacob[a]		
Phillips, Aaron	1780	Anspach, Germany
Phillips, Philip[b]	1807	Charleston

Table 20
(Continued)

Name	*Year Born*	*Place Born*
Sampson, Samuel	1789	St. Edmunds, England
Seixas, Abraham[a]	1786	New York
Simon, Moses[a, c]		
Soria, Isaac[a]		New York
Tobias, Isaac[a]	1796	Charleston

[a]Did not contribute to Beth Elohim in 1823.
[b]Did not contribute to Beth Elohim in 1823 but did in 1819.
[c]This name may be transposed. Moses Simon is otherwise unknown; however, Simon Moses is fairly well documented. He appears in records in South Carolina as early as 1804 and can be found in the federal censuses of 1810, 1820, and 1830 in Charleston. He is also listed in the city directories of 1813, 1822, 1829, 1831, and 1835.
Sources: See the appendix.

giving Forster a permanent appointment. Many did not like his liberal ideas; he had abandoned his Calvinism for Unitarianism. In the dispute that followed the congregation split, with the more traditional group retaining the old building, now the Circular Congregational Church on Meeting Street, and Forster's supporters taking over the Archdale Street building, then the Second Congregational Church, now the Unitarian Church. When Forster fell ill and retired in 1819, the group hired Gilman, who received a warm welcome when he arrived from New England. He enjoyed much success, and by the time he retired in 1854 the congregation had rebuilt its structure and changed its name to the Unitarian Church. In his farewell speech Gilman stated, "I came as an avowed Unitarian, and was expected to unfurl here the banner of Unitarian Christianity." His sermon at the dedication of the new church gloried in the tenets of liberal Christianity.[11]

Silberman rejects European influence on the Charleston reformers, something they mention, and attributes the movement to a dispute in a Congregational church, to which they do not refer. This dispute had, in fact, been resolved a number of years before. Indeed, controversies and schisms occurred in other churches of Charleston. Although some of the Jewish reformers may have remembered the incident in the congregational church, the event would certainly not have prompted them to demand liturgical reforms in the synagogue. The idea is farfetched.

11. Gilman, "Discourse Delivered at the Dedication", and "Farewell to the Old Church" in *The Old and the New*, 59–65.

Table 21
The Members of the Reformed Society: Occupations

Name	*Occupation in 1822*	*Years in Directories*
Abrahams, Levy J.	Not listed	1807, 1816, 1819
Benjamin, Philip	Dry goods store	1819, 1822, 1831, 1835, 1838, 1841, 1849
Cardozo, Isaac N.	None given	1813, 1819, 1822, 1829, 1831, 1835, 1841, 1849, 1852
Carvalho, David Nunes	Watchmaker/jeweler	1813, 1816, 1819, 1822
Cohen, Esdaile P.	Not listed	
Cohen, Jacob	Not listed	1838
Goldsmith, Henry	Deputy register in equity	1819, 1822, 1831, 1835, 1838, 1841, 1852
Goldsmith, Joseph H.	Not listed	1831, 1835
Goldsmith, Morris	Deputy U.S. marshal	1803, 1806, 1816, 1819, 1822, 1829, 1831, 1835, 1841, 1852, 1855, 1859
Harby, Henry Jefferson	Not listed	1829, 1831
Harby, Isaac	Teacher	1809, 1813, 1819, 1822
Harby, Levi M.	Not listed	
Harris, Jacob	Clothing store	1807, 1809, 1813, 1819, 1822, 1831, 1835
Hertz, Jacob E.	Dry goods store	1813, 1816, 1822, 1829, 1831, 1835, 1838, 1841
Hyams, Henry	Dry goods store	1816, 1819, 1822, 1835, 1838, 1841, 1849
Hyams, Moses Kosciusko	Not listed	
Hyams, Samuel	Keeper of jail	1801, 1802, 1803, 1807, 1813, 1816, 1819, 1822, 1829, 1831
Jacobs, Myer	Not listed	1835, 1838
Labatt, Abraham Cohen	Not listed	
Lazarus, Jacob	Merchant	1807, 1813, 1819, 1822
Lazarus, Michael	Merchant	1809, 1813, 1816, 1819, 1822, 1829, 1831, 1835
Levy, Bernard	Not listed	1831, 1835, 1838
Levy, David Cardozo	Not listed	1835, 1838

Table 21
(Continued)

Name	*Occupation in 1822*	*Years in Directories*
Levy, Emanuel	Not listed	1802, 1803, 1806, 1807, 1809, 1813, 1816, 1829, 1831, 1837
Levy, Hayman	Dry goods store	1822
Levy, Lyon	Not listed	1819, 1831, 1835
Levy, Solomon	None given	1790, 1794, 1796, 1806, 1807, 1809, 1813, 1816, 1819, 1822, 1829
Lyon, George	Watch and clockmaker	1822, 1829, 1831, 1835
Moïse, Abraham	Not listed	1829, 1831, 1835, 1838
Moïse, Isaac	Not listed	
Moïse, Jacob	Not listed	
Moïse, Theodore Sydney	Not listed	1829, 1835
Mordecai, Isaac D.	Not listed	
Mordecai, Thomas Whitlock	Not listed	1831, 1835, 1838
Moses, Isaac Clifton	Not listed	1806, 1807, 1816, 1819
Moses, Jacob	Not listed	
Phillips, Aaron	Not listed	1809, 1813, 1829
Phillips, Philip	Not listed	
Sampson, Samuel	Not listed	
Seixas, Abraham	Not listed	1831
Simon, Moses	Not listed	
Soria, Isaac	Not listed	
Tobias, Isaac	Not listed	1835, 1838

Sources: City directories for the years listed.

Political Insecurity

Robert Liberles has noted the social and economic standings of the individuals but concluded that "the Maryland Jew Bill controversy precipitated the Reform initiative in Charleston"—though, he says, this was not the "primary cause." Liberles goes on to state, "American Reform Judaism originated in Charleston because the integration of its Jewry had reached the political plane." The legislation in "nearby Maryland" was designed to give Jews the right to hold office in that state. According to Liberles, its several setbacks "reminded Charleston Jewry that its position was not yet fully secured."[12] The Maryland Jew Bill aroused much controversy when it was debated from 1819 to 1826. Some extracts from articles in a Baltimore newspaper appeared in the *Southern Patriot*, then edited by Jacob Cardozo. The Maryland bill, however, had nothing to do with reform in the synagogue, and the Jews of South Carolina had long enjoyed all the rights of other citizens. No one ever threatened to take them away. The argument has no substance.

Liberles also emphasizes the fact that a number of the reformers later held political offices, including the office of state treasurer, lieutenant governor of Louisiana, and state legislator; however, this was after the fact—much later in some cases. If anything, the reformers' activity in promoting change in the synagogue led them to political involvement rather than the reverse. Had they been under attack, they would more likely have joined their coreligionists in the community in a show of unity, as they had in the past when they felt they had been excluded from events.

European Influence

Barnett Elzas in his *Jews of South Carolina*, published in 1905, wrote that the reform movement was an indigenous one "resulting neither from foreign influence or internal violence."[13] By 1916 he had changed his mind. At that time he published documents regarding the Reformed Society and stated the effort was "directly dependent upon the earlier movement that had taken place in Germany."[14]

The religious changes among Jews had been slow in coming in Europe. Although Protestants split away from Roman Catholicism in the sixteenth century, the Jews, if anything, saw a growing rigidity with the codification of law by Joseph Caro in the *Shulhan Aruh* (The Set Table). They followed "written law" and "oral law." The written law came from the Torah or Pentateuch, the first five books of the Bible that are attributed to Moses. The oral law embodied rabbinical interpretations of the biblical texts as found in the Babylonian Talmud, the Jerusalem Talmud, and other writings. The rabbis taught that both written and oral law had come from God, and the laws could not be changed. Any innovation was a serious offense against the deity.

Changes, however, began to appear during the Enlightenment. The monarchs of the time removed restrictions on Jews, with the result that their communities began to have fewer controls over individuals. Furthermore, it was a tolerant age. Moses Mendelssohn (1729–86) advocated the emergence of the Jews from the ghetto to join the rest of society. One of the things he did was to translate the Torah into German so that Jews who spoke the German dialect of Yiddish could learn High German.

12. Liberles, "Conflict over Reforms," 285.
13 P. 159.

14. *The Sabbath Service*, preface.

Though he firmly believed in keeping Jewish laws, Mendelssohn brought down on his own head the wrath of some rabbis. They charged that rationalism riddled his translation. Furthermore, if the Jews learned German, they would have more contact with gentiles, and having the Torah in German would prevent people from mastering Hebrew. Mendelssohn, however, did not seek to change the faith. Following him, other Jews began to place greater emphasis on the Bible than on talmudic literature. They valued it as a "spiritual treasure" rather than as a legal text. Others questioned the minute regulations affecting daily life that set Jews apart. Some visited churches and came away impressed by the decorum and the services. To make their own ceremonies more understandable, two people made German translations of their prayerbook.

The French Revolution caused greater changes. In 1791 the National Assembly made Jews citizens of France, with freedoms and responsibilities like others. The French extended these privileges to the Batavian Republic (the Netherlands) in 1795, when that area came under French domination. The following year a new Sephardic congregation by the name of Adath Jeshurun in Amsterdam instituted some reforms in the method of worship by eliminating what they considered to be redundant parts of the ritual and by introducing sermons in Dutch.

After Napoleon took over in France, he defeated the Austrians and Prussians and reorganized Europe. The French liberated the Jews in the west German state of Westphalia and in 1808 granted them a consistory to direct Jewish affairs. The consistory appointed rabbis and required them to maintain decorum in the synagogues and preach sermons on special occasions in the vernacular. Also, modifications in the liturgy shortened the services somewhat. In addition, Jewish education underwent changes, with training in secular as well as religious subjects. At the consistory school at Cassel, religious services featured prayers, hymns, and sermons in German. In addition, a confirmation ceremony was borrowed from the Protestants. At Seesen, Israel Jacobson established a temple (as opposed to a synagogue) in 1810 complete with bells, an organ, a choir, a pulpit, German prayers, and a sermon. Traditional rabbis protested to the authorities about these innovations to no avail.

When Napoleon lost his empire, the kingdom of Westphalia disappeared and Jacobson went to Berlin, the capital of Prussia. He held services in his home and later in that of Jacob Herz Beer, a banker. The orthodox rabbis again complained. This time the government of Prussia supported them, and the king issued an order in 1823 that all services must follow traditional ritual and could include no innovations.

Meanwhile, Reform Judaism appeared in Hamburg. In 1817 Edward Kley of Berlin went to Hamburg to head a Jewish school. He soon organized a group of people who favored reforming the services, and by 1818 they had built the Hamburg Temple. Again, the orthodox appealed to the authorities but had no success in stopping religious innovation. This community eventually adopted some of the most far-reaching reforms in Europe.[15]

The innovations among Jews in Europe were known to the reformers in Charleston. In their petition they referred to developments in Holland, Germany, and Prussia, and listed a number of alterations that had recently been adopted in Frankfurt. The Jews of Charleston did not live isolated lives. The city still served as one of the major ports of entry for the United States, and many in the city engaged in international trade. Furthermore, Dutch, German, and Prussian Jews lived in the city—and some of them had only recently arrived. Many of them would have maintained contact with their coreligionists in Europe. The claim that the reformers in Charleston "knew little"[16] about the developments among Jews in Germany cannot be sustained. The reference to the reform movement in Europe appears to have been more than a postscript. The Charleston reformers gave little information about the reforms in Holland, Germany, and Prussia, no doubt, because they expected the *adjunta* to be fully aware of them. Five members of that group had been born in Germany and two in the Netherlands. The developments in Frankfurt had recently occurred and would possibly not be known by the *adjunta*.

15. On European reform, see Meyer, *Response to Modernity*, 100–142; Schwartzman, *Reform Judaism in the Making*, 20–44; Philipson, *The Reform Movement*, 6–33; Blau, *Modern Varieties of Judaism*, 20–39.

16. Liberles, "Conflict over Reforms," 275.

American Factors

Charles Reznikoff in *The Jews of Charleston* stated that the developments in Europe "may have bolstered some Charleston Jews somewhat . . . but the movement in Charleston was native to the place." He says, "in Charleston the Reform movement was inaugurated by a group of American Jewish intellectuals, cultured and world-wise, who were under the influence of the spirit of the age (of which the American Declaration of Independence was another example). In addition, the city itself had a long tradition, preceding the Revolution of religious liberalism and pluralism."[17] Jacob Marcus cites both European and American influences. He notes, however, that "the conditions that made Reform possible in Charleston were true as well of Philadelphia and New York, but the leadership was lacking." In Charleston "the rebellion against the Orthodox was possible because a substantial number of radical intellectuals called Charleston home and among them were several willing to assume leadership."[18]

Marcus's analysis of the development of Reform Judaism is by far the best reasoned. "What influenced the rise of Reform in this country?" he asks. "Above all, events in Europe!" As he points out, less than 1 percent of world Jewry lived in America at the time, and Jewish deists and freethinkers had challenged traditional ideas since the previous century. In America the early nine-

17. P. 124.

18. Marcus, *United States Jewry*, 614–23.

teenth century saw social, intellectual, and religious ferment.[19] Change was the spirit of the times. Individuals in Charleston had been affected by the ideas of John Locke, the Enlightenment, the American Revolution, the United States Constitution, the French Revolution, Thomas Jefferson, Andrew Jackson (who ran for president in 1824), Romanticism, the Protestants, and the residents of Charleston. Innovations had already been made. The synagogue looked like a church, acted much like a church, and the religious leaders had taken the title of "Reverend" and assumed many of the roles of the Protestant pastor or Catholic priest. Furthermore, in 1791 the congregation had translated its service from Hebrew and Spanish into English for the dedication of the Orphan House in Charleston. They also had songs and an oration in English and probably shortened the service as well. Then in 1812 Carvalho had introduced innovations into the service at Beth Elohim. The controversy that followed resulted from the fact that he discontinued the chorus, not that he made changes. In addition, Maurice Mayer, who served as the *hazan* in the 1850s, reported that the records of the congregation showed that an English sermon had been delivered in 1812, very likely at the same time as the chorus.[20]

Although Silberman rejects *Zeitgeist*, the spirit of the times, as too facile an explanation for the development of reform Judaism in Charleston,[21] the reformers on several occasions did refer to the need to adapt to time and place. They had been adapting in Charleston for nearly 130 years. They mixed with the rest of the community from the beginning. They came and went as they wished, engaged in whatever professions they choose, and studied what they wanted. Most of the young people in the Jewish community had been born in Charleston. They were Americans, very likely Americans first and Jews second. Despite the fact that rigid class distinctions existed in Charleston, a person with education and talent, no matter his or her background, could join with the aristocracy. Clubs abounded, including the Philomanthean Society, where Jacob Cardozo and Isaac Harby engaged in discussions and social activities with members of Charleston's elite, including Langdon Cheeves, William Lowndes, Charles Fraser, Rev. Charles Snowden, David Ramsay, and Christopher Gadsden. At the time Harby wrote essays and plays, and operated a school, while Cardozo edited the *Southern Patriot*, Samuel Hart owned one of the two most important bookshops in the city, and Abraham Moïse practiced law.[22]

The Society

The rejection by the *adjunta* of the petition in January 1825 meant that the body intended to make no changes. As far as is known, the reformers never tried

19. Ibid.

20. Mayer, "Geschichte," 104. In both cases, Mayer says, the English sermons were delivered by Germans.

21. Silberman, "American Impact," 93.

22. Moltke-Hansen, "The Expansion of Intellectual Life," 18–20.

to petition them again. Instead, they proceeded to create a separate organization, the Reformed Society of Israelites, on January 16, 1825. Nathaniel Levin in his history of the congregation states that "several members withdrew from the congregation, and joining a larger number who were not members, established a new place of worship."[23]

On February 15, 1825, they adopted a constitution in which they claimed that the organization would be "known and distinguished throughout the world" as the Reformed Society of Israelites. The constitution is a very disappointing document. Much of it deals with petty fines for offenses such as being late to meetings, leaving early, missing a vote, or failing to attend meetings. The document showed more concern for the anniversary dinner than explaining the duties of officers. Only a few articles are important. One provided that any Jewish male could ask to join at the age of seventeen and had to be approved by a favorable vote of three-fourths of the members. Another established the officers of the organization as a president, vice president, secretary, and treasurer. Each served a term of one year. A third article required a three-fourths majority for amending the constitution, which made it harder to change than the 1820 constitution of Beth Elohim, which required approval of only two-thirds of the members. The document, however, said nothing about beliefs, the form of worship, the use of English, or anything else about services. It did mention that as soon as possible the group planned to educate a youth or youths in order to train them to lead divine services—hardly an appropriate item in a constitution.[24]

In order to take actions as a body, especially regarding property, the Reformed Society of Israelites needed to be incorporated. The group petitioned the state legislature for recognition, and the organization became a legal entity on December 20, 1825.[25] The names on the petition for incorporation came in the following order: Aaron Phillips, Michael Lazarus, Isaac Harby, Samuel Hyams, J. N. Cardozo, and D. N. Carvalho. Others are mentioned but not listed. Very likely, Aaron Phillips had served as the president of the organization and Michael Lazarus had been vice president.

The constitution provided that regular elections would be held on the anniversary date of November 21, 1825. Then the group elected Phillips as president, Michael Lazarus as vice president, Morris Goldsmith as secretary, Isaac Mordecai as treasurer, and Abraham Moïse as orator. Isaac Harby served as the chair of the Corresponding Committee.[26]

Isaac Harby and the Reformed Society

The Corresponding Committee, which Harby chaired, included Abra-

23. Levin, "The Jewish Congregation of Charleston," 438.

24. "Constitution of the Reformed Society of Israelites," in Elzas, *The Reformed Society*, 29–43.

25. *Statutes*, 8: 344.

26. Charleston *Mercury*, Nov. 22, 1825.

ham Moïse, Isaac N. Cardozo, D. N. Carvalho, and E. P. Cohen. Like Harby, Cardozo was a writer and editor. Essentially a publicity committee, the group promoted the cause of the Reformed Society. Harby wrote letters to a number of people seeking their approval for the actions taken. His name more than anyone else's became associated with the Reformed Society. Moreover, L. C. Moïse in his *Biography of Isaac Harby* claims that "Mr. Harby was its first appointed spokesman, the first chairman of its most important committee (on correspondence), its third president (1827), and indeed, the leading spirit and greatest moral force of the reformation."[27] Consequently some historians have claimed that Harby was *the* leader of the Reformed Society. There is nothing to substantiate this. Harby, in fact, left the city in 1828 for New York, where he soon died. Furthermore, the "Memoir" written by Abraham Moïse in *A Selection from the Miscellaneous Writings of the Late Isaac Harby* states that he was "*one* of the founders" of the organization, chairman of the Corresponding Committee, and later *a* president.[28]

David N. Carvalho, Abraham Moïse, and Aaron Phillips probably put forth more effort than Harby. Of these, Abraham Moïse seems to have played the greatest role; he has been credited with writing the petition that went to the *adjunta*, and he supposedly wrote the constitution of the society and kept it updated. Furthermore, he was orator in 1825, vice president in 1827, president from 1828 to its demise, and joint editor of the works of Isaac Harby. He also issued a prayerbook for the society, maintained an abiding interest in the organization, and led the Reform movement in Beth Elohim. Nonetheless, Harby was the "soul of the movement."[29]

Harby's ideas probably reflect the thinking of many members of the organization. They can be found in the first anniversary address of the Reformed Society, which he delivered. His speech contains a number of themes. The first dealt with the importance of the movement. "It was almost superfluous," he said, to inform them that the name of the society "alone, forms an era in the history of your race." "The great cause of IMPROVEMENT in Government, in Religion, in Morals, in Literature, is the great cause of mankind." He proclaimed, "In the short revolution of a single year, what a spectacle does your Society present!" Harby compared the association to Martin Luther when he stated that if the Protestant leader had jolted the papacy to its roots, why could not a few Israelites "shake off the bigotry of ages from their countrymen?" He told his audience that their ideas were rapidly spreading throughout the United States, and he would "not wonder if the principles I speak of, were to settle permanently among the Jews of Europe." He continued, "But the consideration of what may be effected

27. P. 39.

28. Moïse and Pinckney, *A Selection from the Miscellaneous Writings*, 28.

29. Mayer, "Geschichte," 173.

abroad, is but of minor importance to the great and *practical* objects we have in view," because it was in Charleston and the United States where they could look for the greatest changes. Even taking into account the hyperbole that nineteenth-century orators used, one must conclude that Harby believed the group had begun a crusade as inevitable as that of the Protestant Reformation. They were not simply changing a few practices in Charleston; they were remaking Judaism.

Next Harby reiterated some of the demands of the group. He went on to explain that the society did not seek to create a new sect, but to improve Judaism by throwing "away Rabbinical interpolations." He claimed that the Bible was the "true legitimate authority." Following this, he traced the history of the Jews and contrasted the situation of those in the United States with their coreligionists in Europe. The time had arrived for them to reassume "their original liberty and happiness."

Then he lashed into the rabbis. The oppression of the Jews could be traced to these "Fabulists and Sophists." They had "tortured the plainest precepts of the Law into monstrous and unexpected inferences" and had "substituted shadow for substance, and form for reality." They had "converted into mystery and absurdity what God intended his people should plainly read and rationally understand, and practically follow." With a few exceptions, the Jews who came to America bowed "beneath the sway of bigotry" and regarded every effort to eliminate rabbinical teachings and ceremonies as "rebellion against the *divine* world." These people did not "understand the necessity of adapting many of the institutions of the great legislator, to the circumstances of the times in which we live, and of the country in which we enjoy our liberties."

This brought Harby to his main point. A "happy few" had been sufficiently enlightened to leave oppression behind to seek liberty. They had found refuge in America. "In this happy land . . . after a few years residence," they

21. Isaac Harby. By an unknown artist. (From Reznikoff and Engelman, *Jews of Charleston* [Philadelphia, 1950].)

A DISCOURSE,

DELIVERED IN CHARLESTON, (S.C.)

ON THE 21ST OF NOV. 1825,

BEFORE THE

Reformed Society of Israelites,

FOR

PROMOTING TRUE PRINCIPLES OF JUDAISM ACCORDING TO ITS PURITY AND SPIRIT,

ON THEIR FIRST ANNIVERSARY.

By ISAAC HARBY, a Member.

———————— " Purus et insons,
" (Ut me collaudem) si et vivo carus amicis,
" Causa fuit PATER."—HOR. *De vera nobilitate.*

CHARLESTON:
PRINTED BY A. E. MILLER,
4, Broad-street.
1825.

22. Title page of the discourse by Harby.

enjoyed the rights of men, something their children had from birth. America was "the land of promise spoken of in our ancient Scriptures." It was "the region to which the children of Israel, if they are wise, will hasten to come." The Jews were not being invited, he said, "to some stony desert or marshy island, or inhospitable clime" or any fixed spot. They could exercise their own free choice and settle where they wanted. The Jews of Charleston were content to live in America and share in the blessings of liberty. This was a land where they could add to the political happiness, power, and glory of the nation. They could liberally educate their children and make them useful citizens. Their countrymen would be "brethren of the same happy family worshipping the same God." They were happy and contented to live here until the annunciation of the Messiah.

The virulent antirabbinical statements have puzzled a number of people. Nothing like this appeared for at least two decades in Europe. There, demands for changes in the worship sometimes had come from rabbis. America had no rabbis, and the reformers did not want them. The first brief mention of these religious authorities appeared at the end of the petition to the *adjunta* when the reformers referred to "Bigotry and Priestcraft." The constitution of the society went somewhat further. Article II claimed that many of the calamities of humankind had "resulted from a blind observance of the ceremonial law, to the neglect of the essential spirit of revealed religion contained in the Law and Prophets," that is, the Bible. Article IV said the primary object of the society was "to devise ways and means, from time to time, of revising and altering such parts of our prevailing system of Worship, as are inconsistent with the present enlightened state of society, and not in accordance with the Five Books of Moses and the Prophets." Harby's comment about the Bible as the source of authority and his characterization of the rabbis only elaborated on what had been stated by the organization before. He went further in his note to this section of his speech by asserting, "The Talmud is called the *traditional* or unwritten law of the Jews. It is not their law. The only law is the written one, found in the Books of Moses." This return to biblical Judaism unfettered by rabbinical interpretations was the "purity and spirit" of the reformers. In the same note Harby indicated that his information on the Jerusalem and Babylonian Talmud came not from reading them but from two French writers, Pierre Bayle, author of *Dictionnaire historique et critique*, and Jacob Christian Basnage, who had written *L'histoire et la religion des juifs depuis Jésus Christ jusqu'à présent*. Harby also referred to the "learned and accurate Basnage" in his speech. Both these Christian authors would have given Harby a jaundiced view of the rabbis. This was, by no means, his conviction alone. The attitude may have come in part from Marannos in London. These Jews had lived for long periods of time in Spain and Portugal disguising themselves as Catholics. They knew their religion only from the Bible, and many resented the rabbis when they came into contact with them. Harby's father had come from

London, but this probably would not have shaped the views of all the innovators. A dispute going on in London between Isaac D'Israeli and the authorities of Bevis Marks synagogue at the time most likely had the greatest impact.

If the rabbis were the enemy, who were the heroes? Harby names three in his speech: Moses Mendelssohn, Baruch Spinoza, and Isaac D'Israeli. Mendelssohn, we have seen, sought to adapt to the area in which he lived and to apply his reason to religion, with the result that the rabbis vigorously assailed him. Baruch Spinoza (1632–77), a Sephardic Jew in Amsterdam, had been expelled from his synagogue for denying the immortality of the soul and maintaining that religions were human in origin. Judaism, according to him, was superfluous—reason alone could determine what was good. Isaac D'Israeli (1766–1848), a Sephardic Jew and freethinker in London, disputed in 1817 with his synagogue about a fine. As a result, he withdrew and had his children, including Benjamin, the future prime minister of England, baptized in the church. In 1833, several years after Harby delivered his discourse, D'Israeli wrote a pamphlet in which he claimed that both written and oral laws were of human origin and should be changed as times required. The Talmud, he said, ought to be placed on the shelf as a curiosity.[30] All three of these men had applied reason to religion, and all had suffered attacks from some of the rabbis. Mendelssohn carefully observed the rites of Judaism and did not believe they should be changed, but the other two broke with the faith and attacked it from without. Of these men, Harby said, "Spinoza stands out like some star 'more fiery from night's blackness'—and MENDELSOHN, more recently, redeems his countrymen and human nature—D'Israeli offers his bright and amiable name to cheer the gloomy scene."

Not only do these references indicate that the leaders of the Reformed Society kept up with religious developments in England and Germany, they demonstrate how radical the reformers had become. They wanted nothing of backward, medieval Europe. The elders at Beth Elohim represented this to them, and, very likely, they directed their barbs at them. The reformers lived in free America, the happy land, where they could worship as they pleased, a right that both the South Carolina and United States constitutions guaranteed them.

Although Harby rejected European religious controls, he fully accepted modern rationalism. For him, "Enlightened ideas are the result of freedom." Faith, he believed, resulted from "rational *demonstration*, not blind acquiescence," and "what the oblivious wing of time may have covered with its shade, the power of reason may perceive and bring to day."

Harby also spoke of another Jewish leader, Mordecai Manual Noah, in his discourse, although he did not give his name. After serving as consul in the Barbary States, Noah returned to New

30. Meyer, *Response to Modernity*, 13–16, 62–64, 171–72.

York, where he began to promote a scheme to establish a Jewish colony at Grand Island on the Niagara River. When he first proposed this, he received criticism from Harby, who wrote that Jews should not live separately but join with the rest of American society. After Noah got the grant to Grand Island, he held dedication ceremonies on September 15, 1825, in Saint Paul's Episcopal Church in Buffalo, the only place large enough for the gathering, where he placed a cornerstone engraved with the Sh'ma on the altar. In what his detractors noted to be a contradiction, Noah proclaimed the "declaration of independence" of the restored Jewish nation "in this free and happy republic." He believed that the "Jews have been destined by Providence to remain a distinct people." He also designated himself as the Judge of Israel, and, among other things, ordered a census and registration of all the Jews in the world and urged people to immigrate to "Ararat," the name he chose for his colony.[31] Both the *Southern Patriot* and the *Courier* of Charleston carried news of this on September 30. On October 4, "Lucian" who, no doubt, was Isaac Harby, ridiculed Noah's actions in the *Courier* as "more than an act of folly; it is an act of insanity." Lucian also said that he had always disputed the propriety of locating a colony of Jews anywhere in the United States where they would be distinguished by different religious habits and customs. This would result in the perpetuation of distinctions and prejudices when they ought to be extinguished. Another letter printed in the *Literary Chronicle and Weekly Review* of London on November 12 has also been attributed to Harby. Although the London editor stated that it came from the Charleston *Courier*, it has not been found there. Harby apparently sent it directly to the editor. In this he was even more scornful of the actions of Noah. He accused him of blasphemy, especially for putting the cornerstone with the Sh'ma on the altar. He said that the proclamation "never could have been written by any Hebrew who respects his religion." Noah, in turn, charged that Harby had little knowledge of the Jewish religion.[32] A month later, when Harby delivered his discourse, he said that America was the promised land and that the Jews were not being invited to a stony land, by which he meant Palestine, nor to a marshy island, by which he meant Grand Island, but they should join the "happy family" of Americans.

In his review of the discourse by Harby and the Constitution of the Reformed Society in the *North American Review*, Samuel Gilman reported, "It has, until lately, been supposed, that the minds of Israelites were so wedded to their religious peculiarities, as to be impenetrable to the spirit of innovation." Who would have expected that there were men in the denomination who could surmount "the proverbial prejudices of their race" and imbibe in

31. Noah, "Ararat Address," 230–52.

32. Sarna, *Jacksonian Jew*, 61–75; *Southern Patriot*, Feb. 3, 1820, Sept. 30, 1825; *Courier*, Sept. 30, Oct. 4, 1825; *Literary Chronicle and Weekly Review* (London), Nov. 12, 1825.

the "liberal spirit of the age." Gilman states that Harby "is a firm 'Jew inwardly,' but is willing to accommodate the 'Jew outwardly' to the conciliatory, compensating, and sacrificing spirit of the age." Gilman concluded that "we cannot but be persuaded, that the spirit of the age, like the voice of Jehovah, will gently and irresistibly convert the present synagogue, with its obsolete ceremonial, its unintelligible language, and its alleged unimpressive influences, into a more rational sanctuary, to which the understandings of ten thousands of votaries shall eagerly resort to be strengthened and enlightened, and their hearts to be warmed, consoled and purified."[33] This article, no doubt, served more than anything else to bring the movement to the approving attention of Protestants, who saw the Jews following the route they had taken three centuries before in their reformation.

Harby apparently sent copies of his discourse to many people. Among those who responded were Edward Livingston, Edward Rutledge, and Thomas Jefferson. Livingston thanked Harby for sending the discourse and reported finding "the most liberal sentiment" in the address. Edward Rutledge pointed out that "reformation in church or state is always attended with difficulties, but the success which has crowned the boldest leaders in both these departments warrant you to proceed." Thomas Jefferson thanked Harby for a copy of the speech and stated, "Nothing is wiser than that all our institutions should keep pace with the advance of time and be improved with the improvement of the human mind." Harby immediately responded to Jefferson's reply that "it is a reward" that the effort to improve his "coreligionaires" had "met the approbation of the good and great."[34]

Subsequent Addresses

The texts of the speeches for the next two anniversary addresses have survived. In these can be seen the reiteration of previous topics but also the expression of a new idea, the need for rites and ceremonies to be useful.[35]

Abraham Moïse delivered the oration on the second anniversary and Isaac N. Cardozo on the third. Neither gave a speech as long or as stirring as Harby's. Moïse began his talk by stating that their ancestors had proudly boasted that they began their rites and ceremonies with songs accompanied by stringed instruments. Apparently choral music accompanied by instrumental music preceded his speech. The group had come together to examine the stages of progress made in the previous year in the "holy work of reformation" and to incite future acts of piety and usefulness. Ap-

33. Gilman's review, "Harby's Discourse on the Jewish Synagogue," 67–79.

34. Livingston to Harby, Dec. 25, 1825, Rutledge to Harby, Mar. 17, 1827, Jefferson to Harby, Jan. 6, 1826, Harby to Jefferson, Jan. 14, 1826, in Moïse, *Biography of Isaac Harby*, 93–97.

35. Meyer, *Response to Modernity*, 231, calls this "very American"; however, Jeremy Bentham's utilitarianism had been around for quite some time.

parently some of the members had begun to waver, because Moïse stated that daily observation showed that some men would not expose themselves to persecution and hatred unless urged by some powerful motive. Then, like his predecessor, Moïse compared the Reform movement to the Christian Reformation, stating that it had been perhaps the greatest era in modern times, which resulted in the gradual conversion of millions of people. He claimed that it had been a moral necessity that compelled the Reformed Israelites to throw off the "yoke of religious bondage" and free themselves from "bigotry and priestcraft." The Jews, he claimed, had lost their conception of God by blindly following the "erroneous doctrines of the Rabbins." The Reformed Society had rescued the dying embers of Judaism, but for this they had gained little glory. This would come, however, when their principles took hold throughout the United Sates. "We claim, then, to be the advocates of a system of rational religion; of substance, not form." The antiquity of rites and ceremonies did not justify them, only their "general utility, the peculiar applicability to the age and country in which we live, to the feeling, sentiments and opinions of Americans."[36]

When his turn came to take the podium on the third anniversary, Isaac Cardozo reaffirmed the necessity of the reforms they had championed. He was, however, somewhat kinder to the rabbis, stating that their interpolations had no support in reason and would fall of themselves. Reforms, on the other hand, prospered least at the place of origin, and the reformer's path was one of more labor than profit. The person not only had to profess his beliefs but to practice them. He was encouraging about progress outside of Charleston. He stated that "the benefits of our institution have . . . been partially felt already abroad." He credited the society for having influenced congregations in the North to have begun readings in English and the Jews in Liverpool to have begun sermons in the vernacular. He appears to be correct in this.[37] Also, the organization had excited attention in Germany, where its changes had been generally praised and its objectives recommended as deserving of all communities of Israelites. Indeed, vowed Cardozo, all religions "under our happy form of government" should be based on rationalism and principles of equality.[38]

OFFICERS OF THE
REFORMED SOCIETY OF ISRAELITES

1825

Aaron Phillips, president
Michael Lazarus, vice president
Morris Goldsmith, secretary
Isaac Mordecai, treasurer

1826

Michael Lazarus, president
Isaac Harby, vice president
Henry M. Hyams, secretary
Isaac Mordecai, treasurer

36. Moïse, "An Address Delivered before the Reformed Society," 122–27.

37. Marcus, *United States Jewry*, 632.

38. Cardozo, *A Discourse Delivered in Charleston Before the Reformed Society*, 128–40.

1827
- Isaac Harby, president
- Abraham Moïse, vice president
- Henry M. Hyams, secretary
- Isaac Mordecai, treasurer

1828
- Abraham Moïse, president
- Isaac N. Cardozo, vice president
- Philip Phillips, secretary
- Joseph Phillips, treasurer

1829
- Abraham Moïse, president
- Isaac N. Cardozo, vice president
- Thomas W. Mordecai, secretary and treasurer

1830
- Abraham Moïse, president
- Isaac N. Cardozo, vice president
- Thomas W. Mordecai, secretary and treasurer

1831
- Abraham Moïse, president
- Isaac N. Cardozo, vice president
- Thomas W. Mordecai, secretary and treasurer

1832
- Abraham Moïse, president
- Isaac N. Cardozo, vice president
- Thomas W. Mordecai, secretary and treasurer

1833–1837?
- Abraham Moïse, president
- Thomas W. Mordecai, secretary and treasurer[39]

39. *Courier*, Nov. 22, 1825, Nov. 22, 1827, Nov. 26, 1828, Nov. 23, 1829, Nov. 24, 1830, Nov. 23, 1831, Nov. 23, 1832; *Southern Patriot*, Nov. 22, 1826; Charleston directory, 1835–36, 1837–38.

Religious Services

At some point, probably in 1825, the members of the Reformed Society began to hold their own religious services and thus became a congregation. According to Maurice Mayer, who served as rabbi at Beth Elohim in the 1850s and who knew some of the people involved in the society, they had a choir, hymns, instrumental music, and the men did not cover their heads.[40] In order to have a permanent place of worship, they appealed to the general public for donations to build a synagogue. They placed notices in the Charleston newspapers during 1826 stating that they had been in operation for nearly two years and donations would be thankfully received. They also set forth four objectives of the organization, these being: (1) to have a considerable portion of the prayers in English, (2) to discontinue observing ceremonies "as partake strongly of bigotry: as owe their origin only to *Rabbinical* institutions," (3) to abolish superfluous prayers, and (4) to read the Pentateuch in Hebrew and English and to have an English discourse. A list of the officers appeared at the end of the announcement; however, the names of the president Aaron Phillips and E. P. Cohen disappeared from the list before the end of October.[41] The group did not raise much money and never constructed a new synagogue. Meanwhile, they met at Seyle's Masonic Hall on Meeting Street.

40. Mayer, "Geschichte, " 172.

41. Charleston *Mercury*, Sept. 2, 1826. The announcement appeared for four months.

For services, they had handwritten copies of their liturgy. At least two have survived; one belonged to Isaac Harby, the other to David N. Carvalho. Carvalho's copy included Hebrew but Harby's did not. Since Carvalho served as the reader of the group and few other people knew Hebrew, the rest did not need it. According to Michael Meyer, "The society's manuscript prayerbook represents the first radical liturgy produced by the Reform movement anywhere, preceding by twenty years the 1845 prayerbook of the Berlin Reform Congregation."[42] Carvalho, Moïse, and Harby have been credited with writing it. In 1830 the society published the prayerbook, though without Hebrew, apparently because no printer in Charleston had the capability of setting the type.[43] Most of the prayerbook was adopted from the Portuguese ritual, but some parts were new, such as the articles of faith, the marriage ceremony, the confirmation ceremony, the service for circumcision, and the ceremony for naming a daughter. At the end, the book contained twenty-eight hymns, all except one being adapted from Christian songs. The preface of the prayerbook stated that the organization contemplated in the future presenting "the Israelites of the United States" an enlarged edition with services for all the holidays and selections from the Hebrew, which had "been unavoidably omitted in the present work." The Sabbath service fulfilled the demands of the Reformed Society. It was much shorter than the older form of worship, taking only eleven pages, and was mostly in English. That which was read in Hebrew was repeated in English. Any person, Jewish or not, could have followed the service. Furthermore, the sermon based on the reading of the Torah was designed to enlighten and guide all in the congregation. Such alterations were anathema to those who believed that nothing should or could be changed.

THE SERVICE ON SABBATH MORNING

Hymn by the Choir in English
Prayer by the Officiating Minister in English
Hymn by the Choir in English
Reading of the 33rd Psalm by the Minister First in Hebrew and Then in English with Responses by the Congregation
Reading of the Sanctification of the Sabbath and the Sh'ma in English by the Minister With Responses by the Congregation
Prayer for the Government in English
Hymn by the Choir in English
Reading of the *Parasa* or portion of the *Torah* by the Minister
Sermon by the Minister in English
Hymn in English
Concluding Prayer in English[44]

42. Meyer, *Response to Modernity*, 231.

43. *The Sabbath Service.* Elzas found two extant copies of this work and reprinted it in New York in 1916. The manuscript by David Nunes Carvalho can be found in the American Jewish Archives. The other was published by Edward L. Cohn as *The Isaac Harby Prayerbook*.

44. This order of service is derived from the prayerbook, Levin's "The Jewish Congregation of Charleston," 438, and Mayer, "Geschichte," 172.

"The most peculiar part of their ritual" was the Ten Articles of Faith, which appeared at the front of the prayerbook. The Reformed Society, however, did "not presume to restrict the faith or conscience of any man." Instead, each person could "believe or reject what his heart and understanding . . . may rationally dictate to be believed or rejected." Levin rightly claimed that these "emanated from *enlarged liberal*, and *enlightened* views" and differed from the creed of Maimonides.[45] Although Judaism had no official dogma, the Thirteen Articles of Faith of Maimonides essentially served that purpose. The two sets of beliefs did differ radically on several points: the divine revelation of the scriptures, the oral law, the concept of rewards and punishments, the promise of a Messiah, and the resurrection of the dead. The compilers of the prayerbook believed the time had arrived to "break in pieces the sceptre of Rabbinical power."[46]

CREED USED BY BETH ELOHIM

Q. What are the fundamental Elements which form the basis of the Jewish faith?
A. The thirteen following:
1. *The existence of God.*—We believe that God exists, who created and sustains the universe.
2. *His unity.*—We believe that God is ONE, and only one, without a second that can in any manner be compared to, or associated with him.
3. *His incorporeality.*—We believe that he is incorporeal—he hath no material figure, neither is he a body. We cannot by any comparison estimate his holiness.
4. *His eternity.*—We believe that he is eternal, without beginning and without end.
5. *His direct superintendence.*—We believe the blessed God reigns *alone* over the universe, and superintends all his creatures without the intermediation of any other power; it is therefore proper to pray to him alone and to no other.
6. *His providence.*—We believe he superintends the actions of mankind, both generally and particularly.
7. *The truth of prophecy.*—We believe that the Lord has communicated his prophetic spirit to those whom he hath chosen, and discovered his mysteries to them.
8. *The prophecy of Moses.*—We believe that our legislator Moses was the prince of prophets, and that none have appeared like unto him.
9. *The delivery of the Law.*—We believe that the law now in our possession was delivered to Moses by God on Mount Sinai.
10. *The permanence of the Law.*—We believe that the law will ever remain permanent as it is, without change or alteration.
11. *Rewards and punishments.*—We believe that God will reward those who fulfil the law, and punish those who transgress it.
12. *The Coming of the Messiah.*—We believe that the Redeemer will come at the time appointed, which is known to

45. Levin, "The Jewish Congregation of Charleston, " 438.

46. In preface of prayerbook, in Elzas, *The Sabbath Service*, 6.

God alone; who will gather the dispersed of Israel, and restore the government up to the house of David.

13. *Resurrection of the dead.*—We believe that those who sleep in the dust will awake, and all who have died will return to life.[47]

ARTICLES OF FAITH OF
REFORMED SOCIETY OF ISRAELITES

I. I believe with a perfect faith, that God Almighty (blessed be his name!) is the Creator and Governor of all creation; and that he alone has made, does make, and will make all things.

II. I believe with a perfect faith, that the Creator, (blessed be his name!) is the only ONE IN UNITY; to which there is no resemblance; and that he alone has been, is, and will be God.

III. I believe with a perfect faith, that the Creator (blessed be his name!) is not corporeal, nor to be comprehended by any understanding capable of comprehending only what is corporeal; and that there is nothing like him in the universe.

IV. I believe with a perfect faith, that the Creator (blessed be his name!) is the only true object of adoration, and that no other being whatsoever ought to be worshipped.

V. I believe with a perfect faith, that the soul of man is breathed into him by God, and is therefore immortal.

VI. I believe with a perfect faith, that the Creator (blessed be his name!) knows all things, and that he will reward those who observe his commands, and punish those who transgress them.

VII. I believe with a perfect faith, that the laws of God, as delivered by Moses in the ten commandments, are the only true foundations of piety towards the Almighty and of morality among men.

VIII. I believe with a perfect faith, that morality is essentially connected with religion, and that good faith towards all mankind, is among the most acceptable offerings to the Deity.

IX. I believe with a perfect faith, that the love of God is the highest duty of his creatures, and that the pure and upright heart is the chosen temple of Jehovah.

X. I believe with a perfect faith, that the Creator (blessed be his name!) is the only true Redeemer of all his children, and that he will spread the worship of his name over the whole earth.[48]

Although the articles of faith were supposedly optional, they were required in the confirmation ceremony. In this ritual a boy born of Jewish parents who was at least thirteen years of age could on any Sabbath make a declaration that he wanted to announce his belief in the Jewish faith. He would go up to the minister's desk, make his declaration "according to the faith and customs of the Reformed Society of Israelites, in whose temple of worship I now stand." The minister would question him if he did this on his free will. When he responded in the affirmative, the minister would ask him to repeat the articles of faith.[49]

47. Appendix 3 of *The State ex rel. A. Ottolengui*, 63–64.

48. Elzas, *The Sabbath Service*, pp. 6–7.

49. Marcus, *United States Jewry*, 628, says that this is no more than an Americanized bar mitzvah.

Decline

The act of confirmation may never have been performed; not long after the prayerbook appeared, the Reformed Society faced hard times. According to Levin, the organization became extinct after a few sickly years.[50] Levin's assessment is somewhat harsh but is basically true. After an enthusiastic beginning by the reformers, who thought they would rock the Jewish world as Luther did the Christians, the movement seems to have faltered. The list of officers indicates, at best, that few wanted to serve and, at worst, that not many were available. No new name appeared between 1828 and 1832. Abraham Moïse kept records on members at the end of the constitution. He indicated that nine had died, fifteen resigned, and one, Philip Benjamin, had been expelled. The reason for the expulsion of Philip Benjamin, the father of Judah Benjamin, is unknown. After this, he apparently took no part in religious affairs.[51] Maurice Mayer gives as one of the reasons for the decline of the movement circumstances that he considered were not appropriate for public disclosure. The expulsion of Benjamin may be involved here.[52] Moïse made his notations regarding the members of the society in 1837 or later, as can be determined by those he indicated as being dead. He was not aware of the deaths of some former members because they had died away from Charleston—Samuel Hyams in Louisiana and Jacob Moïse in Georgia. A number of others about whom little is known probably had moved away as well. The plight of the society grew so bad that the remaining members of the society held a special meeting on May 2, 1833. At that time, they abandoned their dream of building a new synagogue in Charleston and passed a resolution to return the money with interest that had been donated as a result of their fund drive almost five years before.[53] (See Table 22.)

Elzas stated that they apparently wound up their affairs at this meeting. "Thus ended the first great struggle for reform among the Jews of America."[54] However, the group never surrendered its charter, and the city directory for 1835–36 lists it among organizations in Charleston, with Abraham Moïse as president and Thomas Mordecai as secretary. Then the directory for 1837–38 in its "Index to the Different Societies in Charleston" lists the Reformed Society of Israelites still in existence with the same officers. The directory for 1837–38 gives the date of establishment as 1832. The group could have existed as a society, but not as a congregation. On

50. Levin, "The Jewish Congregation of Charleston," 439.

51. He died in Charleston in 1853, by which time his son was already prominent in Louisiana politics. The Death Records of Charleston say that he was buried in the Coming Street Cemetery, but no tombstone was erected for him. At the time he lived on Sans Souci Street in the Charleston Neck area. No will or probate inventory exists for him.

52. Mayer, "Geschichte," 173; Evans, *Judah P. Benjamin*, 10, says that Benjamin was expelled for keeping his shop open on the Sabbath but offers nothing to substantiate this assertion.

53. *Courier*, Sept. 11, 1833.

54. Elzas, *The Reformed Society*, 26, 27.

Table 22
Information on Reformed Society Members Recorded by Abraham Moïse

Name	*Note*	*Died*	*Place Died*
Abrahams, Levy J.	Dead	1829	
Benjamin, Philip	Expelled	1853	Charleston
Cardozo, Isaac N.*	Resigned	1855	Charleston
Carvalho, David Nunes		1860	Baltimore
Cohen, Esdaile P.	Resigned	1856	Baltimore
Cohen, Jacob*		1871	Charleston
Goldsmith, Henry	Resigned	1861	Charleston
Goldsmith, Joseph H.	Resigned	1853	Charleston
Goldsmith, Morris	Resigned	1861	Charleston
Harby, Henry Jefferson*		1851	Charleston
Harby, Isaac	Dead	1828	New York
Harby, Levy			
Harris, Jacob	Dead	1837	Charleston
Hertz, Jacob E.*	Resigned	1846	Charleston
Hyams, Henry		1852	New Orleans
Hyams, Moses Kosciusko	Dead	1836	Pointe Coupée, La.
Hyams, Samuel		1843	Natchitoches, La.
Jacobs, Myer*	Resigned	1861	Charleston
Labatt, Abraham Cohen		1899	Galveston
Lazarus, Jacob	Dead	1834	New York
Lazarus, Michael*	Resigned	1862	Sumter, S.C.
Levy, Bernard*	Resigned	1869	Charleston

the other hand, the compilers could have been using old information. The organization probably ceased to exist by 1835 or 1836, as Abraham Moïse rejoined Beth Elohim no later than February 23, 1836, when he served on a committee with Jacob DeLaMotta, Abraham Tobias, and M. C. Mordecai that drew up the constitution that the congregation approved that year.[55]

55. Preamble, *New Constitution of Beth Elohim*. The preface states that these new laws were "finally adopted and ratified."

The Reformed Society of Israelites showed the extent that the Jews of Charleston, especially those born in the city, felt a part of the American dream. Having little or no training in Hebrew, they found the religious services tedious and without meaning. A number of them were well educated and knew the history not only of their religious group but of the Christians as well. They were aware of the reform developments in Europe. They drank deeply of the intoxicating ideas of the Enlightenment and Jeffersonian democracy. They saw

Table 22
(Continued)

Name	*Note*	*Died*	*Place Died*
Levy, David Cardozo*		1877	Jefferson, N.H.
Levy, Emanuel*	Resigned	1865	
Levy, Hayman		1865	
Levy, Lyon	Resigned	1835	Charleston
Levy, Solomon	Resigned	1839	New York
Lyon, George*			
Moïse, Abraham*		1869	Sumter, S.C.
Moïse, Isaac		1857	Charleston
Moïse, Jacob		1837	Sand Hills, Ga.
Moïse, Theodore Sydney		1885	Natchitoches, La.
Mordecai, Isaac D.*	Resigned	1864	
Mordecai, Thomas Whitlock*	Resigned	1865	
Moses, Isaac Clifton	Dead	1834	Connecticut
Moses, Jacob			
Phillips, Aaron	Dead	1834	Charleston
Phillips, Philip		1884	Washington, D.C.
Sampson, Samuel	Dead	1827	Charleston
Seixas, Abraham	Dead	1834	Charleston
Simon, Moses	Resigned		
Soria, Isaac			
Tobias, Isaac		1860	

*Rejoined Beth Elohim by 1840 and proponent of reform
Sources: Elzas, *The Reformed Society;* Cash Books of Beth Elohim; see also the appendix. Moise did not include Joseph Phillips, who was treasurer in 1828.

themselves as leaders and sought to change their religion, as Luther had done his. But the petition submitted to the *adjunta* did not have the electric effect of Luther's theses. Discontent flared for several years and then smoldered for a few more. The older generation felt comfortable with the ways they had known in another place. As Edward Rutledge pointed out to Harby, reformation is difficult. Few are willing to make a dramatic break with the past and alienate their elders. Harby indicated that "the Jews born in Carolina are mostly of our way of thinking on the subject of worship, and act from a tender regard for the opinions and feelings of their parents, in not joining the society."[56] In time, this conservatism would change.

56. Harby to Gilman, in Gilman, "Harby's Discourse," 74.

CHAPTER 6

The Family

"This is the happy land."
—Myer Moses, 1806[1]

Much of Jewish and southern life centered on the family. Thus Jews in Charleston felt much pressure to marry and raise children. Unfortunately, people seldom record information on the common aspects of life. On the other hand, a considerable amount of data can be derived from official records. This chapter uses the information that is available to gain some idea of the life of the Jewish family in colonial and antebellum Charleston.

Family Names

Charleston had many Jewish families before the Civil War. A few surnames appear fairly often: Cohen (7.65 percent of all Jews in the city had this name), Levy (5.48 percent), Solomon/s (2.91 percent), Hart (2.62 percent), Abrams/Abrahams (2.34 percent), Hyams (2.17 percent), Moïse (2.11 percent), Nathans (2.05 percent), Mordecai (1.66 percent), Lopez (1.43 percent), Canter/Cantor (1.14 percent).[2] These names represent about one-third of the Jews of Charleston. Many surnames can be easily recognized as Spanish and Portuguese: Avila, Cardozo, Carvalho, DaCosta, DaVega, DeLaMotta, Ricardo, and Rodrigues. Germanic names include Belitizer, Berlin, Dessau, Falk, Goldstein, Pearlstein, and Wesel. Some, however, cannot be easily identified as to place of origin. Included among these are Cohen, Israel, Jacobs, Levy, and Moses. Other family names could be mistaken as British, such as Alexander, Barrett, Bush, Davis, Green, Harris, Jones, and Phillips.

Marriage

Just how Jewish men and women began to form families in Charleston and

1. Moses, *An Oration.*

2. This analysis is based on the author's research on family names of all male Jews believed to have resided in Charleston by 1861.

how marriages were arranged is unknown, but there seems to have been considerable social interaction between the two sexes. Social and religious events would have brought them together on many occasions. For the most part, marriages in Charleston took place between people whose families knew one another. Sometimes people from different cities married. This could have resulted when people from different cities visited one another, or when a relative or friend took an active role in arranging the unions. A good example of a person who went to another city, met someone there, fell in love, and married was Jacob Levy, who wed Fanny Yates in Liverpool while on a trip to Europe.[3] Some, though, married without parental approval, as a 1851 letter from Leopold Weiskopf to his brother indicates.[4]

Before a marriage took place, the bridegroom negotiated a marriage settlement with the bride's family or guardians setting forth his agreement to respect and support her and recording the financial settlement being made by both families. The state required marriage settlements, which were supposed to be recorded with the secretary of state if they were to be considered valid.[5] Consequently, many marriage settlements of Jewish couples can be found in the South Carolina Archives. For example, when Abraham M. Seixas married Ritcey Hart, daughter of Joshua Hart, in 1777, he agreed to provide her with £3,500, two slaves, and several articles of silver and furniture. Philip Minis and Mordecai Sheftall served as trustees. The trustees had the responsibility of looking after the welfare of the wife and making sure that the husband lived up to his obligations, as the wife had very few legal rights after marriage.[6] The groom and the trustees negotiated these agreements. Some settlements were in Hebrew but included an English translation. Such was the case when Abraham Jacobs, son of Raphael Jacobs, agreed to marry Shankey Hart, another daughter of Joshua Hart. Each family promised to provide £100, and Jacobs pledged to maintain Miss Hart according to Jewish law.[7] When Joseph DaCosta married Rebecca DePass, the bride's family provided a slave girl, clothes worth £200, and the groom provided £3,000.[8] When Jacob Levy married Fanny Yates, he provided her with $10,000.[9] These agreements were typical.

The brides usually had no official role in the arrangements; however, a single woman of age or a widow could control her own affairs. Thus Catharine Jacobs, a widow and shopkeeper, made a marriage settlement with her future husband Solomon Hyams in 1811. Mrs. Jacobs already owned six slaves and thirty-eight shares in the Planters and

3. Yates, Samuel, and Lazarus Families, manuscript, American Jewish Archives.

4. Leopold Weiskopf to Jacob Weiskopf, Charleston, S.C. Feb. 23, 1851, American Jewish Archives.

5. *Statutes*, 4: 565; 6: 213.

6. MS1.43.

7. MS1.348.

8. MS1.272.

9. Premarital and postnuptial agreements are in the Beth Elohim Archives.

Mechanics Bank, stock in her dry goods store, and a considerable amount of household furniture such as eighteen chairs, ten "elegant pictures," wearing apparel, jewelry, three beds, and three carpets. She assigned her property over to Myer Moses, the trustee, with the understanding she would continue to manage it through him.[10]

The wedding ceremonies usually came a few weeks after representatives from each family concluded the marriage settlements. For example, the contract between Abraham DaCosta and Rebecca Pimiento stated that he would "take to wife the said Rebecca Pemento according to the rites and ceremonies of the Jews" within three months.[11] Most marriages occurred on Wednesday evening. Ancient Jewish practice had called for weddings to take place on that day for virgins and on Thursdays for widows. Many also considered Wednesday to be a lucky day. Only occasionally did weddings take place on other nights such as Sunday. On rare instances widows married on Wednesday, as did Abigail Sampson, widow of Joseph Sampson, in 1834; but more often they wed on Thursday evenings, as did Mrs. Esther Moïse to Hyam Cohen in 1827. The orthodox congregations in the 1840s and 1850s were more likely than the reform congregation to choose Sunday or Tuesday for weddings. Double and triple weddings took place from time to time. In December 1841 Gustavus Poznanski performed weddings for Miriam, Eliza, and Caroline Woolf on the same day, and a week later for Mary Ann and Caroline Suares at the same time.[12]

The Beth Elohim constitutions of 1820 and 1836 showed considerable concern for marriages. They provided that normally only the *hazan* could perform weddings for a fee—in 1820, $5 and in 1836, $10—although exceptions could be made by the president and board of the synagogue.[13] Although great animosity existed in Charleston during the 1840s and 1850s because the city had two Jewish congregations with greatly opposed practices, a number of marriages took place between the two. These presented a problem for the fathers of the brides who, according to the rules of Beth Elohim, had to secure permission from the board and employ the *hazan* for the services. So many people requested exceptions that the board finally ruled that when they granted wavers, the father still had to pay the *hazan* and the *shamass* their usual fees.[14]

Anyone who married contrary to Jewish law could never be recognized as a member of Beth Elohim and could not be buried in the community cemetery. Their children fell under the same ban. Despite this, marriages outside the faith happened from time to time, but the numbers are difficult to determine. Examples would be Sarah DaCosta, daugh-

10. MS6.41–46.

11. MR2M.222.

12. Elzas, *Jewish Marriage Notices*, 20.

13. Rule 19 of the 1820 constitution and article 26 of the 1836 constitution.

14. Minute Book of Beth Elohim, Sept. 24, 1848.

ter of Isaac DaCosta, the first *hazan* of Beth Elohim, who married Davis Mazes (or Maysor), who reportedly came from France with Lafayette. She, however, raised their daughter in her faith. This, no doubt was made easier by the fact that the mother, after the death of her first husband, married a Jew.[15] Another example was Abraham Alexander, the second *hazan*, who married Ann Sarah Huguenin Irby. Of French Huguenot descent, she had previously married, as had Alexander. According to family tradition, the two met during the bombardment of Charleston in the Revolution, when she fainted and he came to her rescue. She enthusiastically adopted Judaism and lived with her husband's son after the death of Abraham Alexander in 1816. In her will, probated in 1835, she asked to be buried in the Jewish cemetery; however, congregation leaders denied her request. Rule 23 of the 1820 constitution forbade accepting proselytes unless the person produced credentials from another congregation where there was a rabbi and a consistory. Ann Alexander's place of burial is unknown. Two of her stepsons also married outside the faith.[16] Members of the DeLyon, Lopez, Moïse, Harby, and Tobias families also married non-Jews. Indeed, the Lopez Cemetery came about because members of that family could not be buried in the regular cemetery. This was despite the fact that David Lopez had built the present structure that houses Beth Elohim. He placed his family's plot next to the Coming Street Cemetery. Eventually, the congregation tore down the wall between the two and incorporated the Lopez Cemetery into the older Coming Street Cemetery.[17] Sephardic Jews appear to have married outside the faith more readily than Ashkenazic ones, and most of the old Sephardic names have disappeared from the city. Had the regulations of Beth Elohim been less stringent on converts and had persons not been forced to leave the synagogue when marrying outside the faith, the numbers lost might have been less.

Marriages between Sephardic and Ashkenazic Jews are also hard to ascertain because many family names could belong to either group. The marriage between Abraham Mendes Seixas and Ritcey Hart could have been between the two groups since the family name of Hart is probably Ashkenazic. Unfortunately, the origin of the Hart family is unknown, and that name could have been adopted by Sephardic people.[18] Also, in such an instance intermarriage could have taken place earlier, and only one person in the past could have been Ashkenazic. Other notices are equally confusing, although the marriage between Abraham DePass and Rachel Derkheim in 1798 does represent a union of the two elements.[19] Certainly tensions existed between the groups, but similar tensions can be found

15. MS2.48; Rezneck, *Unrecognized Patriots*, 38.

16. Stern, *First Jewish Families of America*, 8; W40.354; Alexander, *Notes on the Alexander Family*, 16–18; Elzas, *Jews of South Carolina*, 43–44.

17. Elzas, *Old Jewish Cemeteries*, 99.

18. Elzas, *Jewish Marriage Notices*, 5.

19. Ibid., 7.

among people with other national backgrounds.

People who wanted to marry according to Jewish rites applied to the board of trustees, making the "customary application." "Strangers" or nonmembers had to pay the "customary fees" before being allowed to wed.[20] Whatever the background of the couples, most weddings took place in the synagogue according to the Sephardic practice. The *shamass* had the right, for a fee, to deliver the invitations and erect the *huppah,* or canopy.[21] In 1841 the board resolved that the Standing Committee of Ladies should be requested to provide a canopy and a covering of white for the reading desk at the expense of the congregation.[22] They soon fulfilled the request. Part of the wedding ceremony can be seen in the 1779 wedding of Gershon Cohen and Rebecca Sarzedas. The groom asked Rebecca to be his wife according to the Laws of Moses and promised, "I will endeavour to maintain you in the respectable manner, as is the duty incumbent on a *Yehuda* [Jew] to maintain and respect his lawful wife. I will also give you a dower of two hundred silverlings . . . according to the Laws of Moses, your clothing, food, pocket money & shall live united to you as is the custom of the world." She then consented to become his wife. The groom then gave the bride £750 in addition to the 200 silver coins, making a total of £1,110, and bound himself and his heirs to the marriage contract.[23]

Although the congregation required Jewish weddings to be performed by the *hazan*, Dr. Benjamin A. Rodrigues conducted a wedding ceremony for Esther Clara Rodrigues Monsanto and Joseph Eugene Esdra on April 24, 1839.[24] Within a week the leaders of the synagogue ordered Rodrigues to appear before them. They charged him with violating rule 26 of the 1836 constitution. This regulation stated that, under normal circumstances, no one could perform marriages except for the *hazan*. Even in exceptional cases, as when the *hazan* was ill or absent from the city, application had to be made to the board in advance. Anyone who transgressed this law would be fined $50 and denied his rights and privileges until that amount was paid. The board could not charge Esdra with marrying contrary to the rules of the congregation because he had not joined the synagogue. When Rodrigues appeared, he said he had not violated the constitution because the groom did not belong to the congregation and the ceremony differed from what was laid down in Jewish law. The board, however, did not accept his explanation and fined him $50 and denied him any privileges of the synagogue

20. Examples are Myer Jacobs, who applied for his daughter to marry I. Cohen of Augusta; Elias Abrahams for his daughter to marry Joseph M. Marks; Isaac Segar, "stranger," to marry Miss DeHaan. Minute Book of Beth Elohim.

21. Rule 19, 1820 constitution; article 26, 1836 constitution.

22. Minute Book of Beth Elohim, Aug. 8, 1841.

23. Revolutionary War Pension Application R2108 of Rebecca Cohen, Pension Applications, National Archives.

24. Elzas, *Jewish Marriage Notices*, 18.

until that amount was paid.[25] Rodrigues apparently paid the fine because soon after that he was participating in congregational affairs.

A study of the ages at which people married indicates that the Jewish females who were born and who died in the city were on average twenty-one years of age at the time of their marriage, whereas the men were twenty-nine. The youngest bride was fifteen and the oldest forty-nine at the time of the first marriage. The youngest groom was eighteen and the oldest forty-six. Figures differ little for those born outside Charleston or for whom the place of birth is unknown and who died in the city. The average age for these women at the first marriage was twenty, and the men, thirty-one. The men, in short, tended to be eight to ten years older than their wives.

Not everyone married, of course. Many families had children who never found a spouse or chose to marry. Some, apparently, simply died young, before having had the chance to marry. On the other hand, 10 percent of the females who reached the age of thirty never married. A larger number of men over thirty never married, 13 percent for those who were born and who died in Charleston and 19 percent for those who died in the city but were born elsewhere. The single men and women usually can be found living with relatives, although men sometimes lived in boarding houses, and some single males and females owned or rented their homes. One of the people who did not marry was Grace Peixotto (b. St. Thomas, 1817), the daughter of Solomon Cohen Peixotto, who served as the *hazan* of Beth Elohim for some time, and Rachel Suares Peixotto. According to F. C. Adams, an abolitionist who wrote a scandalous account of Charleston in 1855, she was "a notorious woman, who has kept the worst kind of brothel for years, where harlots of all shades and importations break the quietitude of night with their polluted songs." According to him, she "remained unmolested in her trade of demoralization" and thus "amassed a fortune," which she openly displayed. She made "fine fun" for the "officials and gallants" of the city. Adams's account states that on July 31, 1852, "this mother of crime" appeared before the city council and asked them to pave the lot in front of her brick house on Beresford Street.[26] The brick building still stands, and Grace Peixotto appears in the city directories of 1841, 1855, 1859, and in the Charleston census of 1861. In 1850 she purchased three slaves named Belinda, Judy, and Joe.[27] For many years Beresford Street was noted as the red light district, so much so that after World War II the city changed the name to Fulton in an attempt to alter its image.[28]

25. Minute Book of Beth Elohim, April 30, May 12, 22, 1839. The Esdra and Rodrigues families came from Bordeaux and appear to have been related. In the 1850s Esdra was the secretary of Beth Elohim.

26. Adams, *Manuel Pereira*, 32.

27. MR6C.109.

28. Leland, "Fulton St. House"; Fraser, *Charleston! Charleston!*, 235.

Dwellings

Generally the Jewish families of Charleston lived over shops or other businesses. Some had separate dwelling houses, but this was not the usual case in Charleston. The number of people in a household is given in the censuses; however, not until 1850 did a headcount give the names of all residents at an address. That enumeration shows that a number of households had quite a mixture of people living in them. In addition to the family, this could include older and younger relatives, apparently nonrelated Jews, and others. For example, the household of Henry J. Harby included him, his wife, five children, plus his mother, one of his sisters, and a thirteen-year-old relative by the name of Levy C. Harby, Jr. Martha DeLange had her three children and Hannah Solomons, who is otherwise unknown, in her home. David Seixas had his wife and two children plus Mathias Seixas, who cannot be otherwise identified, Isaac Cardozo, his cousin, and Rachel Seixas, his widowed mother, in his house. Gustavus Poznanski had his wife and four children plus Rachel Barrett, his mother-in-law, and Solomon Barrett, his wife's brother, living with him. The household of Abraham Ottolengui held three generations. In addition to him and his wife and his unmarried children, his son Jacob, his wife, and their sons lived at the same address. The home of Sarah A. Motta contained an even more varied group of people. She operated a boarding house where the following lived: Abraham Lipman, M. Winstock, Solomon Beretz, Mordecai Davis, I. Jones, D. Jacobs, S. Samuel, and R. Solomons. Occasionally Jews lived in non-Jewish households and gentiles in Jewish homes. Thus, Moses Levy, a tavern keeper, and his wife, Eliza, had six people living with them: Maria Prentice who was born in New York, James Brown and Angelica Brown who were born in Washington, D.C., John Riley who was born in Ireland, Maurice [Morris] Levin, a Jew who was born in London, and James Tiplady who was born in Scotland. Apparently they took in roomers, though their place is not listed as a boarding house.

Documents such as marriage settlements, wills, and probate court inventories indicate that most people furnished their houses with chairs, pictures, beds, mattresses, tables, clocks, mirrors, carpets, and such. Other items of value included china, pewter, and especially silverware, silver candlesticks, silver coffee pots, and silver tea pots. A number of people also had books. Although it is difficult to tell if the books were in their shops or among their personal goods, their presence indicates a considerable respect for the written word. The inventory of the estate of Moses Pimienta shows he owned "a lot of Hebrew books" and "a lot of English books,"[29] while that of Solomon Isaacs shows he had "sundry books on curious subjects."[30]

The well-to-do residents lived quite comfortable lives, as attested to by Isaac M. Wise at the time of his visit in 1850. Dr. Benjamin Rodrigues and Poznanski

29. Probate Records, Inventories, Book W, 149, Charleston County.

30. Ibid., Book S, 64.

23. 301 East Bay Street. Built about 1816 for Moses C. Levy. (Photograph by Michael Whittemore.)

24. 44–46 Queen Street. Property of Abraham Sasportas. (Photograph by Michael Whittemore.)

25. 72 George Street. Originally 1 College Street. Home of Abraham Moïse. Now on campus of College of Charleston. (Photograph by Michael Whittemore.)

met him at the dock when he arrived from the north by steamer. He stayed in a home, probably that of Rodrigues, where he "was domiciled in splendid rooms. A negro was placed at my disposal. I was the guest of American aristocrats for the first time in my life."[31] Though Wise's account is often exaggerated, it reveals that those with money seem to have lived quite well in the city.

Children

After marriage, most couples had children within a year or two and continued to have them for several years. Unfortunately, complete information on families is usually lacking.[32] Available data show that a number of women died as a result of childbirth or soon thereafter. For example, Abigail Ancker delivered a child in 1843 and died in 1844, Sarah Cohen Moïse delivered a child in 1818 and died in the same year, and Sarah Moses Hart died as a result of "childbed." Also, four of the women lost children before the infants reached the age of two; for example, Rachel Harby had three infants who did not survive and two other children who seem to have died quite young. (See Table 23.)

31. Wise, *Reminiscences*, 143.

32. Neither the state nor the city kept records of births in the early years. Genealogies also often lack much of this type of information.

26. 69 Meeting Street. Home of M. C. Mordecai. (Photograph by Michael Whittemore.)

Among married women who were born and who died in Charleston by 1861 (39 persons), 15 percent did not have children. Those known to have children delivered on average 5.75. For women who died in Charleston but who are not known to have been born there (58 persons), 14 percent did not have children, and those who did, bore on average 5.98 offspring. Both averages may be low, because children who died early are sometimes not found in genealogies, as the death records of Charleston show. Furthermore, records are less

27. Advertisement of coal by Nathaniel Jacobi. (*Daily Courier*, October 26, 1857.)

likely to have survived of infants who died before the family came to America. It would appear that the average number of children was about six. Some families had more; for example, Rachel Lazarus delivered seventeen children and Lucretia Mordecai eighteen. Male children slightly outnumbered females.

Young male infants, according to the age-old practice, underwent the rite of circumcision on the eighth day after birth. This ceremony could be considered both a religious and "national" duty. Although any Jew could perform this ceremony, a *mohel*, a man especially trained in the ritual and skilled in the surgery, was preferred. The importance of this act to Jews can be illustrated by the fact that the constitutions of 1820 and 1836 required that the third prayer should be made to Philip Hart, the first *mohel* of the congregation. So central to Judaism was this rite that in 1805, when Solomon Hart believed that death drew near, he wrote his will asking that his circumcision instruments be buried with him.[33] And the congregation required that careful records of each circumcision be kept.[34] One other person known for performing this rite was Myer Derkheim. He lived in the city in the early years of the nineteenth century and traveled up and down the East Coast carrying out this ceremony.[35]

At the time of circumcision, the boy received his name. The most common first names for males born in Charleston in 1861 and earlier were Isaac (9.70 percent had this name), Abraham (5.01 percent), Jacob (4.68 percent), David (4.68 percent), Aaron (4.01 percent), Joseph (3.68 percent), Solomon (3.34 percent), Moses (3.01 percent), Benjamin (3.01 percent), and Samuel (2.00

33. W30.863.

34. Rule 23, constitution of 1820. It is not known if Philip Hart and Solomon Hart were related. Neither married.

35. Marcus, *United States Jewry*, 135.

Table 23
Ages of Jewish Women in Antebellum Charleston at
Marriage and Births of First and Last Child

				Age at Time of		
Name	*Year Born*	*Year Married*	*Year Died*	*Marriage*	*Birth of 1st Child*	*Birth of Last Child*
Abrahams, Judith (DeLyon) (Cohen)	1764	1779	1848	15	Unknown	30
Ancker, Abigail Rebecca (Sampson)	1823	1841	1844	18	19	20
Cardozo, Sarah N. (Cohen)	1766	1785	1853	18	19	38
Cohen, Esther (Moses) (Moïse)	1784	1801	1860	17	19	26
Cohen, Leah (Lazarus)	1778	1795	1844	16	22	32
DeLaMotta, Judith (Canter)	1771	1787	1827	16	18	44
Harby, Rachael (Mordecai)	1782	1810	1827	28	29	41
Hyams, Rebecca (Sarzedas)	1781	1798	1852	17	17	Unknown
Lazarus, Mary [Miriam] (Hart)	1792	1812	1828	20	Unknown	29
Moïse, Sarah (Cohen)	1791	1807	1828	16	18	37
Mordecai, Reinah (Cohen)	1784	1802	1853	18	31	34
Moses, Isabella (Myers)	1796	1815	1850	19	23	23
Simpson, Jane (Cohen) (Mordecai)	1789	1808	1843	19	Unknown	Unknown

Note: This table is limited to mothers who were born and died in Charleston by 1861 for whom the date of birth, the date of marriage, and the date of death are known. The ages are approximate and might vary by a year or two.
Sources: See the appendix.

percent). Despite traditions among some Ashkenazic Jews of not naming a son after a living relative and among Sephardic Jews of naming a son after the grandfather, such customs do not appear to have been followed closely. Twenty-nine (22.30 percent) of 130 fathers who had sons born in Charleston gave the sons their names—and this excludes sons born elsewhere. Some of the names were decidedly American in inspiration, including Benjamin Franklin Moïse, Thomas Jefferson Moïse, Henry Jefferson Harby, Oliver Hazard Perry Moses, and Thomas Whitlock Mordecai.

For females the names most popular first name was Sarah (9.50 percent had this name), followed by Rachel (5.37 percent), Rebecca (5.37 percent), Cecile/Cecilia (3.72 percent), Isabel/Isabella/Isabelle (3.72 percent), Caroline (3.31

percent), Cordelia (2.89 percent), Adeline, Catharine/Catherine, Esther, and Judith (2.47 percent each). Some mothers named their daughters for themselves (19 of 124, or 15.32 percent). Girls apparently received no "American" names.

The next important step for boys came when they reached the age of thirteen. By that time, they were supposed to have mastered the reading, or, at least, the pronunciation, of Hebrew and were called to the Torah, that is to say, they could read the Torah and were accepted as an adult. At services on the eve of the Sabbath, they read a passage before the congregation. Thereafter, the individual was obliged to obey all the commandments and could be counted as one of the ten necessary to make up a *minyan*. Known by virtually all Jews today as the *bar mitzvah* (son of the covenant), the Sephardic Jews of Charleston knew this occasion as "Son Minyan." A father in good standing with the congregation could "demand and receive all the customary honors and rights in the Synagogue" for his son upon application to the president of the congregation.[36] Many Jews today have the *bat mitzvah* (daughter of the covenant) for girls, but that institution did not exist in nineteenth-century Charleston.

Unfortunately, many of the young children did not survive for long; many parents experienced the sadness and heartache of witnessing the deaths of their children. The tombstones they erected over the graves of the young reflected their sentiments. Some inscriptions recalled the pleasures the families had enjoyed. The parents of Jacob Barrett, who died at the age of two, erected a monument that read in part: "Closed is the soft ephemeral flower; That never felt a storm. The sunbeam's smile, the zephyr's breath, All that it knew from birth to death." The same parents suffered greater grief when another son, Thaddeus, died at the age of three months. They chiseled their anguish in stone: "Blossom of Heaven! planted here, Yet destined not to bloom, Where all around is cold and sear, And earth a living tomb." Especially sad was the death of Henrietta Hart at the age of eighteen at Patapsco Institute in Maryland. Her family consoled themselves in that "she was not unprepared to die, and that kind friends ministered at her deathbed with most tender affection." Others such as the parents of Octavian Moses, who died at the age of two, accepted the death with resignation: "The Lord giveth and the Lord taketh away. Blessed be the name of the Lord." Some believed the child had gone on to a better place. This was the case for the parents of Isabel Seixas, aged one. They erected a monument with the words: "Though dead to this world, In a brighter abode; They dwell with their Father, Their Friend, and their God." Another family, no doubt mournful for a place left behind not long before, wrote in French: "Içi Repose LEONIE DAVID. Decedée a Charleston, le 12 Septembre, 1858, agée de 10 ans et 10 jours."[37]

36. Rule 18.

37. Elzas, *Old Jewish Cemeteries*, 7, 8, 16, 20, 45, 52.

Education

Children who survived generally received the type of schooling valued by the aristocratic slaveowning society in which they lived. By and large this was a classical education stressing the study of the Latin and Greek languages. South Carolina leaders showed little or no interest in educating the bulk of the white population and, after the Denmark Vesey slave conspiracy, outlawed the education of slaves in order to exert more control over them. Not until 1811 did the state establish Free Schools for whites, but so little money was appropriated that few could operate. Indeed, South Carolina probably had the poorest system of schools in the country. Furthermore, the Free Schools showed a preference for "poor orphans and the children of indigent and necessitous parents," with the result that they became associated with the lower classes. The "academies" and "colleges" catered to the elite. In 1856 Charleston finally established a viable system of public schools, but the Civil War intervened and brought them to an end.[38] The private academies of Charleston for boys usually taught Latin and Greek, modern languages, English, and a few other subjects. The girls' schools emphasized modern languages, music, and needlework.

The Jews of the city showed much concern for secular education, and a number of them operated schools. One of these was Isaac Harby, who established his school at Bedon's Alley in 1809. There he offered courses in elocution, arithmetic, penmanship, grammar, geography, Latin, Greek, composition, and geometry. He also promised to instruct his students "in the principles of virtue & patriotism."[39] Raphael Jacob Moses, who was born in Charleston in 1812, attended the school operated by Harby after his parents discovered he "was not learning anything but mischief" in Bishop John England's school. He found Harby a splendid teacher who, however, did not believe in sparing the rod. A mulberry tree supplied many limbs for the whipping of the boys. By the age of twelve Moses was studying Latin and was about to start learning Greek, "when it suddenly occurred to me that I had absorbed through the skin as much knowledge as I cared to acquire in that way."[40]

Myer M. Cohen conducted his school for both sexes from 1824 to 1828.[41] In 1825 the boys and girls at his academy studied mythology, orthography, grammar, rhetoric, history, geography, and Latin. A visitor to the school stated that the students excelled in their examinations.[42] In addition, Mrs. Hetty Lazarus Moïse operated the Charleston Female Seminary, which she turned over to

38. Anderson, "Public Education in Antebellum South Carolina," 3–11; Jordan "Education for the Community," 99–125.

39. *Daily Courier*, Jan. 1, 1810; Moïse, "Memoir," in Moïse and Pinckney, *A Selection from the Miscellaneous Writings*, 6–11.

40. Marcus, *Memoirs of American Jews*, 1: 146–51.

41. *Daily Courier*, Sept. 28, 1828.

42. *Southern Patriot*, Nov. 16, 1825.

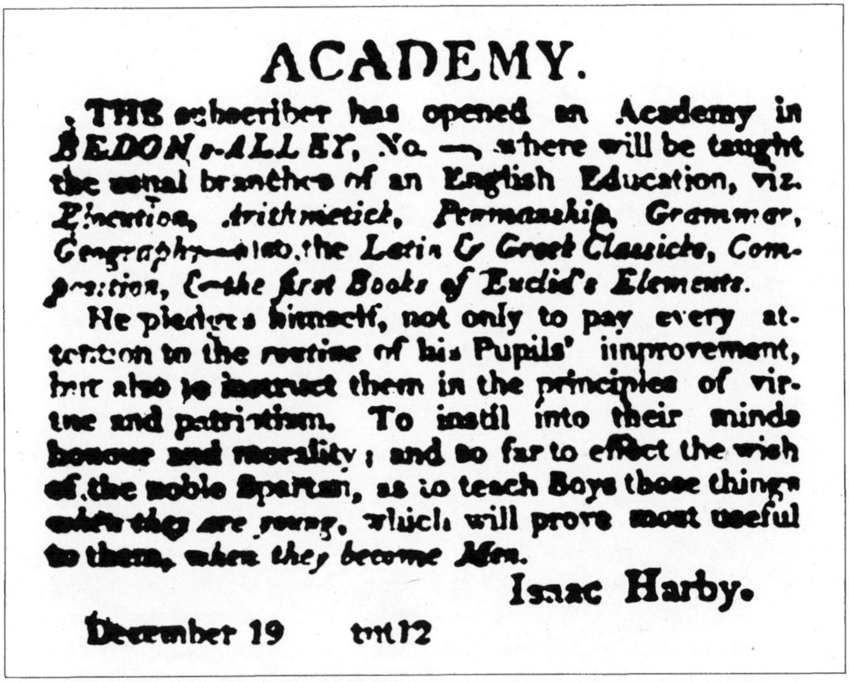

ACADEMY.

THE subscriber has opened an Academy in BEDON's-ALLEY, No. —, where will be taught the usual branches of an English Education, viz. Elocution, Arithmetick, Penmanship, Grammar, Geography—also, the Latin & Greek Classicks, Composition, & the first Books of Euclid's Elements.

He pledges himself, not only to pay every attention to the routine of his Pupils' improvement, but also to instruct them in the principles of virtue and patriotism. To instil into their minds honour and morality; and so far to effect the wish of the noble Spartan, as to teach Boys those things when they are young, which will prove most useful to them, when they become Men.

Isaac Harby.

December 19 [illegible]

28. Advertisement for Isaac Harby's academy. (*Courier*, January 1, 1810.)

Louisa A. Moïse in 1855. The school offered "a complete English education . . . together with French, Spanish, Italian, Music, vocal and instrumental, Drawing and Painting."[43] Other men listed as teachers in city directories are Abraham Ottolengui (1807), Abraham Tongue (1807), David Cardozo (1816), and Jacob Bensadon (1831). In total, the Jews of Charleston became so caught up with the classical system of education that when Poznanski planned to resign in 1850, the congregation sought "a preacher of classical attainments" with a good knowledge of Latin and Greek.[44]

For classical studies beyond the academy level, students could attend the College of Charleston, South Carolina College (now the university), or schools in the Northeast. Judah Benjamin, for example, attended Yale but appears to have been expelled; Judah Barrett Cohen graduated from the College of Charleston. The latter studied several languages and won a medal for oratory while at the college. Not long after his

43. *Daily Courier*, April 15, 1855.

44. Wise, *Reminiscences*, 147.

graduation, the South Carolina Historical Society chose him to deliver the first anniversary address to that organization. He later became a lawyer and worked in New York and Charleston and also edited newspapers in Charleston.[45]

The interest on the part of Jews in higher education developed in the eighteenth century before a college had been established in South Carolina. In 1770, when Rhode Island College moved to Providence and changed its name to honor Nicholas and Joseph Brown, the trustees conducted a fund-raising campaign including a visit by the Reverend Hezekiah Smith to Charleston. The Jews of Charleston especially welcomed him because the college promised to admit religious dissenters. When Israel Joseph, Michael Lazarus, Benjamin Hart, and Moses Lindo gave money, the trustees stated they would welcome Jewish scholars. Lindo promised much more money than the £20 he gave, but nothing further was heard from him.[46]

Work

After completing their education, the males usually went directly to work, often as a clerk in one of the businesses of the city. A few studied law or medicine. Following these apprenticeships, they can often be seen becoming a partner in a business or opening their own shops or practicing a profession. These offspring normally continued to live in their parents' home with the rest of the family and contributed their share. An example of this sort of household would be the home of Nathan Nathans. In the 1850 census he headed a household that included five other males. Levy Nathans (twenty-seven) was a merchant while David (twenty-two), Alexander (eighteen), and Simon (fifteen) were clerks. Jacob (twelve) was too young to work.

Some young men and women continued to live with their parents even after marriage; however, if their own families grew large, they might form their own separate households. Then, as the parents aged, they frequently lived with their children—especially if a spouse died. This appears to be the case of Rachel Seixas (age sixty), who lived in the household of David Seixas (age twenty-seven) in 1850. Some elderly people, especially widows, nevertheless remained the heads of their own households; Catherine Oppenheim, for example, in 1860 had nine other people living in her house.

Many young men moved to find new opportunities. This situation was by no means unique to the Jews of Charleston. One estimate holds that close to half of the white people born in South Carolina after 1800 departed for other localities. The declining economic opportunities in the state, the proclivity for Americans to move, and the opening up of new lands to the west help to account for this

45. Elzas, *Jews of South Carolina*, 270–71.

46. Lindo to Sampson and Solomon Smith, April 17, 1770, Trustees to Lindo, Jan. 1771, Brown University Papers; Marcus, *American Jewry*, 221–22; Goodman, *American Overture*, 61–66; Hühner, "Jews in Connection with the Colleges," 115. Israel Joseph gave £3, Michael Lazarus £1.10, Benjamin Hart £16.9.4, and Moses Lindo £20.

pattern.[47] For the most part the emigrants from South Carolina moved westward into Georgia, Alabama, and Mississippi. The pattern for Jews is somewhat different. For persons known to have been born in Charleston by 1861 and who died elsewhere, the most frequent places of death were Georgia (12.97 percent), New York (12.97 percent), Pennsylvania (3.16 percent), Sumter, South Carolina (7.28 percent), and Louisiana (7.91 percent). Very few died in small communities except residents of South Carolina. For the most part they moved to Savannah, Atlanta, New York City, New Orleans, and Philadelphia. Jews who had been born in Charleston, in fact, died in such diverse places as Barbados, California, Paris, Jamaica, Oregon, and Texas.

Most men who chose to remain in Charleston kept active in business well into old age. When they retired, the city directories list them as "gentlemen" or give no profession for them. Apparently they kept their interest in their firms while allowing others, usually family members, to handle the details.

Remarriage

Not all married couples grew old together, as some spouses died. Men who lost their wives were more likely to remarry than women. The average age at remarriage for them was approximately forty-two years. Although most waited eight or ten years to remarry (one man for thirty-seven years), two remarried within two years after the deaths of their wives. Women who remarried did so on the average at age thirty-one. They tended to wait six to ten years.[48] One woman, Hannah Davis, born in Mannheim, Germany in 1761, first married Hymon Levy, who died in 1791. The following year when she was thirty years of age, she remarried, to Israel DeLieben. Then he died in 1807, and she married again at the age of fifty-two to Moses Davis in 1813. She died at the age of eighty-nine, having survived her third husband by seven years.

Separation and Divorce

Some of the marriages collapsed and resulted in divorce or separation. Divorce has always been possible in Judaism. Although it has been stated that no divorce ever took place in South Carolina prior the Civil War,[49] two Jewish marriages in Charleston ended in divorce. One came about in 1788 when Mordecai Lyon and his wife Binche or Elizabeth Chapman appeared before a *bet din*, or ecclesiastical court, consisting of Israel DeLieben and Israel Myers, "learned men appointed for that purpose." Moses Cohen, Abraham Azuby, Hyam Levy, and Samuel Myers also observed. Apparently others attended be-

47. Rogers, "The Great Population Exodus," 14–27.

48. Information on this is limited for women. Of twenty who remarried, the ages at the time of the second marriage are available for eight and the ages at the time of both marriages for five.

49. Salmon, "Life, Liberty and Dower," 97.

cause the document mentions that "a large concurrence" of the congregation approved the actions taken. All the men known to have been present had been born in Europe and had apparently received training in Jewish customs and practices, especially the two "learned" members and the *hazan,* who had the duty of reviewing the case. DeLieben and Myers were Ashkenazic Jews, while Azuby came from a Sephardic background.

Mordecai Lyon, originally from Poland, came to Charleston during the Revolution. At first he worked as a tailor but appeared to have improved his economic status over the years. Lyon claimed that the "scandalous behaviour" of his wife was such that he could not with any propriety cohabit with her any longer. Indeed, he claimed that Jewish law required that she be divorced. Therefore, Lyon requested the *bet din* to dissolve the marriage and write for him a letter of divorce and separation, or *get*, to be given to his wife in accordance with the statutes of holy law. Furthermore, he stated that his wife had "cordially consented" to such an action and was willing to receive from her husband a letter of divorce and separation. The court, "after strictly framing his just complaints and finding the truth thereof," decided that Elizabeth Chapman had forfeited all the rights and titles of a wife. They granted Lyon's request and wrote a letter of divorce. The authorities then gave the letter of divorce and separation to Lyon who, in turn, delivered it to his wife in the presence of witnesses. By renouncing all her rights and titles as wife, Elizabeth Chapman regained her personal freedom. She could then remarry as she pleased.

On March 23, 1789, the men who had heard and witnessed the case signed a document stating the provisions of the divorce, and the statement was recorded on March 28 with the secretary of state of South Carolina. Nothing indicates they encountered any difficulties with the public authorities in doing this; however, there is no explanation of the delay of over a year before the document is recorded nor of the reason they even turned to the authorities. Ordinarily, the state would not have been involved. They could have submitted the matter to religious authorities in Europe, but, what is more likely, Lyon wished to marry again and wanted to remove any legal barriers that the state might impose. Ordinarily, this would have been strictly a matter of the man, his wife, members of the congregation in Charleston, and Jewish custom.[50]

The *bet din* granted the divorce according to Jewish practices, not secular law. The legal system of South Carolina did not allow for easy divorce and remarriage. One law stated that a marriage was indissoluble when contracted and solemnized in the church, providing there was no precontract that allowed for divorce. Another said that a person committed a felony if he or she married a second husband or wife while the first was still living.[51] Possibly, the state did not interfere with the divorce because the marriage had not been solemnized in a church. Another explanation is that

50. MR2X.632–33.
51. *Statutes*, 2: 476, 508.

the "peculiar institution" of Judaism so baffled the authorities that they allowed the Jews to do things according to their own laws. Lyon married a second time, to Judith Cohen, and he and his wife lived out their days in Charleston.

A second divorce occurred in late 1840. At a meeting of the board of the congregation Gustavus Poznanski reported that "Mr. and Mrs. Prince" had asked him "to give them a *get* or divorce, which the Rev. Gentm. declined" until he consulted the board for its opinion. The trustees ruled that if the *hazan* saw good and sufficient cause according to the Law of Moses, there was "no reason for prohibiting this religious ceremony, & in accordance with this sentiment they hereby sanction the divorce contemplated."[52] Apparently the people involved were George and Sarah Prince, because in 1849 Sarah Prince requested by letter to the trustees of Beth Elohim that her son Samuel be called up on the following Sabbath to read the Torah, as he had reached his thirteenth birthday. The board also received a letter from George Prince denying that Samuel was his son, as the records of the court of chancery would verify. The board ruled that Samuel was a Jew and granted approval for him to be called up.[53]

A number of other people whose marriages did not work out obtained legal separations. When "some unhappy differences" arose between Moses Jacobs and Rebecca Lazarus Jacobs in 1826, they "agreed to and mutually consented to live apart from each other." The articles of separation stated that he "shall not nor will compel her to cohabit with him, nor sue nor disturb any persons that shall receive her into their habitations." They also agreed to equally divide their goods, money, and merchandise in their store on King Street. After that, neither could make claims on the other. In order that Mrs. Jacobs could earn a living, she received the right to trade in her own name.[54] As they had no children, the separation seems to have been fairly simple. On the other hand, a rift in 1852 that involved Solomon Hyams and Caroline Matilda Thompson Hyams was more difficult, as they had a son William Palmedo Hyams. They "mutually consented" to "dissolve the marriage contract between them so far as by law they can do." After that he could not live with her "nor use or frequent her company or conversation at any time." Hyams agreed to pay the trustee of the agreement, John Robinson, $1,000 should he violate any part of the settlement, including troubling or visiting her without her consent. She could do as she wished as if she were a single person, would support herself, and would not make any claims on him. Furthermore, she was given sole right "to retain and keep, educate and protect William Palmedo Hyams, the child of them."[55] The day after the separation settlement was filed, he granted her the rights of a sole trader so that she could legally earn her own living.[56] When

52. Minute Book of Beth Elohim, Nov. 29, 1840.
53. Ibid., July 18, 1849.
54. MR5C.264.
55. MR6F.596.
56. MR6F.600.

Caroline Hyams wrote her will in 1857, she provided that John Robinson should act as the guardian of her son and to be "as a father" if she died. By early 1858 she had expired.[57]

Family Problems

Occasionally other family problems occurred. In June 1839 the trustees of the synagogue reported that serious charges had arrived from Amsterdam regarding Isaac Garretson. According to their information, he had left a wife there in distress many years before. He had lived in Charleston "some years with one who had passed as his wife." The board called him to answer the charges, but the minutes contain no further references to the matter.[58] The charges were possibly false because in April of that year, the Reverend Mr. Poznanski performed a marriage between Garretson's daughter Sarah and L. Hyneman.[59] In another case, a stranger known as Fisher who came to Charleston was accused of having deserted his wife. He died in the city in 1838, and the congregation buried him. After that, word arrived from New York that his name was Liebschith, and that he had left a poor and destitute widow. Liebschith had $80.00 on him at the time of his death. After his burial $14.63 remained. The trustees sent this amount to his widow.[60] A Charleston wife who, at first, refused to follow her husband was Charlotte Canter Sasportas. Her husband, Abraham Sasportas, had been born in France and owned considerable property there.[61] The first wife of Sasportas died in 1778, and he married Charlotte Canter in 1803. In the marriage settlement he provided for $6,000 to be given to his wife should he die. He lived in Charleston until at least 1816, at which time he returned to France. Mrs. Sasportas remained in Charleston. When he wrote his will in 1820, he said about his wife, "I took her without any portion and have generously endowed her in marrying her." He provided a house at 15 Queen Street to her on the condition that she "fixes her residence in France next to her children." Sasportas died in Bordeaux in 1824. Charlotte Sasportas also died in Bordeaux in 1851, apparently having found it in her best interests to live with her family.[62]

Death

Most people in early Charleston did not write wills. The laws of South Carolina were specific on the way property should be divided in cases where people did not make provisions for the distribution of their possessions. The great

57. W41.635.

58. Minute Book of Beth Elohim, June 12, 1839.

59. Elzas, *Jewish Marriage Notices*, 18.

60. Minute Book of Beth Elohim, Sept. 23, Dec. 29, 1838.

61. Abraham Sasportas and Moses Spitzer were members of the French revolutionary Jacobin Club in Charleston. See Kennedy, "A French Jacobin Club in Charleston," 22. Spitzer died under mysterious conditions in December 1795. After he had been missing for ten days, his body was found on Sullivan's Island.

62. W36.1067; MS4.241.

majority of wills written by Jews were drawn up as they lay dying. Those with considerable wealth and those who had not married were more likely to write one, in a few cases years before their demise.

When death came to the Jews of Charleston, they apparently followed Jewish tradition, which placed great emphasis on respect for the deceased. When a person died at home, candles were lit to represent the vestiges of the soul. People remained with the body until the funeral. Obituaries that mention the day of death and the time of the funeral indicate that on occasion two to three days could pass from the time of death until burial—even longer if the deceased had to be brought to Charleston from another city.

Charlestonians seemed to maintain a very strong attachment to the city, even after having left Charleston many years before. After the introduction of railroads, it was not uncommon for residents who had moved away from Charleston to arrange to be returned to the city for interment, some from places as distant as New York. Anyone who belonged to the Jewish congregation could expect to be buried in the cemetery. The families of Jews who were not members would have to seek burial elsewhere.

The funeral services took place in the cemetery following a procession from the home of the deceased to the graveyard. In 1846 M. C. Mordecai proposed that the *hazan* be asked to make an inquiry if it would be incompatible with Jewish beliefs to bring corpses into the synagogue for funeral services, as happened in Christian churches; however, members voted 19 to 6 to table the resolution.[63] Apparently in the early days the Jews carried the funeral bier through the streets, but by 1820 the president of the cemetery took charge of funerals and was responsible for keeping the hearse in good order. He also kept a book listing the plots in the cemetery.[64] The 1836 Constitution provided for a Superintendent of the Cemetery who carried out these duties.[65]

An English visitor to America in 1795 stated that the Jews of Charleston "among other peculiarities in burying their dead" sang a funeral dirge and then, before depositing the corpse in the grave, opened the coffin to place a small bag of earth taken from the grave under the head of the deceased. Then some dust, which was said to be from Jerusalem and carefully kept for the purpose, was placed on the eyes of the dead. This was not only in remembrance of the holy land but of "their expectations of returning thither in God's appointed time."[66] Normally, only the *hazan* could conduct the services, although the trustees allowed some exceptions.

On occasion people did not meet the requirements of membership, and pleas were made that they be allowed Jewish funerals. When strangers died in the city, such a plea could be entered upon

63. Minute Book of Beth Elohim, Nov. 8, 1846.

64. Rule 21, constitution of 1820.

65. Article 38.

66. Winterbotham, *An Historical, Geographical, Commercial, and Philosophical View*, 1: 394.

request of a member. Thus, in 1842 Philip Cohen asked permission to bury a man by the name of I. Goldsmith, who had arrived only about three weeks before. The trustees approved, providing that Cohen paid the usual fee of $25.[67] In 1840 Abraham Ottolengui interceded on behalf of an infant child of Jacob Moses, asking that the child be buried in the graveyard, a request that also was approved.[68] Another person who sought permission to bury a family member was Rachel Lambert. Although she was Jewish, she had married a Christian but had had her son Solomon circumcised according to Jewish law. When Solomon died in 1841 at the age of five, she asked the board to allow him to be buried in the cemetery. Again the board complied.[69]

The Coming Street Cemetery has many tombstones over the graves of the deceased along with memorials along the walls. Family members and friends who placed markers there for adults tended to emphasize their place of origin. Often the epitaphs begin with "a native of Poland," "a native of Bristol, England," or "a native of the state of New York." Without these, the origins of a family would often not now be known. Virtues cited include those of an "indulgent parent, devoting her entire energies to the happiness of her offspring," or service to the Hebrew Benevolent Society, the American Revolution, and to the congregation. Some inscriptions refer to the quickness of death, such as that of David DaVega, who died "of the fever of the climate, after an illness of 42 hours." With its great emphasis on life, Judaism views such a death as a great tragedy. Furthermore, biblical texts say very little about *she'ol*, the place of the dead, which Job (10:21) described as the "land of darkness." Thus, few tombstone inscriptions refer to an existence beyond the grave. An example of one that does is in memory of Sarah C. Moïse, whose relatives hoped "that Heaven has already smiled upon her and that in dying, she has happily exchanged the evanescent pleasures of this world for those of a blissful immortality."[70]

Conversion

On occasion, the ranks of the Jewish population increased when persons returned or converted to the faith. Although the 1820 and 1836 constitutions made this virtually impossible, the 1840 documents must have been silent on the subject. In 1841 Mary Ann Suares sent a message to the board of Beth Elohim that she would like to be allowed to return to "our Holy Religion." Years before she had abandoned the faith and joined a Christian church. She stated that she had repented and desired to return to the Jewish community. The board decided that she would be accepted back if she appeared in the synagogue to express regret and her earnest determination to return and that she

67. Minute Book of Beth Elohim, Jan. 15, 1842.

68. Ibid., Nov. 29, 1840.

69. Ibid., Aug. 15, 1841.

70. Elzas, *Old Jewish Cemeteries*, 5, 6, 9, 10, 11, 29, 30, 45.

publish a notice in the newspapers of the city to that effect. Suares objected to the publication of the notice in the papers but was "willing to undergo any penalty you may feel inclined to inflict." The board relented and allowed her admission.[71] Two months later she married Bernard Levy, a former member of the Reformed Society. She was approximately thirty-five years of age, and he was about fifty-one at the time. Her impending marriage, obviously, was the reason she desired to return to the faith.

In 1847 Miss Ann Buckheister, who had not been born a Jew, expressed a desire to become one. The board required her to be examined by the *hazan* before the board. At the meeting Mr. and Mrs. Henry Davis accompanied her. Poznanski questioned her at length and warned her of the danger she would inflict upon herself from the wrath of the deity should she not be sincere. The *hazan* questioned her on points of faith, and she answered satisfactorily on all counts. She then confessed herself to be "a true believer in the Jewish faith," at which point Poznanski declared her to be qualified, and the board accepted her into the congregation.[72] Later she married David Davis, who apparently was the son of Mr. and Mrs. Henry Davis.

In 1858 Miss Lucia Bull applied to the *hazan*, Maurice Mayer, for instruction in Judaism with the aim of becoming a member of the congregation. Mayer took the matter to the board of trustees, vaguely stating that "This case is surrounded—as you have no doubt already learned—by the most peculiar or rather delicate circumstance." The trustees turned the question over to a committee, but nothing further appears in the minutes.[73]

Thus, from birth to death the life of the family and the Jewish religion were intertwined. Religious ceremonies marked the major milestones in a person's life. On the whole, the families seem to have been close knit, and extended households were common. Like other people, the Jews had family problems from time to time. Their laws allowed them certain means to resolve these difficulties, and a number made use of them. Throughout life and in death they sought to be close to their families and other members of their faith.

71. Minute Book of Beth Elohim, Sept. 13, Oct. 17, 18, 21, 1841.

72. Ibid., May 2, June 9, 1847.

73. Ibid., May 2, 1858.

Chapter 7

Occupations of Men

We enjoy a high privilege. We can unfold a spotless banner. The very birth of our state was noble, no eager spade with unbecoming haste violated the purity of virgin soil to search for glittering metal or precious ore; the civilizing axe of the woodman, the peace-breathing hoe of the farmer, were the simple yet speaking implements; they told of self-denial and bitter sacrifice.

—Asher Cohen, 1858[1]

Although Asher Cohen could speak in glowing terms of the farmer's breaking up the virgin soil of a new land, the city of Charleston lived from the commerce derived from large plantations where African slaves performed the backbreaking labor. Through much of the colonial and antebellum period the city ranked as one of the wealthiest in America. The prosperity of the community induced many to settle there, including the Jews. The affluence resulted from the fact that the city served as the port for the Carolina Low Country. Raw materials from the plantations flowed out, and necessities and luxuries poured in. The Jewish men of Charleston actively participated in almost all aspects of the economy.

The Colonial Era

The first important exports from South Carolina were deerskins and naval supplies such as tar, pitch, and turpentine. Then the colony found a far more important product in rice. Since this staple required large amounts of labor, the plantation owners imported increasing numbers of African slaves. The first boom began after 1730, when the authorities in London allowed the colony to sell rice beyond the British empire. With greater prosperity the city expanded, as new houses and streets appeared on the peninsula. In addition, numerous wharves along the Cooper

1. Toast at anniversary meeting, "The Hebrew Benevolent Society of Charleston," 586.

River attested to the growing commerce. By the middle of the eighteenth century Charleston ranked as one of the great cities in North America; only Philadelphia, New York, and Boston had larger populations. Despite the fact that New York was larger, Charleston exported twice as much tonnage in the 1770s.[2]

A number of Jewish businessmen operated in Charleston during the colonial period. Very little is known about those who lived in the city during the late seventeenth and early eighteenth centuries, but they appear to have been most commonly involved in the import-export business. The earliest advertisement by a Jewish firm appeared in the *South-Carolina Gazette* in 1734, when Jacob Dias Carvallo (Carvalho) and Aaron DeMuttos Gutteres offered liquors for sale. Retail shops such as theirs rarely appear in the official records. On the other hand, the provincial and imperial governments kept accounts on larger businesses from which they collected revenues. The Jewish individuals who seem to have been most active were Isaac DaCosta (1721–83), Solomon Isaacs (d. 1757), and Isaac DePass.[3] As for their rank among fellow importers on the basis of the amount of general merchandise imported, Solomon Isaacs ranked 12th in South Carolina; DaCosta and Farr, 42nd: Isaac DaCosta, 226th: and Philip Hart, 330th.[4] (See Table 24.)

Several of the Jewish merchants owned ships in order to transport their goods. Most, however, did not bother with shipowning, because so many vessels called at the city that the merchants found it more economical to utilize them. Greater profit could be made in buying and selling goods than in transporting them. (See Table 25.)

More is known about Isaac DaCosta than the other colonial merchants. He had businesses in South Carolina and Georgia, and he traded with the northern colonies, the West Indies, West Africa, and Britain. He often worked in a partnership with Thomas Farr but at times operated alone. In 1761–62 he had to spend seven months in Georgia, apparently Savannah, because some of his employees there had been defrauding him. He maintained a keen interest in many goods including rice, indigo, beaver skins, butter, corn, turpentine, deer skins, tanned leather, rum, ship bread, flour, beer, and cider. Along with Farr, he also obtained slaves from the Guinea coast of Africa.[5]

DaCosta worked closely with the Jewish Lopez family of Newport, and much of the information on him results from

2. Much of the information on the economic development of the colony is taken from Sellers, *Charleston Business on the Eve of the American Revolution*, and Rogers, *Charleston in the Age of the Pinckneys.*

3. Moore, "The Largest Exporters of Deer Skins"; Higgins, "Charles Town Merchants and Factors Dealing in the External Negro Trade"; Stumpf, "South Carolina Importers of General Merchandise."

4. Stumpf, "South Carolina Importers of General Merchandise."

5. Isaac DaCosta to Aaron Lopez, Dec. 24, 1761, Sept. 24, Oct. 23, Dec. 22, 1762, Jan. 11, April 12, 1763, July 19, 1764, Lopez Papers, American Jewish Archives.

Table 24
Charleston's Jewish Exporters and Importers, 1735–1775

Names	*Goods*	*Years*	*No. of Cargoes*
Cortissoz & Abrahams[a]	Slaves	1762	1
DaCosta & Farr	General merchandise	1758–62	
DaCosta & Farr	Slaves	1760–63	2
DaCosta & Farr	Deerskins	1755–64	
DaCosta, Isaac	General merchandise	1757, 1762–65	
DaCosta, Isaac	Slaves	1765	1
DePass, Isaac	Slaves	1752	1
Hart, Philip	General merchandise	1758–59	
Isaacs, Solomon	Deerskins	1744–54	
Isaacs, Solomon	General merchandise	1744–56	
Isaacs, Solomon	Slaves	1765	3
Levy, Nathan	Slaves	1772	1

[a] Emanuel Cortissoz and Emanuel Abrahams.

Table 25
Charleston's Jewish Shipowners, 1734–1780

Names	*Year Ship Purchased*
DaCosta, Isaac	1769
DaCosta, Isaac, Thomas Farr, and others	1761 *Carolina Packet*, sloop, 45 tons
DePass, Isaac	1744 *Carolina*, brigantine, 40 tons
Hart, Philip, and Stephen Ketchum	1759 *Philip*, 45 tons
Isaacs, Solomon	1748 *Heron*, sloop, 25 tons
Lindo, Moses	1757 *Lindo Packet*, 30 tons

Sources: Olsberg, "Ship Records in the South Carolina Archives, 1734–1780," 189–209; Thomas Nelson from Isaac DaCosta, Mortgage for a Schooner, Mortgage Book 3A, p. 462, South Carolina Archives.

correspondence they preserved. Moses Lopez visited Charleston in 1742 and returned in 1764. When Lopez arrived in 1764, DaCosta insisted that he stay in the best room in his house. Lopez had anticipated selling his ship the *Hope* but found no buyer; therefore, he advertised for a cargo to be taken to London. First though, he had to sell a variety of goods that he had brought to Charleston. When he discovered that few people wanted the cheap goods in his cargo, he had to auction them for whatever price he could get. Lopez reported that most goods from ships were sold by auctioneers to retailers in this fashion. Retailers came directly to the docks to purchase their supplies and thus eliminated much of the need for warehousing and wholesalers. The retailers, in turn, sold the products to the general public. The biggest buyers were the planters, who insisted on shopping with only one storekeeper. A shopkeeper who did not have goods that a planter wanted would hasten to another shop to purchase them for his customer. Although the planters bought large quantities of goods, they did so on credit, and the retailer had to wait until the first of the year to collect.[6]

When Lopez arrived in Charleston, the city had entered a new phase of economic development with the cultivation of indigo. The plant from which the dye was extracted had been grown in South Carolina since 1741 from seeds brought up from the West Indies. The sea islands of South Carolina and Georgia and the area around Georgetown proved best for its production. After the outbreak of the French and Indian War in 1754, the British cut off goods from the French empire, including indigo, and placed a bounty on its production to encourage growth in their own territories. The new opportunity prompted Moses Lindo, a London Jew, to place an advertisement in the *South-Carolina Gazette* in 1756 stating that he had found Carolina indigo to be of a quality equal to that produced by the French.[7] A few months later he arrived in Charleston and announced that he planned to ship 20,000 pounds of the dyestuff to London early in 1757. He also claimed that he had been allowed to be one of the "best judges" of cochineal, a brilliant scarlet dye derived from insects, and indigo on the Royal Exchange, and that his expertise had been recognized by a committee of the House of Commons.[8] Soon after his arrival Lindo became embroiled in some sort of controversy, and his frequent advertisements in the *South-Carolina Gazette* often served to defend him as much as to promote his business ventures. Indeed, he seems to have been a controversial individual for the rest of his life. On March 3, 1757, he stated that should anyone have demands on him, they could receive their money between the 15th and 25th of that month. At the same time, he declared that he was interested in purchasing a plantation of 500 acres with sixty to seventy slaves. He obviously had financial problems, because at least five disgruntled people to whom he owed money filed civil suits against him that year. In every case where the disposition of the case is indicated, he lost and had to pay his debts.[9] Always looking for opportunities, he developed new dyes in

6. Moses Lopez to Aaron Lopez, April 13, May 3, 8, 18, 23, 1764, in Tobias "Charles Town in 1764."

7. Aug. 19, 1756.

8. Ibid., Nov. 11, Dec. 23, 1756, Jan. 19, 1757.

9. Grimke v. Lindo, JR, 1757, 156; Leger v. Lindo, JR, 1757, 157a; Winborn v. Lindo, JR, 1757, 150a; Dandridge v. Lindo, JR, 1757, 140a. Over the years at least fourteen other suits were filed against him.

1759 from poke berries, which he claimed were as good as those from cochineal. He sent his findings to Solomon DaCosta, the editor of *Philosophical Transactions*, who published them in London.[10]

Despite the enthusiasm for it, Carolina indigo did not rate as high as that from the French possessions. The low reputation of the product was due in part to the quality of the plant and the dye it produced, but also to its poor grading and packing. Thus, in 1762, in order to improve their produce and its market, a group of important people in the province petitioned the governor to appoint Lindo as surveyor and inspector of indigo. The lieutenant governor, several members of the council, ten members of the house, forty-one merchants, and seven indigo planters signed the letter. Governor Thomas Boone followed their advice and appointed Lindo to the position shortly afterward.[11] Inspection of indigo was not required and the position paid no salary, but inspection and grading was necessary to get the best prices. Lindo charged customers a commission for his work. His tenure in this position coincided with the greatest period of export of the product from South Carolina. (See Table 26.)

Table 26

Indigo Exports from South Carolina, 1750–1773

Year	*Pounds*
1750	120,030
1755	193,803
1760	475,847
1765	467,725
1770	483,094
1773	794,150

Source: South-Carolina Gazette, June 21, 1773.

Like rice, indigo required a great deal of labor, and its production resulted in the introduction of more slaves into the colony. Because slaves were cheaper than indentured servants, few of the latter were to be found in Charleston. The only Jew who apparently was indentured, Jonas Phillips, came to Charleston with Lindo.[12]

Lindo served as the official inspector for ten years, at which time he again found himself involved in a number of disputes and resigned his post. Less than a year after Lindo left his position, the governor appointed him as appraiser of all dyes and drugs produced in North America, a title he held until his death in 1774.[13]

In addition to his promotion of indigo, Lindo became involved in a number of other activities. He claimed that he had developed a cure for the yaws, a skin disease resembling syphilis. His

10. *South-Carolina Gazette*, July 29, 1759; Lindo, "An Account of a New Die from the Berries of a Weed in South Carolina."

11. *South-Carolina Gazette*, Sept. 25, 1762; MR2M.120.

12. Phillips, "Family History of the Reverend David Mendez Machado"; Goldberg, *Major Noah*, 8–13.

13. *South-Carolina Gazette*, August 6, 20, 1772; MR2P.526; Sharrer, "Indigo in Carolina"; Winberry, "Reputation of Carolina Indigo."

recipe called for a mixture of poke berries, tobacco, and Roman vitriol, which was to be applied on the sores three times a day. The victim also needed to drink a potion consisting of a mixture of lignum vitae, the bark of a sassafras root, aniseed, and brown sugar.[14] On another instance, he stated he had found a topaz weighing 526 carats, which he had sent to the Queen of England.[15] During his stay in Charleston he obtained a grant for 700 acres on Curratail Creek in the upper part of the colony;[16] however, he never seems to have occupied that land.

Lindo died without a will, and his few possessions were sold at public auction.[17] His reputation, however, endured. His obituary in the *South-Carolina and American General Gazette* referred to him as the "Inspector-General of Indigo in this Province" and stated that he had been "esteemed one of the best Judges of that Dye that ever was in this Country."[18] After his death indigo production sharply fell off and virtually disappeared, although small amounts were grown as late as the twentieth century.

Most of the Jewish men in colonial Charleston operated retail shops and supplied the everyday needs of the citizens or luxuries for the rich. They established their businesses throughout the city, although the most popular places for business were On the Bay, Broad Street, the Wharves, and Elliot Street. In Charleston, retailers held a lower socioeconomic position than did factors or merchants. The factors dealt in the import-export trade, and though they frequently engaged in some of the worst of the abuses of the slave trade, they considered it beneath their dignity to deal with customers in a retail shop. At the top of the social structure were the plantation owners, who gained their wealth almost exclusively from working slaves. They dealt, on the other hand, with retailers. (See Table 27.)

14. *South-Carolina Gazette*, July 28, 1766.

15. Ibid., April 15, 1773.

16. Land Grants, Colonial Series, Oct. 25, 1764, South Carolina Archives.

17. *South-Carolina Gazette*, May 23, 1774.

18. May 6, 1774.

The Early National Period

The onset of the Revolution in 1775 greatly disrupted the economy of Charleston. Many of the Jewish merchants and shopkeepers had to flee the city or found themselves banished. Following the war unsettled conditions continued, and the United States faced economic depression. Many of the traditional markets within the British empire had been lost, and bad weather aggravated an otherwise difficult situation. Not until 1789 did the economy begin to recover. The outbreak of the Napoleonic wars in Europe in 1793 gave new impetus to economic development. Charlestonians sold goods to both the French and the English, and some Jewish merchants such as Abraham Sasportas engaged in privateering.[19] A number of people made great fortunes during these years despite the fact that the indigo market largely collapsed.

19. Jackson, *Privateers in Charleston*, 58–59, 69–79.

Table 27
Jewish Firms Advertising in Charleston Newspapers, 1732–1767

Firm	*Goods Advertised*	*Location(s)*
Carvalho & Gutterez	Spirits and foodstuffs	Church, Elliott St.
Cortissoz, Imanuel	Butter	Market Square
DaCosta & Farr	Fabrics, iron, ironmongery, condiments	Broad St.
DaCosta, Isaac	Dry goods, West Indian dry goods	Broad St.; on the Bay
DeMattos, Moses	Bread, flour	Union St.
DePass, Isaac	Rum, chocolate, cordial waters, sugar	Union St.; Broad St.
Isaacs, Solomon & Co.		On the Bay
Pinto, Isaac	Spirits, rum	On the Bay
Tobias, Joseph	Bread, flour, assorted goods	On the Bay; Elliott's Wharf

Source: Calhoun, Zierden, and Paysinger, "The Geographical Spread of Charleston's Mercantile, Community, 1732–1767," 182–220.

Cotton then became more and more important, and huge amounts were soon departing the wharves of the city. The first two decades of the nineteenth century saw a real boom in rice, cotton, and slaves. (See Table 28.)

One of the leading Jewish businessmen of this time was Philip Hart (1727–96), a merchant and a stock jobber who was born in Germany. There are more records dealing with his career than with that of any other Jew in South Carolina. He took part in 111 civil cases, in 33 of which he was the defendant. After his death, 29 cases were needed to settle his estate. Yet little is known about his career. He never married, and when he died, he left money to relatives, Beth Elohim, the poor, and orphans.[20]

Many of the Jews in postrevolutionary Charleston appear to have been of more humble means than Philip Hart. By 1790 the city directories begin to give a fairly complete listing of the businesses in the city. In that year Jews made up

Table 28
Cotton Exports from Charleston, 1784–1842

Year	*Pounds*
1784	1,200
1790	12,150
1800	17,789,803
1810	93,874,201
1820	127,860,152
1830	298,459,102
1840	539,531,850
1842	785,221,800

Source: Seabrook, *A Memoir on the Origin, Cultivation and Uses of Cotton,* p.7.

20. W26.397.

about 5 percent of the people in the city directory. Fifty percent of these were classified as shopkeepers while 8 percent were brokers, 8 percent vendue masters, and 6 percent merchants. (See the next section for a description of the vendue master's business.) A scattering of other professions can be found. Generally speaking, the pattern holds true for the period up to the 1820s. Some compilers of the directories, however, saw no difference between a merchant and a shopkeeper, thus making it difficult now to know which men had the largest businesses. In addition, directories classify some people as storekeepers and others as shopkeepers, apparently with no distinction meant. Depending on the source, a businessman who sold goods to the highest bidder could also be known as a vendue master, auctioneer, or vendue cryer. (See Table 29.)

After the Revolution, Aaron and David Lopez moved from Newport to Charleston, where they worked as auctioneers, an occupation they found to be the most profitable in the city. Aaron arrived about seven years before David and acquainted himself with local practices. He possessed "the esteem and confidence of all ranks of people." They jointly opened a firm in January 1791 with a considerable amount of goods, the "greatest part of which was knocked off at our first sale." They then filled their stores and "vaults" with many kinds of goods, with the result that business increased each day. David Lopez said they ranked "not second to any other auctioneer in the city, being patronized by many merchants of the first respectability and influence." They also opened a commission store, where they reduced their fees. Other merchants charged a fee for private sales and an additional one if the goods were sold at public auction. The Lopez brothers charged only one, which pleased both the sellers and the buyers,[21] though probably not the other merchants.

Following the War of 1812, rice and cotton continued to bring in huge profits for Charleston planters and exporters. Some Jews became planters, but most continued to engage in commerce, particularly the handling and disposition of imported goods. A considerable number of them had their businesses near the booming wharves. But the good times did not last forever. By 1819 planters had produced an excess of cotton, and prices fell. Other changes soon followed. Robert Fulton inaugurated steamboat navigation in 1806. Rapid development in that field soon meant that trans-Atlantic voyages could be made, with the first port of call being Boston or New York rather than Charleston. Charleston no longer figured so prominently either in shipping or exports.

The Antebellum Period

The generation before the Civil War witnessed the progressive decline of Charleston. By 1828 the Chamber of Commerce recognized that an era may have ended when it reported that

21. David Lopez to Uriah Hendricks, Nov. 24, 1791, Feb. 6, 1792, in Marcus, *American Jewry*, 461–62.

Table 29
The Occupations of Jews Listed in Selected Charleston Directories in the Early National Period

50 Occupations	*1790*	*1801*	*1809*	*1819*
Accountant				3
Auctioneer	4	4	1	3
Baker	1			
Blacksmith	1			
Blockmaker		1		
Boarding house owner		1		1
Boot maker				1
Broker	4	1	1	1
Cabinetmaker				1
Carpenter	1			
Cigar maker	1			
Clerk			4	3
Confectioner				1
Cooper			1	
Crockery store owner				1
Dentist		1	1	
Deputy register				1
Distiller		1	1	1
Druggist	1			
Dry goods store owner				14
Editor				1
Factor	1			1
Grocer		5	1	3
Gunsmith			1	1
Hebrew minister	1	1		
Horse dealer		1		
Interpreter, translator		1	2	1

"Charleston has for several years retrograded" with an unprecedented rapidity.[22] Shifts in trading patterns, federal tariff policies, and a growing antislavery movement all affected the city. On top of these came the Panic of 1837, the Great Fire of 1838, and other sporadic tragedies. South Carolinians became alienated from the nation and began to talk of nullification and then secession. City leaders sought to regain their economic prosperity by promoting economic

22. *Courier*, Mar. 13, 1828.

Table 29
(Continued)

50 Occupations	*1790*	*1801*	*1809*	*1819*
Law enforcement			1	2
Limner	1	1		2
Lumber measurer		1	1	
Mariner		1		
Master of work house		1		
Merchant	3	14	8	24
Mineral water house owner				1
Peddler				1
Physician		1	1	
Planter			1	1
Porter, house				1
Printer			1	
Schoolmaster	1		1	1
Scrivener	3			
Shopkeeper	24	27	54	4
State treasury officer		1		
State treasurer				1
Tailor		1		
Teacher				2
Tobacconist		3		
Vendue cryer		1		3
Vendue master		8		3
Watchmaker				3

Note: As much as possible, directories were chosen that came at ten-year intervals.
Sources: For 1790: *Charleston Directory;* for 1801: *Charleston Directory;* for 1809: Hrabowski, *Directory for the District of Charleston;* for 1819: Schenck and Turner, *Directory for the City of Charleston.*

schemes such as internal improvement and industrialization. They enhanced port facilities and built railroads into the interior, the first being the Charleston and Hamburg line in 1830. But the hinterland had less and less to offer. The lands had been worn out, and planters had moved west. Charleston businessmen also developed their own steamship lines, especially in the coastal trade. Although they had some success, other ports proved more convenient and less costly for exporters because Charlestonians never allowed the railroads to build all the way to the docks. As a result, shipping costs from the terminus to the port made the railroads less competitive than those in other cities. The progressive decline of the city and the growing frustration of the residents eventually culminated in the attack on Fort Sumter in the middle of the harbor and the outbreak of the Civil War.

Jewish merchants took part in the drive to modernize and industrialize. Moses Cohen Mordecai, among many other things, owned steamships for the carrying of goods. He also had a government contract to deliver mail between New York and Charleston. Mordecai named one of his ships, the *Isabel*, for his wife and commissioned a painting of it. Solomon Sampson Solomons, an engineer, directed the building of the North Eastern Railroad, later a part of the Atlantic Coast Line, and became its superintendent. Michael Lazarus promoted steam transportation up and down the rivers and opened navigation by steam up the Savannah River.[23] And Joshua Lazarus, as president of the Gas Light Company in Charleston, lit up the streets and shops of the city. Many others served on boards of railroads, banks, and insurance companies.

Two outstanding Jewish merchants in the antebellum period were Mordecai Cohen (1763–1848) and Moses Cohen Mordecai (1804–88). Mordecai Cohen had arrived in Charleston from Zamosc, Poland, by 1788. The first record of him in South Carolina is a certificate in 1794 of his having taken an oath of allegiance to the United States. Cohen appears in all the city directories from 1794 to 1841 as a shopkeeper, merchant, and planter. He owned much property in upstate South Carolina and in North Carolina as well as in the city and especially suffered from the Great Fire of 1838. His ability and wealth brought him appointments to a number of city boards and corporations such as the Wilmington and Raleigh Railroad. When Lafayette visited the city in 1825, city leaders borrowed his gold and silver plate to help entertain the Frenchman. Many of the documents dealing with his career concern the buying and selling of slaves. He died of old age in Charleston and was buried in the Coming Street Cemetery.[24] Moses Cohen Mordecai was born in Charleston, the son of David Mordecai and Reinah Cohen Mordecai. He married Isabel Rebecca Lyons in 1828, and they had eight children. The directories list his positions as accountant, merchant, and vendue merchant. His shipping business appears to have been his major concern. As he was born in Charleston, he had good connections in the city and served the community in many capacities, on the Board of Health, the Marion Artillery, the Commission of Markets, and the Commission of Pilotage. The people also elected him as an

23. *Daily Courier*, Sept. 20, 1862. He also speculated in Florida land, acquiring 156,000 acres at $1 per acre just north of what is now Miami. Marcus, *United States Jewry*, 172.

24. Tobias, *Hebrew Orphan Society*, 33; W44.356; MR3V.213; MS2.242; Elzas, *Jews of South Carolina*, 188; Marcus, *United States Jewry*, 208.

alderman of the city, as a member of the state House of Representatives, and to the South Carolina Senate. Among other things, he served as a director of the Southwest Railroad, the South Carolina Insurance Company, the Farmers and Exchange Bank, and the Gas Light Company of Charleston.[25]

Most of the Jewish residents of the city during this time, as before, operated small retail businesses. By the 1840s and 1850s they tended to specialize in a few goods instead of offering everything from bridles to butter. They were much more likely to operate a clothing store than any other kind. A growing number, however, worked for other individuals rather than owning their own shops. The number of Jewish accountants and clerks increased. Jewish business firms, especially those involved in the import-export trade or as auctioneers, grew larger and needed more employees. Commonly, several members of a family worked in the same business. Usually the employees were referred to as clerks, although this could cover a wide range of positions. Sometimes a person appeared in one city directory as an accountant and in the next as a clerk. A considerable number of Jews also had jobs in the public sector working as law enforcement officers, assessors, post office employees, and such. Only occasionally did a Jewish man make his livelihood as a blacksmith, blockmaker, carpenter, gunsmith, or seaman. One man, Nathan Bernstein, ran a junk shop in 1855. In addition to the Jewish shopkeepers in Charleston, a number ran country stores in surrounding districts in the Low Country. They became known as "Country Jews," and their presence lasted through much of the twentieth century. (See Table 30.)

Some occupations that have often been thought of as typical of Jewish immigrants, such as peddler or jeweler, are hardly represented in Charleston before 1850, when eastern European Jews began arriving. South Carolina law required peddlers to file a bond with the state treasurer in order to operate legally. Records of such bonds have been found for only three Jewish peddlers,[26] although the city directories from 1790 to 1859 list ten peddlers, six of whom did not appear in Charleston until 1850 or later. These individuals, however, are less likely to appear in the city directories than people who operated shops. Seven jewelers were listed in the directories, but five of these date from 1850 or later.

Another profession that required that a bond be made with the state treasurer was that of vendue master or auctioneer. Apparently this regulation resulted from the fact they took other people's property into their hands for disposition. Of the various businessmen in Charleston, the commission merchants or vendue masters were the most visible. Because they depended on attracting buyers to their places of business at a certain time, they constantly advertised, giving the impression that they constituted a greater part of the economy than

25. Elzas, *Jews of South Carolina*, 196–97.

26. MR3E.303, 3Q.445, 3R.29.

Table 30
The Occupations of Jews Listed in Selected Charleston Directories in the Antebellum Period

65 Occupations	*1829*	*1841*	*1852*
Accountant	7	3	7
Assessor		1	1
Attorney	1	1	5
Auctioneer	3	3	1
Bank cashier		1	2
Blacksmith	1	1	1
Boarding house owner			1
Boots, shoes seller			1
Book auctioneer	1		
Bookbinder		1	
Bookseller			1
Broker	1	1	5
Cabinetmaker	1		2
Carpenter		1	1
Clerk		1	20
Clothing store owner	3	10	4
Coach maker			1
Commission merchant	1	3	11
Corset maker			1
Customs house officer	1	1	3
Daguerreotypist			1
Dentist		1	2
Druggist		2	1
Dry goods store owner	1	4	9
Editor	1	1	1
Factor	1		1
Factory			1
Fancy store owner	2	1	
Fruits dealer		1	1
Gas works president			1
Gauger		1	
Glass stainer			1
Grocer	4	2	3
Hardware store owner		1	1

Table 30
(Continued)

65 Occupations	*1829*	*1841*	*1852*
House and sign painter	1		
Importer		1	
Insurance			1
Ironmonger	1		
Jeweler			2
Law enforcement	4	2	3
Linen store owner	1		
Machinist			1
Mattress maker		1	
Medical student			1
Merchant	5	6	1
Newspaper owner	1		
Packer			1
Painter			1
Physician	1	3	1
Planter	2		1
Post office clerk	2		
Printer		1	
Railroad engineer			1
Seaman			1
Shopkeeper	19		
Silk dyer			1
Soap and candle manufacturer		1	
Tailor		3	1
Tin plate worker	1		
Toy store owner	1		
Umbrella maker			1
Upholsterer	1	1	
Victualer		1	
Watchmaker	1		1
Wholesale dry goods dealer	1		

Note: As much as possible, directories were chosen that came at ten-year intervals.
Sources: For 1829: Cromwell, *Directory of the City of Charleston;* for 1841: Fay, *Charleston Directory;* for 1852: Baggett, *Directory of the City of Charleston.*

they actually did. The best example of the variety of goods handled by vendue masters can be illustrated by a poem by Abraham Mendes Seixas.[27] Though half of it deals with the selling of slaves, the doggerel shows that vendue masters could and would sell most anything. Seixas, who was born in New York, appears in the city directories as a merchant, tallow chandler, and broker. He also served as the *parnass* of the congregation and was warden of the workhouse at the time the verses appeared in the newspaper.[28] Although this poem can be found on a page with other advertisements, it may be a satire, as it appeared only once.

ABRAHAM SEIXAS,
All so gracious,
Once again does offer
His service pure
For to secure
Money in the coffer.

He has for sale
Some negroes, male,
Will suit full well grooms,
He has likewise
Some of their wives
Can make clean, dirty rooms.

For planting, too,
He has a few
To sell, all for the cash,
Of various price,
To work the rice
Or bring them to the lash.

The young ones true,
If that will do,
May some be had of him
To learn your trade
They may be made,
Or bring them to your trim.

The boatmen great,
Will you elate
They are so brisk and free;
What e'er you say,
They will obey,
If you buy them of me.

He also can
Suit any man
With land all o'er the State;
A bargain, sure,
They may procure
If they don't stay too late.

For paper he
Will sure agree,
Bond, note or publick debt;
To sell the same
If with good name
Any buyer can be met.

To such of those
As will dispose
He begs of them to tell;
By not or phiz,
What e'er it is
That they have got to sell.

He surely will
Try all his skill
To sell, for more or less,
The articles
of Beaux and belles,
That they to him address.

A number of people progressed from one position to another. Thomas W. Mordecai began as an accountant but later became a grain merchant and broker. Charles Henry Moïse also started as an accountant but afterward worked as a

27. *South-Carolina State Gazette & Timothy & Mason's Daily Advertiser*, Sept. 9, 1794.

28. Elzas, *Jews of South Carolina*, 43, 82, 92, 93, 106, 128–30, 278.

wholesale grocer, and David Lopez appeared in the directories first as a carpenter, then a builder, and eventually as a factory owner. Mordecai Hyams, who started as a clerk, later became a merchant and ship broker. Isaac Hyams, a peddler, afterward owned his own store and then became a merchant. And Joseph Sampson, a "scribe" or clerk, eventually became a broker and shipping agent.

Medicine

In Charleston a number of Jewish men worked as physicians, dentists, and pharmacists. For training, individuals first had to travel to Europe, as America had no medical schools. Eventually, Americans would be able to attend medical schools in Philadelphia or New York. Finally, the Medical College of South Carolina, the first in the South, began operation in Charleston in 1824.

The earliest Jewish physician whose credentials can be verified is Levi Myers (1768–1827). He was born near Jacksonboro, South Carolina, but his family moved to Georgetown, South Carolina, where he studied medicine for two years under Dr. Hyrne. When Hyrne died, he served as an apprentice under Dr. David Ramsay of Charleston, who encouraged him to study in Britain. After receiving his degree from the University of Glasgow in 1787, Myers returned to the United States, spent some time in New York, and began practice in Georgetown in 1791. He served as apothecary general of the South Carolina militia from 1799 to 1822 and one term in the state legislature. He was the first Jewish doctor to belong to the Medical Society of South Carolina, having joined in 1791. In 1812 he moved to Charleston in order to better educate his children but returned to Georgetown four years later. In 1822 a hurricane struck the South Carolina coast and swept the Myers's house out to sea, drowning the entire family.[29]

A physician with varied interests was Dr. Jacob Canter DeLaMotta (1789–1845). Born in Savannah, the son of Emanuel DeLaMotta and Judith Canter DeLaMotta, he married Charlotte Lazarus in 1835. His family moved to Charleston when he was about twelve years of age, and he spent much of his life there. He studied first under Drs. Alexander Baron, Samuel Wilson, and George Hall of Charleston and then attended the University of Pennsylvania, where he received his degree in 1810. His thesis, *An Investigation of the Properties and Effects of the Spiraea Trifoliata of Linnaeus, or Indian Physic*, was published in Philadelphia that year. He then returned to Charleston, where he became a member of the Medical Society of South Carolina, a necessary step to being accepted in the profession. He worked at the Charleston Dispensary until the War of 1812 broke out. He then joined the Second Regiment of Artillery of the United States Army, which he served as surgeon. In 1814 he received his dis-

29. Waring, *History of Medicine of South Carolina, 1670–1825*, 272–74; Waring, "Chief Medical Officers of the South Carolina Militia," 34–35; David Ramsay to John Eliot, April 23, 1792, copy in American Jewish Archives.

charge in New York and stayed to practice in that city until 1818, when he moved to Savannah. There DeLaMotta practiced with Dr. Moses Sheftall, served as treasurer of the Georgia Medical Society, and took a leadership role in religious affairs. Returning to Charleston in 1823, he set up practice there. The Medical Society of South Carolina elected him as its secretary in the second year of its existence, a post he held for the next decade. In 1833 he became a member of the board of the medical college. He delivered papers before the medical society, published a number of works, served on several boards in the city, became grand commander of the Supreme Council of Scottish Rite Masons, participated in the Union and States' Rights party, acted as president of Shearith Israel, delivered a number of funeral orations, and, among other things, unsuccessfully ran for Congress for the Union and Anti-Test Oath party in 1834. He also had a keen interest in herbs and maintained a botanical garden. In addition, DeLaMotta founded The South Carolina Institution for Correcting Impediments of Speech on Wentworth Street in 1826. A newspaper article from the time states that he permanently cured a drayman from Charleston from stammering in an hour or two. While not busy with other matters, he dispensed medications at Apothecaries Hall, at the corner of Broad and King streets, outside of which he placed a large golden mortar and pestle for advertisement. It became known as the "big yellow bucket." He ran this establishment until his death. The equipment from his pharmacy is now on display in the Charleston Museum.[30]

Another interesting physician was Columbus DaVega (1830–82). Born in Charleston in 1830, the son of Isaac DaVega and Grace Labatt DaVega, he attended local schools. His father died when he was three, and to help support his family he worked at Bancroft's Dry Goods Store while still young. He managed to save enough money to study medicine at night under Dr. C. C. Pritchard. He entered the Medical College of South Carolina, where he received his degree in 1852 at the age of twenty-one. His thesis topic was "A Treatise on Opium," then frequently used as a medicine, in which he carefully states: "I do not presume to advance anything original; but merely to adduce in a summary manner, those facts, which have been recorded by well authenticated writers."

DaVega then began to practice in Charleston; however, physicians educated in America frequently went to Europe for additional training in cities such as Vienna, Paris, and Berlin. DaVega departed for Paris. He studied there with two other doctors from South Carolina, Dr. Courtney King of Charleston and Dr. Edward Berrian Turnipseed of Columbia. Turnipseed received his degree from the medical college the same year as DaVega and King graduated in 1853. Apparently, they traveled together to France.

30. Tobias, "The Many Sided Dr. De La Motta"; Waring, *History of Medicine in South Carolina, 1670–1825*, 208–11; Bennett, *Apothecaries' Hall.*

In 1854 the Russian government recruited the three young doctors from South Carolina to provide medical care in the Crimean War. This war originally involved only Russia and Turkey, but soon Britain, France, and Sardinia-Piedmont entered on the Turkish side in order to stop the expansion of the Russian empire. The Americans served in the war because the Russians offered good pay and the young Americans could gain extensive experience.

DaVega served at Sebastopol throughout its siege and endured the constant bombardment. The noise damaged his hearing, and he suffered from partial deafness for the rest of his life. DaVega became involved in a dispute with German doctors. According to an account by Dr. William Holt, all the American physicians in the Russian service certified that a German doctor had treated him impolitely. DaVega protested to the Russian physician at the main hospital in Sebastopol where he was serving but failed to gain any satisfaction. DaVega then refused to allow the German doctor to enter the rooms where he was treating patients. The German, however, pushed his way in along with assistants. DaVega then took him "by the ear and threw him out." Troubles did not end, and DaVega transferred to another hospital, where he had similar problems. Another American physician, Dr. Stoddard, had to deal with some of the same difficulties with the Germans.

When the Crimean War ended, DaVega returned to Charleston to begin practice again. At the time the Civil War was rapidly approaching. Holt, Turnipseed, and DaVega all served with Confederate forces. DaVega, in fact, was present at the bombardment of Fort Sumter. In the weeks that preceded the outbreak of the Civil War, Charlestonians built a floating battery to be placed in the harbor to attack Fort Sumter. With guns at Fort Moultrie, Fort Johnson, and Morris Island, the Confederates could attack Fort Sumter from all sides. Attached to the battery was a ten-bed hospital apparently designed by DaVega. *Frank Leslie's Illustrated Newspaper* of New York sent an artist to Charleston to sketch the city and its environs as the war approached. The floating battery and its hospital especially fascinated the artist, who in one sketch shows the interior of the hospital. One of the men in the picture is very likely Dr. DaVega. When the bombardment of Fort Sumter began, the Confederates used the floating battery, which took a number of hits; apparently, DaVega's hospital saw considerable use. *The Official Records of the War of Rebellion* indicate that Dr. DaVega served on the battery as well as in other places during the bombardment.[31]

A number of other Jews in Charleston became doctors. Gershon P. Cohen received his degree from the medical college in 1829; however, he appears to

31. Waring, *History of Medicine in South Carolina, 1825–1900*, 48; William Joseph Holt Papers, South Caroliniana Library; photo in *Frank Leslie's Illustrated Newspaper*, Mar. 30, 1861; obituary of DaVega in *News and Courier*, July 15, 1882; Waring, "The Journal of Dr. William Joseph Holt"; Dvoichenko-Markov, "American Doctors in the Crimean War."

have worked elsewhere.[32] Edwin W. Moïse completed his studies at the same institution in 1832, but he moved away to Mississippi and then to New Orleans. He studied law and served as a member and as speaker of the legislature in Louisiana and attorney general in Louisiana.[33] Lawrence Ludlow Cohen graduated from the Medical College of South Carolina in 1838 and practiced in Charleston.[34] Thaddeus Eger Hertz also graduated from the Medical College of South Carolina in 1856 and practiced in Charleston. Joseph H. Goldsmith is listed in the city directory as a physician in 1852, as is Joseph R. Solomons, who received his degree in 1846 and worked as a physician and a dentist. Other physicians receiving medical training in Charleston were Moses Hyams in 1834, Jacob Cohen in 1839, F. J. Moses and A. M. Loryea in 1858.[35] A person who may have been a physician was Andrew Judah. He advertised in the *New York Gazette* of September 7, 1761, as a doctor who had recently arrived in that city. Then on December 31, 1764, he announced in the *South-Carolina Gazette* that he was a physician from London. Later he claimed to be from Amsterdam.[36] Also, the city directory lists Isaac DaCosta as a physician in 1809.

As for pharmacists, Philip Melvin Cohen served for many years supplying a variety of products, from live leeches to hair restorers to worm medicine. In the nineteenth century a qualified pharmacist needed to be trained as a physician. Thus Cohen attended the medical college, where he received his degree in 1836—although he had been licensed the previous year. He operated at a number of addresses. He also served on the City Board of Health for many years and as a director of the Bank of South Carolina.[37] Several other persons can be found listed as pharmacists or physicians: Abraham DeLeon, I. Audler, Philip Augustus Moïse, George Prince, David Sarzedas, and Moses Sarzedas. Most seem, however, to have simply run a shop where medical supplies could be purchased. This certainly was true of Philip Moses, who was listed in the city directories as a butcher, apothecary, and merchant, in that order, and of Joseph Triest, who was listed as a druggist one year but later operated a clothing store.

At least three men worked as dentists. One of these, Zachariah Florance, moved in and out of the city, sometimes leaving his family behind. On the other hand, Benjamin A. Rodrigues, who received his degree from the Medical College of South Carolina in 1834, actively par-

32. Waring, *History of Medicine in South Carolina, 1825–1900*, 352.

33. Ibid., 353; Elzas, *Jews of South Carolina*, 170; *Centennial Memorial of the Medical College of the State of South Carolina*, 117.

34. Waring, *History of Medicine in South Carolina, 1825–1900*, 353; Charleston directory, 1835, 1841.

35. *Centennial Memorial of the Medical College of the State of South Carolina*, 117, 119, 121, 125.

36. Hühner, "Jews in the Legal and Medical Professions," 161.

37. Waring, *History of Medicine in South Carolina, 1825–1900*, 353; Hoch, *History of Pharmacy in South Carolina*, 23, 74.

ticipated in the affairs of Beth Elohim and often supplied money to the board when they had financial troubles. The third, Abraham Alexander Solomons, received his degree from the Medical College of South Carolina in 1835. Although he was licensed as a pharmacist, he worked as a dentist, sometimes with Rodrigues.[38]

Law

The Jews of Charleston showed far less interest in the legal profession than in medicine, perhaps because the profession did not enjoy a very good reputation. Many people perceived lawyers to be generally dishonest. The only attorney for any length of time in the antebellum period was Abraham Moïse. He petitioned to be allowed to practice in 1826 and followed that line of work thereafter. Philip Phillips sought approval from the Court of Appeals to practice in 1829 and very likely became a lawyer in Charleston; however, he moved away to Mobile. There he served as a lawyer and a member of the U.S. House of Representatives in the 1850s. Although Myer M. Cohen is listed as an attorney in 1829, he soon changed his profession, as did Colleton H. Tobias. In the 1840s and 1850s Aaron Moïse, Isaac DaVega, David Henry Mordecai, and Virginius Jenkins Moïse practiced law, in addition to Abraham Moïse.[39]

The Arts

Several Jews in Charleston sought to make a living in the arts; however, this proved difficult. Despite its wealth, the community never placed much value on artists or writers. Indeed, most of the city remained illiterate, the slaves forcibly so, and many of those who had been educated possessed little more than a veneer of culture. A few artists and intellectuals of note did live and work in the city from time to time, people such as Samuel F. B. Morse, John James Audubon, and Robert Mills, but they invariably moved on. The greatest novelist and poet of the city, William Gilmore Simms, was little read even in his own day, and no novel of significance emerged from the city. The Jewish writers and artists rarely if ever made enough from their efforts to support themselves. A number of people tried and, in a more opportune location, might have succeeded.

One of these was Isaac Harby. Born in Charleston in 1788, he attended a classical academy, but at about the age of fifteen left the school. Apparently as a result of some articles he published in a local newspaper, he became an "assistant teacher" at the College of Charleston in 1804. He would have been about sixteen years of age at the time. In 1805 he

38. Hoch, *History of Pharmacy in South Carolina*, 74; *Centennial Memorial of the Medical College of the State of South Carolina*, 117.

39. Petition to Court of Appeals to Practice Law, South Carolina Archives: M. M. Cohen, 1829, 1830; Isaac DaVega, 1846, 1848; Aaron Moïse, Jr., 1842; Abraham Moïse, 1826; Philip Phillips, 1829; Charleston directory, 1813, 1829, 1831, 1835, 1838, 1841, 1849, 1852, 1855, 1859; Morgan, "Philip Phillips," 107–20; Williams, "The Criminal Lawyer," 138–50.

29. Advertisement for a dry goods store. (Dowling, *The Charleston Directory, for 1835–1836* [1835].)

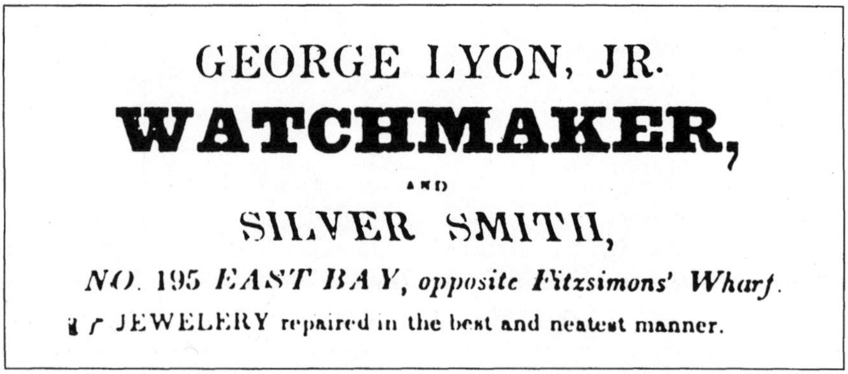

30. Advertisement of a Jewish watchmaker. (Dowling, *The Charleston Directory, for 1835–1836* [1835].)

studied law briefly under Langdon Cheeves but soon gave that up. His father, Solomon Harby, died in 1805, leaving little for his family. As a result Harby had to support the family, which consisted of his mother, two sisters, and four brothers. Financial problems plagued him for the rest of his life.

After the death of his father he began a number of careers. First, he opened a school at Edisto. The city directory of 1809 shows him still at Edisto, but on January 1, 1810, he announced he had opened an academy on Bedon's Alley in Charleston, where the "usual branches of An English Education" would be taught. The directory of 1813 shows that he had moved his school to Beresford Street. He followed that profession at least until 1822, at which time there appears to have been a break for three years. In 1825 he became a free school

31. Apothecaries Hall. Occupied by Jacob DeLaMotta. (From Bennett, *Apothecaries' Hall: A Unique Exhibit at the Charleston Museum* [Charleston, 1923].)

teacher, a position he maintained until he left Charleston in 1828.[40]

Harby also became a playwright. He completed his first play, *Alexander Severus*, in 1805 "between the drudgery of an attorney's office, and the time allotted to repast and rest." This tragedy about one of the Roman emperors consisted of five acts. He took it to Alexander Placide, the foreign-born manager of the Charleston Theatre and a dancing master, who greatly upset Harby when he said "de englese vas not veri coot, dat de play and not de incidents, des avantures, de something to catch de people." At the time, very few plays written by Americans reached production. Theater owners and their audiences preferred English dramas, which the playwrights usually derived from Italian novellas. Harby's work was, in fact, of this genre. Two years later Harby completed his second play, *The Gordian Knot, or Causes and Effects*. He also presented this to Placide and to William Warren of Philadelphia for consideration. Both turned it down. This time,

40. Moïse, "Memoir," in Moïse and Pinckney, *A Selection from the Miscellaneous Writings*, 5–40; *Daily Courier*, Jan. 1, 1810, Feb. 14, 1825, May 27, 1828; Charleston directory, 1809, 1813, 1819, 1822. No record of his being employed by the College of Charleston has been found.

32. Advertisement for fancy goods by von Santen and Baruc. (Gazlay, *City and General Business Directory for 1855* [1855].)

B. A. RODRIGUES M. D.
SURGEON
DENTIST.

HAS INTRODUCED INTO HIS PRACTICE "GOOD-YEAR'S PATENT VULCANITE BASE" FOR ARTIFICIAL TEETH. This work is highly recommended by the most eminent practitioners in the United States and Europe, and especially in cases where metalic plates IRRITATE the mouth.

Specimens can be seen at his Rooms, Meeting-street opposite the Circular Church.

October 12 wsm

J. R. SOLOMONS, M. D.
DENTIST.

HAS REMOVED HIS OFFICE TO HIS RESIDENCE, 5 HORLBECK ALLEY. October 13

33. Announcements about the dental practices of B. A. Rodrigues and J. R. Solomon. (*Courier*, October 15, 1849.)

RHEUMATISM—CURE WARRANTED.

HAYS' LINIMENT is an effectual and certain remedy for Rheumatism, and the Piles. One bottle is sufficient.

The Piles—no cure no pay.—Price $1. It is the positive orders of the proprietors, that every person who will use one bottle of Hays' Liniment, for the Piles, without being cured, shall have the price refunded, on return of the empty bottle to the Agent.

For sale wholesale by Dr. L. S. Comstock, No. 269 Pearl-st., New York, and wholesale and retail by his Agents, P. M. COHEN & CO. Druggists, 61 Broad-street, Charleston, S. C.

☞ Spohn's celebrated Remedy for Headache, and Oldridge's Balm of Columbia for the Hair, for sale a above. Oct 28

34. One of Philip M. Cohen's frequent advertisements of his pharmacy. (*Mercury*, May 6, 1843.)

Office North Eastern Rail Road.
CHARLESTON, April 30, 1857.

ON AND AFTER MONDAY NEXT, THE 4th MAY, this Road will be opened for Passengers and Freight Traffic to Salters.

From the above date, the Passenger Train will leave this City at 7.30 A. M., and returning leave Salters at 2 P. M.

S. S. SOLOMONS,
Engineer and Supt.

April 30 8

35. An announcement by S. S. Solomons, the chief engineer of the North Eastern Rail Road. (*Courier*, May 7, 1857.)

36. The hospital operated by Columbus DaVega. It was attached to the floating battery in Charleston Harbor. (*Frank Leslie's Illustrated Newspaper*, March 30, 1861.)

37. The Levy family's clothing store on King Street. (Gazlay, *City and General Business Directory for 1855* [1855].)

Placide accused Harby of using "false grammar." Just as he was considering burning the play, an actress asked to read it. Her interest and support resulted in its production and subsequent publication on the nights of May 3 and 10, 1810. About a pair of lovers, the drama was based on an English novel by William Henry Ireland called *The Abbess*, which in turn had been based on an Italian novella, *Secreto Maligno*. It was the first play performed in America by a Jewish author. That same year Harby married Rachel Mordecai of Savannah. Together they produced nine children, three of whom died as infants. Harby, at the time of the production of his play, was still only twenty-two years of age.[41]

41. Moïse, "Memoir" in Moïse and Pinckney, *A Selection from the Miscellaneous Writings*, 9–12; Fagin, "Isaac Harby and the Early American Theatre"; Charleston directory, 1806. Harby included the comments made by the theater director in the foreword of his play.

38. The *Isabel*. Owned by M. C. Mordecai. Named for his wife. (Photograph courtesy of Maryland Historical Society.)

Following this, Harby apparently both operated his school and edited newspapers. His first effort at publishing a periodical was *The Quiver*, a weekly that lasted only a short time. In 1814 he founded the *Investigator*, which also quickly died. That same year he acquired the *City Gazette and Commercial Advertiser*. Apparently he changed the title to the *Southern Patriot and Commercial Advertiser*. In 1816 Robert Howard became part owner, and in 1817 Harby sold out to him. While he owned the paper, Harby sought support from John C. Calhoun. He wanted to print the federal laws. When Calhoun replied that South Carolina already had three printers for this purpose, Harby stated that he had not been aware that they had the contract and that "two of them are wonderfully obscure." Should the government need other printers in the future, he would like to have the business as he believed that the government wanted to "patronize its friends and supporters" rather "than those who neither have the boldness nor the ability to do aught in its cause." After leaving the *Southern Patriot*, Harby worked at *The City Gazette and Daily Advertiser* as assistant to the editor, John Gedes, Jr. He also returned to teaching. In 1825 he established *The Examiner*, but it had only a brief existence. He also wrote occasional pieces for the *Charleston Mercury* and other papers. Throughout most of this period he appears to have worked at teaching during the day and at a newspaper at night. He also became involved with the Reformed Society of Israelites beginning in 1824.[42]

In 1819 he managed to complete *Alberti*, his third and last known play. Another drama in five acts, it appeared on the stage with an English actor as producer and a professional cast. This play received great acclaim locally on the nights of April 27 and 30, 1819. During its second performance President James Monroe, who was then visiting the city, attended. As in his other works, Harby based this play on a drama by Alfieri entitled *The Conspiracy of the Pazzi*. In getting the play produced, Harby had to make alterations that he did not like. When he published the work, he restored it as he originally wrote it. In the preface he also defended the criticism that the play was an American production. To this he exclaimed, "I plead guilty. I have even the hardihood openly to acknowledge, nay, be proud of the accident of birth, which has placed me under the protection of laws that I revere, and in the bosom of a country that I love."

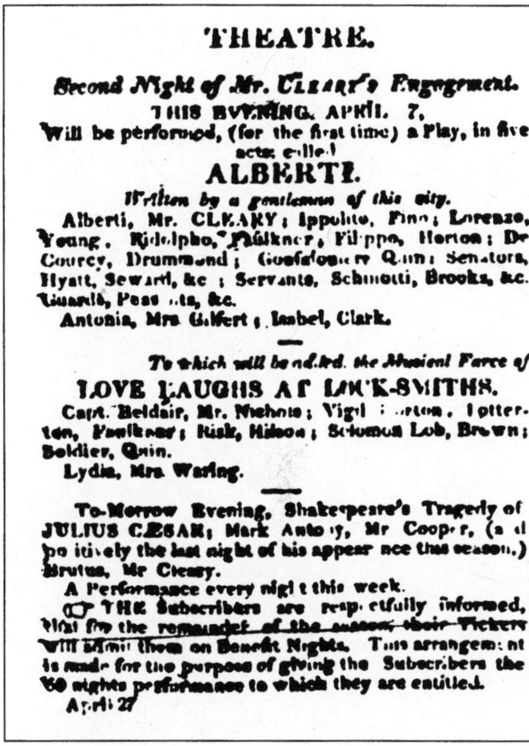

THEATRE.

Second Night of Mr. Cleary's Engagement.

THIS EVENING, APRIL 27,

Will be performed, (for the first time) a Play, in five acts, called

ALBERTI.

Written by a gentleman of this city.

Alberti, Mr. CLEARY; Ippolito, Finn; Lorenzo, Young, Ridolpho, Faulkner, Filippo, Horton; De Courcy, Drummond; [illegible] Quin; Senators, Hyatt, Seward, &c; Servants, Schinotti, Brooks, &c. [illegible], &c.

Antonia, Mrs Gilfert; Isabel, Clark.

To which will be added, the Musical Farce of

LOVE LAUGHS AT LOCK-SMITHS.

Capt. Beldair, Mr. Nichols; Vigil [illegible], Totterton, Faulkner; Risk, Hilson; Solomon Lob, Brown; Soldier, Quin.

Lydia, Mrs Waring.

To-Morrow Evening, Shakespeare's Tragedy of JULIUS CÆSAR; Mark Antony, Mr Cooper, (and positively the last night of his appearance this season.) Brutus, Mr Cleary.

A Performance every night this week.

☞ THE Subscribers are respectfully informed, that for the remainder of the season, their Tickets will admit them on Benefit Nights. This arrangement is made for the purpose of giving the Subscribers the 60 nights performance to which they are entitled.

April 27

39. Advertisement for a play by Isaac Harby. (*Courier*, April 17, 1819.)

In 1827 not long after the death of his wife and with the means of living growing "every day more slender and precarious," Harby wrapped up his affairs in Charleston and set out for New York. He hoped to become a successful playwright "in a large and flourishing city." There he wrote for the *Evening Post* and, along with his sister, Caroline Litchfield Harby, operated a school on Howard Street. But "the scene of his anticipated success soon proved the grave of his intelligence." He died within a few

42. MR3N.460; 4G.400; 4N.298; Brigham, *History and Bibliography of American Newspapers*, 1043; Moïse, *Biography of Isaac Harby*, 6; King, *The Newspaper Press of Charleston*, 77; Harby to Calhoun, July 26, 1815, American Jewish Archives.

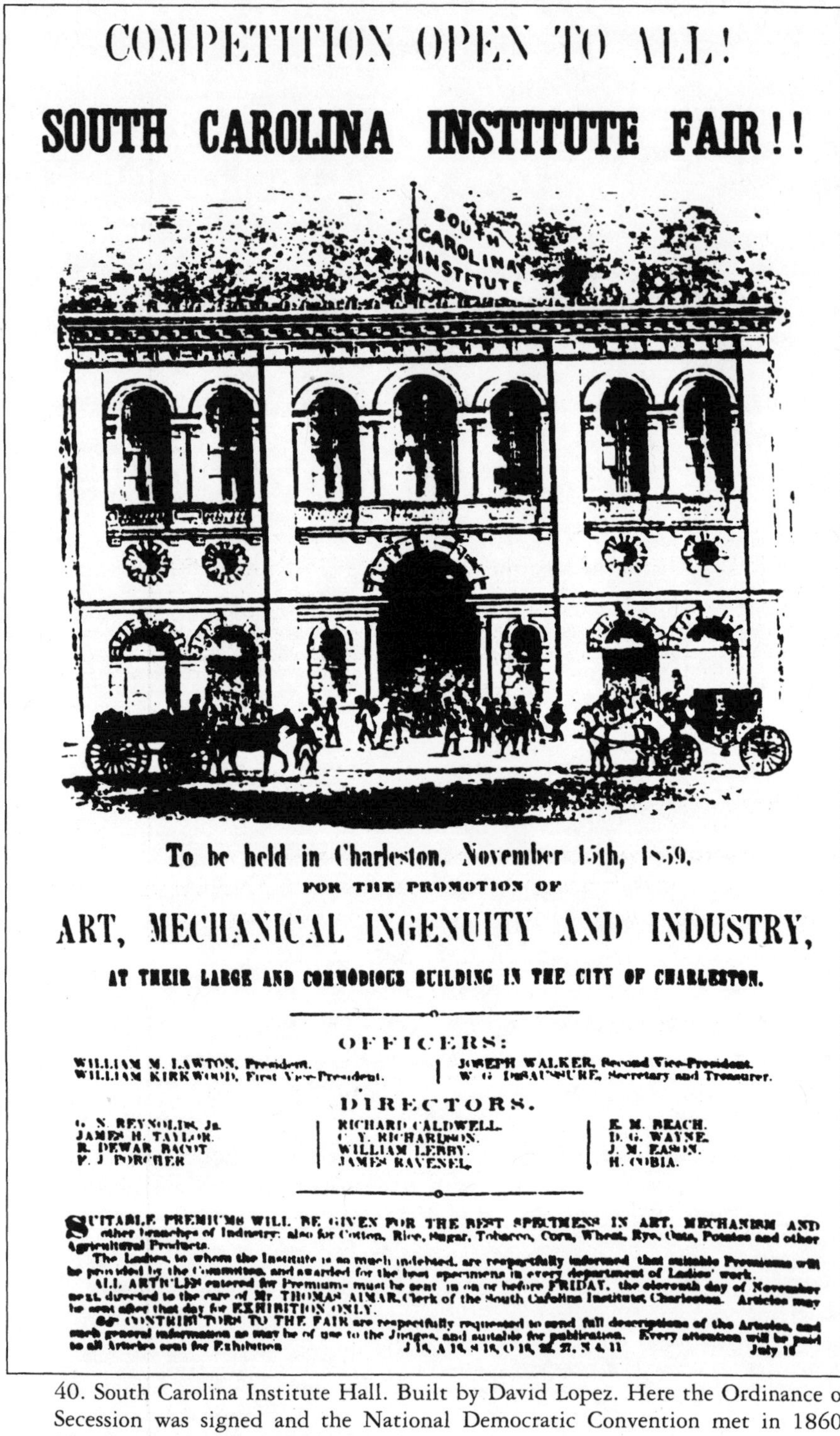

COMPETITION OPEN TO ALL!

SOUTH CAROLINA INSTITUTE FAIR!!

SOUTH CAROLINA INSTITUTE

To be held in Charleston, November 15th, 1859,

FOR THE PROMOTION OF

ART, MECHANICAL INGENUITY AND INDUSTRY,

AT THEIR LARGE AND COMMODIOUS BUILDING IN THE CITY OF CHARLESTON.

OFFICERS:

WILLIAM M. LAWTON, President. | JOSEPH WALKER, Second Vice-President.
WILLIAM KIRKWOOD, First Vice-President. | W. G. DeSAUSSURE, Secretary and Treasurer.

DIRECTORS.

G. N. REYNOLDS, Jr. | RICHARD CALDWELL. | E. M. BEACH.
JAMES H. TAYLOR. | C. Y. RICHARDSON. | D. G. WAYNE.
R. DEWAR BACOT | WILLIAM LEBBY. | J. M. EASON.
F. J. PORCHER | JAMES RAVENEL. | H. COBIA.

SUITABLE PREMIUMS WILL BE GIVEN FOR THE BEST SPECIMENS IN ART, MECHANISM AND other branches of Industry: also for Cotton, Rice, Sugar, Tobacco, Corn, Wheat, Rye, Oats, Potatoes and other Agricultural Products.

The Ladies, to whom the Institute is so much indebted, are respectfully informed that suitable Premiums will be provided by the Committee, and awarded for the best specimens in every department of Ladies' work.

ALL ARTICLES entered for Premiums must be sent in on or before FRIDAY, the eleventh day of November next, directed to the care of Mr THOMAS AIMAR, Clerk of the South Carolina Institute, Charleston. Articles may be sent after that day for EXHIBITION ONLY.

CONTRIBUTORS TO THE FAIR are respectfully requested to send full descriptions of the Articles, and such general information as may be of use to the Judges, and suitable for publication. Every attention will be paid to all Articles sent for Exhibition

J 18, A 18, S 18, O 18, 25, 27, N 4, 11 July 16

40. South Carolina Institute Hall. Built by David Lopez. Here the Ordinance of Secession was signed and the National Democratic Convention met in 1860. (*Courier*, October 27, 1859.)

months. The press in New York and Charleston lamented the loss.[43]

Mordecai Manuel Noah also wrote a play that was performed in Charleston. Entitled *Paul and Alexis; or, The Orphans of the Rhine*, the play came about when Charles Young asked him to write one for his wife in which she could play the leading role. Unfortunately, Noah, who had been actively involved in politics in Charleston, had enemies who gathered and hissed the performance. Not at all original, the play was based on a melodrama by Pixericourt, *Le Pelerin Blanc ou les Orphelins du Hameau*, which, in turn, was based on an earlier play—and that play had been adapted from a still earlier one. Nevertheless, it probably was the second play written by an American that was subsequently performed in England.[44]

Within three months after Isaac Harby left the *Southern Patriot*, the U.S. marshal sold the paper "under execution" to another Jew, Jacob N. Cardozo, as Harby's former partner Robert Howard could not pay his debts. Cardozo, like Harby, was born in America, in this case Savannah; but his family moved to Charleston when he was about eight. According to some sources, he left school at about twelve and worked at a number of jobs; however, the fact that his father served as a schoolteacher and Jacob was the editor of newspapers would indicate he had far more than just the basics in education. Writing interested him all his life. When he was about twenty-four years of age, he joined a literary circle known as the Methulogic Society, which proclaimed its dedication to truth and enlightenment. In 1811 Cardozo delivered the anniversary oration, which he entitled *An Oration on the Literary Character, Delivered on the Anniversary of the Methulogic Society*, which he or the organization subsequently published. In this work he cited literary and scientific leaders as being patriots who led in the fight against tyranny. He pointed out that the French Revolution had gone wrong when Napoleon took over, and that America remained as the hope of civilization. By 1819 he was editing the *Southern Patriot*, and he owned it from January 1823 to April 1845. The paper strongly advocated free trade but only with those countries that opened their ports to American goods. Cardozo succeeded in getting a contract from the federal government to publish for it; however, he lost this business when John Quincy Adams became president. The loss proved very harmful to Cardozo, who appealed to Senator Robert Y. Hayne of South Carolina. At this time the U.S. government still held the mortgage on which Cardozo was making payments. Hayne introduced a bill that reduced the debt and extended the payments

43. Moïse, "Memoir," in Moïse and Pinckney, *A Selection from the Miscellaneous Writings*, 22–24, 40; Fagin, "Isaac Harby and the Early American Theatre," 7–9; Moïse, *Biography of Isaac Harby*, 7–8, 11–14; Kohler, "Isaac Harby, Jewish Religious Leader and Man of Letters"; Harby, *Alberti: A New Play in Five Acts*; Watson, *Antebellum Charleston Dramatists*, 34–41; King, *The Newspaper Press of Charleston*, 77.

44. Goldberg, *Major Noah*, 67–68.

that Cardozo was making to the government for the purchase of the paper.[45]

Extremely interested in economic questions, Cardozo wrote a number of articles for various journals, the most important being "Political Economy—Rent,"[46] and he published two books, *Notes on Political Economy*[47] and *The Tariff: Its True Character and Effects Practically Illustrated*.[48] His writings show far more optimism than that of the English classical economists of his time such as Thomas Malthus. He believed that America had unlimited opportunities. For him, technology was the key to the future, and he advocated industrialization and saw danger in the South's relying too much on cotton. Though he defended the southern way of life, including slavery, he apparently did not own any slaves himself. Furthermore, although denouncing the tariffs that harmed South Carolina commerce, he believed that they caused less harm than the destruction of the Union would.[49] Unfortunately, few southerners heeded his advice.

Cardozo's economic writings brought him little or no profit. Thus he continued to work in the newspaper business. He sold the *Southern Patriot* in 1845 and established the *Charleston Evening News*, which first appeared in October of that year. Then in the autumn of 1847 he sold the *Evening News* but continued to write for it until the Civil War. After 1861 he lived mostly in Savannah, but at the time he wrote his *Reminiscences of Charleston* in 1866, he was residing in Charleston and was eighty years of age. In fact, he continued to contribute to the Savannah *Morning News* until a year before his death in 1872.[50]

Several other Jews of Charleston sought to inform the public and make a living in doing so. Two Jews compiled city directories, Eleazer Elizer in 1803 and Morris Goldsmith in 1831. Also, Samuel Hart sold and published books, and Bernard Levy, Joseph A. Levy, Fisher Moses, Emanuel Levy, and Noah Ellis worked as printers.[51]

Of Charleston's Jews in the visual arts, the first known individuals are Joshua Canter (1767–1826) and John Canter (1782–1823), both sons of Jacob and Rebecca DeLaMotta Canter. Joshua appears to have been born in Copenhagen; John was born in St. Croix. The former appears in the city directories as early as 1790 as a limner (drawer), drawing teacher, and portrait and miniature painter. John, who began his career by 1809, worked as a limner and portrait painter. He reportedly was the "drawing master" at the College of Charleston in 1806. His tombstone inscription indicates that he "was known in the city as an artist of no inferior standing." A

45. MR4R.353; 4Z.245, 246; Elzas, *Jews of South Carolina*, 176–77; Dorfman, *The Economic Mind in American Civilization*, 2: 853.

46. *Southern Review* (Feb. 1828): 192–218.

47. Charleston, 1826.

48. Charleston, 1830.

49. Leiman, *Jacob N. Cardozo*.

50. King, *The Newspaper Press in Charleston*, 77–78; *News and Courier*, Sept. 2, 1873.

51. Charleston directory, 1784, 1802, 1803, 1806, 1809, 1813, 1816, 1829, 1831, 1837–38, 1841, 1852, 1855. Goldsmith also served as a law enforcement officer and was noted for his diligent pursuit of pirates and smugglers. Marcus, *American Jewry*, 91.

41. John Canter's portrait of Leah Lazarus Cohen. (Gibbes Art Museum/ Carolina Art Association.)

work attributed to John Canter, which shows considerable ability, is a portrait of Leah Lazarus Cohen in the Gibbes Art Gallery in Charleston.

One artist who was born in Charleston was Theodore Sydney Moïse (1808–85). He learned to paint from his aunt Penina Moïse. The city directory of 1829 shows him to be an accountant, whereas the one in 1835 lists his profession as a portrait painter; however, he also cleaned and repaired old pictures and executed ornamental penmanship for albums. He married for the first time in Charleston in 1836 but left the city sometime after that for New Orleans. He spent most of his career there, where he painted portraits of the city's leaders.

42. Theodore Moïse's Portrait of Mordecai Cohen. (Gibbes Art Museum/ Carolina Art Association.)

His best works include portraits of Henry Clay, which is in the Metropolitan Museum in New York, and of Andrew Jackson, which is in the City Hall in New Orleans. The Gibbes Art Gallery in Charleston owns a portrait of Mordecai C. Cohen that is attributed to Moïse.

Another Charleston-born artist was Solomon Nunes Carvalho (1815–94). In 1838 he ran a dry goods store in Charleston, but by 1852 he had become a daguerrotypist or photographer. He lived and worked in Charleston, Baltimore, Philadelphia, and New York. In 1853 John C. Frémont, who had attended the College of Charleston (but was expelled) and who later became the first Republican candidate for president of the United States, asked Carvalho to join in an expedition across the Rockies to California. Carvalho, who lived in Charleston at the time, served as the official photographer and wrote the only account of the journey. He was the first photographer to accompany a scientific expedition. He is, however, better known for his portraits of Abraham Lincoln and Brigham Young.

Lawrence L. Cohen (b. 1836), apparently the son of the pharmacist Philip Melvin Cohen, showed talent quite early in life and studied painting at an art school in Dusseldorf, Germany. He had returned to Charleston by 1859, at which time the directory shows him as a clerk. Like other Jews of the city, he supported the Confederacy and painted the Confederate flag, which was raised over Fort Sumter after it was taken by the southerners. Nothing is known about him after this point.[52]

All in all, most of the Jews of Charleston made a comfortable living. A few of them lived extremely well, although a small number survived on charity. They were mostly lower-middle-class shopkeepers; however, some also entered the professions and the arts. No laws, quotas, or other impediments barred them from happily taking part in any profession they wanted.

---

52. *Courier*, Feb. 28, 1836; *Occident* (1852–53), 174; Charleston directory 1790, 1794, 1802, 1803, 1806, 1807, 1809, 1813, 1816, 1819, 1822, 1829, 1835, 1837–38, 1852; *Southern Patriot*, Nov. 8, 13, 1826; Rosenthall, "Jewish Artists in Early Charleston"; Gutmann, "Jewish Participation in the Visual Arts," 21–30; Carvalho, *Incidents of Travel and Adventure in the Far West*; Sturhahn, *Carvalho: Artist-Photographer-Patriot*.

CHAPTER 8

Women and Work

"Then continue lovely woman to tread the path of Virtue; teach to your children early lessons of Piety and Religion, so will you insure to your selves the satisfaction of having done your duty."

—Myer Moses, 1806[1]

"On an equality with man in this happy land, she shows herself worthy of her station by emulating him in every good enterprise in which she can properly embark."

—Nathaniel Levin, 1842[2]

Jewish and antebellum southern traditions regarding women had much in common. Women had distinct roles apart from men. Jewish women sat separately from men in the synagogue: their chief duties were in the home. Jewish male attitudes toward women and their place in society in Charleston can be seen in speeches made by Myer Moses in 1806 and Nathaniel Levin in 1842; both were sons of Englishmen and both had been born in South Carolina. Moses, in an oration to the Hebrew Orphan Society, proclaimed, "Hail woman! . . . a star, which shoots forth to all mankind . . . which can shine upon, and brighten the gloomy object of its care." He stated that "there exists no cure more potent than the kind affection and persuasive language of woman," but "the whitened stock" could become blasted forever if "the foul tongue of Slander" should lay "hold of the character of your sex."[3] Nathaniel Levin spoke in 1842 in honor of the retirement of Sally Lopez from the operation of the Sunday school. He said that a woman was "delicate in her constitution, mild and beneficent in her disposition, warm in her affections, and lovely in all her actions." She was "the guardian and ornament of the social compact." In addition, "her domestic virtues confer on home all its comforts

1. Moses, *An Oration*, 31.

2. Levin, "Address Delivered Before the Society for the Instruction of Jewish Youth," 164.

3. Moses, *An Oration*, 29–31.

and allurements." Men were "her superiors in knowledge and the reasoning faculties," "naturally hardy in constitution, and rugged and boisterous in temper." Yet they turned to women "to seek relief" from their conflicts and oppressive strength, and they could not be "other than depressed, where woman is not exalted." "Wisely" had the Supreme Creator ordained "that she should be a *companion* to man."[4]

As is usually the case, reality differed from the ideas of such men as Levin. The Jewish women of Charleston did far more than adorn the homes and console the "rugged and boisterous" men. They played a much greater role than the southern Jewish man would have liked to admit, and nowhere was this truer than in business.

The Status of Women in Business

Both as a royal province and as a new American state, South Carolina followed English legal procedures regarding the status of women. A single adult woman, or *feme sole*, either unmarried or a widow, could handle her own affairs. A married woman, or *feme covert*, came under the control of her husband and had no property rights except to a dower unless her husband allowed her to be a sole trader. She then enjoyed all rights as if she were single. In Charleston between the years 1766 and 1827 a considerable number of Jewish women took the path as sole traders.[5] A considerable number of other women operated businesses while single or widowed. Indeed, Jewish women could be found behind the counter far more often than on the pedestal.

A married woman had to acquire the rights of a sole trader from her husband. An example of how this was done is provided by Solomon Levi, who in 1766 recorded a document that stated that his wife Sarah should "immediately . . . become a sole Trader within the province." She was to remain such during her coverture "without any interruption, hindrance, disturbance or molestation by him." Furthermore, she could keep all profits and advantages that might arise from her business, and the stock and utensils that she used should be for her sole use. She would be in "no ways liable to the debts of him . . . nor be subject to his control." In addition, her goods could not be taken from her because of his debts. Nor should her property be subject to his control.[6] Normally wives also received the right to write a will, but Sarah Levi was not given this privilege.

Why They Engaged in Business

The amount of information about the Jewish sole traders in South Carolina varies considerably from person to person. In order to understand the women's business activities, one must look not only at them but at their husbands, the

4. Levin, "Address Delivered Before the Society for the Instruction of Jewish Youth," 162–64.

5. After this time, far fewer records are available.

6. MR2M.433.

commercial activities of the spouses, and their families. Unfortunately, little of note has been written about women in business, and virtually nothing on sole traders. Therefore, comparisons cannot readily be made with other women in Charleston or with sole traders in other communities. Jewish women, however, seem to have engaged in business more than other women.

The husband's profession may explain why a few women became free traders. For example, Ann Sarah Huguenin Irby Alexander's husband worked as a treasury clerk, a clerk in the custom's house, and an auditor at the custom's house. He is also listed as having a shop. Very possibly she ran the shop while he did his bookkeeping. Also, Hannah Levy DeLieben's husband was both a vendue master (auctioneer) and a shopkeeper. She possibly became a sole trader to manage the shop, although she seems to have been a strong-willed woman who may have demanded the right to trade in her own name. Sarah Derkheim helped support her family while her husband journeyed up and down the East Coast to perform circumcisions. Also, some wives whose husbands ran shops may have become sole traders so they could operate the businesses while their husbands traveled.

Several women became sole traders after their husbands encountered serious economic and legal problems. In these cases the men may well have turned the business over to their wives as a legal maneuver to avoid losing their property. But the men may also have realized that their wives could handle matters better than they. Or the wives may have asserted themselves and insisted that the husbands give them control. Whoever initiated the action, the husbands rarely appear in the records after declaring their wives sole traders. In some cases the men could have left South Carolina with or without their families.

One of the women who seems to have taken over control of business affairs was Rebecca DeMendes Benjamin, the wife of Philip Benjamin and the mother of Judah Benjamin, who later became the secretary of state for the Confederacy. The family had lived in the West Indies and Wilmington, North Carolina, before arriving in Charleston. By 1822 Philip Benjamin operated a dry goods store in Charleston, and in 1823 he bought a building on King Street. But he quickly had to mortgage this building. Then he faced suits in the Court of Common Pleas for failure to repay loans of $201 and $580. When he could not comply with court orders to honor his debts, he had to allow the sheriff to sell his building. But his troubles did not end; two other suits were filed against him, one for the failure to repay $269.50 and another for failure to repay $1095.00. Clearly, Benjamin was in desperate financial straits. In July 1827 he granted his wife the status of a sole trader, and the court cases against him stopped. Indeed, except for entries in the city directory and his death notice in the city records, little is known about him after that.[7]

Another woman who seems to have

7. RMC Book M4, 231, 271; T 9, 486; Caldwell v. Benjamin, JR, 1826, 25a; Dawson v. Benjamin, JR, 1827, 11a; Marks v. Benjamin, JR, 1828, 40a; Anger & Black v. Benjamin, JR, 1827, 12a.

taken over control of her husband's business affairs because of mismanagement or misfortune was Rachel Moses Cohen. In 1820 her husband, Moses Cohen, was sued for $3,895.12. In 1822 he was charged with the failure to repay loans of $7,223.84, $817.06, and $954.76. He lost all these and agreed to pay the amounts plus court costs. Then, in August 1822, he granted his wife the status of a sole trader. After that no other suits were filed against him. Nor is there any further mention of her.[8]

Gershon Cohen fared even worse. He was the defendant in thirteen suits between 1790 and 1795. Within a month after he lost the last suit, he made his wife, Rebecca Sarzedas Cohen, a sole trader. Following that he was sued only once more—three years later.[9] Frances Pollock, wife of Levy Pollock, may have taken over her husband's affairs under the same circumstances. When he and Henry Lazarus fell into debt, they had to turn their assets over to J. C. Moses & Co., and Milliken Primrose & Co. Following this Frances Pollock became a sole trader.[10] Also, Judith Alberga Suares married Jacob Suares in Kingston, Jamaica. He preceded her to Charleston. When she arrived in 1799, he made her a sole trader, stating that she wanted to carry on a business for herself; however, the fact that he had recently lost a civil suit may be the true reason.[11]

Two women appear to have become sole traders so that their husbands might protect property from being seized. In 1804 Mathias Hart made a declaration that I. M. Hart had laid claim to a number of articles of furniture that his wife Elizabeth Hart had brought with her from New York. Mathias Hart stated that these goods belonged to his wife and her children and had been in her possession before and after she left New York. Three days later, he made her a sole trader.[12] This is the last time the couple is to be found in the records. A second example is that of Rachel Florance. On January 25, 1804, Ivey Smith filed a suit against Zachariah Florance claiming that he had swapped a slave named Doll for a boy slave named Lewis. When the boy died, Smith claimed he had been deceived by Florance and demanded repayment. In a case that was not finally decided until 1808, Smith won. Florance had to pay $400 plus interest and court costs.[13] On July 27, 1804, about six months after Smith filed suit against him, Florance granted his wife Rachel the status of sole trader and turned over for her use a small

8. State Bank v. Cohen, JR, 1820, 156a; Corse v. Cohen, JR, 1822, 68a; Benson v. Cohen, JR, 1822, 90a; Drege v. Cohen, JR, 1811, 9a.

9. The first of these was Shoolbred v. Gershon Cohen and Jacob Jacobs, JR, 1790, 187a, and the last was Hammett v. Nathan Hart & Co. (Gershon Cohen & Nathan Hart), JR, 1795, 292a; Sasportas v. Cohen, JR, 1798, 201a.

10. MR4Q.196. This assignment for the benefit of their creditors is dated Jan. 26, 1819. The deed for the sole tradership is dated 1819.

11. Narr v. Suares, JR, 1799, 706a. The case was decided on June 19, 1799. He made his wife sole trader on July 25, 1799.

12. MR3V.113, July 9, 1804; MR3V.114, July 12, 1804.

13. Smith v. Florance, JR, 1808, 88a.

amount of stock and capital, including three slaves. In 1811 her status reverted to that of a *feme covert* by a new document, which she signed.

Just how frequently men failed to manage their affairs well and turned them over to their wives is unknown. Possibly it happened more often than the examples above reflect. It is likely that creditors saw the futility of suing others.

For Jewish people, the possibility exists that the men turned over affairs to their wives so they could spend their time in study. This explanation, however, is doubtful in the case of Charleston. A number of those whose wives became sole traders were of Sephardic stock. They did not share the eastern European traditions of intense study and likely had little formal training in Jewish thought. When an ecclesiastical court granted Mordecai Lyon a divorce in 1788, Israel DeLieben and Israel Myers, "learned men" in religious questions, heard the divorce case.[14] These were probably the two most knowledgeable men about Jewish law in the city. This is the same Israel DeLieben who married Hannah Levy Hart DeLieben (later Davis). Despite his knowledge of Jewish ways, he was quite active in business affairs. Men such as he did not emigrate to North America to close themselves up in a study.

Women who had previously been married were able to negotiate a better status for themselves than younger brides. A good example of a woman who seems to have been quite successful at handling her own affairs was Hannah Levy Hart DeLieben Davis. She married three times. By the time of her second marriage she was a sole trader, a position she also held during her third marriage. In fact, the marriage settlement for her third marriage provided that Moses Davis should turn over $20,000, a huge sum in those days, for her use. When he did not pay, the trustees, who had the responsibility for looking after her interests, sued him. The court ruled in favor of the trustees, and Davis had to pay his wife the amount plus costs.[15] Surely, the household was not a happy one. Another woman who came to her second marriage with considerable property was Catherine Jacobs Hyams.[16] Solomon Hyams granted her sole tradership five days after the marriage settlement was negotiated.

Another reason why a man might give up his rights to his wife could be illness. Judith Hays Sarzedas, after the death of her first husband, married Jacob Jacobs, a vendue master in Charleston. In June 1796 he wrote his will, and in November 1796 he made his wife a sole trader. Within a year he died.[17] The evidence suggests that he was ill when he turned affairs over to his wife. The same is possibly true for Esther Rodrigues, the wife of Moïse Rodrigues. Both were born in Bordeaux, France, and probably emigrated to Charleston together. She became a sole trader in 1824. Her husband is listed in the city directories in

14. MR2X.632.

15. Lazarus & Hart v. David, JR, 1820, 205a.

16. MS6.41.

17. W26.640.

1825 and 1829 as living on Orange and King streets, but in neither case is a profession given. Normally only older men were so listed. He died in 1830.

Two women went into business because they had no choice. To do so, they had to be assisted by men other than their husbands. One was Sarah Hart, who had married Leo Hart. He made her a sole trader in 1796, and she is to be found in the city directories of 1802 and 1803 operating a shop on Queen Street in Charleston. Then in 1809 her brother Solomon Nathan, a merchant, provided goods and merchandise for her and her child, who had been left in a state of indigence for some time. With these she was to carry on a business.[18] Another was Rachel Florance. Her husband, who as noted above had given and revoked sole tradership status for her, must have left his wife and seven children in Charleston while he lived elsewhere. On May 8, 1817, when he was away in Philadelphia, he gave his wife power of attorney to sell a mulatto slave named William.[19] On July 10, 1817, Jacob Lazarus, Jr., who had been closely associated with him, "moved by love of humanity and sentiments of friendship" toward the family, gave Rachel $8,000 and the slave William, which he had obviously purchased. He provided that she could invest in a dry goods store, slaves, bank stock, or household furniture as she wished.[20] Zachariah Florance returned to the city; he is listed in the 1822 directory as working as a dentist on King Street. Rachel Florance is listed at the same address running a dry goods store. After that, neither appears in the records of South Carolina.

Women Helping Women

Women who had already been involved in business could establish other women in business. This certainly was the case with Judith Hyams. Hannah Hyams, who became a sole trader in 1807 and operated a dry goods store on King Street, transferred her goods and merchandise to Judith Hyams (either her daughter or daughter-in-law) in 1821 so that she might take over her business.[21] At the same time Henry Hyams granted his wife a deed of sole tradership. It appears also that Sarah Ares D'Azevedo Motta was set up in business by her mother, Rachel Woolf D'Azevedo. The father of Sarah Motta, Isaac D'Azevedo, a vendue master died in 1805. His wife then opened a shop.[22] And in 1809 Sarah Motta became a sole trader. She was born in 1789, and so we know that she was only fifteen years of age at the time of her marriage and twenty when she became a sole trader. In the federal census of 1810 she is shown as the head of her household, with three young females also residing there.

A woman who followed in her mother's footsteps was Sarah Moses Woolf, who became a sole trader in 1822. She was the daughter of Mary Moses, who had also been a free dealer.

18. MR4C.66.
19. MR40.67.
20. MR40.68.
21. MR4U.333.
22. Charleston directory, 1806, 1813, 1829.

In some families going into business seems to have been a tradition with the women.

Women thus seem to have become sole traders for a variety of reasons. Some did so at the urging of the husbands; others, at the urging of other women. At still other times, third parties were involved. When women acquired these rights, they could go their own ways—and some seem to have done just that.

Ages at Which Women Became Sole Traders

Though biographical data on the women who were sole traders are limited, some generalizations can be made about their ages. Four of fifteen were married for the first time before the age of twenty. In fact, the average age of eight sole traders at the first marriage was twenty. Also the average age when they became a sole trader for the first time (excluding Hannah Davis) was forty-four, slightly more than double the age at marriage. (See Table 31.)

Sole Traders' Businesses

Once a woman became a free dealer, she typically ran a dry goods store or a cloth store—which could be the same. The type of establishments run by quite a few of the women are known. Frequently they are shown to have operated different kinds of establishments from time to time, even from year to year. (See Table 32.) Furthermore, they moved practically every year. As renters, they appear to have been looking for the best possible location. On the whole the economic lives for sole traders seem to have been precarious. Although such brief designations as "dry goods store" and "shop" or "store" do not give an accurate account of what these women sold, a number of inventories provide much more information.

GOODS TURNED OVER TO REINAH TOBIAS DELYON IN 1766

1 set of scales and weights
1/2 dozen stockings
20 yards of cloth
10 yards of cloth
1 set of measures[23]

GOODS PROVIDED FOR JUDITH SUARES IN 1799

12 pieces of Indian chintz
10 pieces of Indian muslin pieces
12 dozen kid gloves
6 silver spoons with forks
2 large soup spoons
6 silver tea spoons
1 pair silver candle sticks
1 silver teapot
6 mahogany tables
20 chairs
1 large bedstead
1 gold necklace
4 pairs of gold earrings[24]

ITEMS IN DRY GOODS STORE OF CATHERINE HYAMS AT THE TIME OF HER MARRIAGE IN 1811

(In addition she owned household items, six slaves—Mary, Celia, Dina and child, Hannah, Eggy, and York—and 38 shares

23. MR2M.420.
24. MR3M.218.

Table 31
The Ages of Jewish Sole Traders in Early Charleston

Name	*Age at Marriage*	*Age on Becoming Sole Trader*
Cohen, Rachel	14	45
Cohen, Rebecca	18	32
DeLieben, Hannah	31 (2nd)	42
Davis, Hannah	52 (3rd)	61
DeLyon, Reinah	21	25
Hyams, Catherine	26 (2nd)	26
Hyams, Judith	17	25
Lazarus, Esther	—	22
Moses, Deborah	34	37
Moses, Rachel Harris	—	47
Motta, Sarah	15	20
Rodrigues, Esther	—	48
Mordecai (Simpson), Jane	19	19
Suares, Judith	26	30
Woolf, Sarah Moses	—	30

Source: See the appendix.

Table 32
The Types of Businesses of Jewish Sole Traders in Early Charleston

Business	*Name*
Boarding house	Esther Barrett, Abigail Seixas
Clothing store	Rebecca Benjamin, Elizabeth Harris
Cloth store	Reinah DeLyon, Hannah Hyams, Judith Hyams, Susannah Moses, Judith Suares
Dry goods store	Rachel Florance, Catherine Jacobs Hyams
Fruiterer	Abigail Seixas
Hat store	Elizabeth Harris
Shop or store	Esther Barrett, Elizabeth Harris, Sarah Hart, Catherine Jacobs Hyams, Hannah Hyams, Celia Jacobs, Deborah Moses, Jane Mordecai

Sources: City directories.

in Planters and Mechanics Bank)

1,625 yards calico
350 yards of Negro Cloth
50 pieces cloth
300 handkerchiefs
100 yards cloth
55 yards cloth
95 yards Chambray
176 yards Cotton
50 cotton shirts
50 oznaburg
10 pieces cotton cashmere
126 pocket handkerchiefs
52 yards black satin
16 yards striped silk
50 boxes cotton balls
65 yards cloth
84 yards cloth
20 pieces ribbon
80 pair black stockings
20 pair white stockings
10 pair white stockings
120 yards white flannel
20 great coats
10 pair pantaloons
50 handkerchiefs
63 yards cloth
20 yards cloth
10 muslin shawls[25]

GOODS PROVIDED FOR JUDITH HYAMS BY HANNAH HYAMS IN 1821

100 pairs of pantaloons
60 waistcoats
50 shirts
5 body coats
75 pieces of calico
150 yards of waistcoating
8 pieces of Bombay cloth
15 pieces of cambric cloth
150 yards of cashmere
10 pieces of linen
5 pieces of check cloth
100 yards of broadcloth
20 gross of buttons
5 dozen handkerchiefs
8 dozen handkerchiefs of a coarse quality
3 dozen pairs of stockings
100 yards of Muslin cloth [26]

Legal Rights

When a woman received the rights of a sole trader, she could be completely independent of her husband. Even if he did not want her to, she could take advantage of her situation. Some seem to have seized the opportunity, if not immediately, then after some time. This appears to have been true of Rebecca DeMendes Benjamin, who ran her own shop in Beaufort, South Carolina, while her husband seems to have remained in Charleston. When a suit was filed against her in 1839, the sheriff attempted to find her in Charleston. He left a notice "at the usual and most notorious place of the defendant's residence," but she was not in the city. One of the documents in the case indicates that she resided in New York, but when she signed an agreement in the case, she was at Beaufort, South Carolina.[27] This is supported by a statement made in 1898 when a woman reported that Mrs. Benjamin had operated a store in Beaufort that the women of the city espe-

25. MS6.41.

26. MR4U.333.

27. Lloyd v. Benjamin, JR, 1839, 32a.

cially liked since she dealt in goods "ordinarily found in a fair town or village store."[28] Rachel Florance and Sarah Ares D'Azevedo Motta may also have taken advantage of their status as sole traders to assert their independence. Although the husband of Sarah Motta is missing from the 1820 census, he seems to have been in the city; he is listed in the directories of 1819, 1822, 1825, and 1829. Further evidence to support his presence in the city is the fact that when he died in 1839, a monument was placed over his grave, but it does not name her as his spouse. This family is all the more interesting because Rachel D'Azevedo twice sued Motta. She lent him $1200, at an unspecified rate, which he did not repay. She therefore took him to civil court and won in 1827. At that time he signed a note agreeing to pay the debt plus costs. Seven years later she again sued him, this time for $1398, which he admitted he had owed since 1827, likely the $1200 he had agreed to pay plus interest.[29]

A number of the sole traders took others to the Court of Common Pleas; however, they were more likely to be defendants. As plaintiffs, sole traders could sue in their own names, which they did; however, when they were defendants, their husbands were named along with them—though they were not liable for the deeds of their wives. Eight of the women who were sole traders became involved in legal battles; typically, over money they borrowed which they later could not repay. They were then taken to court. In almost all cases the plaintiffs presented proof such as signed notes, and the defendants were then ordered to pay the full amount, plus interest and costs. In some instances, probably those who were the worst off financially, they had to pay only one-half the amount. Sole traders who found themselves taken to court were Rebecca Benjamin, Rebecca Cohen, Frances Emanuel, Elizabeth Harris, Frances Josephs, and Rachel Lazarus.[30] Those who were plaintiffs were Frances Emanuel, Elizabeth Harris, Catherine Hyams, Rachel Lazarus, and Sarah Woolf.[31]

Clearly, the most interesting case involved Frances Emanuel. In 1828 she and her husband Isaac Emanuel sold a house on King Street and their residence on George Street, including all books, furniture, and silver plate, to James Little for $5,000. They then moved into a house owned by John Hunter. But Hunter soon claimed they had not paid a year's rent in the amount of $200, which was two months overdue. He

28. *News and Courier*, Jan. 14, 1898.

29. D'Azevedo v. Motta, JR, 1827, 329a; D'Azevedo v. Motta, JR, 1834, 224a.

30. Lloyd v. Benjamin, JR, 1837, 32a; Aertsen & Co. v. Cohen, JR, 1799, 136a; Firth v. Emanuel, JR, 1827, 121a; Little v. Emanuel, JR, 1831, 116a; Caldwell v. Emanuel, JR, 1833, 125a; Pinckney & Izzard v. Harris, JR, 1826, 220a; Moses v. Josephs, JR, 1827, 248a; Cohen & Mordecai v. Josephs, JR, 1827, 249a.

31. Emanuel v. Ellis, JR, 1827, 123a; Emanuel v. Hunter, JR, 1830, 67a; Harris v. Sampson, JR, 1825, 355a; Catherine Hyams v. Hannah Hyams, JR, 1826, 243a; Lazarus v. Gaillard & Egar, JR, 1821, 39a; Rachel Lazarus v. Benjamin Lazarus, JR, 1836, 91a; Woolf v. Carvalho, JR, 1839, 69a.

therefore empowered William Ardrion to enter Frances Emanuel's house and "to make distress of all such goods and chattels as are upon the premises." On July 30, 1828, Ardrion seized a carpet, a bookcase, a safe, a side board, a looking glass, a mirror, two dining tables, and an easy chair. Frances Emanuel then took Little and Ardrion to court, charging that they had wrongfully taken these items and sued him for $200, which she claimed to be the value of the goods. The jury awarded her $100 plus damages. The following year, however, James Little sued her for $800, which she had borrowed from him and not repaid. She confessed judgment and paid this amount plus costs.[32]

A number of the sole traders bought, sold, were given, or gave away slaves. Since most families had two to four household servants, this is not surprising. Slavery, indeed, may have made it easier for a woman to engage in trade because she could turn household responsibilities over to others. Unfortunately, the records on the buying and selling of slaves are incomplete. Although such transfers of property should have been recorded, it is obvious that most were not. The record, for example, reveals the selling or willing of slaves whose acquisition by their owners was never recorded. The following women handled slave transactions: Ann Alexander sold one slave; Hannah DeLieben (later Davis) bought seven slaves on four occasions; Elizabeth Harris purchased slaves on two occasions; Rachel Levy Hart sold a slave and gave six away; Catherine Jacobs Hyams owned six slaves when she married and sold four; Judith Hyams purchased three slaves from Ann J. Horry, who stipulated they had to be taken out of the state; Celia Jacobs sold three slaves and gave one away; Hannah Levy purchased two slaves; Sarah Mordecai sold one slave; Judith Suares bought and sold two slaves; and Sarah Woolf bought four slaves and sold one. One woman, Hannah Davis (formerly Hannah DeLieben), however, purchased nine slaves in 1822–23. Then in 1823–24 she sold eight. Since the names of those sold match those purchased, Hannah Davis was clearly making money by buying and selling slaves.[33]

The sole traders legally could hold their status for life unless they agreed to give it up. Some seem to have maintained their rights. However, it is difficult to know how long most remained separate traders. Few sole traders show up in the city directories, and when they do, they are usually to be found only for a year or two. This pattern is understandable if they were assisting their husbands in the management of their businesses; some may have taken on the role of separate trader for a short term

32. MR5I.61; Emanuel v. Hunter, JR, 1830, 67a; Little v. Emanuel, JR, 1831, 116a.

33. MR3I.188; 3Q.720; 3T.91, 98, 432; 4V.393; 5A.77; 4F.182; 4C.320; 4X.98; 4Y.461; MS6.41; MR4B.283; 4V.371; 4X.291; 5A.77; 5K.475; 4B.102; 4N.364; 4V.371; 3S.447; 3M.338; 3P.498; 4A.262; 4D.200; 5G.158; 4X.210, 211, 212, 273, 306, 320, 380; 5A.37, 62, 80, 170, 172, 202, 203.

while the family's finances were being straightened out. Most do not show up in official records for a long period of time.

One of the rights granted to sole traders was that of disposing of property by a will. A number of the women appear to have died in Charleston before their husband but did not make wills and did not have a probate court inventory made of their property. Obviously, they were not considered independent and separate traders at the time of their deaths. On the other hand, five of the business women did make wills. One was Ann Alexander, who died in 1835. Having been made a sole trader in 1791, she held that status for forty-two years. Another was Sarah C. Levy, who died in 1822. She referred to herself in the will as a free trader. She had held that status for ten years. A third was Deborah Cohen Moses, who died in 1848 and had been a free dealer, as she states it, since 1813, a period of thirty-five years. During this time there were no entries in the city directory for her and no transactions recorded in official records. A fourth person, Rachel Miriam Harris Moses, died in 1810 after having been a sole trader for nine years. In her will she stated that she was a shopkeeper. She never appeared in the city directory although she did appear in other records. The fifth person was Rachel Lazarus. In her will she left considerable property and money to her relatives. Although she does not mention it in the will, she had been a sole trader for sixty-two years. She also never appeared in the city directory but did carry out a number of activities that were recorded in official documents. Thus, it appears that some women kept their status through life, and three of the five who wrote wills referred to it. It would seem that the failure to be listed in the city directory or to show up in official records does not mean that a woman did not engage in business.

The Loss of Free-Trading Status

For two women, however, tenure as free traders was short. Elizabeth Florance, wife of Levy Florance, became a sole trader in 1813 only to have her status revoked in 1815. In 1818 she regained sole-trading status, but she and her husband disappear from the records by 1822. Rachel Florance, possibly no relation, became a free trader in 1804, but her status was revoked in 1811. Despite this, Jacob Lazarus, Jr., set her up in business in 1817, and she is found in the city directory in 1825 operating a dry goods store at the same address her husband had worked as a dentist in 1822. Although these two women had their free dealerships taken away, their husbands could not have done it without their consent. Either the women freely agreed to the revocation, or they were pressured into agreeing. Both signed or marked the documents revoking their status.

The Ability to Write

Not all the women could sign their legal documents. Jane Cohen Mordecai (later Simpson), Rose Levi, and Sarah Levi signed their names in Hebrew.

Frances Emanuel, Elizabeth Florance, Catherine Hyams, Hannah Hyams, Celia Jacobs, Judith Jacobs, Mary Moses, Rachel Moses, Susannah Moses, and Judith Suares only made marks. Many of the others could sign their names, although the deeds that granted them sole tradership did not require their signatures.

Working Mothers

The deeds granting women sole tradership frequently mentioned that they were being granted with love and affection toward the wife but with special concern for the future generation. Many of the husbands seemingly were interested in the welfare of their children and believed that by giving their wives independent status they could contribute to the well-being of all. Eighteen of the women had young children at the time or after they became sole traders. Of these, only six are known to have had children after becoming a free dealer. Some of the others were beyond the childbearing years; some had no children, and information is lacking on the rest. Although a woman who worked outside the household could help the family, it is doubtful that women such as Rachel Lazarus with seventeen children had much spare time. (See Table 33.)

Table 33
Jewish Sole Traders in Charleston Known to Have Children

Name	*Number of Children* *Total*	*Born After Mother Became Sole Trader*
Benjamin, Rebecca	8	0
Cohen, Rachel	7	0
DaVega, Sarah	2	0
DeLyon, Reinah	4	0
Florance, Rachel	7	0
Harris, Elizabeth	4	0
Hart, Rachel	4	3
Hyams, Judith	10	3
Lazarus, Esther	2	0
Lazarus, Rachel	17	10
Levy, Sarah	4	1
Moses, Deborah	3	0
Moses, Rachel	2	0
Moses, Sarah	4	0
Rodrigues, Esther	1	0
Seixas, Abigail	4	0
Suares, Judith	5	5
Woolf, Sarah	11	4

Sources: See the appendix.

The Jewish sole traders in Charleston achieved their status for a variety of reasons and engaged in a number of business enterprises. Typically, running dry goods stores suited their needs. Once in business, they appear to have taken over their husbands' affairs and managed them better. Or so it would appear: the men are rarely sued after they give their wives the status of sole traders. But like women of any period who work outside the home, they had to balance their family responsibilities with the business. Legally the women were not subject to their husbands' control, but the extent of freedom seems to have varied according to the wishes of the women. Apparently, if they were content with their marriages, the wives did not assert themselves much. On the other hand, if things did not go well, the woman had no obligation to return to coverture. She could leave or run her own affairs. In some instances the acquisition of the rights of a sole trader appears to have been tantamount to a separation. For most, however, it seems to have been a short-term convenience that could be ignored with the passage of time.

Two other women may have been sole traders, although the evidence is confusing. One of these was Hannah A. Moses Abrahams, who married Alexander Hezekiel Abrahams. She is listed in the city directory of 1835 as running a dry goods store, but she dealt in slaves between 1845 and 1854[34] and is listed as the head of the household in the 1840 census. Nevertheless, the 1861 census of the city of Charleston shows Alexander Abrahams to be in the city as the head of his company. The other is Amelia Henry, who married Joel Henry. She died before her husband and is shown in the city directory in 1822 as a midwife. This profession would not involve contracts, and a person would not have to be a sole trader to perform this service. But she bought and sold slaves on her own right, which indicates that she possibly had the status of sole trader.[35]

Other Working Women

In addition to those who became sole traders, a number of women earned their living in the marketplace. They generally left far fewer records behind and are more difficult to identify. As a rule the directories list them only a few times, indicating that they did not succeed or gave up their businesses or had such small businesses that they failed to be noticed. Unmarried women could operate businesses as they wished, although few appear to have taken the opportunity.[36]

One unmarried woman, Penina Moïse (1797–1880, became a writer. Born in Charleston, the daughter of Abraham Moïse and Sarah Moïse, she left school at an early age to help the family's finances. She remained at home with family members for the rest of her life. Moïse wrote hundreds of poems and hymns, many of them after she became blind. The first known of these was published in a Charleston newspaper, the *Southern Patriot*, in 1819. In addition to Charleston newspapers, her poems appeared in *Godey's Lady's Book* in Philadelphia, the

34. MR6A.434; 6B.603; 6D.100.

35. MR4P.153; 4S.200; 4X.289, 421; 5A.506.

36. According to Charleston directories, the following women operated businesses in these years: Rebecca Harris, fruit shop, 1835 and 1837; Jane Sampson, clothing, 1829 and 1831; Sarah Sampson (1767–1827), dry goods, 1831; and Sarah Solomons, clothing and mattresses, 1813, 1816, 1819, and 1822.

Rebecca Harris was the daughter of Hyam Harris and Catherine N. Harris. She was made a denizen in 1824 (MR4Z.383) and was involved in a number of civil suits in her own name (JR, 1828, 194a; Jr, 1832, 261a; JR, 1834, 180a). Sarah Sampson bought two slave girls in 1820 (MR4P.322,350). Records indicate that in 1798 a house and lot were put in trust for Sarah Solomons and others (MR 3V.313), and she sold slaves in 1825 and 1835 (MR5D.43, 50.594).

FIVE DOLLARS
Will be paid for the apprehension of my Negro Girl SALLY, about 14 years old. Had on, when she went away, a black cambric frock, checked apron, and woollen tippet. She may perhaps change her dress. She walks a little stooping, and talks countryfied. She has little or no hair, it has fallen out—large white teeth. She was lately purchased from Thomas S. West, who lives four miles from Four Hole Bridge, by me. The above reward will be paid on delivering her to the master of the Work House, or to the subscriber. LEAH MOSES.
Dec 12 3

43. Advertisement for a runaway slave owned by a woman. (*Mercury*, December 12, 1833.)

CHARLESTON FEMALE SEMINARY.

MRS H. L. MOISE having relinquished school keeping, the duties of this Seminary has been assumed by Mrs. LOUISA A. MOISE, assisted by competent Teachers. Every effort will be made to merit the reputation it has ever sustained. As hitherto, all the Branches comprising a complete English education will be taught, together with French, Spanish, Italian, Music, vocal and instrumental, Drawing and Painting.
Terms made known by application at the Seminary, 20 1-2 Pitt street. thl 12 thl April 12

44. Advertisement for school operated by Louisa A. Moïse. (*Daily Courier*, April 15, 1858.)

Commercial Times in New Orleans, *Heriot's Magazine* in Charleston, *The Occident* in Philadelphia, the *Washington Union* and the *Home Journal* in New York, and the *Daily Times* in Boston. In 1833 she published in Charleston a book of sixty poems entitled *Fancy's Sketch Book*. This is the first book of poems by an American Jewish female. Also, in 1845 when William Gilmore Simms edited a work entitled *The Charleston Book: A Miscellany of Prose and Verse*, she was asked to contribute a poem and a short story. Her works dealt with many subjects, frequently Jewish ones. She also composed sixty of the seventy-four

Table 34
Jewish Widows Who Operated Businesses in Early Charleston

Name	*Occupation*	*Years Listed in Directory*
Abrahams, Judith DeLyon Cohen	Store owner	1803, 1813, 1816, 1822
Alexander, Rachel	Fruit Store owner	1801, 1802, 1803, 1813, 1816
Canter, Rebecca DeLaMotta	School owner	1837
D'Azevedo, Rachel Woolf	Dry goods seller	1806, 1807, 1809, 1813, 1829
Hart, Bella Levy	Dry goods seller	1816
Hyams, Rebecca Sarzedas	Dry goods seller	1816, 1819, 1831
Labatt, Catherine	Dry goods seller	1816
Lopez, Priscilla[a]	Dry goods seller	1813, 1816, 1819, 1822, 1831, 1835
Marks, Sarah Harris	Shop owner	1809
Moïse, Rebecca Levy	Dry goods seller	1852
Moses, Elizabeth	Slopshop owner	1816
Moses, Rachel	Shop owner	1819
Woolf, Rachel Andrew Moses	Shop owner	1790, 1801, 1802, 1803, 1806, 1807

[a]Lopez had three civil suits filed against her (JR, 1825, 197a; JR, 1826, 311a: JR, 1827, 305a).

songs for *Hymns Written for the Service of Hebrew Congregation Beth Elohim of Charleston, S.C.* (Charleston, 1842). Over the years the hymnbook was enlarged and eventually contained 190 of her works. The third edition of the Reform *Union Hymnal* of 1932 still had thirteen hymns by her. Though her works are not considered to rank with the greatest of the nineteenth century, she did make an important contribution, especially in religious music. She worked as a teacher for many years.[37]

37. See also Charleston Section, Council of Jewish Woman, *Secular and Religious Works of Penina Moïse*; Solomon Breibart, "Penina Moïse, Southern Jewish Poetess."

Women were more likely to engage in business after the deaths of their husbands. Their economic situation probably forced them to take on jobs. (See Table 34.) As a group, the women who were not sole traders but engaged in business were far less active than the sole traders. (See Table 35.) Yet some who were widows for a long period seem to have conducted a considerable amount of business. For the most part, however, their shops were small. Altogether, the women played a considerable role in the economic life of Charleston; they may have been more active in the economy than Jewish women in the city in the late twentieth century.

Table 35
Jewish Business Women of Unknown Status in Early Charleston

Name	*Occupation*	*Years Listed in Directory*
Abendanone, Zippora	Shopkeeper	1803
Abrahams, Mrs. M.	Goods and clothing dealer	1837
Cohen, Hannah	Fruit dealer	1852, 1855, 1859
Emanuel, Flora	Shop owner	1806, 1807
Jacobs, Hannah	Shop owner	1806
Levin, Elizabeth[a]	Store owner	1819
Levy, Ann	Dry goods dealer	1807
Levy, Bella[b]	Shop owner	1802
Levy, Eliza[c]	Shop owner	1802
Levy, Rose (d.1812)	Shop owner	1801
Moses, Esther[d]	Shop owner	1816, 1819, 1822
Moses, Mrs. R. F.	Upholsterer	1829
Sampson, Abigail	Dry goods dealer	1831
Tobias, Judith[e]	Store owner	1806, 1807, 1809

[a]Lewis Levin was at 223 King Street; she was at 221.
[b]This could be Bella Levy Hart.
[c]There are several women by this name at that time.
[d]There are three women by this name in the city in 1822.
[e]There are two women by this name.

JEWISH WOMEN WHO WERE SOLE TRADERS

Ann Sarah Huguenin Irby Alexander, 1791 (MR3A.64)
Esther Barrett, 1797 (MR3H.471)
Rebecca DeMendes Benjamin, 1827 (MR5E.163)
Rachel Moses Cohen, 1822 (MR3H.417)
Rebecca Sarzedas Cohen, 1793 (MR3G.112)
Naomi DaCosta, 1793 (MR3C.346)
Sarah [Sol] J. Moses DaVega, 1797 (MR3H.361)
Hannah Levy Hart DeLieben Davis
as Hannah DeLieben, 1803 (MR3S.52)
as Hannah Davis, 1823 (MR4Y.162)
Miriam Davis, 1824 (MR4W.424)
Reinah Tobias DeLyon, 1766 (MR2M.430)
Sarah Derkheim, 1800 (MR3R.300)
Frances Emanuel, 1823 (MR4Y.272)
Elizabeth Florance, 1813 (MR4G.155)
revoked, 1815 (MR4H.286)
granted again, 1818 (MR4N.508)
Rachel Florance, 1804 (MR4C.501)
revoked, 1811 (MR4O.68)
Hetty Goldsmith, 1825 (MR3W.73)

Elizabeth Harris, 1822 (MR4E.76)
Elizabeth Hart, 1804 (MR3V.114)
Rachel Levy Hart, 1806 (MR3W.629)
Sarah Hart, 1796 (MR3I.38)
Catherine Jacobs Hyams, 1811 (MR4E.130)
Hannah Hyams, 1807 (MR3Y.241)
Judith Hyams, 1821 (MR4U.333)
Celia Jacobs, 1808 (MR3Y.480)
Judith (Katy) Hays Sarzedas Jacobs, 1796 (MR3I.120)
Abigail Audler Joseph, 1818 (MR4N.511)
Esther Lyons Lazarus, 1808 (MR3Z.366)
Rachel DeTorres Lazarus, 1785 (MR2Y.45)
Sarah Levi, 1766 (MR3F.358)
Rose Levi, 1796 (MR2M.432)
Hannah Levin, 1807 (MR3Y.207)
Hannah Levy, 1820 (MR4T.335)
Patience Levy, 1773 (MR2P.456)
Sarah (Sally) C. Levy, 1812 (MR4E.534)
Mary Ann Lyon, 1820 (MR4U.85)
Sarah Mordecai, 1804 (MR3U.70)
Deborah Cohen Moses, 1813 (MR4G.259)
Rachel Miriam [Mary] Harris Moses, 1801 (MR3Q.467)
Sarah Machado Moses, 1792 (MR3B.94)
Susannah Moses, 1823 (MR4Z.278)
Sarah Ares D'Azevedo Motta, 1809 (MR4B.48)
Frances Pollock, 1819 (MR4R.235)
Esther Rodrigues, 1824 (MR4G.396)
Bella Myers Sarzedas, 1809 (MR4B.2)
Abigail Valencia Seixas, 1814 (MR4G.424)
Jane Cohen Mordecai Simpson, 1808 (MR3Z.349)
Hetty Solomon, 1806 (MR3W.718)
Judith Alberga Suares, 1799 (MR3M.218)
Sarah Moses Woolf, 1822 (MR4Y.100)

CHAPTER 9

Reform in Beth Elohim and Schism

"This synagogue is our *temple*, this city our *Jerusalem*, this happy land our *Palestine*."

—Gustavus Poznanski, 1841[1]

". . . all, too, were Americans to the core."

—Isaac M. Wise, when he visited Charleston in 1850[2]

After the members of the Reformed Society of Israelites withdrew from Beth Elohim, "the vestry experienced much inconvenience and perplexity in managing their financial affairs." Thus, for a number of years they could not afford to employ a permanent *hazan*. Despite this, according to Nathaniel Levin, they "adhered firmly to the ancient usages," relying on their faith to get them through the difficult times. By 1835 their economic status improved, and they sought a minister to lead the congregation.[3] Meanwhile, New York had replaced Charleston as the city having the most Jews. New York had six congregations while Philadelphia had three. Germans constituted the bulk of the Jewish newcomers to America, and the reform ideas in Germany continued to affect developments in the Jewish communities in the United States.[4] Soon, the reform movement in Charleston took on a new life. The desire for further change on the part of some, however, resulted in the community's being split into warring factions.

First Reforms in the Synagogue

As noted in earlier chapters, the congregation adopted a new constitution in 1836. At first glance, this document

1. *Courier*, Mar. 20, 1841.
2. Wise, *Reminiscences*, 144.

3. Levin, "The Jewish Congregation of Charleston," 439.
4. Tarshish, "The Charleston Organ Case," 419–20.

appears to be staunchly opposed to change in the method of worship. The first article provided that "in order to guard against innovations, it is hereby understood, that it shall not be in the power of any Parnass or administration, to introduce any alteration in the mode of worship of the Synagogue, except as may be specified in this Constitution." Article 15 required three-quarters of the members to adopt changes. In addition, article 12 forbade any member from joining any society that had adopted or shall adopt "innovations in our sacred religion, alterations in the form of worship, as practiced heretofore, or changes in the Mosaical or Rabbinical Laws." Furthermore, if any person who was not a member aided, joined, or assisted such an organization, he would be denied the privilege of joining the congregation. Reformers, it appears, would not be tolerated. A closer reading of the regulations reveals that important changes had been made. Abraham Moïse, who had been one of the most important figures in the Reformed Society of Israelites, helped write this constitution, which is a compromise between the reformers and the orthodox. The prohibition against joining societies that promoted innovations went into force with the new constitution and was not retroactive. Also, the ban against the introduction of innovations was directed against the president and board. So long as further changes would require approval of three-fourths of the members of the congregation, the leaders could not revert to old practices. Furthermore, article 11 required the *hazan* to have not only "all requisite ability in Hebrew learning and scholarship" but also to be "competently qualified in the English language." It was "made his duty on the Sabbath . . . to pronounce a Discourse, and offer up a suitable address to the Almighty, both in the English language." He should say the rest of the service as customary. Also, the constitution ended the irksome practice of public offerings that were then deducted from the annual dues. As of 1836 these offerings "shall be charged in addition to the subscription; except by those who have had *Mizvot*, and then *one*, only shall be allowed, to be deducted from the amount of subscription" (article 9). Reform had come to Beth Elohim; two of the major innovations in the liturgy proposed in the petition of the Convention of Israelites of 1824 had been adopted.

Because the constitution went into effect in September 1836, that year marks the beginning of Reform Judaism in Beth Elohim, the first congregation, after the Reformed Society of Israelites, to adopt reform principles in America. After that came Har Sinai Society of Baltimore, which adopted the Hamburg Temple prayerbook in April 1843, Emanu-El of New York (1845), and Ashe Emeth of Albany (1850).[5]

Gustavus Poznanski

The congregation also sought a full-time *hazan*. Its leaders, headed by Nathan Hart and Handel Moses Hertz, both German born, insisted on obtain-

5. Schwartzman, *Reform Judaism in the Making*, 89–90.

ing a man "who was strict in his observance of all the Mosaical and Rabbinical laws."[6] During their search they found a likely candidate in Gustavus Poznanski, a *shohet* or ritual slaughterer in New York, who had to follow stringent rabbinical laws in performing his duties. Born in Storchnest, Russian Poland, about 1805, Poznanski had been educated in Hamburg, Germany, a city rife with reform ideas; however, he seems not to have been affected by them at the time. He led services on occasion at Shearith Israel synagogue in New York and assisted during the High Holy Days of Rosh ha-Shanah and Yom Kippur.[7] Nathan Hart had met him before his selection and recommended him for the position. The congregation sent Samuel Valentine and Alexander H. Abrahams to New York to "make proper inquiries" about his suitability.[8] Shearith Israel provided Poznanski with a certificate attesting to the fact that his actions had been praiseworthy.[9]

Valentine and Abrahams found Poznanski to be a "rigid Rabbinist," and the congregation elected him as *hazan* on October 9, 1836, for a probationary term of two years. Poznanski arrived in January 1837 and proved himself so satisfactory that the congregation elected him *hazan* for life in May 1838—before his two-year probation period expired. According to Jacob DeLaMotta, who contradicts the assessment of Levin, "religious zeal and devotional conduct" had been quite lax before the arrival of Poznanski. People arrived late, left early, and often paid little attention to the services. Some openly violated the Sabbath and did not observe the holy days. Poznanski's "respectful demeanour and proficiency in his clerical duties, resulted in a great improvement in the services. His sermons and prayers in English commanded attention, and those who had often missed services now attended." Furthermore, interest in the Hebrew language increased. Poznanski also lived as the observant would want him. When he first came to the city he boarded in the home of H. M. Hertz. After his continuous appointment, he married Esther Barrett, daughter of Isaac Barrett and Rachel DaVega Barrett of Charleston, on December 12, 1838.[10]

Rebuilding

After the Great Fire of April 1838 the congregation met for a while in the Hebrew Orphan Society building and then completed the Tabernacle as a temporary place of worship in September 1838. Meanwhile, they set about raising funds to build a new synagogue. Appeals went out not only to the Jewish residents of the city but to other congregations as well. The circular that went to Amsterdam stated that the Charles-

6. State v. Ancker, in *Reports of Cases*, 252.
7. DeSola Pool, *An Old Faith in the New World*, 247, 400.
8. State v. Ancker, in *Reports of Cases*, 252.
9. DeSola Pool, *An Old Faith in the New World*, 430.

10. *State ex rel. A. Ottolengui*, 7–8, 35; Levin, "The Jewish Congregation of Charleston," 439; DeLaMotta, "The Congregations of Charleston," 600–603.

ton congregation sought funds "with melancholy emotions, and peculiarly painful reflections."[11] The minutes of the congregation show that contributions came in from congregations in Alabama, Beaufort, Camden, Cincinnati, Columbia, London, Philadelphia, and Vicksburg, with the largest amounts from London and Columbia. Local individuals, some of them former members of the Reformed Society of Israelites such as David Cardozo Levy and Thomas W. Mordecai, also contributed, the greatest amount being $200 by Nathan A. Cohen. The total collected was $1870; the bulk of the $32,500 cost of rebuilding came from the insurance on the old structure. Cyrus L. Warner, an architect in New York, drew up the plans, and David Lopez, a member of the congregation, built the structure. The synagogue, which still stands today, measured 80 by 56 feet with a 15-foot portico of six Doric columns. Built of Quincy marble, it stood on a 3-foot base and rose to a height of 46 feet. The eastern foundation of the building rested on the foundation of the building that burned. Built on an east-west axis so that worshipers would face Jerusalem, the building ran parallel to Hasell Street. The entrance lay to the west. The interior featured marble floors, a mahogany ark behind columns in Corinthian style modeled on the Monument of Lysicrates in Athens, a dome with a large bronze chandelier donated by Jacob Barrett, and a gallery supported by Ionic columns. Above the ark in black marble and in gilt letters were placed the words "Know Before Whom Thou Standest," and over the 18-foot-high entrance was installed a marble tablet bearing the Sh'ma with the unusual translation, "Hear O Israel the Lord our God is the sole Eternal Being." The Decalogue, an abbreviated version of the Ten Commandments in Hebrew in gilt on black marble tablets, rose above everything at the front of the interior. The elevated *taba* was to be found near the entrance. Made of polished mahogany, it featured bronze embellishments.

Because the building ran parallel to the street, Joshua Lazarus wanted a portico along the street side of the building. When he failed to convince the board, twenty-five members of the congregation petitioned for a meeting on this subject. At the gathering the motion failed by a vote of thirty-two opposed to twenty in favor. Therefore, the builders followed the original plan, and the exterior of the building has remained largely unchanged since then. It stands as one of the finest examples of neoclassical architecture in Charleston. The ceremony for laying the cornerstones took place on Thursday, January 3, 1840.[12]

11. Original in Portuguese Jewish Archives, Amsterdam. Copy in American Jewish Archives. The circular was signed by Joshua Lazarus (chairman of the committee), Nathan Hart, H. M. Hertz, Abraham Ottolengui, and Isaiah Moses (trustees), and S. Valentine (secretary).

12. Minute Book of Beth Elohim, Jan. 17, Mar. 4, 17, April 3, 14, Sept. 19, 25, Oct. 2, 27, 29, Nov. 3, 1839; July 5, Nov. 19, 29, Dec. 13, 1840; Feb. 21, Mar. 17, 1841; Levin, "The Jewish Congregation of Charleston," 491–95.

45. The 1838 Tabernacle. The building no longer exists. (Photograph courtesy of Beth Elohim Synagogue.)

The Controversy over the Organ

At the July 14, 1840, meeting of the board of trustees the president called "the attention of the Board to a very important subject." He had received a petition signed by thirty-eight members requesting that a meeting of the congregation be called "to consider the Propriety of erecting an Organ in the Synagogue." This petition set off a series of charges and confrontations that resulted in further reforms at Beth Elohim.

Like the members of the Reformed Society of Israelites, the petitioners expressed concern for the future. They had, they said, "a deep interest in our religion" and were anxious to use every "laudable and sacred mode by which the rising generation may be made to conform to, and attend our holy worship." They pointed out that organs had been made part of the services in Prague, in Germany, and in the south of France, and that they "would be the last to ask for an innovation in any respect to the uses and formula of the services." An organ had also been used at the consecration of Mikve Israel in Savannah in 1820. Dr. Jacob DeLaMotta, who acted

46. Exterior of Beth Elohim. (Photograph by Michael Whittemore.)

47. Interior of Beth Elohim. (Photograph courtesy of Beth Elohim Synagogue.)

as one of the leaders against the organ in Beth Elohim and who led the orthodox in their early years, had praised its use then. He said: "The ceremony of consecration, was according to the usual custom, and accompanied with occasional Hebrew tunes from a well-toned organ that gave fine effect to the Psalms selected; at the same time revived an ancient custom; and now adopted in some synagogues in Europe of having music on particular occasions."[13] The board ruled by a vote of four to one, with Joshua Lazarus being in opposition, that such a proposal violated the constitution's requirement that services be held according to the Minhag Sephardim. They, however, agreed to call a general meeting of the congregation for Sunday, July 26.[14]

Apparently initiated by J. C. Levy, whose name appears first on the list,[15] the issue had been under discussion for some time, for on July 14, 1840, the board met to consider action against Jacob Simon Jacobs, who on the previous Sabbath insulted the *hazan* by making "use of improper & unbecoming language in synagogue." The board summoned him to appear, which he did the following day. Jacobs stated that he had not intentionally insulted Poznanski but was speaking "in general terms, against all Polanders" who were inclined to help "to introduce an organ in the synagogue." The board did not find his explanation satisfactory, found him guilty, and severely reprimanded him.[16] Obviously, Poznanski had spoken in favor of the use of an organ and stirred the wrath of Jacobs, who later served as a minister of congregation Shearith Israel. Such opposition as that expressed by Jacobs ran deep. To opponents, the use of an organ represented not only an innovation but an opening for further reform: they knew that in Germany the use of an organ usually meant that other reforms followed.

Ninety members attended the congregational meeting on July 26. First, they requested that Poznanski be allowed to attend and speak on the subject. A heated debate followed, but by a vote of fifty-six to thirty-one the meeting agreed to bring him in. The *hazan* "to the surprise of the old Jews . . . had joined the innovators"[17] and spoke in favor of the idea of the introduction of an organ in the synagogue and gave the opinions of several authorities that Jewish law permitted such. After answering many questions, he asked to leave the meeting and not be present at the debate. Then Abraham Moïse made a motion that "an Organ shall be procured and erected in the new Synagogue to be purchased by voluntary contributions, and not drawn from congregational funds." Nathan Hart, the president of

13. DeLaMotta, *Discourse Delivered at the Consecration of the Synagogue of the Hebrew Congregation of Mikva Israel.*

14. Minute Book of Beth Elohim, July 14, 1840.

15. The first names on the petition were J. C. Levy, Mordecai Cohen, Aaron Moïse, M. Jacobs, M. C. Mordecai, and Abraham Tobias.

16. Minute Book of Beth Elohim, July 14, 15, 1840.

17. *The State ex rel. A. Ottolengui*, 8.

the board, ruled the motion out of order by claiming that it violated article I of the constitution, which established the Minhag Sephardim as the mode of worship. M. C. Mordecai than appealed to override the chair's ruling, and when the question was called, forty persons supported the chair and forty-seven voted against him. By making this an ordinary motion rather than a constitutional issue, they could make changes with only a majority of votes. When they took a vote on whether to introduce the organ, the proposal passed by forty-six yeas to forty nays.[18] The proponents of the organ had offered to supply the organ without cost to the congregation to protect the instrument should the vote be reversed in the future. Thus, in September, Mordecai Cohen promised to pay $350 for the organ. He said that he had not been particularly in favor of it, but if the *hazan* had stated it did not violate Jewish law, he would support it. The following month the congregation adopted the maxim "Praise him with stringed instruments & organs," which they placed over the organ.[19]

Though both sides in the issue could find rabbis and interpretations to support their cause, the organ had traditionally not been used in synagogues. Its introduction represented an unacceptable innovation to those who wished to maintain rituals as they had always known them. Although musical instruments had been used in the temple in Jerusalem, most rabbis believed that because of the destruction of the temple, joy had been banished from services. As long as Jews considered themselves to be in exile, they should not employ musical instruments. Those opposed to the organ in Charleston tried to reverse the decision in August, but they failed. The issue had been decided.[20]

The Remnant of Israel

The minority felt so strongly about the use of an organ that they withdrew from Beth Elohim and organized a new congregation, Shearith Israel or the Remnant of Israel. They purchased land for the purpose of building a synagogue. Apparently, they began to hold their own services shortly after the July vote. They certainly existed by September 1840. Annual dues for the preceding year at Beth Elohim had to be paid by the beginning of the Jewish New Year. "None of them subscribed anew, or made any contributions." And they "made no subsequent claim of membership, and were not summoned to meetings, or otherwise treated as members."[21] Meanwhile the seceders received two severe blows with the deaths of Nathan Hart, the president of Beth Elohim but a supporter of Shearith Israel, and H. M. Hertz, also a trustee of Beth

18. Minute Book of Beth Elohim, July 26, 1840. State v. Ancker in *Reports of Cases* has a number of errors on details, especially the people involved.

19. Minute Book of Beth Elohim, Sept. 26, Oct. 4, 1840.

20. Plaut, *The Rise of Reform Judaism*, 34–36; Idelsohn, *Jewish Music*, 232–33, 320–29; Minute Book of Beth Elohim, Aug. 5, 1840.

21. State v. Ancker, in *Reports of Cases*, 254.

Elohim and a proponent of orthodoxy. Both died in September of country fever. The acting *hazan* of Shearith Israel for the first two years, Dr. Jacob DeLa-Motta, delivered a funeral oration for Hart. In the speech DeLaMotta extolled the virtues of Hart and pointed out that though the deceased had come from Germany, he adopted the Sephardic form of worship and "constantly and strenuously advocated the observance of the Ceremonial Law." Hart "could not yield to innovations or improvement" that might weaken the observances.[22] Hertz bequeathed $100 to the "Society of Israelites" that had been "just established for separate Service according to the ancient custom of our Nation."[23] Both men contacted the trustees before they died, stating that they did not want Poznanski to preside at their funerals, and the board reluctantly agreed, though they regarded "it an indignity offered our Rev. Minister."[24]

Abraham Ottolengui (1790–1850), who had been rejected as *hazan* in 1806 because of his youth, replaced Hart as the president of Beth Elohim. One of his first important duties was presiding over a meeting to amend the constitution to deal with the seceders. The gathering took place on Sunday, November 1, at 10:00 A.M. without the seceders. Instead of amending the 1836 constitution, the members of the congregation adopted a new one, which they voted on article by article and accepted in its entirety. The new constitution increased the board from five to seven members and required those who habitually attended religious services at any place other than Beth Elohim to pay $100 per year if they wished to remain members of the congregation. Regular members had to pay only $15. They also denied those who failed to pay their dues for two years the right of burial in the cemetery and required all funerals to be conducted by the *hazan* of Beth Elohim. Abraham Moïse and Ralph Woolf, both of whom had wanted the organ in the synagogue, now joined the board of trustees. The reformers clearly had control and wished to exclude the traditionalists.[25]

Further Reforms

After adopting the new constitution, the board exercised its power to make changes in the method of worship. They initiated an English prayer of the *hazan*'s choosing and had him repeat a portion of the Hebrew prayers in English.[26] When the trustees decided to place the Ten Commandments and the Articles of

22. DeLaMotta, *On the Private and Religious Character of the Late Mr. Nathan Hart*.

23. W42.187, written Sept. 19, 1840.

24. Minute Book of Beth Elohim, Sept. 7, 26, 1840.

25. Minute Book of Beth Elohim, Oct. 27, Nov. 1, 2, 1840; State v. Ancker, in *Reports of Cases*, 255–57. New members admitted from October 1840 through August 1841 were M. Loovis, E. Levy, E. Sampson, Aaron Alexander, Bernard Levy, I. Woolf, Moses Aarons, Marks Solomons, D. D. Sarzedas, Judith Suares, Joseph E. Esdra, and M. Heydenfeld. Of these, only Bernard Levy appears to have belonged to the Reformed Society.

26. Minute Book of Beth Elohim, Nov. 8, 1840.

Faith on the walls of the synagogue, they consulted Poznanski, who altered the code of Maimonides regarding the coming of a Messiah, the resurrection of the dead, and the restoration of the temple.[27] Poznanski's version read: "We believe that the Messiah announced by the prophets is not come—the prophecies in relation to his coming not being fulfilled," whereas the older version stated: "We believe that the Redeemer will come at the time appointed, which is known to God alone; who will gather the dispersed of Israel, and restore the government up to the house of David."[28] This wording marked an important and exceedingly controversial change for the congregation.

Next, the board began to concentrate on making arrangements for the consecration of the new synagogue. They invited many Jewish religious leaders as well as state and local officials. As the building neared completion, the organ arrived, and the "Hebrew Harmonic Society," which consisted of fifty-five men and one woman (Rachel Lazarus), granted it to the synagogue as a loan. They placed it on the gallery at the western end of the synagogue.[29]

The consecration took place amid great festivities on March 19, 1841. Such a large crowd arrived that many could not be accommodated. The trustees, escorted by six of the oldest members of the synagogue and followed by the *parnass* and *hazan*, carried the scrolls from the Tabernacle to the new building. The *shamas* opened the outer doors, and they entered. The *hazan* next sounded the *shofar*, or ram's horn, four times and the choir began to sing the 118th Psalm. Other ceremonies included placing the scrolls in the ark and lighting the perpetual lamp. In the services they used three hymns that had been written by members of the congregation, Penina Moïse, J. C. Levy, and Columbus Moïse. The *Courier* published all three. The last stanza of the hymn written by Penina Moïse read:

Here, Oh Supreme! our humble
  invocation;
Our country, kindred, and the stranger
  bless!
Bless too this sanctuary's consecration,
Its hallowed purpose of our hearts
  impress.
Still, still, let choral harmony,
Ascend before thy throne;
While echoing seraphim reply
The Lord our God is One![30]

The lack of English hymns in Judaism meant that new ones had to be written. Usually the writers used Protestant tunes for which they composed suitable words. Penina Moïse, in writing this hymn and later ones for Beth Elohim, "was the first Jewish woman after many centuries to contribute toward the synagogue ritual."[31]

27. State v. Ancker, in *Reports of Cases*, 257–58; Minute Book of Beth Elohim, Feb. 21, Mar. 7, 1841.

28. Appendices 2 and 3 of *The State ex rel. A. Ottolengui*, 63–64.

29. Minute Book of Beth Elohim, Dec. 27, 1840, Feb. 14, 21, Mar. 7, 1841.

30. *Daily Courier*, Mar. 20, 1841.

31. Idelsohn, *Jewish Music*, 320.

Whereas choral harmony may have prevailed at the consecration, the speech of Poznanski brought greater discord because the *hazan* "spoke chiefly in vindication, on grounds of both reason and scripture, of the restoration of instrumental music" as an aid to worship. He also justified "the reformed practice of conducting certain portions of the service in the vernacular language of the people instead of a tongue unintelligible to most of them." He then spoke of "the plentitude of civil and religious privileges, enjoyed by the House of Israel in this land of liberty and equal right." Then in the climax of his speech he proclaimed, "this synagogue is our *temple*, this city our *Jerusalem*, this happy land our *Palestine*, and as our fathers defended with their lives *that* temple, *that* city and *that* land, so will their sons defend *this* temple, *this* city, and *this* land." The *Courier*, in its account of the events, entitled its article "The Rebuilding of the Temple" and spoke approvingly of the changes being made at Beth Elohim.[32] The traditionalists had been correct when they feared that the introduction of the organ meant other innovations would follow. The Jewish community of Charleston was never again unified in one synagogue.

Following the consecration the trustees thanked Poznanski for his speech and asked for a copy to publish; however, he "declined for various reasons" to give them the text. The board also hired Charles A. DaCosta as the organist, as he had proved his abilities in playing, instructing the choir, and composing music necessary for the ceremonies. DaCosta thus became the first organist for a Jewish synagogue in America.[33] Also, in order to introduce more decorum in services, the group banned children in arms from attending the synagogue and boys under thirteen from reading the Haftarah, the books of the prophets, which followed the reading of the Torah.[34]

On July 28, 1841, the congregation held a general meeting that sixty members attended, at which time Abraham Moïse made a motion "that the form of service adopted by the Board of Trustees up to the present period is acceptable to this meeting and will be regarded as established and permanent." Furthermore, "any changes in the Hebrew" contemplated by the board should be submitted to the congregation for consideration. The only person voting against these resolutions was Thomas W. Mordecai. Another resolution changed the constitution to protect the organ. It could be used on all occasions, and no president, presiding officer, board of trustees, "or any administration whatever" could stop or suspend the use of the organ unless three-fourths of the members agreed. Isaiah Moses cast the only vote against this.[35] Thus, the congregation attempted to consolidate the

32. *Daily Courier*, Mar. 20, 1841.

33. Minute Book of Beth Elohim, Mar. 21, April 5, May 3, 1841. Since DaCosta had been a prominent Jewish name in Charleston, it is possible he was Jewish or half Jewish.

34. Minute Book of Beth Elohim, Mar. 21, April 5, 1841.

35. Ibid., July 28, 1841.

reforms made to this point, but not wishing to allow the board to go further without their approval, they insisted that the members should approve any alterations in the use of Hebrew in the Sabbath services. Obviously, some resistance to further changes had developed within the body. Despite these resolutions, the board authorized the *hazan* to repeat in English such portions as he deemed proper of the funeral and wedding services.[36]

The changes taking place at Beth Elohim and sentiment for reform elsewhere in the country prompted Louis Salomon and Isaac Leeser, both orthodox Jewish ministers, to call for a meeting to be held in Philadelphia to create a national organization of synagogues. This proposal resulted in strong opposition on the part of the nascent reform movement and Sephardic Jews in America, who feared domination by German Orthodox elements. The trustees of Beth Elohim received a circular from Leeser but refused to accept the idea. The board stated that the regulations had been drawn up by a small portion of the Israelites in the country without their consent. The trustees resolved that all such efforts to create any ecclesiastical authority whatsoever were "alien to the spirit and genius of the age in which we live and are wholly inconsistent with the spirit of American Liberty." They also concluded that such a movement "from its very nature must be hostile to the march of improvement, or the progress of enlightened and rational reform." The trustees then called for a general meeting to make known their opposition. The congregation approved the resolutions by a large majority.[37] Abraham Moïse also told Leeser that he had assembled those who agreed with him first, concocted a plan, and then wanted others to join with them. "This of itself, would be sufficient, in my opinion, to keep away all Jews south of the Potomac." It would be useless for Beth Elohim to send delegates because "it is well known that we are at present, the only open and avowed reformers in the United States." He assured Leeser that public opinion was on the side of change and that their adversaries were like the opponents of Martin Luther who refused to grant reasonable and moderate suggestions, with the result being that "their whole scheme" was "overwhelmed and crushed."[38] Obviously, the congregation, led by Moïse, saw itself bringing about a profound change in Judaism. Martin Luther remained the example that the reformers wished to emulate, and they still sought to adapt to the time and place in which they lived—the American South before the Civil War.

The vituperation characteristic of American politics at the time could be found also in the conflicts between the two religious groups in Charleston. Someone challenged the legitimacy of the birth of Poznanski. As a result, the

36. Ibid., Aug. 8, 1841.

37. Ibid., Aug. 8, 10, 1841; Buchler, "The Struggle for Unity," 26–27.

38. Moïse to Leeser, Aug. 12, 1841, in Moïse, *Biography of Isaac Harby*, 83–89.

leaders of the congregation in Storchnest sent an affidavit to Charleston certifying that his father, Joseph Poznanski, had married Sarah, his mother, who was "a virtuous Jewish virgin" at the time, that the marriage had taken place according to Jewish laws, and that Gustavus and others were legitimate children.[39] What opponents had hoped to gain by their accusation is unclear; perhaps they sought to deny his Jewishness, but the rumor evidently became so widespread that Poznanski saw it necessary to write to Poland for the certificate. Since it took three months for the affidavit to arrive from Poland, the charges must have circulated three months before that, or about the time that Poznanski made his consecration speech at the synagogue.

Despite the attacks, reform continued, and Poznanski seems to have taken over leadership of the movement. In November 1841 the trustees appointed a committee to consult with the *hazan* about boys being confirmed "on becoming minian," that is, reaching maturity and being counted as part of the *minyan*. They also ordered 400 copies of the hymnbook to be published.[40]

The two congregations did cooperate on one matter, the appointment of a *shohet* to supervise the butchering of animals. Beth Elohim proposed to Shearith Israel that they share the expense, to which the latter agreed. Not long afterward Myers Breslau, whom they had employed, discovered meat that was marked as kosher but that had not been certified at the butcher stall of Moses Goldsmith in the market. Goldsmith said he did not know how it occurred, but that it could have been done by one of his employees. Breslau took the issue to the trustees of Beth Elohim, who decided there had been a gross neglect, although there was no positive evidence of how it had taken place. They therefore instructed the *shohet* not to kill with Goldsmith again.[41]

Resistance to Further Reform

Then resistance to further reform developed. On February 20, 1842, a vacancy occurred on the board, and the congregation elected Abraham Tobias by a slight majority. He opposed any more reforms, as did Isaiah Moses, Isaac Woolf, and Solomon Moses. Thereafter, these four constituted a majority thwarting Abraham Ottolengui (president), J. C. Levy (vice president), and Abraham Moïse. At the same meeting Poznanski was accused of introducing a new tune in the synagogue without permission. In response, forty-seven members and fifty-nine ladies of the congregation drew up a petition to keep the song. The trustees nevertheless rejected the motion by a vote of three to four. They did rule that it could be used for holidays, except Yom Kippur, but not on the Sabbath. Then differences developed over the observation of Tikkun, a

39. Minute Book of Beth Elohim, Sept. 26, 1841. The affidavit was dated June 29, 1841.

40. Ibid., Nov. 7, 1841.

41. Ibid., Aug. 8, 22, Nov. 23, 1841.

night-long remembrance held twice a year during which time those attending recited prayers in memory of the destruction of the temple in Jerusalem and called for the restoration of Palestine. The synagogue at Charleston supplied drinks, usually liquor, for these observances. In April the board ruled that the prayers for Tikkun were too long and asked the *hazan* to select ones he thought fitting. They also voted $3 for refreshments. The commemoration of Tikkun would be unnecessary if Charleston were the new Jerusalem and America the new Palestine, as Poznanski had proclaimed. Thus, the question of abolition of Tikkun arose. Solomon Moses moved to do away with it, but such "violent opposition" arose that he withdrew his motion. Moïse then had the matter referred to the congregation. Eighteen members wanted to discontinue it while twenty-eight voted to retain. Then a petition from thirty-seven people asked for the addition of an English-only Sabbath afternoon service to be presided over by the *hazan* in the synagogue. At a congregational meeting Abraham Moïse supported the proposal while Abraham Tobias objected strenuously by arguing that people would attend this service to the entire neglect of the regular one. Tempers flared, and the meeting adjourned without a vote on the matter. Following this, both Tobias and Moïse stated that they intended to resign, but they heeded resolutions that asked them to stay.[42]

Then Poznanski proposed a change that brought matters to a head. On the first day of Pesach (Passover) he advised the congregation that he would cease to observe the second day. In ancient Israel this and other holy days had been celebrated for only one day, but with the dispersion of the Jews around the world, they had begun to hold services for two days as they had been anxious "to keep the right day, at a time when the rule for regulating the calendar had not been as certain, but now had been rendered unnecessary by the progress of astronomical science." Poznanski preached that the second day was unnecessary and inconvenient.[43] This created "great alarm," and a special meeting of the board resulted. They ruled that his proposal had been "calculated to *create discord* & anarchy in a religious body when there should always be *peace & harmony.*" They wrote the *hazan* expressing their concern and demanded to know if he planned to continue "innovations of the established forms of service as observed by us and all the congregations of Jews through the world." Poznanski replied that he had been authorized to make such remarks and did not know his recommendation could cause so much alarm. He therefore asked permission to stop delivering sermons and to cease using any English in the services if that was what the congregation wanted. These did not constitute part of his duties as *hazan*. The board voted by a margin of four to two that his letter was

42. Ibid., Feb. 20, Mar. 20, April 24, May 7, 11, 1842; Jan. 15, 17, 23, 1843; State v. Ancker, in *Reports of Cases*, 259; *State ex rel. A. Ottolengui*, 24.

43. State v. Ancker, in *Reports of Cases*, 259.

not satisfactory and called for another.[44] Clearly, Poznanski knew that the board wanted to keep the reforms that had been made, and he intended to force the issue. The *hazan* kept his promise and eliminated all English from a subsequent service. At another meeting four days later Abraham Tobias asked why the *hazan* had omitted the English portions of the services during the last two holy days. Ottolengui stated that he had advised him to do so. The board then resolved to continue the use of English. Poznanski had made his point. The board also received a second letter from the *hazan* in which he said that with the "sole view of restoring and preserving peace and harmony" he would not (quoting them verbatim) "propose or advise in future lectures, innovations of the established forms of service, as observed by us and all other congregations of Jews through the world." He would continue to do this "until the general desire of the congregation to hear the truth of any religious subject, and to have our holy religion divested of all its errors and abuses" had been expressed to him through the board. Poznanski thereby wanted the congregation rather than the trustees to decide the issue; and the board, having little other choice if it wanted peace and harmony, called a meeting. Fifty-one members attended. Abraham Tobias, no doubt hoping to find that the congregation agreed with him, pressed the issue by moving that "the established services of the congregation embrace all the Mosaic and Rabbinical Laws." His effort nonetheless narrowly failed by a vote of twenty-four to twenty-seven, and the meeting was adjourned without any action having been taken.[45]

The proposal to eliminate the second day "fixed those who had become dissatisfied with changes, in their determination to oppose all further innovations, and to re-establish the ancient forms."[46] They realized that, had two more members voted in favor of the Tobias resolution, the outcome would have been twenty-six to twenty-five, and reform could have been stopped. They now began to work with the seceders to bring them back. They held a meeting on April 30, 1843, where Abraham Alexander presided with the purpose of stopping "the progress of Reform in our Synagogue, and to prevent the destruction of our holy religion." They wanted to restore the "true spirit of our religion, in conformity with the Mosaical and Rabbinical laws, and to reinstate the modes of service" as they had been in the old synagogue. They then issued an invitation for members of Shearith Israel to join with them. Thirty-four agreed to do so provided they restore the service, maintain Mosaical and rabbinical laws,

44. Minute Book of Beth Elohim, April 19, 1843. Voting against the *hazan* were Solomon Moses, Abraham Tobias, Isaiah Moses, and Isaac Woolf. Voting for him were Abraham Moïse and Abraham Ottolengui. J. C. Levy was out of the city.

45. Ibid., April 26, 1843.

46. State v. Ancker, in *Reports of Cases*, 259.

erect a ritual bath, and deny any person known for his reform ideas to officiate at the *taba*, that is, fire Poznanski.[47]

Since four members of the board of trustees constituted a majority of that body, they could vote in new members. On April 30 they wrote Ottolengui, the president, asking him to call a meeting of the vestry the next day. The president responded by stating that instead of calling a board meeting he was convening a general meeting of the congregation, as twenty-five members had requested such. Ottolengui knew that a majority of the congregation, bare as it was, favored reform; and decision making power ultimately rested with the members. He possibly got the twenty-five to sign a petition asking for a meeting after he received the letter from the four board members. The trustees then told Ottolengui that this was a constitutional matter, and such meetings could be called only by the board upon application of one-third of the members—something they did not have. The president ruled that no constitutional matter was involved.

The congregation met on May 2, at which time Jacob N. Cardozo presented a series of resolutions that sought to take power away from the board. The first declared "that the will of the majority is the fundamental principle of all associations in this country, political, social and religious." The second stated that the trustees had been elected with the implied assurance they would conform to the will of the majority. The third pointed out that evidence existed that the board planned to admit those who had seceded from the congregation and that the "established ceremonial" and pastor were to be replaced, thus forcing the majority to submit to the minority. Therefore, the president was "instructed by this congregation not to call together the Board of Trustees, until the opinion and feelings of a majority of the congregation are correctly represented." Tobias argued that this was a constitutional matter and that the meeting was illegal. When Ottolengui ruled against him, Tobias and twenty members walked out.

Despite the fact that the president had ruled that no constitutional matter was involved, the thirty-nine members who remained proceeded to amend the constitution. They provided that any Israelite who was at least twenty-one and who was not under religious disabilities who wanted to become a member should apply by letter to the board. A majority of the board could accept the person as an ordinary member, but to become a *yahid*, or voting member, the congregation had to approve. Furthermore, no changes in the form of worship could be made until approved first by the board

47. The documents can be found in Tarshish, "The Charleston Organ Case," 435–36; however, he does not indicate his source. They are not in the Minute Book. Valentine in his testimony said there were some verbal agreements. *State ex rel. A. Ottolengui*, 21. The attorney general in his arguments (p. 19) pointed out that a "treaty" had been made between the four trustees and the members of Shearith Israel "to subvert the system of worship, to break up the organ, and expel the minister."

and second by three-fourths of the voting members.[48]

Not admitting defeat, the four trustees again tried to get Ottolengui to call a meeting of the board. He still declined to do so. After getting a petition of twenty-five members, including the four members of the board, they met anyway on May 6. Ignoring the constitutional changes regarding the admission of new members, they accepted forty-two men from Shearith Israel, thirty-two as *yahidim* and ten as ordinary members. Not until later did they revoke the constitutional changes made by their opponents.[49] On May 10 they called together "a portion of Israelites, members of Kahal Kadosh Beth Elohim," and fulfilled their promises to the former members of Shearith Israel. Nathaniel Levin offered a resolution that stated, "the present condition of the Jews of Charleston is of the most vital importance to us and to our brethren through the world." Therefore they had a duty to "adhere rigidly to our sacred and ancient forms and customs." The traditionalists aimed, he proclaimed, "to check" the "great and growing evil" brought about by "the progressive inroads" and "to restore concord and harmony."[50]

48. Minute Book of Beth Elohim, May 2, 1843. A number of writers, including Marcus, *United States Jewry*, 424, have stated that Jacob Cardozo was orthodox in his beliefs. He was very much a reformer.

49. Minute Book of Beth Elohim, May 6, 15, 1843.

50. Ibid., May 10, 1843.

The Orthodox in Control

The orthodox now in control began to make other changes. They called a meeting and changed the constitution so that three trustees could call the board together. They also required meetings of the vestry to be held at least once a month and allowed any member to conduct burials. The last they directed against Poznanski, who was required by the 1840 constitution to officiate. They also declared as unconstitutional the changes made on May 2.[51] As the president and vice president had refused to accept these changes, they did not attend the meetings. Since the officers held their positions for life, they could not be removed by the orthodox element. The reform element also did not attend the general meetings. The orthodox banned instrumental music, as it was "obnoxious to the consciences of many Israelites," and ordered Poznanski to return books in his possession.[52] Poznanski, however, refused, stating that he was under the control of the president who had ordered him to retain them. The *hazan*, according to a statement he made several years later, fearing "a disgraceful conflict, and perhaps, bloodshed" in the synagogue, also resigned.[53]

Meanwhile the reformers resisted the development. When the board arrived at the synagogue for a meeting on July 10, they found the gates locked. They

51. Ibid., May 15, 1843.

52. Ibid., June 27, 1843 .

53. Ibid., July 3, 1843. The letter explaining his resignation is in ibid., Jan. 3, 1847.

summoned the president and vice president, but the officers refused to turn over the keys. The orthodox board members then forced entry by "breaking or picking the locks." They also chose Jacob Rosenfeld to officiate as reader "while the controversy exists."[54] Then, to their consternation, Charles DaCosta refused to stop playing the organ at services. At a general meeting of the orthodox element they decided to fire DaCosta and to take possession of the synagogue. At this point they found they had to employ legal counsel.[55]

The Court Battle

The minutes of the congregation stop on August 31, 1843, and do not take up again until August 24, 1846. During this time the matter of who controlled the synagogue went to the courts. While the courts decided the issue, someone worked out a compromise between the "Organ Congregation" and the "Remnants," as they were known. One week the Organ Congregation met in the synagogue, the next week the Remnants. When a group did not have use of the synagogue, it met in a separate room, possibly the Tabernacle, "fitted up for public service." Both employed the Minhag Sephardim, but the Organ Congregation used music, had some prayers only in English, a sermon in English, and the concluding prayer "The Lord Bless Thee and Keep Thee" in both Hebrew and English. The Remnants had a longer service, no organ music, a prayer in English for the government, and an occasional sermon in English. The discourses of Rosenfeld, as reader of the Remnants, were "considered plain and instructive."[56]

The Remnants also organized a separate Sunday school operated by "The Society for the Instruction of Jewish Doctrine." More than sixty women met on May 5, 1844, at which time they adopted a constitution and elected officers. Miss Henrietta Hart served as president, Mrs. Mary Hirsch as vice president, Miss P. Valentine as secretary and treasurer. Five others acted as the trustees and five more as the Benevolence Committee. Five teachers, in addition to Henrietta Hart, taught more than sixty students in six classes.[57] At the end of the first year of operation the school held a public display of the accomplishments of the students. "A very numerous assemblage" of parents, friends of the pupils, and "several of our Christian friends" attended the event. Henrietta Hart read a report of the year's activities "and her timidity and retiring modesty (so lovely a trait in woman's character)" impressed the audience. In her speech she emphasized the importance of teaching the youth so they would remain true to the faith. "Lessons of religious truth," she said, "then sink deep into the mind, and time cannot obliterate, circumstances cannot efface them." She then explained how students won awards

54. Ibid., Aug. 31, 1843.

55. Ibid., July 10, 13, 19, Aug. 27, 1843.

56. DeLaMotta, "The Congregations of Charleston."

57. "New School in Charleston."

and announced that "Master Jefferson Tobias" would be awarded the highest prize. Fifty some students from the age of five to fifteen competed for other trophies by being examined on the five books that had been used in their studies. Following this, several of the pupils recited poems and readings, with Miriam Levin recounting an original poem entitled "An Infant's Prayer." Rosenfeld then delivered a sermon based on the verse "Teach a child in the way that he should go, and when he is old, he will not depart from it." An English hymn concluded the event. The following years similar events took place.[58]

Meanwhile, the death of DeLaMotta deprived the orthodox of another of their leaders and benefactors. He had served as the president and first reader for the Remnants for more than two years but seemed pleased when Rosenfeld took over those duties. After that, he withdrew from public life "and from the unpleasant contentions which agitate the Israelites in Charleston." His own family split over religious matters, "as his female relatives were attached to the new order of things."[59]

The issue of who controlled the synagogue occupied the attention of the courts from 1843 to 1846. The reform group filed charges on October 4, 1843, and a *quo warranto* case resulted, which became known as *The State of South Carolina ex relatione Abraham Ottolengui et al., vs. G. V. Ancker et al.* It came to trial before Judge D. L. Wardlaw on Monday, April 15, 1844, with the relators being the reform group and the defendants being the orthodox. The liberal group had charged that the respondents "were intruders who had exercised the privileges of membership without right and to the injury of the Relators."[60] The attorney general, Henry Bailey, and James L. Petigru represented the relators while Christopher G. Memminger and Mitchell King argued for the defendants. Both sides employed some of the best, and apparently most expensive, lawyers in the city. Tried in the Court of Common Pleas, a civil court with a jury, the case lasted four days. The only witness called was Samuel Valentine, who had served as secretary of both groups. At the conclusion the jury retired and "after a short consultation" ruled in favor of the relators.[61] The admission of the members of Shearith Israel had not been legal. The result was that "the friends of Mr. Poznanski have been left in possession of the congregation property."[62] Not satisfied with the outcome,

58. "Examination of the Society," 136–42; "An Examination of the Pupils," 207–8; "Examination of the Society for the Instruction of Jewish Doctrines," 260–61; "Sunday School Anniversary."

59. "Obituary: Jacob DeLaMotta," 59–60.

60. *State ex rel. A. Ottolengui*, 3.

61. Ibid., 57. Since this was a religious matter, Memminger charged no fee. An orphan who had been raised at public expense until he was adopted, Memminger became a reformer. He was largely responsible for the establishment of public education in Charleston. Later when he was secretary of the treasury of the Confederacy, a Union general referred to him disparagingly as a Jew. Marcus, *United States Jewry*, 574.

62. Leeser, "The Quo Warranto Case," 166.

the orthodox appealed the case in January 1845, citing eleven reasons for doing so. They claimed they had never resigned from Beth Elohim and still held membership there; however, the court noted that they had ceased to pay their dues to Beth Elohim, had taken no part in meetings of the congregation, had done nothing to prevent the 1840 constitution from being passed, had formed another congregation and attended meetings there in violation of article 12 of the 1836 constitution, and had applied for readmission. The court, making its ruling in January 1846, thus refused to set aside the verdict of the jury.[63]

Even if the reformers had lost the case, their movement most likely would have continued. At least eighteen members of the Reformed Society of Israelites still lived in the city and took an active role in congregational affairs. Indeed, of the forty-three members on the list kept by Abraham Moïse, ten signed the petition to install the organ, which means they constituted 27 percent of the signatories. Although five of the former members of the Reformed Society became members of Shearith Israel, none of them signed the organ petition; indeed, they appear not to have belonged to Beth Elohim prior to the schism. This was certainly true for three members of the Goldsmith family. On the other hand, the thirteen remaining former members of the Reformed Society stayed with their reform ideas and participated in the case of *State v. Ancker*, where they constituted 28 percent of the relators. Obviously, most of those who sought change in 1824 firmly held on to their beliefs in the succeeding years and finally met with some success. At the same time a greater number, though willing to accept some modifications in the mode of worship, did not want to make radical revisions in Jewish beliefs and practices. The question of the organ caused the split in the congregation, but the move not to observe the second day of holy days and the questioning of the coming of the Messiah decidedly turned them against reform. Some of those who signed the organ petition apparently believed that this action did not betoken further changes. Seven of them subsequently became members of the minority who opposed further changes and voted to admit members of Shearith Israel. Some therefore can be termed "conservatives" in that they were willing to make a few changes. Even Shearith Israel had sermons and a prayer in English.

One of the issues brought out in the trial by the counsel for the relators was the fact that they were the old members of Beth Elohim whereas the defendants were young. Actually, they were about the same age; the average for the relators was 43.12 years and that of the orthodox was 42.52. But the traditionalists differed from the reformers in that many more of them had been born outside the United States—something the counsel for the relators brought out and for which the opposition accused him of trying to prejudice the jury. When the

63. Leeser, "The Appeal Case of the Charleston Congregation"; State v. Ancker, in *Reports of Cases*, 265–86.

lawyer read a list of the relators to Valentine, he responded that "40 [85 percent] were natives, seven alien. Minority about the same. The Respondents [traditionalists], 15 natives, 26 aliens [63 percent]." Valentine also testified that nine-tenths of the congregation did not understand Hebrew.[64] Thus, the overriding element, as in the 1820s, in accounting for reform is the fact that the advocates had been Americanized and southernized to the extent that much of the Hebrew service seemed incomprehensible. The simpler services of the surrounding Protestant churches in the community offered them models that appealed more to them. Their forefathers had left Europe for a more promising land; they believed they had found the promised land.

Gustavus Poznanski stated in 1847 that few of the Israelites of Charleston really opposed change. Resistance, however, developed on the part of two groups. One, he said, personally disliked him, while the other feared that reforms would go too far.[65] His assessment of the situation seems to be basically valid: personalities seem to have been very much involved. Poznanski possessed charisma. His followers throughout his tenure at the synagogue heaped praise on him and tended to give him a free reign in advocating innovations. He certainly had greater powers than a reader normally exercised. Popular leaders, however, can provoke animosity, which he did when he pushed too far for some people. He reaped their hatred.[66]

Shearith Israel, 1846–1861

Once the courts decided which group should control the synagogue, the orthodox accepted their defeat and went about reorganizing Shearith Israel. In November 1846 they petitioned the legislature for incorporation. The president Samuel Hart, Sr., the seven trustees, the secretary and treasurer Samuel Valentine, and Moses Lopez signed the petition. They also indicated that fifty-two other unnamed Israelites constituted the congregation.[67] When the state approved, the congregation could legally own and manage property. The members wrote a constitution and adopted the Portuguese Minhag, with English sermons being the only deviation from a Hebrew service.[68]

On February 24, 1857, they laid the

64. *State ex rel. A. Ottolengui*, 22.

65. Minute Book of Beth Elohim, Jan. 3, 1847.

66. Jacob Levy wrote an article, "The Reformed Israelites," for the *Southern Quarterly Review* in 1844 in which he stated that, among other things, the ideas for the reformers had been based on Gotthold Salomon's *Twelve Sermons Delivered in the New Temple of Israelites* at *Hamburg*, Louis Salomon's *The Mosaic System*, and Isaac Leeser's *Instructions in the Mosaic Religion*. All these works could be purchased at Levin and Tavel in Charleston; however, it is doubtful they had a great effect on reform in Charleston.

67. Records of the General Assembly, Papers, Petitions, 1846, Petition No. 10, Petition ND No. 233.

68. *Occident*, 4(1846–47): 107–8, 260, 357–58.

foundations for their synagogue on Wentworth Street. Jacob Rosenfeld continued to lead Shearith Israel as he had the Remnants when they worshiped on alternate Sabbaths in Beth Elohim. At the ceremony for laying the foundation stones, Rosenfeld delivered a sermon in which he stressed that his congregation was an orthodox one and the synagogue "was designed to be a house of worship for the remnant of Israel; there to worship Him as in the days of yore, in the holy tongue, in which He revealed His divine will to His servants the prophets." He continued, "Orthodoxy shall be taught here in its true spirit, unsullied by its abuses."[69] The congregation also initiated a circular appealing for funds both for building their synagogue and for paying the debts incurred with the appeals case. Fifty-two families made up the group at the time.[70]

The congregation rapidly moved forward with the construction of the synagogue, which they dedicated on August 13, 1847, the first day of the month of Elul. In the sermon delivered at the consecration, Rosenfeld "set forth the grievances under which they laboured."[71] Indeed, the greatest part of his speech castigated the reformers from the time "innovations began to creep in." The attempts to change the creed were in his view "arrogant, baneful, and preposterous." While at one point he said that "it is for God to judge, not man," he proceeded to denounce the schism. Yet he saw some positive benefits in "that the schism of your Synagogue has been for the wise purpose of arousing you from your lethargy, to guard your religion and public worship from innovations, and of bringing back to the fold those who were indifferent or astray."[72] Obviously, feelings in the community continued to run very deep.

When Leeser had proposed a union of the synagogues in America in 1841, the leaders of Beth Elohim had reacted forcefully against it. In 1848 Leeser called for a convention of Jewish leaders to be held in New York in order to establish uniformity in customs, worship, and education. Rosenfeld favored such a conference; however, he pointed out that in the United States the Jewish clerics did not lead their congregations, but had to follow them. The majority ruled whether they understood an issue or not, or whether they took any interest in matters. Furthermore, the readers had short-term appointments and had no real power. Invitations should therefore be sent out to congregational officers, who could then choose to send their ministers.[73] Soon after this Rosenfeld wrote a long poem entitled "Israel's Union" promoting the idea. Two stanzas read:

> Our minister are powerless, are nought
> but serving men,
> Our religious schools a mock'ry, synagogues forsaken;

69. "Rev. Mr. Rosenfeld's Address," 75–79.

70. "The Congregation Shearith Israel," 49–50.

71. *Occident*, 5(1847–48): 371.

72. "Discourse by Rosenfeld," 325–36.

73. Rosenfeld, "The Proposed Assembly," 563–65.

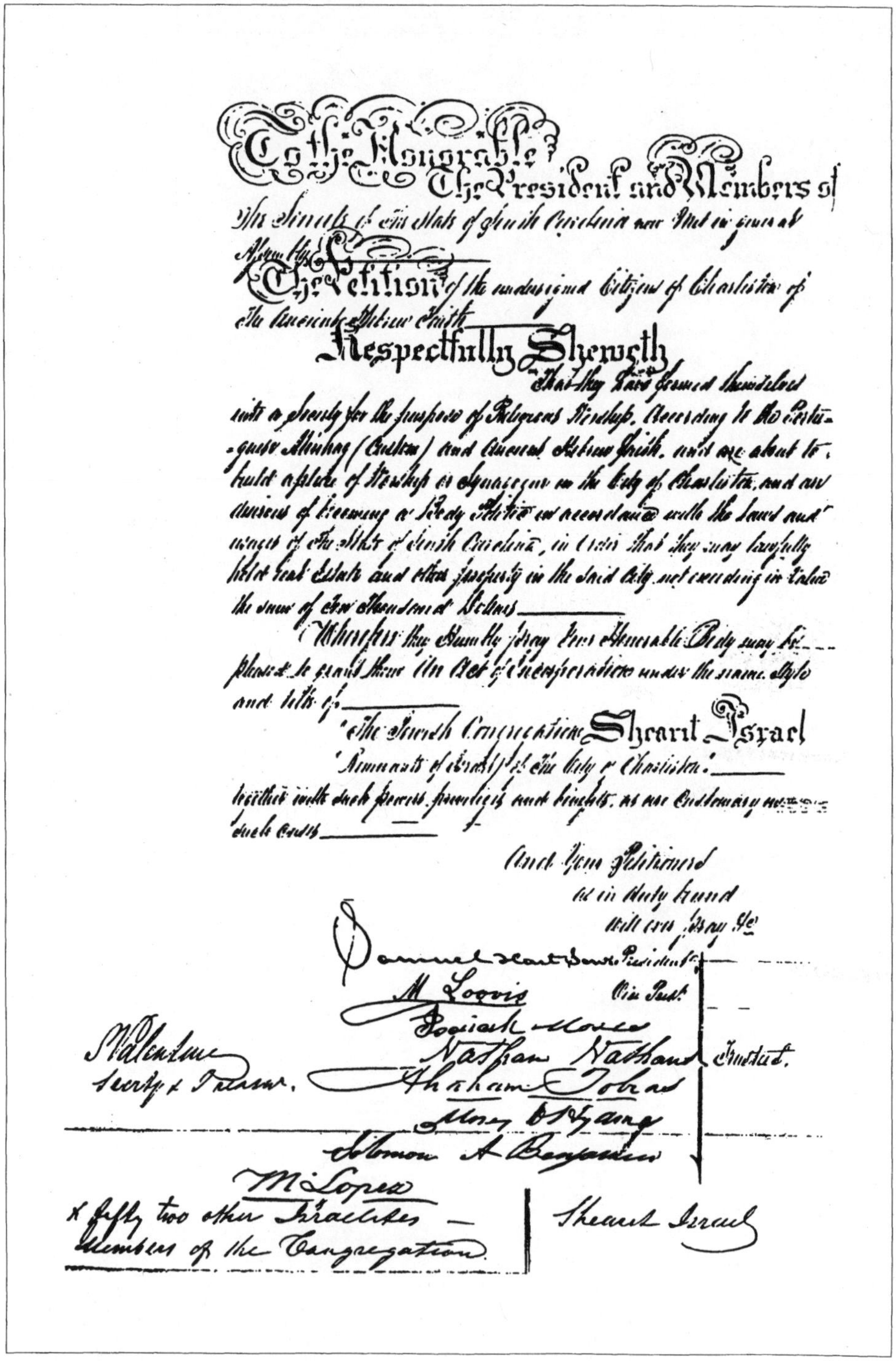

To the Honorable The President and Members of the Senate of the State of South Carolina now Met in General Assembly

The Petition of the undersigned Citizens of Charleston of the Ancient Hebrew Faith

Respectfully Sheweth

That they have formed themselves into a Society for the purpose of Religious Worship. According to the Portuguese Minhag (Custom) and Ancient Hebrew Faith. and are about to build a place of Worship or Synagogue in the City of Charleston, and are desirous of becoming a Body Politic in accordance with the Laws and usages of the State of South Carolina, in Order that they may lawfully hold Real Estate and other property in the said City not exceeding in Value the sum of Ten Thousand Dollars

Wherefore they Humbly pray Your Honorable Body may be pleased to grant them An Act of Incorporation under the name, Style and title of

"The Jewish Congregation Shearit Israel

'Remnants of Israel' of the City of Charleston"

together with such powers, privileges and Rights, as are Customary in such Cases

And Your Petitioners
as in duty bound
will ever pray &c

Samuel Hart Senr. President
M Lopes Vice Presdt.
Josiah Moses
Nathan Nathans — Trustees
Abraham Tobias
Moses D Hyams
Solomon A Benjamin

S Valentine
Secty & Treasur.

M Lopez
& fifty two other Israelites — Members of the Congregation

Shearit Israel

48. Petition of Shearith Israel to incorporate. (South Carolina Archives.)

49. Shearith Israel Synagogue (1847–1866). Later the building became a Catholic church. No longer in existence. (Photograph courtesy of Beth Elohim Synagogue.)

And all those laws, and wise commands, preserved with so much care
By our sage and pious fathers, are practiced now so rare.
Why, in this land that free us made,
Does Israel thus retrograde?
Because Jeshurun has grown fat, therefore we speculate,
Freedom has refined our taste, taught us to violate.
No *unison* 'mongst us is found, as in those days of yore,
When oppression made us pious, united us the more.
Some are reformed, and wisdom boast,
Some orthodox, indifferent most.[74]

Rosenfeld believed that freedom brought perils. His solution would have been centralized control, something that has never been achieved in American Judaism and something that was anathema to native-born southern Jews in 1849.

In 1850 Dr. Morris J. Raphall, one of the outstanding orthodox leaders of the

74. Rosenfeld, "Israel's Union."

time, notified Samuel Hart, Sr., the president of Shearith Israel, that he intended to visit Charleston. Hart called together the trustees of the congregation, who set up a committee of five to take care of Raphall while he was in the city. Hart wrote Raphall an effusive letter that referred to him as an "erudite editor," a "truly pious divine," and a "most gifted lecturer" who had accomplished more for the British Jews than "any Israelite of the present day."[75] The leaders of Shearith Israel considered it a high honor to welcome such a supporter among their midst. The trustees of Beth Elohim felt quite differently. When they heard that Raphall was coming to Charleston, they called a special meeting of the board. They advised the officers to take what action they deemed correct.[76]

Raphall pleased the orthodox of Charleston all the more when he delivered an oration on "The Constancy of Israel." In this address he pointed out that the Jews had maintained their religion through the centuries despite captivity in Egypt and Babylon and many other hardships. He attacked the reformers by stating, "We are to yield to prosperity what we refused to adversity. We are to sit down contented in these United States of America—here is our Jerusalem. We are to give up the restoration of Israel for we are already free citizens. Such are the doctrines propounded from the pulpit by men, who in the words of the Psalmist, 'take counsel together against the Lord and his Messiah.'" He went on to proclaim that the Messiah would come "without fail." Raphall struck a theme as Rosenfeld had done in his consecration speech, that the freedom of Jews in America led to "folly" on the part of a "handful of Jews."[77] This fear has been an element in American Judaism since that time. A free society where persecution did not exist loosened bonds and prevented rabbinical control. Though the orthodox did not long for a return to ghettoes, they felt uneasy in the modern world. They turned their anger toward those who sought to adapt to the world in which they lived. The visit and message of Raphall so buoyed the traditionalists that they published his address and advertised it for sale in the local newspapers.

While Raphall railed against the reformers, Isaac M. Wise, a native of Bohemia and then the minister of a synagogue in Albany, New York, enjoyed a "grand dinner at the house of the parnass" of Beth Elohim, where a "circle of ladies" used "all manner of feminine wiles" to attract his attention.[78] He, too, had come to the city, not, however, so much to encourage the reformers but to seek employment. Poznanski had resigned, and the congregation of Beth Elohim had invited him for an interview. He already had spoken at Beth Elohim. The discourse of Raphall, in fact, answered both the consecration speech of Poznanski and the inaugural sermon of Wise at Charleston.

While Wise grew heady "in paradise,"

75. "Dr. Raphall in Charleston."

76. Minute Book of Beth Elohim, Jan. 8, 1850.

77. Raphall, *The Constancy of Israel*.

78. Wise, *Reminiscences*, 145.

a Jewish editor, no doubt Cardozo, entered the room and reported that he had just heard the speech of Raphall, who "had completely demolished the reform movement." The editor had written down enough of the speech that Wise went into the adjoining room to look it over. "The ball was now set rolling." In the following days each man spoke a number of times, each attacking the arguments of the other before large audiences. On the evening of Purim, the Jewish festival in remembrance of the salvation of Jews in the Persian Empire, the two met. They became friendly that evening, even though Raphall told Wise that if he retraced his steps he could render Judaism great service rather than harm. At the same time Wise told Raphall, "we will see within ten or 20 years what will be left in America of Jewish orthodoxy."[79]

Wise felt overshadowed when Raphall and Poznanski held a public debate. Wise wrote that it "was a foolish and purposeless procedure," but it had been decided upon before his arrival, and "the comedy had to be enacted." Lined up on one side were Poznanski, Wise, and their supporters, while on the other were Raphall and his. Raphall, "a rotund little man with a black velvet skullcap," sat beside Poznanski "in full dress, stiff, cold, and self satisfied." Contemptuous of everyone but himself, Wise, during the debate, wrote a "German poem, which I refrained from publishing because I did not wish to encroach on Heine's preserve." Wise then observed that both men "began to murder Talmudical passages," which they knew only from secondary sources. The debate had no structure and no judges. In the opinion of Wise, Poznanski worsted Raphall, who grew excited and spoke with great violence. Then Raphall "glowed with holy zeal" and turned to Wise and demanded: "Do you believe in the personal Messiah? Do you believe in the bodily resurrection?" Wise responded with a loud "No." Raphall then quickly gathered up his books and stormed from the hall, accompanied by his supporters. He departed during the week, but Wise stayed for the following Sabbath to deliver a sermon.[80]

Wise had not merely refrained from supporting the idea of a Messiah, he had flatly rejected the concept. No other issue at the time could so incite anger among the orthodox. Wise soon found out how much his words had disturbed others. Raphall and the leaders of Shearith Israel published what Wise called a "bull of excommunication" in the *Occident*, stating that since he no longer believed in the personal Messiah or in the bodily resurrection, he was no longer fit to be a Jewish religious leader and should be fired from his position in Albany. A series of articles in the Jewish weekly *Asmonen* also bitterly attacked him, and Leeser refused to print many

79. Ibid., 145–46.

80. Ibid., 148–49. According to one source, Raphall asked Poznanski "if he believed in the Bible, i.e., the Law and the Prophets, he, in the presence of both congregations, replied after a long hesitation, Y-e-s,—several of his own congregation inferring, from his evasion and long consideration, that he did not fully believe." Carvalho, "The Congregation Beth Elohim," 207.

commentaries that he submitted to the *Occident*. Then Louis Spanier, the president of his congregation, fired him. When Wise refused to obey his orders, the president attacked him in the middle of services and a fight soon engulfed the entire synagogue. The sheriff and a posse had to be summoned, and Wise soon found himself ousted from his synagogue and the leader of his supporters in a break-off congregation in Albany. Four years later he went west to Cincinnati, where after the Civil War he created the basic organizations of Reform Judaism in America.[81]

Unfortunately, no records of Shearith Israel have survived except those that were printed. As a result, little of the history subsequent to 1850 can be reconstructed. The congregation did maintain an interest in Palestine; and when Rabbi Aaron Selig, a "missionary from Jerusalem," arrived in the city, the members of Shearith Israel resolved to contribute $1 each per year for the relief of the needy in Jerusalem and Hebron. Although not all fulfilled their promise, they donated $22 in 1850 for the Holy Land. For them, these contributions not only signified acts of charity but further reinforced the concept of the bodily resurrection of the dead and the return to Palestine. Isaac Leeser praised them for their efforts. The trustees of Beth Elohim, however, informed the agent of their "inability of contributing to aid in his laudable mission."[82]

When Rosenfeld accepted another position, Shearith Israel advertised for a new minister and on June 1, 1851, appointed Ellis Lyons for a two-year period.[83] According to Isaac Leeser, who visited the city in early 1852, the congregation flourished, and worship services were well attended; however, Lyon resigned his position soon after that.[84] The congregation met on June 13, 1852, and asked Leeser to become a candidate for the position. He, however, declined. Instead, they hired Solomon Jacobs, who began his duties on Rosh ha-Shanah. Leeser judged him "a safe expounder of our faith," and the congregation found him so pleasing that a year later they raised his salary from $1,000 to $1,500. Despite this, Jacobs resigned in 1857, and Henry Samuel Jacobs of Richmond replaced him after the high holy days. He served until 1861.[85]

One of the tactics used by the members of Beth Elohim to try to keep people from seceding was to deny them burial in the congregational cemetery. The orthodox therefore acquired land adjacent to the Coming Street Cemetery and began their own. A wall separated the two until the congregations merged in 1866, at which time they joined the two cemeteries. Burials began there as early as August 1843 after the death of Rebecca

81. Wise, *Reminiscences*, 152–60; *Occident*, 8(1850–51): 366; Heller, *Isaac M. Wise*.

82. *Occident*, 7(1849–50): 477, 8(1850–51): 199; Minute Book of Beth Elohim, Dec. 16, 1850, Jan. 5, 1821.

83. *Occident*, 9(1851–52): 226.

84. Ibid., 10(1852–53): 174; 224.

85. Ibid., 461; Leeser, "The Rev. Solomon Jacobs." Leeser printed the correspondence. A letter from the *yahidim* and members of the congregation included thirty-five names. They probably are the bulk of the congregation; "Rev. Solomon Jacobs," 271; *Occident*, 15(1857–58): 202, 357.

Emily Ancker. The congregation, however, did not hold its consecration service until 1858, at which time Henry Jacobs delivered an oration.[86]

Despite differences between the two congregations, they cooperated in organizations such as the Hebrew Benevolent Society and when their coreligionists came under attack outside the United States. At the meeting of the Benevolent Society in 1858, the officers came from both groups, and the ministers from each congregation offered blessings over the food.[87]

Beth Elohim, 1843–1861

During the court case the two congregations continued to war against one another. In June 1844 another attack on the character of Poznanski came from the pen of Rev. S. M. Isaacs of New York. Apparently, Isaacs charged that Poznanski had acted without authority of the congregation, had desecrated the Sabbath, and, moreover, possessed some character defects. This so aroused the supporters of the *hazan* that they called a meeting at the tabernacle on June 12, 1844. They passed resolutions in his favor supporting his "foregiving spirit," which he had exhibited despite the "persecution of some of our co-religionists." He had permitted "all controversial assaults upon him to pass without reply." Furthermore, he, after resigning, had agreed to serve as minister without compensation. They published their proceedings in the Charleston *Courier* along with a notice that they had inserted in the November 17, 1843, issue of the *Southern Patriot*. The latter announced that they had procured his services as a *hazan* on alternate Sabbaths. Additionally, they resolved that "in the private character and deportment of the Rev. G. Poznanski, all his co-worshippers, but more particularly the youth of the Congregation, have an example to cherish worthy of their imitation."[88] "Many orthodox Jews" of Charleston responded to the notice of these events, which Isaac C. Cohen had sent to the *Occident* for publication. They charged Poznanski with having desecrated the Sabbath, divided "a once happy and united congregation into broken fragments," and introduced "those *German neologistic doctrines of faith*, which are not *even original with him*, and are only calculated to produce a generation of deists." They would have preferred that he remained in retirement.[89]

The charges against Poznanski did not deter him and his supporters. He continued to serve the "Organ Congregation." In January 1847 he submitted his resignation, stating that "our reform was firmly established by the decision of the tribunals of the country" and that his resignation would help the congregation financially and reunite families. A new minister would not have personal prejudices against him and could work more effectively. The board adjourned in

86. Elzas, *Old Jewish Cemeteries*, 84, 85; Valentine, "Consecration of the 'Beth Chayim.'"

87. "The Hebrew Benevolent Society of Charleston, South Carolina, " 571–89.

88. *Southern Patriot*, Nov. 17, 1843; *Courier*, June 14, 1844; "Rev. Mr. Poznanski."

89. "Rev. Mr. Poznanski," 210–12.

order to consider his request and at a subsequent meeting decided to refer the matter to the congregation. The members of Beth Elohim viewed this prospect with considerable alarm and passed a resolution stating that his retirement would be disastrous to them and to the cause of reform. Their concern induced the *hazan* to remain at his post, but by November of that same year he had made up his mind, and he asked the board to reconsider. Another public meeting resulted, and this time the membership submitted and appointed a committee of five with Poznanski as the chair to find a new *hazan*. In the interim Poznanski would continue to lead services.[90]

Finding a replacement proved difficult. The committee advertised the position in the United States, France, and Germany. They received four applications and recommended Dr. Julius Landsberger of Breslau, Prussia, for the position. He came highly recommended by Abraham Geiger, one of the leading reformers in Germany. In rather extensive correspondence Landsberger posed a number of questions about the terms of employment, the cost of living, the climate, and the "sanitary conditions" of the city. Several months after the congregation decided to employ him, they read in a journal that Landsberger had accepted a position in Europe.[91]

The committee had to begin its work anew. Again they advertised in the United States and Europe. This was when Isaac M. Wise, who is discussed earlier in this chapter, came to their attention. Their first application for the position was his. Although no one on the search committee personally knew him, they had read some of his articles in the *Occident*. He appeared to be a man of great learning and high moral character. In his letter Wise asked that the probationary period be extended to five years and the congregation furnish a house for him "in a manner as would comport with the dignity of his position." He expressed willingness to come to the city on a visit. The committee recommended hiring him upon a successful interview and furnishing his house, but they thought the probationary period should be kept at two years.[92] The congregation thereupon issued an invitation to Wise. Thus, the stage was set for his confrontation with Raphall.

Wise traveled by train and steamer to Charleston. On the boat from Wilmington, North Carolina, he wrote his sermon entitled "Bible Theology," which he delivered at Beth Elohim. In this speech he stated that the theology of the Bible rested on the will of God, which was ruled by rationalism. In Charleston, Poznanski coached him on his manners. He should sit still with his hands folded in public and speak slowly and deliberately, in other words, fashion himself according to the Charleston pattern. Poznanski asked to read his discourse in order to remove any "Germanisms" that

90. Minute Book of Beth Elohim, Jan. 3, 6, 10, Nov. 11, 14, 1847.

91. Ibid., Sept. 24, Oct. 14, Dec. 24, 1848; May 10, Nov. 4, 1849.

92. Ibid., Feb. 5, 1850.

might be included in it; however, Wise retorted, "If there are, you would substitute Polisms for them." When time came to deliver his speech, Wise at first felt terrified of the audience but quickly recovered his ego and thought to himself, "I am your teacher and master; I speak and you listen." Later came the debates with Raphall. Wise returned to Albany "thoroughly Americanized" and fully convinced that he could "satisfy a cultured audience." He had made new friends and felt energized. A few days later he received a telegram from Beth Elohim offering him the position. He was "much taken with Charleston" and the reform principles of the congregation. He would be among people of like mind. He accepted the offer and handed in his resignation at Albany. Many in his congregation sought to retain him. Then his wife, learning of the prevalence of yellow fever in Charleston, persuaded him to remain in Albany.[93]

Again the congregation felt they had been betrayed by a candidate for the post and wrote Wise of their "feelings of mortification & disappointment" and asked him to return the $149.31 that had been incurred in bringing him to Charleston. Poznanski then offered to continue to serve—but without compensation. The trustees, however, insisted on paying him. Only four days after learning of the rejection by Wise, the trustees voted to bring in the second person on their list, Julius Eckman of Richmond. The congregation concurred with the board and hired him.[94]

Meanwhile, Beth Elohim held a retirement celebration for Poznanski. Joshua Lazarus sent copies of articles reporting the proceedings in the Charleston *Evening News* to Isaac Leeser of the *Occident*, who had recently been in Charleston. Aaron Moïse, Sr., who served as the chair of the Committee on Arrangements, provided an engraved silver pitcher to the *hazan* and delivered a laudatory oration. In his reply, Poznanski, among other things, noted the personal attack that had been made on him in 1844 and the response of his supporters. He also stated that though he knew of no intentional offense on his part to the members of Shearith Israel, he begged their forgiveness. Then Gustavus Poznanski Lazarus, on behalf of the young people of the congregation, presented the *hazan* with a second engraved silver pitcher and delivered another speech, to which Poznanski also replied. Poznanski remained in the community and became a member of Beth Elohim.[95]

The congregation lost another leader on December 12, 1850, when Abraham Ottolengui died. He had been the president of the congregation since the death

93. Wise, *Reminiscences*, 143–53; Minute Book of Beth Elohim, Mar. 12, April 7, 24, 1850.

94. Minute Book of Beth Elohim, April 28, May 29, June 2, 1850.

95. *Occident*, 8(1850–51): 249–55; *Charleston Evening News*, June 17, 1850. When he returned to New York, he rejoined Shearith Israel. At first the trustees did not want to provide him seats, but eventually relented. DeSola Pool, *An Old Faith in a New World*, 430.

of Nathan Hart in 1840 and had led the members of Beth Elohim through their most difficult years. The board of trustees passed resolutions honoring him and draped the synagogue in "suitable badges of mourning for the space of thirty days." They also placed a black border around the pages of the minute book where these resolutions were inscribed. In his will he left $1500 to Beth Elohim as the "Ottolengui Fund," the income from which was to be used for aid to the poor. Each year needy Jews of Charleston applied for assistance and, subject to the board of trustees, received it.[96] Joshua Lazarus served as president of the congregation until the Civil War.

Julius Eckman had a short tenure. Born in Germany, he had received a diploma "under the seals of the Rabbinates of Berlin and Prenzlaw" and had been examined at the Royal Frederick Wilhelm College at Berlin. Thus, he apparently was the first ordained rabbi of Beth Elohim. All acknowledged his erudition in ancient and modern languages;[97] however, he quickly alienated the reform members of the congregation. They understood him to be a reformer when he was hired. Indeed, he wrote a letter to Poznanski from Richmond while he was under consideration stating, "Your modification of the creed . . . is quite correct. . . . About the *Messiah, &c.*, this is bordering on the ideal. What is it good to [wrangle?] about terms which have not, since two thousand years been determined." He then went on to indicate that if "more serious changes are contemplated," he would like to know about them before embarking on such an important undertaking.[98] But he soon began to make, in the view of Isaac Leeser of the *Occident*, "many and blessed exertions to restore religion to its former orthodox standard among his flock."[99] Solomon N. Carvalho, one of his supporters but a member of Shearith Israel, said he sought "to reform *his congregation* by causing them to observe our religion and its ceremonies, and not to reform *our religion*."[100] Eckman claimed that his "views were *fully* and *plainly* expressed" at the time of his hiring and that he was elected "contrary to his expectations."[101] He allowed the organ and some prayers in English, but Leeser urged him to renounce all the changes that had been made at Beth Elohim.[102] Eckman seems to have tried. Among other things, he published articles entitled "On the Resurrection" and "On the Origin and Purpose of the Synagogue."[103] A bitter

96. Minute Book of Beth Elohim, Dec. 15, 1850, Jan. 12, 1851, Sept. 24, 1851; *Occident*, 8(1850–51): 578–80; W45.796.

97. Carvalho, "The Congregation Beth Elohim," 203–8; Leeser, "Rev. Dr. Eckman."

98. Eckman to Poznanski, April 26, 5610 [1850], in Cardozo, "The Congregation Beth Elohim," 318.

99. *Occident*, 9(1851–52): 59. Some orthodox observers noted that his change was not different from that of Poznanski.

100. "Minister of the Congregation Beth Elohim," 93. The correspondent used "N" as his name.

101. Eckman, "Beth Elohim Congregation," 141–42.

102. *Occident*, 9(1851–52): 144.

103. Ibid., 148–54; 10(1852–53): 134–44.

struggle broke out again within the congregation between what Carvalho called the "radicals" and the "conservatives." Carvalho and Jacob N. Cardozo wrote defiant articles in which they made incorrect statements.[104] According to Carvalho, Poznanski tried to dictate to Eckman from the beginning, and the latter denounced the former *hazan* to the *parnass* "not only as an infidel, but inimicably disposed to the very institution of Judaism."[105] The "radicals" soon had had enough, and eighteen of them, led by Cardozo, demanded Eckman's resignation, claiming that had they noted any faltering during his interview "on all the points of Reform which have been adopted for the last Ten Years," this would have "proved fatal to the Revd. Gentleman's occupying the office." Eckman had attacked individuals "for supposed defection from the religion of our forefathers." The "conservatives" submitted another petition signed by thirteen members and four nonmembers asking Eckman not to resign. The central issue in their dispute was the Poznanski version of Maimonides' creed on the wall of the synagogue, which sidestepped the question of the coming of a Messiah. It also contained no reference to the resurrection of the dead and the restoration of Palestine. The opponents stated, at this time and during the trial in 1844, that they had not read the creed for several years! The board ruled that Eckman should not make any allusions directly or indirectly to the creed. Not long afterward the board ordered him not to offer private services for burials, marriages, or circumcisions for any Jew or stranger in the city, as this violated the constitution of the synagogue. Then in November a petition from fifteen "friends of Eckman" asked the board to remove the creed from the synagogue. The list contains a curious group of names, two former members of the Reformed Society of Israelites, three petitioners for the organ, six relators in *State v. Ancker*, one former member of the minority in Beth Elohim, and one defendant in *State v. Ancker*. Perhaps they sought only "peace and harmony," which they claimed, especially people such as Abraham Moïse and J. E. Hertz. The board delayed making a decision on the matter but finally resolved that it "would be productive of angry feeling and excitement instead of peace and harmony" to remove the creed. Four days later a general meeting of the congregation met to receive the resignation of Eckman, who stated he could not continue to "perform *clerical functions*" when he had been hired to "do *religious duties*." By a vote of twenty-three to three they accepted his proposed departure. After doing that, they voted unanimously to erase the creed from the wall and inscribe the Sh'ma instead.[106] Ap-

104. Ibid., 9(1851–52): 203–8, 312–22.

105. Carvalho, "The Congregation Beth Elohim," 206.

106. Minute Book of Beth Elohim, May 4, June 1, Nov. 23, 30, Dec. 4, 1851. G. V. Ancker by this time was a member of Beth Elohim, not Shearith Israel. On Dec. 8, 1851, they made a final settlement with Charles DaCosta, who had served since the consecration of the synagogue.

parently glad to rid themselves of Eckman, they did take a latitudinarian attitude on the creed. No one had to accept either the old version or the Poznanski one, and no one would be offended by having to read either on the walls of the place of worship.

Neither of the ministers who followed Poznanski had supported reform to the extent that the majority of the congregation did. Therefore, in the new search for a *hazan*, the congregation decided to explicitly state not only the qualifications needed for the position but further information on the congregation. In doing this the congregation summarized the changes that had been made at Beth Elohim, carefully pointing out that the congregation used the organ, that sermons and some prayers were in English, that hymns and psalms could be in English and Hebrew, that the Torah was read through every three years (rather than in one, which was the usual practice), that the Haftarah and some of the Hebrew portions of the service had been omitted, that the second days of holidays were not observed, and that various other "improvements" had been made in the services. In order to allow time to find a suitable candidate, the congregation decided to appoint a temporary reader, choosing Moses Rubenstein of New York for this task.[107]

Two candidates applied for the permanent position. One of them, Isaac M. Wise, was not considered. The congregation asked the other, Maurice Mayer, to visit. The congregational minutes break off on April 11, 1852, and do not resume again until April 5, 1857, at which time Maurice Mayer had just accepted the permanent position of reader, which indicates that the congregation had extended the probationary period to five years. The lack of any other news of the congregation in the *Occident* during this same period indicates that the congregation had, at last, settled down.[108]

Apparently the conservatives left Beth Elohim for Shearith Israel because financial crises and low membership plagued the Beth Elohim for the next two years. Strapped for funds, the board could not pay its mortgage. When the board assessed each member, several persons resigned from the congregation, causing a further loss in income. The congregation sold two lots next to the burial ground to try to make ends meet. Congregation business proved almost impossible to conduct because so few people attended meetings that quorums could not be filled. Furthermore, the trustees could not pay the minister. By January 1858 Mayer threatened to resign unless they could pay him on time. Meanwhile, members of the congregation began to complain about his comments "on doctrinal points" that had been "in conflict with the cherished principles of some of the members," which caused them to stop attending services. Some demanded that he write out his sermons, which would prevent him from giving in to his impulses.

107. Ibid., Dec. 7, 10, 29, 1850, Feb. 3, 1851.

108. Ibid., Mar. 14, April 4, 11, 1851; April 5, 1857; *Occident*, 10(1852–53): 224.

Next the trustees found that the *hazan* had been studying law, a profession they thought to be incompatible with the duties of a religious leader. Even worse to the thinking of some, he had taken an oath in court without covering his head. When the board chastised him for this, he replied that if they were to be consistent, they should remove the organ, reinstate the second day of festivals, "in a word abolish all reforms." This dispute aroused enough people that a quorum of eighteen could be raised at a general meeting. They ordered the *hazan* to withdraw his letter and to take oaths with his head covered.[109]

Eventually the congregation managed to pay its mortgage after it received several large donations and sold 50 feet of property on the west end of the synagogue lot to Kerrison and Leiding, but the troubles with Mayer continued. In the fall of 1858 he asked permission to leave the city because of the unhealthy conditions there and the fact he had been ill for ten weeks. The board took no action because a quorum had not been present at a general meeting. Mayer proceeded to New York. As a result, the board stopped his pay temporarily. By March 1859 Mayer indicated he might have to use legal means to obtain his salary. Finally in September he offered a letter of resignation, and the board accepted it.[110]

Two months later they appointed Abraham Harris as *hazan*, and he began his duties in February 1860. After the Civil War broke out with the firing on Fort Sumter in the Charleston harbor, the trustees became concerned with the safety of the seal of the congregation, the constitution, and sundry other items, including a copy of the contract awarded to David Lopez to build the synagogue. They put these in the hands of Mordecai Cohen, then the president of the congregation, for safekeeping. Then Harris announced he would resign at the end of 1861, the war apparently being the reason.[111]

A Third Synagogue

Further competition for Beth Elohim came in 1854 when a group of Polish Jews organized a third synagogue in the city. New arrivals from Eastern Europe did not take to the Sephardic ritual and pronunciation of either Beth Elohim or Shearith Israel and rejected the innovations made at Beth Elohim. They began to meet some time that year—very likely before the Jewish New Year. They formally organized on September 30, 1855, with Nathan I. Rosenband as president, Baruch Wolf Frank as vice president, Abraham I. Mintz as secretary, and Abraham Livingstain as treasurer. The congregation became known as Berith Shalome, now Brith Shalom–Beth Israel. At the time the group consisted of forty or fifty members. They established their cemetery by at least

109. Minute Book of Beth Elohim, January 3, 5, 6, 8, April 22, May 2, June 6, 7, 13, July 4, 1858.

110. Ibid., July 20, Aug. 20, Sept. 5, 1858; Mar. 1, 1859.

111. Ibid., Nov. 23, 1859; Feb. 12, 1860; Aug. 4, Oct. 6, 1861.

1856 to the north of the city near Magnolia Cemetery. The first person buried there was "Isaac Son of Isaiah who drowned in a river in the country and [was] brought here for burial."[112]

Thus, by 1861 the Jewish community of Charleston was divided into three congregations, one Polish and two Sephardic. At the same time the nature of the community was changing, with more and more of the old families moving away and eastern Europeans replacing them. The ministers of both the Sephardic congregations resigned by the end of the year. The nation was also divided and poised to engage in a bloody conflict. The happy times had passed. The outbreak of the Civil War thus marked the end of an era for the Jewish people of the city, as it did for all other residents. (See Table 36.)

112. *Brith Shalom Beth Israel, 130th Anniversary, 30th Anniversary Merger*; Elzas, *Jewish Cemeteries of Congregation Berith Shalome*; *Occident*, 14(1856–57): 263.

Table 36

Participants in Key Events in the Jewish Community in Charleston, 1840–1843

Key: RS = Member of Reformed Society of Israelites; Or = signed petition to install organ in the synagogue; Mi = in minority in Beth Elohim, voted to admit members of Shearith Israel; SI = admitted from Shearith Israel; Ox = Orthodox, defendant in *State v. Ancker;* Rf = Reformer, proponent of reform in *State v. Ancker;* Cr = signed petition to remove the creed in 1851.

Name	*Birthplace and Year*	*RS*	*Or*	*Mi*	*SI*	*Ox*	*Rf*	*Cr*
Abrahams, Alexander H.	1801 Germany		x	x				
Abrahams, Elias	1787 England			x				
Alexander, Abraham, Jr.	1771 England		x	x				
Ancker, Gustavus Vasa			x		x	x		
Barnett, Woolf	England				x	x		
Barrett, Jacob							x	
Benjamin, Solomon A.	1807 England				x	x		
Breslau, Moses	Prussia						x	
Cardozo, Isaac Nunes	1793 Charleston	x	x				x	
Cardozo, Jacob Nunes	1786 Savannah						x	
Carvalho, Emanuel Nunes	1817 Charleston			x				
Cohen, Aaron Nathan	1777 England						x	
Cohen, Augustus Philip	1810 Charleston						x	
Cohen, David Daniel	1802 Charleston					x		
Cohen, David Lopez	1820 Georgetown						x	
Cohen, H. C.			x	x				
Cohen, Henry S.	1817			x				
Cohen, Hyam	1788 Charleston		x				x	
Cohen, Isaac S.	1801						x	x
Cohen, Jacob				x				

Table 36
(Continued)

Name	*Born*	*RS*	*Or*	*Mi*	*SI*	*Ox*	*Rf*	*Cr*
Cohen, Jacob, Jr.		x	x				x	
Cohen, Lawrence L.	1815 Charleston						x	
Cohen, Marx Edwin	1810 Charleston		x				x	
Cohen, Mordecai	1763 Poland		x				x	
Cohen, Nathan A.	1805 England				x	x		
Cohen, Philip	1781 Charleston						x	
Cohen, Philip Melvin	1808 New York		x				x	
Cohen, Solomon	1816 Georgetown						x	
Davis, Henry					x	x		
Davis, Moses	1759 Germany				x	x		
DeHaan, L.				x				
Frankford, Simon					x	x		
Goldsmith, Henry	1805 England	x			x	x		
Goldsmith, Joseph H.	1813 Charleston	x			x	x		
Goldsmith, Morris	1778 England	x			x	x		
Harby, Henry Jefferson	1799 Charleston	x					x	
Harris, Abraham J.	1816 Charleston		x					
Harris, George					x	x		
Harris, Isaac	1805 Charleston						x	x
Harris, Z.			x					
Hart, Hyman N.	1816 Charleston				x	x		
Hart, Samuel	1805 Charleston				x	x		
Hart, Samuel Nathan	1808 Charleston				x	x		
Hendricks, Joseph					x	x		
Hertz, Isaac Eger	1812 Charleston						x	x
Hertz, Jacob E.	1776	x	x				x	
Hyams, Henry	1793 England	x			x	x		
Hyams, Mordecai	1828 Charleston				x	x		x
Hyams, Moses David	1798 Charleston		x	x				
Jacobs, Jacob Simon	1794 Denmark				x	x		
Jacobs, Myer	1791 England	x	x				x	
Joseph, Jacob	1805 S.C.		x	x				
Joseph, Joseph J.			x	x				
Lazarus, Benjamin Dores	1800 Charleston		x				x	
Lazarus, Joshua	1796 Charleston						x	
Lazarus, Joshua E. P.	1821 Charleston				x	x		
Lazarus, Michael	1786 Charleston	x	x				x	
Levin, Jacob	1802 England			x				
Levin, Lipmann T.	1818 Charleston				x	x		
Levin, N. [?]				x				
Levin, Nathaniel	1816 S.C.			x				
Levy, Bernard	1789 Charleston	x	x				x	

Table 36
(Continued)

Name	*Born*	*RS*	*Or*	*Mi*	*SI*	*Ox*	*Rf*	*Cr*
Levy, David Cardozo	1805 Charleston	x					x	
Levy, Elias P.	1791 Charleston		x				x	
Levy, Elias, Jr.				x				x
Levy, Emanuel	1794 Charleston	x	x				x	
Levy, Isaac A.	1809 Charleston				x	x		
Levy, Jacob C.			x					
Levy, Levine L.	1805 England				x	x		
Levy, M. A.				x				
Levy, Reuben			x		x	x		
Lipman, Abraham	1778 England						x	
Loovis, Martin				x				
Lopez, Moses	1796 Charleston		x					
Lyon, George [Lyons]		x					x	
Mairs, Levy	1801 Germany				x	x		
Moïse, Aaron	1783 Haiti						x	
Moïse, Aaron	1820 Charleston		x				x	
Moïse, Abraham	1799 Charleston	x	x				x	x
Moïse, Abraham	1809 Charleston						x	x
Moïse, Columbus	1809 Charleston						x	
Mordecai, Benjamin	1809 Charleston						x	x
Mordecai, Isaac	1799 Charleston	x					x	
Mordecai, Moses Cohen	1804 Charleston		x				x	
Mordecai, Thomas Whitlock	1806	x	x				x	
Moses, Andrew Jackson	1815						x	
Moses, Daniel L.				x				
Moses, Isaiah	1772 Germany			x				
Moses, Levy	1773 Germany				x	x		
Moses, Levy J.	1808 Columbia			x				
Moses, Oliver Hazard Perry	1813 Charleston		x				x	
Moses, Reuben	1765 England				x	x		
Moses, Solomon	1783 England							
Nathans, Moses H.	S.C.				x	x		
Nathans, Nathan	1782 England				x	x		
Oppenheim, Hertz Wolff	1786 Germany		x				x	x
Ottolengui, Abraham	1790 Charleston						x	
Ottolengui, Jacob	1819 S.C.						x	x
Rodrigues, Benjamin A.	1815 Charleston		x				x	
Sampson, Jacob H.	1821				x	x		
Sampson, Joseph	1801 England				x	x		
Sampson, Samuel	1818 S.C.	x	x		x	x		
Schwabe, L. H.					x			
Schwerin, Julius	1812 Prussia			x				

Table 36
(Continued)

Name	*Born*	*RS*	*Or*	*Mi*	*SI*	*Ox*	*Rf*	*Cr*
Silverston, M.					x	x		
Solomons, Abraham Alexander	1816 Charleston		x					
Solomons, Mordecai			x				x	
Sommers, Edward	1801 Germany				x	x		
Suares, Abraham	1800				x			
Suares, Jacob Edgar	1810 Beaufort				x	x		
Tobias, Abraham	1793 Charleston		x	x				
Valentine, Samuel	1794 Prussia			x				
Weinberg, W.					x	x		
Woolf, Isaiah	1782 England			x				
Woolf, Ralph			x					
Zachariah, Jonathan	1798 Poland				x	x		

Note: Because of the use of initials and abbreviations in the minutes and errors in the court records, some individuals listed here may be incorrectly identified.
Sources: Minute Books of Beth Elohim; see also the appendix.

Afterword

At the anniversary banquet for the Hebrew Benevolent Society in Charleston in 1858, no toast was offered for the United States or the president. Instead, Asher Cohen made a toast in honor of South Carolina. The allegiance of the Jews, like those of many other Charlestonians, had shifted from the nation to the state. Among other things, Cohen said:

> Carolina, Carolina, Heaven's blessings attend her,
> While we live, we will love and cherish and defend her,
> Though the scorner may sneer at, and witling defame her,
> Our hearts swell with gladness, whenever we name her.[1]

His sentiments matched those of other Jews of the city. They proudly demonstrated their enthusiasm for their state, which had given them so much. From the first arrival of Jews in Charleston, they had adopted the ways of life of the other inhabitants, including, on the part of some, the modification of their religious practices and beliefs. Many of them fought and quite a number died during the Civil War trying to preserve the way of life they had enjoyed. Except in religion, the Jews differed very little from other white residents of the city. There is no reason to expect them to have been otherwise.

1. "Hebrew Benevolent Society of Charleston, South Carolina," 587.

Appendix

This appendix represents an attempt to identify all the Jews who lived in Charleston through 1861. It is also a substitute for notes in the text for biographical information on individuals. Many of the conclusions made in this book were based on data concerning numerous people. To have provided a note citing the sources for the data on each person would have taken hundreds of pages. An alphabetized listing of all the people that indicates the sources used for each seemed the best solution. Anyone wishing to locate information on any person can thus consult this list.

The reader should be warned that the information on a person often differs from one source to another. I used what I considered to be the most accurate sources. Moreover, some people, no doubt, have duplicate entries because of the use of initials in some sources and of full names in others, or because some people had more than one name. Also, bad spelling or illegible writing presented problems. Some people listed here might not have been Jewish, and some Jewish people from Charleston have probably been left out.

Identifying many of the Jews of Charleston was a difficult task. Family names cannot always be trusted. Fortunately, a great deal of genealogical and historical work has been done that can be utilized. Barnett Elzas investigated the history of the Jewish community and included many names in *The Jews of South Carolina*. In addition, he visited every Jewish cemetery in the state and recorded the tombstone inscriptions. Sources in Charleston that were especially helpful in identifying people were the death records, wills, and the cash books of Beth Elohim synagogue. The death records often give fairly complete information on a person, although they cannot always be trusted. Cemetery records and histories of other communities also supplied names of Charleston residents. Then there were family histories. By far the most important of these is the monumental *First Jewish Families of America* by Malcolm Stern, which lists the genealogies of many of the families who lived in Charleston. Public records such as those in the South Carolina Archives, the federal censuses, and city directories helped identify people. A person who appeared to be Jewish could often be found in association with others who were known to be Jews by doing such things as witnessing a will, having power of attorney, or living at the same address. The federal censuses until 1850 gave only the names of the heads of households and the number of people living at the address. Beginning in 1850 and 1860, however, the censuses list all the people in the households along with their ages and places of birth.

Knowing whether or not a person lived in the city and when could also be a problem. Very few records were complete, and families often moved about. For a particular family, decisions often had to be made about each person. For example, if a child was born in Charleston, the assumption was made that the parents lived in the city at the time even though they might not appear in any other records. The date of the birth of the child could thus be assigned to the parents as their first date in South Carolina, provided there were no earlier dates available. Also, if the place of birth was given for a first child and that place was Charleston and the place of birth for a fourth child was Charleston, it was assumed that the second and third children lived in the city—the place of birth, however, was not listed as Charleston for the second and third children, as the family could have been out of the city for a while. Obviously, compiling this appendix required many months of poring over genealogical charts.

Assigning dates for people who are known to have lived in Charleston was difficult. Some families moved about, especially in South Carolina. Therefore, the first date found for them in the state is used although in some cases they did not reside in Charleston for many years. If a record says that a person was born in South Carolina, that date is used even if the person never shows up in other public or synagogue records. For people who moved to Charleston from other areas, the date given is the first one found in some account. Most men show up in records within a year or so after they have arrived in the city. Their wives, however, may never appear in synagogue or public records. In such cases, the date of arrival of the husband is used for the wife if the two were married at the time the man appeared in the records. Some people, however, never show up in the records. This is especially true for underage children who were born in Charleston but whose dates of birth are unknown. Many of these people died or moved away without leaving any trace except in family histories. As a result, no dates can be given for them. The bulk of the people in the list without a date fall into this category. In addition, some adults are known to have lived in the city, but no trace of them in local records can be found. Most often the information for them comes from a source that states something to the effect that they lived in

Charleston in the 1790s. These individuals are listed as having resided in the city, but no precise date can be given for them.

I believe that what follows is a good group picture of the Jews of colonial and antebellum Charleston, even though some individuals may be out of focus.

Each entry consists of three parts: the name, personal information, and sources. The following abbreviations are used in the entries for the personal information:

b. = date of birth
d. = date of death
SC: = first date found in South Carolina
f. = name of father
m. = name of mother
mr. = spouse for first marriage
mr2. = spouse for second marriage
mr3. = spouse for third marriage
Rf: = references. In some cases all sources are listed. In others only a few of many. Those listed here are the ones most important for vital statistics on a person.

Abbreviations used in the entries to indicate the sources of the information are listed and explained at the end of the Introduction.

Aaron, David A. SC: 1803. Rf: MR3V.177

Aarons, ———. SC: 1789. Rf: SFF1

Aarons, Jacob. SC: 1785. Rf: SFF1, 179; EM6; E279; RB1

Aarons, Joseph. SC: 1778. Rf: MR2V.208

Aarons, Levi. d. 1792, SC: 1786. Rf: SFF1

Aarons, Moses. b. 1778, d. 1842, SC: 1811. Rf: DR, E32, 167; 1830C; 1840C; D1822, 1831, 1835

Aarons, Solomon. b. 1731, d. 1821, SC: 1780. Rf: DR, E106, 132, 277, 279; 1790C; D1794; RB1

Aaronson, Woolf. SC: 1800. Rf: CB1800

Abendanone, David. SC: 1800. Rf: EC104, T32, 1810C; SCA1800–09; D1803

Abendanone, Grace. SC: 1807, f. Joseph Abendanone, mr. Hyam Abendanone, 1807. Rf: SFF1; EM8; W45.810

Abendanone, Hyam. SC: 1800, mr. Grace Abendanone, 1807. Rf: SFF1; EM8, E132; 1800C; 1820C; D1802

Abendanone, Isaac. SC: 1792. Rf: MR3B.404

Abendanone, Jacob. SC: 1809. Rf: E132; D1809

Abendanone, Joseph. b. 1750, d. 1815, SC: 1785. Rf: SFF1; W29.673; W21.774; 1790C; 1800C; D1790, 1794, 1801, 1802, 1803, 1806, 1807, 1809

Abendanone, Zippora. SC: 1803. Rf: W30.844; D1803

Abraham, David. SC: 1807. Rf: D1807

Abrahams, ———. b. 1824, d. 1864, SC: 1857. Rf: DR

Abrahams, ———. b. 1831, d. 1849, SC: 1831. Rf: DR

Abrahams, ———. [Mrs. Judah]. SC: 1802. Rf: D1802, 1806

Abrahams, Abraham. b. 1789, d.

1809, SC: 1809. Rf: E132, 167, 279; *City Gazette & Daily Advertiser*, Sept. 27, 1809; D1809

Abrahams, Adolphus Alexander H. b. 1830, d. 1872, SC: 1830, f. Alexander Hezekiel Abrahams, m. Hannah Moses Abrahams, mr. Kate A. Abrahams, 1864. Rf: EC71; SFF5, 210; T32; 1850C; 1860C; D1852, 1855

Abrahams, Alexander Hezekiel. b. 1801, d. 1871, SC: 1821, f. Hezekiel Abrahams, mr. Hannah A. Moses Abrahams, 1829. Rf: DR; EC70; E167; T32; SFF5, 210; T32; 1850C; 1860C; 1861C; D1835, 1838, 1841, 1849

Abrahams, Benjamin. SC: 1825. Rf: JR1825

Abrahams, Catherine Cohen. b. 1795, d. 1851, SC: 1815, mr. Elias Abrahams, 1815. Rf: SFF4; EM10; *SP*, Jan. 19, 1815; 1850C

Abrahams, Cecilia Bush Solomons. b. 1848, d. 1920, SC: 1848, f. Lizer Solomons, m. Perla Sheftall Solomons, mr. Edmund H. Abrahams, 1870. Rf: SFF5, 278

Abrahams, Edmund H. b. 1838, d. 1890, SC: 1838, f. Alexander Hezekiel Abrahams, m. Hannah Moses Abrahams, mr. Cecilia Solomons Abrahams, 1870. Rf: SFF5; E238; 1850C

Abrahams, Edward Sebring H. b. 1849, d. 1908, SC: 1849, f. Alexander Hezekiel Abrahams, m. Hannah Moses Abrahams, mr. Nellie I. Solomons Abrahams, 1872, mr2. Fanny Joseph Abrahams, 1876. Rf: SFF5l; 1850C; 1860C

Abrahams, Elias. b. 1787, d. 1851, SC: 1813, f. Emanuel Abrahams, m. Judith Mordecai Abrahams, mr. Catherine Cohen Abrahams, 1815. Rf: DR; EC94; SFF4; *SP*, Jan. 19, 1815; 1850C; D1816, 1819, 1822, 1829, 1831, 1835, 1838, 1841, 1849, 1852

Abrahams, Elias. b. 1835, d. 1862. Rf: EBS3

Abrahams, Emanuel. b. 1748, d. 1802, SC: 1772, mr. Judith Mordecai Abrahams. Rf: SFF4; 1790C; W28.354 (his); D1790, 1794

Abrahams, Hannah A. (Moses). b. 1809, d. 1875, SC: 1809, f. Isaiah Moses, m. Rebecca Phillips Moses, mr. Alexander Hezekeil Abrahams, 1829. Rf: DR; EC60; SFF5, 210; 1840C; 1850C; 1860C; 1861C; D1835, 1838

Abrahams, Hester. SC: 1820. Rf: 1820C

Abrahams, Hezekiel Moses. b. 1844, d. 1872, SC: 1844, f. Alexander Hezekiel Abrahams, m. Hannah A. H. Moses Abrahams. Rf: SFF5; EC70; 1850C; 1860C

Abrahams, Hyam. b. 1767, d. 1802, SC: 1794, f. Abraham Isaac Abrahams, m. Esther Louisa Abrahams. Rf: EC77; SFF4; E133; RB3

Abrahams, Isaac. b. 1767, d. 1849, SC: 1783. Rf: E133, 279; D1807; RB4

Abrahams, Israel. SC: 1803. Rf: E133; D1803

Abrahams, Jacob. SC: 1790. Rf: E133, 279; W26.397; 1790C; 1810C;

D1790, 1794, 1796, 1801, 1802, 1803, 1806; RB4

Abrahams, Jacob Melvin. b. 1837, d. 1865, SC: 1837, f. Alexander Hezekiel Abrahams, m. Hannah Moses Abrahams, mr. Eudora R. Sampson Abrahams, 1862. Rf: SFF5; EM32

Abrahams, Joseph. b. 1749, d. 1795, SC: 1780, mr. Rebecca DeLyon Abrahams, mr2. Judith DeLyon Cohen, 1791. Rf: SFF7; E103, 277; *OJCS*69; RB4

Abrahams, Judah. SC: 1780. Rf: E91, 277; D1790

Abrahams, Judith (DeLyon) (Cohen). b. 1764, d. 1848, SC: 1764, f. Isaac DeLyon, m. Rinah Tobias DeLyon, mr. Moses Liepman Cohen, 1779, mr2. Joseph Abrahams, 1791. Rf: DR; EC40; SFF7, 57; D1803, 1813, 1816, 1819, 1822; RB4

Abrahams, Judith Mordecai. d. 1794, SC: 1772, mr. Emanuel Abrahams, 1779. Rf: SFF4; EC40

Abrahams, Kate (Abrams). f. Alexander Abrams, m. Elizabeth Joseph Abrams, mr. Adolphus Alexander H. Abrahams, 1864. Rf: SFF4, 5

Abrahams, Levy J. d. 1829, SC: 1807, f. Mordecai Abrahams, m. Sarah Levy Abrahams, mr. Theodotia Armistead Abrahams. Rf: SFF4; E133; SP, April 10, 1830; D1807, 1809, 1816, 1819

Abrahams, Melvina H. b. 1835, d. 1836, SC: 1835, f. Alexander Hezekiel Abrahams, m. Hannah Moses Abrahams. Rf: SFF5

Abrahams, Moïse [Moses]. SC: 1796. Rf: E133; T32; D1794, 1796, 1801, 1802, 1806, 1807

Abrahams, Moses. d. 1833, SC: 1821. Rf: EP; CB1821

Abrahams, Philip. SC: 1768. Rf: EP; SC *Gazette*, May 9, 1768; RB5

Abrahams, Rachel. b. 1794, d. 1849, SC: 1814, f. Joseph Abrahams, m. Judith DeLyon Cohen Abrahams. Rf: EC40; SFF7; CB1814; RB5

Abrahams, Rebecca DeLyon. b. 1733, d. 1788, SC: 1785, mr. Joseph Abrahams. Rf: *OJCS*69; SFF7, 57

Abrahams, Robert Brown. b. 1847, d. 1854, SC: 1847, f. Alexander Hezekiel Abrahams, m. Hannah Moses Abrahams. Rf: SFF5; 1850C

Abrahams, Samuel. b. 1775, d. 1848, SC: 1809, f. Abraham Isaac Abrahams, m. Elkaly Esther Louzada Abrahams. Rf: SFF4; D1809, 1813, 1819

Abrahams, Sarah. b. 1836, SC: 1836, f. Alexander Hezekiah Abrahams, m. Hannah Abrahams. Rf: 1850C

Abrahams, Theodore H. b. 1834, SC: 1834, f. Alexander Hezekiel Abrahams, m. Hannah Moses Abrahams. Rf: SFF5; E167, 223; T32; 1850C; 1860C; D1852

Abrahamson, J. J. SC: 1830. Rf: W46.199; D1849

Abrams, Abram. b. 1805, SC: 1852, mr. Hannah Abrams. Rf: 1860C

Abrams, Alexander H. b. 1818, SC: 1818, f. Elias Abrams, m. Catherine Cohen Abrams, mr. Elizabeth Joseph Abrams, 1844. Rf: SFF4; EM1; 1850C; 1861C; D1849, 1855

Abrams, Edward. b. 1852, SC: 1852,

f. A. Abrams, m. Hannah Abrams. Rf: 1860C

Abrams, Eliza. b. 1813, d. 1824, SC: 1824. Rf: DR

Abrams, Elizabeth F. (Joseph). SC: 1844, f. Lizer Joseph, m. Sarah Joseph, mr. Alexander Abrams, 1844. Rf: SFF4, 139; EM21

Abrams, Emanuel. SC: 1795. Rf: MR3F.229; JR1798

Abrams, Ephraim. SC: 1780. Rf: RB5

Abrams, Ezekiel. b. 1845, SC: 1845, f. A. Abrams, m. Hannah Abrams. Rf: 1860C

Abrams, Hannah. b. 1834, SC: 1834, mr. A. Abrams. Rf: 1860C

Abrams, Isaac. f. Elias Abrahams, m. Catherine Cohen Abrahams, mr. Mary Davis Abrams. Rf: SFF4

Abrams, Isabel. f. Elias Abrahams, m. Catherine Cohen Abrahams. Rf: SFF4

Abrams, Jacob. SC: 1800. Rf: 1800C

Abrams, Jacob. d. 1818, f. Elias Abrahams, m. Catherine Cohen Abrahams. Rf: SFF4

Abrams, Mary Davis. f. Ansel Davis, m. Sarah Davis, mr. Isaac Abrams. Rf: SFF4, 48

Abrams, Moïse. b. 1736, d. 1809, SC: 1800. Rf: EC58; E133, 279; W31.178; RB5

Abrams, Mordecai. f. Elias Abrahams, m. Catherine Cohen Abrahams, mr. Rosalie Densel Abrams. Rf: SFF4

Abrams, Moses [Julian]. f. Elias Abrahams, m. Catherine Cohen Abrahams, mr. Cecile Myers Abrams. Rf: SFF4

Abrams, Solomon. b. 1825, d. 1864. Rf: EBS3

Aguilar, Joseph. SC: 1804. Rf: E133

Albergo, Judah. SC: 1800. Rf: E133

Alexander, ———. b. 1840, d. 1842, SC: 1840. Rf: DR

Alexander, Aaron. b. 1812, d. 1876, SC: 1812, f. Abraham Alexander, Jr., m. Hannah Aarons Abraham Alexander, mr. Sarah Moses Alexander, 1836. Rf: DR; SFF8, 9, 210; E171; EC41; W40.354; 1830C; T32; MS13.279

Alexander, Abraham. b. 1743, d. 1816, SC: 1767, f. Joseph Raphael, mr2. Ann Sarah Huguenin Irby Alexander, 1784. Rf: EC40; SFF8; E43–44, 102, 133, 145, 277, 299; 1790C; 1800C; 1820C; D1790, 1794, 1803, 1806, 1807, 1809, 1813, 1816

Alexander, Abraham, Jr. b. 1771, d. 1844, SC: 1800, f. Abraham Alexander, Sr., mr. Hannah Aarons Alexander, 1801. Rf: EC40, SFF1, 8; E133, 167, 279; W40.354; D1801, 1802, 1803, 1806, 1813, 1831, 1835

Alexander, Alexander. d. 1803, SC: 1787, mr. Rachel Anderson Alexander, 1767. Rf: W29.546 (his); *SCHM*56.45–59; *SCM*3; D1782, 1785, 1790, 1794, 1796, 1802

Alexander, Alexander. b. 1813, SC: 1813, f. Abraham Alexander, m. Hannah Aarons Alexander. Rf: SFF8, 9; AF18; D1822

Alexander, Amanda. b. 1839, d. 1840, SC: 1839, f. Aaron Alexander, m. Sarah Alexander. Rf: EP

Alexander, Ann Sarah Huguenin Irby. d. 1835, SC: 1784, mr. ———

. b. 1851, d. 1852, SC:
ob Barrett, m. Hetty J.
Barrett. Rf: EC7;

SC: 1797, mr.
rrett. Rf: MR3H.417;
19, 1822
a. f. Jacob Barrett
1), m. Hetty
Barrett. Rf: SFF17
. Ottolengui. b. 1818,
: 1834, f. Abraham
, m. Sarah Jacobs
, mr. Jacob Barrett,
DR; EC7, 8; EM15;
; W45.796
. b. 1791, d. 1834, SC:
Rachel J. DaVega
15. Rf: EC10; SFF17,
BS39; CB1814;
19, 1822, 1829, 1831
b. 1838, d. 1871, SC:
ob Barrett, m. Hetty
Barrett. Rf: DR; EC8;
223; SFF17
. 1792, d. 1871, SC:
Hetty J. Ottolengui
34. Rf: DR; EM15;
187; EC7, 8; SFF17,
; 1850C; D1835,
, 1855, 1859
. 1848, d. 1883, SC:
ob Barrett, m. Hetty J.
Barrett, mr. Sarah
1874. Rf: SFF17, 252;

. 1856, d. 1858, SC:
C7
SC: 1802. Rf: E133,
FF17; D1803
SC: 1837. Rf:

Barrett, Lawrence. b. 1844, d. 1845, SC: 1844, f. Jacob Barrett, m. Hetty J. Ottolengui Barrett. Rf: EC8; SFF17

Barrett, Mary Beatrice. f. Jacob Barrett, m. Hetty J. Ottolengui Barrett. Rf: SFF17

Barrett, Rachel J. (DaVega). b. 1801, d. 1865, SC: 1815, f. Moses DaVega, m. Sol DaVega, mr. Isaac Barrett, 1815. Rf: SFF17, 45; EM10; EC10; W51.567 (hers); 1850C; D1835, 1838, 1849

Barrett, Sarah (Poznanski). b. 1844, d. 1874, SC: 1844, f. Gustavus Poznanski, m. Esther Barrett Poznanski, mr. Jacob Barrett, 1874. Rf: DR; EC48; SFF17, 252; 1850C

Barrett, Solomon. SC: 1796, mr. Esther Barrett. Rf: SFF17; MR3H.417; E279; W25.317; 1790C; D1796; RB10, 11

Barrett, Solomon I. b. 1822, d. 1850, SC: 1822, f. Isaac B. Barrett, m. Rachel J. DaVega Barrett. Rf: DR; EC10; SFF17; 1850C; D1849

Barrett, Solomon Judah. b. 1807, d. 1836, f. Judah Barrett. Rf: SFF17

Barrett, Starr. b. 1699, d. 1820, SC: 1788. Rf: EC30; EP; *SP*, Jan. 14, 1820; D1819

Barrett, Thaddeus. b. 1847, d. 1847, SC: 1847, f. Jacob Barrett, m. Hetty J. Ottolengui Barrett. Rf: EC8; SFF17

Bartlett, Sarah (Melhado). mr. Cosam E. Bartlett, 1818. Rf: EP

Baruc, Bernard S. b. 1828, d. 1904, SC: 1855, f. Sigismund Baruc, m. Nanette Baruc, mr. Mathilda R. Oppenheim Baruch, 1855. Rf:

Irby, mr2. Abraham Alexander, 1784. Rf: EL; E44; SFF8; W40.354 (hers); *AF*16–18

Alexander, Catherine. b. 1820, d. 1885, SC: 1820, f. Abraham Alexander, m. Hannah Aarons Alexander. Rf: SFF8; *AF*18

Alexander, Hannah (Aarons). b. 1789, d. 1865, SC: 1789, f. Levi Aarons van Blitz, mr. Abraham Alexander, 1801. Rf: SFF1, 8; EC41, 74; 1850C; 1861C; D1855

Alexander, Joseph. b. 1802, d. 1813, SC: 1802, f. Abraham Alexander, m. Hannah Aarons Alexander. Rf: EC74; SFF8

Alexander, Joseph Albert. b. 1837, d. 1894, SC: 1837, f. Aaron Alexander, m. Sarah Moses Alexander, mr. Sallie Nathans Solomons Alexander, 1874. Rf: SFF9

Alexander, Joseph Raphael. SC: 1760. Rf: SFF8

Alexander, Judah. b. 1742, d. 1804, SC: 1790, f. Joseph Raphael Alexander. Rf: SFF8; 1800C; E133; D1790, 1801, 1802, 1803; RB5

Alexander, Judah. b. 1829, SC: 1849, f. Abraham Alexander (1771–1844), m. Hannah Aarons Alexander. Rf: 1850C; AF18; D1849

Alexander, Leah. b. 1842, d. 1842, SC: 1842, f. Aaron Alexander, m. Sarah Alexander. Rf: EP

Alexander, Moses. b. 1778, d. 1808, SC: 1800, f. Abraham Alexander. Rf: EC47; SFF8; E133; D1802, 1803; RB7

Alexander, Rachel (Anderson). b. 1757, d. 1827, SC: 1767, mr. Alexander Alexander, 1767. Rf: DR; EC71; 1800C; *SCM*3; D1801, 1802, 1803, 1813

Alexander, Rebecca Ella Solomons. b. 1856, d. 1938, SC: 1856, f. Abraham Alexander Solomons, m. Cecilia Moses Alexander, mr. Julius Mortimer Alexander, 1873. Rf: SFF9, 278; *AF*112

Alexander, S. b. 1829, d. 1858, SC: 1850. Rf: DR

Alexander, Sally Nathans (Solomons). b. 1854, d. 1923, SC: 1854, f. Solomon Sampson Solomons, m. Esther Nathans Solomons, mr. Joseph Albert Alexander, 1874. Rf: SFF9, 277; 1860C

Alexander, Sarah. SC: 1832, f. Abraham Alexander, m. Hannah Aarons Alexander. Rf: SFF8; W40.354

Alexander, Sarah (Harris) (Sampson). b. 1801, d. 1833, SC: 1801, f. Jacob Harris, m. Elizabeth Harris, mr. Alexander Sampson, mr2. Alexander Alexander. Rf: SFF9, 94

Alexander, Sarah (Moses). b. 1813, d. 1892, SC: 1813, f. Isaiah Moses, m. Rebecca Phillips Moses, mr. Aaron Alexander, 1836. Rf: SFF8, 9, 210; *AF*59–61; MS13.279

Allen, F. SC: 1819. Rf: CB1819

Amesquita, Raphael DaCosta. b. 1753, d. 1821, SC: 1801. Rf: DR; EC71; E133; D1819

Amram, Rosa Rosenfeld. f. Jacob Rosenfeld, m. Leonara Moses Rosenfeld, mr. Emile Amram. Rf: SFF210

Ancker, Abigail Rebecca (Sampson). b. 1823, d. 1844, SC: 1823, f.

Joseph Sampson, m. Abigail Sampson, mr. Gustavus V. Ancker, 1841. Rf: EC85; SFF11, 259; EM19

Ancker, Alfred. b. 1854, d. 1855, SC: 1854. Rf: DR

Ancker, Catherine (Hyams). b. 1834, SC: 1834, f. Moses David Hyams, m. Susannah Jackson Hyams, mr. Samuel P. Ancker, 1853. Rf: SFF11, 120; 1850C

Ancker, Clothilde. f. Samuel P. Ancker, m. Catherine Hyams Ancker. Rf: SFF11

Ancker, Florence. b. 1859, d. 1859, SC: 1859. Rf: DR

Ancker, Gustavus. SC: 1842, f. Samuel P. Ancker, m. Catherine P. Hyams, mr2. Theresa Kehrer Ancker. Rf: SFF11

Ancker, Gustavus Vasa. SC: 1841, f. Adolph Ancker, m. Hetty Pettigrew Ancker, mr. Abigail Rebecca Sampson Ancker, 1841, mr2. Hannah Hyams Ancker. Rf: SFF11, 120; 1850C; 1861C; T32; E167, 238; EC85; EM19; *Courier*, Dec. 11, 1861; D1841, 1855, 1859

Ancker, Gustavus Vasa. b. 1857, d. 1860, SC: 1857. Rf: DR

Ancker, Hannah (Hyams). f. Moses David Hyams, m. Susannah Jackson Hyams, mr. Gustavus V. Ancker. Rf: SFF11, 120

Ancker, Joseph Theodore. b. 1843, d. 1844, SC: 1843, f. Gustavus V. Ancker, m. Hannah Hyams Ancker. Rf: EC85; SFF11

Ancker, Mitchell. f. Samuel P. Ancker, m. Catherine Hyams Ancker, mr. Leah Adelsheimer Ancker. Rf: SFF11

Ancker, Moses. f. Samuel P. Ancker, m. Catherine Hyams Ancker, mr. Catherine Loeb Ancker. Rf: SFF11

Ancker, Pinckney. f. Samuel P. Ancker, m. Catherine Hyams Ancker. Rf: SFF11

Ancker, Rebecca Emily. b. 1842, d. 1843, SC: 1843, f. Gustavus V. Ancker, m. Abigail Sampson Ancker. Rf: SFF11; EC85

Ancker, Samuel P. b. 1817, d. 1903, SC: 1859, f. Adolph Ancker, m. Hetty Pettigrew Ancker, mr. Catherine Hyams Ancker, 1853. Rf: SFF11, 120; E238; *Courier*, Dec. 11, 1861; D1859

Ancker, Samuel P. b. 1857, f. Samuel P. Ancker, m. Catherine Hyams Ancker, mr. Sarah Kahn Ancker, 1885. Rf: SFF11

Ancker, Susan. b. 1856, d. 1856, SC: 1856. Rf: DR

Ancker, Theodore. b. 1854, d. 1855, SC: 1854, f. Gustavus V. Ancker, m. Hannah Hyams Ancker. Rf: DR; SFF11

Andrews, Abraham. mr2. Nellie (Nettie) Abrahams Andrews, 1761. Rf: SFF12

Andrews, Nellie [Nettie] (Abrahams). mr. Abraham Andrews, 1761. Rf: SFF12

Andrews, Zalegman. b. 1805, SC: 1844, f. Joseph Andrews, m. Sallie Salomon Andrews, mr. Esther Abrams Andrews, 1844. Rf: SFF4, 12

Apple, J. b. 1826, d. 1876. Rf: DR

Areagh, Judah. SC: 1794. Rf: MR3D.411

Ashim, Leopold Nathaniel. b. 1849, d. 1857, SC: 1857, f. Simon Ashim, m. Matilda Adelaide Jacobi Ashim. Rf: EC92; E167; JF7

Ashim, Mathilda Adelaide (Jacobi). b. 1829, SC: 1847, f. Wolf Jacob Jacobi, m. Priscilla Rebecca Jacobi, mr. Simon Ashim, 1847. Rf: EM23; SFF117; JF7

Ashim, Simon. SC: 1853, mr. Mathilda Adelaide Jacobi Ashim, 1847. Rf: EM23; E167; JF7; D1855

Audler, Ezekiel. d. 1829, SC: 1814. Rf: E133; *SP*, Oct. 15, 1829; CB1814

Audler, I. SC: 1839. Rf: E167; Min. April 14, 1839

Audler, Myer. SC: 1817. Rf: E133

Audler, Rosina (Florance). SC: 1827, f. Zachariah Levy Florance, m. Sarah Florance, mr. E. Audler, 1827. Rf: EM13; SFF74

Audler, Shane. SC: 1838, m. Rebecca Solomons, Rf: SCA1838

Audler, Solomon. SC: 1821, mr. Helene Barnett. Rf: E133; SFF74; CB1821

Avila, Abraham. SC: 1697. Rf: EL; E20, 21, 277

Azuby, Abraham. b. 1738, d. 1805, SC: 1784, mr. Esther Azuby. Rf: SFF13; E133, 279, 288, 290–92; 1790C; D1790, 1796, 1801

Azuby, Esther. b. 1754, d. 1805, SC: 1784. Rf: EC83; W30.855 (hers)

Bahr, Emmie (Baruc). b. 1858, SC: 1858, f. Bernard S. Baruc, m. Mathilda R. Oppenheim Baruc, mr. Herman Bahr. Rf: SFF17

Barnard, Alexander. SC: 1805, f.

E167, 223; EC36; EM28; SFF27, 235; 1861C; D1855, 1859

Baruc, Mathilda R. (Oppenheim). b. 1830, d. 1877, SC: 1830, f. Hertz Wolf Oppenheim, m. Catherine Moses Oppenheim, mr. Bernard S. Baruc, 1855. Rf: SFF235; EC36; EM28; 1850C

Baruc, Nannie. b. 1856, d. 1861, SC: 1856, f. Bernhard S. Baruc, m. Mathilda R. Oppenheim Baruc. Rf: EC36; SFF17

Baruch, Bernhard. b. 1844, d. 1879, f. Joseph Baruch, m. Hanchen Baruch. Rf: EC77; SFF17

Baruch, Deborah (Sampson). b. 1852, SC: 1852, f. Joseph Sampson, m. Esther Cohen Sampson, mr. Herman Baruch, 1874. Rf: SFF17, 259

Baruch, Frederika Cohen. b. 1848, d. 1878, mr. Albert Baruch. Rf: EC77; DR; SFF17

Baruck, Solomon. SC: 1790. Rf: D1790

Baum, Elkan. b. 1820, d. 1882, SC: 1855. Rf: E167; EG1; D1855

Baum, Herman. SC: 1855. Rf: D1855

Baum, Jacob. b. 1799, d. 1854, SC: 1854. Rf: EC89; D1855

Baum, Jacob. b. 1853, d. 1881, SC: 1853, f. E. Baum, m. H. Baum. Rf: EG1

Baum, John A. SC: 1855. Rf: D1855

Baum, John S. SC: 1855. Rf: D1855

Baum, Leonora M. (Cohen). b. 1837, d. 1851, SC: 1837, f. Hartwig Cohen, m. Deborah Marks Cohen, mr. Mannes Baum, 1856. Rf: SFF34; EM29; EC28; 1850C

Baum, Mannes. SC: 1856, mr. Leonora M. Cohen Baum, 1856. Rf: SFF34; EM29

Baum, Rosa. d. 1858, SC: 1858, mr. Jacob Baum. Rf: EC89

Baum, Sarah Deborah. b. 1857, SC: 1857, f. Mannes Baum, m. Leonora Cohen Baum. Rf: SFF34

Bayless, Rosa (Lewis). b. 1819, f. David Lewis, m. Rachel Lewis, mr. John Clarke Bayless. Rf: SFF172

Beckwith, Belle (Cohen). b. 1845, SC: 1845, f. Jacob Cohen, m. Sarah Barrett Cohen, mr. George Beckwith. Rf: SFF36; 1850C; 1860C

Belitizer, Caroline. b. 1822, SC: 1850, mr. Isaac Belitizer. Rf: 1850C

Belitizer, Isaac. b. 1814, SC: 1850, mr. Caroline Belitizer. Rf: E167; 1850C; D1852

Belitizer, Jacob. b. 1839, SC: 1850, f. Isaac Belitizer, m. Caroline Belitizer. Rf: E224; 1850C

Belitizer, Theodore. b. 1843, SC: 1850, f. Isaac Belitizer, m. Caroline Belitizer. Rf: E167, 224; 1850C

Benedict, Isabel (Levy). b. 1850, SC: 1850, f. Orlando Levy, m. Catherine Browers Levy, mr. Ludwig Benedict, 1873. Rf: SFF163; 1850C

Benedix, Isaac. b. 1760, d. 1804, SC: 1787. Rf: EL; E279; *OJCS*69

Benjamin, Catherine (Woolfe). SC: 1832, m. Rebecca Woolfe, mr. Solomon Benjamin, 1832. Rf: EM14

Benjamin, David. b. 1829, d. 1894, SC: 1855. Rf: EC45; E167, 238; DR; *Courier* Dec. 11, 1861; D1855

Benjamin, Dores. SC: 1787. Rf: W22.191, 1787; SCA1789
Benjamin, J. SC: 1807. Rf: CB1807
Benjamin, Judah Philip. b. 1811, d. 1884, SC: 1820, f. Philip Benjamin, m. Rebecca DeMendes Benjamin, mr. Natalie St. Martin Benjamin, 1833. Rf: E185–87, 221; SFF18
Benjamin, L. A. SC: 1839. Rf: Min. April 8, 1839
Benjamin, Philip. b. 1780, d. 1853, SC: 1820, f. Judah Benjamin, mr. Rebecca De Mendes Benjamin. Rf: DR; E133, 163, 185, 186; SFF18, 309; 1850C; D1819, 1831, 1835, 1838, 1841, 1849
Benjamin, Rebecca (De Mendes). d. 1847, SC: 1820, f. Solomon De Mendes, m. Eva Levy De Mendes, mr. Philip Benjamin. Rf: E185, 186; SFF18
Benjamin, Samuel. SC: 1790. Rf: D1790
Benjamin, Solomon A. b. 1807, d. 1877, SC: 1831, mr. Catherine Woolf Benjamin, 1832. Rf: EM14; EBS3; E167; DR; D1835, 1838, 1841, 1849, 1852, 1855, 1859
Bensadon, Jacob. SC: 1830. Rf: 1830C; D1831, 1835
Bensadon, Judah. d. 1852, SC: 1841, f. Jacob Bensadon, m. Abigail Jacobs Bensadon, mr. Leah Hyams Bensadon, 1841. Rf: SFF119, 131; E167, 206; EM19; D1849
Bensadon, Leah (Hyams). d. 1891, SC: 1841, f. Henry Hyams, m. Judith Hyams, mr. Judah Bensadon, 1841. Rf: EM19; SFF119, 131
Bentschner, David. b. 1842, d. 1900, SC: 1860, f. Wolff Bentschner, m. Esther Falk Bentschner, mr. Hannah Bentschner, 1869. Rf: DR; EM34; JF8
Bentschner, Esther (Falk). b. 1800, d. 1874, SC: 1857, mr. Wolff Bentschner. Rf: DR; JF8
Bentschner, Hanna (Jacobi). b. 1827, d. 1897, f. Neuman Hirsch Jacobi, m. Sarah Moses Jacobi, mr. David Bentschner, 1869. Rf: DR; EM34; JF5
Bentschner, Hester. b. 1800, d. 1873, SC: 1856. Rf: DR
Bentschner, Isaac. b. 1834, d. 1854, SC: 1854, f. Wolff Bentschner, m. Esther Falk Bentschner. Rf: EC92; E167; JF8
Bentschner, Isidor Wolff. b. 1832, d. 1852, SC: 1852, f. Wolff Bentschner, m. Esther Falk Bentschner. Rf: DR; EC93; E167; JF8; D1852
Bentschner, Jacob. b. 1836, d. 1854, SC: 1854, f. Wolff Bentschner, m. Esther Falk Bentschner. Rf: EC92; E167; JF8
Bentschner, Salomon. f. Wolff Bentschner, m. Esther Falk Bentschner, mr. Faletta David Bentschner, 1874. Rf: JF8
Bentschner, Wolff. b. 1802, d. 1858, SC: 1858, mr. Esther Falk Bentschner. Rf: ENJC3; JF8
Benzakin, Joseph. SC: 1786, mr. Rebecca Benzakin (later Hyams). Rf: E279; SCA1786–93
Beretz, Solomon. b. 1810, SC: 1850. Rf: 1850C
Berge, Mortiz. b. 1808, d. 1838, SC: 1838. Rf: EC17; W41.817
Bergen, Morris. Rf: E167

Berlin, Fannie (Nathans). b. 1835, SC: 1835, f. Nathan Nathans, m. Sarah N. Hertz Nathans, mr. Ralph Berlin, 1847. Rf: SFF231; EM23; 1850C; MS16.429

Berlin, Rachel M. (Baruc). b. 1860, SC: 1860, f. Bernard S. Baruc, m. Mathilda R. Oppenheim Baruc, mr. Simon Berlin. Rf: SFF17

Berlin, Ralph. b. 1835, SC: 1847, mr. Fannie Nathans Berlin, 1847. Rf: E167; EM23; SFF231; MS16.429; D1849, 1852

Bernard, Laura (Levy). f. Orlando R. Levy, m. Catherine Bowers Levy, mr. ——— Bernard. Rf: SFF163

Bernard, Levy. Rf: E167

Bernard, M. SC: 1800. Rf: E133

Bernard, S. B. SC: 1842. Rf: 1850C; T32

Bernstein, ——— F. [Burnstine]. b. 1841, d. 1858, SC: 1858. Rf: DR

Bernstein, Alfred. b. 1856, SC: 1856, f. Nathan Bernstein, m. H. Bernstein. Rf: 1860C

Bernstein, Elizabeth. b. 1860, SC: 1860, f. Nathan Bernstein, m. H. Bernstein. Rf: 1860C

Bernstein, H. b. 1810, d. 1838, SC: 1838. Rf: DR

Bernstein, H. b. 1831, SC: 1860, mr. Nathan Bernstein. Rf: 1860C

Bernstein, Nathan. b. 1828, SC: 1855, mr. H. Bernstein. Rf: E167; 1860C; 1861C; D1855

Bernstein, Philip. b. 1859, d. 1881. Rf: DR

Blank, Hanna D. b. 1836, d. 1858, SC: 1858. Rf: EBS3

Blank, Hanna Rachel. b. 1859, d. 1860, SC: 1859. Rf: DR; EBS3

Blank, Isiah. b. 1820, d. 1867. Rf: EBS3

Blank, Josiah. Rf: E167

Blank, Rachel. b. 1800, d. 1858, SC: 1858. Rf: EBS3

Boas, B. b. 1834, d. 1860, SC: 1860. Rf: DR

Borck, Roschen. d. 1858, SC: 1858, mr. Moses Borck. Rf: ENJC3

Bork, Joseph. SC: 1855. Rf: *BS-BI*

Brady, Adeline J. (Moses). b. 1826, SC: 1826, f. Isaiah Moses, m. Rebecca Phillips Moses, mr. Adolph J. Brady, 1845. Rf: SFF210; EC89; EM22; *AF*57

Brady, Adolph J. SC: 1845, mr. Adeline J. Moses Brady, 1845. Rf: EC89; EM22; SFF210

Brady, Rosa Rebecca. b. 1845, d. 1849, SC: 1849, f. Adolph J. Brady, m. Adeline Brady. Rf: EC89; SFF210

Bramson, Jacob. SC: 1821. Rf: E133; CB1821

Brandon, David Pereyra. SC: 1805, mr. Maria Rodrigues DePass Brandon, 1813. Rf: E133, 145; EM10; SFF58; D1809, 1819

Brandon, Maria (Rodrigues) (DePass). SC: 1813, mr. Samuel DePass, mr2. David Pereya Brandon, 1813. Rf: EM10; SFF58

Brandon, Moses. SC: 1814. Rf: SCA1814

Bravo, ———. SC: 1811. CB1811

Bren, Adelaide (Rosenfeld). b. 1849, SC: 1849, f. Jacob Rosenfeld, m. Leonora Moses Rosenfeld, mr. Robert Bren. Rf: SFF210; 1850C

Breslau, Moses. b. 1770, d. 1840, SC: 1840. Rf: Min. Jan. 26 1840; DR

Breslau, Myers. d. 1845, SC: 1824. Rf: DR; E167

Broadman, J. b. 1768, d. 1841, SC: 1841. Rf: DR

Buley, Jacob. SC: 1807. Rf: CB1807

Bush, David. SC: 1800. Rf: E279

Bush, Jacob. b. 1837, d. 1854, SC: 1854. Rf: DR

Bush, Levy. SC: 1857, mr. Minna Bush. Rf: EC91; D1855

Bush, Minna. d. 1857, SC: 1857, mr. Levy Bush. Rf: EC91

Calder, Phila (Lazarus). d. 1806, f. Aaron Lazarus, m. Esther Cohen Lazarus, mr. William Calder. Rf: SFF151

Canter, Abraham. d. 1858, SC: 1800, f. Jacob Canter, m. Rebecca DeLaMotta. Rf: E133, SFF28; W48.238 (his); T32; CB1800; D1809; RB16

Canter, Benjamin. SC: 1802. Rf: E133; D1813

Canter, David. b. 1776, d. 1829, SC: 1791, f. Jacob Canter, m. Rebecca DeLaMotta Canter. Rf: SFF28; E133, 279; *SP*, Nov. 16, 1826; D1802; RB16, 17

Canter, David Emanuel. b. 1828, d. 1829, SC: 1828, f. Emanuel Canter, m. Rebecca DeLaMotta Canter. Rf: DR; SFF28

Canter, Emanuel. b. 1766, d. 1829, SC: 1766, f. Jacob Canter, m. Rebecca DeLaMotta Canter, mr. Rebecca DeLaMotta Canter. Rf: DR; SFF28; E133, 279; T33; W43.834; W46.90; D1794, 1802, 1803, 1809, 1813, 1816, 1819, 1822, 1829

Canter, Emanuel. SC: 1831. Rf: D1831, 1835, 1838

Canter, Emanuel DeLaMotta. b. 1824, d. 1889, SC: 1824, f. Emanuel Canter, m. Rebecca DeLaMotta Canter. Rf: DR; SFF28; W45.810; W43.838

Canter, Esther (DePass) (DaCosta). f. Ralph Depass, m. Leah DePass, mr. Samuel DaCosta, 1792, mr2. Isaac Canter, 1797. Rf: SFF28, 44, 58; *OJCS*47

Canter, Hannah. b. 1783, d. 1826, f. Jacob Canter, m. Rebecca DeLaMotta Canter. Rf: SFF28

Canter, Isaac. b. 1769, d. 1810, SC: 1800, f. Jacob Canter, m. Rebecca DeLaMotta Canter, mr. Esther DePass DaCosta Canter, 1797. Rf: SFF28; E133, 145; D1803, 1806

Canter, Jacob. f. Isaac Canter, m. Esther DePass Canter. Rf: SFF28

Canter, Jacob. b. 1741, d. 1785, SC: 1785, mr. Rebecca DeLaMotta Canter. Rf: SFF28; EC29; E133; RB17

Canter, Jacob. b. 1770, SC: 1790, f. Jacob Canter, m. Rebecca DeLaMotta Canter. Rf: T33; SFF28; D1790, 1794, 1802, 1803, 1809, 1819

Canter, Jacob DeLaMotta. f. Emanuel Canter, m. Rebecca DeLaMotta Canter. Rf: SFF28

Canter, John. b. 1782, d. 1823, SC: 1800, f. Jacob Canter, m. Rebecca DeLaMotta Canter. Rf: DR; EC29; SFF28; 1820C; CB1800; D1809, 1813, 1816, 1819, 1822; RB17

Canter, Joshua. f. Isaac Canter, m. Esther DePass Canter, mr. Eliza Williams Canter, 1842. Rf: SFF28

Canter, Joshua. b. 1767, d. 1826, SC: 1790, f. Jacob Canter, m. Rebecca

Irby, mr2. Abraham Alexander, 1784. Rf: EL; E44; SFF8; W40.354 (hers); *AF*16–18

Alexander, Catherine. b. 1820, d. 1885, SC: 1820, f. Abraham Alexander, m. Hannah Aarons Alexander. Rf: SFF8; *AF*18

Alexander, Hannah (Aarons). b. 1789, d. 1865, SC: 1789, f. Levi Aarons van Blitz, mr. Abraham Alexander, 1801. Rf: SFF1, 8; EC41, 74; 1850C; 1861C; D1855

Alexander, Joseph. b. 1802, d. 1813, SC: 1802, f. Abraham Alexander, m. Hannah Aarons Alexander. Rf: EC74; SFF8

Alexander, Joseph Albert. b. 1837, d. 1894, SC: 1837, f. Aaron Alexander, m. Sarah Moses Alexander, mr. Sallie Nathans Solomons Alexander, 1874. Rf: SFF9

Alexander, Joseph Raphael. SC: 1760. Rf: SFF8

Alexander, Judah. b. 1742, d. 1804, SC: 1790, f. Joseph Raphael Alexander. Rf: SFF8; 1800C; E133; D1790, 1801, 1802, 1803; RB5

Alexander, Judah. b. 1829, SC: 1849, f. Abraham Alexander (1771–1844), m. Hannah Aarons Alexander. Rf: 1850C; AF18; D1849

Alexander, Leah. b. 1842, d. 1842, SC: 1842, f. Aaron Alexander, m. Sarah Alexander. Rf: EP

Alexander, Moses. b. 1778, d. 1808, SC: 1800, f. Abraham Alexander. Rf: EC47; SFF8; E133; D1802, 1803; RB7

Alexander, Rachel (Anderson). b. 1757, d. 1827, SC: 1767, mr. Alexander Alexander, 1767. Rf: DR; EC71; 1800C; *SCM*3; D1801, 1802, 1803, 1813

Alexander, Rebecca Ella Solomons. b. 1856, d. 1938, SC: 1856, f. Abraham Alexander Solomons, m. Cecilia Moses Alexander, mr. Julius Mortimer Alexander, 1873. Rf: SFF9, 278; *AF*112

Alexander, S. b. 1829, d. 1858, SC: 1850. Rf: DR

Alexander, Sally Nathans (Solomons). b. 1854, d. 1923, SC: 1854, f. Solomon Sampson Solomons, m. Esther Nathans Solomons, mr. Joseph Albert Alexander, 1874. Rf: SFF9, 277; 1860C

Alexander, Sarah. SC: 1832, f. Abraham Alexander, m. Hannah Aarons Alexander. Rf: SFF8; W40.354

Alexander, Sarah (Harris) (Sampson). b. 1801, d. 1833, SC: 1801, f. Jacob Harris, m. Elizabeth Harris, mr. Alexander Sampson, mr2. Alexander Alexander. Rf: SFF9, 94

Alexander, Sarah (Moses). b. 1813, d. 1892, SC: 1813, f. Isaiah Moses, m. Rebecca Phillips Moses, mr. Aaron Alexander, 1836. Rf: SFF8, 9, 210; *AF*59–61; MS13.279

Allen, F. SC: 1819. Rf: CB1819

Amesquita, Raphael DaCosta. b. 1753, d. 1821, SC: 1801. Rf: DR; EC71; E133; D1819

Amram, Rosa Rosenfeld. f. Jacob Rosenfeld, m. Leonara Moses Rosenfeld, mr. Emile Amram. Rf: SFF210

Ancker, Abigail Rebecca (Sampson). b. 1823, d. 1844, SC: 1823, f.

Joseph Sampson, m. Abigail Sampson, mr. Gustavus V. Ancker, 1841. Rf: EC85; SFF11, 259; EM19

Ancker, Alfred. b. 1854, d. 1855, SC: 1854. Rf: DR

Ancker, Catherine (Hyams). b. 1834, SC: 1834, f. Moses David Hyams, m. Susannah Jackson Hyams, mr. Samuel P. Ancker, 1853. Rf: SFF11, 120; 1850C

Ancker, Clothilde. f. Samuel P. Ancker, m. Catherine Hyams Ancker. Rf: SFF11

Ancker, Florence. b. 1859, d. 1859, SC: 1859. Rf: DR

Ancker, Gustavus. SC: 1842, f. Samuel P. Ancker, m. Catherine P. Hyams, mr2. Theresa Kehrer Ancker. Rf: SFF11

Ancker, Gustavus Vasa. SC: 1841, f. Adolph Ancker, m. Hetty Pettigrew Ancker, mr. Abigail Rebecca Sampson Ancker, 1841, mr2. Hannah Hyams Ancker. Rf: SFF11, 120; 1850C; 1861C; T32; E167, 238; EC85; EM19; *Courier*, Dec. 11, 1861; D1841, 1855, 1859

Ancker, Gustavus Vasa. b. 1857, d. 1860, SC: 1857. Rf: DR

Ancker, Hannah (Hyams). f. Moses David Hyams, m. Susannah Jackson Hyams, mr. Gustavus V. Ancker. Rf: SFF11, 120

Ancker, Joseph Theodore. b. 1843, d. 1844, SC: 1843, f. Gustavus V. Ancker, m. Hannah Hyams Ancker. Rf: EC85; SFF11

Ancker, Mitchell. f. Samuel P. Ancker, m. Catherine Hyams Ancker, mr. Leah Adelsheimer Ancker. Rf: SFF11

Ancker, Moses. f. Samuel P. Ancker, m. Catherine Hyams Ancker, mr. Catherine Loeb Ancker. Rf: SFF11

Ancker, Pinckney. f. Samuel P. Ancker, m. Catherine Hyams Ancker. Rf: SFF11

Ancker, Rebecca Emily. b. 1842, d. 1843, SC: 1843, f. Gustavus V. Ancker, m. Abigail Sampson Ancker. Rf: SFF11; EC85

Ancker, Samuel P. b. 1817, d. 1903, SC: 1859, f. Adolph Ancker, m. Hetty Pettigrew Ancker, mr. Catherine Hyams Ancker, 1853. Rf: SFF11, 120; E238; *Courier*, Dec. 11, 1861; D1859

Ancker, Samuel P. b. 1857, f. Samuel P. Ancker, m. Catherine Hyams Ancker, mr. Sarah Kahn Ancker, 1885. Rf: SFF11

Ancker, Susan. b. 1856, d. 1856, SC: 1856. Rf: DR

Ancker, Theodore. b. 1854, d. 1855, SC: 1854, f. Gustavus V. Ancker, m. Hannah Hyams Ancker. Rf: DR; SFF11

Andrews, Abraham. mr2. Nellie (Nettie) Abrahams Andrews, 1761. Rf: SFF12

Andrews, Nellie [Nettie] (Abrahams). mr. Abraham Andrews, 1761. Rf: SFF12

Andrews, Zalegman. b. 1805, SC: 1844, f. Joseph Andrews, m. Sallie Salomon Andrews, mr. Esther Abrams Andrews, 1844. Rf: SFF4, 12

Apple, J. b. 1826, d. 1876. Rf: DR

Areagh, Judah. SC: 1794. Rf: MR3D.411

Ashim, Leopold Nathaniel. b. 1849, d. 1857, SC: 1857, f. Simon Ashim, m. Matilda Adelaide Jacobi Ashim. Rf: EC92; E167; JF7

Ashim, Mathilda Adelaide (Jacobi). b. 1829, SC: 1847, f. Wolf Jacob Jacobi, m. Priscilla Rebecca Jacobi, mr. Simon Ashim, 1847. Rf: EM23; SFF117; JF7

Ashim, Simon. SC: 1853, mr. Mathilda Adelaide Jacobi Ashim, 1847. Rf: EM23; E167; JF7; D1855

Audler, Ezekiel. d. 1829, SC: 1814. Rf: E133; *SP*, Oct. 15, 1829; CB1814

Audler, I. SC: 1839. Rf: E167; Min. April 14, 1839

Audler, Myer. SC: 1817. Rf: E133

Audler, Rosina (Florance). SC: 1827, f. Zachariah Levy Florance, m. Sarah Florance, mr. E. Audler, 1827. Rf: EM13; SFF74

Audler, Shane. SC: 1838, m. Rebecca Solomons, Rf: SCA1838

Audler, Solomon. SC: 1821, mr. Helene Barnett. Rf: E133; SFF74; CB1821

Avila, Abraham. SC: 1697. Rf: EL; E20, 21, 277

Azuby, Abraham. b. 1738, d. 1805, SC: 1784, mr. Esther Azuby. Rf: SFF13; E133, 279, 288, 290–92; 1790C; D1790, 1796, 1801

Azuby, Esther. b. 1754, d. 1805, SC: 1784. Rf: EC83; W30.855 (hers)

Bahr, Emmie (Baruc). b. 1858, SC: 1858, f. Bernard S. Baruc, m. Mathilda R. Oppenheim Baruc, mr. Herman Bahr. Rf: SFF17

Barnard, Alexander. SC: 1805, f. Solomon Barnard. Rf: W30.959 (his); E133

Barnet, Barnet. SC: 1801. Rf: E133

Barnet, Moses. SC: 1818. Rf: E133; EB1819

Barnett, Cordelia (Harris) (Woolf). f. Jacob Harris, m. Elizabeth Harris, mr. Ralph Woolf, 1837, mr2. Lewis S. Barnett, 1851. Rf: EC88; SFF16, 94, 305

Barnett, John. SC: 1855. Rf: T32

Barnett, Lewis S. b. 1822, d. 1856, SC: 1856, f. Samuel Barnett, m. Sarah Barnett, mr. Cordelia Harris Woolf, 1851. Rf: EC88; SFF16, 94

Barnett, Minnie (Loryea). b. 1853, d. 1925, SC: 1853, f. Aaron Loryea, m. Jane Hart Loryea, mr. Joseph Barnett, 1881. Rf: SFF179; 1860C

Barnett, Woolf. SC: 1802. Rf: D1802

Barnett, Woolf. SC: 1840, mr. Selina Rebecca Russell Barnett, 1847, mr2. Rachel Joel Barnet. Rf: E167; SFF16; Min. July 25, 1840

Barnett, Zelda Loryea. b. 1829, d. 1882, SC: 1850, f. Isaac Loryea, m. Esther Loryea, mr. B. J. Barnett, 1850. Rf: SFF179; EM24

Barns, ——— [born Simon]. SC: 1702. RB159

Barrett, ———[no. 1]. b. 1835, d. 1835, SC: 1835. Rf: EC8; SFF27

Barrett, ———[no. 2]. b. 1835, d. 1835, SC: 1835, f. Jacob Barrett, m. Hetty Ottolengui Barrett. Rf: EC8; SFF17

Barrett, Abraham. SC: 1803. Rf: E133

Barrett, Amanda. f. Jacob Barrett, m. Hetty Ottolengui Barrett. Rf: SFF17

Barrett, Barrett. b. 1851, d. 1852, SC: 1851, f. Jacob Barrett, m. Hetty J. Ottolengui Barrett. Rf: EC7; SFF17

Barrett, Esther. SC: 1797, mr. Solomon Barrett. Rf: MR3H.417; D1806, 1819, 1822

Barrett, Eugenia. f. Jacob Barrett (1792–1871), m. Hetty Ottolengui Barrett. Rf: SFF17

Barrett, Hetty J. Ottolengui. b. 1818, d. 1886, SC: 1834, f. Abraham Ottolengui, m. Sarah Jacobs Ottolengui, mr. Jacob Barrett, 1834. Rf: DR; EC7, 8; EM15; SFF17, 234; W45.796

Barrett, Isaac B. b. 1791, d. 1834, SC: 1814, mr. Rachel J. DaVega Barrett, 1815. Rf: EC10; SFF17, 45; T32; TBS39; CB1814; D1816, 1819, 1822, 1829, 1831

Barrett, Isaac J. b. 1838, d. 1871, SC: 1838, f. Jacob Barrett, m. Hetty Ottolengui Barrett. Rf: DR; EC8; E133, 167, 223; SFF17

Barrett, Jacob. b. 1792, d. 1871, SC: 1792, mr. Hetty J. Ottolengui Barrett, 1834. Rf: DR; EM15; E133, 167, 187; EC7, 8; SFF17, 234; 1840C; 1850C; D1835, 1838, 1849, 1855, 1859

Barrett, Jacob. b. 1848, d. 1883, SC: 1848, f. Jacob Barrett, m. Hetty J. Ottolengui Barrett, mr. Sarah Poznanski, 1874. Rf: SFF17, 252; EC48; DR

Barrett, Jacob. b. 1856, d. 1858, SC: 1858. Rf: EC7

Barrett, Judah. SC: 1802. Rf: E133, 245, 246; SFF17; D1803

Barrett, Judith. SC: 1837. Rf: SCA1837

Barrett, Lawrence. b. 1844, d. 1845, SC: 1844, f. Jacob Barrett, m. Hetty J. Ottolengui Barrett. Rf: EC8; SFF17

Barrett, Mary Beatrice. f. Jacob Barrett, m. Hetty J. Ottolengui Barrett. Rf: SFF17

Barrett, Rachel J. (DaVega). b. 1801, d. 1865, SC: 1815, f. Moses DaVega, m. Sol DaVega, mr. Isaac Barrett, 1815. Rf: SFF17, 45; EM10; EC10; W51.567 (hers); 1850C; D1835, 1838, 1849

Barrett, Sarah (Poznanski). b. 1844, d. 1874, SC: 1844, f. Gustavus Poznanski, m. Esther Barrett Poznanski, mr. Jacob Barrett, 1874. Rf: DR; EC48; SFF17, 252; 1850C

Barrett, Solomon. SC: 1796, mr. Esther Barrett. Rf: SFF17; MR3H.417; E279; W25.317; 1790C; D1796; RB10, 11

Barrett, Solomon I. b. 1822, d. 1850, SC: 1822, f. Isaac B. Barrett, m. Rachel J. DaVega Barrett. Rf: DR; EC10; SFF17; 1850C; D1849

Barrett, Solomon Judah. b. 1807, d. 1836, f. Judah Barrett. Rf: SFF17

Barrett, Starr. b. 1699, d. 1820, SC: 1788. Rf: EC30; EP; *SP*, Jan. 14, 1820; D1819

Barrett, Thaddeus. b. 1847, d. 1847, SC: 1847, f. Jacob Barrett, m. Hetty J. Ottolengui Barrett. Rf: EC8; SFF17

Bartlett, Sarah (Melhado). mr. Cosam E. Bartlett, 1818. Rf: EP

Baruc, Bernard S. b. 1828, d. 1904, SC: 1855, f. Sigismund Baruc, m. Nanette Baruc, mr. Mathilda R. Oppenheim Baruch, 1855. Rf:

E167, 223; EC36; EM28; SFF27, 235; 1861C; D1855, 1859

Baruc, Mathilda R. (Oppenheim). b. 1830, d. 1877, SC: 1830, f. Hertz Wolf Oppenheim, m. Catherine Moses Oppenheim, mr. Bernard S. Baruc, 1855. Rf: SFF235; EC36; EM28; 1850C

Baruc, Nannie. b. 1856, d. 1861, SC: 1856, f. Bernhard S. Baruc, m. Mathilda R. Oppenheim Baruc. Rf: EC36; SFF17

Baruch, Bernhard. b. 1844, d. 1879, f. Joseph Baruch, m. Hanchen Baruch. Rf: EC77; SFF17

Baruch, Deborah (Sampson). b. 1852, SC: 1852, f. Joseph Sampson, m. Esther Cohen Sampson, mr. Herman Baruch, 1874. Rf: SFF17, 259

Baruch, Frederika Cohen. b. 1848, d. 1878, mr. Albert Baruch. Rf: EC77; DR; SFF17

Baruck, Solomon. SC: 1790. Rf: D1790

Baum, Elkan. b. 1820, d. 1882, SC: 1855. Rf: E167; EG1; D1855

Baum, Herman. SC: 1855. Rf: D1855

Baum, Jacob. b. 1799, d. 1854, SC: 1854. Rf: EC89; D1855

Baum, Jacob. b. 1853, d. 1881, SC: 1853, f. E. Baum, m. H. Baum. Rf: EG1

Baum, John A. SC: 1855. Rf: D1855

Baum, John S. SC: 1855. Rf: D1855

Baum, Leonora M. (Cohen). b. 1837, d. 1851, SC: 1837, f. Hartwig Cohen, m. Deborah Marks Cohen, mr. Mannes Baum, 1856. Rf: SFF34; EM29; EC28; 1850C

Baum, Mannes. SC: 1856, mr. Leonora M. Cohen Baum, 1856. Rf: SFF34; EM29

Baum, Rosa. d. 1858, SC: 1858, mr. Jacob Baum. Rf: EC89

Baum, Sarah Deborah. b. 1857, SC: 1857, f. Mannes Baum, m. Leonora Cohen Baum. Rf: SFF34

Bayless, Rosa (Lewis). b. 1819, f. David Lewis, m. Rachel Lewis, mr. John Clarke Bayless. Rf: SFF172

Beckwith, Belle (Cohen). b. 1845, SC: 1845, f. Jacob Cohen, m. Sarah Barrett Cohen, mr. George Beckwith. Rf: SFF36; 1850C; 1860C

Belitizer, Caroline. b. 1822, SC: 1850, mr. Isaac Belitizer. Rf: 1850C

Belitizer, Isaac. b. 1814, SC: 1850, mr. Caroline Belitizer. Rf: E167; 1850C; D1852

Belitizer, Jacob. b. 1839, SC: 1850, f. Isaac Belitizer, m. Caroline Belitizer. Rf: E224; 1850C

Belitizer, Theodore. b. 1843, SC: 1850, f. Isaac Belitizer, m. Caroline Belitizer. Rf: E167, 224; 1850C

Benedict, Isabel (Levy). b. 1850, SC: 1850, f. Orlando Levy, m. Catherine Browers Levy, mr. Ludwig Benedict, 1873. Rf: SFF163; 1850C

Benedix, Isaac. b. 1760, d. 1804, SC: 1787. Rf: EL; E279; *OJCS*69

Benjamin, Catherine (Woolfe). SC: 1832, m. Rebecca Woolfe, mr. Solomon Benjamin, 1832. Rf: EM14

Benjamin, David. b. 1829, d. 1894, SC: 1855. Rf: EC45; E167, 238; DR; *Courier* Dec. 11, 1861; D1855

Benjamin, Dores. SC: 1787. Rf: W22.191, 1787; SCA1789

Benjamin, J. SC: 1807. Rf: CB1807

Benjamin, Judah Philip. b. 1811, d. 1884, SC: 1820, f. Philip Benjamin, m. Rebecca DeMendes Benjamin, mr. Natalie St. Martin Benjamin, 1833. Rf: E185–87, 221; SFF18

Benjamin, L. A. SC: 1839. Rf: Min. April 8, 1839

Benjamin, Philip. b. 1780, d. 1853, SC: 1820, f. Judah Benjamin, mr. Rebecca De Mendes Benjamin. Rf: DR; E133, 163, 185, 186; SFF18, 309; 1850C; D1819, 1831, 1835, 1838, 1841, 1849

Benjamin, Rebecca (De Mendes). d. 1847, SC: 1820, f. Solomon De Mendes, m. Eva Levy De Mendes, mr. Philip Benjamin. Rf: E185, 186; SFF18

Benjamin, Samuel. SC: 1790. Rf: D1790

Benjamin, Solomon A. b. 1807, d. 1877, SC: 1831, mr. Catherine Woolf Benjamin, 1832. Rf: EM14; EBS3; E167; DR; D1835, 1838, 1841, 1849, 1852, 1855, 1859

Bensadon, Jacob. SC: 1830. Rf: 1830C; D1831, 1835

Bensadon, Judah. d. 1852, SC: 1841, f. Jacob Bensadon, m. Abigail Jacobs Bensadon, mr. Leah Hyams Bensadon, 1841. Rf: SFF119, 131; E167, 206; EM19; D1849

Bensadon, Leah (Hyams). d. 1891, SC: 1841, f. Henry Hyams, m. Judith Hyams, mr. Judah Bensadon, 1841. Rf: EM19; SFF119, 131

Bentschner, David. b. 1842, d. 1900, SC: 1860, f. Wolff Bentschner, m. Esther Falk Bentschner, mr. Hannah Bentschner, 1869. Rf: DR; EM34; JF8

Bentschner, Esther (Falk). b. 1800, d. 1874, SC: 1857, mr. Wolff Bentschner. Rf: DR; JF8

Bentschner, Hanna (Jacobi). b. 1827, d. 1897, f. Neuman Hirsch Jacobi, m. Sarah Moses Jacobi, mr. David Bentschner, 1869. Rf: DR; EM34; JF5

Bentschner, Hester. b. 1800, d. 1873, SC: 1856. Rf: DR

Bentschner, Isaac. b. 1834, d. 1854, SC: 1854, f. Wolff Bentschner, m. Esther Falk Bentschner. Rf: EC92; E167; JF8

Bentschner, Isidor Wolff. b. 1832, d. 1852, SC: 1852, f. Wolff Bentschner, m. Esther Falk Bentschner. Rf: DR; EC93; E167; JF8; D1852

Bentschner, Jacob. b. 1836, d. 1854, SC: 1854, f. Wolff Bentschner, m. Esther Falk Bentschner. Rf: EC92; E167; JF8

Bentschner, Salomon. f. Wolff Bentschner, m. Esther Falk Bentschner, mr. Faletta David Bentschner, 1874. Rf: JF8

Bentschner, Wolff. b. 1802, d. 1858, SC: 1858, mr. Esther Falk Bentschner. Rf: ENJC3; JF8

Benzakin, Joseph. SC: 1786, mr. Rebecca Benzakin (later Hyams). Rf: E279; SCA1786–93

Beretz, Solomon. b. 1810, SC: 1850. Rf: 1850C

Berge, Mortiz. b. 1808, d. 1838, SC: 1838. Rf: EC17; W41.817

Bergen, Morris. Rf: E167

Berlin, Fannie (Nathans). b. 1835, SC: 1835, f. Nathan Nathans, m. Sarah N. Hertz Nathans, mr. Ralph Berlin, 1847. Rf: SFF231; EM23; 1850C; MS16.429

Berlin, Rachel M. (Baruc). b. 1860, SC: 1860, f. Bernard S. Baruc, m. Mathilda R. Oppenheim Baruc, mr. Simon Berlin. Rf: SFF17

Berlin, Ralph. b. 1835, SC: 1847, mr. Fannie Nathans Berlin, 1847. Rf: E167; EM23; SFF231; MS16.429; D1849, 1852

Bernard, Laura (Levy). f. Orlando R. Levy, m. Catherine Bowers Levy, mr. ——— Bernard. Rf: SFF163

Bernard, Levy. Rf: E167

Bernard, M. SC: 1800. Rf: E133

Bernard, S. B. SC: 1842. Rf: 1850C; T32

Bernstein, ——— F. [Burnstine]. b. 1841, d. 1858, SC: 1858. Rf: DR

Bernstein, Alfred. b. 1856, SC: 1856, f. Nathan Bernstein, m. H. Bernstein. Rf: 1860C

Bernstein, Elizabeth. b. 1860, SC: 1860, f. Nathan Bernstein, m. H. Bernstein. Rf: 1860C

Bernstein, H. b. 1810, d. 1838, SC: 1838. Rf: DR

Bernstein, H. b. 1831, SC: 1860, mr. Nathan Bernstein. Rf: 1860C

Bernstein, Nathan. b. 1828, SC: 1855, mr. H. Bernstein. Rf: E167; 1860C; 1861C; D1855

Bernstein, Philip. b. 1859, d. 1881. Rf: DR

Blank, Hanna D. b. 1836, d. 1858, SC: 1858. Rf: EBS3

Blank, Hanna Rachel. b. 1859, d. 1860, SC: 1859. Rf: DR; EBS3

Blank, Isiah. b. 1820, d. 1867. Rf: EBS3

Blank, Josiah. Rf: E167

Blank, Rachel. b. 1800, d. 1858, SC: 1858. Rf: EBS3

Boas, B. b. 1834, d. 1860, SC: 1860. Rf: DR

Borck, Roschen. d. 1858, SC: 1858, mr. Moses Borck. Rf: ENJC3

Bork, Joseph. SC: 1855. Rf: *BS-BI*

Brady, Adeline J. (Moses). b. 1826, SC: 1826, f. Isaiah Moses, m. Rebecca Phillips Moses, mr. Adolph J. Brady, 1845. Rf: SFF210; EC89; EM22; *AF*57

Brady, Adolph J. SC: 1845, mr. Adeline J. Moses Brady, 1845. Rf: EC89; EM22; SFF210

Brady, Rosa Rebecca. b. 1845, d. 1849, SC: 1849, f. Adolph J. Brady, m. Adeline Brady. Rf: EC89; SFF210

Bramson, Jacob. SC: 1821. Rf: E133; CB1821

Brandon, David Pereyra. SC: 1805, mr. Maria Rodrigues DePass Brandon, 1813. Rf: E133, 145; EM10; SFF58; D1809, 1819

Brandon, Maria (Rodrigues) (DePass). SC: 1813, mr. Samuel DePass, mr2. David Pereya Brandon, 1813. Rf: EM10; SFF58

Brandon, Moses. SC: 1814. Rf: SCA1814

Bravo, ———. SC: 1811. CB1811

Bren, Adelaide (Rosenfeld). b. 1849, SC: 1849, f. Jacob Rosenfeld, m. Leonora Moses Rosenfeld, mr. Robert Bren. Rf: SFF210; 1850C

Breslau, Moses. b. 1770, d. 1840, SC: 1840. Rf: Min. Jan. 26 1840; DR

Breslau, Myers. d. 1845, SC: 1824. Rf: DR; E167

Broadman, J. b. 1768, d. 1841, SC: 1841. Rf: DR

Buley, Jacob. SC: 1807. Rf: CB1807

Bush, David. SC: 1800. Rf: E279

Bush, Jacob. b. 1837, d. 1854, SC: 1854. Rf: DR

Bush, Levy. SC: 1857, mr. Minna Bush. Rf: EC91; D1855

Bush, Minna. d. 1857, SC: 1857, mr. Levy Bush. Rf: EC91

Calder, Phila (Lazarus). d. 1806, f. Aaron Lazarus, m. Esther Cohen Lazarus, mr. William Calder. Rf: SFF151

Canter, Abraham. d. 1858, SC: 1800, f. Jacob Canter, m. Rebecca DeLaMotta. Rf: E133, SFF28; W48.238 (his); T32; CB1800; D1809; RB16

Canter, Benjamin. SC: 1802. Rf: E133; D1813

Canter, David. b. 1776, d. 1829, SC: 1791, f. Jacob Canter, m. Rebecca DeLaMotta Canter. Rf: SFF28; E133, 279; *SP*, Nov. 16, 1826; D1802; RB16, 17

Canter, David Emanuel. b. 1828, d. 1829, SC: 1828, f. Emanuel Canter, m. Rebecca DeLaMotta Canter. Rf: DR; SFF28

Canter, Emanuel. b. 1766, d. 1829, SC: 1766, f. Jacob Canter, m. Rebecca DeLaMotta Canter, mr. Rebecca DeLaMotta Canter. Rf: DR; SFF28; E133, 279; T33; W43.834; W46.90; D1794, 1802, 1803, 1809, 1813, 1816, 1819, 1822, 1829

Canter, Emanuel. SC: 1831. Rf: D1831, 1835, 1838

Canter, Emanuel DeLaMotta. b. 1824, d. 1889, SC: 1824, f. Emanuel Canter, m. Rebecca DeLaMotta Canter. Rf: DR; SFF28; W45.810; W43.838

Canter, Esther (DePass) (DaCosta). f. Ralph Depass, m. Leah DePass, mr. Samuel DaCosta, 1792, mr2. Isaac Canter, 1797. Rf: SFF28, 44, 58; *OJCS*47

Canter, Hannah. b. 1783, d. 1826, f. Jacob Canter, m. Rebecca DeLaMotta Canter. Rf: SFF28

Canter, Isaac. b. 1769, d. 1810, SC: 1800, f. Jacob Canter, m. Rebecca DeLaMotta Canter, mr. Esther DePass DaCosta Canter, 1797. Rf: SFF28; E133, 145; D1803, 1806

Canter, Jacob. f. Isaac Canter, m. Esther DePass Canter. Rf: SFF28

Canter, Jacob. b. 1741, d. 1785, SC: 1785, mr. Rebecca DeLaMotta Canter. Rf: SFF28; EC29; E133; RB17

Canter, Jacob. b. 1770, SC: 1790, f. Jacob Canter, m. Rebecca DeLaMotta Canter. Rf: T33; SFF28; D1790, 1794, 1802, 1803, 1809, 1819

Canter, Jacob DeLaMotta. f. Emanuel Canter, m. Rebecca DeLaMotta Canter. Rf: SFF28

Canter, John. b. 1782, d. 1823, SC: 1800, f. Jacob Canter, m. Rebecca DeLaMotta Canter. Rf: DR; EC29; SFF28; 1820C; CB1800; D1809, 1813, 1816, 1819, 1822; RB17

Canter, Joshua. f. Isaac Canter, m. Esther DePass Canter, mr. Eliza Williams Canter, 1842. Rf: SFF28

Canter, Joshua. b. 1767, d. 1826, SC: 1790, f. Jacob Canter, m. Rebecca

DeLaMotta Canter. Rf: SFF28; E133, 140, 279; W46.90; W45.810 (his); *SP*, Nov. 8, 13, 1826; D1790, 1794, 1801, 1802, 1803, 1806, 1807, 1809, 1813, 1816, 1819, 1822; RB17

Canter, Joshua. b. 1827, SC: 1827, f. Emanuel Canter, m. Rebecca DeLaMotta Canter. Rf: SFF28

Canter, Judith. b. 1827, d. 1890, SC: 1828, f. Emanuel Canter, m. Rebecca DeLaMotta Canter. Rf: DR; SFF28

Canter, Rachel. d. 1856, SC: 1835, f. Jacob Canter, m. Rebecca DeLaMotta Canter. Rf: SFF28; W46.90 (hers); D1835, 1852, 1855

Canter, Ralph. f. Isaac Canter, m. Esther DePass Canter, mr. Sarah DaCosta, 1823. Rf: SFF28

Canter, Rebecca (DeLaMotta). b. 1786, d. 1873, SC: 1837, mr. Emanuel DeLaMotta. Rf: SFF28; *OJCS*39; D1837, 1849

Canter, Rebecca (DeLaMotta). d. 1835, SC: 1796, f. Isaac DeLaMotta, m. Sarah DeLaMotta, mr. Jacob Canter. Rf: SFF28, 54; 1830C; D1819, 1831

Canter, Samuel. SC: 1807. Rf: D1807

Canter, Sarah. SC: 1813. Rf: D1813

Canter, Sarah (DaCosta). f. Joseph DaCosta, m. Rebecca DePass DaCosta, mr. Ralph Canter, 1823. Rf: SFF28, 44

Cantor, Jacob. d. 1821, SC: 1784. Rf: DR; E133, 143, 279; EL; 1790C; D1785, 1796, 1806, 1807

Cantor, Manning. SC: 1807. Rf: E143; D1807

Cardozo, Aaron. b. 1802, d. 1804, SC: 1802, f. David Nunez Cardozo, m. Sarah Cohen Carodozo. Rf: SFF29

Cardozo, Abraham Nunez. d. 1762, SC: 1750, mr. Hannah Allan Cardozo, 1759. Rf: Salley, *St. Phillips*, 154; E32, 39, 277; *SCM*38

Cardozo, David Nunez. b. 1753, d. 1835, SC: 1775, f. Aaron Nunez Cardozo, m. Sarah Nunez Cardozo, mr. Leah Benjamin Cardozo, 1779, mr2. Sarah Cohen Cardozo, 1785. Rf: EC11; SFF29, 36; E84, 87, 92, 95, 133; T146; W40.272 (his); D1796, 1801, 1802, 1803, 1806, 1807, 1809, 1813, 1816, 1819, 1829, 1831; RB17

Cardozo, David Nunez. b. 1804, d. 1804, SC: 1804, f. David Nunez Cardozo, m. Sarah Cohen Cardozo. Rf: SFF29

Cardozo, Frances Nunez. b. 1788, d. 1849, SC: 1788, f. David Nunez Cardozo, m. Sarah Cohen Nunez. Rf: EC12; SFF29; DR; W40.272

Cardozo, Hannah Allan. SC: 1759, mr. Abraham Nunez Cardozo, 1759. Rf: Salley, *St. Phillips*, 154; RB17

Cardozo, Isaac N. b. 1793, d. 1855, SC: 1793, f. David Nunez Cardozo, m. Sarah Cohen Cardozo. Rf: DR; EC12; SFF29; E95, 143, 161, 163, 164, 167, 179, 204; T33; 1850C; D1813, 1819, 1822, 1829, 1831, 1835, 1841, 1849, 1852; RB18

Cardozo, Jacob Nunes. b. 1786, d. 1873, SC: 1794, f. David Nunez Cardozo, m. Sarah Cohen Cardozo. Rf: E133, 141, 167, 172, 176–79, 206, 258; SFF29; *OJCS*40;

D1813, 1819, 1829, 1831, 1835, 1838, 1841, 1849, 1852

Cardozo, Joseph. SC: 1817, mr. Celina Hunter Cardozo, 1817. Rf: 1820C; SCHM66.112–24; EP; D1822

Cardozo, Judith Nunez. b. 1790, d. 1854, SC: 1854, f. David Nunez Cardozo, m. Sarah Cohen Cardozo. Rf: EC12; SFF29; W40.272

Cardozo, Leah. b. 1797, d. 1802, SC: 1797, f. David Nunez Cardozo, m. Sarah Cohen Cardozo. Rf: SFF29

Cardozo, Leah (DeTorres). b. 1765, d. 1780, f. Todros Benjamin, m. Rachel Benjamin, mr. David N. Cardozo, 1779. Rf: SFF62

Cardozo, Samuel Nunez. SC: 1767. Rf: E45, 277; RB18

Cardozo, Sarah N. (Cohen). b. 1766, d. 1853, SC: 1766, f. Isaac Cohen, m. Judith Lyon Cohen, mr. David Nunez Cardozo, 1785. Rf: SFF29, 36; E2; EC12; DR; W40.272; 1840C; D1841; RB18, 27

Carvalho, Caroline A. (Woolf). b. 1824, d. 1904, SC: 1841, f. Isaac Woolf, mr. Emanuel Nunes Carvalho, 1841. Rf: SFF30, 305; EM20, 46

Carvalho, David Nunes. b. 1784, d. 1860, SC: 1809, f. Solomon Nunez Carvalho, m. Judith Henriques Pimentel, mr. Sarah D'Azevedo Carvalho, 1814. Rf: E133, 158, 161, 163, 167, 187; SFF30; T33; CB1809; D1813, 1816, 1819, 1822

Carvalho, David Nunes. b. 1842, d. 1843, SC: 1842, f. Emanuel Nunes Carvalho, m. Caroline A. Woolf Carvalho. Rf: EC46; SFF30

Carvalho, David Nunes. b. 1848, d. 1925, SC: 1852, f. Solomon Nunes Carvalho, m. Sarah Miriam Solis Carvalho, mr. Annie Abrams Carvalho, 1878. Rf: SFF30

Carvalho, Emanuel Nunes. b. 1770, d. 1817, SC: 1807, f. Solomon Nunes Carvalho, m. Judith H. Pimentel Carvalho, mr. Sarah Moreira Carvalho, 1790. Rf: SFF30; E133, 146, 167, 187, 292; CB1809; *SP*, April 3, 1821

Carvalho, Emanuel Nunes. b. 1817, d. 1883, SC: 1817, f. David Nunes Carvalho, m. Sarah D'Azevedo Carvalho, mr. Caroline A. Woolf Carvalho, 1841. Rf: SFF30, 305; EC46; D1841

Carvalho, Isaac. b. 1835, d. 1835, SC: 1835, f. David Nunes Carvalho, m. Sarah D'Azevedo Carvalho. Rf: SFF30

Carvalho, Isaac Woolf Nunes. b. 1848, f. Emanuel Nunes Carvalho, m. Caroline A. Woolf Carvalho. Rf: SFF30

Carvalho, Jacob Dias. SC: 1735. Rf: E26–27; JR1737; RB19

Carvalho, Jacob Solis. b. 1852, d. 1937, SC: 1852, f. Solomon Nunes Carvalho, m. Sarah Miriam Solis Carvalho, mr. Suzanne Walker. Rf: SFF30

Carvalho, Julia. b. 1819, d. 1887, SC: 1819, f. David Nunes Carvalho, m. Sarah D'Azevedo Carvalho. Rf: SFF30

Carvalho, Sarah. f. Emanuel Nunes Carvalho, m. Caroline A. Woolf Carvalho. Rf: SFF30

Carvalho, Sarah. b. 1823, d. 1842, SC: 1823, f. David Nunes Carvalho,

m. Sarah D'Azevedo Carvalho. Rf: SFF30

Carvalho, Sarah Miriam (Solis). b. 1824, d. 1894, f. Jacob da Silva Solis, m. Charity Hays da Silva Solis, mr. Solomon Nunes Carvalho, 1845. Rf: SFF30, 274

Carvalho, Sarah (Moreira). d. 1831, SC: 1811, f. Benjamin Rodrigues Moreira, mr. Emanuel Nunes Carvalho, 1790. Rf: SFF30

Carvalho, Sarah Nunes (D'Azevedo). b. 1793, d. 1864, SC: 1814, f. Benjamin D'Azevedo, m. Judith D'Azevedo, mr. David Nunes Carvalho, 1814. Rf: SFF30, 51; W43.556; D1838

Carvalho, Solomon Nunes. b. 1815, d. 1897, SC: 1815, f. David Nunes Carvalho, m. Sarah D'Azevedo Carvalho, mr. Sarah Miriam Solis Carvalho, 1845. Rf: E167, 187; SFF30; D1838, 1852

Cary, Julia Augusta (Moïse). b. 1835, d. 1892, SC: 1835, f. Isaac Moïse, m. Hetty Lopez Moïse, mr. William Standerwick Cary, 1874. Rf: SFF197; 1850C

Chapman, Edwin. b. 1827, d. 1868, SC: 1860, f. Moses Chapman, m. Hannah Levy Chapman. Rf: EC77; W51.866 (his); SFF308

Chumaceiro, Eudora (Sampson) (Abrahams). f. Samuel Sampson, m. Catherine Goldsmith Sampson, mr. Jacob M. H. Abrahams, 1862, mr2. Joseph H. M. Chumaceiro, 1872. Rf: SFF259

Clapperman, ———. SC: 1819. Rf: CB1819

Cohen, ———. f. Moses Cohen, m. Rachel Moses Cohen. Rf: SFF36

Cohen, ———. d. 1848 SC: 1848. Rf: DR

Cohen, ———. b. 1828, d. 1856, SC: 1828. Rf: DR

Cohen, ———. b. 1834, d. 1858, SC: 1858. Rf: DR

Cohen, ———. b. 1842, d. 1842, f. Isaac S. Cohen, m. Virginia J. Davis Cohen. Rf: SFF36

Cohen, ———. b. 1844, d. 1848, SC: 1844. Rf: DR

Cohen, ———. b. 1848, d. 1849, SC: 1848, f. Marx Edwin Cohen, m. Armida Harby Cohen. Rf: EC32; SFF35, 93

Cohen, ———. b. 1858, d. 1858, SC: 1858, f. Melvin M. Cohen, m. Eliza Virginia Moïse Cohen. Rf: SFF39; EC22

Cohen, ——— Mordica. b. 1775, d. 1844, SC: 1775. Rf: DR

Cohen, Aaron. f. David Lopez Cohen, m. Sarah C. Moïse Cohen. Rf: SFF36

Cohen, Aaron. b. 1808, d. 1862, SC: 1808, f. Moses Cohen, m. Rachel Moses Cohen. Rf: SFF36

Cohen, Aaron. b. 1828, SC: 1828. Rf: 1850C

Cohen, Aaron Nathan. B. 1777, d. 1862, SC: 1838, mr. Rachel Cohen. Rf: EM19, 20; E167, 247; SFF38, 1840C; T33; D1838, 1859

Cohen, Aaron Nathan. SC: 1850, f. Aaron Nathan Cohen, m. Rachel Cohen, mr. Fanny Cohen, 1850. Rf: SFF34, 38; EM24; E239; D1852, 1855, 1859

Cohen, Abraham. b. 1739, d. 1800, SC: 1750, f. Moses Cohen, m. Dinah Comgile Cohen. Rf: SFF35;

E34, 106, 127, 133, 242, 243, 277

Cohen, Abraham. b. 1782, d. 1809, SC: 1800, mr. Rachel Harby Cohen. Rf: SFF93, W31.294 (his); CB1800

Cohen, Abraham Sarzedas. f. Gershon Cohen, m. Rebecca Sarzedas Cohen. Rf: SFF38

Cohen, Abram. b. 1826, d. 1833, f. Jacob Cohen, m. Rachel Lopez Cohen. Rf: SFF36

Cohen, Adela (Isaacks). b. 1832, d. 1890, SC: 1832, f. Abraham Isaacks, m. Rebecca Cohen Isaacks, mr. Daniel Seixas Cohen, 1854. Rf: SFF38, 120

Cohen, Andrew Jacob. b. 1833, d. 1890, SC: 1833, f. Esdaile P. Cohen, m. Frances Hays Cohen, mr. Clotilda Florance Cohen, 1854. Rf: SFF31, 74

Cohen, Ansley Davis. b. 1848, d. 1916, SC: 1848, f. Isaac S. Cohen, m. Virginia J. Davis Cohen, mr. Caroline Moïse Cohen, 1880. Rf: SFF36; E225; 1850C

Cohen, Armida (Harby). b. 1820, d. 1895, SC: 1820, f. Isaac Harby, m. Rachel Mordecai Harby, mr. Marx Edwin Cohen, 1838. Rf: SFF35, 93; EM17; MJSC15

Cohen, Arthur. f. Philip Melvin Cohen, m. Cordelia Moïse Cohen, mr. ——— Blackwell. Rf: SFF39

Cohen, Arthur N. SC: 1845. Rf: EM22; E225

Cohen, Asher D. b. 1838, d. 1904, SC: 1838, f. David Daniel Cohen, m. Mary Hart Cohen, mr. Miriam Hart Cohen, 1865. Rf: SFF35; W50.415; E167, 225, 262; T33; 1860C

Cohen, Augustus Philip. b. 1810, d. 1882, SC: 1810, f. Philip Cohen, m. Eleanor Moses Cohen. Rf: DR; EC63; SFF38, 39; 1850C; 1860C; D1841, 1859

Cohen, Barnet A. b. 1769, d. 1839, SC: 1800, f. Moses Cohen, mr. Bella A Cohen. Rf: E133, 143; EC5, 6; SFF39; T33; D1806, 1807, 1819; RB21

Cohen, Bella. b. 1785, d. 1863, SC: 1785. Rf: EC39; 1850C; SFF309; D1852

Cohen, Bella A. b. 1792, d. 1836, SC: 1836, mr. Barnet A. Cohen. Rf: EC5; SFF39

Cohen, Bella (Moses). d. 1862, f. Myer Moses, m. Rachel Andrews Moses, mr. Solomon Cohen, 1786. Rf: SFF35, 205

Cohen, Benjamin. SC: 1800. Rf: E133; CB1800

Cohen, Blume. d. 1836, SC: 1836, mr. C. H. Cohen. Rf: EP

Cohen, C. Henry. b. 1854, SC: 1854, f John Jay Cohen, m. Cornelia Ann Jacobs Cohen. Rf: E269–70

Cohen, Caroline (Harris). b. 1813, d. 1838, SC: 1838, f. Jacob I. Harris m. Elizabeth Harris, mr. Henry Cohen, 1837. Rf: SFF38, 94; EC47; EM17

Cohen, Caroline R. b. 1838, d. 1898, SC: 1838, f. Henry I. Cohen, m. Caroline Harris Cohen. Rf: EC47; SFF38; DR

Cohen, Casper. SC: 1841. Rf: D1841

Cohen, Cecil. b. 1860, f. Joseph Cohen, m. Sarah Barrett Cohen. Rf: SFF36

Cohen, Cecilia Eliza (Levy). b. 1830, d. 1916, SC: 1830, f. David Cardoza Levy, m. Anna Maria Moses Levy, mr. Israel Cohen, 1850. Rf: SFF32, 164

Cohen, Cecilie (Bentschner). b. 1831, d. 1894, SC: 1845, f. Wolff Bentschner, 1855. Rf: DR; EM27; JF2, 8; SCA1845; 1860C

Cohen, Celia. b. 1756, d. 1830, SC: 1803. Rf: D1803, 1807

Cohen, Clara (Harris). b. 1760, d. 1817, SC: 1797, f. Jacob Harris, m. Elizabeth Harris, mr. Nathan A. Cohen. Rf: EC68

Cohen, Clara (Harris). b. 1812, SC: 1850, mr. Nathan A. Cohen. Rf: 1850C; SFF38, 94

Cohen, Clotilda (Florance). b. 1832, d. 1915, f. Jacob Levy Florance, m. Hannah Levy Lyons Florance, mr. Andrew Jacob Cohen, 1854. Rf: SFF31, 74

Cohen, Cordelia. f. Melvin M. Cohen, m. Elizabeth Moïse Cohen. Rf: SFF39

Cohen, Cordelia S. (Moïse). b. 1810, d. 1869, SC: 1810, f. Cherie Moïse, m. Esther Moses Moïse, mr. Philip Melvin Cohen, 1832. Rf: SFF39, 195; EC59, 60, 62; EM14; DR; 1850C; 1860C

Cohen, Cornelia Ann (Jacobs). b. 1823, SC: 1823, f. Myer Jacobs, m. Rebecca Lazarus Jacobs, mr. Jacob I. Cohen, 1839. Rf: EM18; SFF39, 132; 1860C

Cohen, Cornelius. f. John Jay Cohen, m. Cornelia Ann Jacobs Cohen. Rf: SFF39

Cohen, David. d. 1784, SC: 1784. Rf: W21.435 (his)

Cohen, David Daniel. b. 1802, d. 1860, SC: 1802, f. Mordecai Cohen, m. Leah Lazarus Cohen, mr. Mary Hart Cohen, 1830. Rf: SFF35, 98, 151; E167; EC84; W49.697 (his); 1830C; 1840C; 1860C; T33; *SP*, Mar. 1, 1830; D1829, 1831, 1835, 1838, 1841, 1849, 1852, 1855, 1859

Cohen, David Daniel, Jr. b. 1832, d. 1890, SC: 1832, f. David Daniel Cohen, m. Mary Hart Cohen, mr. Gertrude H. Samuel Cohen, 1870. Rf: SFF35, 260; E225; 1860C; D1852

Cohen, David Lopez. b. 1820, d. 1893, SC: 1820, f. Jacob Cohen, m. Rachel Lopez Cohen, mr. Sarah C. Moïse Cohen, 1842. Rf: SFF36, 195; E167; EM21

Cohen, Deborah (Marks). b. 1801, d. 1888, SC: 1850, f. Samuel Manel Marks, m. Sarah Harris Marks, mr. Rev. Hartwig Cohen, 1824. Rf: SFF34, 185; 1850C

Cohen, E. A. SC: 1835. Rf: D1835

Cohen, Edward. mr. Jeanette Elias Cohen, 1867. Rf: SFF63; E225

Cohen, Eleanor (Moses). b. 1778, d. 1857, SC: 1850, f. Myer Moses, m. Rachel Andrews Moses, mr. Philip Cohen, 1799. Rf: DR; SFF39, 205; EC61; W48.95 (hers); 1850C

Cohen, Eleanor Moses (Hart). SC: 1795, f. Moses Hart, m. Sally Hart, mr. Solomon I. Cohen, 1797. Rf: SFF97; W25.317

Cohen, Eleanor S. b. 1776, d. 1849, SC: 1849, mr. Solomon I. Cohen, 1791. Rf: EC38; SFF36

Cohen, Elijah. b. 1800, SC: 1850. Rf: 1850C

Cohen, Eliza. b. 1800, d. 1811, SC: 1811, f. Mordecai Cohen, m. Leah Lazarus Cohen. Rf: EC76; SFF35

Cohen, Elizabeth (Cohen). b. 1833, d. 1873, SC: 1850, f. Nathan Aaron Cohen, m. Rachel Cohen, mr. Leopold Cohen, 1851. Rf: EM24; SFF38, 1850C

Cohen, Ellen Loria (Mordecai). b. 1837, d. 1915, SC: 1837, f. Moses Cohen Mordecai, m. Isabel Rebecca Lyons Mordecai, mr. Jacob I. Cohen, 1868. Rf: SFF203, 32; 1850C; 1860C

Cohen, Emanuel. SC: 1784. Rf: W22.115

Cohen, Emma. b. 1790, d. 1876. Rf: DR

Cohen, Esdaile P. b. 1792, d. 1856, SC: 1818, mr. Frances Hays Cohen, 1829. Rf: SFF31; EM14; Gregorie, *Sumter*, 94; T33; 1820C (Sumter); *SP*, Sept. 3, 1829

Cohen, Esther. f. Melvin m. Cohen, m. Virginia Elizabeth Moïse Cohen. Rf: SFF39

Cohen, Esther (Moses) (Moïse). b. 1784, d. 1860, SC: 1784, f. Myer Moses, m. Rachel Andrews Moses, mr. Cherry Moïse, 1801, mr2. Hyam Cohen, 1827. Rf: DR; EC57; SFF38, 195, 205; EM14; SCA1819–33

Cohen, Esther (Sampson). b. 1818, d. 1846, SC: 1843, f. Samuel Sampson, m. Amelia Sampson, mr. Henry Cohen, 1843. Rf: EM21; SFF38, 259; MS15.362

Cohen, Eudora Esther. b. 1840, d. 1841, SC: 1840, f. Philip Melvin Cohen, m. Cordelia Moïse Cohen. Rf: DR; EC59; SFF39

Cohen, Eva. f. Isaac S. Cohen, m. Virginia J. Davis Cohen. Rf: SFF36

Cohen, Fanny. b. 1845, SC: 1845. Rf: 1850C; 1860C

Cohen, Fishel Hartwig. b. 1842, SC: 1850, f. Hartwig Cohen, m. Deborah Marks Cohen. Rf: SFF34; E239; 1850C

Cohen, Flora. b. 1794, d. 1838, SC: 1838, mr. H. C. Cohen. Rf: EC18

Cohen, Frances (Cohen). b. 1828, d. 1921, SC: 1828, f. Hartwig Cohen, m. Deborah Marks Cohen, mr. Aaron N. Cohen, Jr., 1850. Rf: EM24; SFF34, 38; 1850C

Cohen, Frances (Hays). b. 1790, d. 1865, SC: 1829, f. Michel Solomon Hays, m. Abigail Hays, mr. Esdaile P. Cohen, 1829. Rf: EM14; SFF31, 106; *SP*, Sept. 3, 1829

Cohen, Francis. SC: 1767. Rf: E45

Cohen, Franklin. b. 1853, d. 1855, SC: 1853. Rf: DR

Cohen, George Nathan [Gabriel]. mr. Grune Jacobi Cohen. Rf: JF1

Cohen, Gershon. b. 1748, d. 1802, SC: 1771, f. Uri Cohen, mr. Rebecca Sarzedas Cohen, 1779. Rf: EC59; SFF38, 262, EM5; 1790C; 1800C; D1782, 1790

Cohen, Gershon. SC: 1790, mr. Cecile Mordecai Cohen. Rf: SFF202; E167; D1790, 1794, 1796, 1801

Cohen, Gershon P. d. 1852, SC: 1842, f. Philip Cohen, m. Eleanor Moses Cohen, mr. Mary Thomas. Rf: SFF39; E133; W48.95

Cohen, Gertrude M. (Samuel). b.

1849, d. 1890, f. Morris Samuel, m. Fanny Cohen Samuel, mr. David D. Cohen, 1870. Rf: SFF35, 260

Cohen, Grace (Seixas). b. 1794, d. 1866, f. Benjamin Mendes Seixas, m. Zipporah Levy Seixas, mr. Jacob I. Cohen, 1815. Rf: SFF38, 266

Cohen, Grune (Jacobi). b. 1790, d. 1876, SC: 1851, mr. George Nathan [Gabriel] Cohen. Rf: JF1

Cohen, Gustavus. b. 1843, SC: 1843, f. Nathan A. Cohen, m. Clara Harris Cohen. Rf: SFF38; 1850C

Cohen, H. C. SC: 1842, mr. Flora Cohen. Rf: EC18; E167; MS15.248 (1842)

Cohen, Hannah. b. 1816, SC: 1850. Rf: DR; W49.609; 1850C; 1860C; D1852, 1855, 1859

Cohen, Hannah. b. 1840, SC: 1860. Rf: 1860C

Cohen, Harby H. b. 1810, SC: 1810. Rf: 1850C; D1852

Cohen, Hartwig. b. 1784, d. 1861, SC: 1815, f. Fishel Cohen, m. Sarah Cohen, mr. Deborah Marks Cohen, 1824. Rf: EC28; E133, 167, 292; SFF34, 185; 1850C; D1831, 1841, 1855, 1859

Cohen, Henrietta Yates (Levy). b. 1818, SC: 1837, f. Jacob Clarisse [Clavius] Levy, m. Fanny Yates Levy, mr. Octavus Cohen, 1837. Rf: SFF35, 169; Yates, Samuel and Lazarus; MS13.365

Cohen, Henry. SC: 1800. Rf: E133, 237

Cohen, Henry. b. 1854, SC: 1854, f. Jacob I. Cohen, m. Cornelia Ann Jacob Cohen. Rf: SFF39

Cohen, Henry B. b. 1841, SC: 1841, f. Nathan A. Cohen, m. Clara Harris Cohen. Rf: 1850C; SFF38

Cohen, Henry S. b. 1817, d. 1855, SC: 1835, f. Aaron Nathan Cohen, m. Rachel Cohen, mr. Caroline Harris Cohen, 1837, mr2. Esther Sampson Cohen, 1843. Rf: SFF38, 94, 259; EM17; EC47; EJCC4; MS15.362; D1835, 1841

Cohen, Herbert. b. 1846, d. 1847, SC: 1847, f. Marx Edwin Cohen, m. Armida Harby Cohen. Rf: EC32; SFF35, 93

Cohen, Hortense (Solomons). b. 1855, SC: 1860, f. Solomon Sampson Solomons, m. Esther Nathans Solomons. Rf: 1860C; SFF277

Cohen, Hyam. b. 1788, d. 1850, SC: 1788, f. Gershon Cohen, m. Rebecca Sarzedas Cohen, mr. Esther Moses Moïse Cohen, 1827. Rf: E133; EC57; SFF38, 196, 205, 1830C; 1850C; T33; D1829, 1831, 1835, 1838, 1841; RB23

Cohen, Hyam. b. 1843, d. 1850, SC: 1843, f. Philip Melvin Cohen, m. Cordelia Moïse Cohen. Rf: SFF39; 1860C

Cohen, Isaac. d. 1787, SC: 1784, f. Moses Cohen, m. Dinah Comgile Cohen, mr. Judith Cohen Lyon. Rf: SFF35; W22.115 (his); RB23

Cohen, Isaac. SC: 1794. Rf: D1794

Cohen, Isaac. b. 1793, d. 1871, SC: 1793, f. Moses Cohen, m. Rachel Moses Cohen, mr. Rebecca Benjamin Sheftall Cohen, 1816. Rf: SFF36, 212, 267; *OJCS*40

Cohen, Isaac A. b. 1798, d. 1819, SC: 1798. Rf: EC29; SP, Oct. 7, 1819

Cohen, Isaac Barrett. b. 1840, d. 1865,

SC: 1840, f. Jacob Cohen, m. Sarah Barrett Cohen, mr. Pauline Barrett Cohen. Rf: SFF17, 36; EC81; E225; 1850C; D1859

Cohen, Isaac S. b. 1801, d. 1865, SC: 1822, f. Solomon I. Cohen, m. Eleanor S. Cohen, mr. Virginia J. Davis Cohen, 1840. Rf: SFF36; EM19; E167, 238; EC38; T33; TBS40; 1850C; D1849, 1855, 1859

Cohen, Isabelle. b. 1849, SC: 1850, f. Isaac S. Cohen, m. Virginia J. Davis Cohen. Rf: SFF36; 1850C

Cohen, J. Hays. SC: 1838. Rf: D1838, 1852

Cohen, J. S. SC: 1837. Rf: E167; D1855

Cohen, Jacob. b. 1796, d. 1871, SC: 1796, f. Solomon Cohen, mr. Rachel Lopez Cohen, 1816, mr2. Sarah Barrett Cohen. Rf: SFF17, 35, 176; EC81; DR; E134, 144, 167; 1820C: 1830C; 1840C; 1850C; 1860C; 1861C; D1838, 1841

Cohen, Jacob. SC: 1818, f. Jacob Cohen, m. Rachel Lopez Cohen, mr. Rebecca Phillips Cohen, 1836, mr2. Phila Moïse Cohen, 1841. Rf: EM16; EM19; E207; SFF36, 176, 195; D1838, 1841, 1849, 1852

Cohen, Jacob. d. 1885, f. Joseph Cohen, m. Sarah Barrett Cohen. Rf: SFF36

Cohen, Jacob A. d. 1800, SC: 1796. Rf: W28.7 (his); MR3R.207; D1796; RB23, 24

Cohen, Jacob Barrett. b. 1835, d. 1885, SC: 1835, f. Jacob Cohen, m. Sarah Barrett Cohen, mr. Marie Young Cohen, 1862. Rf: E167, 206, 225; SFF36; DR; T33; 1850C; D1855, 1859

Cohen, Jacob Cohen. b. 1738, d. 1790, SC: 1772, f. Leipman Cohen, Rf: *OJCS*71

Cohen, Jacob D. SC: 1809. Rf: E134

Cohen, Jacob H. SC: 1850, f. Nathan A. Cohen, m. Clara Harris Cohen. Rf: 1850C; SFF38, 94

Cohen, Jacob H. SC: 1855, mr. Julia Jones Cohen, 1856. Rf: EM28; E167, 239; SFF137; D1855

Cohen, Jacob I. b. 1744, d. 1823, SC: 1776, mr. Elizabeth Whitlock Cohen, 1782, mr2. Rachel Jacobs Cohen, 1807. Rf: SFF32; E84, 95; *SP*, Oct. 18, 1823; D1794

Cohen, Jacob I. b. 1784, d. 1849, SC: 1784, f. Gershon Cohen, m. Rebecca Sarzedas Cohen, mr. Grace Seixas Cohen, 1815. Rf: SFF38, 266; D1829

Cohen, Jacob J. b. 1741, d. 1808, SC: 1780, f. Moses Cohen, m. Dinah Comgile Cohen. Rf: EC62; E91; SFF35; W31.178 (his); *SCHM*33.282; *SCHM*56.45–49; D1790, 1794, 1796, 1801, 1802, 1803, 1806; RB23

Cohen, Jacob, Jr. SC: 1838. Rf: D1838

Cohen, Jeanette (Elias). b. 1846, d. 1868, SC: 1846, f. David Elias, m. Eleanor A. Cohen Elias, mr. Edward Cohen, 1867. Rf: SFF63; EJCC4

Cohen, Jessica. f. Isaac S. Cohen, m. Virginia J. Davis Cohen. Rf: SFF36

Cohen, Jessie. b. 1842, d. 1843, SC: 1843, f. Philip Melvin Cohen, m.

Cordelia Moïse Cohen. Rf: EC62; SFF39

Cohen, John J. b. 1806, d. 1884, SC: 1806, f. Philip Cohen, m. Eleanor Moses Cohen, mr. Cornelia Ann Jacobs Cohen, 1839. Rf: SFF39, 132, 205; E270; EM18; W48.95; 1850C; 1860C; D1855, 1859

Cohen, John J. b. 1849, SC: 1849, f. John Jay Cohen, m. Cornelia Ann Jacobs Cohen, mr. Julia Russell Cohen. Rf: SFF39; 1860C

Cohen, Jonas. b. 1788, d. 1826, SC: 1818. Rf: EC63; E134

Cohen, Joseph. d. 1822, SC: 1800. Rf: E134; 1810C; W30.855; CB1800; D1802, 1803, 1806, 1807, 1813

Cohen, Joseph. SC: 1850, f. Jacob Cohen, m. Sarah Barrett Cohen, mr. Sarah Barrett Cohen, 1858. Rf: T33; EC95; E167, 226; EM30; SFF17, 36; 1850C; D1859

Cohen, Joseph Joel. SC: 1853, mr. Rachel Alexander Cohen, 1853. Rf: EM26; SFF8

Cohen, Judah. SC: 1823. Rf: E134; 1850C

Cohen, Judith (Cohen). SC: 1783, f. Isaac Cohen, m. Rinah Tobias Lyon Cohen, mr. Moses Cohen, 1779. Rf: *OJCS*42

Cohen, Julia (Jones). b. 1838, SC: 1856, f. Israel Jones, m. Eliza Jones, mr. Jacob H. Cohen, 1856. Rf: SFF137; EM28

Cohen, Julius. b. 1839, SC: 1839, f. Nathan A. Cohen, m. Clara Harris Cohen. Rf: 1850C; SFF38; D1859

Cohen, L. mr. Leah Tobias Cohen. Rf: SFF298

Cohen, Laura. b. 1844, SC: 1844, f. Nathan A. Cohen, m. Clara Harris Cohen. Rf: 1850C; SFF38

Cohen, Lavinia (Cohen). f. Nathan A. Cohen, m. Clara Harris Cohen, mr. Jacob S. Cohen. Rf: SFF34, 38, 202

Cohen, Lawrence L. b. 1836, SC: 1836, f. Philip Melvin Cohen, m. Cordelia Moïse Cohen, mr. Savannah Crawford Cohen. Rf: SFF39; 1850C; 1860C; *Courier* Dec. 11, 1861; D1859

Cohen, Lawrence Ludlow. b. 1815, d. 1847, SC: 1815, f. Philip Cohen, m. Eleanor Moses Cohen, mr. Miriam Louisa DeLeon Cohen, 1840. Rf: EM19; EC62; SFF39; DR; T33; D1835, 1841

Cohen, Lawrence Ludlow. b. 1842, d. 1870, SC: 1850, f. Lawrence Ludow Cohen, m. Miriam Louisa DeLeon Cohen. Rf: E226; EC61; SFF39; 1850C

Cohen, Leah (Lazarus). b. 1778, d. 1844, SC: 1778, f. Marks Lazarus, m. Rachel Benjamin Lazarus, mr. Mordecai Cohen, 1795. Rf: SFF35, 151; EC32, 76

Cohen, Leah (Tobias) (Harby). b. 1809, SC: 1809, f. Joseph Tobias, m. Rachel Aarons Tobias, mr. Henry Jefferson Harby, mr2. L. Cohen. Rf: SFF93, 298

Cohen, Leopold. b. 1819, d. 1849, SC: 1849. Rf: DR; EC90; E167

Cohen, Leopold. SC: 1855, mr. Elizabeth Cohen Cohen, 1851. Rf: E238, 265; EM24; SFF38; D1849, 1855, 1859

Cohen, Leopold. b. 1849, SC: 1849. Rf: 1850C; 1860C

Cohen, Levi. SC: 1800, mr. Sarah

Judith Solomons Cohen. Rf: E279; SFF278

Cohen, Lewis. SC: 1818. Rf: E134; *SCHM*66.112; T33

Cohen, Lewis [Louis]. b. 1832, d. 1914, SC: 1855, f. George Nathan Cohen, m. Grune Jacobi Cohen, mr. Cecilia Bentschner Cohen, 1855. Rf: EM27; DR; T33; *SCHM*66.112–24; 1850C, 1860C; D1855, 1859

Cohen, Lily. f. Isaac S. Cohen, m. Virginia J. Davis Cohen. Rf: SFF36

Cohen, M. Isaac. b. 1858, d. 1858, SC: 1858. Rf: DR

Cohen, McDuff. b. 1840, d. 1909, SC: 1840, f. David Daniel Cohen, m. Mary Hart Cohen. Rf: DR; E168, 226, 265; SFF35, 98; T33; W48.277; W49.697

Cohen, Madison. d. 1809, SC: 1809, f. Abraham Cohen, m. Rachel Harby Cohen. Rf: SFF93; W31.294; D1809

Cohen, Malachi A. SC: 1801. Rf: MR4H.304; MR3R.259

Cohen, Manuel. b. 1834, d. 1865, SC: 1845. Rf: DR

Cohen, Margaret. SC: 1807, mr. Jacob I. Cohen. Rf: RB25; D1807

Cohen, Mariam Edith. b. 1860, d. 1863, f. Isaac S. Cohen, m. Virginia J. Davis Cohen. Rf: SFF36

Cohen, Marx Edwin. b. 1810, d. 1882, SC: 1810, f. Mordecai Cohen, m. Leah Lazarus Cohen, mr. Armida Harby Cohen, 1838. Rf: SFF35, 93; EM17; E168, 188; W44.356; D1855, 1859

Cohen, Marx Edwin. b. 1839, d. 1865, SC: 1839, f. Marx Edwin Cohen, m. Armida Harby Cohen. Rf: DR; EC30; E226; SFF35

Cohen, Mary (Hart). b. 1811, d. 1861, SC: 1830, f. Nathan Hart, m. Rachel Hart Hart, mr. David Daniel Cohen, 1830. Rf: SFF35,98; EM14; W48.277; W49.697; 1860C; *SP*, Mar. 1, 1830

Cohen, Mary Jane. b. 1834, d. 1856, SC: 1834, f. David Daniel Cohen, m. Mary Hart Cohen. Rf: DR; EC84; SFF35

Cohen, Melvin M. SC: 1855. Rf: D1855, 1859

Cohen, Melvin M. b. 1846, SC: 1850, f. Philip Melvin Cohen, m. Cordelia Moïse Cohen, mr. Virginia Elizabeth Moïse Cohen. Rf: SFF39, 195, 197; EC22; E168; EM29; 1850C

Cohen, Michael. f. David Daniel Cohen, m. Mary Hart Cohen. Rf: SFF35

Cohen, Michael. SC: 1802. Rf: D1802, 1803

Cohen, Miriam. b. 1783, SC: 1783. Rf: 1850C

Cohen, Miriam (Hart). b. 1840, SC: 1840, f. Samuel Nathan Hart, m. Isabel Lazarus Hart, mr. Asher D. Cohen, 1865. Rf: SFF35, 98

Cohen, Miriam Louise (DeLeon). b. 1822, d. 1869, SC: 1840, f. Abraham DeLeon, m. Isabella Nones DeLeon, mr. Lawrence Ludlow Cohen, 1840. Rf: SFF39, 55; EC61, 62; EM19; W48.95; 1850C

Cohen, Mordecai. b. 1763, d. 1848, SC: 1788, mr. Leah Lazarus

Cohen, 1795. Rf: DR; EC32; E134, 143, 168, 279; SFF35, 151; W44.356 (his); D1794, 1801, 1802, 1803, 1806, 1807, 1809, 1816, 1819, 1822, 1829, 1831, 1835, 1838, 1841

Cohen, Moses. b. 1709, d. 1762, SC: 1749, mr. Dinah Comgile Cohen. Rf: SFF35; EC81

Cohen, Moses. b. 1747, d. 1790, SC: 1772, f. Liepman Cohen, mr. Judith DeLyon Cohen, 1779. Rf: EP; *OJCS*42; SFF57; D1790; RB25

Cohen, Moses. b. 1768, d. 1829, SC: 1796, f. Isaac Cohen, m. Judith Cohen Lyon Cohen, mr. Rachel Moses Cohen, 1791. Rf: SFF36, 212; EM6; D1796, 1801, 1802, 1803, 1807, 1809, 1813, 1816, 1819, 1822

Cohen, Moses Sheftall. b. 1821, d. 1892, f. Isaac Cohen, m. Rebecca Sheftall Cohen, mr. Virginia Zipporah Seixas Cohen, 1847. Rf: SFF36, 266, 267

Cohen, Myer M. b. 1804, d. 1887, SC: 1824, f. Philip Cohen, m. Eleanor Moses Cohen. Rf: E142, 168, 207, 134, 189; SFF39, 205; W48.95; T33; D1829, 1831, 1835

Cohen, N. E., Jr. SC: 1859. Rf: D1859

Cohen, Nancy. b. 1817, d. 1838, SC: 1838. Rf: EP

Cohen, Nathan A. b. 1805, d. 1876, SC: 1827, f. Aaron Nathan Cohen, m. Rachel Cohen, mr. Clara Harris Cohen, 1827. Rf: SFF38, 94; EM14; E168; T33; 1850C; D1829, 1831, 1835, 1838, 1841, 1849, 1852, 1855, 1859

Cohen, Octavus. b. 1814, d. 1876, SC: 1814, f. Solomon Cohen, m. Bella Moses Cohen, mr. Henrietta Yates Levy Cohen, 1837. Rf: EM16; SFF35, 169

Cohen, Octavus. b. 1850, d. 1858, SC: 1850, f. Jacob Cohen, m. Sarah Barrett Cohen. Rf: EC95; SFF36; 1850C; 1860C

Cohen, Octavus. b. 1860, d. 1927, SC: 1860, f. Joseph Cohen, m. Sarah Barrett Cohen, mr. Rebecca Florence Ottolengui Cohen, 1889, mr2. Jennie Foster Cohen. Rf: SFF36, 234

Cohen, P. L. b. 1820, SC: 1820. Rf: 1850C

Cohen, P. Wineman. b. 1825, SC: 1825. Rf: 1850C

Cohen, Percival. f. David Lopez Cohen, m. Sarah C. Moïse Cohen. Rf: SFF36

Cohen, Phila (Moïse). b. 1818, d. 1883, SC: 1818, f. Aaron Moïse, m. Sarah Cohen Moïse, mr. Jacob Cohen, 1841. Rf: SFF195; EM19; DR

Cohen, Philip. b. 1781, d. 1866, SC: 1781, f. Gershon Cohen, m. Rebecca Sarzedas Cohen, mr. Eleanor Moses Cohen, 1799. Rf: EC61, 62; SFF38, 39, 205; EM7; 1800C; 1820C; 1830C; 1850C; SFF309; D1801, 1802, 1807, 1809, 1813, 1819, 1822, 1831, 1849, 1855, 1859

Cohen, Philip. b. 1843, SC: 1843, f. Isaac S. Cohen, m. Virginia J. Davis Cohen, mr. Harriet Lizzy Lieber Cohen, 1878. Rf: SFF36; 1850C

Cohen, Philip Jacob. d. 1790, SC:

1772, f. Liepman Cohen. Rf: EP; E91, 92, 278

Cohen, Philip Lawrence. b. 1846, SC: 1846, f. John J. Cohen, m. Cornelia Jacobs Cohen, mr. Ellen G. Wright. Rf: SFF39; E226; 1860C

Cohen, Philip Melvin. b. 1808, d. 1879, SC: 1829, f. Philip Cohen, m. Eleanor Moses Cohen, mr. Cordelia Moïse Cohen, 1832. Rf: DR; SFF39, 195; E168; EM14; EC59, 60; W48.94; 1840C; 1850C; 1860C; D1829, 1835, 1838, 1841, 1852, 1855, 1859

Cohen, Philip Percival. b. 1844, d. 1848, SC: 1844, f. Philip Melvin Cohen, m. Cordelia Moïse Cohen. Rf: DR; EC59; SFF39

Cohen, Philip S. b. 1810, d. 1837, SC: 1829, f. Solomon I. Cohen, m. Eleanor S. Cohen. Rf: SFF36; E168; D1829, 1835

Cohen, Philippa. d. 1851, SC: 1851, f. Philip Melvin Cohen, m. Cordelia S. Moïse Cohen. Rf: EC60; DR

Cohen, Priscilla. b. 1815, d. 1860, SC: 1860, f. Philip Cohen, m. Eleanor Moses Cohen. Rf: DR; EC61; SFF39; W48.95

Cohen, Priscilla. b. 1822, d. 1833, f. Jacob Cohen, m. Rachel Lopez Cohen. Rf: SFF36

Cohen, Rachel. b. 1838, f. Jacob Cohen, m. Sarah Barrett Cohen. Rf: SFF36

Cohen, Rachel. b. 1847, SC: 1847. Rf: 1850C; 1860C

Cohen, Rachel A. b. 1790, d. 1851, SC: 1851, mr. Aaron Nathan Cohen. Rf: SFF38; EJCC4

Cohen, Rachel (Alexander). b. 1817, d. 1888, SC: 1850, f. Abraham Alexander, m. Hannah Aarons Alexander, mr. Joseph Joel Cohen, 1853. Rf: SFF8; EM26; 1850C; D1838

Cohen, Rachel B. H. b. 1801, d. 1866, SC: 1801, f. Philip Cohen, m. Eleanor Moses Cohen. Rf: DR; EC61; SFF39; W48.95

Cohen, Rachel (Harby). b. 1791, d. 1812, SC: 1791, f. Solomon Harby, m. Rebecca Moses Harby, mr. Abraham Cohen. Rf: SFF93; W31.294

Cohen, Rachel (Lopez). b. 1794, d. 1833, SC: 1794, f. David Lopez, m. Priscilla Moses Lopez, mr. Jacob Cohen, 1816. Rf: SFF35, 36, 176; EM11; W32.521; LF2

Cohen, Rachel (Moses). b. 1777, d. 1848, SC: 1777, f. Abraham Moses, m. Mary Moses, mr. Moses Cohen, 1791. Rf: MR3H.417; *OJCS*42; SFF36, 212; EM6; W26.476; D1801, 1831, 1835

Cohen, Rebecca. b. 1791, SC: 1791, f. Gershon Cohen, m. Rebecca Sarzedas Cohen. Rf: SFF38; 1820C; D1819, 1822

Cohen, Rebecca. f. Solomon I. Cohen, m. Eleanor S. Cohen. Rf: SFF36

Cohen, Rebecca Benjamin (Sheftall). b. 1798, d. 1881, f. Moses Sheftall, m. Elkaleh Bush Sheftall, mr. Isaac Cohen, 1816. Rf: SFF36, 267

Cohen, Rebecca Florence (Ottolengui). b. 1856, d. 1938, SC: 1856, f. Israel Ottolengui, m. Rosalie C. Moïse Ottolengui, mr. Octavus Cohen, 1889. Rf: SFF36, 234; DR

Cohen, Rebecca (Phillips). b. 1807, d.

1840, SC: 1836, f. Zalegman Philipps, m. Arabella Philipps, mr. Jacob Cohen, Jr., 1836. Rf: EC15; EM16; SFF36, 243

Cohen, Rebecca (Sarzedas). b. 1761, d. 1840, SC: 1761, f. Abraham Sarzedas, m. Caty Hays Sarzedas, mr. Gershon Cohen, 1779. Rf: MR3G.112; SFF38, 262; EM5; E92; W45.675; D1802, 1803, 1806

Cohen, Rinah H. b. 1799, d. 1876, SC: 1850, f. Solomon Jacob Cohen, m. Eleanor S. Cohen. Rf: DR; EC38; SFF36; W45.675

Cohen, Rosa. b. 1834, d. 1837, f. Hartwig Cohen, m. Deborah Marks Cohen. Rf: SFF34

Cohen, Rosa Ellen. d. 1833, f. Jacob Cohen, m. Rachel Lopez Cohen. Rf: SFF36

Cohen, Rosa Ellen. b. 1839, d. 1847, SC: 1847, f. Jacob Cohen, m. Sarah Barrett Cohen. Rf: SFF36; EC95

Cohen, Rosa Ellen. b. 1859, d. 1867, f. Jacob Cohen, m. Sarah Barrett Cohen. Rf: EC95; SFF36

Cohen, Rosalie L. b. 1832, d. 1893, SC: 1832, f. David Daniel Cohen, m. Mary Hart Cohen. Rf: SFF35; DR; W48.277; 1860C

Cohen, Samuel. SC: 1852. Rf: D1852

Cohen, Samuel J. b. 1779, d. 1827, SC: 1804. Rf: DR; 1820C; E134, 168; 1820C; D1807, 1816, 1819, 1822

Cohen, Sanford. b. 1851, SC: 1851, f. John Jay Cohen, m. Cornelia Ann Jacobs Cohen. Rf: SFF39; 1860C

Cohen, Sarah (Barrett). b. 1809, d. 1885, SC: 1809, f. Jacob Barrett, m. Hetty J. Ottolengui Barrett, mr. Jacob Cohen, 1858. Rf: SFF17, 35, 36; EM30; EC95; DR; 1850C; 1860C

Cohen, Sarah Cohen (Moïse). f. Aaron Moïse, m. Sarah Cohen Moïse Cohen, mr. David Lopez Cohen, 1842. Rf: SFF36, 195

Cohen, Sarah Henrietta. d. 1836, f. Jacob Cohen, m. Sarah Barrett Cohen. Rf: SFF36

Cohen, Sarah Judith (Solomons). b. 1815, SC: 1815, f. Israel Solomons, m. Eleanor Joseph Solomons, mr. Levi Cohen. Rf: 1850C; SFF278

Cohen, Selina. b. 1818, SC: 1818. Rf: 1850C

Cohen, Septima. b. 1829, f. Jacob Cohen, m. Rachel Lopez Cohen. Rf: SFF36

Cohen, Solomon. b. 1757, d. 1835, SC: 1800, f. Moses Cohen, m. Dinah Comgile Cohen, mr. Bella Moses Cohen, 1785. Rf: SFF35, 205; CB1800; D1801, 1802, 1803, 1806, 1807, 1809, 1813, 1822, 1831

Cohen, Solomon. b. 1816, d. 1862, SC: 1816, f. Jacob Cohen, m. Rachel Lopez Cohen. Rf: SFF36; 1850C; D1838, 1841, 1849

Cohen, Solomon I. b. 1777, d. 1850, SC: 1777, f. Isaac Cohen, m. Judith Cohen, mr. Eleanor S. Moses Hart Cohen, 1797. Rf: EC38; EM7; SFF36; W45.675 (his); W22.115; 1800C; 1810C; T34; D1809

Cohen, Thadeus. d. 1853, SC: 1853. Rf: DR

Cohen, Theodore. b. 1837, SC: 1837,

f. Nathan A. Cohen, m. Clara Harris Cohen. Rf: 1850C

Cohen, Virginia Elizabeth (Moïse). SC: 1850, f. Isaac Moïse, m. Hetty Lopez Moïse, mr. Melvin M. Cohen, 1857. Rf: SFF39, 176, 197; EM29; 1850C

Cohen, Virginia J. (Davis). b. 1820, d. 1895, SC: 1820, f. Ansley Davis, mr. Isaac S. Cohen, 1840. Rf: DR; EC38; EM19; SFF36; 1850C

Cohen, Virginia Jacqueline. b. 1845, d. 1850, SC: 1845, f. Isaac S. Cohen, m. Virginia J. Davis Cohen. Rf: EC38; SFF36; DR; 1850C

Cohen, Virginia Seixas. b. 1849, d. 1933, SC: 1849, f. Moses Sheftall Cohen, m. Virginia Zipporah Seixas Cohen. Rf: SFF36

Cohen, Virginia Zipporah (Seixas). b. 1824, d. 1889, SC: 1824, f. Abraham Seixas, m. Rachel Nunes Carodozo Seixas, mr. Moses Sheftall Cohen, 1847. Rf: SFF36, 266

Cohen, William Bentschner. b. 1860, d. 1934, f. Louis Cohen, m. Cecilie Bentschner Cohen, mr. Sarah Jacobi Cohen, 1886. Rf: JF2

Cohen, Wolf. SC: 1803. Rf: E134; CB1809

Cohen, Zalegman. b. 1840, d. 1841, f. Jacob Cohen, Jr., m. Rebecca Phillips Cohen. Rf: SFF36

Cohen, Zipporah. d. 1838, f. Aaron Nathan Cohen, m. Rachel Cohen. Rf: SFF38

Cohn, Bertha (Pecare). SC: 1842, mr. Jacob Cohn, 1842. Rf: EM20

Cohn, Jacob. SC: 1842, mr. Bertha Pecare Cohn, 1842. Rf: EM20

Cohn, Sophia M. b. 1831, d. 1856, SC: 1855. Rf: DR

Coleman, Sylvester. SC: 1805. Rf: T34; CB1805

Collis, Sarah (Hyams). SC: 1850, f. David Hyams, m. Rebecca Hyams, mr. ——— Collis. Rf: SFF120; 1850C; W51.842

Collis, Septima Maria (Levy). b. 1834, d. 1912, f. David Cardoza Levy, m. Anna Maria Moses Levy, mr. Charles T. H. Collis. Rf: SFF164

Corre, Jacob. SC: 1805. Rf: E134; T34

Cortissoz, Emanuel. SC: 1762. Rf: *SCHM*65.205–17; E43, 278

Culp, Emma Eger (Hertz). b. 1853, SC: 1853, f. Isaac Eger Hertz, m. Nellie Sheftall Cohen Hertz, mr. J. B. Culp. Rf: 1860C; SFF117

DaCosta, Aaron. SC: 1802, f. Isaac DaCosta, Jr. Rf: SFF44; E134, 279; W21.774

DaCosta, Abraham. d. 1786, SC: 1749, f. Joseph DaCosta, m. Sarah Cohen DaCosta, mr. Rebecca Morales Pimienta DaCosta, 1765. Rf: SFF44; E32, 37, 103, 278; *OJCS*72; *SCHM*53.13; W11.301; *SCM*56; MR2M.222

DaCosta, Charles A. d. 1852, SC: 1841. Rf: W46.149

DaCosta, Isaac. b. 1721, d. 1783, SC: 1749, f. Joseph DaCosta, m. Sarah DaCosta, mr. Sarah Pimienta DaCosta. Rf: SFF44; *SCHM*65.205; *SCHM*74.207; *SCHM*34.83

DaCosta, Isaac. b. 1746, d. 1809, SC: 1769, f. Abraham DaCosta, m. Rebecca Pimienta DaCosta. Rf: SFF44; EC106; E91; 1790C;

*SCHM*45.45; T34; D1794, 1796, 1802, 1809

DaCosta, Isaac. d. 1830, SC: 1790, f. Joseph DaCosta, m. Rebecca DePass DaCosta, mr. Jane Samuel DaCosta, 1807. Rf: SFF44; EM9; *SP*, June 19, 1830; D1790, 1796, 1801

DaCosta, Jane (Samuel). b. 1788, d. 1861, f. Hyman Samuel, m. Rebecca Samuel, mr. Isaac DaCosta, 1807. Rf: SFF44; EM9

DaCosta, Joseph. b. 1759, d. 1809, SC: 1759, f. Isaac DaCosta, m. Sarah Pimienta DaCosta, mr. Rebecca DePass DaCosta, 1786. Rf: SFF44; *SCHM*53.13; W24.89; W22.94; E37, 116, 278; *SCM*56; MS1.272; D1794, 1801, 1802, 1803, 1806, 1807

DaCosta, Moses. f. Isaac DaCosta. Rf: SFF44

DaCosta, Naomi. SC: 1749, mr. Abraham DaCosta. Rf: MR3C.346

DaCosta, Rebecca. f. Isaac DaCosta. Rf: SFF44

DaCosta, Rebecca (DePass). SC: 1786, f. Raphael DePass, mr. Joseph DaCosta, 1786. Rf: SFF44, 58; EM6

DaCosta, Rebecca Morales (Pimienta). SC: 1766, f. Moses Pimienta, m. Leah Morales Pimienta, mr. Abraham DaCosta. Rf: SFF44; *OJCS*72; W21.774; W11.301; E32, 38; MR2M.227

DaCosta, Rebecca Salvador Mendes. d. 1781, SC: 1786, f. Francis Salvador, m. Rachel Mendes DaCosta, mr. Moses de Jacob Mendes DaCosta, 1742. Rf: W29.666 (hers)

DaCosta, Samuel. b. 1762, d. 1794, SC: 1790, f. Isaac DaCosta, m. Sarah Pimienta DaCosta, mr. Esther DePass DaCosta, 1792. Rf: E37, 106, 278; SFF44; *OJCS*74; 1790C; D1790; RB28, 29

DaCosta, Sarah (Pimienta). d. 1793, SC: 1790, f. Moses Pimienta, m. Leah Morales Pimienta, mr. Isaac DaCosta. Rf: E37, 39, 117; SFF44; W25.89 (hers); W11.301; 1790C; D1790

Daniels, Henry. SC: 1818. Rf: E134

D'Aquilar, Rebecca Gomez. SC: 1796. Rf: MR3P.379; SCA1799–1801; D1796

D'Aquilar, Sarah. SC: 1796. Rf: SCA1796–1801

DaVega, Abraham. SC: 1829. Rf: D1829

DaVega, Abraham. b. 1823, SC: 1823, f. Isaac DaVega, m. Grace Labatt DaVega, mr. Eliza J. McClure DaVega, 1857. Rf: SFF45; SCA1829–38

DaVega, Amanda. b. 1831, d. 1838, SC: 1831, f. Isaac DaVega, m. Grace Labatt DaVega. Rf: SFF45; EC11

DaVega, Benjamin Franklin. b. 1819, f. Isaac DaVega, m. Grace Labatt DaVega. Rf: SFF45

DaVega, Celina. b. 1835, SC: 1835. Rf: 1860C

DaVega, Columbus. b. 1830, d. 1882, SC: 1830, f. Isaac DaVega, m. Grace Labatt DaVega. Rf: DR; EC48; E168, 206, 226; SFF45; 1860C; D1852, 1859

DaVega, David. b. 1818, d. 1822, SC: 1818, f. Isaac DaVega, m. Grace Labatt DaVega. Rf: EC30; SFF45

DaVega, Grace (Labatt). b. 1799, d. 1872, SC: 1799, f. David Labatt, m. Catherine Labatt, mr. Isaac DaVega, 1815. Rf: SFF45, 148; DR; EC49; 1860C; D1838, 1852, 1859

DaVega, Isaac. b. 1796, d. 1835, SC: 1815, f. Moses DaVega, m. Sol DaVega, mr. Grace Labatt DaVega, 1815. Rf: SFF45, 148; EM11; T34; 1820C; D1816, 1819, 1822, 1831, 1835, 1859

DaVega, Isaac. b. 1825, SC: 1849, f. Isaac DaVega, m. Grace Labatt DaVega, mr. Sarah J. Moses DaVega, 1857. Rf: EM29; E134, 168, 205; T34; D1849, 1852, 1855

DaVega, Moses. d. 1833, SC: 1788, mr. Sarah [Sol] DaVega. Rf: EC64; SFF45; 1820C; MR3H.361; D1801, 1802, 1803, 1806, 1807, 1809, 1819, 1831; RB31

DaVega, Moses. b. 1816, d. 1838, SC: 1835, f. Isaac DaVega, m. Grace Labatt DaVega. Rf: EC11; SFF45; D1835, 1838

DaVega, Sarah J. (Moses). SC: 1857, mr. ——— Moses, mr2. Isaac DaVega, 1857. Rf: EM29; SFF45

DaVega, Sarah [Sol]. b. 1771, d. 1828, SC: 1758, mr. Moses DaVega. Rf: EC28; SFF45

David, ———. b. 1861, d. 1861, SC: 1861. Rf: DR

David, Abraham. b. 1859, d. 1860, SC: 1859, f. Joseph David, m. Matilda David. Rf: DR; 1860C

David, Berrin. b. 1852, SC: 1860, f. Joseph David, m. Matilda David. Rf: 1860C

David, Dinah Comgile (Cohen). SC: 1763, mr. Moses Cohen, mr2. Joseph David, 1763. Rf: SFF35; RB31

David, Jacob. SC: 1807. Rf: 1810C; E134; D1807, 1809, 1813, 1819

David, Jacob. b. 1854, SC: 1860, f. Joseph David, m. Matilda David. Rf: 1860C

David, Joseph. SC: 1763, mr. Dinah Comgile Cohen David, 1763. Rf: SFF35; E45; RB31

David, Joseph. b. 1820, SC: 1860, mr. Matilda David. Rf: 1860C; *Courier* Dec. 11, 1861

David, Leonie. b. 1848, d. 1858, SC: 1858. Rf: EC45

David, Mary Ann. b. 1840, SC: 1860, f. Joseph David, m. Matilda David. Rf: 1860C

David, Matilda. b. 1820, SC: 1860, mr. Joseph David. Rf: 1860C

David, R. L. b. 1821, d. 1877, SC: 1861. Rf: DR; EC71; E168, 238; T34

David, Woolf. b. 1846, SC: 1860, f. Joseph David, m. Matilda David. Rf: 1860C

Davids, Benjamin. d. 1831, SC: 1831. Rf: W39.903 (his)

Davis, ———. b. 1809, d. 1849, SC: 1849. Rf: DR

Davis, Anna (Abrahams). SC: 1844, f. Elias Abrahams, m. Catherine Cohen Abrahams, mr. Solomon Davis, 1844. Rf: SFF4, 49; EM21

Davis, Anna Lucretia (Buckheister). SC: 1847, mr. David Davis, 1848. Rf: EM23; Min. May 2, June 9, 1847

Davis, Ansley S. b. 1848, d. 1906, f.

Solomon Davis, m. Anna Abrahams Davis, mr. Armida Moses. Rf: SFF49, 207; MJCS13

Davis, Armida (Moses). b. 1850, d. 1902, f. Andrew Jackson Moses, m. Octavia Harby Moses, mr. Ansley S. Davis. Rf: SFF49, 207; MJSC13

Davis, Benjamin. d. 1837, SC: 1837. Rf: DR; W39.903 (his)

Davis, Charles L. f. Solomon Davis, m. Anna Abrahams Davis, mr. Julia Minzheimer Davis. Rf: SFF49

Davis, D. b. 1849, d. 1853, SC: 1853. Rf: DR

Davis, David. SC: 1805. Rf: E134

Davis, David M. SC: 1848, mr. Anna Lucretia Buckheister Davis, 1848. Rf: EM23; E168; 1850C

Davis, Dinah (Joel). SC: 1854, f. David Joel, m. Catharine Joel, mr. Henry Davis, 1854. Rf: EM27

Davis, George. SC: 1818. Rf: E134; MR5T.249,359

Davis, Hannah (Levy) (Hart) (DeLieben). b. 1761, d. 1850, SC: 1809, f. Mordecai Levy, m. Mary Levy, mr. Hymon Levy (d. 1791), mr2. Israel DeLieben (d. 1807), 1792, mr3. Moses Davis, 1813. Rf: MR3S.52, MR4Y.162; DR; EC97; EM10; SFF98; 1810C; W48.476 (hers); D1809; RB116

Davis, Henry. SC: 1824, mr. Miriam Davis. Rf: W45.682; MR4X.178, 220, 424; MR5A.118, 380

Davis, Henry. SC: 1830, mr. Dinah Joel Davis, 1854. Rf: EM27; 1830C; 1840C; 1850C

Davis, Hyman. SC: 1822. Rf: W42.366; W35.759

Davis, Israel. SC: 1800. Rf: E134, 288; 1800C; 1810C; T34; D1801, 1802, 1803, 1806, 1807, 1809

Davis, Joseph. SC: 1850. Rf: E168; 1850C; MR5B.483

Davis, Miriam. SC: 1824, mr. Henry Davis. Rf: MR4W.424; W45.682

Davis, Mordecai. b. 1829, SC: 1850. Rf: BS-BI; 1850C

Davis, Mordecai. b. 1830, d. 1830, SC: 1830. Rf: EP

Davis, Moses. b. 1759, d. 1843, SC: 1809, mr. Hannah Hart DeLieben Davis, 1813. Rf: EC97; E134, 168; EM10; SFF98; T34; CB1809

Davis, Rebecca. b. 1858, d. 1858, SC: 1858. Rf: DR

Davis, Sarah. b. 1823, d. 1824, SC: 1823. Rf: DR

Davis, Solomon. b. 1818, d. 1876, SC: 1844, mr. Anna Abrahams Davis, 1844. Rf: SFF49; EM21

Davis, Solomon. SC: 1846, f. Solomon Davis, m. Anna Abrahams Davis, mr. Florence Solomons Davis. Rf: SFF49; W45.682; D1849

D'Azevedo, Benjamin. b. 1764, d. 1828, SC: 1805, f. Moses Cohen D'Azevedo, m. Sarah Farro D'Azevedo, mr. Judith de Abraham de Paz D'Azevedo, 1789. Rf: SFF51; E133, 291; D1816

D'Azevedo, Isaac Cohen. b. 1759, d. 1805, SC: 1794, f. Moses Cohen D'Azevedo, m. Sarah Farro D'Azevedo, mr. Rachel de Abraham Salom, 1784. Rf: E154; EC82; SFF51; T34; 1800C; D1794, 1796, 1801, 1802, 1803

D'Azevedo, Judith de Abraham de Paz. mr. Benjamin D'Azevedo, 1789. Rf: SFF51

D'Azevedo, Rachel de Abraham Salom (Woolf). b. 1768, d. 1843, SC: 1806, f. Jacob Woolf, m. Sarah Woolf, mr. Isaac Cohen D'Azevedo, 1784. Rf: SFF51, 305; 1810C; W43.556 (hers); W30.855; W38.545; D1806, 1807, 1809, 1813, 1829, 1838

DeHaan, Isaac. b. 1843, d. 1843, SC: 1843, f. S. L. DeHaan. Rf: EP

DeHaan, Samuel L. SC: 1838. Rf: Min. Sept. 23, 1838; W42.366; EM20; E168

DeLaMotta, Charlotte. b. 1809, d. 1833, SC: 1809, f. Emanuel DeLaMotta, m. Judith Canter DeLaMotta. Rf: SFF54

DeLaMotta, Charlotte (Lazarus). b. 1804, d. 1894, SC: 1804, f. Marks Lazarus, m. Rachel Benjamin Lazarus, mr. Jacob Canter DeLaMotta, 1835. Rf: DR; EC56; EM15; SFF54, 151

DeLaMotta, Emanuel. b. 1760, d. 1821, SC: 1800, f. Isaac DeLaMotta, m. Sarah DeLaMotta, mr. Judith Canter DeLaMotta, 1787. Rf: DR; EC55; E134; SFF54; 1810C; T34; SP, May 17, 19, 1821 (eulogy); D1801, 1802, 1803, 1806, 1807, 1809, 1813, 1819; RB16

DeLaMotta, Emanuel. b. 1803, d. 1838, SC: 1830, f. Emanuel DeLaMotta, m. Judith Canter DeLaMotta. Rf: SFF54; 1830C

DeLaMotta, Isaac. b. 1726, d. 1794, SC: 1801, mr. Sarah DeLaMotta. Rf: SFF54; T34

DeLaMotta, Isaac. b. 1750, d. 1802, f. Isaac DeLaMotta, m. Sarah DeLaMotta, mr. Sarah Canter DeLaMotta, 1796. Rf: SFF54; EC56; E279; RB123

DeLaMotta, Jacob. b. 1801, d. 1856, SC: 1801, f. Isaac DeLaMotta, m. Sarah Canter DeLaMotta. Rf: SFF54; D1829, 1831, 1835

DeLaMotta, Jacob Canter. b. 1789, d. 1845, SC: 1807, f. Emanuel DeLaMotta, m. Judith Canter DeLaMotta, mr. Charlotte Lazarus DeLaMotta, 1835. Rf: SFF54; E141, 144, 168, 172, 179–81, 190, 206; EC56; EM15; T34; D1841

DeLaMotta, Jacob Emanuel. b. 1836, f. Jacob Canter DeLaMotta, m. Charlotte Lazarus DeLaMotta, mr. ——— Hoffman. Rf: SFF54

DeLaMotta, Judith (Canter). b. 1771, d. 1827, SC: 1771, f. Jacob Canter, m. Rebecca DeLaMotta Canter, mr. Emanuel DeLaMotta, 1787. Rf: DR; EC55; SFF28, 54; *SP*, Sept. 1, 1827 (eulogy); D1822

DeLaMotta, Julia. d. 1839, SC: 1839, f. Jacob Canter DeLaMotta, m. Charlotte Lazarus DeLaMotta. Rf: DR; EC56; SFF54

DeLaMotta, Juliet. f. Jacob Canter DeLaMotta, m. Charlotte Lazarus DeLaMotta. Rf: SFF54

DeLaMotta, Moses. b. 1755, d. 1800, f. Isaac DeLaMotta, m. Sarah DeLaMotta. Rf: SFF54

DeLaMotta, Rachel. b. 1815, d. 1874, SC: 1815, f. Emanuel DeLaMotta, m. Judith Canter DeLaMotta. Rf: DR; SFF54

DeLaMotta, Sarah. b. 1728, d. 1790, SC: 1775, mr. Isaac DeLaMotta. Rf: SFF54; MR2W.5

DeLaMotta, Sarah (Canter). b. 1776, d.

1828, SC: 1796, f. Jacob Canter, m. Rebecca DeLaMotta Canter, mr. Isaac DeLaMotta, 1796. Rf: SFF28, 54; *OJCS*45; D1816; RB17

DeLange, Jonas Lucas. b. 1826, d. 1852, SC: 1826. Rf: DR; EC22; E168; D1849, 52

DeLange, Judah. b. 1835, SC: 1835, f. Lucas DeLange, m. Martha DeLange. Rf: 1850C

DeLange, L. S. Rf: E168

DeLange, Leo H. b. 1822, SC: 1822, f. Lucas DeLange, m. Martha DeLange. Rf: SFF53; 1850C; D1841

DeLange, Lucas. b. 1792, d. 1828, SC: 1829, mr. Martha DeLange. Rf: DR; EC64; SFF53; D1829

DeLange, Martha. b. 1800, SC: 1800, mr. Lucas DeLange. Rf: SFF53; 1850C; DB1848; D1831, 1841

DeLange, Rinah M. b. 1765, d. 1835, SC: 1835. Rf: DR

DeLange, Simon J. b. 1832, d. 1857, SC: 1832, f. Lucas DeLange, m. Martha DeLange. Rf: SFF53; E168; 1850C

DeLeon, Abraham. d. 1761, mr. Esther Nunez DeLeon, 1732. Rf: SFF57

DeLeon, Abraham. b. 1790, d. 1847, SC: 1809, f. Jacob DeLyon, m. Hannah Hendricks DeLyon, mr. Isabella (Bilha) Nones DeLeon, 1815. Rf: DR; EC23; E96, 144, 194, 206, 245; SFF55; D1813

DeLeon, Adelaide. b. 1805, d. 1839, SC: 1805, f. Jacob DeLeon, m. Hannah Hendricks DeLeon. Rf: SFF55; MR5G.176; MR4Y.147; EJCC1

DeLeon, Alberg (Abram). b. 1857, d. 1940, SC: 1857, f. Harmon Hendricks DeLeon, m. Caroline Agnes Moïse DeLeon, mr. Amanda Moïse DeLeon, 1881. Rf: SFF55

DeLeon, Almeria. b. 1836, d. 1882, SC: 1836, f. Abraham DeLeon, m. Isabella Moïse Abraham. Rf: 1860C; SFF55

DeLeon, Amanda (Moïse). b. 1858, d. 1899, SC: 1858, f. Benjamin Franklin Moïse, m. Amanda Isabel Jacobs Moïse, mr. Albert DeLeon, 1881. Rf: DR; SFF55, 196

DeLeon, Anna (Moses). d. 1915, f. Oliver Hazard Perry Moses, m. Anna DeLeon Moses. Rf: SFF207

DeLeon, Benjamin. b. 1854, d. 1910, SC: 1854, f. Harmon Hendricks DeLeon, m. Caroline Agnes Moïse DeLeon, mr. Elinor (Nell) Jones DeLeon. Rf: SFF55; 1860C

DeLeon, Benjamin Nones. b. 1823, d. 1853, SC: 1823, f. Abraham DeLeon, m. Isabella Nones DeLeon. Rf: EC23; SFF55

DeLeon, Caroline Agnes (Moïse). b. 1828, d. 1889, SC: 1828, f. Abraham Moïse, m. Caroline Agnes Moses Moïse, mr. Harmon Hendricks DeLeon, 1851. Rf: DR; EC23; SFF55, 196; 1850C; 1860C

DeLeon, Charles Moses. b. 1854, d. 1876, SC: 1854. Rf: DR; EC23

DeLeon, Edwin. b. 1816, d. 1891, f. Mordecai Hendricks DeLeon, m. Rebecca Lopez DeLeon, mr. Ellen Mary Nowlan DeLeon, 1858. Rf: LF7

DeLeon, Hannah (Hendricks). b. 1767, d. 1839, SC: 1839, f. Uriah Hendricks, m. Eve Esther Gomez

Hendricks, mr. Jacob DeLeon, 1789. Rf: EJCC11; SFF55, 110
DeLeon, Harmon. b. 1860, d. 1928, SC: 1860, f. Harmon Hendricks DeLeon, m. Caroline Agnes Moïse DeLeon. Rf: MJSC19; SFF55
DeLeon, Harmon Hendricks. b. 1829, d. 1901, SC: 1829, f. Abraham DeLeon, m. Isabella Nones Abraham DeLeon, mr. Caroline Agnes Moïse DeLeon, 1851. Rf: DR; SFF55, 56; EC22, 23; EM25; E168; 1860C; D1855, 1859
DeLeon, Henrietta. f. Jacob DeLeon, m. Hannah Hendricks DeLeon. Rf: SFF55
DeLeon, Hettie. b. 1833, d. 1891, SC: 1833, f. Abraham DeLeon, m. Isabella Moïse Abraham. Rf: 1860C; SFF55
DeLeon, Isaac. b. 1738, SC: 1775, f. Abraham DeLeon. Rf: SFF55
DeLeon, Isabel Nones. b. 1828, d. 1896, SC: 1828, f. Abraham DeLeon, m. Isabella Moïse Abraham. Rf: 1860C; SFF55; D1841
DeLeon, Isabella (Bilha) (Moïse). b. 1792, d. 1871, SC: 1860, f. Abraham Moïse, mr. Abraham DeLeon, 1815. Rf: DR; SFF55; 1860C
DeLeon, Israel. SC: 1796. Rf: D1796
DeLeon, Jacob. b. 1764, d. 1828, SC: 1796, f. Abraham DeLeon, mr. Hannah Hendricks DeLeon, 1789. Rf: SFF55; SCA1799–1825; T34; E84, 86, 95–96, 134, 277–79; D1796, 1801, 1802, 1803, 1806, 1807, 1813, 1822
DeLeon, Jacob, Jr. SC: 1796. Rf: D1796
DeLeon, Louisa. b. 1795, d. 1872, SC: 1813, f. Jacob DeLeon, m. Hannah Hendricks DeLeon. Rf: SFF55; MR4C.847, 4Y.146, 147
DeLeon, Mary. b. 1838, SC: 1838, f. Abraham DeLeon, m. Isabella Moïse DeLeon. Rf: 1860C; SFF55
DeLeon, Moïse. b. 1860, d. 1866, SC: 1860. Rf: DR
DeLeon, Mordecai Hendricks. b. 1791, d. 1848, SC: 1809, f. Jacob DeLeon, m. Hannah Hendricks DeLeon, mr. Rebecca Lopez DeLeon. Rf: DR; SFF55; EP; EJCC11; T34; D1813, 1822
DeLeon, Moses. SC: 1821. Rf: CB1821
DeLeon, Perry (Moses). b. 1841, d. 1922, SC: 1841, f. Oliver Hazard Perry Moses, m. Anna DeLeon Moses. Rf: SFF207; E227
DeLeon, Rebecca. b. 1801, d. 1851, SC: 1823, f. Jacob DeLeon, m. Hannah Hendricks DeLeon. Rf: SFF55; MR5A.3, 4W.421
DeLeon, Rebecca (Lopez). b. 1794, d. 1868, SC: 1794, f. David Lopez, m. Priscilla Moses Lopez, mr. Mordecai Hendricks DeLeon. Rf: SFF55, 176; W44.416
DeLeon, Uriah. b. 1806, d. 1883, SC: 1821, f. Jacob DeLeon, m. Hannah Hendricks DeLeon. Rf: SFF55; MR4V.180
DeLieben, Israel. b. 1748, d. 1807, SC: 1790, mr. Hannah Levy Hart DeLieben Davis, 1792. Rf: SFF98; W24.946; SCA1790–1807; D1801, 1802, 1803, 1806; RB32
DeLong, Abraham. SC: 1839. Rf: Min. April 14, 1839
DeLong, Leo. SC: 1839. Rf: Min. Aprll 14, 1839; E168

DeLong, Martha. SC: 1829, f. Leo H. DeLong. Rf: W38.545

DeLyon, Abraham. b. 1733. Rf: RB102; SFF57

DeLyon, Abraham I. d. 1835, SC: 1766, f. Isaac DeLyon, m. Rinah Tobias DeLyon, mr. Sarah Sheftall DeLyon, 1785, mr2. Hannah Sheftall DeLyon. Rf: SFF57; SCA1767–1809; MS1.224; RB102

DeLyon, Hannah. f. Isaac DeLyon, m. Rinah Tobias DeLyon. Rf: SFF57

DeLyon, Hannah (Sheftall). b. 1773, d. 1843, f. Levi Sheftall, m. Sarah DeLaMotta Sheftall, mr. Abraham DeLyon, 1827. Rf: SFF57, 267

DeLyon, Isaac. b. 1739, SC: 1762, f. Abraham DeLyon, m. Esther Nunes DeLyon, mr. Reinah Tobias DeLyon, 1762. Rf: "House Journal, 1783–84," p. 54; E44, 103, 134, 278; SFF57; T34; D1790, 1794; RB102

DeLyon, Isaac. b. 1786, d. 1856, f. Abraham DeLyon, m. Sarah Sheftall DeLyon. Rf: SFF57

DeLyon, Leonora (DeLaMotta). b. 1800, d. 1819, SC: 1800, f. Isaac DeLaMotta, m. Sarah Canter DeLaMotta, mr. Levi Sheftall DeLyon, 1818. Rf: SFF57; EM11; *OJCS*45; RB124

DeLyon, Levi Sheftall. b. 1791, d. 1863, SC: 1819, f. Abraham I. DeLyon, m. Sarah Sheftall DeLyon, mr. Leonora DeLaMotta DeLyon, 1818, mr2. Rebecca DeLaMotta DeLyon, 1820. Rf: SFF54, 57; *SP*, Aug. 24, 1820; CB1819

DeLyon, Rebecca (DeLaMotta). b. 1798, d. 1829, SC: 1798, f. Isaac DeLaMotta, m. Sarah Canter DeLaMotta, mr. Levi Sheftall DeLyon, 1820. Rf: SFF57; *SP*, Aug. 24, 1820, Feb. 18, 1829; RB124

DeLyon, Reinah (Tobias). b. 1741, SC: 1766, f. Joseph Tobias, m. Leah D'Oliveira Tobias, mr. Isaac DeLyon, 1762. Rf: SFF57, 298

DeLyon, Sarah. f. Abraham I. DeLyon, m. Sarah Sheftall DeLyon, mr. 1806. Rf: SFF57

DeLyon, Sarah (Sheftall). b. 1769, d. 1825, f. Levi Sheftall, m. Sarah DeLaMotta Sheftall, mr. Abraham DeLyon, 1785. Rf: SFF56, 267

DeMattos, Moses. SC: 1739. Rf: E27, 277; EL; MR2E.110

DePalacios, Joseph. SC: 1781, mr. Penina Harris DePalacios, 1785. Rf: E91, 278; EM5; W21.774; EP; MR2V.208; *SCM*63; RB138

DePalacios, Penina (Harris). d. 1785, SC: 1785, mr. Nathan Harris, mr2. Joseph DePalacios, 1785. Rf: EM5; *SCM*63; MR2V.208

DePass, Abraham. SC: 1784, f. Jacob DePass, m. Ribca de Samuel Torres DePass, mar. Rachel DeLaMotta DePass, 1784, mr2. Rachel Derkheim DePass, 1798. Rf: SFF54, 58; EM7; E134, D1802

DePass, Hannah (Hart). SC: 1813, mr. Joseph DePass, 1813. Rf: SFF58; EM10

DePass, Isaac [also DePaz]. SC: 1738. Rf: E27, 277; SFF58; *SCHM*65.205; *SCHM*74.207; RB138

DePass, Jacob Samuel. b. 1798, d.

1869, SC: 1820, f. Samuel DePass, m. Maria Rodrigues DePass, mr. Eliza Perriman DePass, mr2. Harriet Porter DePass. Rf: SFF58; 1820C

DePass, Joseph. b. 1786, SC: 1808, f. Ralph DePass, m. Leah DePass, mr. Hannah Hart DePass, 1813. Rf: SFF58; SCA1799–1813; D1813

DePass, Leah. d. 1796, SC: 1796, mr. Ralph Depass, 1796. Rf: SFF58; MR3F.440; D1796

DePass, Rachel (DeLaMotta). b. 1768, d. 1786, SC: 1784, f. Isaac DeLaMotta, m. Sarah DeLaMotta, mr. Abraham DePass, 1784. Rf: SFF54

DePass, Rachel (Derkheim). SC: 1798, f. Myer Derkheim, m. Sarah Derkheim, mr. Abraham DePass, 1798. Rf: SFF58, 59; EM7

DePass, Ralph. b. 1740, d. 1812, SC: 1785, f. Jacob DePass, m. Ribca de Samuel Torres DePass, mr. Leah DePass, 1796, mr2. Sarah Judah DePass, 1798. Rf: SFF58; EM6; E134, 279; SCA1785–99; T34; MS3.338; *SCM*63; D1794, 1801, 1802, 1803, 1806, 1807; RB139

DePass, Sarah (Judah). b. 1760, d. 1842, SC: 1799, f. Hillel Judah, m. Abigail Seixas Judah, mr. Ralph DePass, 1798. Rf: SFF58, 140; MS3.338; *SCM*63

Derkheim, David. f. Myer Derkheim, m. Sarah Derkheim. Rf: SFF59

Derkheim, Eliezer. b. 1789, f. Myer Derkheim, m. Sarah Derkheim. Rf: SFF59

Derkheim, Eliza. f. Myer Derkheim, m. Sarah Derkheim. Rf: SFF59

Derkheim, Mayer Salomon. b. 1799, f. Myer Derkheim, m. Sarah Derkheim. Rf: SFF59

Derkheim, Mordecai [Marcus]. b. 1788, f. Myer Derkheim, m. Sarah Derkheim. Rf: SFF59

Derkheim, Moses. b. 1774, f. Myer Derkheim, m. Sarah Derkheim. Rf: SFF59

Derkheim, Myer. b. 1748, d. 1818, SC: 1800, f. Moses Derkheim, mr. Sarah Derkheim. Rf: SFF59; E279; EM7; 1800C; MR3R.300; D1801

Derkheim, Sarah. b. 1754, d. 1828, SC: 1800, mr. Myer Derkheim. Rf: SFF59; MR3R.300; RB32

DeSaussure, Louisa Alice (Moïse). b. 1844, SC: 1844, f. Abraham Moïse, m. Abigail Louisa Lopez Moïse, mr. John M. DeSaussure. Rf: SFF195

Deshon, Daniel. mr. Pauline Barrett Cohen Deshon, 1870. Rf: SFF17, 36; EM34

Deshon, Pauline (Barrett) (Cohen). f. Jacob Barrett, mr. Isaac B. Cohen, mr2. Daniel Deshon, 1870. Rf: EP; SFF17, 36; EM34

Dessau, Jacob H. SC: 1843, mr. Lavenia T. Zachariah Dessau, 1843. Rf: EM21

Dessau, Lavenia T. (Zachariah). SC: 1843, f. Jonathan Zachariah, mr. Jacob H. Dessau, 1843. Rf: EM21

Dessau, Rebecca. b. 1838, SC: 1850. Rf: 1850C

Dessauer, M. H. d. 1858, SC: 1858. Rf: DR; ENJC4

DeYoung, Moses. b. 1795, d. 1824, SC: 1819. Rf: DR; E134

Dibble, Eliza Emma (Ottolengui). b.

1852, d. 1895, SC: 1860, f. Jacob Ottolengui, m. Eliza Emma Jacobs Ottolengui, mr. Marion W. Dibble, 1876. Rf: SFF234; 1860C

Dinkins, Sarah Ann (Moïse). b. 1824, d. 1905, SC: 1859, f. Jacob Moïse, m. Rebecca Cohen Moïse, mr. Thomas W. Dinkins, 1859. Rf: SFF196; EM30

Dittenhoefer, Abram J. b. 1836, SC: 1836, f. Isaac Dittenhoefer, m. Babetta Dittenhoefer, mr. Sophie Englehart Dittenhoefer. Rf: E274; Schappes 394

Dittenhoefer, Babetta. SC: 1836, mr. Isaac Dittenhoefer. Rf: Schappes, 394

Dittenhoefer, Isaac. d. 1860, SC: 1836, mr. Babetta Dittenhoefer. Rf: E274; Schappes, 394

D'Oliveira, David Lopez. d. 1763, SC: 1749, f. Jacob Lopez D'Oliveira, m. Judica Velma d'Oliveira. Rf: SFF298; E30, 32, 278; W6.635

D'Oliveira, Isaac. d. 1734, f. Jacob Lopez d'Oliveira, m. Judica Velma d'Oliveira. Rf: SFF298

D'Oliveira, Jacob Lopez. d. 1751, SC: 1751, mr. Judica Velha d'Oliveira, 1717. Rf: SFF298; W6.635 (his); E30, 38, 278

D'Oliveira, Judica Velha. mr. Jacob Lopez d'Oliveira, 1717. Rf: SFF298

Dorres, Benjamin. SC: 1779. Rf: E278; SCA1779–90

Douglas, Sarah Ann (Tobias). b. 1833, SC: 1859, f. Isaac Tobias, m. Isabella Cowen Tobias, mr. Campbell Douglas, 1853. Rf: SFF298; W49.496

Drey, Nathan. b. 1821, d. 1848, SC: 1848. Rf: EC24

Droutman, ———. b. 1859, d. 1860, SC: 1860. Rf: DR

Droutman, Bernard. b. 1857, d. 1858, SC: 1857. Rf: DR

Droutman, T. SC: 1824. Rf: E168

Drucker, Caroline. b. 1857, d. 1858, SC: 1858, f. Levy Drucker, m. Rebecca Cohen Drucker. Rf: EJCC4; SFF38

Drucker, Levy. SC: 1853, mr. Rebecca Cohen Drucker, 1853. Rf: EM26; EC51; SFF38

Drucker, Moses. b. 1814, d. 1871. Rf: DR; T34

Drucker, Rebecca (Cohen). SC: 1853, f. Aaron Nathan Cohen, m. Rachel Cohen, mr. Levy Drucker, 1853. Rf: EM26; EC51

Dublin, Henry. b. 1821, d. 1893, SC: 1855. Rf: EBS4; E168; D1855

Dublin, Julia. b. 1851, d. 1872. Rf: EBS4

Dublin, Rebecca. b. 1821, d. 1882. Rf: DR; EBS4

Dublin, Samuel. b. 1850, d. 1864. Rf: EBS4

Dyer, Francis Polock (Ellis) (Abrahams). b. 1799, d. 1868, SC: 1821, f. Jacob Abrahams, mr. Myer J. Ellis, 1821, mr2. John M. Dyer, 1831. Rf: SFF6, 64; EM12; *SP*, Sept. 7, 1821

Eckman, Julius. SC: 1850. Rf: E168, 218, 292

Ehrlich, Fannie. b. 1828, d. 1903, mr. Morris Ehrlich. Rf: DR; EBS4

Ehrlich, Morris. d. 1874, SC: 1851, mr. Sarah Ehrlich, 1851, mr2. Fannie Ehrlich. Rf: DR; EBS4; EC89; 1861C; MS17.488

Ehrlich, Sarah. b. 1817, d. 1851, SC: 1851, mr. Morris Ehrlich, 1851. Rf: EC89; W45.682; MS17.488

Einstein, Judith (Lewis). b. 1818, d. 1883, SC: 1818, f. David Lewis, m. Rachel Lewis, mr. Lewis Einstein, 1838. Rf: SFF172, 173

Elias, Eleanor A. (Cohen). d. 1885, SC: 1845, f. Aaron Nathan Cohen, m. Rachel Cohen, mr. David Elias, 1845. Rf: SFF38, 63; EM22

Elias, Emily (Weinberg). mr. Woolf Elias, 1868. Rf: EM34

Elias, Levy. b. 1799, d. 1877, SC: 1830, mr. Rosa L. Elias. Rf: SFF63; EJCC4

Elias, Levy. b. 1808, d. 1858, SC: 1858. Rf: DR

Elias, Lewis. b. 1844, d. 1908, f. Levy Elias, m. Rosa L. Elias, mr. Rachel Loeb Elias, 1876. Rf: DR; SFF63; EC51; T34

Elias, Marian (Elias). b. 1842, d. 1913, f. Levy Elias, m. Rosa L. Elias, mr. Louis Elias. Rf: DR; EC18, 19; SFF63

Elias, Rachel (Loeb). b. 1851, d. 1894, mr. Lewis Elias. Rf: DR; EC51; SFF63

Elias, Raphael. b. 1847, d. 1907, SC: 1847, f. Levy Elias, m. Rosa L. Elias, mr. Kate I. Schriver Elias, 1883. Rf: DR; SFF63

Elias, Rosa L. b. 1819, d. 1868, mr. Levy Elias. Rf: EJCC4; SFF63

Elizer, Eleazer. b. 1761, d. 1821, SC: 1791, f. Isaac Elizer, m. Riche Isaacks Elizer. Rf: DR; SFF63; E128, 134, 141, 279; SCA1791; D1803, 1813, 1816, 1819

Elizer, Elisha. SC: 1806. Rf: E134, 142; D1807

Elizer, Eliza. SC: 1802. Rf: D1802

Elizer, Frances. b. 1774, d. 1796, f. Isaac Elizer, m. Riche Isaacks Elizer. Rf: SFF63

Elizer, Hannah. b. 1763, d. 1822, SC: 1822, f. Isaac Elizer, m. Riche Isaacks Elizer. Rf: DR; SFF63

Elizer, Isaac. d. 1807, SC: 1796, mr. Riche Isaacks Elizer, 1758. Rf: SFF63, 120; E134; SCA1797; D1796, 1803; RB34

Elizer, Moses. SC: 1780. Rf: E102, 278; Const., 1820, rule 20

Elizer, Priscilla. b. 1767, d. 1796, SC: 1796, f. Isaac Elizer, m. Riche Isaacks Elizer. Rf: SFF63; RB34

Elizer, Riche (Isaacks). b. 1733, d. 1796, SC: 1800, f. Abraham Isaacks, m. Hannah Mears Isaacks, mr. Isaac Elizer, 1758. Rf: SFF63, 120; RB68

Elkins, Louis. SC: 1805. Rf: CB1805

Ellis, Esther (Levin). SC: 1825, mr. Noah J. Ellis, 1825. Rf: EM13

Ellis, Moses J. SC: 1831. Rf: D1831

Ellis, Myer J. b. 1794, d. 1829, SC: 1818, f. Josiah Ellis, mr. Francis Polock Ellis, 1821. Rf: SFF64; EM12; E134; *SP*, Sept. 7, 1821

Ellis, Noah J. SC: 1821, f. Josiah Ellis, mr. Esther Levin Ellis, 1825. Rf: SFF64; EM13; SCA1821; *SP*, Mar. 11, 1825; D1831

Emanuel, Adeline m. (Jacobs) b. 1821, d. 1862, SC: 1821, f. Myer Jacobs, m. Rebecca Lazarus Jacobs, mr. Lafayette Gomez Emanuel, 1861. Rf: DR; SFF66, 132; EM31; 1850C; 1860C

Emanuel, Armida (Cohen). b. 1855, d. 1913, SC: 1855, f. Marx Edwin Cohen, m. Armida Harby Cohen, mr. Solomon Emanuel, 1880. Rf: MJCS15; SFF35, 66

Emanuel, Charlotta. b. 1841, SC: 1850, f. N. Emanuel, m. Sarah Emanuel. Rf: 1850C

Emanuel, Emanuel F. SC: 1800. Rf: E134; D1809

Emanuel, Esther (Alexander). b. 1841, d. 1871, f. Alexander Alexander, m. Sarah Harris Sampson Alexander, mr. Solomon Emanuel, 1869. Rf: SFF9, 66

Emanuel, Flora. SC: 1806. Rf: D1806, 1807

Emanuel, Flora (Emanuel). b. 1817, d. 1889, SC: 1817, f. Nathan Emanuel, m. Sarah Gomez Emanuel, mr. Nathan Emanuel, 1839. Rf: DR; EC6; SFF66

Emanuel, Frances. SC: 1821, mr. Isaac Emanuel. Rf: MR4Y.272; SCA1821

Emanuel, H. SC: 1850. Rf: E239; 1850C

Emanuel, Henrietta. b. 1830, d. 1852, SC: 1852. Rf: DR; EC107

Emanuel, Henrietta Eugenia (Simpson). d. 1836, SC: 1835, f. Michael Simpson, m. Nancy Emanuel, mr. Nathan Emanuel, 1835. Rf: EM16; SFF66, 272

Emanuel, Isaac. SC: 1726. Rf: WIM (1722–26), p. 557

Emanuel, Isaac. SC: 1804, mr. Frances Emanuel. Rf: E134; 1810C; 1820C; 1830C; SCA1804; D1809, 1813, 1816, 1819, 1822, 1829, 1831

Emanuel, Joel. SC: 1852. Rf: D1852

Emanuel, Joseph [Joel]. SC: 1790. Rf: E168; SFF66; SCA1803; D1790

Emanuel, Michael. d. 1801, SC: 1800. Rf: EC78; E134; SFF66; CB1800

Emanuel, Miriam. b. 1787, d. 1801, SC: 1801. Rf: EC81

Emanuel, N. b. 1794, SC: 1849, mr. Sarah Emanuel. Rf: 1850C; D1849

Emanuel, Nathan. SC: 1803, f. Michael Emanuel, mr. Sarah Gomez Emanuel, 1816. Rf: SFF66; CB1805; E143; D1807, 1809

Emanuel, Nathan. b. 1812, d. 1888, SC: 1851, f. Solomon Emanuel, mr. Henrietta Simpson Emanuel, 1835, mr2. Flora Emanuel Emanuel, 1839. Rf: DR; EC92; E168, 205; SFF66; D1852

Emanuel, Plowden Weston. b. 1861, d. 1881, SC: 1861, f. Nathan Emanuel, m. Flora Emanuel Emanuel. Rf: DR; EC63; SFF66

Emanuel, Rosetta. b. 1840, SC: 1850, f. N. Emanuel, m. Sarah Emanuel. Rf: 1850C

Emanuel, Sarah. b. 1805, SC: 1850, mr. N. Emanuel. Rf: 1850C

Emanuel, Sarah (Gomez). b. 1793, d. 1852, SC: 1825, f. Isaac Gomez, m. Abigail Lopez Gomez, mr. Nathan Emanuel, 1816. Rf: EC92; SFF66, 85; SCA1825

Emanuel, Solomon. b. 1841, d. 1921, SC: 1841, f. Nathan Emanuel, m. Flora Emanuel Emanuel, mr. Esther Alexander Emanuel, 1869, mr2. Armida Cohen Emanuel, 1880. Rf: MJSC15; SFF66

Emanuel, Solomon. b. 1843, SC: 1850, f. N. Emanuel, m. Sarah Emanuel. Rf: 1850C

Emboden, A. SC: 1821. Rf: CB1821

Engelberg, Henrietta (Simmons). SC: 1847, mr. Myer Engelberg, 1847. Rf: EM23

Engelberg, Myer. SC: 1847, mr. Henrietta Zimmons Engelberg, 1847. Rf: EM23; E168; 1850C

Epstein, David. SC: 1855. Rf: 1861C; T34; EJCC4; D1855, 1859

Epstein, Elizabeth (Wolf). b. 1837, d. 1892, SC: 1861, f. S. Wolf, mr. Philip Epstein, 1861. Rf: EM31; EJCC4

Epstein, I. SC: 1859. Rf: D1859

Epstein, Isabella. b. 1835, SC: 1860. Rf: 1860C

Epstein, N. b. 1826, SC: 1860. Rf: 1860C

Epstein, Phillip. b. 1837, SC: 1858, mr. Elizabeth Wolf Epstein, 1861. Rf: EM31; 1861C; T34; *SCHM*66.112; 1860C

Epstein, Rachel. b. 1858, SC: 1858. Rf: 1860C

Epstein, Solomon. b. 1853, SC: 1853. Rf: 1860C

Esdra, ——— (1). f. Joseph Eugene Esdra, m. Esther Clara Esdra. Rf: SFF115

Esdra, ——— (2). f. Joseph Eugene Esdra, m. Esther Clara Esdra. Rf: SFF115

Esdra, A. M. (Mrs.). b. 1800, d. 1854, SC: 1854, mr. Adolphe Esdra. Rf: EC50

Esdra, Adolphe. mr. Mrs. A. M. Esdra. Rf: EC50

Esdra, Aurelia. b. 1843, d. 1877, SC: 1843, f. Eugene Esdra, m. Esther Clara Esdra. Rf: DR; EC21; SFF115

Esdra, Esther Clara (Rodrigues Monsanto). SC: 1839, mr. Joseph Eugene Esdra, 1839. Rf: EM18; E168, 238; EC21; SFF115

Esdra, Joseph Eugene. b. 1816, d. 1878, SC: 1835, mr. Esther Clara Rodriguez Esdra, 1839. Rf: DR; EM18; EC21, 22; E168; SFF115; *Courier* Dec. 11, 1861; D1835, 1859

Esdra, Joseph Eugene. b. 1851, d. 1854, SC: 1854, f. Joseph Eugene Esdra, m. Esther Clara Esdra. Rf: EC22; SFF115

Esdra, Pauline. b. 1813, d. 1841, SC: 1841. Rf: DR; EC21; SFF115

Esdra, Zoe. b. 1818, d. 1894. Rf: DR; D1841

Etting, Elkan. SC: 1800. Rf: E134; CB1800

Ezekiel, Emanuel. SC: 1806. Rf: E134

Fabian, H. SC: 1854. Rf: T34

Fabian, Henrietta H. b. 1824, d. 1886, SC: 1841. Rf: DR; D1841

Falk, Abraham. b. 1828, d. 1913, SC: 1852, mr. Henrietta Abrahams Falk, 1855. Rf: DR; EC70; EM28; E168; T34; TBS39; 1860C; D1852, 1855, 1859

Falk, David Beauregard. b. 1861, d. 1916, SC: 1861, f. Abraham Falk, m. Henrietta Abrahams Falk, mr. Sarah Judith Solomons Falk, 1883. Rf: SFF5

Falk, George. SC: 1855. Rf: E168; D1855, 1859

Falk, Georgiana Sarah (Jacobi). b. 1836, d. 1858, SC: 1850, f. Wolf Jacob Jacobi, m. Priscilla Rebecca Jacobi, mr. Zachariah Falk, 1857. Rf: ENJC4; SFF117; EM30; JF7; 1850C

Falk, Henrietta (Abrahams). b. 1832, d. 1884, SC: 1832, f. Alexander

Hezekiel Abrahams, m. Hannah Moses Abrahams, mr. Abraham Falk, 1855. Rf: EM28; SFF5; 1850C; 1860C

Falk, Isaac L. SC: 1855. Rf: D1852, 1855, 1859

Falk, Isaiah M. b. 1858, SC: 1858, f. Abraham Falk, m. Henrietta Abrahams Falk, mr. Janie Solomons Falk, 1880. Rf: SFF5; 1860C

Falk, Joshua A. b. 1856, d. 1857, SC: 1857, f. Abraham Falk, m. Henrietta Abrahams Falk. Rf: SFF5; EC86

Falk, Mary. SC: 1859. Rf: D1859

Falk, Sarah. d. 1854, SC: 1854. Rf: EC86

Falk, Zachariah. SC: 1855, mr. Georgiana Sarah Jacobi Falk, 1857. Rf: SFF117; EM30; E168; JF7; D1855, 1859

Fiegel, Julius. SC: 1855, mr. Theresa Klauber Fiegel, 1857. Rf: EM29; D1855

Fiegel, Theresa (Klauber). SC: 1857, mr. Julius Fiegel, 1857. Rf: EM29

Flaum, Anna. b. 1841, d. 1907, mr. Julius Flaum. Rf: DR; EC91

Flaum, Julius. SC: 1861, mr. Anna Flaum. Rf: EC91; 1861C

Flonacher, Isaac. SC: 1848. Rf: CB1848

Florance, Benjamin. f. Zacharia Levy Florance, m. Sarah Levy Florance, mr. Rebecca Kursheedt Florance, 1836. Rf: SFF74

Florance, Elizabeth. SC: 1813, mr. Levy Florance. Rf: MR4G.155; MR4N.508; D1816

Florance, Frances M. (Cohen). b. 1833, d. 1913, f. Esdaile P. Cohen, m. Frances Hays Cohen, mr. Washington Z. Florance, 1854. Rf: SFF31, 74

Florance, Henry. f. Zachariah Levy Florance, m. Sarah Levy Florance, mr. Mary Levy. Rf: SFF74

Florance, Jacob Levy. b. 1803, d. 1867, SC: 1819, f. Zachariah Levy Florance, m. Sarah Levy Florance, mr. Hannah Levy Florance. Rf: SFF74; E134; SCA1834

Florance, Lavinia. f. Zachariah Levy Florance, m. Sarah Levy Florance. Rf: SFF74

Florance, Levy. SC: 1811, mr. Elizabeth Florance. Rf: MR4G.155 4N.508; E134; D1819, 1822

Florance, Lewis. SC: 1816, f. Zachariah Florance, m. Sarah Levy Florance. Rf: SFF74; E134; D1816

Florance, Rachel [Sarah]. SC: 1804, mr. Zachariah Florance. Rf: MR4O.68; SFF74; D1819

Florance, William. b. 1805, d. 1882, SC: 1805, f. Zachariah Levy Florance, m. Sarah Levy Florance, mr. Myrtilla Seixas Florance, 1834. Rf: SFF74

Florance, Zachariah Levy. d. 1832, SC: 1800, mr. Rachel [Sarah] Florance. Rf: MR3C.173, 4C.501, 4O.68; SFF74; T35; D1801, 1802, 1803, 1806, 1807, 1809, 1813, 1822

Forbes, Caroline (DeLeon). b. 1855, d. 1942, SC: 1855, f. Harmon Hendricks DeLeon, m. Caroline Agnes Moïse DeLeon, mr. Robert Sheldon Forbes, 1885. Rf: SFF55, 56; 1860C

Frank, Baruch Wolf. SC: 1855. Rf: *BS-BI*

Frank, Joseph. b. 1794, d. 1830, SC: 1830. Rf: EP

Frank, Joseph. b. 1859, d. 1898, SC: 1859. Rf: DR

Frankford, Harriet (Cohen). SC: 1841, f. Aaron Nathan Cohen, m. Rachel Cohen, mr. Simon Frankford, 1841. Rf: SFF38; EM20

Frankford, Simon. SC: 1838, mr. Harriet Cohen Frankford, 1841. Rf: SFF38; EM20; E168; Min. Nov. 26, 1838

Franks, David. SC: 1743, f. Jacob Franks. Rf: E25, 277

Frideburg, J. SC: 1848. Rf: E207

Frideburg, Philip. SC: 1807, mr. Sarah Frideburg. Rf: E135; 1820C; MR4V.170

Frideburg, Sarah M. SC: 1821, mr. Philip Frideburg. Rf: MR4V.170; SCA1821

Friedlander, Isaac. SC: 1846, mr. Priscilla Valentine Friedlander, 1846. Rf: EM22; MS16.423; D1849

Friedlander, M. J. b. 1784, d. 1838, SC: 1838. Rf: EC63; E168

Friedlander, Priscilla (Valentine). SC: 1846, f. S. Valentine, mr. Isaac Friedlander, 1846. Rf: EM22; MS16.423

Furst, Daniel H. b. 1810, d. 1867, SC: 1840. Rf: DR; E168; 1861C; D1841

Furst, Israel A. SC: 1800. Rf: MR3Q.325; E168

Furth, Joseph. b. 1794, d. 1838, SC: 1838. Rf: EP

Furth, Joseph. SC: 1831. Rf: E168, 238; *Courier* Dec. 11, 1861; D1831

Garretson, Isaac. d. 1839, SC: 1838. Rf: Min. April 14, 1839; EM18; E168; MS14.217; D1838

Goldberg, Aaron. b. 1845, SC: 1845, f. Jacob Goldberg, m. Miriam Goldberg. Rf: 1850C

Goldberg, David. d. 1842, SC: 1842, mr. Ricke Goldberg. Rf: W42.391 (his)

Goldberg, Jacob. b. 1812, SC: 1850, mr. Miriam Goldberg. Rf: 1850C

Goldberg, Miriam. b. 1816, SC: 1850, mr. Jacob Goldberg. Rf: 1850C

Goldberg, Moses. b. 1826, SC: 1850. Rf: 1850C

Goldberg, Rachel. b. 1841, SC: 1850, f. Jacob Goldberg, m. Miriam Goldberg. Rf: 1850C

Goldberg, Rebecca. b. 1843, SC: 1850, f. Jacob Goldberg, m. Miriam Goldberg. Rf: 1850C

Goldberg, Reuben. b. 1847, SC: 1847, f. Jacob Goldberg, m. Miriam Goldberg. Rf: 1850C

Goldberg, Ricke. SC: 1842, mr. David Goldberg. Rf: W42.391

Goldman, L. Jacob. b. 1799, d. 1879, SC: 1861. Rf: DR; EC81; 1861C

Goldsmidt, Jonas. b. 1805, d. 1842, SC: 1842. Rf: EC25; E168

Goldsmith, ———. b. 1785, d. 1828, SC: 1785. Rf: DR

Goldsmith, Abigail. b. 1823, SC: 1823. Rf: 1850C

Goldsmith, Abraham. SC: 1802. Rf: W32.706; 1820C; *SCHM*66.112; SCA1809; D1802, 1803, 1806, 1819, 1822, 1831, 1835

Goldsmith, Abraham Alexander. b. 1840, d. 1906, SC: 1860, f. Moses Goldsmith, m. Eleanor Alexander Goldsmith, mr. Rose Hilzheim Goldsmith, 1863, mr2. Anna

Sampson Goldsmith. Rf: DR; SFF84; E135, 168, 227; EC77, 97; 1860C

Goldsmith, Cordelia D. b. 1815, d. 1902, SC: 1855. Rf: DR; SCA1855

Goldsmith, Cecilia D. b. 1826, SC: 1826. Rf: 1850C; 1860C

Goldsmith, Eleanor (Alexander). b. 1814, d. 1885, SC: 1814, f. Abraham Alexander, m. Hannah Aarons Alexander, mr. Moses Goldsmith, 1837. Rf: DR; EC98; SFF8, 84; *AF*18; 1860C

Goldsmith, Frances (Phillips). b. 1790, d. 1848, SC: 1835, f. Jacob Phillips, m. Hannah Isaacs Phillips, mr. Isaac Goldsmith. Rf: EC98; SFF84, 247; *AF*62; 1830C; 1840C; D1822, 1835, 1841

Goldsmith, Hannah. b. 1748, d. 1828, SC: 1748, mr. Abraham Goldsmith. Rf: DR; *City Gazette*, April 21, 1828

Goldsmith, Hannah (Sampson). f. Samuel Sampson, m. Catherine Goldsmith Sampson, mr. Abraham Alexander Goldsmith. Rf: SFF84, 259

Goldsmith, Henry. b. 1805, d. 1861, SC: 1821. Rf: DR, E142, 168; 1840C; 1850C; 1860C; D1819, 1822, 1831, 1835, 1838, 1841, 1852

Goldsmith, Hetty [Esther]. SC: 1803, mr. Samuel Goldsmith. Rf: MR3W.073; MR3X.193

Goldsmith, Isaac Moses. b. 1774, d. 1821, SC: 1803, mr. Frances Phillips Goldsmith. Rf: DR; E135; SFF84; D1816, 1819, 1822

Goldsmith, Isaac Phillip. b. 1842, d. 1864, SC: 1859, f. Moses Goldsmith, m. Eleanor Alexander Goldsmith. Rf: E228; SFF84; D1859

Goldsmith, Jacob. b. 1848, SC: 1848. Rf: 1860C

Goldsmith, Joseph H. b. 1813, d. 1853, SC: 1813. Rf: DR; 1850C; D1831, 1835, 1841, 1852

Goldsmith, Joseph J. f. Isaac Moses Goldsmith, m. Frances Phillips Goldsmith. Rf: EC99; SFF84

Goldsmith, Joseph J. b. 1852, SC: 1852, f. Moses Goldsmith, m. Eleanor Alexander Goldsmith. Rf: SFF84; 1860C

Goldsmith, Julia A. b. 1852, SC: 1852. Rf: 1860C

Goldsmith, Mary A. b. 1833, SC: 1833. Rf: 1860C

Goldsmith, Mikell Myers. b. 1847, d. 1864, SC: 1847, f. Moses Goldsmith, m. Eleanor Alexander Goldsmith. Rf: SFF84; EC99; E228; 1860C

Goldsmith, Morris. b. 1778, d. 1861, SC: 1803, mr. Sarah Goldsmith. Rf: DR; 1810C; 1820C; 1830C; 1840C; 1850C; 1860C; 1861C; E135, 142, 161, 163; EM25; SCA1805; D1803, 1806, 1816, 1819, 1822, 1829, 1831, 1835, 1841, 1852, 1855, 1859

Goldsmith, Moses. b. 1815, d. 1884, SC: 1815, f. Isaac M. Goldsmith, m. Frances Phillips Goldsmith, mr. Eleanor Goldsmith, 1839. Rf: DR; EC98; SFF84; 1840C, 1860C; 1861C; *Courier* Dec. 11, 1861; D1855, 1859

Goldsmith, Raphal Benjamin. b. 1850, d. 1852, SC: 1850, f. Moses

Goldsmith, m. Eleanor Alexander Goldsmith. Rf: EC98; SFF84
Goldsmith, Rebecca. SC: 1829. Rf: SCA1829–39
Goldsmith, Rose (Hilzheim). b. 1844, d. 1898, f. Marcus Hilzheim, m. Henrietta Alexander N. Hilzheim, mr. Abraham Alexander Goldsmith, 1863. Rf: DR; EC77; EM32; SFF8
Goldsmith, Rosy. b. 1812, d. 1813, SC: 1813, f. Morris Goldsmith, m. Sarah Goldsmith. Rf: EC74
Goldsmith, Samuel. SC: 1804, mr. Hetty Goldsmith. Rf: MR3W.073; E135; D1806
Goldsmith, Sarah. b. 1785, d. 1828, SC: 1813, mr. Morris Goldsmith. Rf: EC74; *SP*, Dec. 26, 1828
Goldsmith, Solomon. SC: 1804. Rf: E135
Goldsmith, W. Henry. f. Moses Goldsmith, m. Eleanor Alexander Goldsmith. Rf: SFF84
Goldstein, Aaron. b. 1832, d. 1854, SC: 1854. Rf: EC92; E168
Goldstein, Abraham. b. 1843, SC: 1855, f. Jacob Goldstein, m. Hannah Goldstein. Rf: 1860C; D1855, 1859
Goldstein, Adeline. b. 1841, d. 1906. Rf: DR
Goldstein, Charlotte. b. 1832, SC: 1860, mr. David Goldstein. Rf: 1860C
Goldstein, David. b. 1827, d. 1874, SC: 1860, mr. Charlotte Goldstein. Rf: 1860C; DR
Goldstein, David. b. 1853, SC: 1860, f. Jacob Goldstein, m. Hannah Goldstein. Rf: 1860C
Goldstein, Fanny. b. 1850, SC: 1860, f. Jacob Goldstein, m. Hannah Goldstein. Rf: 1860C
Goldstein, Hannah. b. 1822, SC: 1860, mr. Jacob Goldstein. Rf: 1860C
Goldstein, Harriett. b. 1824, d. 1889, SC: 1854. Rf: DR
Goldstein, Henrietta. b. 1859, SC: 1860, f. Jacob Goldstein, m. Hannah Goldstein. Rf: 1860C
Goldstein, Isadore. SC: 1855. Rf: D1855, 1859
Goldstein, Jacob. b. 1821, d. 1881, SC: 1855, mr. Hannah Goldstein. Rf: DR; EC80; E168; 1860C; 1861C; D1855, 1859
Goldstein, Philip. b. 1837, d. 1858. SC: 1858, f. David Goldsmith. Rf: ENJC4
Goldstein, S. SC: 1859. Rf: D1859
Gollinger, ———. b. 1824, SC: 1860, mr. Herman Gollinger. Rf: 1860C
Gollinger, Augusta. b. 1859, SC: 1860, f. Herman Gollinger. Rf: 1860C
Gollinger, Bertha. b. 1819, d. 1889, SC: 1819. Rf: DR
Gollinger, Hannah. b. 1857, d. 1901, SC: 1860, f. Herman Gollinger. Rf: EBS4; 1860C
Gollinger, Herman. b. 1825, d. 1883, SC: 1860. Rf: DR; 1860C
Gollinger, M. H. b. 1855, d. 1861, SC: 1861. Rf: EBS5
Gollinger, Simon. b. 1855, SC: 1860, f. Herman Gollinger. Rf: 1860C
Gomez, Elias. SC: 1792. Rf: E135, 279; MR3D.109; D1794; RB44
Gomez, Isaac D. C. SC: 1805. Rf: E135
Gomez, Jacob. SC: 1796. Rf: E135; D1796, 1803, 1806, 1807; RB45

Gomez, Lewis. SC: 1802. Rf: E135, 142; D1802, 1803
Gomez, Phillip H. SC: 1802. Rf: E135; D1802, 1809
Gomez, Rebecca D. SC: 1801. Rf: MR3P.380
Goodman, Amelia (Harris). b. 1813, d. 1888, f. Hyam Harris, m. Catherine Nathan Harris, mr. Daniel Goodman, 1828. Rf: SFF94
Goodman, J. I. SC: 1804. Rf: CB1804
Goodman, M. SC: 1804. Rf: E135; CB1804
Gottschalk, Frances (Mordecai). b. 1845, d. 1927, SC: 1845, f. Benjamin Mordecai, m. Clara Polock Mordecai, mr. Felix Gottschalk. Rf: SFF202; 1860C
Gouthalk, Isaac. b. 1799, d. 1859, SC: 1859. Rf: DR
Green, David. SC: 1818. Rf: E135
Greenburg, S. SC: 1857. Rf: Min. Sept. 16, 1857
Gutteres, Aaron DeMuttos. SC: 1734. Rf: E26, 27, 277; SCA1737
Haas, Adolph Godchaux. b. 1833, d. 1858, SC: 1858, mr. Hester Hyams Haas, 1858. Rf: DR; ENJC4; EM30; SFF120
Haas, E. b. 1821, d. 1877, SC: 1857. Rf: DR
Haas, Ernestine (Straus). mr. Daniel Haas, 1866. Rf: EM33
Haas, Hester (Hyams). b. 1837, SC: 1837, f. Moses David Hyams, m. Susannah Jackson Hyams, mr. Adolph G. Haas, 1858. Rf: EM30; SFF120; W51.842; 1850C; 1860C
Halsy, I. SC: 1838. Rf: Min. Sept. 23, 1838
Hamberg, Len (Goodman). b. 1849, d. 1877, SC: 1849, mr. Charles Hamberg, 1867. Rf: EM33; EJCC3
Hamilton, Emma (Levy). b. 1832, d. 1873, f. John Clarisse Levy, m. Fanny Yates Levy, mr. Samuel Prioleau Hamilton, 1851. Rf: SFF169; Yates, Samuel and Lazarus
Hannay, Hannah. b. 1756, d. 1840, SC: 1821. Rf: DR; EC31; CB1821
Harby, ———(1). f. Isaac Harby, m. Rachel Mordecai Harby. Rf: SFF93
Harby, ———(2). f. Isaac Harby, m. Rachel Mordecai Harby. Rf: SFF93
Harby, ———(3). f. Isaac Harby, m. Rachel Mordecai Harby. Rf: SFF93
Harby, Abraham. b. 1835, SC: 1835. Rf: 1850C; D1855
Harby, Caroline de Litchfield. b. 1801, d. 1876, SC: 1801, f. Solomon Harby, m. Rebecca Moses Harby. Rf: DR; EC111; SFF93; E168; 1850C
Harby, Charles. f. Henry Jefferson Harby, m. Leah Tobias Harby. Rf: SFF93
Harby, George Washington. b. 1797, d. 1862, SC: 1797, f. Solomon Harby, m. Rebecca Moses Harby, mr. Mary Olivia Lucas Harby, 1828, mr2. Marie Ulalie Pouillot Harby, 1835. Rf: SFF93; E135, 190–91; T35
Harby, Henry Jefferson. b. 1799, d. 1851, SC: 1799, f. Solomon Harby, m. Rebecca Moses Harby, mr. Leah Tobias Harby. Rf: DR;

EC110; SFF93, 298; 1840C; 1850C; D1829, 1831, 1841, 1849, 1852; RB49

Harby, Henry Jefferson. b. 1843, d. 1852, SC: 1843, f. Henry Jefferson Harby, m. Leah Tobias Harby. Rf: DR; EC111; SFF93; 1850C

Harby, Horace. b. 1846, d. 1905. Rf: MJSC13

Harby, Isaac. b. 1788, d. 1828, SC: 1788, f. Solomon Harby, m. Rebecca Moses Harby, mr. Rachel Mordecai Harby, 1810. Rf: E99; SFF93; D1809, 1813, 1819, 1822

Harby, Isaac. b. 1833, SC: 1833, f. Henry Jefferson Harby, m. Leah Tobias Harby. Rf: SFF93; 1850C; D1852

Harby, Jacob DeLaMotta. b. 1848, d. 1916, SC: 1848, f. Levi Charles Harby, m. Leonora R. DeLyon Harby, mr. Lee Cohen Harby, 1869. Rf: SFF93; MJSC19

Harby, Julian. b. 1815, f. Isaac Harby, m. Rachel Mordecai Harby. Rf: SFF93

Harby, Leah (Tobias). b. 1810, SC: 1810, mr. Henry J. Harby. Rf: 1850C

Harby, Lee (Cohen). b. 1849, d. 1918, f. Marx Edwin Cohen, m. Armida Harby Cohen, mr. Jacob DeLa-Motta Harby, 1869. Rf: EM34; SFF35, 93

Harby, Leonora R. (DeLyon). SC: 1841, mr. Levi Charles Harby, 1841. Rf: SFF93

Harby, Levi Charles. b. 1793, d. 1870, SC: 1793, f. Solomon Harby, m. Rebecca Moses Harby, mr. Leonora R. DeLyon Harby, 1842. Rf: SFF93; E144; RB93

Harby, Levy C., Jr. b. 1837, SC: 1837. Rf: 1850C

Harby, Rachael (Mordecai). b. 1782, d. 1827, SC: 1782, f. Samuel Mordecai, m. Catherine Mordecai, mr. Isaac Harby, 1810. Rf: DR; SFF12, 93; *SP*, April 4, 1827, eulogy.

Harby, Rebecca (Moses). b. 1768, d. 1854, SC: 1768, f. Myer Moses, m. ——— Frangipini Moses, mr. Solomon Harby, 1787. Rf: EC111; SFF93, 205; 1850C; D1807, 1829, 1831, 1835

Harby, Samuel. b. 1813, d. 1862, f. Isaac Harby, m. Rachel Mordecai Harby, mr. Frances Levy Harby, 1842, mr2. Sarah Levy Harby, 1851. Rf: SFF93

Harby, Samuel DaCosta. b. 1795, d. 1799, SC: 1795, f. Solomon Harby, m. Rebecca Moses Harby. Rf: SFF93; RB49

Harby, Solomon. b. 1762, d. 1805, SC: 1781, f. Isaac Harby, m. Frangi-pani, mr. Rebecca Moses Harby, 1787. Rf: SFF93, 205; E135, 172, 279; D1801, 1802, 1803

Harby, Solomon. b. 1811, SC: 1811, f. Henry Jefferson Harby, m. Leah Tobias Harby. Rf: SFF93; 1850C

Harby, Solomon. b. 1811, d. 1830, SC: 1811, f. Isaac Harby, m. Rachel Mordecai Harby. Rf: SFF93; *SP*, Sept. 14, 1830

Harby, Tobias. b. 1836, d. 1860, SC: 1836, f. Henry Jefferson Harby, m. Leah Tobias Harby. Rf: DR; EC111; SFF93; W49.650

Harby, Washington. b. 1840, d. 1841, SC: 1840. Rf: DR

Harris, ———. b. 1785, d. 1860, SC: 1860. Rf: DR

Harris, A. b. 1780, d. 1841, SC: 1780. DR

Harris, Aaron. b. 1822, d. 1869, f. Hyam Harris, m. Catharine Nathan Harris, mr. Hariette Lynn Harris, 1856. Rf: SFF94

Harris, Abraham. SC: 1835. Rf: DR; E168, 219, 292; D1835, 1838

Harris, Abraham Hyam. b. 1805, d. 1868, SC: 1818, f. Hyam Harris, m. Catharine Nathan Harris. Rf: SFF94

Harris, Abraham J. b. 1816, d. 1871, SC: 1816. Rf: DR; E168, 23; T35; 1861C; SCA1860

Harris, Alexander. b. 1817, d. 1869, f. Hyam Harris, m. Catharine Nathan Harris, mr. E. J. Thompson Harris, 1857. Rf: SFF94

Harris, Andrew. SC: 1785. Rf: E135, 279; SCA1785–1812; D1794, 1801, 1803, 1807; RB49

Harris, Catherine (Nathan). b. 1781, d. 1845, f. Moses Nathan, m. Amelia Nathan, mr. Hyam (Henry) Harris, 1799. Rf: SFF94, 228

Harris, Clara. b. 1736, d. 1822, SC: 1822. Rf: DR

Harris, Elizabeth. b. 1778, d. 1858, SC: 1811, mr. Jacob Harris. Rf: SFF94; EM14; D1806, 1809, 1813, 1816, 1829

Harris, Esther. SC: 1818. Rf: *State v. Rebecca M. Harris, Esther Harris &Abraham Harris*, 1818

Harris, George. SC: 1840. Rf: E168; 1840C

Harris, Hannah (Leman). b. 1814, d. 1878, SC: 1851, mr. Isaac Harris, 1851. Rf: DR; EC90; EM25; 1860C

Harris, Henry. SC: 1782. Rf: "House Journal, 1783–1784," pp. 84, 253; E99, 278; RB49

Harris, Henry. d. 1809, f. Hyam Harris, m. Catharine Nathan Harris. Rf: SFF94

Harris, Hyam (Henry). d. 1828, SC: 1800, f. Abraham Harris, mr. Catharine Nathan Harris, 1799. Rf: SFF94; SCA1811; D1807, 1816, 1819, 1822; RB49

Harris, Isaac. b. 1805, d. 1869, SC: 1805, mr. Hannah Leman Harris, 1851. Rf: EC89; E168, 238; EM25; 1850C; 1860C; 1861C; D1831, 1835, 1838

Harris, Jacob. b. 1766, d. 1837, SC: 1797, mr. Elizabeth Harris. Rf: SFF94; E135; EM16; SCA1811; D1807, 1809, 1813, 1819, 1822, 1831, 1835; RB50

Harris, Jacob. d. 1811, SC: 1811, f. Hyam Harris, m. Catharine Nathan Harris. Rf: SFF94; SCA1811

Harris, Levy Judah. b. 1815, d. 1891, SC: 1838, f. Hyam Harris, m. Catharine Nathan Harris, mr. Rebecca Myers Harris, 1857. Rf: SFF94, 240; D1838

Harris, Mordecai. SC: 1783. Rf: E278

Harris, Morris. b. 1837, d. 1914, SC: 1861. Rf: DR; E228, 263

Harris, Moses. SC: 1780. Rf: E91, 92, 106, 135, 278; RB50

Harris, Moses. b. 1807, d. 1877, f. Hyam Harris, m. Catharine Nathan Harris, mr. Marie A. C. Lamarlere Harris, 1833. Rf: SFF94

Harris, Nathan. SC: 1778, mr. Penina Harris. Rf: MR2V.208
Harris, Noah. SC: 1857. Rf: Min. Sept. 5, 1858
Harris, Penina. SC: 1778, mr. Nathan Harris. Rf: MR2V.208
Harris, Rachel A. b. 1829, d. 1885, SC: 1829. Rf: DR
Harris, Rebecca. b. 1801, d. 1883, SC: 1814, f. Hyam Harris, m. Catharine Nathan Harris. Rf: SFF94; CB1814; D1838
Harris, Rebecca (Myers). SC: 1818, f. Eleazer Myers, m. Rachel Myers, mr. Levy Judah Harris, 1857. Rf: SFF94, 240
Harris, Z. SC: 1835. Rf: E168, 246; D1835
Hart, ———. d. 1744, SC: 1744. Rf: E28, 277
Hart, ———. b. 1848, d. 1848, SC: 1848, f. Samuel Nathan Hart, m. Isabel Lazarus Hart. Rf: SFF98
Hart, Abraham Levy. SC: 1796, f. Levy Hart. Rf: SCA1803; SFF97
Hart, Adelaide Fanny (Samuel). b. 1852, f. Morris Samuel, m. Fanny Cohen Samuel, mr. Nathan S. Hart, 1871. Rf: SFF98, 260
Hart, Alexander. b. 1807, d. 1877, SC: 1829, f. Simon Moses Hart, m. Rachel Levy Hart, mr. Augusta Georgia Canter Hart, 1842. Rf: SFF97; D1829
Hart, Alexander Moses. d. 1797, SC: 1797, f. Moses Hart, m. Sally Hart. Rf: E279; SFF97; W26.207 (his); W26.397
Hart, Bella (Levy). b. 1762, d. 1851, SC: 1788, f. Mordecai Levy, m. Mary Cohen Levy, mr. Daniel Hart. Rf: EC35; SFF98, 99; EP; W31.441; SCA1813; 1850C; D1816, 1829, 1831, 1835, 1841
Hart, Bernard. b. 1814, d. 1843, SC: 1814, f. Simon Moses Hart, m. Rachel Levy Hart, mr. Irma Jacobs Hart. Rf: SFF97; E279
Hart, Betsey. SC: 1797, f. Moses Hart, m. Sally Hart. Rf: SFF97; W26.607
Hart, Caroline E. b. 1808, d. 1890, SC: 1808, f. Daniel Hart, m. Bella Levy Hart. Rf: DR; EC34; SFF99; W48.27
Hart, Caspar. b. 1828, d. 1874, SC: 1859, mr. Pauline Hart. Rf: DR; 1860C; D1852
Hart, Daniel. d. 1811, SC: 1792, f. ——— Hart of Mannheim, mr. Bella Levy Hart. Rf: SFF98, 99; EM9; EC35; E117, 135, 168; 1800C; 1810C; W46.21; D1794, 1801, 1802, 1803, 1806, 1807, 1809
Hart, Daniel. b. 1854, SC: 1860, f. Caspar Hart, m. Pauline Hart. Rf: 1860C
Hart, Daniel Samuel. b. 1839, d. 1877, SC: 1839, f. Samuel Nathan Hart, m. Isabel Lazarus Hart, mr. Priscilla Lopez Hart, 1860. Rf: DR; EC52; E229; SFF98, 176; T35
Hart, David. SC: 1800. Rf: CB1800; SCA1803–17
Hart, Elizabeth. SC: 1804, mr. Mathias Hart. Rf: MR3V.113; SCA1804–09; D1813, 1816
Hart, Emanuel. SC: 1814. Rf: MR4I.300
Hart, Ephraim. SC: 1783. Rf: E279
Hart, Esther. b. 1740, SC: 1761, mr. Moses Hart. Rf: SFF98

Hart, Esther. SC: 1768, f. Joshua Hart, m. Rebecca Hart. Rf: SFF98

Hart, Esther Eudora (Ezekiel). b. 1812, d. 1841, f. Joseph Ezekiel, m. Leah Levy Ezekiel, mr. Samuel Hart, 1833. Rf: SFF99, 169

Hart, Gerstine. b. 1851, SC: 1860, f. Caspar Hart, m. Pauline Hart. Rf: 1860C

Hart, Godfrey. b. 1837, SC: 1850. Rf: 1850C

Hart, Hannah. SC: 1800. Rf: SCA1800–13

Hart, Hart Moses. b. 1764, d. 1795, SC: 1795, f. Moses Hart, m. Sally Hart. Rf: EC58; E279; SFF97; W25.317 (his)

Hart, Hart Moses. SC: 1803. Rf: 1810C; SCA1803

Hart, Henrietta. b. 1804, d. 1897, SC: 1804, f. Daniel Hart, m. Bella Levy Hart. Rf: DR; EC34; SFF99; 1861C

Hart, Henrietta. b. 1843, d. 1860, SC: 1860, f. Samuel Nathan Hart, m. Isabel Lazarus Hart. Rf: EC50; SFF98

Hart, Henry. b. 1797, d. 1834, SC: 1797, f. Simon Moses Hart, m. Rachel Levy Hart. Rf: SFF97

Hart, Henry. b. 1845, d. 1865, f. Samuel Nathan Hart, m. Isabel Lazarus Hart. Rf: SFF98

Hart, Hyman N. b. 1816, d. 1859, SC: 1816, f. Nathan Hart, m. Rachel Hart, mr. Hetty Maria Gomez Hart, 1841. Rf: SFF98; T35; Min. April 14, 1839; W48.476; W46.21; W48.277; 1850C; D1849, 1855; RB52

Hart, Hymon N. d. 1791, SC: 1791, f. Hart of Mannheim, mr. Hannah Levy Hart DeLieben Davis, 1761. Rf: SFF98; E279; W24.946; 1790C

Hart, Isabel (Lazarus). b. 1820, d. 1893, SC: 1820, f. Jacob Lazarus, m. Miriam Hart Lazarus, mr. Samuel Nathan Hart. Rf: DR; EC49; SFF98, 99; W48.476

Hart, Israel. b. 1852, d. 1859, SC: 1852, f. Samuel Nathan Hart, m. Isabel Lazarus Hart. Rf: DR; EC50; SFF98

Hart, Israel Daniel. b. 1861, d. 1901, SC: 1861, f. Daniel Samuel Hart, m. Priscilla Lopez Hart, mr. Rosalie Levy Hart, 1889. Rf: SFF98

Hart, Jacob J. SC: 1855. Rf: D1855

Hart, Joseph. SC: 1802. Rf: E135; W31.441; D1803, 1806, 1809

Hart, Joseph. b. 1813, d. 1819, SC: 1819, f. Simon Moses Hart, m. Rachel Levy Hart. Rf: SFF97; *SP*, Aug. 6, 1819

Hart, Josephine. SC: 1823. Rf: MR4Y.461

Hart, Joshua. d. 1787, SC: 1762, f. Moses Hart, m. Esther Hart, mr. Rebecca Hart. Rf: EM5, 6; SFF98; E43, 65, 278; W11.301; SCA1758–89

Hart, Joshua. b. 1843, d. 1901, f. Samuel Nathan Hart, m. Isabel Lazarus Hart, mr. Myrtilla Florance Jackson Hart, 1884. Rf: DR; EC34; SFF98

Hart, Leo. SC: 1774, mr. Sarah Hart. Rf: MR3I.38; E135; W38.545

Hart, Levy. SC: 1811, mr. Abigail Minis Sheftall Hart, 1818. Rf: T35; EM11; E135, 168

Hart, Lewis. b. 1846, SC: 1846, f.

Hyman N. Hart, m. Hetty Maria Gomez Hart, mr. Annie Hart. Rf: SFF98; 1850C

Hart, Louisa. SC: 1823. Rf: MR4Y.461

Hart, Mathias. d. 1809, SC: 1803, mr. Elizabeth Hart. Rf: MR3V.113; E135

Hart, Michael. SC: 1773. Rf: W22.94; SCA1773–75

Hart, Miriam. SC: 1824, f. Leo Hart. Rf: W38.545; W50.415; D1841

Hart, Moses. SC: 1761, mr. Esther Hart. Rf: SFF98, E40, 278; 1820C; D1819; RB54

Hart, Moses. SC: 1780, mr. Sally Hart. Rf: SFF97; SCA1780

Hart, Naphtali H. SC: 1763. Rf: E135, 168, 279; RB54

Hart, Naphtali H. b. 1800, d. 1832, SC: 1800, f. Daniel Hart, m. Bella Levy Hart, mr. Sarah Moses Hart, 1823. Rf: DR; EC33; EM13; SFF99; SCA1819–27; D1822

Hart, Nathan. SC: 1774. Rf: SCA1774; RB55

Hart, Nathan. b. 1784, d. 1840, SC: 1802, f. Samuel Hart, mr. Rachel Hart, 1807. Rf: DR; EM9; SFF98; EC33; E135; T39; SCA1813; D1806, 1807, 1809, 1816, 1819, 1829, 1831, 1835, 1838, 1841

Hart, Nathan. b. 1848, d. 1897, SC: 1850, f. Hyman N. Hart, m. Hetty Maria Gomez Hart. Rf: SFF98; 1850C

Hart, Nathan Samuel. b. 1841, SC: 1841, f. Samuel Nathan Hart, m. Isabel Lazarus Hart, mr. Adelaide Fanny Samuel Hart, 1871. Rf: SFF98

Hart, Pauline. b. 1832, SC: 1860, mr. Caspar Hart. Rf: 1860C

Hart, Philip. b. 1727, d. 1796, SC: 1750. Rf: EC58; SFF97; E32; W26.397 (his); *SCHM*74.254; *SCHM*56.45; 1790C; D1794

Hart, Philip Levy. SC: 1826, f. Levy Hart. Rf: T35; SFF97; W26.397; D1829

Hart, Priscilla (Lopez). b. 1839, d. 1882, SC: 1839, f. David Lopez, m. Catherine Dobyns Hinton Lopez, mr. Daniel Samuel Hart, 1860. Rf: DR; EC52; EM31; SFF98, 176; 1850C

Hart, Rachel. SC: 1806, mr. Samuel Hart. Rf: MR3W.629; D1807

Hart, Rachel (Hart). b. 1790, d. 1869, SC: 1790, f. Daniel Hart, m. Bella Levy Hart, mr. Nathan Hart, 1807. Rf: DR; EM9; SFF99; 1861C

Hart, Rachel (Levy). b. 1800, SC: 1800, mr. Simon Moses Hart. Rf: SFF97; 1850C

Hart, Rebecca. d. 1788, SC: 1766, mr. Joshua Hart. Rf: SFF98

Hart, Rosetta. f. Samuel Nathan Hart, m. Isabel Lazarus Hart. Rf: SFF98

Hart, Samuel. SC: 1767, mr. Rachel Hart. Rf: SFF98; MR3W.629; SCA1767–1806; D1802

Hart, Samuel. b. 1805, d. 1896, SC: 1805, f. Daniel Hart, m. Bella Levy Hart, mr. Esther Eudora Ezekiel Hart, 1833. Rf: EC34; SFF99, 169; E158; SCA1839; T35; 1850C; D1849, 1852, 1855

Hart, Samuel M. SC: 1801. Rf: T35; D1806, 1816, 1819, 1822, 1829, 1831

Hart, Samuel Nathan. b. 1808, d.

1880, SC: 1808, f. Nathan Hart, m. Rachel Hart, mr. Isabel Lazarus Hart. Rf: DR; SFF98; EM15; D1835, 1849, 1852, 1855

Hart, Sarah. SC: 1774, mr. Leo Hart. Rf: MR3I.038; 1800C; D1802, 1803

Hart, Sarah. b. 1784, d. 1874, SC: 1845. Rf: DR; EBS5; 1850C

Hart, Sarah (Moses). b. 1805, d. 1825, SC: 1806, f. Joseph Moses, mr. Naphtali Henry Hart, 1823. Rf: DR; EC67; SFF99; EM13

Hart, Simon Moses. b. 1763, d. 1840, SC: 1790, f. Moses Hart, m. Sally Hart, mr. Rachel Levy Hart. Rf: SFF97; 1790C; 1800C; 1810C; E135; D1790, 1801, 1803, 1807, 1809, 1813

Hart, Solomon. b. 1775, d. 1805, SC: 1803. Rf: E135; W30.863 (his)

Hart, Susan. b. 1794, SC: 1860. Rf: 1860C

Hass, Daniel. mr. Ernestine Strauss Hass, 1866. Rf: EM33

Heilbrun, Joseph. SC: 1858, mr. Lizzie L. Sommers Heilbrun, 1858. Rf: EM30

Heilburn, Lizzie L. (Sommers). SC: 1858, f. E. Sommers, mr. Joseph Heilburn, 1858. Rf: EM30

Hendricks, Esther (Phillips). b. 1794, f. Jacob Phillips, m. Hannah Isaacs Phillips, mr. Isaac Hendricks. Rf: SFF247; AF62

Hendricks, Frances (Mayer) (Solomons). b. 1827, d. 1866, f. Sampson Solomons, m. Molsey Joseph Solomons, mr. Raphael Mayer, 1854, mr2. Benjamin F. Hendricks, 1859. Rf: EC15; SFF277

Hendricks, Joseph. SC: 1820. Rf: E168; 1820C; SCA1831

Hendricks, Rachel (Sampson). SC: 1852, f. Samuel Sampson, m. Catherine Goldsmith Sampson, mr. Isaac Hendricks, 1852. Rf: EM26; SFF259

Hendricks, Sarah. SC: 1805. Rf: CB1805

Henriques, Moses. SC: 1839. Rf: SCA1839

Henriques, Sarah (Seixas). f. Isaac Mendes Seixas, m. Abigail Valencia Seixas, mr. Elias Henriques. Rf: SFF263

Henry, Aaron. SC: 1779. Rf: RB62

Henry, Amelia [Ann]. b. 1755, d. 1825, SC: 1755, mr. Joel Henry. Rf: DR; SFF115; SCA1818; *SP*, July 28, 1825, eulogy; D1822

Henry, Anna (Myers). SC: 1809, f. Levy Myers, m. Frances Minis Myers, mr. Isaac Henry. Rf: SFF114, 216; CB1809

Henry, Bernard. SC: 1807. Rf: T35; E135, 169

Henry, Catherine. d. 1812, SC: 1793, mr. Jacob Henry. Rf: SFF115; SCA1793

Henry, Cordelia. f. Jacob Henry. Rf: SFF115

Henry, Denah. f. Jacob Henry. Rf: SFF115; MR5D.266

Henry, Esther. b. 1787, d. 1823, SC: 1823, mr. Jacob Henry. Rf: DR; SFF115

Henry, Esther Lucile (Esdra). SC: 1836, mr. Philip Jacob Henry, 1836. Rf: EM16; SFF115

Henry, Jacob P. SC: 1790, f. Joel Henry, m. Amelia Henry, mr. Catherine Henry, mr2. Esther

Henry. Rf: SFF115; E135; T35; 1800C; 1810C; 1820C; 1830C; D1790, 1794, 1796, 1801, 1802, 1803, 1806, 1809, 1813

Henry, Jane Caroline. SC: 1842, mr. Joel Henry. Rf: SFF115

Henry, Joel. SC: 1820, mr. Amelia Henry. Rf: SFF115; 1820C (in Sumter); E135; SCA1839

Henry, Joel. d. 1830. SC: 1809, f. Jacob Henry, mr. Jane Caroline Henry. Rf: SFF115; E135

Henry, Judah. f. Jacob Henry. Rf: SFF115

Henry, Marie. SC: 1814, f. Levy Myers, m. Francis Minis Myers, mr. Jacob Henry, 1814. Rf: SFF114, 216; MS6.360

Henry, Marks. SC: 1821. Rf: CB1821

Henry, Maurice L. SC: 1801, mr. Miriam Solomons Henry, 1807. Rf: EM8; E135, 145

Henry, Miriam (Solomons). SC: 1807, mr. Maurice L. Henry, 1807. Rf: EM8

Henry, Morris C. SC: 1811. Rf: CB1811

Henry, Philip Jacob. b. 1808, d. 1842, SC: 1836, f. Jacob Henry, mr. Esther Lucile Esdra Henry, 1836. Rf: EC21; EM16; E169; SFF115; 1840C; Min. April 14, 1839

Henry, Samuel. SC: 1834, f. Jacob Henry. Rf: SFF115; SCA1834

Henry, Sarah. f. Jacob Henry. Rf: SFF115

Hertz, Albert Eger. b. 1829, SC: 1829, f. Jacob Hertz, m. Rebecca Mordecai Hertz, mr. Maria S. Solana Hertz, 1854. Rf: EM27; SFF117; 1850C; D1849, 1852

Hertz, Alexander. b. 1763, d. 1822, SC: 1804. Rf: DR; EC83; E135; SFF117; SCA1807; D1822

Hertz, Edwin Eger. b. 1819, d. 1867, SC: 1819, f. Jacob Hertz, m. Rebecca Mordecai Hertz, mr. Francis Sheftall Cohen Hertz, 1848. Rf: EM23; SFF117

Hertz, Emma Eger. b. 1817, d. 1832, SC: 1832, f. Jacob Hertz, m. Rebecca Mordecai Hertz. Rf: EC13; SFF117

Hertz, Esther (Peixotto). b. 1811, d. 1853, SC: 1839, f. Solomon Cohen Peixotto, m. Rachel Suares Peixotto, mr. Lewis Hertz, 1839. Rf: EM18; SFF240

Hertz, Fannie Sheftall. b. 1856, d. 1856, SC: 1856, f. Isaac Eger Hertz, m. Nellie Sheftall Cohen Hertz. Rf: DR; EC13; SFF117

Hertz, Fannie Sheftall (Cohen). f. Isaac Cohen, mr. Edwin Eger Hertz, 1848. Rf: EM23; SFF117

Hertz, Frederick Eger. b. 1829, d. 1868, SC: 1829, f. Jacob Hertz, m. Rebecca Mordecai Hertz, mr. Rebecca S. Cohen Hertz. Rf: SFF117; *OJCS*, 47; 1850C; D1849, 1852, 1855

Hertz, H. E. b. 1817, d. 1872, SC: 1817. Rf: DR; 1860C

Hertz, Handel Moses. b. 1780, d. 1840, SC: 1802, mr. Isabella Hertz. Rf: EC51, 73; SFF117; E135, 169; 1820C; W42.187 (his); D1813, 1816, 1822, 1831, 1835, 1838, 1841

Hertz, Henrietta. b. 1830, SC: 1830. Rf: 1850C

Hertz, Isaac Eger. b. 1812, d. 1877, SC: 1812, f. Jacob Hertz, m. Rebecca Mordecai Hertz, mr.

Nellie Sheftall Cohen Hertz, 1850. Rf: DR; EM24; SFF117; T35; EC13; E169, 238, 1850C; 1860C; *Courier* Dec. 11, 1861; D1835, 1838, 1841, 1849, 1855, 1859

Hertz, Isaac Eger. b. 1859, d. 1860, SC: 1859, f. Isaac Eger Hertz, m. Nellie Sheftall Cohen Hertz. Rf: DR; EC13; SFF117; 1860C

Hertz, Isabella. b. 1769, d. 1824, SC: 1769, mr. Handel Moses Hertz. Rf: EC73; SFF117; *City Gazette*, Jan. 30, 1824

Hertz, Jacob E. b. 1776, d. 1846, SC: 1809, mr. Rebecca Mordecai Hertz, 1810. Rf: DR; EC13, 14; E135, 169; SFF117; 1820C; 1830C; 1840C; D1813, 1816, 1822, 1829, 1831, 1835, 1838, 1841

Hertz, James E. SC: 1841. Rf: W47.742; D1841, 1852

Hertz, Levy. SC: 1800. Rf: MR3Q.325

Hertz, Lewis. SC: 1833, mr. Esther Peixotto Hertz, 1839. Rf: EM18; SFF240; E169; 1840C; W41.817; D1841

Hertz, Nellie Cohen. b. 1857, d. 1858, SC: 1858, f. Isaac Eger Hertz, m. Nellie Sheftall Cohen Hertz. Rf: EC13; SFF117

Hertz, Nellie Sheftall (Cohen). b. 1831, d. 1865, SC: 1850, f. Isaac Cohen, mr. Isaac Eger Hertz, 1850. Rf: EM24; SFF117; *OJCS*47; 1850C; 1860C

Hertz, Rebecca (Mordecai). b. 1791, d. 1833, SC: 1810, f. Joseph Mordecai, m. Esther Marache Mordecai, mr. Jacob Hertz, 1810. Rf: EC13; SFF117, 200

Hertz, Thaddeus Eger. b. 1832, d. 1880, SC: 1832, f. Jacob Hertz, m. Rebecca Mordecai Hertz, mr. Louisa E. Jenkins Hertz, 1878. Rf: DR; SFF117; E169; 1850C; D1852, 1855, 1859

Heydenfeldt, Jacob. d. 1825, SC: 1808, f. Solomon Heydenfeldt, mr. Esther Desirée DePass Heydenfeldt, 1815. Rf: SFF58; E135

Heydenfeldt, Solomon. b. 1816, d. 1890, SC: 1816, f. Jacob Heydenfeldt, m. Esther D. DePass H. Mannahan, mr. Sarah Jones Heydenfeldt, 1844, mr2. Katherine Collins. Rf: SFF58; E169, 191, 206; EM19

Hill, Fanny (Phillips). b. 1840, f. Philip Phillips, m. Eugenia Levy Phillips, mr. Charles P. Hill. Rf: SFF24

Hilzheim, Alexander Marcus. b. 1846, d. 1864, f. Marcus Hilzheim, m. Henrietta A. Naumann Hilzheim. Rf: EC42; SFF8

Hilzheim, Henrietta (Alexander) (Naumann). b. 1806, d. 1886, SC: 1806, f. Abraham Alexander, m. Hannah Aarons Alexander, mr. William Naumann, 1827, mr2. Marcus Hilzheim. Rf: DR; EC42; EM14; SFF8

Hilzheim, Marcus. b. 1807, d. 1882, mr. Henrietta A. Naumann Hilzheim. Rf: DR; EC42; SFF8

Hirsch, Harriet (Mordecai). b. 1845, d. 1868, SC: 1845, f. Thomas Whitlock Mordecai, m. Lucretia Cohen Mordecai, mr. Isaac Willard Hirsch, 1866. Rf: DR; EM33; SFF201; 1850C; 1860C

Hirsch, Isaac Willard. b. 1844, d. 1925, mr. Harriet Mordecai Hirsch, 1866. Rf: DR; SFF201

Hirsch, John M. b. 1801, d. 1874, SC: 1841, mr. Miriam R. Woolf Hirsch, 1841. Rf: DR; EM20; SFF305

Hirsch, Melvin J. b. 1841, d. 1903, mr. Nettie Louise Levin Hirsch, 1866. Rf: DR; EM33; SFF153

Hirsch, Miriam R. (Woolf). d. 1857, SC: 1841, f. Isaac Woolf, m. Sarah Moses Woolf, mr. John M. Hirsch, 1841. Rf: EM20; SFF305

Hirsch, Nettie Louise (Levin). f. M. Levin, m. Eliza T. Woolf Levin, mr. Melvin J. Hirsch, 1866. Rf: EM33; SFF153

Hoffman, Gustave. b. 1823, d. 1890, mr. Henrietta Hoffman. Rf: EBS5

Hoffman, Henrietta. b. 1824, d. 1889, SC: 1860, mr. Gustave Hoffman. Rf: DR; EBS5

Hoffman, Julius. b. 1845, d. 1897. Rf: EBS5

Hoffman, Rachel. SC: 1857, f. Eleazer Myers, m. Rachel Peixotto Myers, mr. A. J. Hoffman, 1857. Rf: SFF240

Hoffman, Rudolph. b. 1850, d. 1874, SC: 1852. Rf: DR; EBS5

Holz, Michaelis. SC: 1857, mr. Minna Holz. Rf: EBS5

Holz, Minna. b. 1822, d. 1857, SC: 1857, mr. Michaelis Holz. Rf: EBS5

Hoppenheim, Emil M. b. 1860, SC: 1860, f. Joseph Hoppenheim, m. Hannah Hoppenheim. Rf: 1860C

Hoppenheim, Frances. b. 1855, SC: 1855, f. Joseph Hoppenheim, m. Hannah Hoppenheim. Rf: 1860C

Hoppenheim, Hannah. b. 1827, SC: 1827, mr. Joseph Hoppenheim. Rf: 1860C

Hoppenheim, Hertz. b. 1850, SC: 1850, f. Joseph Hoppenheim, m. Hannah Hoppenheim. Rf: 1860C

Hoppenheim, Joseph J. b. 1851, SC: 1851, f. Joseph Hoppenheim, m. Hannah Hoppenheim. Rf: 1860C

Hoppenheim, Joseph W. b. 1824, d. 1860, SC: 1824, mr. Hannah Hoppenheim. Rf: EBS5; 1860C

Hoppenheim, Kate. b. 1857, SC: 1857, f. Joseph Hoppenheim, m. Hannah Hoppenheim. Rf: 1860C

Housseau, Dorthea (Abramowitch). SC: 1852, mr. Simond Housseau, 1852. Rf: EM26

Housseau, Simond. SC: 1852, mr. Dorthea Abramowitch Housseau, 1852. Rf: EM26

Huchet, Elonide (Esdra). SC: 1839, mr. Eugene Huchet, 1839. Rf: EM18

Hyams, ———. f. Henry Hyams, m. Judith Hyams. Rf: SFF119

Hyams, ———. f. Henry Hyams, m. Judith Hyams. Rf: SFF119

Hyams, ———. f. Moses David Hyams, m. Susanna Jackson Hyams. Rf: SFF120

Hyams, ———. f. Moses David Hyams, m. Susannah Jackson Hyams. Rf: SFF120

Hyams, ———. b. 1828, d. 1829, SC: 1828, f. David Hyams, m. Rebecca Sarzedas Hyams. Rf: DR; SFF120

Hyams, Adelaide (Jones). b. 1839, SC: 1839, f. Israel J. Jones, mr. Hamilton Hyams, 1855. Rf: EM28; SFF120; 1860C

Hyams, Andrew Jackson. b. 1818, d. 1870, SC: 1818, f. Samuel Hyams, m. Miriam Levy Hyams. Rf: SFF119

Hyams, Augustus M. b. 1847, d. 1892, SC: 1847, f. Moses David Hyams, m. Susannah Jackson Hyams. Rf: SFF120; W51.842; 1860C

Hyams, Catherine (Jacobs). b. 1785, d. 1831, SC: 1811, mr. Samuel Jacobs, 1805, mr2. Solomon M. Hyams, 1811. Rf: DR; MR4E.120; EC37; EM8; SFF119, 131; D1831

Hyams, Daniel. b. 1789, d. 1839, SC: 1818. Rf: DR; 1830C; E135; D1835, 1838

Hyams, David. SC: 1798, f. Moses Hyams, m. Judith Isaacks Hyams, mr. Rebecca Hyams, 1798. Rf: SFF44, 119; T35; D1801, 1802, 1803, 1806, 1807, 1809, 1813; RB63

Hyams, David. SC: 1808, f. Solomon M. Hyams. Rf: SFF119; W42.635

Hyams, Eleanor. b. 1857, SC: 1857. Rf: 1860C

Hyams, Eleazer Levy. b. 1810, d. 1860, SC: 1810, f. Samuel Hyams, m. Miriam Levy Hyams. Rf: SFF119; D1831

Hyams, Elizabeth. b. 1809, d. 1843, SC: 1809. Rf: DR

Hyams, Elizabeth. b. 1843, SC: 1843, f. Moses David Hyams, m. Susannah Jackson Hyams. Rf: SFF120

Hyams, Elizabeth [2]. b. 1857, SC: 1835, f. Moses David Hyams, m. Susannah Jackson Hyams. Rf: 1860C

Hyams, Florence. b. 1859, SC: 1859, f. Moses David Hyams, m. Susannah Jackson Hyams. Rf: 1860C

Hyams, Gustavus. b. 1847, SC: 1847, f. Moses D. Hyams, m. Susannah J. Hyams. Rf: 1850C

Hyams, H. P. f. Henry Hyams, m. Judith Hyams. Rf: SFF119

Hyams, Hamilton. b. 1833, SC: 1850, f. Moses David Hyams, m. Susanna Jackson Hyams, mr. Adelaide Jones Hyams, 1855. Rf: SFF120; EM28; T35; 1850C; 1860C; 1861C; D1852, 1855, 1859

Hyams, Hamilton. b. 1857, d. 1858, SC: 1857. Rf: DR

Hyams, Hannah. b. 1763, d. 1827, SC: 1807, mr. Isaac Hyams. Rf: DR; MR3Y.241; SCA1807; D1807, 1816

Hyams, Henry. b. 1793, d. 1852, SC: 1809, f. Solomon, m. Hyams, mr. Judith Hyams. Rf: SFF119: EM22, 23; SCA1813; CB1809; D1816, 1819, 1822, 1835, 1838, 1841, 1849

Hyams, Henry. b. 1859, SC: 1859, f. Mordecai Hyams, m. Josephine Joseph, mr. Viola Straus Hyams. Rf: SFF119; 1860C

Hyams, Henry Michael. b. 1806, d. 1875, SC: 1806, f. Samuel Hyams, m. Miriam Levy Hyams, mr. Laurel Smith Hyams. Rf: SFF119

Hyams, Isaac. b. 1762, d. 1830, f. Moses Hyams, m. Judith Isaacks Hyams, mr. Catherine Hyams. Rf: SFF119

Hyams, Isaac. SC: 1801, mr. Hannah

Hyams. Rf: 1820C; SCA1801–07; D1813, 1819, 1822

Hyams, Isaac D. b. 1829, d. 1837, SC: 1837, f. Moses David Hyams, m. Susanna Jackson Hyams. Rf: EC37; SFF120

Hyams, Isaac Leo. d. 1846, f. Moses David Hyams, m. Susanna Jackson Hyams. Rf: SFF120

Hyams, Isaac Robert. b. 1827, f. Henry Hyams, m. Judith Hyams. Rf: SFF119

Hyams, Jacob. b. 1797, d. 1825, SC: 1825. Rf: DR

Hyams, Josephine (Josephs). b. 1836, d. 1906, SC: 1836, f. Levy L. Josephs, m. Isabelle Joseph Josephs, mr. Mordecai Hyams, 1855. Rf: EM26; SFF119, 139; SCA1857; MS8.390; 1850C; 1860C

Hyams, Judith. b. 1796, d. 1883, SC: 1796, mr. Henry Hyams. Rf: MR3Y.480; EJCC6; SFF119

Hyams, Judith. b. 1800, d. 1840, SC: 1800, f. Samuel Hyams, m. Miriam Levy Hyams. Rf: SFF119

Hyams, Julia. SC: 1836, f. Solomon M. Hyams. Rf: SFF119; W41.635; MS16.248

Hyams, Leah. SC: 1836, f. Solomon M. Hyams. Rf: SFF119; W41.635; MS16.246, 248

Hyams, Mary A. SC: 1813. Rf: SCA1813

Hyams, Miriam (Levy). b. 1779, d. 1821, SC: 1806, f. Eleazer Levy, m. Judith Levy, mr. Samuel Hyams. Rf: DR; EC110; SFF119; *SP*, Jan. 22, 1821, eulogy; D1806

Hyams, Mordecai. b. 1787, d. 1817, SC: 1812, f. Solomon H. Hyams. Rf: SFF119; *SP*, Sept. 30, 1817; W41.635; SCA1816; E135; D1816

Hyams, Mordecai. b. 1828, d. 1907, SC: 1828, f. Henry Hyams, m. Judith Hyams, mr. Josephine Joseph Hyams, 1855. Rf: EM28; 1840C; 1850C; 1860C; 1861C; MS18.390; D1852, 1855, 1859

Hyams, Moses. SC: 1836, f. Solomon M. Hyams. Rf: SFF119; W41.635

Hyams, Moses David. b. 1798, d. 1868, SC: 1798, f. David Hyams, m. Rebecca Sarzedas Hyams, mr. Susannah Jackson Hyams. Rf: DR; EC36, 37; SFF120; 1840C; 1850C; 1860C; 1861C; T35; W51.841 (his); D1831, 1835, 1838, 1841, 1849, 1852, 1855, 1859

Hyams, Moses David. b. 1842, SC: 1842, f. Moses D. Hyams, m. Susanna Jackson Hyams, mr. E. A. Way Hyams, 1867. Rf: SFF120; W51.842; 1850C; 1860C

Hyams, Moses Kosciusko. b. 1798, d. 1836, SC: 1798, f. Samuel Hyams, m. Miriam Levy Hyams. Rf: SFF119; T35

Hyams, Pauline (Baum). b. 1837, SC: 1837, mr. Pinckney A. Hyams, 1857. Rf: EM29; SFF120; 1860C

Hyams, Pinckney A. b. 1830, d. 1860, SC: 1830, f. Moses David Hyams, m. Susanna Jackson Hyams, mr. Pauline Baum Hyams, 1857. Rf: EM29; SFF120; W51.842; T35; 1850C; D1855, 1859

Hyams, Rachel. f. Henry Hyams, m. Judith Hyams. Rf: SFF119

Hyams, Rebecca (Benzakin). SC: 1792,

mr. Joseph Benzakin, mr2. Solomon Hyams. Rf: JR1792.83

Hyams, Rebecca (Sarzedas). b. 1781, d. 1852, SC: 1781, f. David Sarzedas, m. Sarah DaCosta Sarzedas, mr. David Hyams, 1798. Rf: DR; SFF44, 120; 1850C; SCA1793; D1816, 1819, 1831, 1849

Hyams, Rosina [Rosetta]. b. 1841, d. 1841, SC: 1841, f. Moses David Hyams, m. Susanna Jackson Hyams. Rf: DR; SFF120

Hyams, Samuel. b. 1766, d. 1843, SC: 1800, f. Moses Hyams, m. Judith Isaacks Hyams, mr. Miriam Levy Hyams. Rf: SFF119; EC110; 1800C; 1810C; 1820C; 1830C; SCA1802; D1801, 1802, 1803, 1807, 1813, 1816, 1819, 1822, 1829, 1831; RB63

Hyams, Samuel Myers. b. 1813, SC: 1813, f. Samuel Hyams, m. Miriam Levy Hyams. mr. ——— Gainie. Rf: SFF119

Hyams, Solomon. b. 1818, SC: 1838, f. Solomon Hyams, mr. Caroline Matilda Thompson Hyams, 1840. Rf: SFF119; W41.635; W48.202; 1850C; D1838, 1849, 1852, 1855, 1859

Hyams, Solomon M., Sr. b. 1753, d. 1837, SC: 1790, f. Moses Hyams, m. Judith Isaacks Hyams, mr. Rebecca Hyams, mr2. Catherine Jacobs Hyams, 1811. Rf: DR; EC37; SFF119; W41.465 (his); EM10, 1820C; 1830C; SCA1792; D1790, 1794, 1801, 1802, 1803, 1816, 1819, 1822, 1831, 1835

Hyams, Susannah (Jackson). b. 1810, d. 1864, SC: 1810, mr. Moses David Hyams. Rf: EC37; SFF120; W51.842; 1850C; 1860C

Hyams, Thaddeus Street. b. 1837, d. 1854, SC: 1837, f. Moses David Hyams, m. Susannah Jackson Hyams. Rf: EC37; SFF120; 1850C

Hyams, William Palmedo. SC: 1855, f. Solomon Hyams, m. Caroline Matilda Thompson Hyams. Rf: SFF119; W48.202

Hyman, Amelia. b. 1826, SC: 1860. Rf: 1860C

Hyman, Asher. b. 1860, SC: 1860. Rf: 1860C

Hyman, Celia Rosa. b. 1834, d. 1902, mr. Moses Hyman. Rf: EBS5

Hyman, Charles. b. 1832, SC: 1860. Rf: 1860C; *Courier* Dec. 11, 1861

Hyman, Daniel B. SC: 1819. Rf: CB1819

Hyman, Eliza (Levin). b. 1783, d. 1870. Rf: EC67

Hyman, Moses. b. 1784, d. 1851, SC: 1851, mr. Celia Rosa Hyman. Rf: DR; EBS5

Hyneman, L. SC: 1839, mr. Sarah Garretson Hyneman, 1839. Rf: EM18; Min. April 14, 1839

Hyneman, Sarah (Garretson). SC: 1839, f. Isaac Garretson, mr. L. Hyneman, 1839. Rf: EM18

Isaacks, Abraham. d. 1835, SC: 1801, f. Jacob Isaacks, m. Rebecca Mears Isaacks, mr. Rebecca Cohen Isaacks. Rf: SFF120; T5; D1806, 1807, 1813; RB65

Isaacks, Abraham Mears. b. 1765, d. 1814, SC: 1800, f. Moses Isaacks, m. Judith Rachel Mears, mr. Rebecca Simson Isaacks, 1806. Rf:

SFF120; EC74; E135; W32.845 (his); SCA1801

Isaacks, Catherine (Cohen). b. 1781, d. 1862, SC: 1781, f. Gershon Cohen, m. Rebecca Sarzedas Cohen, mr. Sampson Mears Isaacks, 1807. Rf: SFF38; 120; EM8

Isaacks, Jochebed. f. Abraham Mears Isaacks, m. Rebecca Simson Isaacks. Rf: SFF120; *AF*107

Isaacks, Judah. f. Abraham Isaacks, m. Rebecca Cohen Isaacks. Rf: SFF120

Isaacks, Judah M. f. Jacob Isaacks, m. Rebecca Mears Isaacs. Rf: SFF120; RB68

Isaacks, Judith. b. 1723, d. 1802, f. Abraham Isaacks, m. Hannah Mears Isaacks. Rf: SFF120; RB68

Isaacks, Judith Rachel (Mears). b. 1747, d. 1819, SC: 1806, f. Judah Mears, m. Jochabed Michaels Mears, mr. Moses Isaacks, 1764. Rf: SFF120, 190; D1806, 1807

Isaacks, M. A. SC: 1814. Rf: CB1814

Isaacks, Moses. b. 1737, d. 1798, SC: 1800, f. Abraham Isaacs, m. Hannah Mears Isaacs, mr. Judith Rachel Mears Isaacks, 1764. Rf: SFF120; W32.845; EM15; E279; RB68

Isaacks, Moses. b. 1807, f. Abraham Mears Isaacks, m. Rebecca Simson Mears. Rf: SFF120

Isaacks, Rachel. b. 1781, d. 1803, f. Jacob Isaacks, m. Rebecca Mears Jacobs. Rf: SFF120; RB68

Isaacks, Rebecca (Cohen). b. 1797, d. 1876, SC: 1797, f. Moses Cohen, m. Rachel Moses Cohen, mr. Abraham Isaacks. Rf: SFF36, 120; W32.845

Isaacks, Rebecca (Mears). f. Judah Mears, m. Jochabed Michaels Mears, mr. Jacob Isaacks, 1760. Rf: SFF120, 190; RB69

Isaacks, Rebecca (Simson). b. 1769, d. 1854, f. Solomon Simson, m. Sarah Mears Simson, mr. Abraham Mears Isaacks, 1806. Rf: SFF120, 272

Isaacks, Sampson Mears. b. 1777, d. 1859, SC: 1804, f. Moses Isaacks, m. Judith Rachel Mears Isaacks, mr. Catherine Cohen Isaacks, 1807. Rf: SFF38, 120; E135; EM8; W45.810

Isaacks, Sarah. f. Abraham Isaacks, m. Hannah Mears Isaacks. Rf: SFF120; RB69

Isaacks, Solomon. SC: 1803. Rf: E135

Isaacks, Washington. f. Abraham Isaacks, m. Rebecca Cohen Isaacks. Rf: SFF120

Isaacs, Abraham. SC: 1809. Rf: D1809, 1819

Isaacs, Alexander. SC: 1849. Rf: E169; SCA1864; D1849, 1852, 1855

Isaacs, Asher. SC: 1757. Rf: W8.14; RB65

Isaacs, Elizabeth. SC: 1804, mr. Samuel Isaacs. Rf: W29.698

Isaacs, Henry. SC: 1765. Rf: E278

Isaacs, Isaiah. SC: 1779. Rf: E84, 95

Isaacs, Jacob. b. 1718, d. 1798, SC: 1830, f. Abraham Isaacks, m. Hannah Mears Isaacs, mr. Rebecca Mears Isaacs, 1760. Rf: SFF120; 1830C

Isaacs, Joshua. SC: 1774. Rf: MR2P.257; RB67

Isaacs, Mary. SC: 1804, mr. Abraham Isaacs. Rf: MR4O.56, 1804

Isaacs, Samuel. d. 1804, SC: 1804, mr. Elizabeth Isaacs. Rf: W29.698; E169

Isaacs, Samuel F. SC: 1824. Rf: E169; SCA1824

Isaacs, Solomon. d. 1757, SC: 1740, f. Joseph Isaacs. Rf: SFF124; E28, W8.14 (his); *SCHM*65.203; *SCHM*74.233; SCA1752

Isaacson, Mordecai. SC: 1811. Rf: CB1811

Isaacson, Rebecca (Lazarus). b. 1808, f. Isaac Lazarus, m. Esther Lyons Lazarus, mr. Morris Isaacson, 1830. Rf: SFF150

Isack, Abraham. d. 1710, SC: 1710. Rf: W1.54 (his); E23, 277

Isear, Abraham. b. 1835, d. 1885, SC: 1861. Rf: EG2; 1861C

Isear, Anna (Mintz). b. 1832, d. 1890, SC: 1857, mr. J. Isear, 1857. Rf: EG2; EM29

Isear, J. A. b. 1823, d. 1889, SC: 1857, mr. Anna Mintz Isear, 1857. Rf: DR; EBS5; EM29

Isenburg, Benjamin. SC: 1855. Rf: D1855

Isenburg, Joseph. SC: 1855. Rf: E169; D1855

Israel, Joseph. SC: 1814. Rf: CB1814

Israel, Morris. b. 1835, d. 1911, mr. Rebecca Israel. Rf: DR; EC27; E169, 263, 265

Israel, Naphtali H. b. 1808, d. 1839, SC: 1838. Rf: DR; EC21; D1838

Israel, Rebecca. b. 1839, d. 1896, SC: 1839, mr. Morris Israel. Rf: DR; EC27

Jackson, Abraham. b. 1813, d. 1814, f. Montague Jackson, m. Hannah Hyams Jackson. Rf: SFF119

Jackson, Hannah (Hyams). SC: 1811, f. Moses Hyams, m. Judith Isaacks Hyams, mr. Montague Jackson, 1811. Rf: EM10; SFF119; EC71

Jackson, Montague. SC: 1806, mr. Hanna Hyams Jackson, 1811. Rf: SFF119; EC71; MR4F.197; D1806, 1813, 1816

Jackson, Noah. b. 1853, d. 1877. Rf: EC79

Jacob, David Cohen. SC: 1809. Rf: CB1809

Jacob, Jacob Simon. SC: 1860, mr. Sarah Jacob, mr2. Mathilda Friedenburg Jacob, 1860. Rf: EBS5; EM31

Jacob, Mathilda (Friedenburg). SC: 1860, mr. Jacob Simon Jacob, 1860. Rf: EM31

Jacob, Sarah. b. 1802, d. 1860, SC: 1860, mr. Jacob Simon Jacob. Rf: DR; EBS5

Jacobi, ———. b. 1835, d. 1871. Rf: DR

Jacobi, Benjamin. SC: 1861. Rf: 1861C

Jacobi, Charlotte (Phillips). b. 1838, d. 1900, f. Casper Phillips, m. Sarah Cohen Phillips, mr. Moritz Jacobi, 1857. Rf: JF1, 5

Jacobi, Edward Jacob. b. 1826, d. 1841, f. Wolf Jacob Jacobi, m. Priscilla Rebecca Barnet Jacobi. Rf: SFF117; JF6

Jacobi, Elizabeth Elenor. b. 1837, d. 1845, SC: 1845, f. Wolf Jacob Jacobi, m. Priscilla Rebecca Barnet Jacobi. Rf: EC24; SFF117; JF7

Jacobi, Moritz [Morris]. b. 1832, d. 1896, SC: 1850, f. Neuman Hirsch Jacobi, m. Sarah Moses Jacobi, mr. Charlotte Phillips Jacobi, 1857. Rf: JF5; E169; 1850C; D1855

Jacobi, Nathaniel. b. 1828, SC: 1850, f. Wolf Jacob Jacobi, m. Priscilla R. Nathan Barnet Jacobi, mr. Rosalie Beuthner Jacobi, 1865. Rf: E238; SFF117; T36; JF6; 1850C; *Courier* Dec. 11, 1861; D1852, 1859

Jacobi, Priscilla Rebecca (Barnett). b. 1807, d. 1841, SC: 1841, f. Nathan Barnet, mr. Wolf Jacob Jacobi. Rf: SFF117; EC24; EBS5; JF6

Jacobi, Samueline (Heydenfeldt). b. 1819, SC: 1819, f. Jacob Heydenfeldt, m. Esther D. DePass H. Hannahan, mr. Abraham Jacobi. Rf: SFF58

Jacobi, Wolf Jacob. b. 1799, d. 1866, SC: 1849, mr. Priscilla Rebecca Barnet Jacobi, mr2. Hester Eger Hertz Jacobi, 1854. Rf: SFF117; 1850C; EBS5; EM27; E169; JF6; D1849, 1852, 1859

Jacobosky, Emma. b. 1816, d. 1892. Rf: DR

Jacobowsky, S. D. SC: 1861. Rf: E238

Jacobs, Abigail. b. 1852, SC: 1860. Rf: 1860C

Jacobs, Abraham. b. 1755, d. 1834, SC: 1785, f. Raphael Jacobs, m. Sarah Simson Jacobs, mr. Shankey Hart Abrahams Jacobs, 1785. Rf: SFF98, 131; EM6; E135, 142, 279; *SCHM*19.176; MS1.348; *SCM*130; D1802

Jacobs, Barnard [Barnett]. b. 1744, d. 1824, SC: 1800, f. Raphael Jacobs, m. Sarah Simson Jacobs, mr. Celia Jacobs. Rf: W38.545; E135; SCA1805–09; D1802, 1803, 1807, 1809

Jacobs, Caroline. SC: 1807. Rf: MS5.283; MS13.431

Jacobs, Cecilia. SC: 1809, mr. Barnard Jacobs. Rf: MR3Y.480; W38.545; 1830C; 1840C; E135; D1813, 1816, 1822, 1831, 1835, 1841, 1849

Jacobs, David. b. 1825, d. 1876, SC: 1850, mr. Rebecca Jacobs. Rf: DR; EC82; E169, 239; 1850C; T36, TBS40; EJCC6; 1850C; 1860C; D1852, 1859

Jacobs, Fisher. SC: 1821. Rf: E135; CB1821

Jacobs, Frederick. SC: 1780. Rf: E92, 278

Jacobs, Frederick C. b. 1834, SC: 1834, f. Myer Jacobs, m. Rebecca Lazarus Jacobs, mr. Louisa Elizabeth Lyons Jacobs, 1862. Rf: SFF132; E169, 230; T36; 1850C; 1860C; D1841, 1855, 1859

Jacobs, H. R. SC: 1861. Rf: T36; E169, 230

Jacobs, Hamilton. b. 1830, SC: 1830. Rf: 1860C

Jacobs, Hannah. SC: 1806. Rf: D1806

Jacobs, Henrietta. f. Myer Jacobs, m. Rebecca Lazarus Jacobs. Rf: SFF132

Jacobs, Henry. b. 1852, SC: 1852, f. David Jacobs, m. Rebecca Jacobs. Rf: 1860C

Jacobs, Henry Samuel. b. 1827, d. 1893, SC: 1859, f. Samuel Jacobs, m. Rebecca Jacobs, mr. Julia Matilda Lyon Jacobs, 1851. Rf:

SFF134; EP; T36; 1860C; *Courier* Dec. 11, 1861; D1859

Jacobs, Hyam. d. 1842, SC: 1800. Rf: E135; 1810C; 1830C; W41.819 (his); SCA1807; D1807, 1809, 1813, 1835

Jacobs, Hyman. b. 1780, d. 1838, SC: 1838. Rf: EP

Jacobs, Isaac. b. 1823, d. 1903, SC: 1839. Rf: DR; Min. April 14, 1839; W42.366; 1861C

Jacobs, Isaiah. SC: 1838, f. Hyam Jacobs. Rf: W41.819; E230

Jacobs, Israel. b. 1714, SC: 1775, mr. Maria C. [Zipporah] Machado Jacobs. Rf: E106, 278; EP; SFF234; SCA1775

Jacobs, Israel. SC: 1838, f. Hyam Jacobs. Rf: W41.819

Jacobs, Jacob. b. 1742, d. 1797, SC: 1763, mr. Caty Hays Sarzedas Jacobs, 1775. Rf: E43, 91, 103, 135, 278; SFF131; EC58; W26.640 (his); 1790C; SCA1776–91; D1782, 1790, 1794, 1796

Jacobs, Jacob. SC: 1794. Rf: D1794

Jacobs, Jacob Simon. b. 1794, SC: 1840, mr. Sarah Jacobs. Rf: E169; 1840C; 1850C; 1860C; D1852

Jacobs, Joseph. SC: 1767. Rf: E45

Jacobs, Joseph. SC: 1842, f. Hyman Jacobs. Rf: W41.819; D1852

Jacobs, Joshua. SC: 1782. Rf: E106

Jacobs, Judith [Caty] (Hays) (Sarzedas). SC: 1796, f. Judah Hays, m. Rebecca Michaels Hays, mr. Abraham Sarzedas, 1753, mr2. Jacob Jacobs, 1775. Rf: MR3I.120; SFF104, 131

Jacobs, Julia Matilda (Lyon). b. 1827, d. 1906, SC: 1860, f. Moses Lyon, m. Abigail Lyon, mr. Henry Samuel Jacobs, 1851. Rf: SFF134; 1860C

Jacobs, Levi. SC: 1818. Rf: E135

Jacobs, Louis. SC: 1839. Rf: E230, 263; SCA1839

Jacobs, Louisa Elizabeth (Lyons). b. 1842, f. Jacob Cohen Lyons, m. Louisa E. Hart Lyons, mr. Frederick C. Jacobs, 1862. Rf: SFF132, 183

Jacobs, M. b. 1803, d. 1833, SC: 1859. Rf: DR; W49.852; W49.1070

Jacobs, Maria Caetana [Zipporah] (Nunes) (Mendes Machado). b. 1714, d. 1799, mr. David Mendes Machado, 1733, mr2. Israel Jacobs. Rf: EP; SFF234

Jacobs, Mary Ann (Audler). SC: 1852, mr. Philip Simon Jacobs, 1852. Rf: EM26

Jacobs, Mathilda. b. 1834, SC: 1860. Rf: 1860C

Jacobs, Miriam. SC: 1838, f. Hyam Jacobs. Rf: W41.819; MR5X.134

Jacobs, Montague. b. 1856, SC: 1856, f. David Jacobs, m. Rebecca Jacobs. Rf: 1860C

Jacobs, Moses. b. 1795, d. 1841, SC: 1823, mr. Rebecca Lazarus Jacobs, 1824. Rf: DR; E135, 169; 1830C; W42.366 (his); MS8.537, 1824; D1831, 1835

Jacobs, Myer. b. 1791, d. 1861, SC: 1811, mr. Rebecca Lazarus Jacobs, 1817. Rf: DR; EC6, 7; E135; SFF132, 151; 1840C; 1850C; 1860C; T36; D1835, 1838, 1841, 1849, 1852

Jacobs, Philip. SC: 1769. Rf: E278; EP; SCA1755

Jacobs, Philip Simon. SC: 1841, mr. Mary Audler Jacobs, 1852. Rf: *SCHM*66.183; E169; EM26; D1841

Jacobs, Rebecca. b. 1824, d. 1904, SC: 1860, mr. David Jacobs. Rf: EJCC6; 1860C; DR; D1859

Jacobs, Rebecca. b. 1857, d. 1858, SC: 1858, f. Henry Samuel Jacobs, m. Julia Matilda Lyon. Rf: DR; ENJC5; EP; SFF134

Jacobs, Rebecca (Lazarus). b. 1791, d. 1869, SC: 1820, f. Marks Lazarus, m. Richa Benjamin Lazarus, mr. Myer Jacobs, 1817. Rf: SFF151, 132; EP; SCA1827–48; EC7; 1850C; 1860C

Jacobs, Reed. SC: 1849, f. Myer Jacobs, m. Rebecca Lazarus Jacobs. Rf: SFF132; D1849

Jacobs, Rosina. b. 1858, d. 1864, SC: 1858, f. David Jacobs, m. Rebecca Jacobs. Rf: EJCC6

Jacobs, S. L. b. 1802, d. 1860, SC: 1860. Rf: DR

Jacobs, Samuel. b. 1767, d. 1810, SC: 1794, f. David Jacobs, m. Richa Simson Jacobs, mr. Catherine Jacobs Hyams, 1805. Rf: SFF119, 131; MR3G.379; SCA1802–08; D1794, 1796, 1807; RB75

Jacobs, Samuel. b. 1849, SC: 1849, f. Henry Samuel Jacobs, m. Julia Matilda Lyon Jacobs. Rf: SFF134; 1860C

Jacobs, Sarah. b. 1786, d. 1861, SC: 1786, f. Abraham Jacobs, m. Shankey Hart Jacobs. Rf: SFF131; SCA1859

Jacobs, Sarah. b. 1800, SC: 1850, mr. Jacob Simon Jacobs. Rf: 1850C

Jacobs, Shankey (Hart). b. 1766, d. 1804, SC: 1766, f. Joshua Hart, m. Rebecca Hart, mr. Abraham Jacobs, 1788. Rf: SFF98; 131; EP; EM6

Jacobs, Shelah. SC: 1809. Rf: MR4C.14

Jacobs, Washington. SC: 1849, f. Myer Jacobs, m. Rebecca Lazarus Jacobs. Rf: SFF132; D1849

Jacobson, Henry. SC: 1861. Rf: 1861C; E230

Jacobson, J. J. b. 1826, SC: 1850. Rf: 1850C

Jacobson, M. L. SC: 1861. Rf: E238; *Courier* Dec. 11, 1861

Jacoby, Bertha. b. 1830, d. 1902, SC: 1860, mr. Seigismond A. Jacoby. Rf: 1860C; DR

Jacoby, Hannah. b. 1853, SC: 1860, f. Seigismond A. Jacoby, m. Bertha Jacoby. Rf: 1860C

Jacoby, Isadore. b. 1851, SC: 1860, f. Seigismond A. Jacoby, m. Bertha Jacoby. Rf: 1860C

Jacoby, Rudolph Robinson. b. 1848, SC: 1860, f. Seigismond A. Jacoby, m. Bertha Jacoby. Rf: 1860C

Jacoby, Seigismond A. b. 1825, d. 1884, SC: 1860, mr. Bertha Jacoby. Rf: DR; EBS6; 1860C; 1861C

Jacubowsky, Simon David. b. 1819, d. 1864, SC: 1860. Rf: DR; EBS6; *Courier* Dec. 11, 1861

Joachimsen, Caroline (Cohen). b. 1841, d. 1914, SC: 1841, f. Marx Edwin Cohen, m. Armida Harby Cohen, mr. Joseph P. Joachimsen, 1863. Rf: MJSC15; SFF35

Johnson, Augusta (Ellis). f. Myer J. Ellis, m. Francis Polock Ellis, mr. Abraham Johnson, 1847. Rf: SFF64

Jonas, Joshua. SC: 1777. Rf: E280; EL; SCA1788, 1790; RB76

Jones, ——— (Nathan). SC: 1792, mr. Abraham Jones, 1792. Rf: EM6

Jones, Abraham. SC: 1790, mr. ——— Nathan, 1792. Rf: EM6; E135; 1830C; 1840C; SCA1792; D1790, 1794, 1822, 1831, 1841; RB76

Jones, Elias. SC: 1792. Rf: W41.819; SCA1792–1828

Jones, Israel. d. 1804. SC: 1794. Ref: SCA1794–1804; D1796, 1803

Jones, Israel. b. 1830, SC: 1850, mr. Sarah A. Henry Jones, 1851. Rf: EM25; 1850C

Jones, Joshua. SC: 1780. Rf: E106; D1794, 1801

Jones, Samuel B. d. 1809, SC: 1763. Rf: EC62; E91, 135, 278; SFF137; 1790C; 1800C; SCA1778–1804; D1794, 1796, 1801, 1802, 1803, 1806, 1807

Jones, Sarah A. (Henry). SC: 1851, f. Morris L. Henry, m. Mariam Henry, mr. Israel Jones, 1851. Rf: EM25

Jones, Solomon I. b. 1808, SC: 1839, mr. Anna Jane Jones. Rf: SCA1839–40; SFF137

Joseph, A. A. b. 1828, SC: 1828. Rf: 1850C

Joseph, Abigail (Audler). SC: 1818, mr. Moses Joseph, 1818. Rf: MR4N.471; EM11

Joseph, Barnet. SC: 1802. Rf: E135

Joseph, Cecilia. b. 1844, SC: 1844. Rf: 1850C

Joseph, Charlotte. b. 1813, SC: 1813. Rf: 1850C

Joseph, Daniel M. b. 1804, d. 1819, SC: 1818, f. Isaac Joseph. Rf: EC30; E135; EP; *SP*, Dec. 2, 1819, eulogy

Joseph, E. C. b. 1836, SC: 1836. Rf: 1850C

Joseph, Elizabeth (Nathans). b. 1837, d. 1858, SC: 1850, f. Nathan Nathans, m. Sarah N. Hertz, mr. S. J. Joseph, 1854. Rf: EM26; SFF231; ENJC6; 1850C

Joseph, Elizer. SC: 1800. Rf: CB1800

Joseph, Emily. b. 1839, d. 1842, f. Joseph Joseph, m. Frances Alexander Joseph. Rf: SFF139

Joseph, F. A. b. 1804, SC: 1804. Rf: 1850C

Joseph, Frances. b. 1830, SC: 1830. Rf: 1850C

Joseph, Frances (Alexander). SC: 1822, f. Abraham Alexander, m. Hannah Aarons Alexander, mr. Joseph Joseph, 1822. Rf: EM13; SFF8, 139

Joseph, Henrietta. b. 1845, SC: 1845. Ref: 1850C

Joseph, Henrietta (Abrams). SC: 1850, f. Elias Abrahams, m. Catherine Cohen Abrahams, mr. Lizar H. Josephs, 1853. Rf: EM26; SFF4, 139; 1850C

Joseph, Henry. SC: 1818. Rf: MS8.351, 1822; E136

Joseph, Isaac. SC: 1816. Rf: EC30, 139; SCA1816–17

Joseph, Israel. b. 1733, d. 1804, SC: 1764, f. Isaac Joseph, mr. Miriam

Levy Joseph. Rf: EC74, 82; SFF98, 139; E117; W29.673 (his); 1790C; 1800C; SCA1767; D1790, 1794, 1802, 1803

Joseph, Jacob. b. 1805, SC: 1805. Ref: 1850C; D1841

Joseph, Jacob. b. 1832, SC: 1832. Rf: 1850C

Joseph, Joseph. b. 1849, SC: 1849. Rf: 1850C

Joseph, Joseph J. SC: 1801, f. Lizer Joseph, m. Sarah Joseph, mr. Frances Alexander Joseph, 1822. Rf: EM13; E169; SFF8, 139; 1820C; 1830C; 1850C; SCA1822–41; D1801, 1802, 1806, 1809, 1816, 1835, 1838, 1841; RB77

Joseph, Lazarus. SC: 1802. Rf: E136; D1802, 1803

Joseph, Lizar. b. 1824, SC: 1824. Rf: 1850C

Joseph, Lizar H. SC: 1851, f. Jacob Judah Joseph, m. Sarah Emanuel Jacob, mr. Sarah Judith Judah Joseph, mr2. Henrietta Abrahams Joseph, 1851. Rf: EG2; *AF*126; E169; EM26; SFF139

Joseph, Maria. b. 1841, SC: 1841. Ref: 1850C

Joseph, Miriam (Levy). b. 1753, d. 1815, SC: 1815, f. Mordecai Levy, m. Mary Cohen, mr. Israel Joseph. Rf: SFF98, 139; EC74

Joseph, Moses. SC: 1818, mr. Abigail Audler Joseph, 1818. Rf: MR4N.571; EM11; E136; 1820C; SCA1818; D1819, 1822

Joseph, Nathan. SC: 1801. Rf: SCA1801–02

Joseph, Rosa. b. 1783, d. 1828, mr. Joseph J. Josephs. Rf: EP

Joseph, Samuel. SC: 1802. Rf: D1802, 1806; RB77

Joseph, Sarah. b. 1823, d. 1824, SC: 1824, f. Joseph Josephs, m. Frances Alexander Josephs. Rf: SFF139; EG2

Joseph, Sarah Judith (Judah). b. 1776, d. 1820, f. Jacob Judah, mr. Lizer Joseph. Rf: *AF*126

Joseph, Solomon. SC: 1839. Rf: SCA1839

Joseph, Solomon M. SC: 1800. Rf: E136

Josephs, Elias. b. 1830, SC: 1830. Rf: 1850C; D1849, 1852

Josephs, Frances L. b. 1795, d. 1827, SC: 1827, mr. Levy L. Josephs. Rf: JR1827, 249a; EP

Josephs, Isabelle (Joseph). SC: 1822, f. Lizer Joseph, m. Sarah Joseph, mr. Levy L. Josephs. Rf: SFF139; MS8.351

Josephs, Jacob Judah. b. 1810, d. 1862, SC: 1810, f. Levy L. Josephs, m. Isabelle Joseph Josephs. Rf: SFF139; 1850C; D1849, 1852

Josephs, Levy L. b. 1795, d. 1827, SC: 1795, mr. Frances L. Josephs, mr2. Isabelle Joseph Josephs. Rf: EP; SFF139; 1820C (Georgetown); E136; SCA1824

Josephs, Lizzie. b. 1845, SC: 1845. Rf: 1860C

Josephs, Samuel J. SC: 1854, mr. Elizabeth Nathans Josephs, 1854. Rf: EM26; SFF231; MS18.249

Josephs, Sarah. b. 1820, SC: 1820. Rf: 1850C

Judah, Andrew. SC: 1764. Rf: E43

Judah, Baruch H. b. 1763, d. 1830, f.

Hillel Judah, m. Abigail Seixas Judah. Rf: SFF140

Judah, Elizabeth. SC: 1791. Rf: SCA1791

Judah, Isaac. SC: 1753. Rf: SCA1753

Judah, Isaac H. b. 1761, d. 1827, f. Hillel Judah, m. Abigail Seixas Judah. Rf: SFF140

Judah, Jacob. b. 1765, SC: 1765, f. Hillel Judah, m. Abigail Seixas Judah. Rf: SFF140; W28.147; E136; 1790C; SCA1789; D1802; RB80

Judah, Samuel. d. 1789, SC: 1774. Rf: SCA1774–89

Kaminski, Charlotte Virginia Emanuel. b. 1840, d. 1881, f. Nathan Emanuel, m. Flora Emanuel Emanuel, mr. Heiman Kaminski, 1867. Rf: DR; SFF66; EC79; Rogers, 472

Keller, Samuel. SC: 1819. Rf: CB1819

Kleber, ———. b. 1789, d. 1849, SC: 1849. Rf: DR

Kohn, H. b. 1787, d. 1882. Rf: DR

Koopman, M. SC: 1852. Rf: E169

Krautman, I. SC: 1848. Rf: Min. Feb. 6, 1848

Krutschnitt, Peninah (Benjamin). b. 1824, d. 1903, f. Philip Benjamin, m. Rebecca DeMendes Benjamin, mr. John Krutschnitt. Rf: SFF18

Labatt, Abraham Cohen. b. 1802, d. 1899, SC: 1802, f. David Labatt, m. Catherine Labatt, mr. Caroline Hyams Labatt, 1825. Rf: EM13; E136; SFF119, 148; SCA1829

Labatt, Amelia [Minky] (Marks). b. 1806, d. 1871, SC: 1806, f. Samuel Handel Marks, m. Sarah Harris Marks, mr. Isaac Cohen Labatt. Rf: SFF148, 185

Labatt, Caroline (Hyams). b. 1802, SC: 1825, f. Samuel Hyams, m. Miriam Levy Hyams, mr. Abraham C. Labatt, 1825. Rf: EM13; SFF119, 148

Labatt, Catherine. b. 1773, d. 1846, SC: 1816, mr. David Labatt. Rf: SFF148; SCA1822–24; D1813, 1816, 1822, 1829, 1831, 1835; RB83

Labatt, Cora. f. David Labatt, m. Catherine Labatt. Rf: SFF148

Labatt, David. SC: 1796, mr. Catherine Labatt. Rf: SFF148; E136, 145, 280; D1796, 1801, 1802, 1803, 1806, 1807; RB83

Labatt, David. f. Abraham Cohen Labatt, m. Caroline Hyams Labatt, mr. Emily B. Labatt. Rf: SFF148

Labatt, Isaac Cohen. b. 1804, d. 1870, SC: 1829, f. David Labatt, m. Catherine Labatt, mr. Amelia (Minky) Marks Harris Labatt. Rf: SFF148, 185; E136, 169; SCA1831; D1829, 1831, 1835, 1838

Labatt, Leon. f. Abraham Cohen Labatt, m. Caroline Hyams Labatt. Rf: SFF148

Lambert, Elizabeth. f. William C. Lambert, m. Rachel DePass Lambert. Rf: SFF58

Lambert, Rachel (DePass) (Moses). SC: 1813, f. Samuel DePass, m. Maria Rodriquez DePass Brand, mr. Fisher Moses, 1824, mr2. William Lambert. Rf: SFF58; EC25, 110, 212; EM13; MR5X.185

Lambert, Rosalie. d. 1835, SC: 1835, f. William C. Lambert, m. Rachel

DePass Moses Lambert. Rf: EC110; SFF58

Lambert, Samuel. f. William C. Lambert, m. Rachel DePass Moses Lambert. Rf: SFF58

Lambert, Solomon. b. 1836, d. 1841, SC: 1836, f. William C. Lambert, m. Rachel DePass Moses Lambert. Rf: DR; EC25; SFF58

Lambert, William C. SC: 1830, mr. Rachel DePass Moses. Rf: SFF58; EC110; 1830C; MR5X.186

Lange, John H. Rf: E169

Lazarus, ———. b. 1788, d. 1788, SC: 1788, f. Marks Lazarus, m. Rachel Benjamin Lazarus. Rf: SFF151

Lazarus, ———. b. 1834, d. 1857, SC: 1857. Rf: DR

Lazarus, Aaron. b. 1777, d. 1841, SC: 1777, f. Marks Lazarus, m. Rachel Benjamin Lazarus, mr. Esther Cohen Lazarus, 1803, mr2. Rachel Mordecai Lazarus, 1821. Rf: SFF38, 151; E136, 280; T36; EP; W44.261; SCA1801–07

Lazarus, Aaron. b. 1840, SC: 1840, f. Gershon Clarendon Lazarus, m. Caroline Jay Jacobs Lazarus. Rf: 1850C; SFF151

Lazarus, Abraham. b. 1827, SC: 1860, mr. Rose Lazarus. Rf: 1860C

Lazarus, Adeline. b. 1802, d. 1865, SC: 1802, f. Marks Lazarus, m. Rachel Benjamin Lazarus. Rf: EC31; SFF151; W44.261; W49.1000; W50.406 (hers); 1850C; 1860C

Lazarus, Albert. b. 1848, d. 1879, SC: 1848, f. Benjamin Dores Lazarus, m. Cornelia Cohen Lazarus, mr. Jane Warner Hart, 1872. Rf: DR; EC22; SFF98, 151; 1850C

Lazarus, Benjamin. b. 1779, d. 1780, SC: 1779, f. Marks Lazarus, m. Rachel Benjamin Lazarus. Rf: EC27; SFF151

Lazarus, Benjamin Dores. b. 1800, d. 1875, SC: 1800, f. Marks Lazarus, m. Rachel Benjamin Lazarus, mr. Cornelia Cohen Lazarus, 1840. Rf: DR; EM18; SFF35, 151; E26; 1850C; SCA1826; D1829, 1831, 1835, 1841, 1849, 1852, 1855, 1859

Lazarus, Benjamin Dores. b. 1842, SC: 1842, f. Benjamin Dores Lazarus, m. Cornelia Cohen Lazarus, mr. Wilhelmina Toomer Lazarus. Rf: SFF151; E231; 1850C; 1861C

Lazarus, Bernard. b. 1827, d. 1832, f. Henry Lazarus, m. Louisa Lazarus. Rf: EP; SFF150

Lazarus, Caroline Jay (Jacobs). b. 1817, SC: 1817, f. Myer Jacobs, m. Rebecca Lazarus Jacobs, mr. Gershon L. Lazarus, 1837. Rf: EM17; SFF132; 151; 1850C; 1860C

Lazarus, Catherine. SC: 1824, m. Frances Lazarus. Rf: SCA1828–32; EC28; D1831

Lazarus, Channah L. b. 1828, d. 1901. Rf: DR; MS4.268

Lazarus, Clara. b. 1822, d. 1822, SC: 1822. Rf: DR

Lazarus, Cornelia. b. 1841, d. 1921, SC: 1841, f. Benjamin Dores Lazarus, m. Cornelia Cohen Lazarus. Rf: DR; SFF151; 1850C

Lazarus, Cornelia (Cohen). b. 1805, d. 1886, SC: 1805, f. Mordecai Cohen, m. Leah Lazarus Cohen, mr. Benjamin Dores Lazarus, 1840. Rf: DR; EC26; SFF35, 151; W44.356; W49.1000; EM18; 1850C

Lazarus, Daniel. b. 1795, d. 1795, SC: 1795, f. Marks Lazarus, m. Rachel Benjamin Lazarus. Rf: EC27; SFF151

Lazarus, Daniel. f. Jacob Lazarus, m. Miriam Hart Lazarus. Rf: SFF99

Lazarus, Edgar Marks. b. 1836, d. 1884, SC: 1836, f. Joshua Lazarus, m. Phoebe Yates Lazarus, mr. Minnie Mordecai Lazarus, 1864. Rf: SFF151; EM32; W49.852; T36; 1850C; 1860C

Lazarus, Edward. b. 1849, SC: 1849, f. Benjamin Dores Lazarus, m. Cornelia Cohen Lazarus, mr. Jennie Harrison. Rf: SFF151; W51.866; 1850C

Lazarus, Emma. b. 1798, d. 1865, SC: 1798, f. Marks Lazarus, m. Rachel Benjamin Lazarus. Rf: EC31; SFF151; W40.365; W44.261; W44.261; EP; 1850C; 1860C

Lazarus, Esther (Cohen). b. 1784, d. 1816, f. Gershon Cohen, m. Rebecca Sarzedas Cohen, mr. Aaron Lazarus, 1803. Rf: SFF38, 151

Lazarus, Esther (Lyons). b. 1786, d. 1846, SC: 1808, f. Eleazer Lyons, m. Hannah Levy Lyons, mr. Isaac Lazarus, 1805. Rf: MR3Z.366; SFF150, 182; E136

Lazarus, Frances. b. 1742, d. 1822, SC: 1822. Rf: DR; EC28

Lazarus, Gershon Clarendon. b. 1804, d. 1868, SC: 1837, f. Aaron Lazarus, m. Esther Cohen Lazarus, mr. Caroline Jay Jacobs Lazarus, 1837. Rf: EM17; SFF132, 151; 1850C; 1860C; 1861C; E169, 204; W49.1070; MS4.268; D1849, 1852, 1855, 1859

Lazarus, Gustavus Poznanski. b. 1842, SC: 1842, f. Gershon Clarendon Lazarus, m. Caroline Jay Jacobs Lazarus. Rf: 1850C; 1860C; SFF151

Lazarus, Henry. SC: 1814, m. Frances Lazarus, mr. Louisa Lazarus. Rf: EC28; EP; SFF150; E136; 1830C; SCA1819–26; D1819

Lazarus, Hetty Maria (Gomez) (Hart). b. 1822, d. 1869, SC: 1850, f. Aaron Lopez Gomez, m. Hetty Hendricks Gomez, mr. Hyman N. Hart, 1841, mr2. Joshua E. P. Lazarus, 1861. Rf: SFF85, 98, 99; E169; 1850C

Lazarus, Isaac. SC: 1804, mr. Esther Lyons Lazarus. Rf: SFF150, 182; E136

Lazarus, Isabel. b. 1855, SC: 1855. Rf: 1860C

Lazarus, Jacob. b. 1781, d. 1834, SC: 1805, mr. Miriam Hart Lazarus, 1812. Rf: EM10; SFF99; E136; 1820C; W31.441; T36; CB1805; SCA1813–27; D1807, 1813, 1819, 1822

Lazarus, Jane Warner (Hart). b. 1851, d. 1874, f. Samuel Nathan, m. Isabel Lazarus Nathan, mr. Albert Lazarus, 1872. Rf: EC22; SFF98, 151

Lazarus, Joseph. SC: 1803. Rf: E136

Lazarus, Joshua. b. 1796, d. 1861, SC: 1796, f. Marks Lazarus, m. Rachel Benjamin Lazarus, mr. Phoebe Yates Lazarus, 1834. Rf: DR; EC6, 27; E136; EM16; W49.1070 (his);

W44.261; 1840C; 1850C; 1860C; T36; SFF151; D1841, 1849, 1852, 1855, 1859

Lazarus, Joshua. b. 1838, SC: 1838, f. Gershon Clarendon Lazarus, m. Caroline Jay Jacobs Lazarus. Rf: 1850C; 1860C; D1859

Lazarus, Joshua E. P. b. 1821, d. 1889, SC: 1821, f. Jacob Lazarus, m. Miriam Hart Lazarus, mr. Hetty Maria Gomez Hart Lazarus, 1861. Rf: SFF99; EC49; W40.415; D1849, 1859

Lazarus, Julia Edith. b. 1830, d. 1873, f. Aaron Lazarus, m. Rachel Mordecai Lazarus. Rf: DR; EC31; SFF151

Lazarus, Lazarus. b. 1860, SC: 1860, f. Abraham Lazarus, m. Rose Lazarus. Rf: 1860C

Lazarus, Lena. b. 1856, SC: 1860, f. Abraham Lazarus, m. Rose Lazarus. Rf: 1860C

Lazarus, Louisa. SC: 1820, mr. Henry Lazarus. Rf: SFF150; SCA1820

Lazarus, Marks. b. 1757, d. 1835, SC: 1757, f. Michael Lazarus, mr. Rachel Benjamin Lazarus, 1776. Rf: DR; EC32, 33; SFF151; W40.339 (his); T36; D1790, 1794, 1801, 1802, 1803, 1807, 1809, 1813, 1816, 1819, 1822, 1829, 1831, 1835

Lazarus, Marx Hubert. b. 1846, d. 1914, SC: 1846, f. Benjamin Dores Lazarus, m. Cornelia Cohen Lazarus, mr. Mordenai Levy Lazarus, 1881. Rf: DR; SFF151; 1850C

Lazarus, Mary [Miriam] (Hart). b. 1792, d. 1828, SC: 1792, f. Daniel Hart, m. Bella Levy Hart, mr. Jacob Lazarus, 1812. Rf: DR; EC76; SFF99

Lazarus, Michael. SC: 1749. Rf: SFF151; E32, 40, 84; SCA1767–75; RB84

Lazarus, Michael. b. 1786, d. 1862, SC: 1786, f. Marks Lazarus, m. Rebecca Benjamin Lazarus. Rf: SFF151; E161; W49.1070(his); W44.261; SCA1818; 1850C; 1860C; 1861C; D1809, 1813, 1816, 1819, 1822, 1829, 1831, 1835, 1841, 1849, 1855, 1859

Lazarus, Michael Washington. b. 1844, SC: 1844, f. Gershon Clarendon Lazarus, m. Caroline Jay Jacobs Lazarus, mr. Mary Beatrice Barrett Lazarus. Rf: 1850C; 1860C; SFF151

Lazarus, Minnie [Rachel] (Mordecai). b. 1839, SC: 1850, f. Moses Cohen Mordecai, m. Isabel Rebecca Lyons Mordeca, mr. Edgar Marks Lazarus, 1864. Rf: EM32: SFF151, 203; 1850C; 1860C

Lazarus, Mordenai Charlotte Blair (Levy). b. 1850, d. 1897, SC: 1850, f. Mordecai M. Lazarus, m. Jane Hart Lazarus, mr. Marks Hubert Lazarus, 1881. Rf: DR; SFF151, 169; W50.415

Lazarus, Moses L. SC: 1818, f. Jacob Lazarus, m. Miriam Hart Lazarus. Rf: SFF99; E136

Lazarus, Phoebe (Yates). b. 1794, d. 1870, SC: 1834, f. Samuel Yates, m. Martha Yates, mr. Joshua Lazarus, 1834. Rf: EC27; EM16; W49.852; SFF151, 308; 1850C; 1860C

Lazarus, Rachel. b. 1781, d. 1785, SC: 1781, f. Marks Lazarus, m. Rachel Benjamin Lazarus. Rf: SFF151

Lazarus, Rachel. b. 1858, SC: 1858, f. Abraham Lazarus, m. Rose Lazarus. Rf: 1860C

Lazarus, Rachel A. b. 1807, d. 1883, SC: 1807, f. Aaron Lazarus, m. Esther Cohen Lazarus. Rf: DR; SFF151; EP; SCA1848

Lazarus, Rachel DeTorres (Benjamin). b. 1762, d. 1847, SC: 1772, f. Todros Benjamin, m. Rachel DeTorres Benjamin, mr. Marks Lazarus, 1776. Rf: DR; EC32, 33; SFF62, 151; E92; W44.261 (hers); 1840C; SCA1801

Lazarus, Rachel (Mordecai). b. 1789, d. 1838, f. Jacob Mordecai, m. Rebecca Myers Mordecai, mr. Aaron Lazarus, 1821. Rf: SFF151, 200

Lazarus, Rosamond. f. Jacob Lazarus, m. Miriam Hart Lazarus. Rf: SFF99

Lazarus, Rose. b. 1830, SC: 1857, mr. Abraham Lazarus. Rf: 1860C, Min. Sept. 16, 1857, Sept. 25, 1859

Lazarus, Rosetta. f. Jacob Lazarus, m. Miriam Hart Lazarus. Rf: SFF99

Lazarus, Simon. SC: 1800. Rf: E136

Lazarus, Solomon. b. 1844, d. 1892, SC: 1844, f. Benjamin Dores Lazarus, m. Cornelia Cohen Lazarus. Rf: EC22; SFF151; E231; 1850C

Lazarus, Solomon David. b. 1793, d. 1808, SC: 1793, f. Marks Lazarus, m. Rachel Benjamin Lazarus. Rf: EC26; SFF151

Lazarus, Walter. b. 1853, SC: 1853, f. Gershon C. Lazarus, m. Caroline Jay Jacobs Lazarus. Rf: 1860C; SFF151

Lazarus, Washington. SC: 1839. Rf: Min. April 14, 1839

Lee, Joseph. SC: 1818, mr. Mariam Myers Lee, 1819. Rf: E136; EM12; 1820C

Lee, Mariam (Myers). SC: 1819, f. Samuel Myers, mr. Joseph Lee, 1819. Rf: EM12

Lee, Samuel. b. 1820, d. 1821, SC: 1820. Rf: DR

Lehman, Hannah. b. 1828, SC: 1850. Rf: 1850C

Leibshith, ———. b. 1784, d. 1838, SC: 1838. Rf: Min. Sept. 23, Dec. 29, 1838

Leidloff, Selina (DaVega). d. 1886, f. Isaac DaVega, m. Sarah J. Moses DaVega, mr. Herman Leidloff, 1881. Rf: SFF45

Leman, ———. b. 1795, d. 1849, SC: 1849. Rf: DR

Lemmon, ———. SC: 1821. Rf: E136; CB1821

Leob, Catharine. b. 1788, d. 1853, SC: 1853, mr. Jacob Leob. Rf: EC26

Leob, Jacob. SC: 1853, mr. Catherine Leob. Rf: EC26

Lesser, Jacob. b. 1837, d. 1862. Rf: DR

Levenburg, Joseph. SC: 1859. Rf: Min. Feb. 13, 1860

Levenston, ———. SC: 1821. Rf: CB1821

Levi, Elias. b. 1804, d. 1866, SC: 1804. Rf: DR

Levi, L. SC: 1827. Rf: TBS40

Levi, Lyon. SC: 1786. Rf: EP

Levi, Rose. SC: 1796, mr. Solomon Levi. Rf: MR3F.358

Levi, Sarah. SC: 1766, mr. Solomon Levi. Rf: MR2M.432

Levi, Solomon. SC: 1766, mr. Sarah Levy. Rf: MR2M.432; E44, 278; W18.1; RB86, 97

Levin, ———. b. 1820, d. 1855, SC: 1855. Rf: DR

Levin, ———. b. 1860, d. 1860, SC: 1860. Rf: DR

Levin, Ann (Sampson). b. 1815, d. 1846, SC: 1839, f. Samuel Sampson, m. Amelia Sampson, mr. Jacob Levin, 1839. Rf: EJCC6; EM17; SFF153, 259

Levin, Anna. b. 1852, SC: 1852, f. Harris Levin, m. Esther Levin. Rf: 1860C

Levin, Charlotte A. (Woolf). b. 1817, d. 1883, SC: 1817, f. Isaac Woolf, m. Sarah Moses Woolf, mr. L. T. Levin, 1844. Rf: DR; SFF153, 305; MS15.453

Levin, Eliza Isabella. b. 1841, d. 1841, SC: 1841, f. Nathaniel Levin, m. Mary Moses Levin. Rf: DR; EC44; SFF153

Levin, Eliza T. (Woolf). b. 1815, d. 1867, SC: 1841, f. Isaac Woolf, m. Sarah Moses Woolf, mr. Moritz Levin, 1841. Rf: DR; EM20; SFF153, 305

Levin, Elizabeth. SC: 1819. Rf: D1819, 1822

Levin, Emanuel. SC: 1800. Rf: E136; SCA1828; CB1819; D1835

Levin, Esther. b. 1813, SC: 1860, mr. Harris Levin. Rf: 1860C, Min. Feb. 13, 1860

Levin, Esther (Davis). f. Solomon Davis, m. Anna Abrahams Davis, mr. Solomon Moses Davis. Rf: SFF49

Levin, Hannah. SC: 1807, mr. Lewis Levin. Rf: MR3Y.207; SFF153

Levin, Hannah. b. 1828, d. 1876, SC: 1856. Rf: DR; EBS6

Levin, Harris A. b. 1838, d. 1872, SC: 1860, mr. Matilda Levin. Rf: 1860C; DR

Levin, Harris D. b. 1805, d. 1881, SC: 1861, mr. Esther Levin. Rf: EBS6; 1860C; 1861C

Levin, Hava Sulka. d. 1858, SC: 1858. Rf: EBS6

Levin, Isabella. b. 1844, d. 1850, SC: 1844, f. Nathaniel Levin, m. Mary Moses Levin. Rf: DR; EP; SFF153

Levin, Jacob. b. 1802, d. 1874, SC: 1822, f. Lewis Levin, mr. Ann Sampson Levin, 1839, mr2. Judith Mordecai Levin, 1850. Rf: EJCC6; SFF153, 203; EM17; MS20.322; D1822, 1835

Levin, Judith (Mordecai). b. 1806, d. 1880, SC: 1806, f. David Mordecai, m. Reinah Cohen Mordecai, mr. Jacob Levin, 1850. Rf: EJCC6; SFF153, 203

Levin, Julian. b. 1847, SC: 1847. Rf: 1850C; 1860C

Levin, Lewis. b. 1765, d. 1817, SC: 1807, mr. Hannah Levin. Rf: EC36; SFF153; E136; D1807, 1816

Levin, Lewis. b. 1793, d. 1829, SC: 1807, f. Lewis Levin, m. Hannah Levin. Rf: SFF153; EP; *SCHM*6.183; SCA1807–29; D1819, 1822

Levin, Lewis. b. 1842, d. 1842, SC: 1842, f. Nathaniel Levin, m. Mary Moses Levin. Rf: EC44; SFF153

Levin, Lewis C. b. 1808, d. 1860, SC: 1808. Rf: E169, 192

Levin, Lewis C. b. 1849, d. 1850, SC: 1849, f. Nathaniel Levin, m. Mary Moses Levin. Rf: EC93; SFF153; 1850C

Levin, Lipmann T. b. 1818, d. 1892, SC: 1818, f. Lewis Levin, m. Hannah Levin, mr. Charlotte A. Woolf Levin, 1844. Rf: DR; EM21; SFF153, 305; MS15.453

Levin, Marion R. b. 1857, d. 1902, SC: 1857. Rf: DR; EP

Levin, Mary (Moses). b. 1819, d. 1887, SC: 1819, f. Solomon Moses, m. Isabella Myers Moses, mr. Nathaniel Levin, 1837. Rf: DR; EC44; EM17; SFF153, 213; W45.682; 1850C; 1860C

Levin, Matilda. b. 1840, SC: 1860, mr. Harris A. Levin. Rf: 1860C

Levin, Miriam. b. 1838, SC: 1838. Rf: 1850C; 1860C

Levin, Moritz. b. 1810, d. 1865, SC: 1840, f. Lewis Levin, m. Hannah Levin, mr. Eliza T. Woolf Levin, 1841. Rf: EM20; SFF153, 305; E169; DR; D1849, 1852, 1855, 1859

Levin, Nathaniel. b. 1816, d. 1899, SC: 1816, f. Lewis Levin, m. Hannah Levin, mr. Mary Moses Levin, 1837. Rf: DR; EM17; SFF153; E33; 1850C; 1860C; SCA1842–43; *Courier* Dec. 11, 1861; D1849, 1852, 1855, 1859

Levin, Nathaniel. b. 1845, d. 1914, SC: 1845. Rf: 1850C; 1860C; DR

Levin, Solomon. SC: 1800. Rf: MR3Q.325

Levin, Solomon. b. 1842, SC: 1842. Rf: 1860C; D1859

Levin, Solomons. SC: 1800. Rf: MR3Q.325

Levin, Woolf. b. 1850, SC: 1860, f. Harris Levin, m. Esther Levin. Rf: 1860C

Levinsohn, ———. b. 1823, d. 1871. Rf: DR

Levinsohn, Jacob. SC: 1859. Rf: 1861C; T37; D1859

Levy, ———. mr. Rachel Moïse Levy. Rf: SFF195

Levy, ———. b. 1809, d. 1834, SC: 1809. Rf: DR

Levy, ———. b. 1828, d. 1829, SC: 1828. Rf: DR

Levy, ———. b. 1849, d. 1849, SC: 1849, f. Mordecai M. Levy, m. Jane Hart Levy. Rf: SFF169

Levy, ———, Mrs. b. 1794, d. 1834, SC: 1794. Rf: DR

Levy, ———, [Mrs. Hart]. SC: 1802. Rf: D1802

Levy, A. SC: 1855. Rf: D1855

Levy, Aaron. SC: 1830. Rf: 1830C; D1831, 1835

Levy, Abigail (Sampson). b. 1805, SC: 1805, mr. Joseph Sampson, mr2. L. L. Levy, 1834. Rf: EM15; SFF259; 1830C; SCA1854

Levy, Abraham L. b. 1796, d. 1829, SC: 1800, f. Lyon Levy, m. Leah Tobias Levy, mr. Rebecca Benjamin Levy, 1826. Rf: SFF18, 163; E136; W40.179; T36; SCA1822–26; D1813

Levy, Alfred L. b. 1823, d. 1827, SC: 1823, f. Lyon Levy, m. Sarah Cardoza Levy. Rf: DR; SFF163

Levy, Alice. b. 1825, d. 1827, f. Hayman Levy, m. Almeria DeLeon Levy. Rf: SFF159

Levy, Almeria (DeLeon). b. 1798, d.

1882, SC: 1819, f. Jacob DeLeon, m. Hannah Hendricks DeLeon, mr. Hayman Levy, 1819. Rf: EM12; SFF55, 159

Levy, Almeria Emma (Moses). b. 1845, SC: 1845, f. Charles Brown Moses, m. Angelina Lazarus Levy, mr. Eugene Henry Levy. Rf: SFF165, 207

Levy, Amanda Fitzalan (Phillips). b. 1812, SC: 1834, f. Aaron Phillips, m. Caroline Lazarus Phillips, mr. Ezra Levy, 1834. Rf: EM15; SFF163, 247; W49.1000

Levy, Angelica (Heydenfeldt). SC: 1841, f. Solomon J. Heydenfeldt, mr. Isaac Levy, 1841. Rf: EM19; SFF167

Levy, Ann. SC: 1807. Rf: D1807

Levy, Anna Maria. b. 1840, d. 1841, f. Lyon Levy, m. Leath Tobias Levy. Rf: SFF163

Levy, Anna Maria (Moses). b. 1805, d. 1899, SC: 1805, f. Isaac Clifton Moses, m. Hannah Lazarus Moses, mr. David Cardoza Levy, 1826. Rf: SFF163, 164, 207

Levy, Barnet. b. 1811, d. 1848, SC: 1811. Rf: E169; EP

Levy, Bella. SC: 1803. Rf: D1803, 1806, 1807

Levy, Belle. d. 1893, f. Orlando R. Levy, m. Catherine Bowers Levy. Rf: SFF163

Levy, Bernard. b. 1789, d. 1869, SC: 1789, mr. Mary Ann Suares Levy, 1840. Rf: DR; EM20; EC83; E136; T36; SCA1833–43; D1831, 1835, 1838

Levy, Calhoun. f. Orlando R. Levy, m. Catherine Bowers Levy. Rf: SFF163

Levy, Caroline Agnes. d. 1834, f. David Cardoza Levy, m. Anna Maria Moses Levy. Rf: SFF164

Levy, Catherine. SC: 1806, mr. Samuel S. Levy. Rf: MR4Y.463

Levy, Catherine (Bowers). b. 1830, SC: 1850, mr. Orlando R. Levy. Rf: SFF163; W47.743; SCA1861; 1850C

Levy, Chapman. b. 1787, d. 1849, SC: 1811, f. Samuel Levy, m. Sarah Moses Levy, mr. Flora Levy, 1818. Rf: EM11; EC110; T26; SCA1808–28; SFF169; RB89

Levy, Charles Ferdinand. b. 1828, d. 1901, SC: 1828, f. Elias Levy, m. Rachel Moïse Levy, mr. Laura Louise Barrett Levy, 1853. Rf: DR; T36; W47.743; SFF17, 163; EM26; E169; SCA1847; 1850C; 1861C; D1852, 1855, 1859

Levy, Charles Ferdinand. b. 1861, d. 1939, SC: 1861, f. Charles Ferdinand Levy, m. Laura Louise Barrett Levy. Rf: SFF163

Levy, Cherry Moïse. b. 1825, SC: 1825, f. Elias Levy, m. Rachel Moïse Levy, mr. Esther Caroline Raphall Levy, 1851. Rf: EM25; SFF163; W47.743; 1850C; SCA1842–46

Levy, Clarence. b. 1830, d. 1872, SC: 1830. Rf: 1860C; DR; D1852, 1859

Levy, Clarence E. b. 1832, d. 1872, SC: 1832, f. Elias Levy, m. Rachel Moïse Levy. Rf: DR; EC19; SFF163; E169, 231; W47.743; 1850C

Levy, Cordelia. b. 1831, d. 1833, SC: 1831, f. Elias Levy, m. Rachel

Moïse Levy. Rf: DR; EC19; SFF163

Levy, Cossman. b. 1813, d. 1838, SC: 1838. Rf: EC18; E169

Levy, David. SC: 1800. Rf: E136, 292; CB1800

Levy, David. b. 1841, d. 1842, SC: 1841, f. Lyon Levy, m. Sarah Cardozo Levy. Rf: DR; SFF163

Levy, David Cardozo. b. 1805, d. 1877, SC: 1805, f. Lyon Levy, m. Sarah Cardozo Levy, mr. Anna Maria Moses Levy, 1826. Rf: SFF163, 164; E163, 169, 193; T37; 1840C; W44.416; SCA1826–47; D1835, 1838, 1841

Levy, David Cardozo. b. 1837, d. 1863, f. David Cardozo Levy, m. Anna Maria Moses Cardozo. Rf: SFF164

Levy, David J. SC: 1855. Rf: D1855

Levy, Edward. b. 1800, SC: 1800. Rf: 1850C; D1852

Levy, Eleanor (Moïse). b. 1824, d. 1890, SC: 1824, f. Aaron Moïse, m. Sarah Cohen Moïse, mr. Lionel Cardoza Levy, 1847. Rf: EM22; SFF163, 164, 195

Levy, Eleazer. SC: 1785. Rf: E136; SCA1785; D1803, 1806

Levy, Elias, Jr. SC: 1835. Rf: D1835, 1841

Levy, Elias P. b. 1791, d. 1856, SC: 1791, f. Lyon Levy, m. Leah Tobias Levy, mr. Rachel Moïse Levy, 1821. Rf: DR; EC19; SFF163, 195; EP; W47.743 (his); T37; 1830C; 1840C; 1850C; SCA1820–51; D1831, 1835, 1838, 1841, 1849, 1852, 1855

Levy, Eliza. b. 1787, SC: 1802, mr. Solomon Levy. Rf: MR4Z.504; D1802

Levy, Eliza. b. 1810, SC: 1850, mr. Moses Levy. Rf: W45.682; 1850C; 1860C; 1861C

Levy, Eliza (Aarons). b. 1786, d. 1857, SC: 1805, f. Levi Arons van Blitz, mr. Simon Levy, 1805. Rf: DR; EM8; EC93; SFF1

Levy, Eliza Henrietta. b. 1821, d. 1822, SC: 1822, f. Chapman Levy, m. Flora Levy. Rf: EC110; SFF169

Levy, Elizabeth Jane. b. 1842, d. 1914, f. Mordecai M. Levy, m. Jane Hart Levy. Rf: DR; SFF169

Levy, Ella. f. Simon Levy, m. Eliza Aarons Levy. Rf: SFF1

Levy, Ellen Alice (Moïse). d. 1893, f. Isaac Moïse, m. Hetty Lopez Moïse, mr. Solomon Lionel Levy, 1846. Rf: SFF163, 197

Levy, Emanuel. b. 1794, d. 1867, SC: 1784. Rf: 1830C; 1850C; E136, 169; W31.441; EP; SCA1820–35; D1802, 1803, 1806, 1807, 1809, 1813, 1816, 1829, 1831, 1838, 1841

Levy, Esther. mr. Joseph Levy. Rf: SFF154

Levy, Esther. SC: 1856, mr. Orlando Levy. Rf: W47.743

Levy, Esther Rachel. SC: 1860. Rf: Min. Feb. 13, 1860

Levy, Ezekiel. SC: 1779. Rf: E106, 278

Levy, Ezra. b. 1810, SC: 1832, f. Lyon Levy, m. Sarah Cardozo Levy, mr. Amanda Phillips Levy, 1834. Rf: EM15; SFF163; E169; W41.683; T37; 1840C; SCA1834–38

Levy, F. C. b. 1856, d. 1858, SC: 1858. Rf: DR

Levy, Fanny (Yates). b. 1797, SC: 1837, f. Samuel Yates, m. Martha Yates, mr. Jacob Clarisse Levy, 1817. Rf: EM11; SFF169, 308; W41.909

Levy, Flora. f. Lyon Levy. Rf: SFF163

Levy, Flora. SC: 1830, mr. Marks Levy. Rf: W46.199

Levy, Flora (Levy). b. 1803, d. 1823, SC: 1818, f. Menachem Levy, mr. Chapman Levy, 1818. Rf: EM11; EJCC11; SFF169; *SP*, June 9, 1823

Levy, Frances. m. Simon Levy, m. Eliza Aarons Levy. Rf: SFF1

Levy, Frances. b. 1812, d. 1837, SC: 1837, f. Lyon Levy, m. Sarah Cardozo Levy. Rf: EC14; SFF163

Levy, Frances. b. 1826, SC: 1826. Rf: 1850C

Levy, Frances (Goldsmith). d. 1905, SC: 1860, f. Moses Goldsmith, m. Eleanor Alexander Goldsmith, mr. Edward S. Levy, 1879. Rf: SFF84; 1860C

Levy, George. b. 1820, d. 1832, f. Hayman Levy, m. Almeria DeLeon Levy. Rf: SFF159

Levy, George J. SC: 1817, mr. Hannah Levy. Rf: E136; MR4T.335; 1820C; T37; SCA1817–35; D1819, 1831, 1855

Levy, Hannah. SC: 1808, mr. George Levy. Rf: MR4T.335; SCA1808–21

Levy, Hannah (Abrahams) (Levy). SC: 1796, mr. Samuel Levy, 1796, mr2. Solomon Levy, 1804. Rf: EM6, 8

Levy, Hart. SC: 1779. Rf: E136, 278, 288; 1800C; SCA1779–92; D1794, 1796, 1801, 1816; RB91

Levy, Hayman. b. 1795, d. 1865, SC: 1809, f. Solomon Levy, m. Rebecca Eve Hendricks Levy, mr. Almeria DeLeon Levy, 1819. Rf: EM12; SFF159; T37; CB1809; D1822; RB91

Levy, Henry. SC: 1840. Rf: SCA1840–41

Levy, Hertz. SC: 1800. Rf: MR3Q.325

Levy, Hesary. b. 1819, d. 1823, SC: 1819. Rf: DR

Levy, Hetty Barrett. b. 1858, d. 1897, SC: 1858, f. Charles Ferdinand Levy, m. Laura Louise Barrett Levy. Rf: SFF163

Levy, Hyam E. SC: 1785. Rf: E280; 1790C; SCA1785–1819; RB91

Levy, Isaac. b. 1769, d. 1806. Rf: EP

Levy, Isaac. b. 1849, d. 1894. Rf: EC18; EP

Levy, Isaac A. b. 1809, d. 1871, SC: 1809, f. Nathan Levy, m. Sarah Levy, mr. Angelique Heydenfeldt Levy, 1841. Rf: EM19; SFF58, 167; D1859

Levy, Isaac Tobias. b. 1792, d. 1811, SC: 1830, f. Lyon Levy, m. Leah Tobias Levy. Rf: SFF163; W40.179

Levy, Isaiah. b. 1801, d. 1825, SC: 1825. Rf: DR

Levy, Israel. SC: 1759. Rf: E42, 278; MR2L.238

Levy, Israel. SC: 1841. Rf: D1841

Levy, J. C. [I. C.]. SC: 1811. Rf: E144, 169, 238; Min. April 14, 1839; W40.359; W44.261; SCA1827–39; D1816, 1819, 1822, 1829, 1831, 1835, 1849

Levy, J. W. b. 1798, d. 1825. Rf: EP; *SP*, Feb. 1, 1826

Levy, Jacob. b. 1793, d. 1814, f. Lyon

Levy, m. Sarah Cardoza Levy, mr. Rachel Moïse Abraham Levy, 1814. Rf: SFF163; W40.179

Levy, Jacob. SC: 1839, mr. Sarah Edwitha Marks Levy, 1839. Rf: SFF165, 185

Levy, Jacob Barrett. b. 1856, d. 1858, SC: 1856, f. Charles Ferdinand Levy, m. Laura Louise Barrett Levy. Rf: SFF163

Levy, Jacob Clarisse [Clavius]. b. 1788, d. 1875, SC: 1788, f. Moses Clava Levy, m. Sarah Levy, mr. Fanny Yates Levy, 1817. Rf: SFF169, 308; E136, 194; EM11; W41.909; D1809, 1813, 1835, 1838; RB92

Levy, Jacqueline Ellen. b. 1816, d. 1896, SC: 1860, f. Elias P. Levy, m. Rachel Moïse Levy. Rf: EC57; E183; SFF163, 195; 1860C

Levy, James D. b. 1843, d. 1845, f. Mordecai M. Levy, m. Jane Hart Levy. Rf: SFF169

Levy, Jane. b. 1838, SC: 1860. Rf: 1860C

Levy, Jane (Hart). b. 1816, d. 1865, SC: 1861, f. Nathan Hart, m. Rachel Hart Hart, mr. Mordecai M. Levy, 1839. Rf: EC48; SFF98, 169; W40.415 (hers); 1861C

Levy, Jeanette (Goldburg). SC: 1844, f. Asher Goldburg, mr. Emanuel Levy, 1844. Rf: MS16.094

Levy, Jonas J. SC: 1818. Rf: E136

Levy, Joseph. b. 1728, d. 1772, SC: 1757, f. Moses [Raphael] Levy, m. Grace Mears Levy, mr. Esther Levy. Rf: SFF154; E42, 278

Levy, Joseph. SC: 1802. Rf: MR3Q.594; RB92

Levy, Joseph A. b. 1810, d. 1835, SC: 1831. Rf: DR; D1831

Levy, Judah B. SC: 1818. Rf: E136

Levy, Juliana. f. Levy Myers, m. Frances Minis Myers. Rf: SFF216

Levy, Laura Louise (Barrett). b. 1837, d. 1912, SC: 1853, f. Jacob Barrett, m. Hetty J. Ottolengui Barrett, mr. Charles Ferdinand Levy, 1853. Rf: DR; SFF17, 163; EM26; W47.743

Levy, Leah. b. 1802, d. 1821, SC: 1802, f. Lyon Levy, m. Sarah Cardozo Levy. Rf: DR; SFF163; *SP*, Aug. 7, 1821, eulogy

Levy, Leah. b. 1838, d. 1871. Rf: EC107

Levy, Leah (Tobias). b. 1771, d. 1799, f. Joseph Tobias, m. Judith Tobias, mr. Lyon Levy, 1790. Rf: SFF163, 298

Levy, Levine L. b. 1805, SC: 1838, mr. Abigail Levy. Rf: 1850C; D1835, 1838, 1849, 1852, 1859

Levy, Levy G. d. 1857, SC: 1857. Rf: EC92

Levy, Lewis. b. 1802, d. 1866, SC: 1846, f. Nathan Levy, m. Sarah Levy. Rf: SFF167; W45.682; E231

Levy, Lionel. SC: 1839. Rf: 1840C; 1850C; E169, 239

Levy, Lionel Cardoza. b. 1827, d. 1885, SC: 1827, f. Lyon Levy, m. Sarah Cardoza Levy, mr. Eleanor Moïse Levy, 1847. Rf: SFF163, 164

Levy, Lionel Cardoza. b. 1847, d. 1906, SC: 1847, f. Lionel Cardoza Levy, m. Eleanor Moïse Levy, mr. Isabel Moses Levy, 1869. Rf: SFF164, 212; E239; W41.683

Levy, Lyon. b. 1764, d. 1835, SC: 1785, mr. Leah Tobias Levy, 1790, mr2. Sarah Cardoza Levy, 1801. Rf: EC14; SFF29, 163, 298; E136; 1800C; 1810C; 1820C; MS1.518; *SCM*151; D1794, 1796, 1801, 1803, 1806, 1807, 1809, 1813, 1819, 1822, 1831; RB93

Levy, Lyon. b. 1803, d. 1835, SC: 1819, f. Lyon Levy, m. Sarah Cardoza Levy. Rf: SFF163; 1820C; W40.179 (his); D1819; 1831, 1835

Levy, M. A. SC: 1843, mr. Sarah A. Levy. Rf: EC93; EP; D1849

Levy, Marcus. b. 1825, d. 1858, SC: 1839. Rf: DR; Min. April 14, 1839

Levy, Marks. b. 1824, d. 1852, SC: 1850, mr. Flora Levy. Rf: EC91; E169; W46.199 (his); 1850C; D1841

Levy, Martha Sarah. d. 1886, SC: 1837, f. Jacob Clarisse Levy, m. Fanny Yates Levy. Rf: SFF169; W41.909 (1837)

Levy, Marx. SC: 1859. Rf: D1859

Levy, Mary Ann (Suares). b. 1806, d. 1897, SC: 1806, f. Jacob Suares, m. Judith Suares, mr. Bernard Levy, 1841. Rf: DR; EM20; EC82; SFF228, 289; D1841

Levy, Mary Hannah. b. 1846, d. 1916, SC: 1859, f. Mordecai H. Levy, m. Jane Hart Levy. Rf: DR; SFF169; W40.415

Levy, Max. b. 1823, d. 1902, SC: 1856. Rf: EP; T37; DR

Levy, Michael. SC: 1779. Rf: E278; SCA1779; RB94

Levy, Miriam (Andrews). b. 1772, d. 1847, SC: 1816, f. Abraham Andrews, m. Nellie Andrews, mr. Reuben Levy. Rf: SFF12; EP; SCA1816

Levy, Mordecai M. b. 1808, d. 1850, SC: 1839, f. Menachem Levy, mr. Jane Hart Levy, 1839. Rf: SFF98, 169; EC84; E136, 280; W50.415; T37

Levy, Moses. f. Simon Levy, m. Eliza Aarons Levy. Rf: SFF1

Levy, Moses. SC: 1804. Rf: CB1804; D1806

Levy, Moses. b. 1803, d. 1804, SC: 1804, f. Nathan Levy, m. Sarah Levy. Rf: EC78; SFF167

Levy, Moses. SC: 1835. Rf: D1835, 1838, 1841, 1852, 1855, 1859

Levy, Moses. b. 1805, SC: 1805, mr. Eliza Levy. Rf: 1840C; 1850C; 1860C; 1861C; D1849, 1852, 1855

Levy, Moses Clava. b. 1750, d. 1839, SC: 1783, mr. Sarah Levy. Rf: DR; "House Journal, 1783–1784," p. 242; SFF169; E117; SCA1791–1837; 1790C; 1800C; 1810C; 1820C, 1830C; D1790, 1794, 1796, 1801, 1802, 1803, 1806, 1807, 1809, 1816, 1819, 1822, 1831, 1835, 1838; RB94, 95

Levy, Nathan. SC: 1772, mr. Patience Levy. Rf: MR2P.456; SCA1772; D1794, 1801, 1802, 1803, 1806, 1807, 1809, 1819, 1822

Levy, Nathan. b. 1758, d. 1827, SC: 1805, mr. Sarah Levy. Rf: DR; MR4E.534; SFF167; W35.759; E129, 136, 278; 1820C; CB1805; D1796

Levy, Nathaniel. b. 1842, SC: 1860. Rf: 1860C

Levy, Olivia. b. 1814, d. 1837, SC:

1837, f. Lyon Levy, m. Sarah Cardozo Levy. Rf: EC14; SFF163; W41.683

Levy, Orlando R. b. 1822, d. 1906, SC: 1822, mr. Esther Levy, mr2. Catherine Bowers Levy. Rf: DR; EP; SFF163; W47.743; 1850C; SCA1858–61; D1855

Levy, Patience. SC: 1773, mr. Nathan Levy. Rf: MR2P.456, 1773

Levy, Penina Septima (Moses). b. 1821, d. 1844, SC: 1844, f. Isaac Clifton Moses, m. Hannah Lazarus Moses, mr. Solomon C. Levy. Rf: EC15; SFF207; EP

Levy, Philippa. b. 1819, d. 1827, SC: 1819, f. Lyon Levy, m. Sarah Cardozo Levy. Rf: DR; SFF163

Levy, Phillip. b. 1807, d. 1819, SC: 1819, f. Lyon Levy, m. Sarah Cardozo Levy. Rf: SFF163; *SP*, June 11, 1819, eulogy

Levy, Polly. b. 1784, SC: 1850. Rf: 1850C

Levy, R. d. 1805, SC: 1804. Rf: EP

Levy, Rachel. b. 1857, d. 1894. Rf: DR; EC18

Levy, Rachel (Elias). f. Levy Elias, m. Rosa L. Elias, mr. Isaac Levy, 1879. Rf: SFF63

Levy, Rachel Hart. b. 1841, d. 1918, SC: 1859, f. Mordecai M. Levy, m. Jane Hart Levy. Rf: DR; SFF169; W50.415

Levy, Rachel (Moïse). b. 1803, d. 1833, SC: 1818, f. Cherry Moïse, m. Esther Moses Levy, mr. Elias P. Levy, 1821. Rf: EC19; EM12; SFF163, 195; EP; SCA1818

Levy, Rachel (Moïse) (Abraham). b. 1795, d. 1872, SC: 1795, f. Abraham Moïse, m. Sarah Moïse, mr. Jacob Levy, 1814. Rf: DR; EC57; E183; SFF195; 1860C; D1835

Levy, Rebecca (Benjamin). b. 1809, SC: 1823, f. Philip Benjamin, m. Rebecca DeMendes Benjamin, mr. Abraham L. Levy, 1826. Rf: SFF18, 163

Levy, Reuben. b. 1759, d. 1828, SC: 1797, mr. Miriam Andrews Levy. Rf: DR; SFF12; 1800C; 1810C; 1820C; SCA1797–1826; D1803, 1806, 1809, 1813, 1816, 1819, 1822; RB95

Levy, Reuben. SC: 1831. Rf: D1831, 1838

Levy, Rochelle E. b. 1847, d. 1849, f. Mordecai M. Levy, m. Jane Hart Levy. Rf: SFF169

Levy, Rose. b. 1727, d. 1812, SC: 1762, mr. Solomon Levy. Rf: EP; SCA1806; D1801

Levy, Samuel. SC: 1741. Rf: RB96; E24; RB96

Levy, Samuel. d. 1802, SC: 1782. Rf: "House Journal 1783–84," pp. 36, 37; E98, 136, 278; EP; 1800C; SCA1783–98; D1794, 1796, 1801, 1802, 1803

Levy, Samuel. b. 1812, SC: 1812. Rf: 1850C

Levy, Samuel. SC: 1845, f. Nathan Levy, m. Sarah Levy, mr. Hannah Hendricks Levy, 1845. Rf: SFF167, 247

Levy, Samuel. b. 1818, d. 1851, SC: 1850, f. Simon Levy, m. Eliza Aarons Levy. Rf: EC93; SFF1; 1850C

Levy, Samuel S. SC: 1801, mr. Catherine Levy. Rf: MR4Y.463;

SCA1806–10; D1801, 1807, 1809, 1813

Levy, Samuel Yates. b. 1827, d. 1887, SC: 1827, f. Jacob Clarisse Levy, m. Fanny Yates Levy, mr. Annabella Myers Yates Levy. Rf: SFF169; W41.909

Levy, Sarah. b. 1767, d. 1858, SC: 1837, mr. Moses Clava Levy. Rf: SFF169; W41.909

Levy, Sarah. b. 1788, d. 1823, SC: 1788. Rf: DR

Levy, Sarah. d. 1841, SC: 1841. Rf: DR

Levy, Sarah A. b. 1809, d. 1855, SC: 1855, mr. M. A. Levy. Rf: EC93; EP

Levy, Sarah (Cardozo). b. 1780, d. 1837, SC: 1780, f. David Nunez Cardozo, m. Leah Benjamin Cardozo, mr. Lyon Levy, 1801. Rf: EC14; SFF29, 163; W40.179; D1816, 1835, 1841

Levy, Sarah Edwintha (Marks). b. 1815, d. 1876, f. Hayman Marks, m. Grace Seixas Judah Marks, mr. Jacob Levy, 1839. Rf: SFF165, 185

Levy, Sarah (Sally) C. b. 1781, d. 1822, SC: 1813, mr. Nathan Levy. Rf: DR; SFF167; DR; W35.759 (hers); *SP*, Aug. 26, 1822, eulogy

Levy, Simon. d. 1857, SC: 1846, mr. Ellen Alice Moïse Levy, 1846. Rf: EM22; EP

Levy, Simon L. d. 1833, SC: 1802, mr. Eliza Aarons Levy, 1805. Rf: 1810C; 1820C; EM8; EC93; E136; SFF1; SCA1809–27; D1802, 1803, 1806, 1807, 1809, 1813, 1816, 1819, 1822

Levy, Simon L. b. 1806, d. 1833, SC: 1806, f. Simon Levy, m. Golah Aarons Levy, mr. Mary Levy. Rf: EP; SFF1

Levy, Solomon. SC: 1757. Rf: EL

Levy, Solomon. b. 1770, d. 1839, SC: 1790, mr. Eliza Levy. Rf: 1810C: 1820C, EP; MR4Z.504; SCA1792–1829; D1790, 1794, 1796, 1806, 1807, 1809, 1813, 1816, 1819, 1822, 1829

Levy, Solomon B. b. 1823, d. 1865, SC: 1861, f. Hayman Levy, m. Almeria DeLeon Levy. Rf: SFF159

Levy, Solomon Lionel. b. 1808, d. 1884, SC: 1808, f. Lyon Levy, m. Sarah C. Levy, mr. Ellen Alice Moïse Levy, 1846. Rf: 1850C; W41.683; SFF163

Levy, Susan. b. 1827, SC: 1827. Rf: 1850C

Levy, Tobias. SC: 1783. Rf: SCA1783–84

Levy, Uriah. SC: 1823. Rf: E136

Levy, Zachariah. SC: 1800. Rf: E136

Lewinson, Ellen (Levy). b. 1855, SC: 1855, f. Charles Ferdinand Levy, m. Laura Louise Barrett Levy, mr. Louis Lewinson, 1896. Rf: SFF163

Lewis, ———. b. 1812, d. 1812, SC: 1812, f. Davis Lewis, m. Rachel Lewis. Rf: SFF172

Lewis, Alexander. b. 1810, d. 1877, SC: 1810, f. David Lewis, m. Rachel Salomon Lewis, mr. Rebecca Powers Lewis, 1833, mr2. Esther Phillipson Lewis, 1854. Rf: SFF172

Lewis, Catherine. b. 1813, d. 1827, SC: 1813, f. David Lewis, m. Rachel Salomon Lewis. Rf: DR; SFF172

Lewis, David. b. 1763, d. 1839, SC:

1804, f. Henry Lewis, m. Judith D'Israeli Lewis, mr. Rachel Salomon Levy, 1809. Rf: SFF162; E136; CB1805

Lewis, Henry. b. 1825, d. 1850, f. David Lewis, m. Rachel Lewis. Rf: SFF172

Lewis, Joseph C. b. 1816, d. 1864, SC: 1861, f. David Lewis, m. Rachel Lewis. Rf: SFF172

Lewis, Moses. b. 1821, f. David Lewis, m. Rachel Salomon Lewis. Rf: SFF172

Lewis, Rachel (Salomon). b. 1794, d. 1831, SC: 1794, f. Moses Salomon, mr. David Lewis, 1809. Rf: SFF172, 173

Lewith, Adolph. SC: 1859. Rf: D1859

Lewith, E. J. SC: 1859. Rf: D1859

Lewith, Henry. b. 1838, d. 1862, SC: 1859. Rf: DR; D1859

Lewith, Magdalena. b. 1805, d. 1890, SC: 1852, mr. R. Joseph Lewith. Rf: DR; EC90; D1859

Lewith, R. Joseph. b. 1807, d. 1852, SC: 1852, mr. Magdalena Lewith. Rf: EC90

Lichtenstein, L. SC: 1840. Rf: Min. July 21, 1840

Lindo, Chs. SC: 1819. Rf: CB1819

Lindo, Moses. b. 1712, d. 1774, SC: 1757. Rf: E44–67; SCA1757–74; RB97

Linley, Rebecca (Hyams) (Bean). f. David Hyams, m. Rebecca Maysor Hyams, mr. ——— Bean, mr2. Archibald Linley. Rf: SFF119, 120

Lipman, Abraham. b. 1778, SC: 1809, mr. Mary Lipman. Rf: 1820C; 1850C; E136, 169; EJCC6; CB1809; SCA1818–22; D1813, 1816, 1819

Lipman, Ezekiel. SC: 1820. Rf: 1820C

Lipman, Jacob. SC: 1819. Rf: D1819

Lipman, Mary. d. 1841, SC: 1821, mr. Abraham Lipman. Rf: EJCC6; SCA1821

Lipman, Ralph. b. 1808, d. 1837, SC: 1820. Rf: EC17; EP; 1820C

Livingstain, Abraham. b. 1815, d. 1880, SC: 1840. Rf: DR; EBS6

Livingstain, Dina. b. 1814, d. 1896. Rf: DR; EBS6

Livingston, Hannah. b. 1794, d. 1864, SC: 1830, mr. Lewis Livingston. Rf: EBS7; 1850C

Livingston, Jacob. b. 1839, d. 1905. Rf: DR; E169, 265

Livingston, Lewis S. b. 1798, SC: 1850, mr. Hannah Livingston. Rf: 1850C

Livingston, Mary. b. 1842, d. 1916. Rf: DR

Lobell, Moses. SC: 1803. Rf: E136

Loeb, Bluhma (Cohen). b. 1858, d. 1941, SC: 1858, f. Louis Cohen, m. Cecilia Bentschner Cohen, mr. Levi Loeb, 1877. Rf: JF2; 1860C

Loeb, Daniel. b. 1822, d. 1885, SC: 1851, mr. Henrietta Loeb. Rf: DR; EC64; W49.609; T37; SCA1851

Loeb, Eliza L. (Goldsmith). b. 1855, d. 1925, SC: 1860, f. Moses Goldsmith, m. Eleanor Alexander Goldsmith, mr. Jacob H. Loeb, 1880. Rf: DR; SFF84; 1860C

Loeb, Henrietta. b. 1821, d. 1895, mr. Daniel Loeb. Rf: DR; EC64

Loeb, Jacob H. b. 1846, d. 1893, SC: 1846, mr. Eliza L. Goldsmith Loeb, 1880. Rf: DR; SFF84; E231, 263

Loevenstein, ———. SC: 1818. Rf: E136

Loewenburg, Bertha. b. 1855, SC: 1855, f. Joseph Loewenburg, m. Rachel Loewenburg. Rf: 1860C

Loewenburg, Delah. b. 1857, SC: 1857, f. Joseph Loewenburg, m. Rachel Loewenburg. Rf: 1860C

Loewenburg, Jacob. b. 1853, SC: 1853, f. Joseph Loewenburg, m. Rachel Loewenburg. Rf: 1860C

Loewenburg, Joseph. b. 1826, SC: 1860, mr. Rachel Loewenburg. Rf: 1860C

Loewenburg, Rachel. b. 1830, SC: 1860, mr. Joseph Loewenburg. Rf: 1860C

Loewenstein, Abraham Levin. b. 1832, d. 1854, SC: 1854. Rf: DR; EC107

Loewentritt, Betty (Goldberg). SC: 1841, mr. G. M. Loewentritt, 1841. Rf: EM19

Loewentritt, G. SC: 1841, mr. Betty Goldbert Loewentritt, 1841. Rf: EM19

Loovis, Adeline (Cohen). SC: 1838, f. H. C. Cohen, mr. M. Loovis, 1838. Rf: EM17

Loovis, Martin. SC: 1838, mr. Adeline Cohen Loovis, 1838. Rf: EM17; E170; T37; MS14.63

Lopez, ———. b. 1811, f. David Lopez, m. Priscilla Moses Lopez. Rf: SFF176

Lopez, A. b. 1843, d. 1843, SC: 1843, f. David Lopez, m. Catherine Dobyns Hinton Lopez. Rf: DR; SFF176

Lopez, Aaron. SC: 1790. Rf: 1790C; W28.147; W25.89; W32.706; E136; T37; SCA1790–1803; D1790, 1794, 1803, 1806, 1807, 1809, 1813; RB98

Lopez, Aaron. b. 1800, d. 1873, SC: 1800, f. David Lopez, m. Priscilla Moses Lopez, mr. Eleanor Cohen Lopez. Rf: SFF176; E205; T37; 1840C; MS8.553; D1838, 1841; RB98

Lopez, Aaron Moïse. b. 1848, d. 1899, SC: 1848, f. David Lopez, m. Rebecca Moïse Lopez, mr. Cordelia Cohen, 1872. Rf: SFF176, 177; 1850C

Lopez, Abram Moïse. b. 1847, d. 1848, SC: 1847, f. David Lopez, m. Rebecca Moïse Lopez. Rf: EC100; SFF176

Lopez, Caroline A. (Moïse). b. 1854, d. 1885, SC: 1854, f. Charles Henry Moïse, m. Theodora Sydney Moïse, mr. Julian Lee Lopez, 1882. Rf: DR; EC101; SFF176, 196; 1860C

Lopez, Catherine Dobyns Hinton. b. 1814, d. 1843, SC: 1814, mr. David Lopez, 1832. Rf: DR; EC99; SFF176

Lopez, Cecile (Ottolengui). b. 1858, d. 1936, SC: 1858, f. Israel Ottolengui, m. Rosalie C. Mose Ottolengui, mr. Edward Hinton Lopez, 1881. Rf: EC101; SFF176, 234

Lopez, Cecilia E. (Cohen). b. 1843, d. 1909, SC: 1843, f. Jacob Cohen, m. Sarah Barrett Cohen, mr. Moses E. Lopez, 1862. Rf: DR; SFF36, 176; 1850C

Lopez, Charles Hinton. b. 1842, d. 1843, SC: 1843, f. David Lopez, m. Catherine Dobyns Hinton Lopez. Rf: EC99; SFF176; EP

Lopez, Columbus. b. 1850, d. 1851, SC: 1850, f. David Lopez, m. Rebecca Moïse Lopez. Rf: DR; EC100; SFF176

Lopez, Cordelia M. (Cohen). b. 1848, d. 1933, SC: 1848, f. Philip Melvin Cohen, m. Cordelia Moïse Cohen, mr. Aaron M. Lopez, 1872. Rf: EC101; SFF39, 176, 177; 1850C; 1860C

Lopez, Daniel. b. 1798, d. 1798, SC: 1798, f. David Lopez, m. Priscilla Moses Lopez. Rf: SFF176

Lopez, David. b. 1750, d. 1811, SC: 1793, f. Moses Lopez, m. Rebecca Rodrigues de Rivera Lopez, mr. Rachel Lopez, mr2. Priscilla Moses Lopez, 1793. Rf: W32.251 (his); SFF175, 176, 205; EC75; 1810C; E122; T37; EP; SCA1795–1812; D1794, 1801, 1802, 1803, 1806, 1807, 1809

Lopez, David. b. 1809, d. 1884, SC: 1809, f. David Lopez, m. Priscilla Moses Lopez, mr. Catherine Dobyns Hinton Lopez, 1832, mr2. Rebecca Moïse Lopez, 1846. Rf: EM22; EC100; SFF176, 195; 1840C; W32.397; W29.673; T37; 1850C; 1861C; SCA1839; DR; D1835, 1841, 1849, 1852, 1855, 1859

Lopez, David. b. 1834, d. 1862, SC: 1834, f. David Lopez, m. Catherine Dobyns Hinton Lopez. Rf: EC99; SFF176; 1850C; D1859

Lopez, David. b. 1860, d. 1872, SC: 1860, f. John Hinton Lopez, m. Maria Cohen Lopez. Rf: DR; SFF176

Lopez, E. H. d. 1877. Rf: DR

Lopez, Edward Hinton. b. 1853, d. 1914, SC: 1853, f. David Lopez, m. Rebecca Moïse Lopez, mr. Sarah Ottolengui Lopez, 1877, mr2. Cecile Ottolengui Lopez, 1881. Rf: EC101; SFF176, 234

Lopez, Eugene. b. 1849, d. 1873, SC: 1849, f. David Lopez, m. Rebecca Moïse Lopez. Rf: DR; EC100; SFF176; 1850C

Lopez, Israel Cohen. b. 1855, d. 1858, SC: 1855, f. John Hinton Lopez, m. Maria Cohen Lopez. Rf: EC101; SFF176

Lopez, John. SC: 1809. Rf: E137, 170; 1810C; D1809, 1813, 1816, 1822

Lopez, John Hinton. b. 1833, d. 1884, SC: 1833, f. David Lopez, m. Catherine Dobyns Hinton Lopez, mr. Maria Cohen Lopez, 1854. Rf: DR; EM27; EC100, 101; E231; SFF32, 176; 1850C; D1855, 1859

Lopez, Joseph. SC: 1803. Rf: E137; SCA1803

Lopez, Julian Lee. b. 1852, SC: 1852, f. David Lopez, m. Rebecca Moïse Lopez, mr. Caroline A. Moïse Lopez, 1882. Rf: SFF176, 196; EC101

Lopez, Kate. b. 1858, d. 1858, SC: 1858, f. John Hinton Lopez, m. Maria Cohen Lopez. Rf: EC101; SFF176

Lopez, Maria (Cohen). b. 1830, d. 1905, f. Benjamin I. Cohen, mr. John Hinton Lopez, 1854. Rf: EM27; SFF176

Lopez, Moses. b. 1796, d. 1849, SC: 1796, f. David Lopez, m. Priscilla Moses Lopez. Rf: DR; EC100; SFF176; W32.521; E137, 170, 187; T37; SCA1826–44; D1849

Lopez, Moses E. b. 1836, d. 1907, SC: 1836, f. David Lopez, m. Catherine Dobyns Hinton Lopez, mr. Cecilia Cohen Lopez, 1862. Rf: DR; SFF36, 176; E232, 265; T37; 1850C

Lopez, Priscilla (Moses). b. 1775, d. 1866, SC: 1775, f. Myer Moses, m. Rachel Andrews Moses, mr. David Lopez, 1793. Rf: DR; EC75; SFF176, 205; W21.521; 1820C; 1860C; SCA1816–27; D1813, 1816, 1819, 1822, 1831, 1835, 1852, 1855, 1859

Lopez, Rebecca Cohen (Moïse). b. 1814, d. 1858, SC: 1814, f. Aaron Moïse, m. Sarah Cohen Moïse, mr. David Lopez, 1846. Rf: EC100; EM22; SFF176, 195; 1850C

Lopez, Samuel. SC: 1800. Rf: SCA1816–34; CB1800; D1829, 1831

Lopez, Sarah. SC: 1801. Rf: D1801

Lopez, Sarah (Ottolengui). b. 1855, d. 1877, SC: 1855, f. Israel Ottolengui, m. Rosalie C. Moïse Ottolengui, mr. Edward Hinton Lopez, 1877. Rf: EC101; SFF176, 234

Lopez, Sarah (Sally). b. 1806, d. 1902, SC: 1806, f. David Lopez, m. Priscilla Moses Lopez. Rf: DR; EC100; SFF176; E182, 262; 1860C

Loryea, Aaron. b. 1821, d. 1911, SC: 1850, f. Isaac Loryea, m. Esther Loryea, mr. Jane Hart Loryea, 1846. Rf: MJSC14; SFF179; E170, 238; EM22; 1850C; 1860C; T37; *Courier* Dec. 11, 1861; D1852

Loryea, Abraham. b. 1839, SC: 1850, f. Isaac Loryea, m. Esther Loryea. Rf: SFF179; 1850C

Loryea, Esther. b. 1801, d. 1890, SC: 1845, mr. Isaac Loryea. Rf: DR; 1861C; SFF179; W47.600

Loryea, Hennie. b. 1859, SC: 1859. Rf: 1860C

Loryea, Isaac. b. 1798, d. 1855, SC: 1849, mr. Esther Loryea. Rf: EC85; SFF179; E170; W47.600; SCA1849; D1849

Loryea, Isaac Moultrie. b. 1857, d. 1919, SC: 1860, f. Aaron Loryea, m. Jane Hart Loryea, mr. Annie R. Loryea. Rf: SFF179; 1860C

Loryea, Jane D. (Hart). b. 1825, d. 1895, SC: 1860, mr. Aaron Loryea, 1846. Rf: EM22; SFF179; MJSC14; 1860C

Loryea, Joseph. SC: 1855, f. Isaac Loryea, m. Esther Loryea. Rf: SFF179; W47.600

Loryea, Joseph H. b. 1848, d. 1929, SC: 1848, f. Aaron Loryea, m. Jane Hart Loryea, mr. Rosabel L. Hyman Loryea, 1879. Rf: SFF179; 1850C; 1860C

Loryea, Louis W. b. 1852, d. 1902, SC: 1852, f. Aaron Loryea, m. Jane Hart Loryea, mr. Wilhelmina V. Bond Loryea, 1889. Rf: SFF179; 1860C

Lowenberg, David. SC: 1861. Rf: E232

Lowenberg, Joseph. b. 1831, d. 1885. Rf: EBS7

Lowenberg, Molcie (Josephs). b. 1841, d. 1910, SC: 1841, f. Levy L. Josephs, m. Isabelle Joseph Josephs, mr. Isaac Lowenberg, 1873. Rf: SFF139; 1850C

Lowenstein, ———. SC: 1843. Rf: *State v. Ancker*
Loyns, Rose. b. 1853, d. 1915, SC: 1853, mr. Louis Loyns. Rf: MJSC18
Luria, Albert Moses. b. 1843, d. 1862, f. Raphael J. Moses, mr. Eliza M. Moses Luria. Rf: E200; *AJA*7, 90–103
Luria, E. b. 1805, d. 1890. Rf: EBS7
Lyon, Abraham. SC: 1790. Rf: 1790C; D1790
Lyon, Daniel. SC: 1821. Rf: CB1821
Lyon, David. SC: 1807. Rf: CB1807
Lyon, Elizabeth Chapman. SC: 1788, mr. Mordecai Lyon. Rf: MR2X.632
Lyon, George [Lyons]. SC: 1835, mr. Mary Ann Lyon. Rf: E170; SCA1829; D1822, 1829, 1831, 1835
Lyon, George, Jr. SC: 1835. Rf: D1836
Lyon, Isaac. SC: 1805. Rf: CB1805
Lyon, Joseph. SC: 1818. Rf: W34.16; E137
Lyon, Judith (Cohen). b. 1748, d. 1815, SC: 1790, mr. Isaac Cohen, mr2. Mordecai Lyon. Rf: SFF35, 36; MSl.525; SCA1790–1811; *SP*, Nov. 22, 1815
Lyon, L. S. D. SC: 1825. Rf: E170, 205
Lyon, Levy. SC: 1795. Rf: E137
Lyon, Mary Ann. SC: 1820, mr. George Lyon. Rf: MR4V.85; SCA1820–25
Lyon, Mordecai. d. 1818, SC: 1782, mr. Elizabeth Chapman Lyon, mr2. Judith Cohen Lyon. Rf: "House Journal, 1783–1784," pp. 36, 37; 1790C; 1800C; 1810C; T37; SCA1790–1818; *SP*, Oct. 22, 1818, eulogy; D1790, 1794, 1796, 1801, 1802, 1803, 1807, 1809
Lyon, Moses Rodriguez. SC: 1794. Rf: E137; SCA1801; D1794
Lyon, Philip. b. 1795, d. 1831, SC: 1831. Rf: EP
Lyon, Solomon D. SC: 1809. Rf: E137
Lyon, William. SC: 1818. Rf: E137
Lyons, ———. b. 1783, d. 1861, SC: 1861. Rf: DR
Lyons, ———. SC: 1820. Rf: 1820C
Lyons, Elizabeth (Wolff). f. Abraham Wolff, mr. Henry Lyons, 1842. Rf: SFF183
Lyons, Ellis. SC: 1852. Rf: E170, 219
Lyons, Emanuel Joseph. SC: 1819. Rf: D1819
Lyons, Henry. b. 1805, d. 1858, SC: 1850, f. Isaac Lyons, m. Rachel Cohen Lyons, mr. Elizabeth Wolff Lyons, 1842. Rf: SFF183; 1850C; EJCC7
Lyons, Isaac. b. 1774, d. 1843, SC: 1805, m. Bilah Lyons, mr. Rachel Cohen Lyons, 1803. Rf: SFF180, 183; 1820C; T37; E137; MR5B.147; D1809, 1813, 1816, 1819
Lyons, Isaac Montgomery. b. 1811, d. 1837, SC: 1811, f. Isaac Lyons, m. Rachel Cohen Lyons. Rf: EJCC7; SFF183; EP
Lyons, Jacob Cohen. b. 1807, d. 1887, f. Isaac Lyons, m. Rachel Cohen Lyons, mr. Louisa E. Hart Lyons. Rf: SFF183; E246
Lyons, Joseph. b. 1785, SC: 1860. Rf: 1860C
Lyons, Joseph. b. 1813, d. 1839, SC: 1813, f. Isaac Lyons, m. Rachel

Cohen Lyons. Rf: SFF183; E137; W45.581; EJCC7; W34.16

Lyons, Mordecai. SC: 1816. Rf: D1816

Lyons, Rachel (Cohen). b. 1770, d. 1838, SC: 1838, mr. Isaac Lyons, 1803. Rf: SFF180, 183; EJCC7

Lyons, Theodore Hart. b. 1817, d. 1837, f. Isaac Lyons, m. Rachel Cohen Lyons. Rf: SFF183

Machado, David Mendes. b. 1695, d. 1747, mr. Maria Caetana Z. Nunez Machado, 1733. Rf: SFF234

Magnus, Rebecca (Alexander). b. 1823, d. 1892, SC: 1823, f. Abraham Alexander, m. Hannah Aarons Alexander, mr. Saul Magnus, 1857. Rf: EM29; SFF8; *AF*18; 1850C

Mairs, Elizabeth. b. 1769, d. 1845, SC: 1810, mr. Simon Mairs. Rf: EC50; SFF184; EP; SCA1810–38; D1835

Mairs, Levy. b. 1801, d. 1849, SC: 1821, f. Simon Mairs, m. Elizabeth Mairs. Rf: DR; EC87; SFF184; E137, 179; SCA1829–39; D1831, 1835, 1838, 1841

Mairs, Seligman. b. 1799, d. 1883, SC: 1850, f. Simon Mairs, m. Elizabeth Mairs. Rf: DR; EC51; SFF184; T37; 1850C

Mairs, Simon. b. 1765, d. 1835, SC: 1803, mr. Elizabeth Mairs. Rf: EC50; SFF184; EM13; E137, 170; 1810C; 1820C; 1850C; W34.16; SCA1809–37; D1809, 1816, 1819, 1822, 1829, 1831

Manassen, Amelia. b. 1826, SC: 1850. Rf: 1850C

Manheim, Israel. SC: 1801. Rf: E137

Manheim, Malky. b. 1800, d. 1855, SC: 1855. Rf: EBS7

Manheim, Solomon. SC: 1800. Rf: E137; CB1800

Mannahan, Esther Desirée (DePass) (Heydenfeldt). SC: 1815, f. Samuel DePass, m. Maria Rodriquez DePass Brand, mr. Jacob Heydenfeldt, 1815, mr2. ——— Mannahan. Rf: SFF58, 167

Mantoue, Benjamin. b. 1839, d. 1906, SC: 1855, mr. Fanny Jacob Mantoue. Rf: DR; EC91; EG8

Marchand, Levy. SC: 1800. Rf: E137

Markess, Joseph. SC: 1782. Rf: E106

Marks, Alexander. b. 1788, d. 1861, SC: 1788, f. Humphrey (Mordecai) Marks, m. Frances Marks, mr. Esther Hart Marks, 1816. Rf: SFF98, 186; E137, 246; SCA1810–21; D1809

Marks, Cecile (Abrahams). b. 1821, d. 1894, SC: 1821, f. Elias Abrahams, m. Catherine Cohen Abrahams, mr. Joseph Hart Marks, 1851. Rf: SFF4, 186

Marks, Deborah. SC: 1816. Rf: D1816, 1819

Marks, Elias. b. 1790, d. 1886, SC: 1790, f. Humphrey Marks, m. Frances Marks, mr. Jane Barham, 1816, mr2. Julia Pierpont Warner, 1853. Rf: SFF186; E137, 142, 195; SCA1818; D1813

Marks, Eliza (Hyams). b. 1808, d. 1837, SC: 1808, f. Samuel Hyams, m. Miriam Levy Hyams, mr. Joseph B. Marks, 1832. Rf: EM15; SFF19, 119

Marks, Esther (Benzeken). SC: 1808, f.

Joseph Benzeken, mr. Mark Marks, 1808. Rf: MR4W.503; SFF19; EM9

Marks, Esther (Hart). b. 1792, d. 1853, SC: 1816, f. Jacob Naphtali Hart, m. Leah Nathan Hart, mr. Alexander Marks, 1816. Rf: SFF98, 186

Marks, Frances. b. 1762, d. 1850, SC: 1818, mr. Humphrey Marks, 1786. Rf: EJCC7; SFF186; SCA1818–25

Marks, Frederick H. SC: 1818, f. Humphrey Marks, m. Frances Marks, mr. Rebecca M. Marks, 1855. Rf: SFF186; SCA1818

Marks, Humphrey [Mordecai]. b. 1760, d. 1838, SC: 1788, mr. Frances Marks. Rf: EJCC7; SFF186; 1800C; 1810C; 1820C; E137, 195, 246, 280; SCA1792–1807; D1794, 1796, 1802, 1803, 1806, 1807, 1809, 1813, 1816, 1819, 1822; RB107

Marks, Hyam. SC: 1800. Rf: E137

Marks, Isaac. b. 1796, d. 1810, SC: 1810, f. Humphrey Marks, m. Frances Marks. Rf: EC77; SFF186

Marks, Isaac D. SC: 1834. Rf: *State v. Isaac D. Marks*, 1834

Marks, Joseph. b. 1771, d. 1840, SC: 1790, mr. Eliza Hyams Marks, 1832. Rf: DR; EM15; 1830C, 1840C; W42.168 (his); SFF19, 119; SCA1818–26; D1790, 1802, 1803, 1807, 1809, 1813, 1816, 1819, 1822, 1829, 1831, 1838, 1841; RB106

Marks, Mark. b. 1778, d. 1834, SC: 1804, mr. Esther Benzeken Marks, 1808. Rf: E137, 142; SFF19; EM9; SCA1811–25; MR4W.503; D1809, 1822, 1831

Marks, S. SC: 1800. Rf: E137

Marks, Samuel Mandel. b. 1762, d. 1804, SC: 1800, f. Isaac Marks, m. Miriam Simpson Marks, mr. Sarah Harris Marks, 1797. Rf: SFF185; E137; 1800C; SCA1803; D1802, 1803, 1806, 1807

Marks, Sarah (Harris). b. 1776, d. 1821, SC: 1808, mr. Samuel Mandel Marks, 1797. Rf: DR; SFF185; 1820C; SCA1808; D1809; RB50

Marks, Solomon. SC: 1805. Rf: E137; MR3Y.5; D1806

Marques, Joseph. SC: 1780. Rf: E94, 278

Massias, Abraham A. b. 1772, d. 1848, SC: 1804. Rf: DR; EC106; E137, 144, 170, 195; T38; W44.353 (his); SCA1836; D1829, 1831

Massias, Solomon H. SC: 1802. Rf: E143; D1802, 1841

Mayer, Isaac. SC: 1843. Rf: *State v. Ancker*

Mayer, Isaac. b. 1840, d. 1843, SC: 1843, f. Isaac Mayer. Rf: EP

Mayer, Maurice. SC: 1852. Rf: E160, 170, 219, 292

Mayer, Sarah Gertrude (Oppenheim). b. 1826, d. 1911, SC: 1826, f. Hertz Wolff Oppenheim, m. Catherine Moses Oppenheim May, mr. Morris Mayer. SFF235; 1850C

Mears, Jochabed (Michaels). f. Moses Michaels, m. Catherine H. Michaels Mears, mr. Judah Mears. Rf: SFF190, 193; *AF*107

Mears, Judah. d. 1762, f. Sampson

Mears, m. Joy Tabitha Franks
Mears, mr. Jochabed Michaels
Mears. Rf: SFF190; EG2
Mears, Solomon. SC: 1805. Rf: CB1805
Melhado, David. SC: 1803. Rf: E137; RB111
Melhado, Emanuel. SC: 1800. Rf: E137; T38; CB1800
Mendes, Aaron. d. 1818, SC: 1802. Rf: E137; EP
Mendis, Jacob. SC: 1797. Rf: E20, 277; *FSSC*159
Meyer, ———. d. 1859, SC: 1859, f. Morris Meyer, m. Sarah Cohen Meyer. Rf: EC73; SFF36
Meyer, Emil Joseph. b. 1826, d. 1857, SC: 1857, mr. Emily Fredericka Oppenheim Meyer, 1857. Rf: EC35; SFF235; E170; EM29; W48.177 (his); Min. Nov. 1, 1857
Meyer, Emil Joseph. b. 1857, d. 1930, SC: 1857, f. Emil Joseph Meyer, m. Emily F. Oppenheim Meyer, mr. Eda Hirschfield Meyer. Rf: SFF235; 1860C
Meyer, Emily Frederika (Oppenheim). b. 1837, d. 1920, SC: 1837, f. Hertz Wolff Oppenheim, m. Catherine Moses Oppenheim, mr. Emil Joseph Meyer, 1857. Rf: SFF235; W46.284; EM29; 1860C
Meyer, Ephraim. b. 1861, d. 1861, SC: 1861. Rf: DR
Meyer, Gottlieb. SC: 1819. Rf: W41.819.
Meyer, Jacob. b. 1810, d. 1875, SC: 1840. Rf: DR; 1861C; *Courier* Dec. 11, 1861
Meyer, Marks. b. 1854, d. 1889. Rf: DR
Meyer, Mordecai. SC: 1766. Rf: W11.301 (1766)
Meyers, Abraham. SC: 1782. Rf: E106
Meyers, Catherine. b. 1857, d. 1858, SC: 1857, f. Morris Meyers, m. Sarah Cohen Meyers. Rf: DR; EC73; SFF36
Meyers, M., Mrs. b. 1783, d. 1870, SC: 1783. Rf: DR
Meyers, Morris. SC: 1848, mr. Sarah Cohen Meyers, 1848. Rf: EM23; SFF36; EC73; E170, 238; 1850C; 1861C
Meyers, Philip. SC: 1790, mr. Frances Solomons Myers, 1827. Rf: 1790C; EM14; TBS40
Meyers, Sarah (Cohen). b. 1810, d. 1852, SC: 1848, f. Solomon I. Cohen, m. Eleanor S. Cohen, mr. Morris Meyers, 1848. Rf: EC38; EM23; SFF36; W45.675
Milhado, Benjamin. SC: 1796, mr. Hannah DePass Milhado, 1796. Rf: EM6; SFF58; 1800C; E137; SCA1799; D1801, 1802, 1803, 1806
Milhado, Hannah DePass. b. 1778, d. 1829, SC: 1796, f. Ralph DePass, m. Leah DePass, mr. Benjamin Milhado, 1796. Rf: EM6; SFF58
Mincks, Samuel. SC: 1696. Rf: EL; *FSSC*163; WIM(1694–1704), 362; RB111
Mindez, Alexander M. H. SC: 1798, f. Moses Harzog Mindez, m. Della M. H. Mindez. Rf: MR3M.178
Mindez, Della M. H. SC: 1798, mr. Moses Harzog Mindez. Rf: MR3M.178
Mindez, Ella M. H. SC: 1798, f. Moses Harzog Mindez, m. Della M. H. Mindez. Rf: MR3M.178

Mindez, Hendel M. H. SC: 1798, f. Moses Harzog Mindez, m. Della M. H. Mindez. Rf: MR3M.178

Mindez, Moses Harzog. SC: 1798, mr. Della M. H. Mindez. Rf: MR3M.178

Minis, Abigail. b. 1775, d. 1835, SC: 1781, f. Philip Minis, m. Judith Polock Minis. Rf: SFF194; SCA1781–94

Minis, Divinah (Cohen). b. 1787, d. 1874, SC: 1803, f. Solomon Cohen, m. Bella Moses Cohen, mr. Isaac Minis, 1803. Rf: EM7; SFF35, 194

Minis, Emily (Tobias). b. 1828, d. 1914, SC: 1828, f. Abraham Tobias, m. Eleanor Lopez Tobias, mr. Theodore Minis, 1848. Rf: SFF194, 298; W47.820

Minis, Isaac. b. 1780, d. 1856, SC: 1780, f. Philip Minis, m. Judith Polock Minis, mr. Divinah Cohen Minis, 1803. Rf: SFF194: EM7; T38; SCA1815

Minis, Judith (Polock). b. 1745, d. 1819, f. Isaac Polock, m. Fanny Isaacks Polock, mr. Philip Minis, 1774. Rf: SFF194, 252

Minis, Philip. b. 1734, d. 1789, SC: 1780, f. Abraham Minis, m. Abigail Minis, mr. Judith Polock Minis, 1774. Rf: SFF194; E91, 92, 278; EM6; SCA1781–86

Mintz, Abraham I. SC: 1855. Rf: *BS-BI*

Mintz, Etel. b. 1818, d. 1883, SC: 1861. Rf: EBS7; E240

Mintz, Joseph. b. 1817, d. 1891, SC: 1851. Rf: EBS7

Mintz, Rebecca. b. 1805, d. 1889. Rf: EBS7

Mintz, W. D. SC: 1861. Rf: E240

Modina, Moses. SC: 1707. Rf: EL; RB115

Moïse, ———. f. Isaac Moïse, m. Hetty Lopez Moïse. Rf: SFF197

Moïse, Aaron. b. 1783, d. 1852, SC: 1791, f. Abraham Moïse, m. Sarah Moïse, mr. Phila Cohen Moïse, 1805, mr2. Sarah Cohen Moïse, 1807. Rf: EC28; SFF38, 195; E137, 170; 1810C; 1820C; 1850C; T38; SCA1803–23; D1807, 1809, 1813, 1816, 1819, 1822, 1829, 1831, 1835

Moïse, Aaron. b. 1820, d. 1880, SC: 1820, f. Aaron Moïse, m. Sarah Cohen Moïse, mr. Elizabeth Clark Lanier Moïse. Rf: SFF195; SCA1842; D1841, 1849

Moïse, Abigail Louisa (Lopez). b. 1810, d. 1890, SC: 1810, f. David Lopez, m. Priscilla Moses Lopez, mr. Abram Moïse, 1835. Rf: EC66; EM15; SFF176, 195; W46.235; 1850C; D1859

Moïse, Abraham. b. 1737, d. 1809, SC: 1791, mr. Sarah Moïse, 1779. Rf: SFF195; E181, 280

Moïse, Abraham. b. 1799, d. 1869, SC: 1799, f. Abraham Moïse, m. Sarah Moïse, mr. Caroline Agnes Moses Moïse, 1827. Rf: EC57; EM14; SFF195, 196; T38; E196, 205; 1850C; 1860C; 1861C; MS9.424; D1829, 1831, 1835, 1838, 1841, 1849, 1852, 1855, 1859

Moïse, Abraham. b. 1809, d. 1852, SC: 1809, f. Aaron Moïse, m. Phila Cohen Moïse, mr. Abigail Louisa Lopez Moïse, 1835. Rf: SFF176, 195; E137, 141, 170,

205; EC62, 66; W46.235; 1850C; D1829, 1831, 1835, 1838, 1849, 1852

Moïse, Abraham H. b. 1857, d. 1861, SC: 1857, f. Charles Henry Moïse, m. Theodora Sydney Moïse. Rf: SFF196; 1860C

Moïse, Algernon Sidney. b. 1840, d. 1842, SC: 1840, f. Abraham Moïse, m. Abigail Louisa Lopez Moïse. Rf: DR; EC66; SFF195

Moïse, Amanda Isabel (Jacobs). b. 1831, d. 1904, SC: 1850, f. Myer Jacobs, m. Rebecca Lazarus Jacobs, mr. Benjamin Franklin Moïse, 1853. Rf: SFF132, 196; EC64, 66; 1850C

Moïse, Benjamin. b. 1790, d. 1824, SC: 1791, f. Abraham Moïse, m. Sarah Moïse, mr. Rebecca Levy Moïse, 1817. Rf: DR; SFF195; *SP*, July 3, 1824; 1820C; T38; SCA1820; D1819, 1822

Moïse, Benjamin Franklin. b. 1830, d. 1887, SC: 1852, mr. Amanda Isabel Jacobs Moïse, 1853. Rf: SFF132, 196; 1861C; EC65, 66; E170, 262, 263; SCA1877; D1852, 1855

Moïse, Benjamin Franklin. SC: 1855, f. Benjamin Franklin Moïse, m. Amanda Isabel Jacobs Moïse, mr. Florence Stella Hart Moïse, 1884. Rf: SFF99, 196; D1855, 1859

Moïse, Camillus. b. 1848, SC: 1848, f. Abraham Moïse, m. Abigail Louisa Lopez. Rf: SFF195; 1850C

Moïse, Camillus T. b. 1817, d. 1844, SC: 1817, f. Aaron Moïse, m. Sarah Cohen Moïse. Rf: DR; EC60; SFF195; E170

Moïse, Caroline Agnes (Moses). b. 1808, d. 1880, SC: 1827, f. Isaac Clifton Moses, m. Hannah Lazarus Moses, mr. Abraham Moïse, 1827. Rf: DR; SFF195, 196, 207; EC57; EM14; SCA1827–51; MS9.424; 1850C; 1860C

Moïse, Catherine. b. 1846, SC: 1846. Rf: 1850C

Moïse, Cecilia A. b. 1790, SC: 1790. Rf: 1850C

Moïse, Cecilia Frances (Moses). b. 1806, d. 1844, SC: 1806, f. Isaac Clifton Moses, m. Hannah Lazarus Moses, mr. Theodore Sidney Moïse, 1836. Rf: EM16; SFF199, 207

Moïse, Cecilia Francis. b. 1855, SC: 1855, f. Charles Henry Moïse, m. Theodora Sydney Moïse. Rf: SFF196; 1860C

Moïse, Cecilia (Woolf). b. 1789, d. 1871, SC: 1789, f. Solomon Woolf, m. Rachel Andrews Moses Woolf, mr. Hyam Moïse, 1807. Rf: EC75; EM9; SFF195, 199, 205; SCA1815–34

Moïse, Charles Henry. b. 1830, d. 1896, SC: 1830, f. Abraham Moïse, m. Caroline Agnes Moses Moïse, mr. Theodora Sydney Moïse, 1853. Rf: MJSC12; SFF196; E170, 194, 263; T38; 1850C; 1860C; D1852, 1855, 1859

Moïse, Charles Henry. b. 1859, d. 1898, SC: 1859, f. Charles Henry Moïse, m. Theodora Sydney Moïse, mr. Celeste Laycock Moïse, 1889. Rf: SFF196; 1860C

Moïse, Cherie. b. 1781, d. 1823, SC: 1791, f. Abraham Moïse, m. Sarah Moïse, mr. Esther Moses Moïse,

1801. Rf: SFF195, 205; MF185–86; EM12; E137, 145, 280; 1810C; T38; SCA1800–22; D1806, 1807, 1809, 1813, 1816, 1819; RB115

Moïse, Cherry. b. 1823, d. 1824, SC: 1823. Rf: DR

Moïse, Columbus. b. 1809, d. 1871, SC: 1809, f. Aaron Moïse, m. Sarah Cohen Moïse, mr. Fanny Emma Levy, 1854. Rf: SFF195, 197; E170, 206, 207; T38; D1829, 1831, 1835

Moïse, David. b. 1849, SC: 1849, f. Abraham Moïse, m. Abigail Louisa Lopez Moïse. Rf: SFF195; 1850C

Moïse, David Calhoun. b. 1847, d. 1887, SC: 1847, f. Isaac Moïse, m. Hetty Lopez Moïse, mr. Cora Washington Tell Moïse. Rf: SFF197; W48.147; 1850C

Moïse, Edwin Henry. b. 1845, d. 1883, SC: 1845, f. Isaac Moïse, m. Hetty Lopez Moïse, mr. Nannie Bell Field Moïse. Rf: SFF197; E232; 1850C

Moïse, Edwin Warren. b. 1810, d. 1868, SC: 1810, f. Hyam Moïse, m. Cecilia Woolf Moïse, mr. Priscilla Lopez Moïse, 1835, mr2. Louise Hubert. Rf: SFF176, 199; EM27; E170, 196; EC19; D1852, 1855

Moïse, Edwin Warren. b. 1832, d. 1902, SC: 1832, f. Abraham Moïse, m. Caroline Agnes Moses Moïse, mr. Esther Lyon Moïse, 1854. Rf: MJSC12; SFF196, 198; EM27; 1850C

Moïse, Ella. b. 1855, d. 1855, SC: 1855, f. Benjamin Franklin Moïse, m. Amanda Isabel Jacobs Moïse. Rf: DR; SFF196

Moïse, Esther (Lyon). b. 1837, d. 1917, SC: 1854, f. George Lyon, m. Rachel Lyon, mr. Edwin Warren Moïse, 1854. Rf: MJSC12; EM27; SFF196, 198

Moïse, Fanny Emma (Levy). b. 1831, d. 1925, SC: 1831, f. David Cardoza Levy, m. Anna Maria Moses Levy, mr. Columbus Moïse, 1854. Rf: SFF164, 197

Moïse, Henrietta. b. 1836, SC: 1836. Rf: 1850C

Moïse, Herbert L. b. 1861, d. 1883, SC: 1861, f. Benjamin Franklin Moïse, m. Amanda Isabel Jacobs Moïse. Rf: DR; EC64; SFF196

Moïse, Hetty (Lopez). b. 1805, d. 1885, SC: 1805, f. David Lopez, m. Priscilla Moses Lopez, mr. Isaac Moïse, 1827. Rf: DR; SFF176, 195, 197; 1850C; 1861C; D1849, 1859

Moïse, Howard Cohen [Clifford]. SC: 1838. Rf: D1838

Moïse, Howard Cohen [Clifford]. b. 1836, d. 1908, SC: 1836, f. Jacob Moïse, m. Rebecca Cohen Moïse, mr. Louise McDonald Moïse, 1865. Rf: SFF196; E232; D1855

Moïse, Hyam. b. 1785, d. 1811, SC: 1791, f. Abraham Moïse, m. Sarah Moïse, mr. Cecilia Woolf Moïse, 1807. Rf: EM9; EC75; SFF196, 199; E137; W30.855; T38; SCA1807–19; D1807, 1809

Moïse, Isaac. b. 1800, d. 1857, SC: 1800, f. Abraham Moïse, m. Sarah Moïse, mr. Hetty Lopez Moïse, 1827. Rf: EC42; SFF195, 197; W48.187 (his); 1850C; 1861C;

E137; T38; SCA1827–28; D1849, 1852, 1855

Moïse, Isaac Randolph [Isaac Edwin]. b. 1843, SC: 1843, f. Isaac Moïse, m. Hetty Lopez Moïse. Rf: SFF197; W48.187; E137, 170, 182, 232; 1850C; D1859

Moïse, Isabel Nones (DeLeon). b. 1858, d. 1927, SC: 1858, f. Harmon Hendricks DeLeon, m. Caroline Agnes Moïse DeLeon, mr. Marion Moïse, 1877. Rf: MJSC12; SFF55, 198; 1860C

Moïse, Jacob. b. 1798, d. 1837, SC: 1798, f. Abraham Moïse, m. Sarah Moïse, mr. Rebecca Catherine Cohen Moïse. Rf: T38; SFF39, 195, 196; MF243; SCA1824–28

Moïse, Jacob. SC: 1855, f. Jacob Moïse, m. Rebecca Cohen Moïse. Rf: SFF196; D1855

Moïse, Jefferson. b. 1856, d. 1860, SC: 1856, f. Benjamin Franklin Moïse, m. Amanda Isabel Jacobs Moïse. Rf: DR; EC66; SFF196

Moïse, Kate. f. Abraham Moïse, m. Abigail Louisa Lopez Moïse. Rf: SFF195

Moïse, Marion. b. 1859, d. 1910, SC: 1859, f. Edwin Warren Moïse, m. Esther Lyon Moïse, mr. Isabel Nones DeLeon, 1877. Rf: SFF55, 198; MJSC12

Moïse, Miriam. b. 1819, d. 1823, SC: 1823. Rf: DR

Moïse, Penina. b. 1797, d. 1880, SC: 1797, f. Abraham Moïse, m. Sarah Moïse. Rf: EC57; SFF195; E176, 181–84; W48.187; SCA1818; 1850C; 1860C

Moïse, Percival Randolph. b. 1828, d. 1849, SC: 1828, f. Aaron Moïse, m. Sarah Cohen Moïse. Rf: DR; EC60; SFF195

Moïse, Philah (Cohen). b. 1787, d. 1805, SC: 1805, f. Gershon Cohen, m. Rebecca Sarzedas Cohen, mr. Aaron Moïse, 1805. Rf: EC59; EM8; SFF38, 195

Moïse, Philip Augustus. b. 1824, d. 1887, SC: 1849, f. Jacob Moïse, m. Rebecca Cohen Moïse, mr. Selina Florance Moïse, 1855. Rf: MJSC16; SFF74, 196; E170, 228; *Courier* Dec. 11, 1861; D1849, 1855

Moïse, Priscilla. b. 1837, d. 1839, SC: 1839, f. Abraham Moïse, m. Abigail Louisa Lopez Moïse. Rf: EC66; SFF195

Moïse, Priscilla (Lopez). b. 1807, d. 1839, SC: 1807, f. David Lopez, m. Priscilla Moses Lopez, mr. Edwin Warren Moïse, 1835. Rf: EC19; SFF176, 199; LF4

Moïse, Rebecca. b. 1838, SC: 1850. Rf: 1850C

Moïse, Rebecca. b. 1861, d. 1912, f. Thomas Jefferson Moïse, m. Rebecca Harby Moïse. Rf: SFF196

Moïse, Rebecca Catherine (Cohen). b. 1800, d. 1884, SC: 1800, f. Philip Cohen, m. Eleanor Moses Cohen, mr. Jacob Moïse. Rf: DR; EC65; SFF39, 195, 196; SCA1850; 1850C; D1835, 1852

Moïse, Rebecca (Levy). mr. Benjamin Moïse, 1817. Rf: SFF195

Moïse, Rebecca (Moses). b. 1841, d. 1918, SC: 1859, f. Andrew Jackson Moses, m. Octavia Harby Moses, mr. Thomas J. Moïse, 1859. Rf: MJSC13; EM30; SFF196, 207

Moïse, Sarah. b. 1762, d. 1842, SC: 1791, mr. Abraham Moïse, 1779. Rf: DR; EC59; SFF195; MF185; 1820C; SCA1808–22; D1816, 1819, 1822

Moïse, Sarah (Cohen). b. 1791, d. 1828, SC: 1791, f. Gershon Cohen, m. Rebecca Sarzedas Cohen, mr. Aaron Moïse, 1807. Rf: DR; EC29; SFF38, 195; SCA1821–23; D1819

Moïse, Sarah Louisa. b. 1836, d. 1837, SC: 1837, f. Abraham Moïse, m. Abigail Louisa Lopez. Rf: EC66; SFF195; EP

Moïse, Sarah Priscilla. b. 1841, SC: 1841, f. Isaac Moïse, m. Hetty Lopez Moïse. Rf: SFF197; W48.187; 1850C

Moïse, Selina (Florance). SC: 1855, f. William Florance, m. Myrtilla Seixas Florance, mr. Philip Augustus Moïse, 1855. Rf: SFF74, 196; EM28

Moïse, Theodora Sydney (Moïse). b. 1837, d. 1925, SC: 1850, f. Theodore Sidney Moïse, m. Cecilia Frances Moses Moïse, mr. Charles Henry Moïse, 1853. Rf: MJSC12; SFF196, 199; 1850C; 1860C

Moïse, Theodore Sydney. b. 1808, d. 1885, SC: 1808, f. Hyam Moïse, m. Cecilia Woolf Moïse, mr. Cecilia Frances Moses Moïse, 1836, mr2. Matilda Jane Vaughn, 1845. Rf: SFF199; EM16; T38; SCA1818; D1829, 1835

Moïse, Theodore Sydney. b. 1861, d. 1889, SC: 1861, f. Charles Henry Moïse, m. Theodora Sydney Moïse, mr. Eloisa Cuellar Moïse, 1882. Rf: SFF196

Moïse, Thomas Jefferson. b. 1826, d. 1869, SC: 1849, f. Jacob Moïse, m. Rebecca Cohen Moïse, mr. Rebecca Harby Moïse, 1859. Rf: EC30; EM65; SFF196, 295; T38; W48.187; W49.1000; 1861C; D1849, 1855, 1859

Molina, Moses. SC: 1785. Rf: W21.774 (his); E33, 280

Monsanta, Rodrigues. SC: 1804. Rf: E137

Morales, Isaac. SC: 1796. Rf: MR3R.583

Morales, Jacob. SC: 1800. Rf: E137; 1800C; D1801, 1802, 1803, 1806

Mordecai, ———. SC: 1819, mr. Mordecai Hyams. Rf: D1819

Mordecai, ———. b. 1801, d. 1846, SC: 1801. Rf: DR

Mordecai, ———. b. 1829, d. 1829, SC: 1829. Rf: DR

Mordecai, ——— [1]. d. 1843, f. Thomas W. Mordecai, m. Lucretia Cohen Mordecai. Rf: SFF201

Mordecai, ——— [2]. f. Thomas W. Mordecai, m. Lucretia Cohen Mordecai. Rf: SFF201

Mordecai, ——— [3]. f. Thomas W. Mordecai, m. Lucretia Cohen Mordecai. Rf: SFF201

Mordecai, ——— [4]. f. Thomas W. Mordecai, m. Lucretia Cohen Mordecai. Rf: SFF201

Mordecai, ——— [5]. f. Thomas W. Mordecai, m. Lucretia Cohen Mordecai. Rf: SFF210

Mordecai, ——— [6]. f. Thomas W. Mordecai, m. Lucretia Cohen Mordecai. Rf: SFF201

Mordecai, ——— [7]. f. Thomas W. Mordecai, m. Lucretia Cohen Mordecai. Rf: SFF201

Mordecai, ——— [8]. f. Thomas W. Mordecai, m. Lucretia Cohen Mordecai. Rf: SFF201

Mordecai, ——— [9]. f. Thomas W. Mordecai, m. Lucretia Cohen Mordecai. Rf: SFF201

Mordecai, Abraham G. b. 1811, d. 1841, SC: 1841, f. Goodman Mordecai, m. Jane Cohen Mordecai. Rf: SFF202; EJCC7

Mordecai, Allen Lewis. b. 1841, d. 1908, SC: 1841, f. Benjamin Mordecai, m. Clara Polock Mordecai, mr. Katherine Marks Mordecai, 1865. Rf: SFF202; 1860C

Mordecai, Arthur Levy. b. 1856, d. 1858, SC: 1856, f. Benjamin Mordecai, m. Clara Polock Mordecai. Rf: DR; EC54; SFF202

Mordecai, Benjamin. b. 1809, d. 1893, SC: 1809, f. Goodman Mordecai, mr. Clara Polock Mordecai, 1838. Rf: SFF202; T38; 1850C; 1860C; 1861C; E170, 221, 222, 238, 261; EL; T38; SCA1847–60; *Courier* Dec. 11, 1861; D1849, 1855, 1859

Mordecai, Catherine [Isabel] (Andrews). SC: 1778, f. Abraham Andrews, m. Nellie Abrahams Andrews, mr. Samuel Mordecai, 1778. Rf: SFF12; EM5; SCA1779

Mordecai, Cecilia. b. 1812, d. 1833, SC: 1833, f. Goodman Mordecai, m. Jane Cohen Mordecai. Rf: EC9; SFF202

Mordecai, Clara Polock. b. 1819, d. 1894, SC: 1819, mr. Benjamin Mordecai, 1838. Rf: SFF202; 1860C

Mordecai, Cornelia. b. 1841, d. 1841, SC: 1841, f. Thomas Whitlock Mordecai, m. Lucretia Cohen Mordecai. Rf: DR; SFF201

Mordecai, Cornelia. b. 1844, d. 1867, SC: 1844, f. Thomas Whitlock Mordecai, m. Lucretia Cohen Mordecai. Rf: DR; SFF201; 1850C; 1860C

Mordecai, David. b. 1781, d. 1818, SC: 1801, f. Mordecai Moses Mordecai, m. Zipporah DeLyon Mordecai, mr. Reinah Cohen Mordecai, 1802. Rf: EC40; SFF203; T38; 1810C; SCA1806–15; D1806, 1807, 1809

Mordecai, David Henry. b. 1818, d. 1899, SC: 1859, f. David Mordecai, m. Reinah Cohen Mordecai. Rf: SFF203; D1859

Mordecai, David Henry. b. 1833, d. 1859, SC: 1833, f. Moses Cohen Mordecai, m. Rebecca Lyons Mordecai. Rf: SFF203; 1850C

Mordecai, Elias Polock. b. 1855, d. 1858, SC: 1855, f. Benjamin Mordecai, m. Clara Polock Mordecai. Rf: DR; EC54; SFF202

Mordecai, Esther Cohen. b. 1843, d. 1909, SC: 1850, f. Thomas Whitlock Mordecai, m. Lucretia Cohen Mordecai. Rf: DR; SFF201; 1850C; 1860C

Mordecai, Esther [Hetty]. b. 1811, d. 1881, SC: 1811, f. Joseph Mordecai, m. Esther Marache Mordecai. Rf: DR; SFF200; 1860C

Mordecai, Esther (Marache). b. 1768, d. 1820, SC: 1803, f. Solomon Marache, m. Rebecca Myers Marache, mr. Joseph Mordecai,

1786. Rf: SFF184, 200; *SP*, Jan. 21, 1820; RB117

Mordecai, Frances {Fanny}. b. 1804, d. 1858, SC: 1804, f. Goodman Mordecai, m. Miriam Rebecca Mordecai. Rf: EJCC7; SFF202

Mordecai, Goodman. SC: 1808, mr. Miriam R. Mordecai, mr2. Jane Cohen Mordecai Simpson, 1808. Rf: MR3Z.349; EM9; EC45; E137; SFF202; SCA1808–12; MS5.410

Mordecai, Goodman. b. 1839, d. 1922, SC: 1839, f. Benjamin Mordecai, m. Clara Polock Mordecai, mr. Ada Jackson Mordecai, 1864. Rf: SFF202; 1860C

Mordecai, Harriet. b. 1810, d. 1873, SC: 1823, f. Joseph Mordecai, m. Esther Marache Mordecai. Rf: DR; 1860C; 1861C; SFF200; D1852

Mordecai, Henrietta. b. 1831, SC: 1831, f. Moses Cohen Mordecai, m. Isabel Rebecca Lyons Mordecai. Rf: 1850C

Mordecai, Henry. b. 1847, d. 1920, SC: 1847, f. Benjamin Mordecai, m. Clara Polock Mordecai, mr. Corrine Harris Mordecai, 1879. Rf: SFF202; 1860C

Mordecai, Hetty. b. 1811, d. 1881, SC: 1811. Rf: DR

Mordecai, Hortensia. b. 1830, SC: 1860, f. Moses Cohen Mordecai, m. Isabel Rebecca Lyons Mordecai. Rf: SFF203; 1860C

Mordecai, Isaac. SC: 1786. Rf: SCA1786–1808; D1809

Mordecai, Isaac. b. 1799, d. 1846, SC: 1799. Rf: DR; EP; 1830C; 1840C; SCA1831–41; D1831, 1835, 1841

Mordecai, Isaac D. b. 1805, d. 1864, SC: 1823, f. David Mordecai, m. Reinah Cohen Mordecai. Rf: SFF203; EC39; E137, 170; T38

Mordecai, Isaac John Randolph. b. 1835, d. 1895, SC: 1850, f. Moses Cohen Mordecai, m. Isabel Rebecca Lyons Mordecai, mr. Emma Brown Mordecai, 1868. Rf: SFF203; E170, 232; 1850C; D1855

Mordecai, Isaac Whitlock. b. 1840, SC: 1840, f. Thomas Whitlock Mordecai, m. Lucretia Cohen Mordecai, mr. Laura H. Taylor Mordecai, 1866. Rf: SFF201; E232; 1850C; 1860C

Mordecai, Isabel. b. 1828, SC: 1850, f. Moses Cohen Mordecai, m. Isabel Rebecca Lyons Mordecai. Rf: SFF203; 1850C

Mordecai, Isabel Rebecca (Lyons). b. 1804, d. 1895, SC: 1850, f. Isaac Lyons, m. Rachel Cohen Lyons, mr. Moses Cohen Mordecai, 1828. Rf: SFF183, 203; 1850C; 1860C

Mordecai, Isabella. b. 1842, SC: 1842, f. Moses Cohen Mordecai, m. Isabella Rebecca Lyons Mordecai. Rf: 1850C; 1860C

Mordecai, J. R. SC: 1859. Rf: D1859

Mordecai, Jacob. SC: 1800, mr. Sarah Mordecai. Rf: MR3U.070; 1800C; SCA1804; D1806, 1807, 1809

Mordecai, Joseph {Joseph D?}. b. 1766, d. 1839, SC: 1808, f. Moses Mordecai, m. Elizabeth Whitlock Mordecai, mr. Esther Marache Mordecai, 1786. Rf: DR; SFF200; 1810C; 1820C; 1830C; SCA1808;

D1809, 1819, 1822, 1829, 1831, 1835

Mordecai, Judith. b. 1796, d. 1820, SC: 1820, f. Joseph Mordecai, m. Esther Marache Mordecai. Rf: EP; SFF200; *SP*, June 6, 1820, eulogy

Mordecai, Laura. b. 1818, d. 1839, SC: 1839, f. Jacob Cohen. Rf: EP

Mordecai, Leah Cohen. b. 1836, d. 1919, SC: 1836, f. Thomas Whitlock Mordecai, m. Lucretia Cohen Mordecai. Rf: DR; SFF201; 1850C

Mordecai, Leon A. b. 1843, d. 1925, SC: 1843, f. Benjamin Mordecai, m. Clara Polock Mordecai. Rf: SFF202; 1860C

Mordecai, Lewis. b. 1815, SC: 1860. Rf: 1860C

Mordecai, Lucretia C. b. 1842, d. 1922, SC: 1842, f. Thomas Whitlock Mordecai, m. Lucretia Cohen Mordecai. Rf: DR; SFF201; 1860C

Mordecai, Lucretia (Cohen). b. 1807, d. 1888, SC: 1807, f. Mordecai Cohen, m. Leah Lazarus Cohen, mr. Thomas Whitlock Mordecai, 1834. Rf: DR; SFF35; 201; EM15; W44.356; 1850C; 1860C; SCA1836–39

Mordecai, Miriam Rebecca. b. 1779, d. 1808, SC: 1808, mr. Goodman Mordecai. Rf: EC45; SFF202

Mordecai, Moses Cohen. b. 1804, d. 1888, SC: 1804, f. David Mordecai, m. Reinah Cohen Mordecai, mr. Isabel R. Lyons Cohen Mordecai, 1828. Rf: SFF183, 203; E170, 196, 206, 261; 1830C; 1840C; 1850C; 1860C; 1861C; SCA1825–52; D1819, 1822, 1829, 1831, 1835, 1841, 1849, 1852, 1855, 1859

Mordecai, Noah. SC: 1810. Rf: E137

Mordecai, Rebecca. SC: 1805. Rf: MR3Y.562

Mordecai, Reinah (Cohen). b. 1784, d. 1853, SC: 1784, f. Moses Cohen, m. Judith DeLyon Cohen, mr. David Mordecai, 1802. Rf: EC40; SFF57, 203, 309; MR5H.219; D1819, 1822, 1829, 1831, 1835

Mordecai, Reinah Cordelia. b. 1815, f. David Mordecai, m. Rinah Cohen Mordecai. Rf: SFF203

Mordecai, Sampson. b. 1783, d. 1826, SC: 1783, f. Samuel Mordecai, m. Catherine Andrews Mordecai. Rf: SFF12; EP; *SP*, Sept. 1, 1826

Mordecai, Samuel. b. 1751, d. 1819, SC: 1779, mr. Catherine [Isabel] Andrews Mordecai, 1778. Rf: SFF12; E91, 100, 278; EM5; MR2S.399; *SCM*178; SCA1779–86

Mordecai, Sarah. SC: 1804, mr. Jacob Mordecai. Rf: MR3U.070; D1809

Mordecai, Solomon Joseph. b. 1790, f. Joseph Mordecai, m. Esther Marache Mordecai, mr. Isabella Jane Kincaid Mordecai, 1817. Rf: SFF200, 201; D1849

Mordecai, Theodore. b. 1812, f. David Mordecai, m. Reinah Cohen Mordecai. Rf: SFF203

Mordecai, Thomas Moultrie. b. 1855, d. 1926, SC: 1855, f. Thomas Whitlock Mordecai, m. Lucretia Cohen Mordecai, mr. Hannah Moses Mordecai, 1890, mr2. Gertrude Agnes Dahl Mordecai, 1893. Rf: DR; SFF201, 210; 1860C

Mordecai, Thomas Whitlock. b. 1806, d. 1865, SC: 1831, f. Joseph Mordecai, m. Esther Marache Mordecai, mr. Lucretia Cohen Mordecai, 1834. Rf: SFF35, 201, 202; 1840C; 1861C; T38; EM15, 33; E163, 164, 170, 233; SCA1836–47; D1831, 1835, 1838, 1841, 1849, 1852, 1859

Mordecai, Thomas Whitlock. b. 1839, d. 1861, SC: 1839, f. Thomas Whitlock Mordecai, m. Lucretia Cohen Mordecai. Rf: DR; SFF201; 1850C; 1860C

Mordecai, Zipporah. b. 1825, d. 1873, SC: 1825, f. David Mordecai, m. Reinah Cohen Mordecai. Rf: SFF203; 1860C

Morris, ———. b. 1815, d. 1851, SC: 1815. Rf: DR

Morris, Aaron. SC: 1810. Rf: E137

Morris, Ainsley. b. 1745, d. 1812, SC: 1812, f. Simpson Morris. Rf: EC41; EP

Morris, Elias. b. 1790, d. 1864, SC: 1852. Rf: DR

Morris, Henry. SC: 1802. Rf: E137; 1820C; SCA1820

Morris, Simpson. SC: 1809. Rf: E137; 1820C; MR5A.200

Morse, Solomon. SC: 1818. Rf: E137

Moses, ——— [1]. f. Israel Moses, m. Deborah Cohen Moses. Rf: SFF212

Moses, ——— [2]. f. Israel Moses, m. Deborah Cohen Moses. Rf: SFF212

Moses, A. DeLeon. b. 1842, d. 1901, SC: 1842, f. Oliver Hazard Perry Moses, m. Anna DeLeon Moses, mr. Eliza Cohen Moses, 1878. Rf: MJSC15; SFF207; E233

Moses, Aaron J. b. 1817, d. 1893, SC: 1817, f. Isaiah Moses, m. Rebecca Phillips Moses, mr. Judith A. Ottolengui Moses, 1844. Rf: DR; T38; SFF210; EC53; EM21; E170, 238, 253; 1861C; EP; SCA1834–47; *Courier* Dec. 11, 1861; D1852, 1855

Moses, Abigail. b. 1750, d. 1825, SC: 1750, mr. Lyon Moses. Rf: DR; SFF213; 1810C (St. Johns); W35.635; SCA1792–1826; D1822

Moses, Abraham. d. 1796, SC: 1769. Rf: E91, 122, 137, 278; SFF212; 1790C; W26.476 (his); SCA1769–96; D1794, 1796

Moses, Abraham. d. 1821, SC: 1800, f. Abraham Moses, m. Mary Moses. Rf: EP; D1801, 1802

Moses, Abraham. b. 1828, f. Isaiah Moses, m. Rebecca Phillips Moses, mr. Annie Jonas Moses. Rf: SFF210, 211

Moses, Addie. f. Charles Brown Moses, m. Angelina Lazarus Moses. Rf: SFF207

Moses, Adeline (Moses). d. 1873, SC: 1850, f. Joseph Moses, m. Rachel Moses, mr. Levy J. Moses, 1832. Rf: DR; SFF210, 211, 213; EM15; W34.16; MS16.154; 1850C

Moses, Agnes (DeLeon). b. 1852, d. 1936, SC: 1852, f. Harmon Hendricks DeLeon, m. Caroline Agnes Moïse DeLeon, mr. Felix Jacob Moses, 1876. Rf: SFF55, 211; 1860C

Moses, Alfred Huger. b. 1840, SC: 1840, f. Levy J. Moses, m. Adeline

Moses Moses, mr. Janette Nathans Moses. Rf: 1850C; SFF211

Moses, Andrew. SC: 1810. Rf: E137; MS14.255; SCA1812

Moses, Andrew Jackson. b. 1815, d. 1877, f. Isaac Clifton Moses, m. Hannah Lazarus Moses, mr. Octavia Harby Moses, 1839. Rf: MJSC15; SFF207; EC16

Moses, Angelina (Lazarus). b. 1809, SC: 1834, f. Aaron Lazarus, m. Esther Cohen Lazarus, mr. Charles Brown Moses, 1834. Rf: SFF151, 207; EC17; MS13.54; SCA1854

Moses, Anna (DeLeon). b. 1816, d. 1888, SC: 1816, f. Abraham DeLeon, m. Isabella Nones Moses DeLeon, mr. Oliver Hazard Perry Moses, 1839. Rf: DR; EC24; SFF55, 207

Moses, Attival. SC: 1779. Rf: RB119

Moses, Barnard. SC: 1780, mr. Esther DeLyon Moses, 1777. Rf: SFF57; E91, 278; 1790C; SCA1781–98; RB119

Moses, Bella. SC: 1784. Rf: MR2V.87

Moses, Catherine. b. 1814, d. 1821, SC: 1814. Rf: DR

Moses, Catherine (Phillips). b. 1809, d. 1885, f. Zalegman Phillips, m. Arabella Solomons Phillips, mr. Montgomery Moses, 1832. Rf: SFF206, 243

Moses, Cecilia. b. 1766, d. 1842, SC: 1812. Rf: EP; W41.783; MR4P.445

Moses, Chapman. SC: 1805. Rf: E137; 1810C; SCA1815–17; D1806, 1807

Moses, Charles Brown. b. 1810, d. 1854, SC: 1810, f. Isaac Clifton Moses, m. Hannah Lazarus Moses, mr. Angelina Lazarus Moses, 1834. Rf: DR; EC16; SFF207; T38; SCA1832–34

Moses, Charles Brown. b. 1848, d. 1852, SC: 1852, f. Charles Brown Moses, m. Angelina Lazarus Moses. Rf: EC17; SFF207

Moses, Clifton. f. Charles Brown Moses, m. Angelina Lazarus Moses, mr. Jones West. Rf: SFF207

Moses, Cornelia Alice (Cohen). SC: 1860, f. John Jay Cohen, m. Cornelia Ann Jacobs Cohen, mr. Franklin J. Moses, 1864. Rf: SFF39, 206; 1860C

Moses, D. L. b. 1831, SC: 1831, mr. Hester A. Moses. Rf: 1860C

Moses, Daniel L. SC: 1815, f. Lyon Moses, m. Abigail Moses. Rf: SFF213; E137, 170, 239; 1840C; CB1815; SCA1826–27; D1835, 1841

Moses, David. SC: 1769. Rf: JR1769

Moses, David L. b. 1845, d. 1882, SC: 1845, f. Oliver Hazard Perry Moses, m. Anna DeLeon Moses. Rf: DR; EC24; SFF207; E233

Moses, David Machado. b. 1785, d. 1858, SC: 1785, f. Philip Moses, m. Sarah Machado Moses, mr. Miriam Seixas Moses, 1832. Rf: SFF212; E137; D1809

Moses, Deborah (Cohen). b. 1776, d. 1848, SC: 1813, f. Jacob Raphael Cohen, m. Rebecca Luria Cohen, mr. Israel Moses, 1810. Rf: MR4G.259; SFF180, 212; W45.581 (hers); SCA1813–37

Moses, Dora (DaVega). f. Isaac DaVega, m. Sarah J. Moses

DaVega, mr. Isaiah Ezra Moses. Rf: SFF45, 210

Moses, Edwin L. b. 1834, d. 1865, SC: 1834, f. Levy Moses, m. Miriam Joseph Moses. Rf: EC96; SFF210; E170, 233; 1850C; 1860C

Moses, Eliazer. SC: 1778. Rf: *SCHM*53.101–12

Moses, Eliza (Cohen). b. 1842, d. 1926, SC: 1842, f. Marx Edwin Cohen, m. Armida Harby Cohen, mr. A. DeLeon Moses, 1878. Rf: MJSC15; SFF35, 207

Moses, Eliza Matilda (Moses). b. 1812, d. 1892, SC: 1812, f. Isaac Clifton Moses, m. Hannah Lazarus Moses, mr. Raphael J. Moses, 1834. Rf: SFF207, 212; W45.581

Moses, Elizabeth. b. 1744, d. 1819, SC: 1768, mr. Henry Moses. Rf: EC110; SCA1768–1808; D1816, 1819

Moses, Esther (DeLyon). b. 1762, SC: 1783, f. Isaac DeLyon, m. Rinah Tobias DeLyon, mr. Barnard Moses, 1777. Rf: SFF57; MS1.626; SCA1783–98

Moses, Esther (Isaacks). b. 1780, d. 1841, SC: 1800, f. Moses Isaacks, m. Judith Rachel Mears Isaacks, mr. Isaac Moses, 1800. Rf: EM7; SFF120, 212; D1816, 1819, 1822

Moses, Esther Mendez (Phillips). b. 1778, d. 1845, SC: 1845, f. Jonas Phillips, m. Rebecca Machado Phillips, mr. Myer Moses, 1803. Rf: EC20; EM7; SFF205, 243

Moses, Ezra I. b. 1833, d. 1877, SC: 1833, f. Isaiah Moses, m. Rebecca Phillips Moses, mr. Sarah H. Levy Moses. Rf: SFF164, 210; *AF*57; 1850C; D1852

Moses, Fanny. b. 1810, SC: 1810. Rf: 1850C

Moses, Felix J. b. 1853, d. 1888, SC: 1853, f. Jacob I. Moses, m. Sarah Ottolengui Moses, mr. Agnes DeLeon Moses, 1876. Rf: SFF55, 211

Moses, Fisher [Fishel]. b. 1783, d. 1827, SC: 1783, f. Philip Moses, m. Sarah Machado Moses, mr. Rachel DePass Moses Lambert, 1824. Rf: DR; EM13; SFF58, 212; D1809, 1813

Moses, Franklin J. b. 1804, d. 1877, SC: 1825, f. Myer Moses, m. Esther Phillips Moses, mr. Jane Dorcas McClenahan Moses, 1828. Rf: SFF205; E100, 137, 197–99, 205, 206, 247, 252; T38

Moses, Grace Aguilar. f. Levy J. Moses, m. Adeline Moses Moses. Rf: SFF211

Moses, H. b. 1820, SC: 1820. Rf: 1860C

Moses, Hannah (Lazarus). b. 1768, d. 1846, SC: 1802, mr. Reuben Moses. Rf: DR; EC88; SFF213; MS4.268

Moses, Hannah (Lazarus). b. 1783, d. 1835, SC: 1783, f. Marks Lazarus, m. Rachael Benjamin Lazarus, mr. Isaac Clifton Moses, 1802. Rf: EC15; EM7; SFF151, 207; SCA1819

Moses, Hannah Maria (Moses). b. 1840, d. 1860, f. Raphael J. Moses, m. Eliza M. Moses, mr. Isaac I. Moses, 1856. Rf: SFF210, 212

Moses, Hart. SC: 1792. Rf: E117, 122, 137, 380; D1794

Moses, Hart J. b. 1807, d. 1860, SC:

1807, f. Joseph Hart Moses, m. Rachel Moses. Rf: DR; EC73; SFF213; W38.1826; SCA1839; 1860C

Moses, Henry. b. 1746, d. 1814, SC: 1782, mr. Elizabeth Moses. Rf: "House Journal, 1783–1784," pp. 36, 37; EC110; E98, 137, 278; T38; 1790C; 1800C; 1810C; SCA1782–1813; D1794, 1796, 1801, 1802, 1803, 1806, 1807, 1809, 1813; RB120

Moses, Henry Clay. b. 1844, SC: 1844, f. Levy J. Moses, m. Adeline Moses Moses, mr. Frances Sampson Moses. Rf: 1850C; SFF211

Moses, Hervey Hall. b. 1849, d. 1850, SC: 1850, f. Jacob I. Moses, m. Sarah Ottolengui Moses. Rf: EC54; SFF211

Moses, Hester [Hetty]. b. 1831, SC: 1831, f. Lyon Moses, m. Abigail Moses. Rf: SFF213; W35.635; 1850C; 1860C

Moses, Hetty. b. 1812, d. 1892, SC: 1830, f. Joseph Moses, m. Rachel Moses. Rf: DR; EC73; 1830C; 1861C; SFF213

Moses, Hetty [Hester] (Simmons). b. 1788, d. 1823, SC: 1788, f. Montague Simons, mr. Simon Moses, 1804. Rf: DR; SFF271; W32.706; MS4.401; D1809, 1819, 1822

Moses, I. H. b. 1810, d. 1860, SC: 1810. Rf: DR

Moses, Isaac. b. 1769, d. 1831, SC: 1769, f. Abraham Moses, mr. Esther Isaacks Moses, 1800. Rf: EM7; SFF212; T38; W26.476; E177, 122, 137, 280; SCA1794–1831; D1819

Moses, Isaac. SC: 1790, f. Isaac Clifton Moses, m. Hannah Lazarus Moses. Rf: SFF207; D1790, 1794, 1796, 1802, 1803

Moses, Isaac C. b. 1837, d. 1850, SC: 1837, f. Raphael J. Moses, m. Eliza M. Moses. Rf: SFF212

Moses, Isaac Clifton. b. 1781, d. 1834, SC: 1802, f. Myer Moses, m. Rachel Andrews Moses, mr. Hannah Lazarus Moses, 1802. Rf: EC15; SFF205, 207; EP; 1810C; 1830C; T38; E137, 141, 163, 233; D1806, 1807, 1816, 1819

Moses, Isaac I. b. 1822, SC: 1822, f. Isaiah Moses, m. Rebecca Phillips Moses, mr. Hannah Maria Moses, 1856, mr2. Mary Alice Moses, 1869. Rf: SFF207, 210, 212

Moses, Isaac L. b. 1794, d. 1807, SC: 1805, f. Lyon Moses, m. Abigail Moses. Rf: EC78; SFF213; CB1805

Moses, Isabel A. b. 1820, d. 1854, f. Isaac Clifton Moses, m. Hannah Lazarus Moses. Rf: SFF207

Moses, Isabel DeLeon (Cohen). b. 1843, d. 1892, SC: 1850, f. Lawrence Ludlow Cohen, m. Miriam Louisa DeLeon Cohen, mr. Zalegman P. Moses, 1866. Rf: EM33; SFF39, 206; 1850C

Moses, Isabella (Myers). b. 1796, d. 1850, SC: 1796, mr. Solomon Moses, 1815. Rf: DR; EC93; SFF213; EP; 1850C

Moses, Isaiah. b. 1772, d. 1857, SC: 1800, mr2. Rebecca Phillips Moses, 1807. Rf: EC87; SFF210,

247; 1800C; 1810C; 1820C; 1830C; 1850C; EM9; E138, 143, 170; T38; SCA1809–54; D1801, 1802, 1803, 1806, 1807, 1809, 1813, 1822, 1829, 1831, 1835, 1849, 1852

Moses, Isaiah. SC: 1804, mr. Sarah Moses. Rf: W33.1436; D1813

Moses, Isaiah Ezra. f. Ezra I. Moses, m. Sarah H. Levy Moses, mr. Dora DaVega Moses. Rf: SFF45, 210

Moses, Israel. b. 1787, d. 1849, SC: 1787, f. Philip Moses, m. Sarah Machado Moses, mr. Deborah Cohen Moses, 1810. Rf: SFF212; E138, 199; W45.481; 1820C; 1830C; T38; SCA1813–32; D1809, 1816, 1822, 1829, 1831, 1835; RB120

Moses, Jacob. SC: 1780, mr. Susannah Moses, Rf: EP; E91, 190, 278; 1820C; SCA1826–27; D1822

Moses, Jacob I. b. 1811, d. 1854, SC: 1811, f. Isaiah Moses, m. Rebecca Phillips Moses, mr. Rinah J. Ottolengui Moses, 1839, mr2. Sarah Ottolengui Moses, 1848. Rf: EC53; SFF210, 211, 234; *AF*53; T38; D1829, 1831, 1838

Moses, Jane. b. 1821, d. 1822, SC: 1821. Rf: DR

Moses, Joseph. b. 1772, d. 1814, SC: 1802, mr. Rachel Moses. Rf: EC73; E138, 170, 238; SFF213; D1802, 1803, 1813; RB121

Moses, Joseph Winthrop. SC: 1830. Rf: 1830C; E138, 170, 206

Moses, Joseph Winthrop. b. 1836, SC: 1836, f. Levy J. Moses, m. Adeline Moses Moses. Rf: SFF211; SCA1858; 1850C

Moses, Josiah. SC: 1819. Rf: SCA1822–29; D1819

Moses, Judah. b. 1848, SC: 1848, f. Levy J. Moses, m. Adeline Moses Moses, mr. Charlotte Baer Moses. Rf: 1850C; SFF211

Moses, Judith (Ottolengui). b. 1816, d. 1883, SC: 1816, f. Abraham Ottolengui, m. Sarah Jacob Ottolengui, mr. Aaron I. Moses, 1844. Rf: DR; EC53; EM21; SFF210, 234; W45.796

Moses, Julius L. b. 1828, d. 1901, SC: 1828, f. Levy Moses, m. Miriam Joseph Moses, mr. Rebecca Jackson Moses, 1859. Rf: DR; EC63; SFF129, 210; W48.476; T39; 1850C

Moses, Leah. SC: 1832. Rf: SCA1832–34

Moses, Levy. b. 1773, d. 1869, SC: 1793, mr. Miriam Joseph Moses, 1809. Rf: DR; EC96; EM9; E138, 170; SFF139, 210; W48.476; 1810C; 1820C; 1850C; 1861C; T39; SCA1793–1838; D1806, 1809, 1816, 1819, 1822, 1829, 1831, 1838, 1841, 1849, 1852

Moses, Levy J. b. 1808, d. 1876, SC: 1808, f. Isaiah Moses, m. Rebecca Phillips Moses, mr. Adeline Moses Moses, 1832. Rf: DR; EM15; SFF210, 211; TBS39; T39; 1850C; 1861C; E170, 205; SCA1832–40; D1835, 1841, 1849, 1852, 1855

Moses, Lyon. b. 1748, d. 1821, SC: 1781, mr. Abigail Lyon Moses. Rf: DR; EC78; SFF213; E117, 121; W35.635 (his); 1790C; 1810C; 1820C; EP; SCA1790–1821; *SP*,

April 26, 1821; D1790, 1794, 1796, 1801, 1802, 1803, 1806, 1807, 1809, 1813, 1816, 1819; RB121

Moses, Lyon Moses. b. 1800, d. 1856, SC: 1800, f. Lyon Moses, m. Abigail Moses. Rf: SFF213; W35.635; 1850C

Moses, Martha. f. Isaac Clifton Moses, m. Hannah Lazarus Moses. Rf: SFF207

Moses, Mary. b. 1830, d. 1838, SC: 1830. Rf: DR

Moses, Mary Alice (Moses). b. 1841, SC: 1841, f. Charles Brown Moses, m. Angelina Lazarus Moses, mr. Isaac I. Moses, 1869. Rf: SFF207, 210, 212

Moses, Mary [Rachael Miriam] Harris. b. 1754, d. 1810, SC: 1801, mr. Solomon Moses. Rf: EC44; MR3Q.407; SFF213; 1810C; W31.391 (hers); SCA1801–10

Moses, Miriam [Mary] Joseph. b. 1791, d. 1863, SC: 1791, f. Israel Joseph, m. Miriam Levy Joseph, mr. Levy Moses, 1809. Rf: EC96; EM9; SFF139, 210; 1850C; 1860C; 1861C; SCA1815–25

Moses, Montefiore Jacob. b. 1841, d. 1878, f. Jacob I. Moses, m. Rinah J. Ottolengui Moses, mr. Rosetta Jonas Moses, 1863. Rf: SFF136, 211

Moses, Montgomery. b. 1808, d. 1886, SC: 1808, f. Myer Moses, m. Esther Phillips Moses, mr. Catherine Phillips Moses, 1832. Rf: SFF205, 206; SCA1830–45

Moses, Mordecai. b. 1803, d. 1805, f. Joseph Moses, m. Rachel Moses. Rf: SFF213

Moses, Mordecai. b. 1842, SC: 1842, f. Levy J. Moses, m. Adeline Moses Moses. Rf: SFF210

Moses, Mordecai Lyons. f. Levy J. Moses, m. Adeline Moses Moses. Rf: SFF211

Moses, Morris. f. Isaiah Moses, mr. Sarah Jonas Moses. Rf: SFF136, 210

Moses, Moses. b. 1818, d. 1856, SC: 1818, f. Isaiah Moses, m. Rebecca Phillips Moses. Rf: SFF210; D1855

Moses, Moses Lyon. SC: 1818. Rf: E183: SCA1827–29; D1835

Moses, Myer. b. 1779, d. 1833, SC: 1779, f. Myer Moses, m. Rachel Andrews Moses, mr. Esther Phillips Moses, 1803. Rf: EC20; EM7; SFF205; 1810C; 1820C; E138, 140, 144, 170, 197; T39; D1806, 1807, 1809, 1813, 1816, 1819, 1822

Moses, Myer [Meyer]. b. 1735, d. 1787, SC: 1767, mr. ——— Frangipini Moses, mr2. Rachel Andrews Moses. Rf: SFF205; SCA1767–93

Moses, Octavia (Cohen). b. 1844, d. 1936, SC: 1844, f. Marx Edwin Cohen, m. Armida Harby Cohen, mr. Altamont Moses, 1871. Rf: MJSC13; SFF35, 206

Moses, Octavia (Harby). b. 1823, d. 1904, SC: 1823, f. Isaac Harby, m. Rachel Mordecai Harby, mr. Andrew Jackson Moses, 1839. Rf: MJCS13; EM18; SFF93, 207

Moses, Oliver Hazard Perry [Perry]. b. 1813, d. 1880, SC: 1813, f. Isaac Clifton Moses, m. Hannah Lazarus Moses, mr. Anna DeLeon Moses,

1839. Rf: DR; EC24; SFF55, 207; 1840C; T39; D1838, 1841

Moses, Ottolengui Aaron. b. 1846, d. 1906, SC: 1846, f. Aaron I. Moses, m. Judith A. Ottolengui Moses, mr. Flora Moses. Rf: SFF210, 211

Moses, P. SC: 1801. Rf: SCA1801–20

Moses, Perry. b. 1844, d. 1862, f. Oliver Hazard Perry Moses, m. Anna DeLeon Moses. Rf: EJCC11; SFF207; MS14.296

Moses, Philip. d. 1799, SC: 1774, mr. Sarah Machado Moses. Rf: EC77; EP; 1790C; W26.476; E91, 102, 206, 238, 278, 280; W27.848 (his); SFF212, 234; SCA1774–92; D1790, 1794, 1796; RB122

Moses, Philip. SC: 1801. Rf: D1801, 1802, 1803, 1806, 1807, 1809, 1816; RB122

Moses, Phineas. b. 1798, d. 1895, f. Isaiah Moses, mr. Elinor Block Moses, 1829. Rf: SFF210

Moses, Pier. SC: 1810, f. Solomon Moses. Rf: SFF213; W31.391

Moses, R. J. SC: 1835, mr. Miriam L. Moses. Rf: SCA1838; D1835, 1838

Moses, Rachel. d. 1780, SC: 1780, f. Myer Moses, m. Rachel Andrews Moses. Rf: SFF205

Moses, Rachel. b. 1781, d. 1860, SC: 1850, mr. Joseph Moses. Rf: DR; SFF213; 1850C; D1819, 1822, 1829

Moses, Rachel (Andrews). SC: 1783, mr. Myer Moses. Rf: SCA1783–1831

Moses, Rachel Woolf. b. 1811, d. 1836, SC: 1811, f. Myer Moses, m. Esther Phillips Moses. Rf: SFF205

Moses, Raphael. b. 1812, d. 1893, SC: 1812, f. Israel Moses, m. Deborah Cohen Moses, mr. Eliza M. Moses, 1834. Rf: SFF207, 212; E170, 199–202; W45.581; MS12.186; SCA1835–48

Moses, Rebecca. b. 1851, d. 1880, SC: 1851. Rf: DR

Moses, Rebecca (Jackson). b. 1836, d. 1888, SC: 1860, f. John Daniel Jackson, m. Sarah Louisa Salomon Jackson, mr. Julius L. Moses, 1859. Rf: DR; SFF129, 210; E170; 1860C

Moses, Rebecca (Phillips). b. 1792, d. 1872, SC: 1807, f. Jacob Phillips, m. Hannah Isaacks Phillips, mr. Isaiah Moses, 1807. Rf: DR; SFF210, 247; EM9; *AF*62, 67; EC87

Moses, Rebecca Phillips. b. 1806, d. 1889, SC: 1806, f. Myer Moses, m. Esther Phillips Moses. Rf: SFF205

Moses, Reuben. b. 1765, d. 1850, SC: 1818, f. Solomon Moses, mr. Hannah Moses. Rf: DR; EC88; SFF213; W45.672 (his); 1830C; 1840C; T38; SCA1819–46; E138; D1819, 1822, 1831, 1835, 1838, 1849

Moses, Rinah J. (Ottolengui). b. 1813, d. 1845, SC: 1839, f. Abraham Ottolengui, m. Sarah Jacobs Ottolengui, mr. Jacob I. Moses, 1839. Rf: EC53; EM18; SFF210, 211, 234

Moses, Rosalie (Davis). b. 1851, d. 1918, f. Solomon Davis, m. Anna Abrahams Davis, mr. Alfred H. Moses. Rf: SFF49, 207

Moses, Rosannah. b. 1838, SC: 1838,

f. Levy J. Moses, m. Adeline Moses Moses. Rf: 1850C; SFF211

Moses, Rynear. f. Jacob I. Moses, m. Rinah J. Ottolengui Moses. Rf: SFF211

Moses, Sally. b. 1791, d. 1809, SC: 1809. Rf: *City Gazette & Daily Advertiser*, Dec. 30, 1809; W33.1436; EP

Moses, Samuel. SC: 1801. Rf: E170; SCA1801–40

Moses, Samuel. SC: 1852. Rf: 1852

Moses, Sarah. b. 1820, d. 1821, SC: 1820. Rf: DR

Moses, Sarah Adeline. b. 1834, d. 1861, SC: 1850, f. Levy J. Moses, m. Adeline Moses Moses. Rf: SFF211; EP

Moses, Sarah Hannah (Levy). b. 1838, d. 1907, f. David Cardoza Levy, m. Anna Maria Moses Levy, mr. Ezra I. Moses. Rf: SFF164, 210

Moses, Sarah (Machado). b. 1747, d. 1810, SC: 1792, f. David Mendes Machado, m. Maria Caetana Nunzez Machado, mr. Philip Moses. Rf: MR3B.094; SFF212, 234; EC77; 1790C; EP; SCA1792–99

Moses, Sarah Matilda. b. 1835, d. 1838, f. Raphael J. Moses, m. Eliza M. Moses Moses. Rf: SFF212

Moses, Sarah (Ottolengui). SC: 1848, f. Abraham Ottolengui, m. Sarah Jacobs Ottolengui, mr. Jacob I. Moses, 1848. Rf: EM23; SFF210, 211, 234; W45.796

Moses, Sarah Rebecca. b. 1851, d. 1880, SC: 1851, f. Aaron I. Moses, m. Judith A. Ottolengui Moses. Rf: DR; EC52; SFF210

Moses, Simeon. f. Isaiah Moses, mr. Jane Joseph Moses, 1827. Rf: SFF210

Moses, Simon. SC: 1804, mr. Hester [Hetty] Simons Moses, 1804. Rf: 1810C; 1820C; 1830C; W32.706; E138, 170; SFF271; MS4.401; SCA1804–36; D1813, 1822, 1829, 1831, 1835

Moses, Simpson. b. 1786, d. 1809. Rf: EP

Moses, Solomon. f. Isaiah Moses. Rf: SFF210

Moses, Solomon. b. 1734, d. 1828, SC: 1794, mr2. Rachel Miriam [Mary] Harris Moses. Rf: DR; EC44; SFF213; TBS40; EP; SCA1799–1826; D1796, 1801, 1802, 1803, 1806, 1807, 1809, 1813, 1819, 1822

Moses, Solomon. b. 1783, d. 1857, SC: 1808, f. Solomon Moses, m. Rachel Miriam (Mary) Moses, mr. Isabella Myers Moses, 1815. Rf: DR; SFF213; E138, 142, 170, 204; 1850C; D1813, 1819, 1822, 1829, 1831, 1835, 1841, 1855

Moses, Susannah. SC: 1824, mr. Jacob Moses. Rf: MR4Z.278

Moses, William Moultrie. d. 1878, f. Jacob I. Moses, m. Rinah Ottolengui Moses, mr. Penina S. Moses Moses, 1865. Rf: SFF211, 212

Moses, Williamson. f. Isaac Clifton Moses, m. Hannah Lazarus Moses. Rf: SFF207

Moss, Amanda Octavia (Levy). b. 1843, d. 1897, f. David Cardoza Levy, m. Anna Maria Moses Levy, mr. Lucien Moss, 1885. Rf: SFF164, 214

Moss, Isabelle (Harris). b. 1819, d.

1907, SC: 1819, f. Hyam Harris, m. Catharine Nathan Harris, mr. Samuel L. Moss, 1838. Rf: SFF94, 214

Moss, Joseph. SC: 1822. Rf: T39; *SCHM*66.183–192; Min. April 14, 1839; D1822, 1831, 1838

Moss, Samuel. SC: 1824. Rf: MR5I.8

Motta, C. SC: 1801. Rf: D1801

Motta, Isaac. SC: 1790. Rf: E138; 1790C; 1800C; W21.774; D1794, 1796, 1802

Motta, Jacob Ares. b. 1781, d. 1839, SC: 1801, mr. Sarah Ares D'Azevedo Motta, 1804. Rf: EC48; SFF51; T39; 1820C; W30.855; W38.545; D1801, 1806, 1807, 1819, 1822, 1829, 1831, 1835, 1838; RB124

Motta, Jane. SC: 1816. Rf: D1816

Motta, Sarah Ares (D'Azevedo). b. 1789, d. 1859, SC: 1789, f. Isaac D'Azevedo, m. Rachel de Abraham Salom d'Azevedo, mr. Jacob Ares Motta, 1804. Rf: DR; SFF51; MR4B.048; 1810C; W43.556; W30.885; MS4.376; SCA1809–53; D1809, 1841, 1849, 1852

Mussius, Abraham. SC: 1732. Rf: EL

Myers, Abraham Solomon. SC: 1800. Rf: CB1800

Myers, Belle. f. Levy Myers, m. Frances Minis Myers. Rf: SFF216

Myers, Belle (Cohen). f. Moses Cohen, m. Dinah Comgile Cohen, mr. Abram Myers. Rf: SFF35, 216

Myers, Caroline. b. 1848, SC: 1848, f. M. Myers, m. Rebecca Myers. Rf: 1850C

Myers, Catherine (Jacobs). SC: 1811, mr. Moses Myers, 1811. Rf: MS6.4

Myers, Eleazer. SC: 1835, mr. Rachel Peixotto Myers, 1839. Rf: SFF240; EM18; E170; 1850C; 1861C; D1835

Myers, Elizabeth. b. 1805, d. 1827, f. Levy Myers, m. Frances Minis Myers. Rf: SFF216

Myers, Esther (Cohen). b. 1748, d. 1826, SC: 1799, f. Moses Cohen, m. Dinah Comgile Cohen, mr. Mordecai Myers. Rf: SFF35, 216; W31.178; SCA1799

Myers, Frances (Minis). b. 1776, d. 1827, SC: 1794, f. Philip Minis, m. Judith Pollock Minis, mr. Levy Myers, 1794. Rf: EM6; SFF194, 216

Myers, Hessie. b. 1807, d. 1827, f. Levy Myers, m. Frances Minis Myers. Rf: SFF216

Myers, Heyward. f. Levy Myers, m. Frances Minis Myers. Rf: SFF216

Myers, I. b. 1840, d. 1843, SC: 1843. Rf: DR

Myers, Isaac. b. 1841, SC: 1841, f. M. Myers, m. Rebecca Myers. Rf: 1850C

Myers, Israel. SC: 1785. Rf: 1790C; 1800C; E138, 143, 280; SCA1785–88; D1790, 1794, 1801, 1802

Myers, J. b. 1843, d. 1843, SC: 1843. Rf: DR

Myers, Joseph. SC: 1790. Rf: 1790C

Myers, Joseph. d. 1787, SC: 1786. Rf: W22.191 (his); SCA1786

Myers, Joshua. f. Eleazer Myers, m. Rachel Peixotto Myers. Rf: SFF240

Myers, Julian. b. 1814, d. 1827, f.

Levy Myers, m. Frances Minis Myers. Rf: SFF216

Myers, Kate. f. Julian Myers, m. Priscilla Tobias Myers. Rf: SFF216

Myers, Levy Julian. b. 1823, d. 1897, SC: 1849, mr. Priscilla Lopez Tobias Myers, 1849. Rf: SFF216, 298; E170, 204, 238; W47.820

Myers, Levy Julian. f. Julian Myers, m. Priscilla Tobias Myers. Rf: SFF216

Myers, Levy [Levi]. b. 1768, d. 1827, SC: 1768, f. Mordecai Myers, m. Esther Cohen Myers, mr. Frances Minis Myers, 1794. Rf: EP; SFF194, 216; E128, 141, 241, 243; D1813

Myers, Lewis. SC: 1802. Rf: E138; 1820C

Myers, Lily. f. Levy Myers, m. Frances Minis Myers. Rf: SFF216

Myers, M. b. 1811, SC: 1849, mr. Rebecca Myers. Rf: 1850C; *Courier* Dec. 11, 1861; D1849

Myers, Michael. b. 1763, d. 1828, SC: 1800, mr. Rachel Phillips Myers, 1802. Rf: DR; SFF247; 1800C; 1820C; EP; T39; E138; D1801, 1802, 1803, 1822

Myers, Mordecai. b. 1727, d. 1788, SC: 1765, mr. Esther Cohen Myers. Rf: EG3; SFF35, 216; E45, 100, 138, 278; SCA1765–84

Myers, Mordicai. b. 1794, d. 1865, SC: 1813, f. Levy Myers, m. Frances Minis Myers, mr. Sarah Henrietta Cohen Myers. Rf: SFF216; D1813

Myers, Moses. SC: 1800. Rf: CB1800

Myers, Moses. b. 1845, SC: 1845, f. M. Myers, m. Rebecca Myers. Rf: 1850C

Myers, Priscilla (Tobias). b. 1823, d. 1902, SC: 1823, f. Abraham Tobias, m. Eleanor Lopez Tobias, mr. Levy Julian Myers, 1849. Rf: EM24; SFF216, 298

Myers, Rachael. b. 1843, SC: 1843, f. M. Myers, m. Rebecca Myers. Rf: 1850C

Myers, Rachel (Peixotto). b. 1814, d. 1843, SC: 1839, f. Solomon Cohen Peixotto, m. Rachel Suarez Peixotto, mr. Eleazer Myers, 1839. Rf: EM18; SFF240; EP

Myers, Rachel (Phillips). b. 1786, d. 1870, f. Jacob Phillips, m. Hannah Isaacks Phillips, mr. Michael Myers, 1802. Rf: SFF247; *AF62*

Myers, Rebecca. b. 1821, SC: 1821, mr. M. Myers. Rf: 1850C

Myers, Rebecca. b. 1840, SC: 1840. Rf: 1850C

Myers, Samuel. SC: 1788. Rf: 1800C; 1810C; MR2X.632; E138, 170, 280; D1790, 1794, 1796, 1801, 1802, 1803, 1806, 1807, 1809, 1813

Myers, Sarah. SC: 1802. Rf: D1802, 1806

Myers, Sarah. b. 1850, SC: 1850, f. M. Myers, m. Rebecca Myers. Rf: 1850C

Myers, Sarah Lopez (Isaacks). b. 1770, d. 1860, f. Moses Isaacks, m. Judith Rachel Mears Isaacks, mr. Judah Myers, 1821. Rf: SFF120, 217

Myers, Solomon. b. 1847, SC: 1850, f. M. Myers, m. Rebecca Myers. Rf: 1850C

Myers, Theodosia. b. 1810, d. 1827, f. Levy Myers, m. Frances Minis Myers. Rf: SFF216

Myers, William W. f. Julian Myers, m. Priscilla Tobias Myers. Rf: SFF216

Naar, Moïse [Moses]. SC: 1801. Rf: E138; MR3M.133; D1802, 1806, 1807

Naar, Mordecai. SC: 1802. Rf: E138; D1802

Nachman, Abraham. b. 1797, d. 1855, SC: 1846, mr. Sprinse Nachman. Rf: EC85; SFF280; SCA1852; D1849, 1852

Nachman, Fanny (Emanuel). b. 1823, d. 1894. Rf: DR; EC107

Nachman, Sprinse. b. 1797, d. 1852, SC: 1852, mr. Abraham Nachman. Rf: EC25

Nathan, ———. b. 1816, f. Henry Nathan, m. Esther Levy Nathan. Rf: SFF228

Nathan, Abraham. d. 1798, SC: 1785. Rf: King, *Newspaper*, p. 49; EP

Nathan, Abraham. b. 1835, SC: 1850. Rf: 1850C

Nathan, Amelia. b. 1819, d. 1895, SC: 1819, f. Henry Nathan, m. Esther Levy Nathan. Rf: DR; EC31; SFF228

Nathan, Ann (Cohen). SC: 1841, f. Aaron Nathan Cohen, m. Rachel Cohen, mr. Myer Nathan, 1841. Rf: SFF38; MS15.85

Nathan, Annie Augusta (Florance). b. 1842, d. 1878, f. William Florance, m. Myrtilla Seixas Florance, mr. Israel Robert W. Nathan, 1859. Rf: SFF74, 227

Nathan, Asher. b. 1826, d. 1895, SC: 1849, f. Henry Nathan, m. Esther Levy Nathan. Rf: SFF228; D1849

Nathan, Asher Moses. b. 1785, d. 1863, SC: 1804, f. Moses Nathan, m. Amelia Nathan, mr. Marguerite Dalton Nathan, 1810. Rf: SFF228; E138

Nathan, Bernard. b. 1789, d. 1869, f. Levy Nathans. Rf: SFF228

Nathan, Cecilia. b. 1844, d. 1872, f. Myer Nathan, m. Ann Cohen Nathan. Rf: EJCC7; SFF38

Nathan, Charlotte. b. 1845, SC: 1845. Rf: 1850C

Nathan, Cordelia A. (Pollock). b. 1853, d. 1925, f. Elias Pollock, m. Sarah Pollock, mr. Henry Huthchinson Nathan, 1873. Rf: DR; EC30; SFF228, 289

Nathan, David. SC: 1800. Rf: E138; 1800; D1801, 1806

Nathan, Ephraim. b. 1841, SC: 1841. Rf: 1850C

Nathan, Esther (Levy). b. 1789, d. 1871, SC: 1789, mr. Henry Nathan, 1815. Rf: EC16; E138; SFF228; EP

Nathan, Eudora M. (Hart). b. 1843, d. 1874, SC: 1843, f. Hyman N. Hart, m. Hetty Maria Gomez Hart, mr. Gratz Nathan, 1867. Rf: SFF98, 226; 1850C

Nathan, Fanny (Cohen). f. Isaac Cohen, m. Judith Lyon Cohen, mr. Solomon Nathan. Rf: SFF36

Nathan, Frank. b. 1829, SC: 1850. Rf: 1850C

Nathan, Henry. b. 1790, d. 1837, SC: 1809, mr. Esther Levy Nathan, 1815. Rf: EC16; EM11; SFF228; E138; 1820C; SCA1822; D1816, 1819, 1822, 1831; RB133

Nathan, Henry Hutchinson. b. 1847, d. 1902, SC: 1847, f. Moses Henry H. Nathan, m. Leah C. Peixotto Nathan, mr. Cordelia A. Pollock

Nathan, 1873. Rf: DR; EC30, 31; SFF228, 289

Nathan, Henry (Hyman). b. 1828, d. 1865, f. Henry Nathan, m. Esther Nathan. Rf: SFF228

Nathan, Hyman. SC: 1855. Rf: D1855

Nathan, Isaac. b. 1838, SC: 1838. Rf: 1850C

Nathan, Isaiah. SC: 1819. Rf: E138

Nathan, Israel. SC: 1820. Rf: 1820C; SCA1823

Nathan, Leah Cohen (Peixotto). b. 1822, d. 1909, f. Solomon Cohen Peixotto, m. Rachel Suares Peixotto, mr. Moses Henry Nathan, 1846. Rf: DR; SFF228, 240

Nathan, Levy. SC:1789. Rf: SFF228

Nathan, Levy Nathan Fisher. b. 1833, f. Henry Nathan, m. Esther Levy Nathan. Rf: SFF228; E170

Nathan, Mordecai. SC: 1703. Rf: E22, 277; SCA1715–16

Nathan, Moses D. SC: 1794. Ref: E138; SCA1794–1817; D1794, 1816, 1817

Nathan, Moses Henry. b. 1821, d. 1875, SC: 1821, f. Henry Nathan, m. Esther Levy Nathan, mr. Leah Cohen Peixotto Nathan, 1846. Rf: DR; EC86; SFF228; E170, 205, 265; T39; 1850C; SCA1843; D1849, 1852, 1855

Nathan, Myer. b. 1799, d. 1863, SC: 1841, mr. Ann Cohen Nathan, 1841. Rf: EM19; SFF38; EJCC7; *SCHM*66.183; 1850C; MS15.85; D1841

Nathan, N. H. SC: 1831. Rf: D1831

Nathan, Rachel. b. 1806, SC: 1850. Rf: 1850C

Nathan, Rebecca. b. 1833, SC: 1833. Rf: 1850C

Nathan, Samuel. b. 1824, d. 1878, SC: 1846, f. Henry Nathan, m. Esther Levy Nathan, mr. Sarah C. Peixotto Nathan, 1846. Rf: SFF228, 240; D1852

Nathan, Samuel C. b. 1853, d. 1880, f. Myer Nathan, m. Ann Cohen Nathan. Rf: EJCC7; SFF38

Nathan, Sarah Cohen (Peixotto). b. 1826, d. 1904, SC: 1846, f. Solomon Cohen Peixotto, m. Rachel Suares Peixotto, mr. Samuel Nathan, 1846. Rf: SFF228, 240; EM22

Nathan, Simon. SC: 1788. Rf: Mort3F.637; D1801

Nathan, Simon. b. 1835, d. 1875, f. Henry Nathan, m. Esther Levy Nathan. Rf: SFF228

Nathan, Solomon. b. 1776, d. 1829, SC: 1799, mr. Fanny Cohen Nathan. Rf: EC66; E138, 170, 280; W38.545 (his); 1800C; EP; SCA1799–1824; D1802, 1803, 1806, 1807

Nathans, Alexander H. b. 1832, SC: 1832, f. Nathan Nathans, m. Sarah N. Hertz Nathans. Rf: SFF231; W47.543; 1850C; D1852

Nathans, Alice Gertrude (Cohen). b. 1847, d. 1900, SC: 1850, f. Isaac Cohen, m. Virginia J. Davis Cohen, mr. Jacob N. Nathans, 1871. Rf: SFF36, 231; EC17; 1850C

Nathans, Amelia. b. 1824, SC: 1824. Rf: 1850C

Nathans, Annabel (Josephs). f. Levy L.

Josephs, m. Isabelle Joseph Josephs, mr. ——— Nathans. Rf: SFF139

Nathans, David. b. 1828, SC: 1828, f. Nathan Nathans, m. Sarah N. Hertz Nathans. Rf: SFF231; E180; 1850C

Nathans, Emily Touro (Moses). b. 1846, SC: 1846, f. Levy J. Moses, m. Adeline Moses Moses, mr. Lewis Nathans. Rf: 1850C; SFF211

Nathans, Esther. b. 1795, SC: 1795. Rf: 1840C; 1850C; D1838

Nathans, Esther (Tobias). f. David DeOliveria Tobias, m. Rachel Russell Tobias, mr. Abraham Nathans, 1851. Rf: SFF229, 298

Nathans, Henrietta. b. 1842, SC: 1842, f. Levy L. Josephs, m. Isabelle Joseph Josephs, mr. James Nathans. Rf: SFF139; 1860C

Nathans, Hester. SC: 1841. Rf: D1841

Nathans, Hutchinson. b. 1847, SC: 1847. Rf: 1850C

Nathans, Isabella. b. 1849, SC: 1849. Rf: 1850C

Nathans, Jacob N. b. 1837, d. 1914, SC: 1850, f. Nathan Nathans, m. Sarah N. Hertz Nathans, mr. Alice Gertrude Cohen Nathans, 1871. Rf: DR; T39; SFF36, 231; E170, 206, 234, 265; W47.543; 1850C; 1860C

Nathans, Leah. b. 1824, SC: 1824. Rf: 1850C

Nathans, Levy. b. 1823, SC: 1823, f. Nathan Nathans, m. Sarah N. Hertz Nathans, mr. Sarah M. Joseph Nathans, 1854. Rf: EM27; SFF231; E170; 1850C; D1849

Nathans, Meyer. SC: 1838. Rf: E170; D1838

Nathans, Moses H. b. 1832, SC: 1832. Rf: 1860C

Nathans, Nathan. b. 1769, d. 1829, SC: 1805. Rf: DR; CB1805; D1807, 1809, 1822, 1829

Nathans, Nathan. b. 1782, d. 1854, SC: 1801, mr. Sarah N. Hertz Nathans. Rf: EC85; SFF117, 231; 1810C; 1830C; 1850C; 1861C; W47.543; EP; SCA1814–54; D1831, 1835, 1838, 1841, 1849, 1852

Nathans, Rachel (Cohen). SC: 1807, f. Moses Cohen, m. Dinah Comgile Cohen, mr. ——— Nathans. Rf: SFF35; W31.178

Nathans, Sarah N. (Hertz). b. 1804, d. 1865, SC: 1804, f. Handel Moses Hertz, m. Isabella Hertz, mr. Nathan Nathans. Rf: EC86; SFF117, 231; W47.543; 1850C; 1860C; 1861C; D1855

Nathans, Simon N. b. 1834, d. 1852, SC: 1834, f. Nathan Nathans, m. Sarah N. Hertz Nathans. Rf: DR; EC86; SFF231; 1850C

Nauman, William. b. 1790, d. 1835, SC: 1827, mr. Henrietta Alexander Nauman, 1827. Rf: EP; SFF8; EM14; E170; 1830C; SCA1830; D1829, 1831, 1835

Nettling, Solomon. SC: 1802. Rf: E138

Noah, Judith. b. 1789, d. 1868, f. Manuel Noah, m. Zipporah Phillips Noah. Rf: SFF232

Noah, Manuel. b. 1755, d. 1822, SC: 1793, mr. Zipporah Phillips

Noah, 1784. Rf: EP; SFF232; E280; SCA1793–94

Noah, Mordecai Manuel. b. 1785, d. 1851, SC: 1807, f. Manuel Noah, m. Zipporah Phillips Noah, mr. Rebecca Esther Jackson Noah, 1827. Rf: SFF129, 232; T39; E51, 94, 138, 141, 278

Noah, Uriah. SC: 1811. Rf: W32.704

Noah, Zipporah (Phillips). b. 1764, d. 1792, f. Jonas Phillips, m. Rebecca Phillips, mr. Manuel Noah, 1784. Rf: SFF232, 243

Nollman, ———. b. 1828, d. 1829, SC: 1828. Rf: DR

Nones, Benjamin. d. 1823, SC: 1780, f. Aaron Nones. Rf: *SCHM*34.81; EP; E84, 96, 97; SCA1783; *SP*, Mar. 10, 1823

Nordhaus, Hannah (Hyams). b. 1838, d. 1916, f. Henry Hyams, m. Judith Hyams, mr. Alexander Nordhaus. Rf: SFF119

Nunez, Anna Maria (Moses). f. Charles Brown Moses, m. Angelina Lazarus Moses, mr. Israel M. Nunez, 1859. Rf: SFF207, 212, 213

Nurwohl, Bertha. d. 1856, SC: 1856. Rf: EBS3; W48.177

Oberndorfer, Frances (Lewis). b. 1823, d. 1875, f. David Lewis, m. Rachel Lewis, mr. Elias N. Oberndorfer. Rf: SFF172

Offen, Jacobus V. SC: 1810. Rf: E138

Oppenheim, Catherine (Moses). b. 1802, d. 1890, SC: 1802, f. Joseph Moses, m. Rachel Moses, mr. Hertz Wolff Oppenheim, 1821. Rf: DR; SFF213, 235; EM12; W46.284; SCA1834; *SP*, May 12, 1811; 1850C; 1860C; 1861C

Oppenheim, Edwin Hertz. b. 1840, d. 1918, SC: 1850, f. Hertz Woolf Oppenheim, m. Catherine Moses Oppenheim. Rf: SFF235; E234; W46.284; 1850C; 1860C

Oppenheim, Hannah A. (Goldsmith). b. 1845, d. 1903, SC: 1860, f. Moses Goldsmith, m. Eleanor Alexander Goldsmith, mr. Samuel H. Oppenheim, 1862. Rf: DR; EM32; SFF84, 235; 1860C

Oppenheim, Henry Hertz. b. 1833, d. 1888, SC: 1833, f. Hertz Woolf Oppenheim, m. Catherine Moses Oppenheim. Rf: SFF235; E170, 234, 265; W46.284; W48.177; 1850C; 1860C; D1841, 1849, 1855

Oppenheim, Herman Detmold Hertz. b. 1841, d. 1896, SC: 1841, f. Hertz Wolff Oppenheim, m. Catherine Moses Oppenheim, mr. Sarah Jonas Oppenheim, mr2. M. L. Prescott. Rf: SFF235; W46.235; 1850C; 1860C

Oppenheim, Hertz Wolff. b. 1786, d. 1853, SC: 1821, f. Wolff Oppenheim, mr. Catherine Moses Oppenheim, 1821. Rf: EC35; SFF235; W46.234; T39; E138, 170, 234; 1850C; 1861C; SCA1824–39; D1829, 1831, 1835, 1838, 1852

Oppenheim, Hester Moses. SC: 1830. Rf: 1830C

Oppenheim, Jacob. f. Hertz Wolff Oppenheim, m. Catherine Moses Oppenheim. Rf: SFF235

Oppenheim, Joseph Hertz. b. 1823, d.

1901, SC: 1823, f. Hertz Wolff Oppenheim, m. Catherine Moses Oppenheim, mr. Hannah Joseph Oppenheim. Rf: SFF235; 1850C; 1860C; 1861C; D1849, 1852, 1855

Oppenheim, Julius Hertz. b. 1835, d. 1903, SC: 1835, f. Hertz Wolff Oppenheim, m. Catherine Moses Oppenheim, mr. Sarah Ann Goldsmith Oppenheim, 1862. Rf: SFF235; EM32; E171, 234; W46.284; 1850C

Oppenheim, Samuel Hertz. b. 1828, d. 1910, SC: 1849, f. Hertz Wolff Oppenheim, m. Catherine Moses Oppenheim, mr. Hannah A. Goldsmith Oppenheim, 1862. Rf: DR; SFF84, 235; W46.284; 1860C; 1861C; E171; EM32; D1849, 1852, 1855

Oppenheim, Sarah Ann (Goldsmith). b. 1841, d. 1913, SC: 1841, mr. Julius H. Oppenheim, 1862. Rf: SFF84, 235; EM32; 1860C

Oppenheim, Wolf. b. 1822, d. 1822, SC: 1822, f. Hertz Wolff Oppenheim, m. Catherine Moses Oppenheim. Rf: DR; SFF235

Ostler, Julia (Hertz). b. 1832, SC: 1850, f. Jacob Hertz, m. Rebecca Mordecai Hertz, mr. Henry Edmund Ostler. Rf: SFF117; 1850C

Ottolengui, Abraham. b. 1790, d. 1850, SC: 1790, f. Mordecai Ottolengui, m. Rinah Ottolengui, mr. Sarah Jacobs Ottolengui. Rf: EC52; SFF234; E171; T39; 1820C; 1830C; 1850C; 1860C; 1861C; W45.796 (his); SCA1812–43; D1807, 1819, 1822, 1831, 1835, 1838, 1841, 1849

Ottolengui, Abraham. b. 1835, d. 1835, f. Abraham Ottolengui, m. Sarah Jacobs Ottolengui. Rf: SFF234; DR; EC53

Ottolengui, Abraham. b. 1844, d. 1850, SC: 1844, f. Abraham Ottolengui, m. Sarah Ottolengui. Rf: DR; EC52

Ottolengui, Abraham. b. 1849, d. 1852, SC: 1850, f. Jacob Ottolengui, m. Eliza Emma Jacobs Ottolengui. Rf: EC54; SFF234; 1850C

Ottolengui, Abraham. b. 1854, d. 1894, SC: 1854. f. Jacob Ottolengui, m. Eliza Emma Jacobs. Rf: DR; SFF234

Ottolengui, Benjamin A. Rodrigues. b. 1861, d. 1937, SC: 1861, f. Daniel Ottolengui, m. Helen R. Rodriguez Ottolengui, mr. May Hall Ottolengui. Rf: SFF234

Ottolengui, Cornelia Alice. b. 1851, d. 1935, SC: 1860, f. Jacob Ottolengui, m. Eliza Emma Jacobs Ottolengui. Rf: MJSC19; SFF234; 1860C

Ottolengui, Daniel. b. 1836, d. 1918, SC: 1836, f. Abraham Ottolengui, m. Sarah Jacobs Ottolengui, mr. Helen Rosalie Rodriguez Ottolengui, 1860. Rf: DR; EM31; SFF234, 254; 1850C; D1859

Ottolengui, Eliza Emma (Jacobs). b. 1819, d. 1899, SC: 1819, f. Myer Jacobs, m. Rebecca Lazarus Jacobs, mr. Jacob Ottolengui, 1848. Rf:

DR; SFF132, 234; EM24; 1850C; 1860C

Ottolengui, Florance Dobney. b. 1859, d. 1928, SC: 1859, f. Israel Ottolengui, m. Rosalie C. Mose Ottolengui. Rf: SFF234

Ottolengui, Helen Rosalie (Rodriguez adopted). b. 1843, d. 1866, SC: 1843, f. Benjamin A. Rodriguez, m. Cecilia Solomons Rodriguez, mr. Daniel Ottolengui, 1860. Rf: SFF234, 254; EM31; 1850C

Ottolengui, Isaac. b. 1822, d. 1824, SC: 1822, f. Abraham Ottolengui, m. Sarah Jacobs Ottolengui. Rf: SFF234

Ottolengui, Israel. b. 1832, d. 1895, SC: 1832, f. Abraham Ottolengui, m. Sarah Jacobs Ottolengui, mr. Rosalie Cecile Moïse Ottolengui, 1854. Rf: DR; EC51, 52; SFF196, 234; E171, 234; T39; 1850C; D1859

Ottolengui, Jacob. b. 1819, d. 1900, SC: 1819, f. Abraham Ottolengui, m. Sarah Jacobs Ottolengui, mr. Eliza Emma Jacobs Ottolengui, 1848. Rf: DR; SFF234; EC54; E171; EM24; 1850C; 1860C; 1861C; T39; TBS40; SCA1845–60; D1849, 1859

Ottolengui, Jessie. b. 1861, d. 1953, SC: 1861, f. Israel Ottolengui, m. Rosalie C. Moïse Ottolengui. Rf: SFF234

Ottolengui, Miriam. f. Abraham Ottolengui, m. Sarah Jacobs Ottolengui. Rf: EC53; SFF234

Ottolengui, Mordecai. f. Abraham Ottolengui, m. Sarah Jacobs Ottolengui. Rf: SFF234

Ottolengui, Mordecai. d. 1794, mr. Rinah Mordecai. Rf: SFF234

Ottolengui, Mordecai H. Abraham. SC: 1851, f. Abraham Ottolengui, m. Sarah Jacobs Ottolengui. Rf: EC52: SFF234; CB1851

Ottolengui, Rachel. b. 1821, SC: 1821, f. Abraham Ottolengui, m. Sarah Jacobs Ottolengui. Rf: SFF234; 1850C

Ottolengui, Rebecca. b. 1826, d. 1826, SC: 1826, f. Abraham Ottolengui, m. Sarah Jacobs Ottolengui. Rf: DR; SFF234

Ottolengui, Rinah. d. 1810, mr. Mordecai Ottolengui. Rf: SFF234

Ottolengui, Rosalie Cecile (Moïse). b. 1835, d. 1914, SC: 1854, f. Jacob Moïse, m. Rebecca Cohen Moïse, mr. Israel Ottolengui, 1854. Rf: DR; EC52; SFF196, 234

Ottolengui, Sarah (Jacobs). b. 1793, d. 1864, SC: 1851, mr. Abraham Ottolengui. Rf: EC52; SFF234; CB1851

Painter, Eliza (Moses). b. 1848, d. 1926, f. Charles Brown Moses, m. Angelina Lazarus Moses, mr. A. R. Painter. Rf: SFF207

Palacios, Joseph. SC: 1778. Rf: MR2V.208

Parmiento, Moses. SC: 1753. Rf: EL; SCA1753–54

Parrish, Isabel (DeLaMotta). f. Jacob Canter DeLaMotta, m. Charlotte Lazarus DeLaMotta, mr. William Parrish. Rf: SFF54

Pearlstein, J. b. 1817, d. 1877, SC: 1856, mr. Janetta Pearlstein. Rf: DR; EBS7, 11

Pearlstein, Mary. b. 1849, d. 1873, SC:

1851, mr. Isaac M. Pearlstein. Rf: DR; EBS7

Pearlstine, Janette. b. 1819, d. 1897, mr. T. Pearlstine. Rf: EBS11

Pearlstine, Tanchum. SC: 1855. Rf: BS-BI

Pecare, Bertha. SC: 1838, f. Rosel Pecare. Rf: W41.817; MS15.248; D1838

Pecare, Jacob. SC: 1838, f. Rosel Pecare. Rf: W42.391; W41.817; E171

Pecare, Myer. SC: 1838, f. Rosel Pecare. Rf: W41.817; E171; MR5Y.411, 421; D1849, 1852

Pecare, Rosel. b. 1799, d. 1838, SC: 1833. Rf: EC17; W41.817 (his)

Pecare, Samuel. SC: 1833. Rf: E171; SCA1833; D1835

Peixotto, ———. b. 1824, d. 1824, SC: 1824, f. Solomon Cohen Peixotto, m. Rachel Suares Peixotto. Rf: SFF240

Peixotto, Caroline (Solomons). b. 1812, d. 1887, f. Solomon Solomons, m. Alice Abrahams Solomons, mr. David E. Cohen Peixotto, 1839. Rf: EJCC7; SFF240, 277

Peixotto, David E. Cohen. b. 1815, d. 1897, f. Solomon Cohen, m. Rachel Suares Peixotto, mr. Caroline Solomons Peixotto, 1839. Rf: EJCC7; SFF240, 277

Peixotto, Grace. b. 1817, SC: 1850, f. Solomon Cohen Peixotto, m. Rachel Suares Peixotto. Rf: SFF240; 1861C; SCA1850; D1855, 1859

Peixotto, Hortense (Levy). d. 1923, mr. Solomon C. Peixotto, 1870. Rf: SFF240

Peixotto, Joshua. b. 1810, SC: 1829, f. Solomon Cohen Peixotto, m. Rachel Suares Peixotto. Rf: SFF240; E171, 207, 246; D1829

Peixotto, Rachael de David de Isaac (Suares). b. 1791, d. 1826, SC: 1826, mr. Solomon Cohen Peixotto, 1809. Rf: DR; SFF240

Peixotto, Rebecca [Ribca]. b. 1820, d. 1837, SC: 1820, f. Solomon Cohen Peixotto, m. Rachel Suares Peixotto. Rf: SFF240

Peixotto, Solomon Cohen. b. 1785, d. 1837, SC: 1818, f. Joshua Cohen Peixotto, m. Esther Levy Maduro Peixotto, mr. Rachel Suares Peixotto, 1809. Rf: EM18; SFF240; E138; 1820C; SCA1831–36; D1831, 1835

Peixotto, Solomon Cohen. b. 1840, d. 1919, f. David E. Cohen Peixotto, m. Caroline Solomons Peixotto, mr. Hortense Levy Peixotto, 1870. Rf: SFF240; E234

Pember, Phoebe (Levy). f. Jacob Clarisse Levy, m. Fanny Yates Levy, mr. Thomas Noyes Pember, 1856. Rf: SFF169

Peraire, Zelmaire (Sasportas). f. Abraham Sasportas, m. Charlotte Canter Sasportas, mr. Edward Peraire. Rf: SFF262; RB153

Perrera, Jacob. SC: 1800. Rf: CB1800

Petska, Barnet. b. 1849, SC: 1850. Rf: 1850C

Petska, David. b. 1824, d. 1849, SC: 1849. Rf: DR; EC90

Petska, Eleanor. b. 1824, SC: 1850. Rf: 1850C

Petska, Lavina. b. 1849, SC: 1849. Rf: 1850C

Petska, Rosa Gesler. b. 1815, SC: 1850. Rf: 1850C

Phillips, Aaron. b. 1780, d. 1834, SC: 1807, mr. Caroline Lazarus Phillips, 1807, mr2. Isabella Lazarus Phillips, 1821. Rf: EM15; EC68; SFF151; T39; 1810C; E138, 163, 171; W40.17 (his); T39; MS5.283, 1807; SCA1807–32; D1809, 1813, 1829

Phillips, Abraham. b. 1788, d. 1813, SC: 1809, f. Jacob Phillips, m. Hannah Isaacks Phillips. Rf: *AF*62; E138; SFF247

Phillips, Adeline (Cohen). b. 1839, d. 1906, SC: 1839, f. Hartwig Cohen, m. Deborah Marks Cohen, mr. Isaac Phillips, 1860. Rf: EM31; SFF34, 249; 1850C

Phillips, Benjamin. SC: 1790, Rf: 1790C; 1810C; 1820C; 1830C; E138, 171, 280; SCA1823; D1796, 1803, 1813; RB140

Phillips, Caroline (Lazarus). b. 1790, d. 1818, SC: 1790, f. Marks Lazarus, m. Rachel Benjamin Lazarus, mr. Aaron Phillips, 1807. Rf: EM8; EC68; SFF151, 247; MS5.283

Phillips, Casper. b. 1814, d. 1883, SC: 1850, mr. Sarah Cohen Phillips. Rf: DR; JF1; 1850C

Phillips, David. SC: 1800. Rf: E138, 280; D1802

Phillips, Eleazer. SC: 1784. Rf: 1790C; SCA1784–1825

Phillips, Eugenia (Levy). b. 1820, d. 1902, SC: 1820, f. Jacob C. Levy, m. Fanny Yates Levy, mr. Philip Phillips, 1836. Rf: SFF169, 247

Phillips, Frances (Cohen). d. 1890, SC: 1837, f. Moses Cohen, m. Rachel Moses Cohen, mr. Jonas Altamont Phillips, 1837. Rf: EM16; SFF36, 243

Phillips, Hannah (Isaacks). d. 1798, f. Jacob Isaacks, m. Rebecca Mears Isaacks, mr. Jacob Phillips, 1785. Rf: SFF120, 247

Phillips, Isabella (Lazarus). b. 1785, d. 1862, SC: 1785, f. Marks Lazarus, m. Rachel Benjamin Lazarus, mr. Aaron Phillips, 1821. Rf: EC69; EM12; SFF151, 247; W49.1000; 1850C; D1835

Phillips, Isidore. b. 1841, d. 1865, SC: 1850, f. Casper Phillips, m. Sarah Cohen Phillips. Rf: JF1; 1850C

Phillips, Jacob. b. 1750, d. 1820, SC: 1780, mr. Hannah Isaacks Phillips, 1785. Rf: SFF120, 247; E138; *AF*62; RB141

Phillips, Jonas. b. 1735, d. 1803, SC: 1756, f. Aaron Phaibush Phillips, m. Phila von Stein Phillips, mr. Rebecca Machado Phillips, 1762. Rf: SFF234, 243; E64, 65, 278; EM7; RB141

Phillips, Jonas Altamont. b. 1806, d. 1862, SC: 1837, f. Zalegman Phillips, m. Arabella Solomons Phillips, mr. Frances Cohen Phillips, 1837. Rf: SFF36, 243; MR5Y.168

Phillips, Joseph. SC: 1827. Rf: E163; SCA1827

Phillips, Julius. f. Casper Phillips, m. Sarah Cohen Phillips. Rf: JF1

Phillips, Leonard. b. 1859, d. 1884, f. Casper Phillips, m. Sarah Cohen Phillips, mr. Flora Benjamin Phillips. Rf: JF2

Phillips, Marion (Levy). SC: 1825, f. Solomon Levy, Sr., mr. E. L. Phillips. Rf: City Gazette, 8 Nov. 1825

Phillips, Mitchell A. f. Casper Phillips, m. Sarah Cohen Phillips, mr. ——— Gollinger Phillips, 1873. Rf: JF1

Phillips, Naphtali. b. 1817, d. 1864, SC: 1807. Rf: EJCC7; EP; E171; SCA1807

Phillips, Nathan. SC: 1779. Rf: RB142

Phillips, Nathaniel. f. Casper Phillips, m. Sarah Cohen Phillips. Rf: JF1

Phillips, Oscar. b. 1818, d. 1818, SC: 1818, f. Aaron Phillips, m. Caroline Lazarus Phillips. Rf: SFF247

Phillips, Philip. b. 1796, SC: 1818, f. Jacob Phillips, m. Hannah Isaacks Phillips. Rf: SFF247; *AF*62; E138; SCA1819–35

Phillips, Philip. b. 1807, d. 1884, SC: 1807, f. Aaron Phillips, m. Caroline Lazarus Phillips, mr. Eugenia Levy Phillips, 1836. Rf: EM16; SFF169, 247; E138, 163, 171, 202–3, 205, 206; T39

Phillips, Rachel. b. 1809, SC: 1850, f. Aaron Phillips, m. Caroline Lazarus Phillips. Rf: SFF247; W41.683; 1850C; 1860C

Phillips, Rebecca (Machado). b. 1746, d. 1831, f. David Mendes Machado, m. Maria C. N. Machado Jacobs, mr. Jonas Phillips, 1762. Rf: SFF234, 243

Phillips, Sarah (Cohen). b. 1817, d. 1861, f. George Nathan Cohen, m. Grune Jacobi Cohen, mr. Casper Phillips. Rf: JF1

Phillips, Sigmund. b. 1855, d. 1922, f. Casper Phillips, m. Sarah Cohen Phillips, mr. Augusta Myer Phillips, 1876. Rf: JF1

Phillips, Solomon. b. 1810, f. Aaron Phillips, m. Caroline Lazarus Phillips. Rf: SFF147

Phillips, William. SC: 1839. Rf: Min. April 14, 1839

Pimienta, Aaron. SC: 1780, f. Moses Pimienta, m. Leah Morales Pimienta. Rf: SFF44; W21.435; W21.774; E280; SCA1780–89; RB143

Pimienta, Joel. SC: 1766, f. Moses Pimienta, m. Leah Morales Pimienta. Rf: SFF44; W11.301; RB143

Pimienta, Leah (Morales). d. 1768, SC: 1750, mr. Moses Pimienta, 1745. Rf: SFF44; W11.301 (hers); SCA1766–79; RB143

Pimienta, Moses. d. 1765, SC: 1750, mr. Leah Morales Pimienta, 1745. Rf: SFF44; W25.89; W11.301; E32, 40, 278; SCA1758–67; RB143

Pincosson, Abraham. b. 1827, d. 1871. Rf: EBS7

Pinkussohn, Abram. b. 1851, SC: 1860, f. Pinkus Pinkussohn, m. Elizabeth Pinkussohn. Rf: 1860C

Pinkussohn, Caroline. b. 1860, SC: 1860, f. Pinkus Pinkussohn, m. Elizabeth Pinkussohn. Rf: 1860C

Pinkussohn, Elizabeth. b. 1830, d. 1894, SC: 1860, mr. Pinkus Pinkussohn. Rf: DR; EBS7; 1860C

Pinkussohn, J. SC: 1835. Rf: T39

Pinkussohn, Jacob. b. 1855, SC: 1855,

f. Pinkus Pinkussohn, m. Elizabeth Pinkussohn. Rf: 1860C
Pinkussohn, L———. b. 1856, SC: 1856, f. Pinkus Pinkussohn, m. Elizabeth Pinkussohn. Rf: 1860C
Pinkussohn, Pinkus. b. 1823, d. 1876, SC: 1859, mr. Elizabeth Pinkussohn. Rf: DR; EBS7; 1860C; 1861C; E171, 238; SCA1862; *Courier* Dec. 11, 1861; D1859
Pinkussohn, Solomon. b. 1853, SC: 1853, f. Pinkus Pinkussohn, m. Elizabeth Pinkussohn. Rf: 1860C
Pinkussohn, Sophie. b. 1858, SC: 1858, f. Pinkus Pinkussohn, m. Elizabeth Pinkussohn. Rf: 1860C
Pinto, David. SC: 1808. Rf: E138; CB1808
Pinto, Isaac. b. 1720, d. 1791, SC: 1760, f. Abraham Pinto, m. Sarah Pinto. Rf: SFF251; E42, 278; EP
Plum, Benjamin. d. 1847, SC: 1847. Rf: EC24; Min. April 4, 1847
Pollock, Cushman. SC: 1780. Rf: RB146
Pollock, Frances. b. 1803, d. 1878, SC: 1819, mr. Levy Pollock. Rf: MR4R.235; EJCC8; SCA1819–23
Pollock, Joseph. SC: 1821. Rf: CB1821
Pollock, Levy. SC: 1792, mr. Frances Pollock. Rf: MR4R.235; 1810C; SCA1792–1819; D1819
Pollock, Samuel. SC: 1780. Rf: E91, 278; *SCHM*53.13–18; SCA1781; RB146
Pollock, Sarah (Suares). b. 1808, d. 1865, f. Jacob Suares, m. Judith Suares, mr. Elias Pollock. Rf: EJCC8; SFF289
Pollock, Solomon. d. 1805, SC: 1781, mr. Jane Nesbitt Pollock, 1783. Rf: EP; E92, 106, 138, 278, 280; 1790C; 1800C; SCA1781–1803; D1790, 1794, 1801, 1802, 1803; RB147
Polock, Adeline (Hyams). SC: 1845, f. Henry Hyams, m. Judith Hyams, mr. Elias C. Polock, 1845. Rf: EM22; SFF119
Polock, Elias C. b. 1806, d. 1895, SC: 1835, mr. Adeline Hyams Polock, 1845. Rf: EJCC8; SFF119; EP; EM22; D1835
Polock, Ella Carson. d. 1905, f. Judah B. Polock, m. Mary Hyams Polock. Rf: SFF119
Polock, Joseph d. 1794, SC: 1794. Rf: RB146
Polock, Judah B. b. 1826, d. 1889, mr. Mary Hyams Polock, 1848. Rf: SFF119
Polock, Levi. b. 1849, d. 1852, f. Elias Polock, m. Adeline Hyams Polock. Rf: SFF119
Polock, Mary (Hyams). SC: 1848, f. Henry Hyams, m. Judith Hyams, mr. Judah B. Polock, 1848. Rf: EM23; EJCC8; SFF119
Pool, Isaac. b. 1773, d. 1813, SC: 1800. Rf: EC75; W32.704 (his); 1800C; SCA1806; D1801, 1802, 1803
Poznanski, Esther G. (Barrett). b. 1820, d. 1870, SC: 1838, f. Isaac Barrett, m. Rachel J. DaVega Barrett, mr. Gustavus Poznanski, 1838. Rf: EM17; EC10; SFF17, 252; W51.467; SCA1848; 1850C
Poznanski, Gershon. b. 1818, d. 1839, f. Joseph Poznanski, m. Sarah Poznanski. Rf: SFF252; E171, 215
Poznanski, Gustavus. b. 1805, d.

1879, SC: 1836, f. Joseph Poznanski, m. Sarah Poznanski, mr. Esther Barrett Poznanski, 1838. Rf: SFF17, 252; E171, 208, 216–19, 292; EC10; EM17; W41.567; W45.741; 1850C; D1849

Poznanski, Gustavus. b. 1842, d. 1862, SC: 1850, f. Gustavus Poznanski, m. Esther Barrett Poznanski. Rf: EC49; E234; SFF252; 1850C; D1859

Poznanski, Hyam. b. 1818, d. 1839, SC: 1839, f. Joseph Poznanski, m. Sarah Poznanski. Rf: DR; EC49; SFF252

Poznanski, Isaac. b. 1840, SC: 1850. Rf: 1850C

Poznanski, Joseph. b. 1841, SC: 1850. Rf: 1850C

Prince, George. b. 1815, d. 1878, SC: 1839, mr. Mary Ann Prince. Rf: DR; EC80; T39; 1840C; 1850C; 1861C; D1841

Prince, Mary Ann (Cortissoz). b. 1821, d. 1880, SC: 1850, mr. ——— Cortissoz, mr2. George Prince. Rf: DR; EC80; 1850C; D1841

Prince, Sarah B. b. 1809, d. 1865, SC: 1861. Rf: EBS8; 1861C

Ramos, Jacob. SC: 1773. Rf: E45, 278; SCA1793

Redlich, I. SC: 1860. Rf: Min. Feb. 13, 1860

Reese, ———. SC: 1819. Rf: E138

Rendet, Tello. SC: 1858. Rf: Min. Sept. 5, 1858

Renner, Jacob. SC: 1791. Rf: RB148

Repplier, Fanny (Levy). f. Jacob C. Levy, m. Fanny Yates Levy, mr. George Repplier. Rf: SFF169

Retlich, J. d. 1850, SC: 1850. Rf: EBS8

Ricardo, Benjamin. SC: 1762, mr. Sarah Ricardo. Rf: 1800C; E138; T40; SCA1799–1805; D1801, 1802, 1803, 1809; RB148

Ricardo, Joseph. SC: 1801. Rf: E138; T40; SCA1802–04

Ricardo, Joseph. b. 1814, d. 1857, SC: 1849. Rf: W48.47 (his); EP; W46.149; D1849

Ricardo, Raphael Israel. SC: 1802, mr. Sarah Hyams Ricardo, 1807. Rf: EM8; SFF119; E138, 142; T40; CB1805; D1806, 1807

Ricardo, Sarah (Hyams). SC: 1807, f. Solomon Hyams, m. Catherine Jacobs Hyams, mr. Raphael Israel Ricardo, 1807. Rf: EM8; SFF119

Rice, A. mr. Hannah Rice. Rf: EBS8

Rice, Hannah. b. 1802, d. 1885, SC: 1850, mr. A. Rice. Rf: DR; EBS8; 1850C

Rice, Theresa. b. 1809, d. 1879. Rf: EBS8

Rich, Arnethena. b. 1838, SC: 1860. Rf: 1860C

Rich, Eva. b. 1815, d. 1886, SC: 1860, mr. Lippman Rich. Rf: DR; EBS8; 1860C

Rich, Hannah. b. 1843, SC: 1860, f. Lippman Rich, m. Eva Rich. Rf: 1860C

Rich, John. SC: 1852. Rf: E238; D1852

Rich, Lippmann. b. 1807, d. 1881, SC: 1860, mr. Eva Rich. Rf: DR; EBS8; E237; 1860C; *Courier* Dec. 11, 1861

Rich, Phillip. b. 1845, SC: 1860, f. Lippman Rich, m. Eva Rich. Rf: 1860C

Richard, Meyer. SC: 1861. Rf: E237, 239

Riesenberg, M. SC: 1840. Rf: Min. July 25, 1840

Riser, Isabel (Naumann). f. William Naumann, m. Henrietta Alexander Naumann, mr. Simon Riser, 1853. Rf: SFF8

Riverra, Abraham R. SC: 1801. Rf: E138; T6

Riz, David. SC: 1709. Rf: EL; RB149

Robinson, D. d. 1858, SC: 1858. Rf: EC108

Robinson, M. d. 1858, SC: 1858. Rf: EC108

Rodrigues, Abraham. SC: 1797, mr. Rebecca Sasportas Rodrigues, 1797. Rf: EM6; E139; 1800C; SFF262; SCA1797–1819; MS3.23; D1801, 1802, 1806, 1809

Rodrigues, Benjamin D. b. 1815, d. 1871, SC: 1815, f. Moïse Rodrigues, m. Esther Rodrigues, mr. Cecilia Solomon Rodrigues, 1835. Rf: DR; E171, 203, 238; EM15, 31; EC17; EP; 1840C; 1850C; SCA1839–67; MS13.74; SFF254, 279; D1835, 1838, 1841, 1849, 1852, 1855, 1859

Rodrigues, Cecilia (Solomons). b. 1816, SC: 1835, f. Mark Solomons, m. Rachel Solomons, mr. Benjamin A. Rodrigues, 1835. Rf: EM15; SFF254, 279; 1850C; MR5Y.302

Rodrigues, Esther. b. 1776, d. 1838, SC: 1798, mr. Moïse Rodrigues. Rf: MR4G.366; SFF254; EC17; SCA1816

Rodrigues, Esther Clara. b. 1836, d. 1839, SC: 1836, f. Benjamin A. Rodrigues, m. Cecilia Solomons Rodrigues. Rf: DR; EC17; SFF254

Rodrigues, Moïse [Moses]. d. 1830, SC: 1806, mr. Esther Rodrigues. Rf: EC26; SFF254; E139, 171; EP; SCA1820–25; D1806, 1807

Rodrigues, Rebecca (Sasportas). SC: 1797, f. Abraham Sasportas, m. Rachel DaCosta Sasportas, mr. Abraham Sasportas, 1797. Rf: EM6; SFF262; MS3.23

Rodrigues, Rudolph T. b. 1836, SC: 1836. Rf: 1850C

Rodriguez, Theodore. d. 1843. Rf: E139, 203; EP

Roos, David. SC: 1852. Rf: E171

Rosenband, Nathan I. b. 1821, d. 1856, SC: 1855. Rf: DR; EBS8

Rosenfeld, Harmon. b. 1845, SC: 1845, f. Jacob Rosenfeld, m. Leonora Moses Rosenfeld. Rf: 1850C; SFF210

Rosenfeld, Isaiah. f. Jacob Rosenfeld, m. Leonora Moses Rosenfeld. Rf: SFF210

Rosenfeld, Isidore. b. 1847, SC: 1847, f. Jacob Rosenfeld, m. Leonora Moses Rosenfeld, mr. Matilda Brady Rosenfeld. Rf: 1850C; SFF210

Rosenfeld, Jacob. b. 1814, SC: 1844, mr. Leonora Moses Rosenfeld. Rf: 1850C; SFF210; MS16.191; D1849

Rosenfeld, Leonora (Moses). b. 1820, SC: 1820, f. Isaiah Moses, m. Rebecca Phillips Moses, mr. Jacob Rosenfeld, 1845. Rf: SFF210; MS16.191; 1850C

Rosenfeld, Levy. f. Jacob Rosenfeld, m.

Leonora Moses Rosenfeld. Rf: SFF210
Rosenthall, Hyam. SC: 1859. Rf: Min. Sept. 25, 1859
Rothchild, M. C. b. 1801, d. 1841, SC: 1841. Rf: DR
Rowman, S. SC: 1861. Rf: Min. Sept. 3, 1861
Rubenstein, Is. SC: 1859. Rf: Min. Sept. 25, 1859
Rubenstein, S. Mendal. b. 1859, d. 1860, SC: 1859. Rf: DR
Russel, Moses. SC: 1818. Rf: E139
Russell, Perla (Sheftall). b. 1788, d. 1850, SC: 1788, f. Levi Sheftall, m. Sarah DeLaMotta Sheftall, mr. Isaac Russell, 1808. Rf: SFF256, 267
Sacedote, Joseph C. SC: 1818. Rf: E139
Sacks, Sarah. SC: 1859. Rf: Min. Feb. 13, 1860
Salmonson, Hester Eger (Hertz) (Jacobi). SC: 1854, f. Jacob Hertz, m. Rebecca Mordecai Hertz, mr. Wolf Jacob Jacobi, 1854, mr2. ——— Salmonson. Rf: EM27; SFF117; JF6
Salomon, Lewis. d. 1835, SC: 1805. Rf: E139; EP; MR3U.463; D1806
Salomon, Moses. SC: 1794. Rf: SFF172
Salomon, Rosalie Alice (Levy). b. 1824, d. 1861, f. Hayman Levy, m. Almeria DeLeon Levy, mr. David Salomon. Rf: SFF159, 257
Salomon, Sarah. b. 1774, d. 1847, SC: 1825. Rf: EC22; W38.545; 1830C; SCA1825–26; D1829, 1831, 1835
Salvador, Francis. b. 1747, d. 1776, SC: 1773, f. Jacob Salvador, m. Esther Dequiros Salvador, mr. Sarah Salvador, 1767. Rf: EC106; SFF258; E45, 68–77, 107–116; SCA1774–79
Salvador, Joseph. b. 1716, d. 1786, SC: 1784, f. Francis Salvador, m. Rachel Mendes DaCosta Salvador, mr. Leonora de Antonio Lopes DaCosta, 1738. Rf: SFF258; E33, 69, 70, 83, 108–118, 280; W22.94 (his); SCA1763–99
Sampson, Abraham Joseph. b. 1842, SC: 1842. Rf: SFF259; E171; 1850C; D1859
Sampson, Amelia. b. 1800, d. 1819, SC: 1819, mr. Samuel Sampson. Rf: SFF259; *SP*, Aug. 14, 1819
Sampson, Catharine. b. 1822, d. 1822, SC: 1822, f. Samuel Sampson. Rf: DR; SFF259; MR5Y.278
Sampson, Catherine (Goldsmith). f. Isaac Goldsmith, m. Frances Phillips Goldsmith, mr. Samuel Sampson, 1838. Rf: SFF84, 259
Sampson, Edwin J. d. 1862, f. Samuel Sampson, m. Catherine Goldsmith Sampson. Rf: SFF259; E171, 235
Sampson, Elias. b. 1764, d. 1824, SC: 1805. Rf: DR; E139; SCA1822–24
Sampson, Emanuel. SC: 1835. Rf: D1835
Sampson, Esther (Cohen). b. 1831, d. 1897, SC: 1841, f. Hartwig Cohen, Deborah Marks Cohen, mr. Joseph Sampson, 1851. Rf: EG3; SFF34, 259; 1850C
Sampson, Eugene. b. 1847, SC: 1847. Rf: 1850C
Sampson, Hannah Francis. b. 1844, d. 1845, SC: 1844, f. Joseph

Sampson, m. Rebecca Sampson. Rf: DR; EP

Sampson, Henry. SC: 1819. Rf: E139, 235; 1820C; *SCHM*66.218; SCA1822–25; D1819, 1822

Sampson, Jacob H. b. 1821, d. 1865, f. Samuel Sampson. Rf: EG3; SFF259; E171

Sampson, Jane. b. 1793, SC: 1829. Rf: 1850C; D1829, 1831, 1835

Sampson, Jane Cohen. b. 1845, SC: 1845. Rf: 1850C

Sampson, Joseph. b. 1801, d. 1830, SC: 1817, mr. Abigail Sampson Levy. Rf: EC72; SFF259; EP; EM15; 1820C; *SCHM*66.218; SCA1822–26; D1819, 1822, 1829

Sampson, Joseph. b. 1813, d. 1886, SC: 1834, mr. Rebecca Goldsmith Sampson, 1839. Rf: DR; *SCHM*66.218; SFF84; 1850C; 1860C; MS14.158; SCA1839–62; D1849, 1855, 1859

Sampson, Joseph. b. 1823, d. 1883, SC: 1823, f. Samuel Sampson, mr. Esther Cohen Sampson, 1851. Rf: SFF259; EM25; E238

Sampson, L. SC: 1839. Rf: Min. April 14, 1839

Sampson, Michael. SC: 1805. Rf: E139

Sampson, Moses. b. 1847, SC: 1847. Rf: 1850C; 1860C

Sampson, Moses L. b. 1850, d. 1876, SC: 1850, f. Joseph Sampson. Rf: DR; EP

Sampson, Rachael. b. 1821, SC: 1821. Rf: 1850C

Sampson, Rebecca (Goldsmith). b. 1814, d. 1882, SC: 1839, f. Isaac Goldsmith, m. Frances Phillips Goldsmith, mr. Joseph Sampson, 1839. Rf: SFF84; 1850C; 1860C; SCA1839

Sampson, Sampson. b. 1826, SC: 1841. Rf: 1850C; D1841, 49

Sampson, Samuel. b. 1789, d. 1827, SC: 1823, mr. Amelia Sampson. Rf: DR; EC71; SFF259; E139

Sampson, Samuel. b. 1818, SC: 1818, f. Samuel Sampson, mr. Catherine Goldsmith Sampson, 1838. Rf: EM17; SFF84, 259; 1840C; 1850C; 1860C; T40; TBS40; D1835, 1838, 1859

Sampson, Samuel. b. 1849, SC: 1849. Rf: 1850C; 1860C

Sampson, Sarah. b. 1767, d. 1827, SC: 1818. Rf: DR; SCA1818

Sampson, Sarah. b. 1840, SC: 1840. Rf: 1850C; 1860C

Sampson, Thomas. SC: 1852. Rf: E171, 204; MR5I.13

Samson, ———. b. 1844, d. 1845, SC: 1844. Rf: DR

Samson, Abigail (Goldsmith). SC: 1831, f. Morris Goldsmith, mr. Samuel Samson, 1851. Rf: EM25; SCA1833–34; D1831

Samson, Samuel. b. 1817, d. 1906, SC: 1851, mr. Abigail Goldsmith Samson, 1851. Rf: DR; EM25, E238; *Courier* Dec. 11, 1861; D1852

Samuel, ———, Mrs. b. 1838, d. 1862, SC: 1859. Rf: DR

Samuel, Hyman [also Samuels]. SC: 1806, mr. Rebecca Alexander Samuel. Rf: SFF44; E139; 1810C; D1806

Samuel, Joshua. SC: 1810. Rf: E139

Samuel, M. b. 1821, SC: 1850. Rf: 1850C; D1852

Samuel, Rebecca (DaCosta). f. Aaron

Alexander DaCosta, mr. Hyman Samuel. Rf: SFF44

Samuel, S. b. 1825, SC: 1850. Rf: 1850C

Samuel, Samuel. b. 1790, SC: 1850, f. Hyman Samuel, m. Rebecca Samuel. Rf: SFF44; 1850C

Samuels, Elizabeth. b. 1820, d. 1865, SC: 1850. Rf: DR; 1850C

Samuels, Moses [also Samuel]. b. 1811, d. 1896, SC: 1859. Rf: DR; E171, 240; 1861C; D1859

Sarzedas, Bella (Myers). b. 1771, d. 1855, SC: 1795, f. Mordicai Myers, m. Esther Cohen Myers, mr. Moses Sarzedas, 1790. Rf: EG3; MR4B.2; SFF216, 262; 1850C; MS1.534; SCA1795–1809; RB125

Sarzedas, David. b. 1760, d. 1841, SC: 1780, f. Abraham Sarzedas, m. Caty Hays Sarzedas, mr. Sarah DaCosta Sarzedas. Rf: DR; SFF44, 262; E91, 92, 139, 141, 278; 1810C; SCA1785–1825; D1794, 1796, 1813, 1819, 1822, 1835

Sarzedas, David. b. 1785, d. 1828, SC: 1785, f. David Sarzedas, m. Sarah DaCosta Sarzedas. Rf: SFF262; 1820C; SCA1815–17; D1822

Sarzedas, Moses. b. 1767, d. 1811, SC: 1790, f. Abraham Sarzedas, m. Caty Hays Sarzedas, mr. Bella (Myers) Sarzedas, 1790. Rf: EP; SFF216, 262; E244, 280; MS1.534; SCA1791–1809; D1794, 1796

Sarzedas, Sarah Ann. d. 1820, SC: 1820, mr. David Sarzedas, Jr. Rf: *SP*, May 11, 1820, eulogy

Sarzedas, Sarah (DaCosta) (Maysor). b. 1767, d. 1816, SC: 1800, f. Isaac DaCosta, m. Sarah DaCosta, mr. David Maysor, 1779, mr2. David Sarzedas. Rf: SFF44, 262; SCA1800; RB29

Sasportas, Aaron. d. 1798, f. Abraham Sasportas, m. Rachel DaCosta Sasportas. Rf: SFF262

Sasportas, Abraham. d. 1824, SC: 1778, mr. Rachel DaCosta Sasportas, 1778, mr2. Charlotte (Leah) Canter Sasportas, 1803. Rf: SFF28, 44, 262; E106, 139, 279; EM 5, 7; W36.1067 (his); 1790C; T40; W25.89; SCA1778–1819; D1790, 1794, 1796, 1806, 1807, 1816

Sasportas, Augustus. SC: 1820, f. Abraham Sasportas, m. Charlotte Canter Sasportas. Rf: SFF262; W36.1067

Sasportas, Charlotte [Leah] (Canter). b. 1783, d. 1851, SC: 1825, f. Jacob Canter, m. Rebecca DeLaMotta Canter, mr. Abraham Sasportas, 1803. Rf: SFF28, 262; SCA1825; RB16

Sasportas, I. SC: 1839. Rf: Min. April 8, 1839

Sasportas, Isaac. b. 1791, d. 1819, SC: 1791, f. Abraham Sasportas, m. Rachel DaCosta Sasportas. Rf: SFF262; SCA1818–25

Sasportas, Rachel (DaCosta). SC: 1778, f. Isaac DaCosta, m. Sarah Pimienta, mr. Abraham Sasportas, 1778. Rf: SFF44, 262; SCA1779–86

Sasportas, Sarah. f. Abraham Sasportas, m. Rachel DaCosta Sasportas. Rf: SFF262

Schirer, ———. SC: 1847. Rf: Min. Aug. 10, 1847

Schlesinger, Virginia (Ancker). b. 1860, d. 1944, f. Gustavus V. Ancker, m. Hannah Hyams Ancker, mr. Alfred Schlesinger, 1884. Rf: SFF11

Schlichter, ———. b. 1794, d. 1839, SC: 1839. Rf: DR

Schur, Barnet. b. 1831, d. 1906, SC: 1850, f. David Schur, m. Bella Schur. Rf: DR; 1850C; D1859

Schur, Bella. b. 1806, SC: 1850, mr. David Schur. Rf: 1850C

Schur, David. b. 1800, d. 1853, SC: 1847, mr. Bella Schur. Rf: DR; 1850C; SCA1847

Schur, Henrietta. b. 1826, SC: 1850, f. David Schur, m. Bella Schur. Rf: 1850C

Schwabe, L. H. SC: 1843. Rf: *State v. Ancker*

Schwerin, Caroline (Suares). b. 1819, d. 1904, SC: 1841, f. Jacob Suares, m. Judith Suares, mr. Julius Schwerin, 1841. Rf: MJSC12; EM20; SFF289; MS15.159

Schwerin, Harman. b. 1852, d. 1895, SC: 1852, f. Julius Schwerin, m. Caroline Suares Schwerin, mr. Cecile F. Moses. Rf: MJSC16; SFF289

Schwerin, Jacob Henry. b. 1845, d. 1849, SC: 1845, f. Julius Schwerin, m. Caroline Suares Schwerin. Rf: DR; SFF289

Schwerin, Julius. b. 1812, d. 1875, SC: 1841, mr. Caroline Suares Schwerin, 1841. Rf: SFF289; EM20; E171

Scriber, Woolf. d. 1838, SC: 1838. Rf: EP

Seaman, Lenard. b. 1833, d. 1859, SC: 1859. Rf: DR

Seckendorf, G. b. 1828, SC: 1850. Rf: 1850C

Seckendorf, Hannah. b. 1805, SC: 1850. Rf: 1850C

Seckendorf, Isaac. b. 1810, SC: 1850. Rf: E171; 1850C

Seckendorf, Marx. SC: 1861. Rf: E238; 1861C

Segar, Elizabeth (DeHaan). SC: 1842, f. Samuel DeHaan, mr. Frank Segar, 1842. Rf: EM20

Segar, Frank. SC: 1842, mr. Elizabeth DeHaan Segar, 1842. Rf: EM20

Segar, Isaac. SC: 1842, mr. ——— DeHaan. Rf: Min. Feb. 2, 1842

Seixas, ———. f. Abraham Mendes Seixas, m. Richea Hart Seixas. Rf: SFF263

Seixas, ———. b. 1853, d. 1853, SC: 1853, f. David Cardozo Seixas, m. Henrietta DeLeon Seixas. Rf: EC20; SFF266

Seixas, Abigail. b. 1783, f. Abraham Mendes Sexias, m. Richea Hart Seixas. Rf: SFF263

Seixas, Abigail Valencia. d. 1819, SC: 1814, mr. Isaac Mendes Seixas. Rf: MR4.242; EC69; SFF263; D1816

Seixas, Abraham. b. 1786, d. 1834, SC: 1825, f. Benjamin Mendes Seixas, m. Zipporah Levy Seixas, mr. Rachel Nunes Cardozo Seixas, 1821. Rf: EC11; SFF266; T40; D1831

Seixas, Abraham DeLeon. b. 1847, d. 1900, SC: 1850, f. David Cardozo Seixas, m. Henrietta DeLeon Seixas, mr. Alice Couch Seixas. Rf: SFF266; 1850C

Seixas, Abraham Mendes. b. 1750, d.

1799, SC: 1777, f. Isaac Mendes Seixas, m. Rachel Levy Seixas, mr. Richea Hart Seixas, 1777. Rf: EC6; EM5; SFF263; E43, 82, 92, 93, 106, 128–30, 278; 1790C; SCA1781–98; MS1.53; D1790, 1796, 1806

Seixas, Abraham Mendes. b. 1810, d. 1867, SC: 1810, f. Isaac Mendes Seixas, m. Abigail Valencia Seixas, mr. Hannah Pardo Seixas, 1841. Rf: SFF263

Seixas, Benjamin. b. 1826, d. 1828, f. Abraham Seixas, m. Rachel Nunes Cardozo Seixas. Rf: SFF266

Seixas, Benjamin Mendes. SC: 1861, f. Isaac Mendes Seixas, m. Abigail Valencia Seixas, mr. Eleanor H. Cohen Seixas, 1865. Rf: SFF263; EM32; E235

Seixas, Caroline. f. Isaac Mendes Seixas, m. Abigail Valencia Seixas. Rf: SFF263

Seixas, David Cardozo. b. 1823, d. 1857, SC: 1848, f. Abraham Seixas, m. Rachel Nunes Cardozo Seixas, mr. Henrietta DeLeon Seixas, 1846. Rf: EC20; SFF55, 266; W48.167 (his); T40l; 1850C; SCA1850–57; D1849, 1852, 1855

Seixas, Eleanor H. (Cohen). b. 1841, d. 1874, SC: 1841, f. Philip Melvin Cohen, m. Cordelia Moïse Cohen, mr. Benjamin B. Seixas, 1865. Rf: SFF39, 265; 1850C; 1860C

Seixas, Fanny [Frances]. b. 1855, d. 1868, SC: 1860, f. David Cardozo Seixas, m. Henrietta DeLeon Seixas. Rf: EC20; SFF266; W48.167; 1860C

Seixas, Fanny Mendes. b. 1787, f. Abraham Mendes Seixas, m. Richea Hart Seixas. Rf: SFF263

Seixas, Florence Augusta (Cohen). b. 1853, SC: 1853, f. Philip Melvin Cohen, m. Cordelia Moïse Cohen, mr. Meyer L. Seixas, 1873. Rf: SFF39, 265

Seixas, George Augustus Hopty. b. 1851, d. 1853, SC: 1851, f. David Cardoza Seixas, m. Henrietta DeLeon Seixas. Rf: EC20; SFF266

Seixas, Grace Mendes. b. 1785, d. 1821, f. Abraham Mendes Seixas, m. Richea Hart Seixas. Rf: SFF263

Seixas, Henrietta (DeLeon). b. 1823, d. 1912, SC: 1823, f. Abraham DeLeon, m. Isabella Nones DeLeon, mr. David Cardozo Seixas, 1846. Rf: DR; EC20; SFF266; W48.167; 1850C; 1860C; SCA1850; D1859

Seixas, Hortensia (Moses). b. 1815, d. 1890, SC: 1815, f. Myer Moses, m. Esther Phillips Moses, mr. Jacob Levy Seixas, 1834. Rf: SFF205, 265

Seixas, Isaac Mendes. b. 1778, d. 1826, SC: 1778, f. Abraham Mendes Seixas, m. Rachel Hart Seixas, mr. Abigail Valencia Seixas. Rf: SFF263; E139; EP; 1810C; T40; SCA1801–10; D1801, 1802, 1807, 1809, 1816, 1819

Seixas, Isabella. b. 1857, d. 1868, SC: 1857, f. David Cardozo Seixas, m. Henrietta DeLeon Seixas. Rf: EC20; SFF266; 1860C

Seixas, Jacob. SC: 1822. Rf: E139; T40

Seixas, James Madison. b. 1829, d.

1889, SC: 1829, f. Abraham Seixas, m. Rachel Nunes Carodozo Seixas, mr. Marie Julia Deslonde Seixas, 1865. Rf: SFF266; E142, 171; EM32; W48.167; D1852

Seixas, Joshua. b. 1781, f. Abraham Mendes Seixas, m. Richea Hart Seixas. Rf: SFF263

Seixas, Lawrence Ludlow. b. 1849, d. 1868, SC: 1850, f. David Cardozo Seixas, m. Henrietta DeLeon Seixas. Rf: SFF266; 1850C; 1860C

Seixas, Mathias. b. 1829, SC: 1829. Rf: 1850C

Seixas, Miriam. b. 1834, d. 1837, SC: 1837, f. Abraham Seixas, m. Rachel Nunes Cardoza Seixas. Rf: EC11; SFF266

Seixas, Moses Mendes. b. 1793, f. Abraham Mendes Seixas, m. Richea Hart Seixas. Rf: SFF263

Seixas, Rachel Nunes (Cardozo). b. 1795, d. 1860, SC: 1795, f. David Nunez Cardozo, m. Sarah Cohen Cardozo, mr. Abraham Seixas, 1821. Rf: EM12; SFF29, 266; W40.272; W48.167; SCA1840; *SP*, April 13, 1821; 1850C; D1835, 1849

Seixas, Richea [Ritcey] (Hart). SC: 1777, f. Joshua Hart, m. Rebecca Hart, mr. Abraham M. Seixas, 1777. Rf: EM5; SFF98, 263; E43; MS1.53

Seixas, S. D. SC: 1849. Rf: D1849

Seixas, Virginia A. b. 1854, d. 1876, SC: 1860, f. David Cardozo Seixas, m. Henrietta DeLeon Seixas. Rf: DR; EC21; SFF266; W48.167; 1860C

Seixas, Zipporah. b. 1795, f. Abraham Mendes Seixas, m. Richea Hart Seixas. Rf: SFF263

Shapira, Louis D. b. 1827, d. 1895. Rf: E235

Sheftall, Abraham. SC: 1819. Rf: CB1819

Sheftall, Benjamin. b. 1771, d. 1835, SC: 1780, f. Levi Sheftall, m. Sarah DeLaMotta Sheftall. Rf: SFF267, 270

Sheftall, Clara (DeLaMotta). f. Emanuel DeLaMotta, m. Judith Canter DeLaMotta, mr. ——— Sheftall. Rf: SFF54

Sheftall, Emanuel. b. 1786, d. 1818, f. Levi Sheftall, m. Sarah DeLaMotta Sheftall. Rf: SFF267

Sheftall, Frances (Hart). b. 1740, d. 1820, SC: 1761, f. Moses Hart, m. Esther Hart, mr. Mordecai Sheftall, 1761. Rf: SFF98, 267

Sheftall, Isaac. b. 1779, d. 1780, SC: 1779, f. Levi Sheftall, m. Sarah DeLaMotta Sheftall. Rf: SFF267

Sheftall, Judith. b. 1781, d. 1854, SC: 1781, f. Levi Sheftall, m. Sarah DeLaMotta Sheftall. Rf: SFF267

Sheftall, Levi. b. 1739, d. 1809, SC: 1766, f. Benjamin Sheftall, m. Hannah Solomons Sheftall, mr. Sarah DeLaMotta Sheftall, 1768. Rf: SFF267; E30, 32, 40, 104, 278; SCA1766–85

Sheftall, Levi. b. 1776, d. 1796, f. Levi Sheftall, m. Sarah DeLaMotta Sheftall. Rf: SFF276

Sheftall, Mordecai. b. 1735, d. 1797, SC: 1761, f. Benjamin Sheftall, m. Perla Sheftall, mr. Frances Hart Sheftall, 1761. Rf: SFF98, 267; E30, 32, 40, 43, 84, 93, 278; SCA1769–88

Sheftall, Mordecai. b. 1783, d. 1856, SC: 1783, f. Levi Sheftall, m. Sarah DeLaMotta Sheftall, mr. Virginia Russell Sheftall, 1832. Rf: SFF267, 268

Sheftall, Moses. b. 1814, d. 1850, f. Moses Sheftall, m. Elkaleh Bush Sheftall. Rf: SFF267

Sheftall, Rachel. b. 1778, d. 1781, f. Levi Sheftall, m. Sarah DeLaMotta Sheftall. Rf: SFF267

Sheftall, Sarah (DeLaMotta). b. 1754, d. 1811, f. Isaac DeLaMotta, m. Sarah DeLaMotta, mr. Levi Sheftall, 1768. Rf: SFF54, 267

Sheftall, Sheftall. b. 1762, d. 1849, SC: 1800, f. Mordecai Sheftall, m. Frances Hart Sheftall. Rf: SFF267; CB1800

Sill, Adeline. b. 1824, d. 1893, SC: 1824, mr. J. M. Sill. Rf: EJCC9

Silverston, M. SC: 1843. Rf: E171; *State v. Ancker*

Simmons, B. M. SC: 1839. Rf: Min. Jul. 24, 1839

Simmons, Billy. d. 1859. Rf: DR

Simon, Michael. SC: 1805. Rf: E139

Simon, Moses. SC: 1825. Rf: E138

Simons, Israel. SC: 1799. Rf: MR3M.218

Simons, Montague. b. 1752, d. 1813, SC: 1780, f. Isaac Simmons. Rf: "House Journal, 1783–1784," pp. 36, 37; SFF271; EC75; W32.706 (his); EP; SCA1785–1812; E98, 139, 278

Simons, Moses. b. 1768, d. 1808, SC: 1782, f. Isaac Simons. Rf: "House Journal, 1783–1784," p. 84; SFF271; EC76; E92, 139, 278

Simons, Sampson. b. 1750, d. 1811, SC: 1780, f. Isaac Simons. Rf: EC45; SFF271; E92, 139, 278; W27.848; 1790C; 1810C; SCA1776–1806; D1790, 1801, 1803, 1806, 1807, 1809

Simons, Samuel. b. 1761, d. 1824, SC: 1772, f. Isaac Simons. Rf: DR; EC67; SFF271; 1790C; 1820C; T40; E139, 240; SCA1785–1824; D1790, 1794, 1802, 1803, 1806, 1807, 1809

Simons, Saul. b. 1757, d. 1809, SC: 1780, f. Isaac Simons. Rf: SFF271; E102, 279

Simons, Solomon. SC: 1809. Rf: CB1809

Simpson, Abraham. SC: 1840. Rf: Min. Jan. 25, 1840

Simpson, Adeline. b. 1810, d. 1852, SC: 1810, f. Michael Simpson. Rf: DR; SFF272

Simpson, Annie B. b. 1820, d. 1905, f. Michael Simpson. Rf: SFF272

Simpson, Catherine. b. 1806, d. 1893, SC: 1825, f. Michael Simpson. Rf: SFF272; SCA1825 (Jacksonboro)

Simpson, Esther (Abrahams) (Andrews). f. Elias Abrahams, m. Catherine Cohen Abrahams, mr. Zalegman Andrews, 1844, mr2. Myer M. Simpson, 1851. Rf: SFF4, 12, 272; EM25

Simpson, Jacob. b. 1768, d. 1824, SC: 1821. Rf: DR; E139; EP

Simpson, Jane (Cohen) (Mordecai). b. 1789, d. 1843, SC: 1789, f. Gershon Cohen, m. Cecile Cohen, mr. Gomez [Goodman] Mordecai, 1808, mr2. Michael Simpson. Rf: DR; EC9; SFF202, 272; EM9; 1840C

Simpson, Joseph. f. Michael Simpson. Rf: SFF272

Simpson, Leonard. f. Michael Simpson. Rf: SFF272

Simpson, Michael. b. 1773, d. 1833, SC: 1806, mr. Nancy Simpson, mr2. Jane Cohen Simpson. Rf: SFF272; EC9, 68; 1830C; CB1806; SCA1814–25

Simpson, Myer M. b. 1823, SC: 1823, f. Michael Simpson, mr. Esther Abrams Simpson, 1851. Rf: SFF272; W45.581; EM25; E171

Simpson, Nancy. b. 1791, d. 1817, SC: 1817, mr. Michael Simpson. Rf: EC68; SFF272

Simpson, Rebecca. b. 1810, d. 1824, SC: 1824. Rf: DR; EP

Simson, Jochebed. b. 1771, d. 1814, f. Solomon Simson, m. Sarah Mears Simson. Rf: SFF272; *AF*107

Sirqui, Joseph. SC: 1804. Rf: E139; CB1805

Sisson, Leila (Lazarus). b. 1848, SC: 1848, f. Gershon Clarendon Lazarus, m. Esther Cohen Lazarus, mr. Vardy Pritchard Sisson. Rf: 1850C; 1860C; SFF151

Sloman, John. SC: 1848. Rf: T40; E238; *Courier* Dec. 11, 1861

Slowman, Abraham. SC: 1819. Rf: E139; CB1819

Slowman, Eliza. SC: 1831. Rf: D1831, 1835, 1838

Smith, Charles Ferninand. d. 1849, SC: 1849, f. Thomas Smith, m. Everleen Smith. Rf: EC111; SFF163

Smith, Everline (Levy). SC: 1856, f. Elias P. Levy, m. Rachel Moïse Levy, mr. Thomas Smith, 1838. Rf: SFF163; EP; W47.743; EC111

Solomon, A. SC: 1838. Rf: D1838

Solomon, A. L. b. 1828, d. 1904, SC: 1861. Rf: EJCC9; E171, 264

Solomon, Chapman. b. 1769, d. 1849, SC: 1801. Rf: SFF273; 1820C; SCA1814–23; D1801, 1802, 1803, 1806, 1807, 1809

Solomon, Erasmus. SC: 1806. Rf: SCA1806

Solomon, Hannah. SC: 1830. Rf: 1830C

Solomon, Hannah (Hyams). b. 1813, d. 1890, SC: 1813, f. Solomon Hyams, m. Catherine Jacobs Hyams, mr. Levy Solomon, 1838. Rf: SFF119, 273; W41.635

Solomon, Isaac. SC: 1780. RB163

Solomon, Jonas. SC: 1822. Ref: D1822

Solomon, Joseph. SC: 1779. Rf: EP; E87, 93, 279; W24.946

Solomon, Joseph. SC: 1801. Rf: D1801, 1802, 1806, 1807

Solomon, Levy. b. 1754, d. 1827, SC: 1783. Rf: RB163

Solomon, Levy. b. 1812, SC: 1805, f. Chapman Solomon, mr. Hannah Hyams Levy, 1838. Rf: SFF273; CB1805

Solomon, Phineas. b. 1802, d. 1850, SC: 1841. Rf: E171, 246; EP; T40

Solomon, Rachel [Hetty]. b. 1799, d. 1855, SC: 1806, mr. Mark Solomon. Rf: MR3W.718; SFF279; E139, 247

Solomon, Samuel. b. 1772, d. 1848, SC: 1772. Rf: DR

Solomon, Sarah. b. 1772, d. 1848, SC: 1772. Rf: DR

Solomon, Zadok. SC: 1780. Rf: E91, 92; 1810C

Solomons, Aaron. b. 1824, d. 1843, SC: 1824, f. Mark Solomons, m. Rachel Solomons. Rf: SFF279

Solomons, Aaron [Solomon]. b. 1791, d. 1851, SC: 1791, f. Joseph Solomons, m. Judith Solomons, mr. Rebecca Solomons. Rf: SFF277; W31.166; E139; 1810C; SCA1811–28; D1809, 1819, 1822, 1838; RB162

Solomons, Abraham A. b. 1851, d. 1852, SC: 1851, f. Abraham Alexander Solomons, m. Cecilia Moses Solomons. Rf: SFF278

Solomons, Abraham Alexander. b. 1816, d. 1899, SC: 1816, f. Israel Solomons, m. Eleanor Joseph Solomons, mr. Cecilia Moses Solomons, 1843. Rf: SFF210, 278; EM21; *AF*108–9; SCA1850; D1838

Solomons, Alexander. b. 1756, d. 1836, SC: 1798, mr. Cecilia Cohen Solomons, 1785. Rf: EC5; SFF202; E139; 1810C; 1820C; 1830C; SCA1798–1808; D1802, 1803, 1806, 1807, 1809, 1813, 1816, 1819, 1822, 1829, 1831, 1835; RB164

Solomons, Alice (Abrahams). b. 1789, d. 1839, SC: 1805, f. Emanuel Abrahams, m. Judith Mordecai Abrahams, mr. Solomon Solomons, 1805. Rf: EC55; EM8; SFF4, 277; W31.166; MR5X.448

Solomons, Andrew. SC: 1798. Rf: MR3V.313

Solomons, Augustus Aurelius. b. 1829, d. 1891, SC: 1829, f. Mark Solomons, m. Rachel Solomons, mr. Kate Cohen Solomons, 1852. Rf: SFF279; D1841

Solomons, Benjamin. SC: 1798. Rf: E139; SCA1798–1827

Solomons, Benjamin. b. 1824, d. 1885, SC: 1824. Rf: DR

Solomons, Bennett. b. 1839, SC: 1860. Rf: 1860C

Solomons, Catey. SC: 1798, mr. Hyam Solomons. Rf: SCA1798

Solomons, Catherine. SC: 1806. Rf: SCA1823–43; D1806, 1816, 1819, 1822

Solomons, Catherine. b. 1806, SC: 1806. Rf: 1860C

Solomons, Cecilia (Cohen). b. 1765, d. 1839, SC: 1785, mr. Gershon Cohen, mr2. Alexander Solomons, 1785. Rf: DR; EC5; EM21; SFF202; EP

Solomons, Cecilia (Moses). b. 1815, d. 1882, SC: 1815, f. Isaiah Moses, m. Rebecca Phillips Moses, mr. Abraham A. Solomons, 1843. Rf: EM21; SFF210, 278; *AF*61

Solomons, Chapman. SC: 1802. Rf: E139; CB1805; D1822

Solomons, Charles. SC: 1798. Rf: MR3V.313

Solomons, David. b. 1821, d. 1847, f. Mark Solomons, m. Rachel Solomons. Rf: SFF279; E171; EP

Solomons, E. b. 1820, d. 1841, SC: 1820. Rf: DR

Solomons, E. J. SC: 1852. Rf: D1852

Solomons, Edward. b. 1822, d. 1895, SC: 1822, f. Mark Solomons, m. Rachel Solomons, mr. Mary Solomons. Rf: MJSC13; SFF279

Solomons, Eleanor (Joseph). b. 1794, d. 1856, SC: 1794, f. Lizer Joseph, m. Sarah Joseph, mr. Israel Solomons, 1814. Rf: SFF278; 1850C; MR5W.154; MS6.323: SFF139, 177; D1835, 1838, 1841

Solomons, Eleazer [Lizer]. b. 1815, d.

1889, SC: 1832, f. Israel Solomons, m. Eleanor Joseph Solomons, mr. Perla Sheftall Solomons, 1847. Rf: EM23; SFF278; E171; 205; G8; D1835, 1838

Solomons, Elias. SC: 1798. Rf: SCA1798

Solomons, Emma. f. Solomon Solomons, m. Alice Abrahams Solomons. Rf: SFF277

Solomons, Esdaile. b. 1817, d. 1840, SC: 1817, f. Mark Solomons, m. Rachel Solomons. Rf: SFF279; EP

Solomons, Esther (Nathans). b. 1832, d. 1893, SC: 1850, f. Nathan Nathans, m. Sarah N. Hertz Nathans, mr. Solomon Sampson Solomons, 1852. Rf: DR; SFF231, 277; 1850C; 1860C

Solomons, Esther Sarah (Ottolengui). SC: 1808, f. Mordecai Ottolengui, m. Rinah Ottolengui, mr. Israel Solomons, 1808. Rf: EM9; SFF234, 277, 278

Solomons, Fanny. b. 1807, SC: 1807, f. Solomon Solomons, m. Alice Abrahams Solomons. Rf: SFF277; W31.166

Solomons, Frances (Joseph). b. 1831, SC: 1831, f. Joseph Joseph, m. Frances Alexander Joseph, mr. Moses Joseph Solomons, 1851. Rf: EM25; SFF139, 278; 1850C

Solomons, Hannah. b. 1812, SC: 1812. Rf: 1850C

Solomons, Hart. b. 1774, d. 1817, SC: 1799, mr. Rebecca Cohen Solomons, 1815. Rf: EC35; W33.1348 (his); EP; E139; 1810C; SCA1799–1811; *SP*, Oct. 19, 1815

Solomons, Henrietta. b. 1820, d. 1838, f. Mark Solomons, m. Rachel Solomons. Rf: SFF279

Solomons, Henrietta S. (Emanuel). b. 1836, SC: 1856, f. Nathan Emanuel, m. Henrietta Emanuel Emanuel, mr. Moses J. Solomons, 1856. Rf: SFF66, 278; EM29

Solomons, Henry. SC: 1843. Rf: *State v. Ancker*

Solomons, Hyam. d. 1801, SC: 1782, mr. Catey Solomons. Rf: "House Journal, 1783–1784," pp. 36, 37; E98, 279; W28.147 (his); SCA1786–97; D1794

Solomons, Isaac. SC: 1810. Rf: 1810C

Solomons, Israel. b. 1770, d. 1830, SC: 1800, f. Solomon Solomons, mr. Esther Sarah Ottolengui Solomons, 1808, mr2. Eleanor Joseph Solomons, 1814. Rf: EG4; EM9; SFF139, 277, 278; *AF*107; E139; MS6.323

Solomons, Israel. b. 1847, d. 1854, SC: 1847, f. Abraham Alexander Solomons, m. Cecilia Moses Solomons. Rf: SFF278

Solomons, Jacob T. b. 1825, d. 1875, SC: 1825, f. Mark Solomons, m. Rachel Solomons. Rf: SFF279

Solomons, Joseph. d. 1808, SC: 1780, f. Solomon Solomons, mr. Judith Moses Solomons. Rf: SFF277; 1800C; W27.848; W31.166 (his); E91, 139, 243, 279; SCA1788–1807; D1796, 1803; RB163

Solomons, Joseph. b. 1809, d. 1832, SC: 1829, f. Solomon Solomons, m. Alice Abrahams Solomons. Rf: EC55; SFF277; 1830C; D1829

Solomons, Joseph J. b. 1858, d. 1867, SC: 1858, f. Solomon Sampson

Solomons, m. Esther Nathans Solomons. Rf: DR; EC36; 1860C; SFF277

Solomons, Joseph R. b. 1824, d. 1887, SC: 1824, f. Mark Solomons, m. Rachel Solomons, mr. Rebecca Solomons, 1857. Rf: DR; MJSC12; E171, 235, 238, 262, 264; EM29, 1850C; 1861C; SCA1861; SFF272, 279; D1849, 1852, 1859

Solomons, Judah. f. Israel Solomons, m. Eleanor Joseph Solomons. Rf: SFF278; E139

Solomons, Judith. b. 1759, d. 1815, SC: 1815, mr. J. Solomons. Rf: *SP*, Nov. 29, 1815

Solomons, Levy [also Levi]. b. 1754, d. 1827, SC: 1783. Rf: DR; EP; E98, 139, 243, 279; "House Journal, 1783–1784," pp. 36–37; SCA1788–1825; D1806, 1807

Solomons, Levy J. SC: 1831. Rf: E171; T40; SCA1834

Solomons, Lewis. SC: 1822. Rf: D1822

Solomons, Mark. b. 1763, d. 1830, SC: 1805. Rf: E139

Solomons, Mark. b. 1787, d. 1837, SC: 1806, mr. Rachel Solomons. Rf: SFF279; E139, 247; 1810C; SCA1806–35; D1807, 1809, 1813

Solomons, Molcie (Joseph). b. 1800, d. 1835, SC: 1800, f. Lizer Joseph, m. Sarah Joseph, mr. Sampson Solomons, 1819. Rf: DR; EC15; SFF139, 27

Solomons, Mordecai. SC: 1835, f. Solomon Solomons. Rf: E171; D1835

Solomons, Moses. SC: 1740, f. Benedictus Solomons, m. Abigail Franks Solomons, mr. Margaret Solomons. Rf: E24, 27, 277; SFF75; SCA1741; RB164

Solomons, Moses. b. 1799, d. 1826, f. Solomon Solomons. Rf: SFF277

Solomons, Moses. SC: 1840. Rf: 1840C; D1849

Solomons, Myer. SC: 1780. Rf: E91, 92, 278, 279; RB164

Solomons, Nathan. SC: 1801. Rf: E139; D1801, 1803

Solomons, Perla (Sheftall). b. 1811, d. 1897, f. Moses Sheftall, m. Elkaleh Bush Sheftall, mr. Eleazer Solomons, 1847. Rf: EM23; SFF267, 278

Solomons, Rachel. SC: 1807, f. Joseph Solomons, m. Judith Solomons. Rf: SFF277; W31.177

Solomons, Rebecca (Audler). SC: 1838, mr. Aaron Solomons. Rf: SCA1838

Solomons, Rebecca (Cohen). SC: 1808, mr. Hart Solomons, 1815. Rf: W33.1348; *SP*, Oct. 19, 1815; SCA1824–46

Solomons, Rebecca (Simpson). b. 1827, d. 1904, SC: 1849, f. Michael Simpson, mr. Joseph R. Solomons, 1857. Rf: EM29; SFF272, 279; D1849

Solomons, Rinah. f. Israel Solomons, m. Esther S. Ottolengui Solomons. Rf: SFF278

Solomons, Sampson. b. 1794, d. 1833, SC: 1819, f. Solomon Solomons, mr. Molcie Joseph Solomons, 1819. Rf: EC15; EP; SFF139, 277; MS8.1

Solomons, Sarah. SC: 1798. Rf: 1810C; 1820; 1840C; SCA1798–

1841; D1813, 1816, 1819, 1822, 1841

Solomons, Sarah (Falk). b. 1859, d. 1938, SC: 1859, f. Abraham Falk, m. Henrietta Abrahams Falk, mr. Isaiah Abraham Solomons, 1884. Rf: SFF5, 278; 1860C

Solomons, Solomon. b. 1784, d. 1836, SC: 1805, f. Joseph Solomons, mr. Alice Abrahams Solomons, 1805. Rf: EC55; EM14; E139; 1810C; 1820C; 1830C; W31.166; SCA1814–25; D1806, 1807, 1809, 1816, 1819, 1822, 1829, 1831; RB164

Solomons, Solomon Sampson. b. 1825, d. 1904, SC: 1825, f. Sampson Solomons, m. Molcie Joseph Solomons, mr. Esther Nathans Solomons, 1852. Rf: DR; E171, 204, 262; T40; 1850C; 1860C; SCA1847; D1859

Solomons, Zipporah Molsey (Solomons). b. 1829, d. 1890, SC: 1848, f. Sampson Solomons, m. Molcie Joseph Solomons, mr. Joseph M. Solomons, 1848. Rf: EM23; SFF277, 278; MS16.511

Somers, Anton. b. 1793, d. 1851, SC: 1851. Rf: DR; EC87

Sommers, Ann (Levy). b. 1811, SC: 1840, mr. Edward Sommers, 1840. Rf: EM19; 1850C

Sommers, Edward. b. 1801, SC: 1840, mr. Ann Levy Sommers, 1840. Rf: EM19; E171; 1850C; 1861C; W43.556; T40; D1852, 1855, 1859

Sommers, Joseph. b. 1833, d. 1867. Rf: EJCC10

Sommers, Levy. b. 1839, SC: 1839, f. Edward Sommers, m. Ann Levy Sommers. Rf: 1850C

Sommers, Lizzy. b. 1837, SC: 1837, f. Edward Sommers, m. Ann Sommers. Rf: 1850C

Soria, Hetty (Cohen). SC: 1826, f. Moses Cohen, m. Rachel Moses Cohen, mr. Isaac Soria, 1826. Rf: EM13; SFF36

Soria, Isaac. SC: 1825, f. Aaron Soria, m. Rachel Mendez Hega Soria, mr. Hetty Cohen Soria, 1826. Rf: SFF280; EM13

Soria, Zipporah (Cohen). b. 1804, d. 1892, SC: 1804, f. Moses Cohen, m. Rachel Moses Cohen, mr. Joseph Soria, 1833. Rf: SFF36, 280

Spencer, A. R. f. Allen R. Spencer, m. Catherine R. Hertz Spencer. Rf: SFF117

Spencer, Allen R. SC: 1850, mr. Catherine R. Hertz Spencer. Rf: SFF117; 1850C

Spencer, Catherine (Hyams). f. David Hyams, m. Rebecca Maysor Hyams. Rf: SFF120

Spencer, Catherine R. (Hertz). f. Jacob Hertz, m. Rebecca Mordecai Spencer, mr. Allen R. Spencer. Rf: EC12; SFF117

Spencer, Florina North. b. 1854, d. 1865, f. Allen R. Spencer, m. Catherine R. Spencer. Rf: EC12; SFF117

Spencer, John. f. Allen R. Spencer, m. Catherine R. Spencer. Rf: SFF117

Spitz, I. A. b. 1797, d. 1819, SC: 1818. Rf: EP; E139

Spitzer, Bernard Moses. d. 1796, SC: 1790. Rf: EP; 1790C; E279; SCA1795; D1790, 1794

Stern, Asher. SC: 1857, f. Seligman Stern, m. Miriam Stern. Rf: W49.609

Stern, Miriam (Lehman). b. 1804, d. 1857, SC: 1857, mr. Seligman Stern. Rf: DR; EC91; W49.609 (hers)

Stern, Seligman. SC: 1857, mr. Miriam Lehman Stern. Rf: EC91; W49.609

Strauss, ———. b. 1857, d. 1858, SC: 1857. Rf: DR

Strauss, Bernard. SC: 1861. Rf: E235; 1861C

Suares, Aaron. b. 1856, d. 1892, SC: 1856, f. Jacob Edgar Suares, m. Isabelle Nathan Suares. Rf: MJSC17; SFF278; E171; 1860C

Suares, Abraham. b. 1800, d. 1864, SC: 1800. Rf: EP; 1850C; SCA1825; D1829, 1831, 1835, 1838, 1849

Suares, Benjamin C. b. 1816, SC: 1838, mr. Harriet Suares. Rf: E171; 1850C; 1860C; 1861C; *Courier* Dec. 11, 1861; D1835, 1838, 1841, 1849, 1852, 1855

Suares, David. b. 1767, d. 1817, SC: 1799. Rf: SFF289; E280; EC68; SCA1799–1815; D1802, 1806, 1807, 1809

Suares, David. SC: 1831. Rf: D1831

Suares, Edward. b. 1847, SC: 1847. Rf: 1850C; 1860C

Suares, Esther. b. 1842, d. 1908, SC: 1842, f. Jacob Edgar Suares, m. Isabelle Nathan Suares. Rf: MJSC17; SFF289; 1850C; 1860C

Suares, Harriet. b. 1822, SC: 1822, mr. Benjamin C. Suares. Rf: 1850C; 1860C; 1861C

Suares, Henry Edgar. b. 1850, d. 1914, SC: 1850, f. Jacob Edgar Suares, m. Isabelle Nathan Edgar. Rf: SFF289; 1860C

Suares, Isaac. d. 1825, SC: 1804. Rf: EP; E139; *SCHM*66.218; 1810C; SCA1810–20; D1809, 1813, 1819

Suares, Isaac. b. 1854, d. 1898, SC: 1860, f. Jacob Edgar Suares, m. Isabelle Nathan Suares. Rf: MJSC17; SFF289; 1860C

Suares, Isabelle (Nathan). b. 1820, d. 1897, SC: 1820, f. Henry Nathan, m. Esther Nathan, mr. Jacob E. Suares, 1839. Rf: MJSC17; EM18; SFF228, 289; 1850C; 1860C

Suares, Jacob. b. 1755, d. 1818, SC: 1799, mr. Judith Suares. Rf: DR; E139, 171, 292; EC96; SFF289; 1820C; T40; SCA1799–1820; D1802, 1803, 1806, 1807, 1819; RB167

Suares, Jacob Edgar. b. 1810, d. 1894, SC: 1820, f. Jacob Suares, m. Judith Suares, mr. Isabelle Nathan Suares, 1839. Rf: MJSC17; SFF289; 1850C; 1860C; 1861C; E139, 171, 235; D1849, 1852, 1855

Suares, Joseph. SC: 1810. Rf: 1810C

Suares, Judith. b. 1770, d. 1853, SC: 1799, mr. Jacob Suares. Rf: MR3M.218; EC96; SFF289; 1830C; 1840C; SCA1799–1828; D1829, 1831, 1835, 1838

Suares, L. P. SC: 1843. Rf: *State v. Ancker*

Suares, Miriam. b. 1845, SC: 1845. Rf: 1850C; 1860C

Suares, Rachel. SC: 1812. Rf: SCA1812–20; D1819

Suares, Rachel. b. 1809, d. 1873, SC:

1809, f. Jacob Suares, m. Judith Suares. Rf: EJCC10; SFF289
Suares, Samuel. b. 1858, SC: 1858, f. Jacob E. Suares, m. Isabelle Suares. Rf: 1860C
Suares, Theodosia Isabelle. b. 1839, SC: 1839. Rf: 1850C
Tabar, Esperanza. SC: 1784. Rf: SFF13; W30.855
Tillman, Mamie (Hyams). b. 1855, d. 1941, SC: 1855, f. Mordecai Hyams, m. Josephine Joseph Hyams, mr. Cassius L. Tillman. Rf: SFF119; 1860C
Tobias, Abraham. b. 1793, d. 1856, SC: 1793, f. Joseph Tobias, m. Rachel Aarons Tobias, mr. Eleanor Lopez Tobias, 1822. Rf: DR; EC86; EM24; SFF176, 298; T41; E139, 143, 204, 296; 1830C; 1861C; SCA1811–46; D1816, 1819, 1822, 1829, 1831, 1835, 1838, 1841, 1849, 1852, 1855
Tobias, Abraham. b. 1857, d. 1860, SC: 1857, f. Thomas Jefferson Tobias, m. Adelaide Hendricks Tobias. Rf: SFF298
Tobias, Adelaide (Hendricks). b. 1830, d. 1878, SC: 1830, f. Uriah Hendricks, mr. Thomas Jefferson Tobias, 1853. Rf: SFF298; EM26
Tobias, Augustus Levy. b. 1825, d. 1879, SC: 1825, f. Isaac Tobias, m. Isabella Cowen Tobias, mr. Sophia St. Amand Tobias, 1850. Rf: DR; SFF298; 1861C; W49.596; SCA1857–59; D1849, 1852, 1855, 1859
Tobias, Colleton H. b. 1831, d. 1862, SC: 1831, f. Isaac Tobias, m. Isabella Cowen Tobias. Rf: SFF298; W49.596; 1860C; D1852, 1855
Tobias, David D'Oliveira. b. 1804, d. 1874, SC: 1825, f. Joseph Tobias, m. Rachel Aarons Tobias, mr. Rachel Russell Tobias, 1820. Rf: SFF298; W33.1055; SCA1825–27
Tobias, David Henry. b. 1860, d. 1907, SC: 1860, f. Joseph Lopez Tobias, m. Rosa Hays Mordecai Tobias, mr. Teresa Fisher Tobias, 1892. Rf: SFF299
Tobias, Eleanor. b. 1857, d. 1857, SC: 1857, f. Joseph Lopez Tobias, m. Rosa Hays Mordecai Tobias. Rf: EC95; SFF299
Tobias, Eleanor (Lopez). b. 1803, d. 1880, SC: 1803, f. David Lopez, m. Priscilla Lopez, mr. Abraham Tobias, 1822. Rf: DR; EC86; SFF176, 298; W47.820; SCA1826–27; D1859
Tobias, Fanny. b. 1856, d. 1922, SC: 1856, f. Thomas Jefferson Tobias, m. Adelaide Hendricks Tobias. Rf: SFF298
Tobias, Henry. SC: 1841. Rf: E171; T41
Tobias, Hortensia. b. 1858, d. 1860, SC: 1858, f. Joseph Lopez Tobias, m. Rosa Hays Mordecai Tobias. Rf: DR; EC96; SFF299; 1860C
Tobias, Isaac. b. 1771, d. 1803, SC: 1797, f. Joseph Tobias, m. Judith Tobias. Rf: SFF298; T41; SCA1797–1801; D1802, 1803
Tobias, Isaac. b. 1796, d. 1860, SC: 1796, f. Joseph Tobias, m. Rachel Aarons Tobias, mr. Isabella Cowen Tobias, 1824. Rf: DR; EC111;

SFF298; W49.596 (his); E139, 171, 280; 1850C; SCA1833–53; D1835, 1838, 1849, 1852, 1859

Tobias, Isabel. b. 1855, d. 1925, SC: 1855, f. Joseph Lopez Tobias, m. Rosa Hays Mordecai Tobias. Rf: DR; SFF299; MR5P.228

Tobias, J. b. 1801, d. 1877, SC: 1801. Rf: DR

Tobias, Jacob. b. 1749, d. 1775, SC: 1767, f. Joseph Tobias, m. Leah D'Oliveira Tobias, mr. Rachel DaCosta, 1775. Rf: EM5; SFF298; E40, 279; W6.635; W18.1; *SCHM*1.135; *SCHM*2.92

Tobias, Jacob. b. 1786, d. 1811, f. Joseph Tobias, m. Rachel Aarons Tobias. Rf: SFF298

Tobias, Joseph. b. 1684, d. 1761, SC: 1737, mr. Leah D'Oliveira Tobias. Rf: SFF298; E24, 32, 33, 38, 40, 277, 279; W6.635; SCA1737–61; RB168

Tobias, Joseph. b. 1745, SC: 1762, f. Joseph Tobias, m. Leah D'Oliveira Tobias, mr. Judith Tobias. Rf: SFF298; W18.1; SCA1762; RB168

Tobias, Joseph. b. 1764, d. 1810, SC: 1764, f. Joseph Tobias, m. Judith Tobias, mr. Rachel Aarons Tobias, 1785. Rf: SFF298; E40, 120, 139, 279; EM6; T41; EP; W33.1055; 1790C; 1810C; D1794

Tobias, Joseph. SC: 1790, f. Joseph Tobias, m. Rachel Aarons Tobias. Rf: SFF298; D1790, 1801

Tobias, Joseph Lopez. b. 1825, d. 1893, SC: 1825, f. Abraham Tobias, m. Eleanor Lopez Tobias, mr. Rosa Hays Mordecai Tobias, 1855. Rf: DR; EC95; EM27; SFF298, 299; W47.820; 1860C; D1849, 1852, 1855, 1859

Tobias, Judith. SC: 1798, f. Joseph Tobias, m. Leah D'Oliveira Tobias. Rf: SFF298; W6.635

Tobias, Judith. d. 1816, SC: 1806, mr. Joseph Tobias. Rf: SFF298; W33.1055; D1806, 1807, 1809, 1813

Tobias, Judith. b. 1798, f. Joseph Tobias, m. Rachel Aarons Tobias. Rf: SFF298

Tobias, Leah (D'Oliveira). b. 1715, d. 1778, SC: 1751, f. Jacob D'Oliveira, m. Judica Velma D'Oliveira, mr. Joseph Tobias. Rf: SFF298; W6.635; W18.1

Tobias, Marion J. b. 1835, d. 1836, SC: 1835, f. Isaac Tobias, m. Isabella Cowen Tobias. Rf: EC110; SFF298

Tobias, Masoad. b. 1740, d. 1798, f. Joseph Tobias, m. Leah D'Oliveira Tobias. Rf: SFF298; E32, 40, 279

Tobias, Masoad. b. 1801, f. Joseph Tobias, m. Rachel Aarons Tobias. Rf: SFF298

Tobias, Orlando Joseph. d. 1852, f. David D'Oliveira Tobias, m. Rachel Russell Tobias, mr. Virginia Judith Nathans Tobias, 1850. Rf: SFF298

Tobias, Rachel (Aarons). b. 1761, d. 1828, SC: 1785, f. Jacob Aarons, mr. Joseph Tobias, 1785. Rf: DR; SFF1, 298; EM6; W33.1055

Tobias, Rachel (DaCosta). SC: 1775, mr. Jacob Tobias, 1775. Rf: EM5; SFF298

Tobias, Rachel (Russell). b. 1798, d.

1887, f. Philip Moses Russell, m. Esther Mordecai Russell, mr. David D'Oliveira Tobias, 1820. Rf: SFF298

Tobias, Rinah. b. 1788, SC: 1810, f. Joseph Tobias, m. Rachel Aarons Tobias. Rf: SFF298; W33.1055; SCA1810

Tobias, Rosa Hays (Mordecai). b. 1832, d. 1897, SC: 1832, f. Moses Cohen Mordecai, m. Isabel Rebecca Lyons Mordecai, mr. Joseph Lopez Tobias, 1855. Rf: DR; SFF203, 298, 299; EC95; EM27; 1850C; 1860C

Tobias, S. J. SC: 1855. Rf: D1855

Tobias, Solomon. b. 1791, SC: 1816, f. Joseph Tobias, m. Rachel Aarons Tobias, mr. Margaret McManus Tobias. Rf: SFF298

Tobias, Thomas Jefferson. b. 1830, d. 1878, SC: 1830, f. Abraham Tobias, m. Eleanor Lopez Tobias, mr. Adelaide Justina Hendricks Tobias, 1853. Rf: DR; EC95; EM26; SFF298; W47.820; D1852, 1859

Tobias, Virginius Jenkins. b. 1827, d. 1895, SC: 1827, f. Isaac Tobias, m. Isabella Cowen Tobias, mr. Josephine Pope Tobias, 1863. Rf: SFF298; 1850C; D1849, 1852, 1855, 1859

Tongue, Abraham. SC: 1802. Rf: E139, 142; D1807

Tongues, Mark. SC: 1792. Rf: E117, 122; 1790C; D1794

Torres, Abraham. b. 1755, d. 1829, SC: 1799, mr. Sarah D'Aquilar Torres, 1800. Rf: DR; EP; 1820C; E139, 154; EM7; SCA1799–1810; D1803, 1806, 1807; RB169

Torres, Benjamin. SC: 1798. Rf: EC109; RB169

Torres, Sarah (D'Aquilar). SC: 1800, mr. Abraham Torres, 1800. Rf: EM7; MR3P.380; SCA1801

Tourne, Esther (Jackson). b. 1814, d. 1896, SC: 1814, f. Montague Jackson, m. Hannah Hyams Jackson, mr. Joseph Etienne Tourne, 1837. Rf: SFF119

Trager, Eva (Jacobs). b. 1857, SC: 1860, f. Henry Samuel Jacobs, m. Julia Matilda Lyon Jacobs. Rf: SFF134; 1860C

Triest, Caroline. b. 1808, d. 1878, SC: 1856, mr. Joseph Triest. Rf: DR; EC39; W49.609

Triest, Joseph. b. 1809, d. 1891, SC: 1855, mr. Caroline Triest. Rf: DR; EC39; E171, 237; D1855, 1859

Triest, Maier. b. 1831, d. 1894, SC: 1850. Rf: DR; E171, 235, 262, 266; EC39; 1850C; D1852, 1855, 1859

Triest, S. Rf: E171

Uhlman, J. H. b. 1827, d. 1845, SC: 1845. Rf: E171; EP

Valance, Moses. SC: 1801. Rf: E140

Valentine, Abraham O. SC: 1806. Rf: E140; SCA1806

Valentine, B. SC: 1839. Rf: Min. April 14, 1839

Valentine, David. SC: 1711. Rf: *Valentine v. Valentine*, JR1711–1712

Valentine, Emanuel. b. 1826, d. 1880, SC: 1826, f. Samuel Valentine, m. Fanny Mairs Valentine. Rf: DR; EC51; SFF184

Valentine, Fanny (Mairs). b. 1807, d. 1870, SC: 1807, f. Simon Mairs, m. Elizabeth Mairs, mr. Samuel Valentine, 1823. Rf: DR; EC88; EM13; SFF184; EP

Valentine, Isaac D. b. 1833, d. 1862, SC: 1859, f. Samuel Valentine, m. Fanny Mairs Valentine. Rf: EC88; SFF184; E171; D1859

Valentine, Isabel. d. 1860, SC: 1860. Rf: EC94

Valentine, Israel. b. 1824, d. 1850, SC: 1824, f. Samuel Valentine, m. Fanny Mairs Valentine. Rf: DR; EC87; SFF184; 1850C

Valentine, Jacob. b. 1829, d. 1891, SC: 1829, f. Samuel Valentine, m. Fanny Mairs Valentine, mr. Louise Valentine. Rf: SFF184; E171, 207, 236; EP; D1849, 1855

Valentine, Judith. SC: 1696, mr. Simon Valentine. Rf: EL; RB171

Valentine, Miriam (Levin). mr. N. Hertz Valentine, 1864. Rf: SFF184; MS19.549

Valentine, N. Hertz [Hertz N.]. b. 1833, d. 1873, SC: 1833, f. Samuel Valentine, m. Fanny Mairs Valentine, mr. Miriam Valentine, 1864. Rf: DR; SFF184; T41; EP; EC50; MS19.549; D1859

Valentine, P. SC: 1844. Rf: *Occident*, 2, p. 164

Valentine, Samuel. b. 1794, d. 1868, SC: 1818, mr. Fanny Mairs Valentine, 1823. Rf: DR; EC88; EM13; SFF184; 1850C; 1861C; E140, 171, 246; T41; SCA1838–39; D1822, 1829, 1831, 1835, 1838, 1841, 1849, 1855, 1859

Valentine, Simon. SC: 1696, mr. Judith Valentine. Rf: EL; *FSSC*327; WIM(1694–1704).129, 362, 428; SCA1696–1711

Vanderveri, Rebecca. b. 1798, d. 1825, SC: 1825. Rf: DR

Vasaski, A. SC: 1861. Rf: Min. Sept. 3, 1861

Vierga, Joseph [Vierra]. b. 1744, d. 1821, SC: 1780; Rf: DR; D1803, 1806, 1809

Waage, Mordecai G. SC: 1802. Rf: E140; T41

Walters, J. SC: 1820. Rf: E172; 1820C; Min. April 14, 1839

Warburg, Levy. SC: 1795. Rf: RB173

Warner, Caroline. b. 1815, SC: 1815. Rf: 1850C

Warner, Jane (Hart). b. 1795, d. 1858, SC: 1795, f. Daniel Hart, m. Bella Levy Hart, mr. William Warner, 1814. Rf: EC34; EM10; SFF99; 1850C; W48.277 (hers)

Warner, William. b. 1778, d. 1848, SC: 1814, mr. Jane Hart Warner, 1814. Rf: EM10; SFF99; 1820C; W48.277; EC34; CB1814; SCA1820; D1819

Waterman, S. A. SC: 1821. Rf: E140; CB1821

Weill, A. mr. Caroline Weill. Rf: EC107

Weill, Alphons Charleston. b. 1851, d. 1854, SC: 1851, f. A. Weill, m. Caroline Weill. Rf: EC107

Weill, Caroline. mr. A. Weill. Rf: EC107

Weinberg, Aaron. b. 1842, SC: 1842, f. B. A. Weinberg, m. Fanny Weinberg. Rf: 1850C

Weinberg, Abraham. b. 1846, SC:

1846, f. B. A. Weinberg, m. Fanny Weinberg. Rf: 1850C

Weinberg, Amelia. b. 1847, SC: 1847, f. B. A. Weinberg, m. Fanny Weinberg. Rf: 1850C

Weinberg, B. A. b. 1800, d. 1890, SC: 1848, mr. Fanny Weinberg. Rf: DR; 1850C; CB1848

Weinberg, Bertha. b. 1785, d. 1874, SC: 1785. Rf: DR

Weinberg, Caroline. b. 1848, SC: 1848, f. B. A. Weinberg, m. Fanny Weinberg. Rf: 1850C

Weinberg, Fanny. b. 1828, d. 1878, SC: 1843, mr. B. A. Weinberg. Rf: DR; EBS9; 1850C; 1861C

Weinberg, Isaac. b. 1850, SC: 1850, f. B. A. Weinberg, m. Fanny Weinberg. Rf: 1850C

Weinberg, Lizzie. b. 1858, d. 1880. Rf: EBS9

Weinberg, W. SC: 1843. Rf: *State v. Ancker*

Weinburg, Joseph L. b. 1858, d. 1859, SC: 1859. Rf: EBS9

Weinglass, Lewis. b. 1803, SC: 1850. Rf: 1850C

Weinnerman, Philip. SC: 1849. Rf: Min. Jan. 7, 1849

Weisbein, Rebecca C. (Hertz). b. 1852, SC: 1860, f. Isaac Eger Hertz, m. Nellie Sheftall Cohen Hertz, mr. David Weisbein, 1875. Rf: SFF36, 117; 1860C

Weiskopf, Anna. b. 1859, SC: 1859, f. Leopold Weiskopf, m. Rose Weiskopf. Rf: 1860C

Weiskopf, Bertha. b. 1856, SC: 1856, f. Leopold Weiskopf, m. Rose Weiskopf. Rf: 1860C

Weiskopf, David. b. 1854, SC: 1854, f. Leopold Weiskopf, m. Rose Weiskopf. Rf: 1860C

Weiskopf, Henry. b. 1852, SC: 1852, f. Leopold Weiskopf, m. Rose Weiskopf. Rf: 1860C

Weiskopf, Leopold. b. 1816, SC: 1851, mr. Rose Weiskopf. Rf: E238; T41; 1860C; 1861C; *Courier* Dec. 11, 1861

Weiskopf, Rose. b. 1829, SC: 1860, mr. Leopold Weiskopf. Rf: 1860C

Weiskopf, Samuel. b. 1857, SC: 1857, f. Leopold Weiskopf, m. Rose Weiskopf. Rf: 1860C

Weissenberger, ———. SC: 1818. Rf: E140

Wells, Miriam (Labatt). f. Abraham Cohen Labatt, m. Caroline Hyams Labatt, mr. J. B. Wells II. Rf: SFF119, 148

Wesel, D. V. SC: 1839. Rf: Min. April 14, 1839; E172

Wetherhahn, Abraham [Wetherhorn]. b. 1845, SC: 1845, f. Marcus Wetherhahn. Rf: 1850C

Wetherhahn, Bertha. mr. Marcus Wetherhahn. Rf: EC95

Wetherhahn, Henry. b. 1847, SC: 1847, f. Marcus Wetherhahn. Rf: 1850C

Wetherhahn, J. Rf: E237

Wetherhahn, L. b. 1838, SC: 1850, f. Marcus Wetherhahn. Rf: 1850C

Wetherhahn, Leopold. b. 1842, d. 1910. Rf: DR

Wetherhahn, Levy. b. 1842, SC: 1842, f. Marcus Wetherhahn. Rf: E236, 266; 1850C

Wetherhahn, Marcus. b. 1812, d. 1873, SC: 1838, mr. Bertha Wetherhorn. Rf: DR; EC95;

1850C; 1861C, Min. Sept. 3, 1861

Wetherhahn, Pena. b. 1842, d. 1915. Rf: DR

Wetherhahn, Philip. b. 1830, d. 1897, SC: 1859, f. Marcus Wetherhahn. Rf: EBS9; 1850C; D1859

Wetherhahn, Sarah. b. 1826, d. 1904. Rf: DR

Wetherhahn, Sigmund M. b. 1858, d. 1891, SC: 1858. Rf: EBS9

Wetherhahn, Sipporah. b. 1805, d. 1855, SC: 1855, mr. Marcus Weatherhahn. Rf: DR; EC94

Wetherhahn, Solomon. SC: 1861. Rf: E237

Whippey, Catherine Francis. b. 1834, d. 1858, SC: 1858, mr. Cornelius Francis Whippey. Rf: DR; EC111; W49.650

Whippey, Cornelius Frances. SC: 1858, mr. Catherine Frances Whippey. Rf: DR; EC111; W49.650

Williams, Annie (Mordecai). b. 1853, SC: 1853, f. Benjamin Mordecai, m. Clara Polock Mordecai, mr. Charles J. Williams. Rf: SFF202; 1860C

Williams, Rebecca. b. 1769, d. 1820, SC: 1820. Rf: DR

Wineberg, ———. b. 1843, d. 1844, SC: 1844, f. B. Wineberg, m. Janetta Wineberg. Rf: EP

Wineberg, Janetta (Nachman). b. 1825, d. 1844, SC: 1844, f. Abraham Nachman, m. Sprinse Nachman, mr. B. Wineberg. Rf: DR; EC25

Wineman, Laura Louise (Jacobs). b. 1826, d. 1909, SC: 1850, f. Myer Jacobs, m. Rebecca Lazarus Jacobs, mr. Philip Wineman, 1852. Rf: DR; EM26; SFF132; EC6; 1850C; 1860C

Wineman, Philip. b. 1825, d. 1895, SC: 1851, mr. Laura Louisa Jacobs Wineman, 1852. Rf: DR; EM26; SFF132; E172, 238, 262, 264; T41; 1860C; *Courier* Dec. 11, 1861; D1855

Wineman, Philip. b. 1854, SC: 1854, f. Philip Wineman, m. Laura Louise Jacobs Wineman. Rf: 1860C

Winstock, M. b. 1825, SC: 1850. Rf: 1850C

Winstock, Rebecca. d. 1860, SC: 1860. Rf: EBS9

Wittkowsky, Susan (Hyams). b. 1841, SC: 1841, f. Moses David Hyams, m. Susanna Jackson Hyams, mr. Adolph Wittkowsky. Rf: SFF120; W51.842; EC37; 1850C; 1860C

Wolf, ———. [Mrs.]. b. 1789, d. 1834, SC: 1834. Rf: DR

Wolf, Jacob. b. 1839, d. 1864. Rf: EBS9

Wolf, Pauline. SC: 1860. Rf: Min. Feb. 13, 1860

Wolf, Sarah. b. 1823, d. 1824, SC: 1823. Rf: DR

Wolfe, Anna. b. 1858, SC: 1858, f. Simon Wolfe, m. Sarah Wolfe. Rf: 1860C

Wolfe, Benjamin. b. 1791, d. 1827, SC: 1827. Rf: DR

Wolfe, Caroline. b. 1860, SC: 1860, f. Simon Wolfe, m. Sarah Wolfe. Rf: 1860C

Wolfe, Cordelia. b. 1820, SC: 1820. Rf: 1850C

Wolfe, Esther. b. 1837, d. 1891, SC: 1860, mr. Simon Wolfe. Rf: EJCO2; 1860C

Wolfe, Jacob. SC: 1769. Rf: *SCHM*65.205–71

Wolfe, Sarah (Cohen). b. 1827, d. 1892, SC: 1827, f. Hartwig Cohen, m. Deborah Marks Cohen, mr. Saling Wolfe, 1845. Rf: EJCC10; EM10; SFF34, 304

Wolfe, Simon. b. 1814, d. 1884, SC: 1860, mr. Sarah Wolfe. Rf: DR; 1861C; EJCO2; EP

Woolf, Catherine. SC: 1832. Rf: SCA1832; MS11.146, D1832

Woolf, Cecile (Mordecai). b. 1848, SC: 1848, f. Benjamin Mordecai, m. Clara Polock Mordecai, mr. Henry M. Woolf. Rf: SFF202; 1860C

Woolf, Clarence Reuben. b. 1838, d. 1867, SC: 1838, f. Isaac Woolf, m. Sarah Moses Woolf. Rf: DR; SFF305; W45.682; 1850C

Woolf, Emma C. SC: 1846, f. Isaac Woolf, m. Sarah Moses Woolf. Rf: SFF305; W45.682

Woolf, Henry. SC: 1790. Rf: E280; 1790C; MR3I.74; SCA1797–99; D1794, 1796

Woolf, Isaac. b. 1782, d. 1870, SC: 1806, f. Jacob Woolf, m. Sarah Woolf, mr. Sarah Moses Woolf, 1809. Rf: DR; EM10; SFF213, 305; W45.682; T41; EC46; 1830C; 1840C; 1850C; 1861C; SCA1809–43; D1831, 1835, 1838, 1841, 1849, 1855

Woolf, J. C. SC: 1794. Rf: SCA1794

Woolf, Levi. b. 1810, d. 1810, SC: 1810. Rf: EC44; SFF305

Woolf, Miriam. SC: 1814. Rf: SCA1814

Woolf, Rachel (Andrews) (Moses). b. 1753, d. 1835, SC: 1790, f. Abraham Andrews, mr. Myer Moses, mr2. Solomon Wool, 1789. Rf: DR; EC19; SFF12, 205; EP; 1790C; 1800C; SCA1792–1830; D1790, 1801, 1802, 1803, 1806, 1807, 1831, 1835

Woolf, Ralph. SC: 1834, f. Isaac Woolf, m. Sarah Moses Woolf, mr. Cordelia Harris Woolf, 1837. Rf: SFF94, 305; EM16; E172; SCA1834–37; MS13.338; D1835, 1838

Woolf, Rebecca. SC: 1830. Rf: 1830C; 1840C; SCA1830–34; D1831

Woolf, Sarah. b. 1738, d. 1831, SC: 1799. Rf: EC46; SCA1799–1829; D1831

Woolf, Sarah (Moses). b. 1792, d. 1869, SC: 1829, f. Solomon Moses, m. Rachel Miriam (Mary) Moses, mr. Isaac Woolf, 1809. Rf: DR; EC46; EM10; SFF213, 305; 1850C; 1861C; D1829, 1831, 1835, 1838

Woolf, Solomon. SC: 1783, mr. Rachel Andrews Moses Woolf, 1789. Rf: SFF12, 205; "House Journal, 1783–1784, pp. 84, 253; SFF12, 205; E280; MS1.450; W28.354; W22.191; SCA1784–92; RB174

Woolf, Solomon Jackson. b. 1829, d. 1830, SC: 1829, f. Isaac Woolf, m. Sarah Moses Woolf. Rf: DR; SFF305

Woolf, Theodosia. b. 1820, d. 1824, f. Isaac Woolf, m. Sarah Moses Woolf. Rf: SFF305

Woolf, Theodosia Rodolph. b. 1833, d. 1838, f. Isaac Woolf, m. Sarah Moses Woolf. Rf: SFF305

Wright, Eliza (Marks). SC: 1822, f. Joseph Marks, m. Eliza Hyams Marks, mr. Alexander Walter Wright, 1822. Rf: *SP*, Nov. 12, 1822

Zachariah, Amelia. SC: 1850, mr. Jonathan Zachariah. Rf: 1850C

Zachariah, Jonathan. b. 1798, SC: 1850, mr. Amelia Zachariah. Rf: E172, 237; W45.682; 1850C; EM1; *Courier* Dec. 11, 1861

Zacharias, Ephraim P. SC: 1855. Rf: *BS-BI*; 1860C

Zacharias, Esther. SC: 1860. Rf: 1860C

Zacharias, Hanchen. SC: 1860. Rf: 1860C

Zacharias, Isidore. SC: 1849. Rf: 1860C; D1849

Zacharias, Jane. SC: 1860. Rf: 1860C

Zacharias, Mina. SC: 1860. Rf: 1860C

Zacharias, Moses L. b. 1831, d. 1867, SC: 1860, mr. Yetta Zacharias. Rf: EBS10; 1860C; 1861C

Zacharias, R. d. 1858, SC: 1858. Rf: EBS10

Zacharias, Robert. SC: 1860. Rf: 1860C

Zacharias, Rosa Sally. b. 1849, d. 1858, SC: 1858. Rf: EBS10

Zacharias, Rosalia. b. 1820, d. 1896, SC: 1860. Rf: EBS10; 1860C

Zacharias, Selig. b. 1821, d. 1893, SC: 1861. Rf: DR; EBS10; 1860C; 1861C

Zacharias, Simon. SC: 1860. Rf: 1860C

Zacharias, Solomon. d. 1858, SC: 1858. Rf: EBS10

Zacharias, Yetta. b. 1831, SC: 1860, mr. Moses Zacharias. Rf: 1860C

Zemach, Abraham. SC: 1801. Rf: E140

Glossary

Although some of these terms would be known to people of the Jewish faith, people of other religions might not be familiar with their meanings. In addition, several are used by Sephardic Jews only, especially words such as *adjunta* and *yahid*.

Hebrew plurals are generally indicated by the suffix *-im* or *-ot*.

adjunta, ajunta, junta—governing body; trustees of a synagogue; vestry

adjunto, ajunto, junto—member of a board of trustees

anno mundi—(Latin) in the year of the world; date from creation

Bet Din, Beth Din (House of Judgment)—an ecclesiastical court

gabbai, gabbay—treasurer

haham—rabbi

hazan—reader; leader of prayers; minister

heikhal—ark; cabinet where scrolls are kept

mikva, mikvah—ritual bath

Minhag Sephardim—the Sephardic form of worship

minyan—ten males over the age of thirteen needed for prayers

Mishnah—ancient compilation of Jewish law

mohel—one who performs circumcisions

parnas, parnass—president of congregation

rabbi—my master; my teacher

Rosh ha-Shanah—New Year

Shabat, Shabbat—Sabbath

shamas, shamass—sexton; beadle

Sh'ma—Deuteronomy 6:4: "Hear, O Israel, the Lord Our God is One."

shofar—ram's horn

shohet—ritual butcher

shomar, shomer—watchman

taba(h), Teba(h)—reading desk

Talmud—rabbinical interpretations of Mishnah

Torah—the five books of Moses

yahid, yachid, yechid—member of a congregation with the right to vote

Yom Kippur—Day of Atonement

Bibliography

UNPUBLISHED SOURCES

American Jewish Archives, Cincinnati, Ohio

Circular of Beth Elohim to Amsterdam for Rebuilding in 1838.

Descendants of David Lopez and Priscilla Moses.

Frances Sheftall to Mordecai Sheftall, March 3, 1780; August 20, 1780.

Isaac DaCosta to Aaron Lopez, December 24, 1761; September 24, October 23, December 22, 1762; January 11 April 12, 1763; July 19, 1764, Lopez Papers.

Isaac Harby to John C. Calhoun, July 26, 1815.

Jacobi Genealogy by Svend Jacobi.

John Joachim Zubly to Isaac DaCosta, [1770].

Leopold Weiskopf to Jacob Weiskopf, February 23, 1851.

Letter of Abigail Minis, January 15, 1780.

Letter of Frances Sheftall, no date.

Letters from Bevis Marks to the Parnassim of Beth Elohim, March 19, May 8, July 3, 25, 1806. Extracts from Congregation Bevis Marks Relating to American Jewish Synagogue Affairs, 1806–1838.

Minutes of the Trustees of the New Burial Ground, Charleston, S.C., 1798.

Payroll Records of Samuel Marks during His Service in the Revolutionary War, South Carolina, 1779–1780.

Sketch of DeLeon Family by Perry DeLeon.

Yates, Samuel and Lazarus Families, Manuscript History.

American Jewish Historical Society, Waltham, Massachusetts.

Minutes of a meeting of Isaac DaCosta, Abraham DaCosta, Isaac DaCosta, Jr., Isaac DeLeon, and Jacob Tobias, January 25, 1775.

Beth Elohim Archives, Charleston, South Carolina

Cash Book, 1800, 1801, 1803–1814, 1805, 1807, 1809, 1811, 1814,

1815, 1819, 1823, 1848–1861, 1852–1853.
Minute Book, 1838–1843, 1846–1852, 1857–1866.

Brown University, Providence, Rhode Island

Brown University Papers.

Charleston County, Charleston, South Carolina

Death Records.
McCrady Plats.
Probate Inventories.
Register of Mesne Conveyance Books.
Will Books.

National Archives, Washington, D.C.

Census Reports, 1800, 1810, 1820, 1830, 1840, 1850, 1860.
Pension Applications.

Public Record Office, London, England

Shaftesbury Papers.

South Carolina Archives, Columbia, South Carolina

Accounts Audited of Claims Growing out of the Revolution.
Bills of Sale.
Charleston District, Court of Common Pleas, Judgement Rolls.
Colonial Plats.
Conveyances.
Court of Appeals, Petitions to Practice Law.
Court of Appeals in Equity, Petitions to Practice Law.
Court of Appeals in Law, Petitions to Practice Law.
Court of Common Pleas, Judgement Rolls.
Court of Common Pleas, Summary Process Rolls.
Court of Equity, Petitions to Practice Law.
Court of General Sessions, Bills of Indictment.
General Assembly Papers, Petitions.
Land Grants, Colonial Series.
Marriage Settlements.
Memorials.
Miscellaneous Records.
Mortgages.
Register of Limited Partnerships.
Renunciations of Dower.
Wills, Inventories, and Miscellaneous Records.

South Carolina Historical Society, Charleston, South Carolina

Diary of Jacob F. Schirmer.

South Caroliniana Library, Columbia, South Carolina

A. Ottolengui to Judge Bay, October 9, 1829.
William Joseph Holt Papers.

PUBLISHED SOURCES

Periodicals

Charleston Evening News, Charleston, S.C.
Charleston Gazette, Charleston, S.C.
City Gazette, Charleston, S.C.
City Gazette & Commercial Daily Advertiser, Charleston, S.C.
Courier, Charleston, S.C.
Daily Courier, Charleston, S.C.

Gazette of the State of South-Carolina, Charleston, S.C.
Jewish Chronicle, London, England.
Literary Chronicle and Weekly Review, London, England.
Mercury, Charleston, S.C.
News and Courier, Charleston, S.C.
New York Gazette, New York, New York.
Occident and American Jewish Advocate, Philadelphia, Pa.
Rembrancer, London, England.
Royal Gazette, Charleston, S.C.
Royal South-Carolina Gazette, Charleston, S.C.
South-Carolina and American General Gazette, Charleston, S.C.
South-Carolina Gazette, Charleston, S.C.
South-Carolina Gazette and Country Journal, Charleston, S.C.
South-Carolina Gazette and General Advertiser, Charleston, S.C.
South Carolina State Gazette & Timothy & Mason's Daily Advertiser, Charleston, S.C.
South-Carolina Weekly Gazette, Charleston, S.C.
Southern Patriot, Charleston, S.C.
Sunday Times and Noah's Weekly Messenger, New York, New York.
Times, Charleston, S.C.
Universal Magazine, London, England.

City Directories

Baggett, J. H. *Directory of the City of Charleston for the Year 1852*. Charleston, S.C., 1851.
Clarke's Charleston Directory; With a Large and Elegant Plan of the City. Charleston, S.C., 1796.
Cromwell, O. *Directory or Guide to the Residences and Places of Business of the Inhabitants of the City of Charleston and its Environs for the Year 1829*. Charleston, S.C., 1829.
Dowling, Daniel J. *The Charleston Directory; and Register for 1835–1836*. Charleston, S.C., 1835.
———. *Register for 1837 and 1838*. Charleston, S.C., 1837.
Elizer, Eleazer. *A Directory for 1803*. Charleston, S.C., 1803.
Fay, T. C. *Charleston Directory and Stranger's Guide for 1840 and 1841*. Charleston, S.C., 1840.
Folker, Joseph. *A Directory of the City and District of Charleston: And Stranger's Guide*. Charleston, S.C., 1813.
Gazlay, David M. *The Charleston City and General Business Directory for 1855*. Charleston, S.C., 1855.
Goldsmith, Morris. *Directory and Strangers' Guide for the City of Charleston and its Vicinity From the Fifth Census of the United States*. Charleston, S.C., 1831.
Honour, John H. *A Directory of the City of Charleston and Neck for 1849*. Charleston, S.C., 1849.
Hrabowski, Richard. *Directory for the District of Charleston*. Charleston, S.C., 1809.
Mears and Turnbill, *Charleston Directory Containing the Names of the Inhabitants*. Charleston, S.C., 1859.
Milligan, Jacob. *The Charleston Directory and Revenue System*. Charleston, S.C., 1790.
———. *The Charleston Directory.* Charleston, S.C., 1794.
Motte, Abraham. *Charleston Directory and Strangers' Guide for the Year 1816*. Charleston, S.C., 1816.

Negrin, J. J. *Negrin's Directory and Almanac for the Year 1806*. Charleston, S.C., 1806.

———. *Negrin's Directory for the Year 1807*. Charleston, S.C., 1807.

———. *New Charleston Directory and Stranger's Guide, for the Year 1802*. Charleston, S.C., 1802.

Nelson, John Nixon. *Nelson's Charleston Directory, and Strangers Guide for 1801*. Charleston, S.C., 1801.

Schenck, James R., and Charles H. Turner. *Directory and Stranger's* Guide for *the City of Charleston. Also Directory for Charleston Neck for the Year 1819*. Charleston, S.C., 1819.

———. *The Directory and Stranger's Guide, for the City of Charleston; Also a Directory for Charleston Neck for the Year 1822*. Charleston, S.C., 1822.

Tobler, John. *South-Carolina Almanack, for the Year of Our Lord 1782; Being Second After Leap Year. Containing the Lunations; Eclipses; Rising and Setting of the Sun; Rising and Setting of the Moon and Stars: Aspects: Judgement of the Weather, &tc, &tc, &tc*. Charleston, S.C., 1782.

———. *South Carolina and Georgia Almanack for 1785*. Charleston, S.C., 1784.

ARTICLES AND BOOKS

Acts of Privy Council of England, Colonial Series. Vol. 4. London, 1911.

Adams, Francis Colburn. *Manuel Pereira; or, The Sovereign Rule of South Carolina. With Views of Southern Laws, Life, and Hospitality*. n.p., 1853.

Adams, Hannah. *History of the Jews from the Destruction of Jerusalem to the Nineteenth Century*. 2 vols. Boston, 1812.

Alexander, Henry Aaron. *Notes on the Alexander Family of South Carolina and Georgia and Connections*. Atlanta, 1954.

Altman, Alexander. *Moses Mendelssohn: A Biographical Study*. London, 1973.

Anderson, J. Perrin. "Public Education in Ante-bellum South Carolina." *Proceedings of the South Carolina Historical Association* (1933), 3–11.

Andreano, Ralph Louis, and Herbert D. Werner. "Charleston Loyalists: A Statistical Note." *South Carolina Historical Magazine* 60 (1959): 164–68.

"The Appeal Case of the Charleston Congregation in the Case of the State ex Relatione A. Ottolengui, vs. G. V. Ancker and others. —Charleston, Feb. —1846." *Occident* 3 (1845–46): 615–26; 4 (1846–47): 50–55, 157–62.

Archdale, John. *A New Description of That Fertile And Pleasant Province of Carolina*. London, 1707.

Ash, John. *The Present State of Affairs in Carolina*. London, 1706. Reprinted in A. S. Salley, *Narratives of Early Carolina, 1650–1708*, pp. 269–76. New York, 1911.

"B. Mordecai v. M. J. Jacobi, January, 1859." *Reports of Cases at Law, Argued and Determined in the Court of Appeals and Court of Errors of South Carolina. From January, 1859; to May, 1860; Both Inclusive,* ed. J. S. G. Richardson, 12:547–49. Charleston, S.C., 1860.

Baldwin, Agnes Leland. *First Settlers of*

South Carolina, 1670–1700. Easley, S.C., 1985.

Bancroft, Frederic. *Slave Trading in the Old South.* Baltimore, 1931.

Bargar, B. D. *Royal South Carolina, 1719–1763.* Columbia, S.C., 1970.

Barnwell, Joseph W. "The Evacuation of Charleston by the British in 1782." *South Carolina Historical Magazine* 11 (Jan. 1910): 1–26.

Barnwell, Robert Woodward, Jr. "Addressers of Clinton and Arbuthnot." *Proceedings of the South Carolina Historical Society* (1939): 44.

"Benevolent Society." *Occident* 5 (1847–48): 310.

Benjamin, I. J. *Three Years in America, 1859–62.* 2 vols. Philadelphia, 1956.

Bennett, John. *Apothecaries' Hall: A Unique Exhibit at the Charleston Museum. An Ancient Drug-Shop Whose Business Survived Plagues, War, Great Fires, and Earthquakes.* Charleston, S.C., 1923.

Benwell, J. *An Englishman's Travels in America: His Observances of Life and Manners in the Free and Slave States.* London, 1853.

Berman, Jeremiah J. "The Trend in Jewish Religious Observances in Mid-Nineteenth Century America." *Publications of the American Jewish Historical Society* 37 (1947): 31–53.

Blau, Joseph L. *Judaism in America: From Curiosity to Third Faith.* Chicago, 1976.

———. *Modern Varieties of Judaism.* New York, 1964.

Blau, Joseph L., and Salo W. Baron. *The Jews of the United States: A Documentary History, 1790–1840.* New York, 1965.

Breibart, Solomon. "Penina Moïse, Southern Jewish Poetess." In *Jews of the South: Selected Essays from the Southern Jewish Historical Society,* ed. Samuel Proctor and Louis Schmier, pp. 31–41. Macon, Ga., 1984.

———. "The Rev. Mr. Gustavus Poznanski: First American Jewish Reform Minister." Charleston, S.C., 1979. Pamphlet.

———. "Some Places in Charleston, S.C. of Jewish Interest." n.p., n.d. Pamphlet.

———. "The Synagogues of Kahal Kadosh Beth Elohim, Charleston." *South Carolina Historical Magazine* 80 (1974): 215–35.

———. "Two Jewish Congregations in Charleston, S.C., before 1791: A New Conclusion." *American Jewish History* 69 (1980): 360–63.

Brewster, Lawrence Fay. *Summer Migrations and Resorts of South Carolina Low-Country Planters.* Durham, N.C., 1947.

Brigham, Clarence Saunders. *History and Bibliography of American Newspapers, 1690–1820.* New York, 1947.

Brith Shalom Beth Israel: 130th Anniversary, 30th Anniversary Merger, January 13, 1985, 20 Teveth, 5745. Charleston, S.C., 1985.

Buchler, Joseph. "The Struggle for Unity: Attempts at Union in American Jewish Life, 1654–1868." *American Jewish Archives* 2 (1949): 21–46.

Calhoun, Jeanne A., Martha A. Zierden, and Elizabeth A. Paysinger. "The Geographical Spread of Charleston's Mercantile Community, 1732–1767." *South Carolina Historical Magazine* 86 (1985): 182–220.

Cardozo, Isaac N. *A Discourse Delivered in Charleston (S.C.) on the 21st Of Nov. 1827 Before the Reformed Society of Israelites for Promoting True Principles of Judaism According to Its Purity and Spirit*. Charleston, S.C., 1827

Cardozo, Jacob N. "The Congregation Beth Elohim." *Occident* 9 (1851–52): 313–22.

———. *Notes on Political Economy.* Charleston, S.C., 1826.

———. *An Oration on the Literary Character. Delivered on the Anniversary of the Methulogic Society, 1st October 1811*. Charleston, S.C., 1811.

———. *A Plan of Financial Relief. Addressed to the Legislature of Georgia and Confederate States Congress*. Atlanta, 1863.

———. "Political Economy—Rent." *Southern Review,* February 1828; pp. 192–218.

———. *Reminiscences of Charleston.* Charleston, S.C., 1866.

———. *The Tariff: Its True Character and Effects Practically Illustrated*. Charleston, S.C., 1830.

Carolina Art Association. *American Jewish Art and History in the South, 1697–1900. Presented by the Carolina Art Association and the Charleston Arrangements Committee in Honor of the Sixty-Second Annual Meeting of the American Jewish Historical Society.* Charleston, S.C., 1964.

Carvalho, Emanuel Nunes. *A Key to the Hebrew Tongue*. Philadelphia, 1815.

Carvalho, Solomon N. "The Congregation Beth Elohim of Charleston." *Occident* 9 (1851–52): 203–8, 354–65.

———. *Incidents of Travel and Adventure in the Far West: with Col. Fremont's Last Expedition Across the Rocky Mountains; Including Three Months Residence in Utah and a Perilous Trip Across the Great American Desert, to the Pacific*. New York, 1857.

Catalogue of the Medical Graduates of the University of Pennsylvania. Philadelphia, 1839.

Catterall, Helen Tunnicliff. *Judicial Cases Concerning American Slavery and the Negro.* 4 vols. Washington, D.C., 1926–36.

Centennial Memorial of the Medical College of the State of South Carolina, 1824–1924. Charleston, S.C., 1924.

"Charity Sermon by the Rev. S. Jacobs." *Occident* 10 (1852–53): 414.

Charleston Section, Council of Jewish Women. *Secular and Religious Works of Penina Moïse*. Charleston, S.C., 1911.

Chomsky, William. "Hebrew Grammar and Textbook Writing in Early Nineteenth-Century America." In *Essays in American Jewish History,* ed. Bertram Korn, pp. 123–45. Cincinnati, 1958.

Chyet, Stanley F. "The Political Rights of the Jew in the United States, 1776–1840." *American Jewish Archives* 10 (1958): 14–75.

———. "Reflections on Southern-Jewish Historiography." *Turn to the South: Essay on Southern Jewry,* ed. Nathan M. Kaganoff and Melvin I. Irofsky, pp. 13–20. Waltham,

Mass., and Charlottesville, Va., 1979.

"City Council of Charleston v. S. A. Benjamin." *South Carolina Law Reports. Reports of Cases Argued and Determined in the Court of Appeals, November 1847–May 1848,* pp. 508–36. Columbia, S.C., 1848.

"City Council of Charleston v. Solomon Cohen, Jr." *South Carolina Law Reports, Cases at Law Argued and Determined in the Law Court of Appeals and Court of Errors of South Carolina from November, 1843, to May, 1844, Both Inclusive*, ed. R. H. Spears, 2: 342–50. Charleston, S.C., 1860.

City of Charleston. *Digest of Ordinances of the City Council of Charleston, from the Year 1783 to October 1844. To Which are added the Acts of the Legislature which Relate Exclusively to the City of Charleston*. Charleston, S.C., 1844.

Clarke, Philip G., Jr. *Anglicanism in South Carolina, 1670–1976*. Easley, S.C., 1976.

Clinton, Sir Henry. *The American Rebellion, Sir Henry Clinton's Narrative of His Campaigns, 1775–1782, With An Appendix of Original Documents,* ed. William Bradford Willcox. New Haven, Conn., 1954.

Cohen, Caroline Myers. *Records of the Myers, Hays, and Mordecai Families from 1707 to 1913*. Washington, D.C., 1913.

Cohen, Judah Barrett. *Judaism and the Typical Jew: An Address Delivered Before the Jews of Charleston, S.C., on the Celebration of the Centennial Anniversary of the Birthday of Sir Moses Montefiore at the Hasel Street Synagogue, October 1884*. Charleston, S.C., 1884.

———. "Oration Delivered on the First Anniversary of the South Carolina Historical Society, June 28, 1855." *Collections of South Carolina Historical Society* 2 (1858): 104–17.

Cohen, Meyer M. *Notices of Florida and the Campaigns*. Charleston, S.C., 1836.

Cohen, Robert. "The Demography of Jews in Early America." *Modern Jewish Fertility,* ed. Paul Ritterband, pp. 144–59. Leiden, 1981.

Cohn, Edward L. *The Isaac Harby Prayerbook*. Charleston, S.C., 1974.

Coker, P. C. *Charleston's Maritime Heritage, 1670–1865*. Charleston, S.C., 1987.

Cole, David. "A Brief Outline of the South Carolina Colonial Militia System." *Publications of the South Carolina Historical Society* (1954): 14–23.

"The Congregation of Shearith Israel of Charleston." *Occident* 5 (1847–48): 49–50.

Constitution, 1776. Charles Town, S.C., 1776.

Constitution, 1778. Charles-Town, S.C., 1778.

Constitution, 1790. Charleston, S.C., 1790.

Constitution of the Hebrew Congregation of Kaal Kadosh Beth-Elohim or House of God, Charleston (S.C.). Charleston, S.C., 1820.

Constitution of Reformed Society of Israelites. for Promoting True Principles of Judaism According to its Purity and Spirit. Charleston, 1825.

Courtney, E. S. *Eulogy on the Hon. William Crafts*. Charleston, S.C., 1826.

Defoe, Daniel. *Party-Tyranny.* London, 1705. Reprinted in A. S. Salley, ed., *Narratives of Early Carolina, 1650–1708*, pp. 223–64. New York, 1911.

Dalcho, Frederick. *An Historical Account of the Protestant Episcopal Church in South Carolina*. Charleston, S.C., 1820.

Dawson, J. L., and H. W. DeSaussure. *Census of the City of Charleston, South Carolina for the Year 1848*. Charleston, S.C., 1849.

"Death of an Old Servant." Charleston *Daily Courier*, December 12, 1859.

DeLaMotta, Jacob. "The Congregations of Charleston." *Occident* 1 (1843–44): 600–604; 2 (1844–45): 26–28.

———. *Discourse Delivered at the Consecration of the Synagogue of the Hebrew Congregation of Mikva Israel in the City of Savannah, Georgia*. Savannah, Ga., 1820.

———. *An Eulogium to the Memory of Dr. Samuel Wilson, Delivered by Appointment in the First Presbyterian Church, Before the Charleston Medical Society on Emulation, and a Numerous Assemblage of Citizens on the 10th Day of April, 1827*. Charleston, S.C., 1827.

———. *Funeral Address Pronounced in the Synagogue Previous to the Interment of the Relics of the Rev. Gershon Mendes Seixas.* New York, 1816.

———. *An Investigation of the Properties and Effects of the Spiraea Trifoliata of Linnaeus, or Indian Physic*. Philadelphia, 1810.

———. *On the Private and Religious Character of the Late Mr. Nathan Hart*. Charleston, S.C., 1840.

———. *An Oration on the Causes of Mortality Among Strangers During the Late Summer and Fall*. Savannah, Ga., 1820.

DeSola Pool, David and Tamar DeSola Pool. *An Old Faith in the New World: Portrait of Shearith Israel, 1654–1954*. New York, 1955.

Dorfman, Joseph. *The Economic Mind in American Civilization*. 2 vols. New York, 1946.

"Dr. Raphall in Charleston." *Occident* 8 (1850–51): 48–51.

Drayton, John. *Memoirs of the American Revolution*. 2 vols. Charleston, S.C., 1821.

Duffy, John. *Epidemics in Colonial America*. Baton Rouge, La., 1953.

———. "Yellow Fever in Colonial Charleston." *South Carolina Historical Magazine* 52 (1951): 189–97.

Dunn, Richard S. "The English Sugar Islands and the Founding of South Carolina." *South Carolina Historical Magazine* 72 (1971): 81–93.

Dvoichenko-Markov, E. "American Doctors in the Crimean War." *Journal of the History of Medicine* 9 (1954): 362–67.

Eckman, Julius. "Beth Elohim Congregation of Charleston, South Carolina." *Occident* 9 (1851–52): 141–44.

———. "On the Origin and Purpose of Synagogues." *Occident* 10 (1852–53): 134–44.

———. "On the Resurrection." *Occident* 9 (1851–52): 148–54, 256–64, 348–53.

Elzas, Barnett A. *Documents Relative to a*

Proposed Settlement of Jews in South Carolina in 1748. Charleston, S.C., 1903.

———. *Jewish Cemeteries at Columbia, S.C.* Charleston, S.C., 1910.

———. *Jewish Cemeteries of Congregation Berith Shalome at Charleston, S.C.* Charleston, S.C., 1910.

———. *Jewish Cemetery at Georgetown, S.C.* Charleston, S.C., 1910.

———. *Jewish Marriage Notices from the Newspaper Press of Charleston, S.C. (1775–1906)*. New York, 1917.

———. *The Jews of South Carolina*. Philadelphia, 1905.

———. *The Jews of South Carolina: Record of the First Naturalization in the Province*. Charleston, S.C.: n.d.

———. *Judaism—An Exposition.* Charleston, S.C., 1896

———. *Leaves from My Historical Scrapbook*. Charleston, S.C., 1907.

———. *New Jewish Cemetery of K.K. Beth Elohim at Charleston, S.C.* Charleston, S.C., 1910.

———. *Old Jewish Cemeteries at Charleston, S.C.* Charleston, S.C.: 1903.

———. *The Organ in the Synagogue—An Interesting Chapter in the History of Reform Judaism in America*. Charleston, S.C., 1902.

———. *The Reformed Society of Israelites of Charleston, S.C.* New York, 1916.

Engelman, Uriah Z. "Jewish Education in Charleston, South Carolina during the Eighteenth and Nineteenth Centuries." *Publications of the American Jewish Historical Society* 42 (1952–53): 43–67.

———. "Jewish Statistics in the U.S. Census of Religious Bodies (1850–1936)." *Jewish Social Studies* 9 (1947): 127–74.

Evans, Eli N. *Judah P. Benjamin: The Jewish Confederate*. New York, 1987.

Evening Service of Roshashanah and Kippur, or the Beginning of the Year and the Day of Atonement. New York, 1761.

"Examination of the Pupils of the School for Instruction of Jewish Youth, Charleston, S.C." *Occident*, 4 (1846–47): 207–8.

"Examination of the Society for the Instruction of Jewish Doctrine." *Occident* 3 (1845–46): 136–43.

"Examination of the Society for the Instruction of Jewish Doctrines, at Charleston, S.C." *Occident* 5 (1847–48): 260–61, 308–10.

Extracts from the Journals of the Provincial Congresses, 1775–1776, ed. William E. Hemphill. Columbia, S.C.,1960.

Ezekiel, Herbert T., and Gaston Lichtenstein. *The History of the Jews of Richmond from 1769 to 1917*. Richmond, Va., 1917.

Fagin, N. Bryllion. "Isaac Harby and the Early American Theatre." *American Jewish Archives* 8 (1956): 3–13.

Farley, M. Foster. "The Mighty Monarch of the South: Yellow Fever in Charleston and Savannah." *Georgia Review* 27 (Spring 1973): 56–70.

"Fifty-Sixth Anniversary of the Hebrew Benevolent Society of Charleston, S.C." *Occident* 6 (1848–49): 41–48.

Ford, Frederick A. *Census of the City of Charleston for the Year* 1861. Charleston, S.C., 1861.

Fraser, Charles. *Reminiscences of Charleston*. Charleston, S.C., 1854.

Fraser, Walter J., Jr. *Charleston! Charles-*

ton!: The History of a Southern City. Columbia, S.C.,1989.

Friedenberg, Albert M. "Calendar of American Jewish Cases (1793–1904)." *Publications of the American Jewish Historical Society* 12 (1904): 87–99.

———. "The Jews and American Sunday Laws." *Publications of the American Jewish Historical Society* 11 (1903): 101–15.

Friedenwald, Herbert "Note Relative to Jews Keeping Their Stores Open on Sundays in the District of Charleston, S.C. " *Publications of the American Jewish Historical Society* 5 (1897): 202ff.

Friedman, Lee M. "Jacob Mears [of Jamaica] and Simon Valentine of Charleston, South Carolina." *Publications of the American Jewish Historical Society* 61 (1951): 77–82.

"From the 2nd Volume of Minutes Books of the Cong: Shearith Israel in New York." *Publications of the American Jewish Historical Society* 21 (1913).

Gerber, David A. "Anti-Semitism and Jewish-Gentile Relations in American Historiography and the American Past." In David A. Gerber, ed., *Anti-Semitism in American History,* pp. 3–56. Urbana, Ill., 1986.

Gibbes, R. W. *Documentary History of the American Revolution, 1776–1782.* New York, 1857.

Gilman, Samuel. "Harby's Discourse on the Jewish Synagogue." *The North American Review,* July 1826, pp. 67–79.

———. *The Old and the New: Or Discourses and Proceedings at the Dedication of the Re-moddled Unitarian Church in Charleston, S.C. on Sunday, April 2, 1854, Proceeding by the Farewell Discourse.* Charleston, S.C., 1854.

Goldberg, Isaac. *Major Noah: American-Jewish Pioneer.* Philadelphia, 1944.

Goodman, Abram Vossen. *American Overture: Jewish Rights in Colonial Times.* Philadelphia, 1947.

———. "South Carolina from Shaftesbury to Salvador." In *Jews in the South,* ed. Leonard Dinnerstein and Marydale Palsson, pp. 29–42. Baton Rouge, La., 1973.

Goodman, Paul. *Bevis Marks in History: A Survey of the External Influences of the Congregation Sahar Asamain Bevis Marks London.* Oxford, 1934.

Gregorie, Anne King. *History of Sumter County, South Carolina.* Sumter, S.C., 1954.

Grinstein, Hyman B. *The Rise of the Jewish Community of New York, 1654–1860.* Philadelphia, 1947.

Grollman, Earl A. "Dictionary of American Jewish Biography in the Seventeenth Century." *American Jewish Archives* 2 (1950): 3–10

Gutmann, Joseph. "Jewish Participation in the Visual Arts of Eighteenth and Nineteenth Century America." *American Jewish Archives* 15 (1963): 21–57.

Hagy, James W. "From the Crimea to Charleston: The Career of Columbus DaVega." *Bulletin of Kahal Kadosh Beth Elohim.* Charleston, S.C., February 1989. Reprinted in *Southern Jewish Historical Society Newsletter,* Fall 1989.

———. "Her Scandalous Behavior: A

Jewish Divorce in Charleston, S.C., 1788." *American Jewish Archives* 61 (1989): 185–98.

Haley, K. H. D. *The First Earl of Shaftesbury.* New York, 1968.

Hamilton, James, Jr. *An Account of the Late Intended Insurrection Among a Portion of the Blacks of this City. Published by the Authority of the Corporation of Charleston.* Charleston, S.C., 1822.

Harby, Isaac. *Alberti: A New Play in Five Acts.* Charleston, S.C., 1819.

———. *A Discourse, Delivered in Charleston on the 21st of November 1825 Before the Reformed Society of Israelites, for Promoting True Principles of Judaism According to Its Purity and Spirit on Their First Anniversary.* Charleston, S.C., 1825.

———. *The Gordian Knot; or Causes & Effects, a Play in Five Acts.* Charleston, S.C., 1810.

Harris, Ray Baker. *Eleven Gentlemen of Charleston, Founders of the Supreme Council, Mother Church of the World, Ancient and Accepted Scottish Rite of Masonry.* Washington, D.C., 1959.

Hebrew Benevolent Society of Charleston. *Constitution and By-Laws 1795–1900.* Charleston, S.C., 1900.

"Hebrew Benevolent Society of Charleston, South Carolina." *Occident* 16 (1858–59): 571–89.

Hebrew Orphan Society of Charleston. *Constitution of Hebrew Orphan Society of Charleston.* Charleston, S.C., 1887.

"Hebrew Society for the Instruction of Jewish Youth in Charleston." *Occident* 3 (1845–46): 94–96.

Heitman, Francis Bernard. *Historical Register and Dictionary of the United States Army, from Its Organization, September 29, 1789 to March 2, 1903.* Washington, D.C., 1903.

Heller, James G. *Isaac M. Wise: His Life, Work and Thought.* New York, 1965.

Hemperley, Marion R. ed. "Federal Naturalization Oaths, Charleston, South Carolina, 1790–1860." *South Carolina Historical Magazine* 66 (1965): 112–24, 183–92, 218–28.

Hewatt, Alexander. *An Historical Account of the Rise and Progress of the Colonies of South Carolina and Georgia.* 2 vols. Spartanburg, S.C., 1962 (reprint).

Heyl, Erik. *Early American Steamers.* Buffalo, N.Y., 1953.

Higgins, W. Robert. "Charles Town Merchants and Factors Dealing in the External Negro Trade, 1735–1775." *South Carolina Historical Magazine* 65 (1964): 205–17.

Hirsch, Arthur Henry. *The Huguenots of Colonial South Carolina.* Durham, N.C., 1928.

Hoch, J. Hampton. *The History of Pharmacy in South Carolina.* Charleston, S.C., 1951.

Hough, Franklin Benjamin. *The Siege of Charleston by the British Fleet and Army Under the Command of Admiral Arbuthnot and Sir Henry Clinton, Which Terminated with the Surrender of that Place on the 12th of May 1780.* Albany, N.Y., 1867.

Hühner, Leon. "Jews in Connection with the Colleges of the Thirteen Original States Prior to 1800." *American Jewish Historical Society Publications* 19 (1910): 101–24.

———. "Jews in the Legal and Medical Professions in America Prior to 1800." *Publications of the Jewish Historical Society* 22 (1914): 147–65.

———. "Jews in the War of 1812." *Publications of the Jewish Historical Society* 26 (1918): 173–200.

———. "The Jews of South Carolina from the Earliest Settlement to the End of the American Revolution." *Publications of the Jewish Historical Society* 12 (1904): 39–61.

———. "Some Additional Notes on the History of the Jews of South Carolina." *Publications of the American Jewish Historical Society* 19 (1910): 151–56.

Hymns Written for the Service of Hebrew Congregation Beth Elohim of Charleston, S.C. Charleston, S.C., 1842.

Hymns Written for the Use of Hebrew Congregations. Charleston, S.C., 1856.

Idelsohn, Abraham Z. *Jewish Music in its Historical Development*. New York, 1944.

"In the Case of the State ex relatione A. Ottolengui, vs. G.V. Ancker and others.—Charleston, Feb. 1846." *Occident* 3 (1845–46): 615–26.

"The Israelites of South Carolina." *Occident* 12 (1854–55): 496–510.

Jackson, Melvin H. *Privateers in Charleston, 1793–1796: An Account of a French Palatinate in South Carolina.* Washington, D.C., 1969.

"The Jewish Authorities on Reform." *Occident* 2 (1854–55): 245–54, 288–95.

"John Waddell v. M. C. Mordecai, May, 1835." *Reports of Cases at Law, Argued and Determined in the Court of Appeals of South Carolina*, ed. W. H. Hill, 2: 366–72. Charleston, S.C., 1857.

Jones, Charles C., Jr. "The Settlement of the Jews in Georgia." *Publications of the American Jewish Historical Society* 1 (1892): 5–12.

Jordan, Laylon Wayne. "Education for the Community: Christopher G. Memminger and the Origination of Common Schools in Antebellum Charleston." *South Carolina Historical Magazine* 83 (1984): 99–115.

———. "Police Power and Public Safety in Antebellum Charleston: The Emergence of New Police, 1800–1860." *South Atlantic Urban Studies* 3 (1979): 122–40.

Journal of the Commissioners for Trade and Plantations from January 1711/12 to December 1749. London, 1931.

Journals of the Commons House of Assembly, 1745–1746, ed. J. H. Easterby. Columbia, S.C., 1956.

Journals of the Commons House of Assembly of South Carolina, For the Four Sessions of 1693, ed. A. S. Salley. Columbia, S.C., 1907.

Journals of the Commons House of Assembly of South Carolina for the Two Sessions of 1697, ed. A. S. Salley. Columbia, S.C. , 1913.

Journals of the House of Commons, From November the 7th, 1693 to November the 23rd 1697. Vol. 9. London, England, 1803.

Journals of the House of Representatives, 1783–1784, ed. Theodora J. Thompson. Columbia, S.C., 1977.

Journals of the House of Representatives, 1791, ed. Michael E. Stevens and Christine M. Allen. Columbia, S.C., 1985.

Journals of the Privy Council, 1783–1789, ed. Adele Stanton Edwards. Columbia, S.C., 1971.

Kennedy, L. H., and T. Parker. *An Official Report of the Trials of Sundry Negroes Charged with an Attempt to Raise an Insurrection in the State of South Carolina*. Charleston, S.C., 1822.

Kennedy, Michael L. "A French Jacobin Club in Charleston, South Carolina, 1792–1795." *South Carolina Historical Magazine* 92 (1991): 4–22.

King, William L. *The Newspaper Press of Charleston, S.C.* Charleston, S.C., 1872.

Klebaner, Benjamin Joseph. "Public Poor Relief in Charleston, 1800–1860." *South Carolina Historical Magazine* 55 (1954): 210–20.

Kohler, Max J. "Isaac Harby, Jewish Religious Leader and Man of Letters." *Publications of the American Jewish Historical Society* 32 (1931): 35–53.

———. "Phases in the History of Religious Liberty in America, with Special Reference to the Jews." *American Jewish Historical Quarterly* 11 (1903): 53–73.

Korn, Bertram Wallace. *The American Reaction to the Mortara Case, 1858–1859*. Cincinnati, Ohio, 1957.

———. "Factors Bearing upon the Survival of Judaism in the Ante-Bellum Period." *American Jewish History Quarterly* 53 (1964): 341–51.

———. "Jews and Negro Slavery in the Old South, 1789–1865." In *Jews in the South,* ed. Leonard Dinnerstein and Marydale Palsson. Baton Rouge, La., 1973.

———. *Jews and Slavery in the Old South, 1789–1865*. Elkins Park, Pa., 1961.

Lambert, Robert Stansbury. *South Carolina Loyalists in the American Revolution*. Columbia, S.C., 1987.

Leeser, Isaac. "The Appeal Case of the Charleston Congregation." *Occident* 3 (1845–46): 615–26; 4 (1846–47): 50–55, 103–6, 157–62.

———. "The Quo Warranto Case at Charleston." *Occident* 2 (1844–45): 166.

———. "Rev. Dr. Eckman and His Congregation." *Occident* 9 (1851–52): 209–21.

———. "The Rev. Solomon Jacobs." *Occident* 10 (1852–53): 399–403.

———. "Testimonial of the Members of the Hebrew Benevolent Society of Charleston, South Carolina, to their President, S. Valentine." *Occident* 13 (1855–56): 38–45.

Leiman, Melvin M. *Jacob N. Cardozo: Economic Thought in the Antebellum South*. New York, 1966.

Leland, Jack. "Fulton St. House One of Last Relics of Red Light District." *News and Courier*, October 27, 1986.

Levasseur, A. *Lafayette in America in 1824 and 1825; or Journal of a Voyage to the United States*. 2 vols. Philadelphia, 1829.

Levett, Ella Pettit. "Loyalism in Charleston, 1761–1784." *Proceedings of the South Carolina Historical Association* (1936): 3–17.

Levin, Nathaniel. "Address Delivered Before the Society for the Instruction of Jewish Youth, in Charleston, S.C., on the Anniversary of the Society, February, 1842." *Occident* 1 (1843–44): 162–74.

———. "The Jewish Congregation of Charleston." *Occident* 1 (1843–44): 336–42, 384–90, 434–40, 491–96.

Levy, B. H. *Savannah's Old Jewish Community Cemeteries*. Macon, Ga., 1983.

Levy, Jacob. "The Reformed Israelites." *Southern Quarterly Review* 6 (April 1844): 312–60.

Liberles, Robert. "Conflict over Reforms: The Case of Congregation Beth Elohim, Charleston, South Carolina." In *The American Synagogue: A Sanctuary Transformed*, ed. Jack Wertheimer, pp. 274–96. New York, 1987.

Lindo, Moses. "An Account of a New Die from the Berries of a Weed in South Carolina." *Philosophical Transactions* 53 (1763): 238–39.

Lovett, Ella Pettit. "Loyalism in Charleston, 1761–1784." *Publications of the South Carolina Historical Society* (1936): 3–17.

McGrady, Edward. *History of South Carolina under the Proprietary Government, 1670–1719*. New York, 1897.

Marcus, Jacob Rader. "The American Colonial Jew: A Study in Acculturation." In *The American Jewish Experience*, ed. Jonathan D. Sarna, pp. 6–17. New York, 1986.

———. *The American Jewish Woman: A Documentary History*. Cincinnati, Ohio, 1981.

———. *American Jewry. Documents: Eighteenth Century. Primarily Hitherto Unpublished Manuscripts*. Cincinnati, Ohio, 1959.

———. *The Colonial American Jew, 1492–1776*. 3 vols. Detroit, Mich., 1970.

———. *Early American Jewry: The Jews of Pennsylvania and the South, 1655–1790*. Philadelphia, 1953.

———. *An Index to Scientific Articles on American Jewish History*. New York, 1971.

———. *Memoirs of American Jews, 1775–1865*. 3 vols. Philadelphia, 1955–56.

———. "The Periodization of American Jewish History." *Publications of the American Jewish Historical Society* 47 (1958): 125–33.

———. *To Count a People: American Jewish Population Data, 1585–1984*. Lanham, Md., 1990.

———. *United States Jewry, 1776–1985*. Vol. 1. Detroit, Mich., 1989.

Mayer, Maurice. "Geschichte des religiösen Umschwunges unter den Israeliten Nordamerikas." *Sinai* 1 (1856): 101–7, 171–81, 197–205, 241–45.

Melnick, Ralph. "Billy Simmons: The Black Jew of Charleston." *American Jewish Archives* 32 (1980): 3–8.

Mendelssohn, Moses. *Jerusalem: A Treatise on Ecclesiastical Authority and Judaism*. 2 vols. London, 1838.

Merrens, Roy H. *The Colonial South Carolina Scene: Contemporary Views, 1697–1774*. Columbia, S.C., 1972.

Meyer, Michael A. *Response to Modernity: History of the Reform Movement in Judaism*. Oxford, 1988.

Mielziner, Ella McKenna Friend. *Moses Mielziner, 1823–1903: A Biography with a Bibliography of His Writings*. New York, 1931.

"Minister of the Congregation Beth Elohim, Charleston, S.C." *Occident* 9 (1851–52): 92.

Moïse, Abraham. "An Address Delivered Before the Reformed Society of Israelites, on its Second Anniversary, November, 1826." In Lucius Clifton Moïse, *Biography of Isaac Harby, With An Account of the Reformed Society of Israelites, Charleston, S.C.*, pp. 122–27. Columbia, S.C., 1931.

Moïse, Abraham, and Henry L. Pinckney. *A Selection from the Miscellaneous Writings of the Late Isaac Harby, Esq.* Charleston, S.C., 1829.

Moïse, Harold. *The Jewish Cemetery at Sumter, S.C.: A Transcription of the Names and Dates on the Tombstones, 1874–1912*. Sumter, S.C., 1942.

———. *The Moïse Family of South Carolina*. Columbia, S.C., 1961.

Moïse, Lucius Clifton. *Biography of Isaac Harby, with an Account of the Reformed Israelites of Charleston, S.C.* Columbia, S.C., 1931.

Moïse, Penina. *Fancy's Sketch Book.* Charleston, S.C., 1833.

Moltke-Hansen, David. "The Expansion of Intellectual Life: A Prospectus." In Michael O'Brien and David Moltke-Hansen, eds. *Intellectual Life in Antebellum Charleston*. Knoxville, Tenn., 1986.

Moore, W. O., Jr. "The Largest Exporters of Deer Skins from Charleston, 1735–1775." *South Carolina Historical Magazine* 74 (1973): 144–50.

Morais, Sabato. "Mickve Israel Congregation of Philadelphia." *Publications of the American Jewish Historical Society* 1 (1893): 13–24.

Morgan, David T. "Eugenia Levy Phillips: The Civil War Experiences of a Southern Jewish Woman." In *Jews of the South: Selected Essays from the Southern Jewish Historical Society*, ed. Samuel Proctor and Louis Schmier. Macon, Ga., 1984.

———. "Judaism in Eighteenth-Century Georgia." *Georgia Historical Quarterly* 58 (1974): 41–54.

———. "Philip Phillips, Jurist and Statesman." In *Jews of the South: Selected Essays from the Southern Jewish Historical Society*, ed. Samuel Proctor and Louis Schmier. Macon, Ga., 1984.

Morris, Richard B. "Civil Liberties and the Jewish Tradition in Early America." *Publications of the American Jewish Historical Society* 46 (1956): 20–39.

Moses, Herbert A. *The Early Minutes of the Sumter Society of Israelites*. Sumter, S.C., 1936.

Moses, Myer. *An Oration Delivered Before the Hebrew Orphan Society on the 15th of October, 1806*. Charleston, S.C., 1807.

New Constitution of the Hebrew Congregation of Kaal Kadosh Beth Elohim or House of God. Charleston, S.C., 1837.

"New School in Charleston." *Occident* 2 (1844–45): 163–64.

"News Items: Beth-Elohim Congregation of Charleston." *Occident* 15 (1857–58): 105–6.

"News Items: Charleston." *Occident* 4 (1846–47): 107–8.

"News Items: Charleston." *Occident* 5 (1847–48): 371.

"News Items: Charleston." *Occident* 9 (1851–52): 59.

"News Items: Charleston." *Occident* 9 (1851–52): 226.

"News Items: Charleston." *Occident* 14 (1856–57): 549.

"News Items: Charleston.—The Congregation Shearith Israel." *Occident* 15 (1857–58): 357.

"News Items: Charleston, S.C." *Occident* 10 (1852–53): 173–74.

"News Items: Charleston, S.C." *Occident* 11 (1853–54): 377.

"News Items: Charleston, S.C." *Occident* 15 (1857–58): 202.

"News Items: Charleston, S.C." *Occident* 16 (1858–59): 263.

"News Items: Charleston, South Carolina." *Occident* 10 (1852–53): 224.

"News Items: Shearith Israel Congregation of Charleston." *Occident* 7 (1849–50): 477.

"News Items: Shearith Israel Congregation of Charleston." *Occident* 8 (1850–51): 199.

Noah, Mordecai Manuel. "Ararat Address." *Publications of the American Jewish Historical Society* 21 (1913): 230–52.

———. *A Letter Addressed to the Members of the Legislature of South Carolina Examining the Claims and Qualifications of Dewitt Clinton to the Presidency of the United States*. Charleston, S.C., 1812.

Noel, W., ed. *Calendar of State Papers, Colonial Series, 1669–1774*. 27 vols. London, 1860–1926.

"Obituary: Abraham Ottolengui." *Occident* 8 (1850–51): 528–30.

"Obituary: Jacob DeLaMotta." *Occident* 3 (1845–46): 59–66.

O'Brien, Michael, and David Moltke-Hansen, eds. *Intellectual Life in Antebellum Charleston*. Knoxville, Tenn., 1985.

"Old Billy." *American Jewish Archives* 15 (1963): 3–5.

Olsberg, R. Nicholas. "Ship Records in the South Carolina Archives, 1734–1780." *South Carolina Historical Magazine* 74 (1973): 189–209.

Oppenheim, Samuel. "The Jews and Masonry in the United States Before 1810." *Publications of the American Jewish Historical Society* 19 (1910): 1–94.

Parker, Mattie Erma Edwards. *North Carolina Charters and Constitutions*. Raleigh, N.C., 1963.

Pease, Jane H., and William H. Pease. "The Blood-Thirsty Tiger: Charleston and the Psychology of Fire." *South Carolina Historical Magazine* 79 (1978): 281–95.

———. *The Web of Progress: Private Values and Public Styles in Boston and Charleston, 1828–1843*. New York, 1985.

Peck, Abraham J. "That Other Peculiar Institution: Jews and Judaism in the Nineteenth Century South." *Modern Judaism* 7 (1987): 99–114.

Perrin, Anderson J. "Public Education in Antebellum South Carolina." *Proceedings of the South Carolina Historical Association* (1937): 3–11.

Philipson, David. "The Progress of the Jewish Reform Movement in the United States." *Jewish Quarterly Review* 10 (1897): 52–99.

———. *The Reform Movement in Judaism.* New York, 1931.

Phillips, N. Taylor. "Family History of the Reverend David Mendez Machado." *Publications of the American Jewish Historical Society* 2 (1894): 45–61.

Pinckney, Henry L. *A Report; Containing a Review of the Proceedings of the City Authorities from the 4th September, 1837 to the 1st August, 1835.* Charleston, S.C., 1838.

———. *A Report Relative to the Proceedings for the Relief of the Sick Poor, During the Late Epidemic. . . . 5th of November 1838.* Charleston, S.C., 1838.

Plaut, W. Gunther. *The Rise of Reform Judaism: American and European Sources.* New York, 1965.

"Poll Lists, Charleston Municipal Elections, 1787." *South Carolina Historical Magazine* 56 (1955): 45–49.

Proceedings of a Public Meeting of the Citizens of Charleston Held at the City Hall, on the 28th August, 1840; in Relation to the Persecution of the Jews in the East. Also the Proceedings of a Meeting of the Israelites of Charleston Convened at the Hall of the Hebrew Orphan House on the Following Evening, in Reference to the Same Subject. Charleston, S.C., 1840.

Proceedings of the Citizens and City Council of Charleston, in Relation to the Destruction of the Steamboat Home. Charleston, S.C., 1837.

Proctor, Samuel, and Louis Schmier, eds. *Jews of the South: Selected Essays from the Southern Jewish Historical Society.* Macon, Ga., 1984.

Pyburn, Nita Katharine. "The Public School System of Charleston before 1860." *South Carolina Historical Magazine* 61 (1960): 86–98.

"R. W. Habersham v. B. A. Rodrigues, January, 1842." *South Carolina Law Reports. Cases at Law Argued and Determined in the Law Court of Appeals and Court of Errors of South Carolina from November, 1842, to May, 1843, Inclusive,* ed. R. H. Spears, 1: 294–99. Charleston, S.C., 1860.

Raisin, Jacob S. *Centennial Booklet: Commemorating the Introduction of Reform Judaism in America at Kahal Kadosh Beth Elohim at Charleston, S.C., Organized 1750.* Charleston, S.C., 1925.

Ramsay, David. *The History of South Carolina from Its First Settlement in 1670 to the Year 1808.* 2 vols. Charleston, S.C., 1809.

Raphall, Morris J. *The Bible View of Slavery. A Discourse.* New York, 1861.

———. *The Constancy of Israel—A Discourse Delivered Before the Congregation Shearit Israel, Charleston, S.C.* Charleston, S.C., 1850.

"Records Kept by Colonel Isaac Hayne." *South Carolina Historical Magazine* 11 (1910): 92–110.

Reese, George H. *The Cornwallis Papers: Abstracts of Americana.* Charlottesville, Va., 1970.

"Reform Movement among the Jews." *Nation* 4 (June 18, 1868): 488–89.

Report of Interments in the City of Charleston from 1834–1846. Charleston, S.C., 1846.

"Rev. Dr. Eckman at Augusta." *Occident* 10 (1852–53): 92–95.

"Rev. Mr. Poznanski." *Occident* 2 (1844–45): 210–12.

"Rev. Mr. Rosenfeld's Address at Charleston." *Occident* 5 (1847–48): 75–79.

"Rev. S. Jacob of Charleston." *Occident* 10 (1852–53): 461–62

"Rev. Solomon Jacobs, of Charleston." *Occident* 11 (1853–54): 271.

Rezneck, Samuel. *Unrecognized Patriots: The Jews in the American Revolution*. Westport, Conn., 1975.

Reznikoff, Charles, and Uriah Z. Engelman. *The Jews of Charleston: A History of an American Jewish Community.* Philadelphia, 1950.

Ritterband, Paul, ed. *Modern Jewish Fertility.* Leiden, 1981.

Rivers, William James. *A Sketch of the History of South Carolina to the Close of the Proprietary Government by the Revolution of 1719*. Charleston, S.C., 1856.

Rogers, George C., Jr. *Charleston in the Age of the Pinckneys*. Norman, Okla., 1969.

———. *The History of Georgetown, South Carolina*. Columbia, S.C., 1970.

Rogers, Tommy W. "The Great Population Exodus from South Carolina." *South Carolina Historical Magazine* 68 (1967): 14–27.

Rosen, Robert N. *A Short History of Charleston*. San Francisco, 1982.

Rosenbloom, Joseph R. *A Biographical Dictionary of Early American Jews: Colonial Times through 1800*. Lexington, Ky., 1960.

Rosendale, Simon W. "An Act Allowing Naturalization of Jews in the Colonies." *Publications of the America Jewish Historical Society* 1 (1893): 93–98.

———. "An Early Ownership of Real Estate in Albany, New York, By a Jewish Trader." *Publications of the American Jewish Historical Society* 3 (1895): 61–71.

Rosenfeld, Jacob. "Discourse Delivered by the Rev. Jacob Rosenfeld, at the Consecration of the Orthodox Synagogue, Charleston, S.C., on Friday the 1st Day of Elul, 5607, 13th of August, 1847." *Occident* 5 (1847–48): 325–36.

———. "Israel's Union: A Vision." *Occident* 7 (1849–50): 362–66.

———. "The Proposed Assembly. Letter from Rev. Jacob Rosenfeld of Charleston." *Occident* 6 (1848–49): 563–65.

Rosenthall, William A. "Jewish Artists in Early Charleston." *Jewish Art and Culture in Early America*, pp. 16–18. Charleston, 1981.

Rosenwaike, Ira. "An Estimate and Analysis of the Jewish Population of the United States in 1790." *Publications of the American Jewish Historical Society* 50 (1960): 23–68.

———. "The Jewish Population of the United States as Estimated from the Census of 1820." *American Jewish Historical Quarterly* 53 (1963): 138–51.

———. *On the Edge of Greatness: A Portrait of American Jewry in the Early National Period.* Cincinnati, Ohio, 1985.

Roth, Cecil. "A Description of America 1785—A Letter from Joseph Salvador." *American Jewish Archives* 17 (1965): 27–33.

Rubin, Saul Jacob. *Third to None: The Saga of Savannah Jewry, 1733–1983.* Savannah, Ga., 1983.

Rubinger, Naphtali J. "A Dismissal in Albany." *American Jewish Archives* 24 (1972): 160–83.

The Sabbath Service and Miscellaneous Prayers, Adopted by the Reformed Society of Israelites, Founded in Charleston, South-Carolina, November 21, 1825. Charleston, S.C., 1830.

Salley, A. S. "The Fundamental Constitutions of Carolina." *Publications of the South Carolina Historical Association* (1934): 25–31.

———. *Narratives of Early Carolina, 1650–1708.* New York, 1911.

———. *President Washington's Tour Through South Carolina.* Columbia, S.C., 1932.

Salley, A. S. and D. E. Huger Smith, eds. *Register of St. Phillips Parish, Charles Town, South Carolina.* Columbia, S.C., 1971.

Salmon, Marylynn. "Life, Liberty, and Dower: The Legal Status of Women after the American Revolution." In *War, Women, and Revolution*, ed. Carol R. Berkin and Clara M. Lovett. New York, 1980.

Salomon, Gotthold. *Twelve Sermons Delivered in the New Temple of the Israelites at Hamburgh*, trans. Anna Maria Goldsmid. Charleston, S.C., 1841.

Samuel, Wilfred S. "A Review of the Jewish Colonists in Barbados in the Year 1680." *Transactions of the Jewish Historical Society of England* 13 (1932): 1–111.

Sarna, Jonathan D., ed. *The American Jewish Experience.* New York, 1986.

———. *Jacksonian Jew: The Two Worlds of Mordecai Noah.* New York, 1981.

Schappes, Morris U. *A Documentary History of the Jews in the United States.* New York, 1971.

Schwartzman, Sylvan. *Reform Judaism in the Making.* New York, 1955.

Scott, Edwin J. *Random Recollections of a Long Life.* Columbia, S.C., 1884.

Seabrook, Whitemarsh B. *A Memoir on the Origin, Cultivation and Uses of Cotton From the Earliest to the Present Time.* Charleston, S.C., 1844.

Sellers, Leila. *Charleston Business on the Eve of the American Revolution.* Chapel Hill, N.C., 1934.

Sharrer, G. Terry. "Indigo in Carolina, 1671–1796." *South Carolina Historical Magazine* 72 (1971): 94–103.

"Shearith Israel Congregation, Charleston." *Occident* 12 (1854–55): 258–59.

Shecut, J. L. E. W. *Medical and Philosophical Essays. Containing Topographical, Historical and Other Sketches of the City of Charleston.* Charleston, S.C., 1819.

Sheftall, John McKay. "The Sheftalls of Savannah: Colonial Leaders and Founding Fathers of Georgia Judaism." In *Jews of the South: Selected Essays from the Southern Jewish Historical Society*, ed. Samuel Procter and Louis Schmier. Macon, Ga., 1984.

Silberman, Lou H. "American Impact: Judaism in the United States in the Early Nineteenth Century." In *Tradition and Change in Jewish Experience*, ed. A. Leland Jamison, pp. 89–105. Syracuse, N.Y., 1978.

Simms, William Gilmore, ed. *The Charleston Book, A Miscellany of Prose and Verse.* Charleston, S.C., 1845.

Simonhoff, Harry. *Jewish Notables in*

America, 1776–1865: Links of an Endless Chain. New York, 1956.

Simons, Robert Bentham. "Regimental Book of Captain James Bentham, 1778–1780." *South Carolina Historical Magazine* 53 (1952): 13–18, 101–12, 161–71, 230–40.

Simons, Thomas Y. *A Report on the History and Causes of the Strangers or Yellow Fever of Charleston: Read Before the Board of Health*. Charleston, S.C., 1830.

Smith, W. Roy. *South Carolina as a Royal Province, 1719–1776*. New York, 1903.

Smyth, Thomas. *Two Discourses on the Occasion of the Great Fire in Charleston, On Friday Night, April 27, 1838*. Charleston, S.C., 1838.

The State ex rel. A. Ottolengui et al. vs. G. V. Ancker et al: Report of the Evidence and Arguments of Counsel, by a Member of the Charleston Bar. Charleston, S.C., 1844.

"The State ex relatione Abraham Ottolengui and others vs. G. V. Ancker and others." In *Reports of Cases at Law, Argued and Determined in the Court of Appeals and Court of Errors of South Carolina, 1845 to December 1846*, ed. J. S. G. Richardson, 2: 245–86. Columbia, S.C., 1846.

"The State v. Jacob Meyer." *South Carolina Law Reports. Cases at Law Argued and Determined in the Law Court of Appeals and Court of Errors of South Carolina, From November 1842 to May 1843, Both Inclusive*, ed. R. H. Spears, 1: 285–89. Charleston, S.C., 1860.

The Statutes at Large of South Carolina, ed. Thomas Cooper and David McCord. 10 vols. Columbia, S.C., 1836–1941.

Steen, Ivan D. "Charleston in the 1850's: As Described by British Travellers." *South Carolina Historical Magazine* 71 (1970): 36–45.

Stern, Malcolm. "The 1820's: American Jewry Comes of Age." In *A Bicentennial Festschrift for Jacob Rader Marcus*, ed. Bertram W. Korn, pp. 69–97. New York and Waltham, Mass., 1976.

———. "Charleston's First Jews." *Southern Jewish Historical Newsletter*, Fall 1988.

———. *The First Jewish Families of America, 600 Genealogies*. Cincinnati, Ohio, 1979.

———. "New Light on the Jewish Settlement of Savannah."*American Jewish Historical Quarterly* 52 (1963): 169–99.

———. "Reforming of Reform Judaism—Past, Present, Future." *American Jewish Historical Quarterly* 63 (1973): 111–37.

Stoesen, Alexander. "The British Occupation of Charleston, 1780–81." *South Carolina Historical Magazine* 63 (1962): 71–82.

Strock, Sol M. "Switzerland and the Jews." *Publications of the American Jewish Historical Society* 11 (1903): 7–99.

Stumpf, Stuart Owen. "Implications of King George's War for the Charleston Mercantile Community." *South Carolina Historical Magazine* 77 (1976): 161–88.

———. "South Carolina Importers of General Merchandise, 1735–

1765." *South Carolina Magazine of History* 84 (1983): 1–10.

Sturhahn, Joan. *Carvalho: Artist-Photographer-Patriot*. New York, 1976.

"Sunday Laws in South Carolina." *Occident* 5 (1847–48): 593–99.

"Sunday Laws in South Carolina: Review of Judge O'Neal's Opinion." *Occident* 6 (1848–49): 36–39.

"Sunday School Anniversary at Charleston, South Carolina." *Occident* 12 (1854–55): 253–57.

Tanakh: A New Translation of The Holy Scriptures According to the Traditional Hebrew Texts. Philadelphia, 1985.

Tarshish, Allan. *Bicentennial Anniversary in Charleston*. Cincinnati, Ohio, 1950.

———. "The Charleston Organ Case." *American Jewish Historical Quarterly* 54 (1965): 411–49.

Thomas, J. P. *The Carolina Tribute to Calhoun*. Columbia, S.C.,1857.

Thomas, Jno. P., Jr. "The Barbadians in Early South Carolina." *South Carolina Historical Magazine* 31 (1930): 75–92.

Tobias, Thomas J. "Charles Town in 1764." *South Carolina Historical Magazine* 67 (1966): 63–74.

———. *The Hebrew Benevolent Society of Charleston, S.C., Founded 1784, The Oldest Jewish Charitable Society in the United States*. Charleston, S.C., 1965.

———. *The Hebrew Orphan Society of Charleston, S.C., Founded 1801: An Historical Sketch.* Charleston, S.C., 1957.

———. "Joseph Tobias of Charles Town: Linguister." *Publications of the American Jewish Historical Society* 49 (1959): 33–38.

———. "The Many Sided Dr. De La Motta." *American Jewish Historical Quarterly* 52 (1963): 200–19.

———. "This Cemetery We Rededicate." *American Jewish Historical Quarterly* 53 (1964): 352–70.

———. "Tombstones That Tell a Story: Charleston's Historic Coming Street Cemetery." *Journal of the Southern Jewish Historical Society* 2 (1958): 2–8.

"Token of Respect to Rev. Mr. Poznanski." *Occident* 8 (1850–51): 249–55.

Uhlendorf, Bernhard Alexander. *The Siege of Charleston With An Account of the Province of South Carolina: Diaries and Letters of Hessian Officers from the Von Jungkenn Papers in the William L. Clements Library.* Ann Arbor, Mich., 1938.

"Uncle Billy: The First Carrier." *Centennial Edition: The News and Courier* (Charleston, S.C., 1903), p. 11.

United States, Census Department. *Heads of Families at the First Census of the United States in the Year 1790: South Carolina*. Washington, D.C., 1908.

Valentine, Samuel. "Consecration of the 'Beth Chayim' of the Congregation 'Shearith Israel,' Charleston, S.C." *Occident* 15 (1857–58): 479–84.

"Violation of Sunday Laws at Charleston." *Occident* 4 (1846–47): 588–96.

Wallace, David Duncan. *The History of South Carolina.* Vol. 1. New York, 1934.

———. *South Carolina: A Short History*

1520–1948. Chapel Hill, N.C., 1951.

Waring, Joseph I. "Chief Medical Officers of the South Carolina Militia." *South Carolina Historical Magazine* 71 (1970): 33

———. *A History of Medicine in South Carolina, 1670–1825*. Columbia, S.C., 1964.

———. *A History of Medicine in South Carolina, 1825–1900*. Columbia, S.C., 1967.

———. "The Journal of Dr. William Joseph Holt in the Crimean War." *Journal of the South Carolina Medical Association* 62 (1966): 24–28.

Watson, Charles S. *Antebellum Charleston Dramatists*. Tuscaloosa, Ala., 1976.

Webber, Mabel L. "Joseph Smith's Diary, 1780–1781." *South Carolina Historical Magazine* 33 (1932): 1–83, 281–96.

Weir, Robert M. *Colonial South Carolina: A History*. Millwood, N. Y, 1983.

White, Carleton. *Narrative of the Loss of the Steam Packet Home on a Voyage from New York to Charleston.* New York, 1837.

Williams, Jack Kenny. "The Code of Honor in Ante-Bellum South Carolina." *South Carolina Historical Magazine* 54 (1953): 113–26.

———. "The Criminal Lawyer in Ante-Bellum South Carolina." *South Carolina Historical Magazine* 56 (1955): 138–50.

Wilson, Teresa E., and Janice L. Grimes. *Marriage and Death Notices from the Southern Patriot, 1815–1830*. 2 vols. Easley, S.C., 1986.

Winberry, John S. "Reputation of Carolina Indigo." *South Carolina Historical Magazine* 80 (1979): 242–50.

Winterbotham, William. *An Historical, Geographical, Commercial, and Philosophical View of the American United States and of the European Settlements in America and the West-Indies*. 4 vols. London, 1795.

Wise, Isaac M. *Reminiscences*. Cincinnati, Ohio, 1901.

Wolf, Edwin, and Maxwell Whiteman. *The History of the Jews of Philadelphia from Colonial Times to the Age of Jackson*. Philadelphia, 1976.

Wolf, Lucien. *The History and Genealogy of the Jewish Families of Yates and Samuel of Liverpool*. London, 1901.

Index

Note: A number of individuals have the same name and cannot always be distinguished from one another; for example, twelve people have the name of Jacob Cohen. Thus, names that may represent two or more people are marked with an asterisk. A number of names in the index do not conform to those in the appendix as some individuals cannot always be fully identified in documents.

ABOUT THE AUTHOR

James William Hagy is Professor of History at the University of Charleston, South Carolina. He obtained his doctorate from the University of Georgia.